Winston Churchill
The struggle for survival, 1940–1965

By the same author

THE ANATOMY OF COURAGE

WINSTON CHURCHILL
bust by Oscar Nemon
*Reproduced by gracious permission of
Her Majesty the Queen*

Winston
CHURCHILL

The struggle for survival
1940-1965

Taken from the diaries of

LORD MORAN

Distributed by
HERON BOOKS

This edition published by
Heron Books, London
by arrangement with
Constable & Company
10–12 Orange Street
London WC2

© Trustees of Lord Moran. Nutley
Publications Ltd 1966

Printed in Switzerland

Contents

v

Contents

vi

Illustrations

To
DOROTHY

who has been given back to me
and to

JOHN & GEOFFREY

who in their different ways
are not unlike her

Acknowledgments

I have to thank Her Majesty the Queen for permission to print her letter to Mr. Churchill. I am grateful to General Eisenhower and to Mr. Max Aitken for permission to use letters.

I wish to express my thanks to Mr. Richard Church for his help in keeping this book within manageable proportions. I am grateful to Professor Terence Spencer of Birmingham University for his valuable advice while I was writing this book. I have been able to turn to him whenever a doubtful point arose.

Mr. Henry Laughlin of Houghton, Mifflin Co., of Boston, U.S.A., has followed my story as it unfolded, and I have found his sustained interest heartening. Mr. Craig Wylie has read the text and has given me the benefit of his careful judgment. I have, too, been fortunate in my London publisher, Mr. Ben Glazebrook of Constable and Co. He has met me at every point and has made things easy for me. And here may I pay tribute to Mr. Denis Hamilton's warm encouragement.

I have to thank the late Professor Una Ellis-Fermor and Professor Muriel Bradbrook for criticism and counsel. I have come to rely on the frank criticism of my son, John Wilson: at every stage he has helped me to settle points of difficulty.

I would like to thank my wife and Miss Marian Dean for the time and care they have given to correcting the proofs.

In expressing my thanks to publishers for allowing me to make quotations, I wish to underline my debt to Cassell and Co. for permission to use words from Sir Winston's books.

When I put down my pen, I wish to be sure that I have reported faithfully those who have talked to me about him. I trust that in checking those conversations I have forgotten no one.

Preface

It happened that in both the German Wars I was plucked out of a busy life and left with time on my hands. In the First War I found myself in the trenches in France, where for nearly three years, apart from a battle or two, it was my task to help the men of my battalion to see the business through, although they were better fitted for war than I was. To fill the day and to save myself from the awful sameness of those years of trench warfare I began to keep a diary.

It was not a diary in the ordinary sense of the word. My job was to keep men in the line. What was happening in men's minds? How were they wearing? Those were the only questions that seemed to matter during my years with the battalion in France, and in my diary I set out to find the answers. Entry after entry was taken up with reflections on morale, which after a lapse of thirty years found their way into print in *The Anatomy of Courage*.

In the Second War, in May 1940, a few days after Mr. Churchill became Prime Minister, he accepted me, though without enthusiasm, as his doctor. When I began to travel with him my practice vanished; it did not return, and I was able to give all my time to my unusual task. In a sense it was not unlike my job in the First War, only I was concerned now with the effects of stress and strain on a single individual, Winston Churchill.

He came to me more than once in the last years of the war complaining of exhaustion, and it was plain that he was nearly burnt out. But it was after the war, when he was fighting inch by inch to keep his place in political life in the face of a series of strokes, that he was really in need of help. 'It is the state of my mind that troubles me,' he complained. 'You have studied these things. Surely you ought to be able to do something for it.'

Winston knew that if he was to help me he must not keep anything back, and it became my custom as I drove away from No. 10

or Chequers or Chartwell to note, sometimes on the back of an envelope, anything that he said which might help me to get to the bottom of his troubles. From these notes I wrote out the conversations with Winston the same night. They are printed as they were recorded at the time. I have not touched them since.

I had at that time no thought of writing for publication, and the diary in its original form contained much that could not be properly published for many years. I think it was Brendan Bracken who first pressed me to turn my diary into a book. Brendan knew that the incidents which give excellence to biography are of a 'volatile and evanescent kind, such as soon escape the memory.' He was searching for Winston's Boswell, and he was troubled because most of those who might have caught the tang of his talk were gone. 'Mind you, my dear doctor, it's not going to be easy. You won't get much from his letters.' A grin told me that something was coming. 'You see, Charles, Winston is preoccupied with getting the record straight for posterity.' When I did nothing, Brendan tried to bring things to a head by sending me to Winston's solicitor, Mr. Moir, to talk about the business side. I did not respond, but Brendan did not give up. A few days before he died he sent for me. He wanted to guide my pen, and for an hour and a half he spoke about Winston until he had to stop to get his breath.

Brendan found an ally in Smuts, though the artist in Winston made little appeal to him. He would, indeed, grow impatient with Winston's flippancy when the talk touched on religion. Smuts had few heroes, but to him Winston was the one indispensable man, the only man with ideas. Smuts's cool, scientific habit of mind turned to measurements. He was concerned that history should be informed about the size of the man, the measure of his achievement. One day I was summoned to the Hyde Park Hotel and given my orders.

I was not impressed by this pleading. It did not seem to me that Winston's place in history needed a footnote by his doctor. It was in this mood that, a long time later, I attended a dinner at Caius College, Cambridge, to celebrate its foundation six centuries earlier. I sat next to Dr. G. M. Trevelyan. I did not know him, and neither of us, I suppose, is at our ease with strangers. For a long time we sat in silence. Then, perhaps, it occurred to him that I was a guest from London. At any rate, he fired a question at me about Churchill as if he were not interested in my answer. When I replied he turned his chair towards me, and for half an hour directed at me a stream of questions. I dealt with them as best I might. 'This is history,' he said. 'You ought to get it on paper.' I tried to tell him that the trouble was that I was Winston's doctor. He interrupted me, and,

xvi

taking me, as it were, by the scruff of the neck, proceeded to tell me that I knew some facts about Winston which were not known to others, and that it was my duty to make them available to posterity. 'It is inevitable that everything about this man will be known in time. Let us have the truth.'

I was shaken by Trevelyan's insistence that a knowledge of these particular facts might disarm criticism of Winston's conduct of affairs in the last year of the war, and that if I did not record them, no one else could. It was surely not fair to Winston to withhold these extenuating circumstances. But so deeply ingrained in my mind was a binding obligation to preserve a decent reticence after seeing patients that I was still reluctant to try to write about Winston while I was his doctor.

It was not until some years later that I came to see that it is not possible to follow the last twenty-five years of Winston's life without a knowledge of his medical background. It was exhaustion of mind and body that accounts for much that is otherwise inexplicable in the last year of the war—for instance, the deterioration in his relations with Roosevelt. Masefield ascribed the diffuseness of Winston's *The Second World War* to the same reason. It is certain that the onset of old age and the succession of strokes explain in part why he was not more effective as Leader of the Opposition, and later as First Minister of the Crown. While Winston counted politically these details are part of history and ought not to be left out of his story. It is as plain that only a doctor can give the facts accurately.

After his retirement in April, 1955, Winston made little effort to hide his distaste for what was left to him of life, and the historian might conclude that this reveals a certain weakness in moral fibre. Such strictures will, however, carry little weight unless due allowance is made for the way in which his will was sapped by old age and disease. It is therefore proper, and only fair to him, that the reader should be given the details of his mounting decrepitude.

When, however, Winston ceased to count in politics, when in a sense he could no longer be said to be responsible, I began to question whether there was any purpose in preserving a chronicle of his failing powers. During the last five years of his life I continued from habit to make notes in my case-book, but apart from the two alarming accidents when he broke his spine and fractured his femur, the short entries in my diary add little to the record. I have thought it proper to omit the painful details of the state of apathy and indifference into which he sank after his resignation, because they are no longer of historical significance, and so I bring my story to an end five years before his death.

Winston, as I shall tell, once asked me whether he ought to have retired earlier. I did not answer, but in turn myself asked a question: 'What will be said in fifty years' time of the part I have played?' I was, I think, alone in urging him to hang on, though I knew that he was hardly up to his job for at least a year before he resigned office. His family and his friends pressed him to retire; they feared that he might do something which would injure his reputation. I held that this was none of my business. I knew that he would feel that life was over when he resigned, and that he would be unhappy when there was no purpose in his existence. It was my job as his doctor to postpone that day as long as I could.

It was said of Chatham that his countrymen were so conscious of what they owed to him that they did not want to hear about his faults. That may be true of Winston Churchill. And yet he is already a part of history. A biographer, it is said, is on his oath, and once I decided to write this book its nature could not be in doubt; I cannot tamper with the facts any more than I could fake an experiment in the laboratory. In extreme old age a man is still sensitive to praise or blame, but he has come to see that if he can get at the truth much will be forgiven him.

'However, all things of this nature must be submitted, as this is, with great deference to the judgment of the equal reader.'[1]

---

[1] Clarendon, *History of the Rebellion*, preface to 1st Edition.

Book one

This Star of England

May 1940–February 1945

Small time, but in that small most greatly lived
This star of England: fortune made his sword.

HENRY V

Part one

The Riddle of the War

Chapter one

The New War

May 24, 1940

Winston Churchill is 65. He has just been appointed Prime Minister, and I have become his doctor, not because he wanted one, but because certain members of the Cabinet, who realized how essential he has become, have decided that somebody ought to keep an eye on his health.

It was in these rather ambiguous circumstances that I made my way this morning to Admiralty House,[1] wondering how he would receive me. Though it was noon, I found him in bed reading a document. He went on reading while I stood by the bedside. After what seemed quite a long time, he put down his papers and said impatiently:

'I don't know why they are making such a fuss. There's nothing wrong with me.'

He picked up the papers and resumed his reading. At last he pushed his bed-rest away and, throwing back the bed-clothes, said abruptly:

'I suffer from dyspepsia, and this is the treatment.'

With that he proceeded to demonstrate to me some breathing exercises. His big white belly was moving up and down when there was a knock on the door, and the P.M. grabbed at the sheet as Mrs. Hill came into the room.

Soon after I took my leave. I do not like the job, and I do not think the arrangement can last.

*

The next entry in my diary is dated January, 1941. One day in that month, when I called at the Annexe[2] at Storey's Gate, the man

---

[1] Mr. Churchill continued to live for some weeks after he became Prime Minister in the rooms he had occupied as First Lord of the Admiralty.

[2] Fortified Office of the Ministry of Defence (see also p. 78).

at the door said that Mrs. Churchill wanted to see me before I saw the Prime Minister. She said that he was going to Scapa.[1]

'When?'

'Today at noon. There is a blizzard there, and Winston has a heavy cold. You must stop him.'

I went to his room and said my piece. He became very red in the face, and throwing off the bed-clothes, shouted, 'What damned nonsense! Of course I am going.'

I went back to Mrs. Churchill to report progress. 'Well,' she said shortly, 'if you cannot stop him, the least you can do is to go with him.' I had nothing with me, but the P.M. lent me a greatcoat with a broad astrakhan collar. He said it would keep out the wind. The purpose of the visit was ostensibly to bid farewell to Lord Halifax, who was about to take up his office as our Ambassador in Washington. But I suspect that the Prime Minister's real purpose was to have a look at the Fleet at Scapa. Facing sheets of driving snow and sleet which caught the breath, I found it difficult to share his enthusiasm. As for Lord Halifax, even in those Arctic surroundings, he had the aspect of an Italian primitive.

On the return journey, Tom Johnston[2] dined us at the Station Hotel at Glasgow, and I sat next to Harry Hopkins,[3] an unkempt figure. After a time he got up and, turning to the P.M., said:

'I suppose you wish to know what I am going to say to President Roosevelt on my return. Well, I'm going to quote you one verse from that Book of Books in the truth of which Mr. Johnston's mother and my own Scottish mother were brought up: "Whither thou goest, I will go; and where thou lodgest, I will lodge: thy people shall be my people, and thy God my God." ' Then he added very quietly: 'Even to the end.'

I was surprised to find the P.M. in tears. He knew what it meant. Even to us the words seemed like a rope thrown to a drowning man.

*

There is no other entry in my diary until December, 1941. There is nothing about the great events which happened during those months, when England stood alone and the Prime Minister touched the peak of his achievement. He did not talk to me about them, though I visited him regularly. When I entered his room, he would put down his papers reluctantly. 'Cannot you see,' he seemed to say, 'that I am very busy and want to get on with my work?' He was fit

---

[1] The naval base in the Orkney islands used by the Home Fleet in both world wars.

[2] Tom Johnston, Secretary of State for Scotland, 1941–5.

[3] Harry Hopkins, President Roosevelt's closest adviser and confidant.

and well and did not need me. He grudged every second that was taken from his work. My visits became shorter and shorter—a few perfunctory questions and I was out of his room.

*

December 12, 1941

Mr. Churchill has been panting to meet the President ever since he heard of Pearl Harbour,[1] so today we are bound for Washington. This morning, about noon, he pulled himself out of a launch and was piped aboard the *Duke of York* as she lay at anchor at Greenock; his feeling for a naval occasion had been partly met by a yachting cap over a double-breasted blue reefer coat. I gave him time to be received on the quarter-deck before I followed, and sensed at once the ordered peace of a great battleship.

December 20, 1941

Since we left the protection of the Clyde, we have been battened down for eight days, listening to the dull pounding of the great seas on the ship's ribs. Everyone here takes whatever comes as it comes, save Lord Beaverbrook,[2] whose undisciplined spirit chafes at the confinement. He hates the hours we spend round the table when lunching or dining. The P.M. does the talking, of course, and Max does his best to listen. It is not easy for him; his life has not prepared him for this sort of thing. The people he gathers round him at Cherkley are not interested in books; their conversation is earthy and full of the frailty of man. Max never seems to tire of the shabby drama of some men's lives, their infidelities and their passions: that is what he means by good talk. Winston, on the other hand, speaks as he writes. There are brilliant descriptive passages that fall on Max's ears as prosy stuff, interminably long-winded; he often wonders if it will ever come to an end. Besides, Max does not like playing second fiddle to anyone. At Cherkley he is king.

Winston for his part is too much taken up with his own thoughts to notice Max's fretting. If Max is particularly argumentative—well, what of that? It is just Max's way. Moreover, the astute little man is at pains to hide his feelings. If he is restless as he endures this tribulation, at any rate he keeps a close guard on his tongue when the P.M. is present. He knows—no one better—that Winston is his only friend in politics, and he intends to keep that friend, even if it

[1] On December 7, 1941, Japanese aircraft, launched from aircraft-carriers, attacked Pearl Harbour, the headquarters of the American Pacific Fleet, in the Hawaiian islands. This act of pure aggression brought the United States into the war.   [2] Max Beaverbrook, then Minister of Supply.

means playing the part of patient listener, a role for which he is not equipped by nature. You can see his grey face, devoid of colour, sourly surveying his plate for a long time. Suddenly the P.M. will pause in the monologue:

'What do you say, Max? Don't you agree?'

'Oh, yaas,' Max hurriedly chimes in.

Chimes is, of course, the least appropriate verb I could have hit upon. It is rather as if he were trying to spit out something which has an unpleasant taste.

The P.M. is not affected, as Max is, by being sealed below decks. Tonight he embarked on a long *post-mortem* on Dakar.[1] When he had done, someone asked how, just before Dakar, the Vichy ships from Toulon had succeeded in passing through the Straits of Gibraltar under the nose of our Navy. It was, the P.M. said, because three things had gone wrong; that all three should happen together was an extraordinary coincidence. First, a warning message came to the Foreign Office, but it came during a raid and the deciphering people had retired to their dug-out. On their return after the 'All Clear' they dealt with priority stuff, and this message was not marked 'priority.' Secondly, an officer at the Admiralty with whom rested the decision whether to wake the First Lord or not did not do so, and action which could have been taken at 2 a.m. was not taken until 11 a.m.

Max pushed back his chair and stretched out his legs; his whole aspect gave an impression of a spent runner. 'Thirdly,' Winston went on, 'the man in command at Gibraltar did nothing.'

Max pulled himself together.

'And the Prime Minister,' he said in a loud voice, 'accepted blame and criticism for all this himself and blamed no one.'

The Prime Minister required no encouragement to continue. He began to talk about Stalin and his demand for Lithuania. Winston would never be a party to countries being given over to Communism. This was not entirely new to his audience, and they settled down to hear more. Harriman,[2] however, intervened. At this juncture, Max permitted himself a noisy yawn. Harriman paused. It was fatal. He had lost his chance. 'De Gaulle,' the P.M. broke in, 'has perhaps done his best, but it amounts to very little.'

Poor Max! After all, their styles of conversation have a good deal

---

[1] The French naval base on the coast of Senegal in French West Africa. In September Free French forces, led by General de Gaulle and supported by the Royal Navy, attempted a landing at Dakar in an effort to secure the base against the Axis. The attempt failed, and Churchill was severely criticized by the Press for having been easily persuaded by de Gaulle to back the expedition.

[2] Averill Harriman, Roosevelt's special representative in the United Kingdom.

in common. Both of them mean the same thing by the word 'conversation.' They bat, and the other fellows field. Max is very sensitive to his audience: he talks to impress them; pretty women put him on his mettle, but they are not expected to contribute to the talk. Winston talks to amuse himself; he has no thought of impressing anybody. He requires no help, least of all from women. His subjects come from the past; some are set pieces, such as the Boer War or the charge of the 21st Lancers at Omdurman.

Max is only concerned with the bare drama of events. He is a miser about words. But Winston feasts on the sound of his adjectives; he likes to use four or five words all with the same meaning, as an old man shows you his orchids; not to show them off, but just because he loves them. The people in his stories do not come to life; they are interred in a great sepulchre of words. His incidents soon lose their sharp edges; they do not linger in the memory. So it happens that his audience, tired by the long day, only wait for the chance to slip off to bed, leaving Winston still talking to those who have hesitated to get up and go.

To say that the P.M. does not seem any the worse for wear from the tedious days below deck is an understatement. He is a different man since America came into the war. The Winston I knew in London frightened me. I used to watch him as he went to his room with swift paces, the head thrust forward, scowling at the ground, the sombre countenance clouded, the features set and resolute, the jowl clamped down as if he had something between his teeth and did not mean to let go. I could see that he was carrying the weight of the world, and wondered how long he could go on like that and what could be done about it. And now—in a night, it seems—a younger man has taken his place. All day he keeps to his cabin, dictating for the President a memorandum on the conduct of the war. But the tired, dull look has gone from his eye; his face lights up as you enter the cabin. A month ago, if you had broken in on his work, he would have bitten off your head. And at night he is gay and voluble, sometimes even playful.

The P.M., I suppose, must have known that if America stayed out there could only be one ending to this business. And now suddenly the war is as good as won and England is safe; to be Prime Minister of England in a great war, to be able to direct the Cabinet, the Army, the Navy, the Air Force, the House of Commons, England herself, is beyond even his dreams. He loves every minute of it.

But there are moments when the old craving for adventure stirs in him. It is not at all his idea of war to see it through in the security of Whitehall; he wants to see for himself what is happening at the

Front. It is not unreasonable, he will pout, to want to go into things there. Whereas for Max there is no comfort in a sniff of danger. If he makes himself fly the Atlantic, he fears for his life, although, he says, he prefers 'one night of terror' to 'a week of boredom' in a ship. When there is nothing else to worry about, he will imagine he has some new disease that is bound to kill him in the end. For years he has kept a book in which he enters with meticulous accuracy every fluctuation in his health.

The P.M. knows, of course, that there will be stupid people who will say that he ought to stay in London at the centre of things, but he scarcely gives them a thought. His plan is simple. First, he decides what he would like to do, and then he experiences no difficulty in finding good reasons for doing it.

Besides, this trip requires no excuse. When Winston told me this he got so excited that he began to lisp:

'We were at dinner at Chequers on Sunday when I lifted the lid of the pocket wireless which Harriman gave me. The nine o'clock news had started. At the end there was something about the Japanese attacking American shipping. It wasn't very clear, and I didn't realize what had happened when Sawyers [1] came into the room. He said: "It's quite true. We heard it ourselves outside. The Japs have attacked the Americans." '

Since that moment it has never been out of his mind that America's entry into the war might mean a change in her strategy:

'They may concentrate upon Japan and leave us to deal with Germany. They have already stopped the stream of supplies that we were getting.'

Washington, December 22, 1941

After nine days' racket I cannot get the sound of the great seas out of my head. Before we anchored in Chesapeake Bay the P.M. was talking about steaming up the Potomac to Washington. Now he was like a child in his impatience to meet the President. He spoke as if every minute counted. It was absurd to waste time; he must fly. Portal,[2] Harriman, Max and I came with him. The rest of the party followed by train.

Our Lockheed was over the lights of Washington in three-quarters of an hour. It gave me a sense of security; we were a long way from the war and the London black-out. On landing I let the P.M. have a start before I got out. Looking around, I noticed a man propped against a big car, a little way off. The P.M. called me and

---

[1] Churchill's valet.   [2] Air Marshal Portal, Chief of Air Staff.

introduced me. It was President Roosevelt. Even in the half-light
I was struck by the size of his head. I suppose that is why Winston
thinks of him as majestic and statuesque, for he has no legs to speak
of since his paralysis. He said warmly that he was very glad to welcome me. I was a doctor, and he immediately began to speak of
the casualties at Pearl Harbour, many of them with very bad burns.
He made me feel that I had known him for a long time. Halifax
took me in his car to the Mayflower Hotel, while Max went with
the P.M. to the White House.

It was nearly midnight and I had gone to my room when a page
brought a message from the P.M. to say that he wanted to see me at
the White House. I went in one of the President's cars, but when we
arrived at the gate the guards ran out from the lodge and flashed
their torches on the driver's pass. They looked at me doubtfully
before they allowed the car to enter the grounds. A black servant
opened the door with a friendly smile.

I was taken up some stairs to the P.M.'s bedroom, which I found
deserted. It smelt of cigar smoke and I tried to open the window.
The crumpled bed-clothes were thrown back, and the floor was
strewn with newspapers, English and American, just as the P.M.
had thrown them away when he had glanced at the headlines; it
would have been the first thing he would have done when they took
him to his room, for he always wants to know what the papers are
saying about him. I had plenty of time to catch up with the news,
for it was an hour and a half before the P.M. came out of the
President's room. He looked at me blankly; he had forgotten that
he had sent for me.

'I am sorry I have kept you waiting.'

'Is there anything wrong?' I asked.

'The pulse is regular,' he said with a whimsical smile.

He wanted to know if he could take a sleeping pill. He must
have a good night. No; there was nothing else he needed. Already
his thoughts were back in the President's room. When I left him
I said he could take two reds,[1] for I could see he was bottling up his
excitement. Max took me down in the lift.

'I have never seen that fellow in better form. He conducted the
conversation for two hours with great skill.'

Max, too, was agog; he lives on his nerves. The P.M. had been
able to interest the President in a landing in North Africa. Indeed,
according to Max, the President was very forthcoming; he said he
would like to send three American divisions to Ulster. That had
gone down well.

[1] Barbiturate sleeping pills.

December 23, 1941

I told the P.M. what Max had said. Winston was full of Pearl Harbour.

'Well,' he said, 'when heads of states become gangsters, something has got to be done.'

December 24, 1941

This evening, as the light began to fail, 30,000 people gathered round a Christmas tree in the grounds of the White House. They sang hymns; then there was a sermon, and then speeches by the P.M. and the President. Winston spoke with emotion:

'Let the children have their night of fun and laughter. Let the gifts of Father Christmas delight their play. Let us grown-ups share to the full in their unstinted pleasures before we turn again to the stern task and the formidable years that lie before us, resolved that, by our sacrifice and daring, these same children shall not be robbed of their inheritance or denied their right to live in a free and decent world. And so, in God's mercy, a happy Christmas to you all.'

When the P.M. came in from the balcony he told me that he had had palpitations during the ceremony; he made me take his pulse.

'What is it, Charles?'

'Oh, it's all right.'

'But what is it?' he persisted.

'A hundred and five.'

He was a little taken aback.

'It has all been very moving,' he lisped with excitement. 'This is a new war, with Russia victorious, Japan in, and America in up to the neck.'

Afterwards Harry Hopkins, who is living in the White House, took me to his bedroom. His lips are blanched as if he had been bleeding internally, his skin yellow like stretched parchment and his eyelids contracted to a slit so that you can just see his eyes moving about restlessly, as if he was in pain. He looks like a Methodist minister, but he brought me whisky and oysters, with which I was toying diplomatically when Mrs. Roosevelt burst in with a lot of parcels. We talked about the ceremony, and Harry was full of praise for the P.M.'s speech. I saw Winston later and told him that Harry had said it was interesting to hear two great orators with such different methods.

'I don't know about oratory,' the P.M. retorted, 'but I do know what is in people's minds and how to speak to them.'

Does he know what is in people's minds? Though he may have

learnt by long experience the feel of an audience, he knows nothing of their lives, their hopes and aspirations. When he speaks it is to express his ideas; he says a piece. In England, outside the House of Commons, all audiences are much the same to him; they differ only in size. Whereas Roosevelt, if Hopkins is right, when he is preparing a speech, wastes little time in turning phrases; he tries to say what is in his mind in the shortest and simplest words. All the time he gives to that particular speech is spent in working out what each individual in his audience will think about it: he always thinks of individuals, never of a crowd. His whole purpose in speaking is to try to bring them over to his point of view.

Since 1940 we do not think of the P.M. as handicapped by living apart from the people. His countrymen have come to feel that he is saying what they would like to say for themselves if they knew how. He still says a piece, but for perhaps the first time in his life he seems to see things through the eyes of the average man. He still says what he is feeling at the moment, but now it turns out that he is speaking for the nation.

December 25, 1941

The President took the P.M. to church this morning.

'It is good for Winston,' he said, 'to sing hymns with the Methodies.'

Winston thought so too.

'I am glad I went,' he said to me. 'It's the first time my mind has been at rest for a long time. Besides, I like singing hymns.'

The P.M. is going to Ottawa in a few days, and he wants me to go with him:

'Of course, Charles, I am not afraid of being ill, but I must keep fit for my job.'

He made a little affectionate gesture. He is full of the address which he is to make to Congress tomorrow. He showed me a quotation from the 112th Psalm, which the aged Lord Selborne had sent him:

'He shall not be afraid of evil tidings: his heart is fixed, trusting in the Lord.'

He likes the words and is going to use them. I was reading the psalm when he said:

'Come along, Charles. We will go to the President.'

He led the way to a small room, where the President was making cocktails for his English visitors, the three Chiefs of Staff, Martin[1]

[1] John Martin, Principal Private Secretary to Churchill.

and myself. The P.M. took the Bible from me and read his quotation to the President, who liked it. Then at eight o'clock we went down to a room where there was a plan for the dinner table. It was a family party, all members of one of the two branches of the Roosevelt family, but there must have been forty or fifty names on the plan. Everybody stood in a circle and Mrs. Roosevelt went round and shook hands. We then went in to dinner. The President said there would be no speeches, but he just wanted to remind us that the King and Queen had dined there two and a half years ago, and this had been a beginning of the coming together of the two English-speaking races, which would go on after the war. He then proposed the health of Sir John Dill,[1] whose birthday it was, and 'absent relatives.' When dinner was over we saw a film, a history of the war up to the present time.

The P.M. was silent and preoccupied. Perhaps he was turning over in his mind tomorrow's speech to Congress. It was a tremendous occasion, he told me; he could remember nothing quite like it in his time. The two democracies were to be joined together and he had been chosen to give out the banns. In what mood, he wondered, would he find the Senate? He knew, of course, that some of the senators were not at all friendly to the British. Would they perhaps show it? This morning he decided that what he was going to say to them was all wrong. At any rate, he had to finish his speech before he went to bed. He yawned wearily. He would be glad when it was all over. It must be getting late. He got up and asked the President to excuse him. 'I must prepare for tomorrow,' he said. It would take him, he thought, until about two o'clock. Smiling vaguely at the company, he withdrew.

When he had gone, we resumed our seats, and sheets of music were given to each of us. Then a fellow in a uniform like a bandmaster's came in and conducted while we sang carols, beginning with 'O Come, All Ye Faithful.' At the end they wheeled away the President in his chair after he had waved 'Good night' to us. He had been like a schoolboy, jolly and carefree. It was difficult to believe that this was the man who was taking his nation into a vast conflict in which, until Pearl Harbour a few days ago, she had no thought of being engaged.

December 26, 1941

After breakfast I went to the White House to pay my daily visit to the P.M. Martin said he was buried in his speech, so I did not

---

[1] Sir John Dill, Head of British Joint Staff Mission to Washington.

SIR CHARLES WILSON
(Lord Moran)

LORD BEAVERBROOK

ask to see him. He went on working at it until they told him he
would be late for Congress. Then we set off from the back entrance
of the White House, dashing through the streets with the siren
wailing and two G-men on each of the running boards, their pockets
bulging with revolvers, ready to jump off in a second if anything
happened. A few people lining the streets waved and cheered,
though without fervour. At the Capitol I was about to walk up the
stairs when the P.M. caught sight of me and called me into the lift.
He took me with him to a small room to wait for his call. There he
sat arranging his thoughts as he gazed at the floor. Once he got up
and paced rapidly up and down the room, mumbling to himself; then
he stopped, and, looking down at me, he said, with his eyes popping:

'Do you realize we are making history?'

They came for him and I slipped into my seat. The P.M. began
effectively and at once got on terms with his audience:

'I cannot help reflecting that if my father had been American and
my mother British, instead of the other way round, I might have got
here on my own.'

When the laughter was dying down, it would break out again,
and this, coming right at the beginning, convinced him that he had
got a grip on things. There was great cheering when he mentioned
China and a loud shout when, speaking of the Japanese, he said with
passion:

'What sort of people do they think we are?'

At this, Congress rose as one man and stood cheering as if they
would never stop. They think of Japan just as we think of Germany.
But when the P.M. said: 'If we had kept together after the last war,
if we had taken common measures for our safety, this renewal of the
curse need never have fallen upon us,' there was less applause, and
when he went on: 'Five or six years ago it would have been easy,
without shedding a drop of blood, for the United States and Great
Britain to have insisted on fulfilment of the disarmament clauses of
the treaties which Germany signed after the Great War,' Congress
listened in silence. Nor did he seem to touch his hearers when he
vituperated Hitler and Mussolini, any more than people at home
like this side of his oratory. Nevertheless, taken as a whole, it was
Winston at his best.

There was a great scene at the end. The Senators and Congressmen stood cheering and waving their papers till he went out.

I met him in the small room where he had awaited the summons
to address the American people. He was sweating freely, but he said
it was a great weight off his chest. He laughed with one of the
Senators, almost noisily, so that people looked round.

On my return to the White House I found him pacing up and down the garden. He said he had been doubtful about his speech overnight; he had not liked it. When he awoke he thought it was all right, but before he got up he was sure it would be just right.

'I hit the target all the time,' he said.

'Yes; but they listened in silence when you said, "If we had acted together after the last war . . ." I don't think they would have taken that at all, even a few months ago.'

He went on to express concern that he never met anyone but the President. He ought, he said, to see some of the other members of the Administration. Men like Cordell Hull,[1] he realized, resent everything being done at the White House, behind closed doors, between the President and the P.M., without so much as a word to them. He was afraid that when he left they would do their best to undo what he had done. He is thinking about giving a dinner at the Embassy to these people when he returns from Ottawa.

December 27, 1941

The P.M. seems so preoccupied with his mission of good fellowship to America in general and to the President in particular that I decided not to bother him by calling this morning. When I got back to the hotel at ten o'clock, after a stroll through the streets, I found an urgent message. I was wanted at the White House. Would I go at once. I took a taxi.

'I am glad you have come,' the P.M. began.

He was in bed and looked worried.

'It was hot last night and I got up to open the window. It was very stiff. I had to use considerable force and I noticed all at once that I was short of breath. I had a dull pain over my heart. It went down my left arm. It didn't last very long, but it has never happened before. What is it? Is my heart all right? I thought of sending for you, but it passed off.'

There was not much to be found when I examined his heart. Indeed, the time I spent listening to his chest was given to some quick thinking. I knew that when I took the stethoscope out of my ears he would ask me pointed questions, and I had no doubt that whether the electro-cardiograph showed evidence of a coronary thrombosis or not, his symptoms were those of coronary insufficiency. The textbook treatment for this is at least six weeks in bed. That would mean publishing to the world—and the American newspapers would see to this—that the P.M. was an invalid with a crippled heart and a doubtful future. And this at a moment when America has just

[1] Cordell Hull, Secretary of State in President Roosevelt's Administration.

come into the war, and there is no one but Winston to take her by the hand. I felt that the effect of announcing that the P.M. had had a heart attack could only be disastrous. I knew, too, the consequences to one of his imaginative temperament of the feeling that his heart was affected. His work would suffer. On the other hand, if I did nothing and he had another and severer attack—perhaps a fatal seizure—the world would undoubtedly say that I had killed him through not insisting on rest. These thoughts went racing through my head while I was listening to his heart. I took my stethoscope out of my ears. Then I replaced it and listened again. Right or wrong, it seemed plain that I must sit tight on what had happened, whatever the consequences.

'Well,' he asked, looking full at me, 'is my heart all right?'

'There is nothing serious,' I answered. 'You have been overdoing things.'

'Now, Charles, you're not going to tell me to rest. I can't. I won't. Nobody else can do this job. I must. What actually happened when I opened the window?' he demanded. 'My idea is that I strained one of my chest muscles. I used great force. I don't believe it was my heart at all.'

He waited for me to answer.

'Your circulation was a bit sluggish. It is nothing serious. You needn't rest in the sense of lying up, but you mustn't do more than you can help in the way of exertion for a little while.'

There was a knock at the door. It was Harry Hopkins. I slipped away. I went and sat in a corner of the secretaries' room, picking up a newspaper, so that they would not talk to me. I began to think things out more deliberately. I did not like it, but I determined to tell no one. When we get back to England, I shall take him to Parkinson, who will hold his tongue.

December 28, 1941

When Max heard the P.M. speak against Marshall's[1] proposal of one supreme commander of the Allied forces, he began to concoct one of those little schemes in which he is an adept. He went to Harry Hopkins and they arranged a meeting between Marshall and the Prime Minister. This took place today, and Winston was soon won over by Marshall's arguments. Two days ago the P.M. was sure that the plan was neither workable nor desirable. Now his doubts are dispelled; it has become plain to him that it is a trump card.

I wish Winston would be more sensible about things. The pace here is prodigious. Usually when he has an important speech on

[1] General George Marshall, Chief of Staff of the U.S. Army.

17

the stocks he lives with it for forty-eight hours. During that time he is on edge, his temper is short and he is best left to himself. But these historic pronouncements to Congress and to the Parliament at Ottawa have to be ground out in odd moments when he is not needed in conference and when he is not closeted with the President. Sometimes the night is nearly over before he goes to bed. It is true that he seems to revel in every moment of the long day, but little things, straws in the wind, warn me that a price must be paid for flouting Nature. I dread Ottawa.

We left the White House this evening by the back entrance. The President and Harry Hopkins came to the door to see us off. The P.M. asked me to drive with him in his car to the station. As we drove out of the grounds he opened the window of the car. He was short of breath.

'There seems no air,' he said, 'in this car. Is it a stuffy night, Charles?'

And then he put his hand on my knee.

'It is a great comfort to have you with me,' he said.

He has used these words twice in four days; the first time was before the heart attack. This is something new; it has not happened before.

December 29, 1941

On our arrival at Ottawa, the big fur-hatted Canadian Mounted Police kept back with difficulty the vast, enthusiastic crowds which pushed good-humouredly towards the P.M. and soon enveloped him. The atmosphere of Ottawa after Washington is like Belfast after Dublin. We drove to Government House through streets banked with snow. After a hot bath, Winston seemed his usual self, and we lunched with the Canadian Cabinet, a ceremony that lasted for two hours. There was still dinner at Government House to be got through, and then a reception. However, so far nothing untoward has happened. Whenever we are alone, he keeps asking me to take his pulse. I get out of it somehow, but once, when I found him lifting something heavy, I did expostulate. At this he broke out:

'Now, Charles, you are making me heart-minded. I shall soon think of nothing else. I couldn't do my work if I kept thinking of my heart.'

The next time he asked me to take his pulse I refused point-blank.

'You're all right. Forget your damned heart.'

He won't get through his speech tomorrow if this goes on.

December 31, 1941

Winston's speech, particularly his attack on Vichy, roused the Canadians, though it was not up to the Washington standard. At one point he talked in his variation of the French tongue. And then he told them how he had warned the French Government that Britain would fight on alone whatever France did, and how Weygand had gone to the French Cabinet and said:

'In three weeks England will have her neck wrung like a chicken.'

The P.M. paused.

'Some chicken. Some neck!' He spat out his contempt.

Gust after gust of delighted laughter ended in applause, which went on for a long time.

At night we dined with Mackenzie King.[1] I got there early. He had been my patient in London, and did not hesitate to speak his mind. I found him restive about the P.M. He said that there were many men winning the war and confessed that he was 'rather put off by a strain of violence in the Prime Minister.' I argued that it is no more than a certain lack of restraint, but it was plain that this was no passing mood.

Wilson[2]: 'You have known Winston for a long time?'

Mackenzie King: 'Yes; I have. I first met him when he was going round Canada on a lecture tour.'

Wilson: 'That can't have been long after the Boer War.'

Mackenzie King: 'No. I found him at his hotel drinking champagne at eleven o'clock in the morning.'

'The great thing in politics,' said our host later, 'is to avoid mistakes.' I could almost see the P.M. sniffing as Mackenzie King, looking at us through his pince-nez, which were tethered to a button-hole by a long black ribbon, made this pronouncement. King had never been a man to take risks, and this prudent outlook no doubt accounts for some lack of fervour on the P.M.'s part. The two men are, of course, quite friendly, but the P.M. is not really interested in Mackenzie King. He takes him for granted.

I cannot help noticing Winston's indifference to him after the wooing of the President at the White House. There the P.M. and the President seemed to talk for most of the day, and for the first time I have seen Winston content to listen. You could almost feel the importance he attaches to bringing the President along with him, and in that good cause he has become a very model of restraint and self-discipline; it is surely a new Winston who is sitting there

[1] Mackenzie King, Prime Minister of Canada.
[2] Sir Charles Wilson became Lord Moran in 1943.

quite silent. And when he does say anything it is always something likely to fall pleasantly on the President's ear. But here, in Ottawa, he does not seem to bother.

We go back to Washington tomorrow.

January 1, 1942

I sometimes wonder if the P.M. feels the full weight of the decisions he has to make. I have not been present at the meetings, but I cannot help being there in spirit. It is as if Winston has a family of twelve children and there is not enough food for all of them—some of them must starve to death. He has to decide which.

But these decisions are at least taken when everyone who counts is here in Washington. The Americans are worried about what will happen after we disperse. It was to decide this that the P.M. came to Washington: he wanted to show the President how to run the war. It has not worked out quite like that. On the 29th, the day after we left Washington for Ottawa, the Chiefs of Staff of both countries met. The discussion was heated until they at last decided that there should be two committees, one in London, the other in Washington. There was no hope of agreement on any other basis. But this did not suit the President. He wanted one committee in Washington, and after what Hopkins calls 'a hell of a row' he got what he wanted.

It is, of course, an unequal contest. Our Chiefs of Staff miss Brooke,[1] whom we had left in London picking up the threads. The peace-loving Dill is no substitute. What he lacks is the he-man stuff. That is why he is no longer C.I.G.S. And Winston is only half-hearted in their support; he is just now possessed with one idea to the exclusion of all others. He feels he must bring the President into the war with his heart set on victory. If that can be done, nothing else matters. Nor is Max very helpful. He has not much use for our sailors and soldiers, and likes showing off to the Americans his influence with the P.M. But after all Marshall remains the key to the situation. The P.M. has a feeling that in his quiet, unprovocative way he means business, and that if we are too obstinate he might take a strong line. And neither the P.M. nor the President can contemplate going forward without Marshall.

Florida, January 5, 1942

The P.M. decided to come here because he did not want to tax the hospitality of the President, who likes to get away over the week-

[1] General Sir Alan Brooke became Chief of the Imperial General Staff late in 1941.

end to Hyde Park.[1] It was a thoughtful move to give the White House a respite, and we are seeing Winston in a new role.

General Marshall brought us in his own plane from Washington to Florida. The air here is balmy after the bitter cold of Ottawa—oranges and pineapples grow here. And the blue ocean is so warm that Winston basks half-submerged in the water like a hippopotamus in a swamp.

Florida, January 9, 1942

The P.M. was on his best behaviour in Washington. Now he is suffering from a sharp reaction. He does not like making important decisions, especially when he finds himself lined up with the Americans against his own Chiefs of Staff, and the strain mounts when they are interspersed by important pronouncements that will be read, sentence by sentence, over the world. Nor has he yet forgotten what he calls his 'pump,' though he has given up feeling his pulse. At any rate, he has had plenty of time here to work off steam.

Nothing seems to be right. Perhaps it is the close atmosphere; anyway, the P.M. is in a belligerent mood. He told us that he had sent a stiff telegram to Curtin, the Prime Minister of Australia. The situation in Malaya was making Australia jumpy about invasion. Curtin was not satisfied with the air position. He had renewed his representations to London in blunt terms. The P.M. fulminated in his reply. London had not made a fuss when it was bombed. Why should Australia? At one moment he took the line that Curtin and his Government did not represent the people of Australia. At another that the Australians came of bad stock. He was impatient with people who had nothing better to do than to criticize him.

The significance of this outburst was not lost on me. I did not worry about the Australians. I knew that he had been persuaded to tone down the cable before it was sent. Besides, he liked them as men and respected them as fighting soldiers. But this was a bulletin, signed by himself, which said more plainly than bulletins usually do what it meant: that this particular patient needed rest. He was just hitting out blindly, like a child in a temper. But I knew that he had not the slightest intention of taking his doctor's advice.

The P.M. was still glowering at his plate. He had not yet come to the end of his grievances. It had been suggested to him that the Archbishop of York [2] should be the new Archbishop of Canterbury; yet he, the Archbishop, went about talking of Christian revolution

---

[1] Birthplace and family home of President Roosevelt, a small town on the east side of the Hudson River, some eighty miles north of New York.

[2] Archbishop Temple.

and stuff of that kind. Winston sniffed; he would take his time about the appointment.

The news from London did not help matters. The *Queen Elizabeth* and the *Valiant* had been put out of action, and we had lost command of the Mediterranean. To get him in a sunnier mood, I asked him about Hess, whereupon the P.M., throwing off his ill humour, launched out into a description of Hess's motives.[1]

Someone asked the P.M. whether the Philippines would have to surrender. He smiled.

'That depends on the strength of the forces defending and of the forces attacking.'

Attempts to pump the P.M. never get anywhere: if he is going to be indiscreet, he does not want anyone's help.

Lunch with Madame Balsan.[2] When we left, Winston mused a little, and then said half to himself: 'Wealth, taste and leisure can do these things, but they do not bring happiness.'

Tomorrow we go back to Washington.

January 14, 1942

The Americans have got their way and the war will be run from Washington, but they will not be wise to push us so unceremoniously in the future. Our people are very unhappy about the decision, and the most they will agree to is to try it out for a month. They were, however, brought back to good humour by the final figures of the production estimates. Harry gave me some figures which meant something even to me: 100,000 aircraft in 1943 for 45,000 in 1942, and 75,000 tanks in 1943 for 45,000 in 1942. The P.M. gives Max most of the credit; Harry hands it to the President. I would bracket them together: to set a seemingly impossible target requires a particular cast of mind, and they have both got that kind of mind. I think Winston, more than anyone here, visualizes in detail what this programme means to the actual conduct of the war. He is drunk with the figures.

January 15, 1942

To Bermuda this morning by air. I was strolling in the garden of Government House when I learnt that there was a conference going on indoors to decide whether we should return by air or by the ship. At that moment the P.M. came up to me and, putting his arm through mine, said:

[1] Rudolph Hess, deputy to Hitler, flew alone from Augsburg and landed in Scotland on May 10, 1941. He was treated as a prisoner of war. When he was freed after the war, Lord Moran was sent by Mr. Attlee to Nuremberg to report on Hess's sanity.

[2] Former Duchess of Marlborough, later married to M. Jacques Balsan.

'We are returning by air. They are fixing up the details now. But we cannot all go in the flying-boat. I am sure, Charles, you won't mind returning in the ship.'

I was completely taken by surprise, but as he spoke I knew I must not give way. There flashed through my mind the mishap at the White House when he tried to open the bedroom window. I had kept this to myself, and if I let him go alone and anything happened to him in the air I alone was responsible. It would be my doing. Apart from this, my own position would become impossible. I had been the target of a good deal of criticism because I had come on this journey while President of the College.[1] I had always met this criticism by arguing that looking after the Prime Minister's health was even more important than doing my job as President. But if he should cross the Atlantic alone, and I follow by sea a week or so later, what would become of my argument? I disengaged my arm and made for the house. I heard the P.M. say something soothingly, but I took no notice. I found the Chiefs of Staff in a room in conference. I broke into their discussion without ceremony. 'I believe,' I said, 'it has been decided to return by air, and that it is suggested the Prime Minister fly and I come by sea.' I made it plain that I could not agree. And with that I withdrew. I hated to be so abrupt, but I could not go into a long rigmarole with these people.

January 16, 1942

We left Bermuda today in a flying-boat, R.M.A. *Berwick*. In mid-Atlantic they brought the P.M. a bulletin. He read it and, leaning towards me, put his hand on my knee.

'Do you realize we are fifteen hundred miles from anywhere?'

'Heaven is as near by sea as by land,' I reminded him.

'Who said that?' he asked.

'I think it was Sir Humphrey Gilbert.'

He looked at the bulletin again. We have still nine hours to go, but we have enough fuel for fifteen.

*

I learnt afterwards that we were fortunate that night. We lost our way and turned north only just in time to avoid the German batteries outside Brest. In another five minutes we should have been over them. Then, when we approached the English coast from Brest, we were mistaken for an enemy bomber, and fighter aircraft came out to intercept us. However, they missed us.

[1] The Royal College of Physicians.

Chapter two

Lord Beaverbrook resigns

January 17, 1942

As the train carried the Prime Minister towards London, he sat for a time with his white hands laid out on his thighs, his head poked forward, absorbed in thought. The five weeks that he had been out of the country had not been wasted, he felt; the close friendship he had established with President Roosevelt had smoothed out every difficulty.

'I have done a good job of work with the President,' he said yesterday. 'We got on together. I think we shall soon see dividends. I am sure, Charles, the House will be pleased with what I have to tell them.'

When, however, he picked up a pile of morning papers, he was pained to find that the country did not share his satisfaction. On the contrary, public opinion seemed to be baffled by the way things had gone wrong; the nation was frankly puzzled and worried. He put down the *Manchester Guardian* with an angry gesture.

'There seems to be plenty of snarling,' he said in a tired voice.

January 27, 1942

It has been an uneasy ten days since we landed, and I know the P.M. feels that, if there must be a debate in the House of Commons, it is a good thing to get it over. He told me that when he rose today he knew at once that he had a critical House.

He began by admitting that there had been many blunders. As far as military secrecy would permit, he believed in telling the House everything, for it had always been his policy to discount future calamities by describing the immediate outlook in the darkest terms. It seemed that the blacker he painted the picture, the more their hearts went out to this courageous man. He, at any rate, told them the truth: they had not forgotten Baldwin.[1] The P.M. some-

[1] Stanley Baldwin, Prime Minister, 1923–4, 1924–9, 1935–7.

how made them feel that they were partners in that heroic struggle, though taking, himself, the fullest personal responsibility for whatever went wrong:

'If we have handled our resources wrongly, no one is so much to blame as I.'

Besides, his main theme struck the House as reasonable. Caught unprepared, we had only just managed to keep our heads above water. We could not be armed everywhere:

'If we had started to scatter our forces over these immense areas in the Far East we should have been ruined.'

The House was silent, but reconciled to the hard truth of the Prime Minister's argument. He told me that he felt they were with him as he drew towards the end: he had spoken for nearly two hours:

'Although I feel the broadening swell of victory and liberation bearing us and all the tortured peoples onwards safely to the final goal, I must confess to feeling the weight of the war upon me even more than in the tremendous summer days of 1940.'

January 29, 1942

As the P.M. prepared for bed tonight, his feeling of relief at the rout of his critics was expressed rather more freely:

'H—— is a silly bastard. There are about half a dozen of them; they make a noise out of all proportion to their importance. The House knows this, but unfortunately people abroad take them too seriously; they do a lot of harm. You know how they voted? Four hundred and sixty-four to one.'

His voice rose as if he would like to annihilate his detractors. The wind fell as quickly as it had risen. After all, the majority was only what he had expected.

January 30, 1942

This morning there was a message from the President, whose birthday it is, which gave the P.M. great pleasure. 'It is fun,' it said, 'to be in the same decade with you.'

*

It would appear from my diary that the Prime Minister's Parliamentary triumph was only a momentary gleam in a dark winter. February in particular dealt him some hard blows. Something more than a vote of confidence was required to put the Government on its feet. The country needed a tonic, and the only tonic that would do any lasting good was a resounding victory. What the country got was the disaster of Singapore.[1] Political tension grew, and with it a demand for a strengthening of the Government.

My diary records:

'The P.M. hates being told what to do, though he knows that he will have to bow to the storm. But if he must change his Ministers, he is determined that he will do it in his own way. I think, from what I hear, that he has decided to make a change that has long been in his mind. He wants Lord Beaverbrook to organize production. Nothing "that dynamic little man" does—and he is pretty erratic at times—can shake the P.M.'s faith in his genius.'

The political figures with whom Winston Churchill had grown up in politics, John Morley, Arthur Balfour, Asquith and Lord Rosebery, were all dead; Max was almost the last of those who had lived with him through the shocks and strains of the First World War, when the members of his present Cabinet were quite unknown. It comforted the P.M. to talk to Max and to compare their troubles with those they had had to overcome in the First World War. It had long been in his mind to combine the Ministries of Aircraft Production and of Supply in one Ministry of War Production. Max was to be the Minister; there, surely, he would have abundant scope for his genius.

The Ministers of the various departments concerned took a rather different view of the Prime Minister's proposal. They were frankly horrified by the thought of having to work under or with Lord Beaverbrook. Max was quite aware of their hostility and—this influenced him more—of his own limitations. By his own peculiar methods, he knew he could get a tremendous drive in any department that he took over. But it did not last. At every turn he seemed to upset those with whom he had to work, and though he could bluff through, he was never sure that he was right. And so, when he found that no one had any confidence in his judgment or wanted to work under him, he seemed to lose faith in himself.

How easy it would be in a vast undertaking of this kind to make a single error of judgment which might have catastrophic consequences! Beaverbrook's vivid imagination already pictured the glee of his enemies at his public exposure and downfall. A profound

---

[1] The fall of Singapore on February 15, 1942, was described by Churchill as 'the worst disaster and largest capitulation in British History.' Despite the rapid advance of the Japanese in the Malayan peninsula, it was thought that the island could hold out indefinitely. However, the defences, built in 1921, were designed only to meet an attack from the sea. The defence of the besieged island became impossible when the Japanese cut the water supply, which came from Johore on the mainland.

dejection of spirit took possession of him; his attacks of asthma grew more frequent and more severe; his distaste for office became an obsession. And yet he could not bring himself to say 'No' to the Prime Minister. On February 4 he was appointed Minister of War Production.

The fall of Singapore on February 15 stupefied the Prime Minister. He had begun to talk about Malaya when he was in Florida, and I recall how one day in the middle of January I found him in a positively spectacular temper. He had just learnt from Wavell[1] that the defences of Singapore—the work of many years—were built only to meet attacks from the sea. Many of the guns could only fire seaward. It had never entered his head, he complained, that the rear of the fortress was quite unprotected against an attack from the land.

'Why didn't they tell me about this? Oh, no; it is my own fault. I ought to have known. I could have asked. I cannot understand it. Did no one realize the position?'

There was another and more crucial question, to which the Prime Minister could find no answer. How came 100,000 men (half of them of our own race) to hold up their hands to inferior numbers of Japanese? Though his mind had been gradually prepared for its fall, the surrender of the fortress stunned him. He felt it was a disgrace. It left a scar on his mind. One evening, months later, when he was sitting in his bathroom enveloped in a towel, he stopped drying himself and gloomily surveyed the floor: 'I cannot get over Singapore,' he said sadly.

Winston's dejection over the surrender of 100,000 men was the result of one of those hunches that came to him in which he appeared to stumble on the truth before it was seen by others: he knew that the surrender of Singapore was something more than a reverse. I think he wondered if it were a portent.

It is the will to fight that counts in war. That, in some measures, was missing at Singapore. Wavell, after visiting the garrison, had reported to the Prime Minister on February 11, 1942:

'Morale of some troops is not good, and none is as high as I should like to see.'

Singapore was a symptom of a malady which broke out during the war in various places from time to time. When the chance came, I asked some of the soldiers at the top how far the infection had spread. There was a discussion about the comparative merits of the soldier in the two wars that was not reassuring. I was left to turn

[1] General Sir Archibald Wavell, Allied Supreme Commander in the Far East except the Pacific.

over in my mind the social implications to a nation of a decay in its martial spirit.

Meanwhile, things were far from well with the newly appointed Minister of War Production. Lord Beaverbrook did not give up his search for a way out of his dilemma. He was still stalling, and day after day he used all his astuteness to block any attempt by the Prime Minister to bring things to a head. At last the P.M. reached the end of his patience. He sent to Lord Beaverbrook a proof of the White Paper defining the Ministry of War Production with a note. He had given time and thought to a plan that would be agreeable to Lord Beaverbrook and to those with whom he would have to work. There followed an abrupt intimation that this was the Prime Minister's last word. The letter ended with a sad warning. If Lord Beaverbrook insisted on resigning at a time when everything was at stake, he ought to realize that it would do grave hurt to his country and to his own name.

This letter left Lord Beaverbrook no way out. There was nothing for it but to accept the Prime Minister's plans, and on February 10 the White Paper was presented to the House by the P.M. Then, in the third week of February, when everything seemed settled, Lord Beaverbrook resigned. He persisted that he was a sick man, but that was no reason why he and the Prime Minister should not part friends.

February 26, 1942.

My dear Winston,

I am leaving this Office today and going to the place I came from. And now I must tell you about twenty-one months of high adventure, the like of which has never been known.

All the time, everything that has been done by me has been due to your holding me up.

You took a great chance in putting me in, and you stood to be shot at by a section of Members for keeping me here.

It was little enough I gave you, compared with what you gave me. I owe my reputation to you. The confidence of the public really comes from you. And my courage was sustained by you. These benefits give me a right to a place in your list of lieutenants who served you when you brought salvation to our people in the hour of disaster.

In leaving, then, I send this letter of gratitude and devotion to the leader of the nation, the saviour of our people, and the symbol of resistance in the free world.

Yours affectionately,

Max.

The P.M. showed me the letter—'a very nice letter'—saying: 'I like him very much.' With a stroke of the pen, Max had won back all the lost ground. Soon after it was noticed that Lord Beaverbrook's health had taken a sharp turn for the better.

That Beaverbrook was determined to resign is plain, but the motive for his going is more open to doubt. Six days after Mr. Churchill became Prime Minister, I wrote to Lord Beaverbrook congratulating him on his appointment as Minister of Aircraft Production. He replied briefly the same day:

May 16, 1940.

Dear Wilson,

I am disappointed that you, a doctor, did not reproach me for taking this monstrous risk with my health.

Although I do not need anybody to tell me I am a fool for bending my old shoulders to this burden, I know it very well myself.

With kindest regards,
Yours sincerely,
Beaverbrook.

Only Lord Beaverbrook would embark on his stupendous task in that mood. And yet I wonder if it was as simple as this. Could it be that he was staking out a claim in advance that if he wanted to throw in his hand at any time the state of his health must be accepted as a reasonable and proper explanation for his resignation?

Nearly a year went by, and then in the spring of 1941 I find in my diary a copy of a long letter to Max,[1] bearing the date, April 18, 1941. Max said his job was finished. I said it had only begun. I told him plainly that I had made it clear to the P.M. that there was no health reason why he should not go on doing his job.

Max replied the next day. It is a strange letter.[2] To justify his resignation, he sets out his infirmities—he was quite unrepentant—but those who know him will pay more attention to a postscript in which he complains that the P.M. did not ask his advice and looked upon him as a quarrelsome fellow.

But nothing happened. Six months later, his resignation as again in the air. This time his health was not mentioned. Lord Beaverbrook said that he did not think we were helping Russia enough. Unless more vigorous steps were taken, he would have to reconsider his position. To this threat of resignation, the Prime Minister dryly replied: 'We shall all have to reconsider our position.'

However, four months later, Russia appeared to have dropped out

[1] See Appendix 1.   [2] See Appendix 1.

of the picture: in February, 1942, Beaverbrook blamed his asthma for his resignation. Woodrow Wyatt, in his book, *Distinguished for Talent*,[1] suggests another explanation:

'Singapore, to the shame of Britain, fell on the 15th February. It was the blackest hour of the war. Churchill's prestige was on the recoil and the country was turning against him.

'Beaverbrook . . . chose this exact moment to make a resignation that for once he would not withdraw. It took effect on the 19th February, four days after the fall of Singapore. He estimated that Churchill would be driven from power by a dispirited and resentful country. He thought himself the automatic next choice. . . .

'He believed the country would demand him.'

As his doctor, I had been familiar with Lord Beaverbrook's asthma for many years, and I did not accept it then as an adequate explanation of his resignation. It is true that his attacks became more frequent and more severe in times of strain, but he did not allow them to interfere with anything in which he was interested. It may be that after the fall of Singapore, as Wyatt suggests, Lord Beaverbrook caught a brief glimpse of himself as First Minister of the Crown. But there is no reason to think that this was at the back of his mind when he was on the point of resigning in the spring of 1941, and again in the autumn. Looking back, I still believe that it was his own profound mistrust of himself that haunted him in office. If he found that he was not up to his job, he must get out of it before he made some disastrous mistake.

In a sense, he was the architect of his own misfortunes. With all his astuteness, his uncanny skill in probing motives, he could never understand the mind of the average Englishman. And the average Englishman could not understand him.

When Max had disposed of himself in this fashion, I hoped the P.M. would be left in peace, but my diary in March of that year is full of imprecations on the head of Franklin Roosevelt, of all men. I was concerned with his views of India only in so far as they contributed to the burden the Prime Minister bore in the spring of 1942, for I could not help noticing that a difference of opinion with the President or Max Beaverbrook took more out of him than a major disaster in the field.

The dispute began during the visit to Washington after Pearl Harbour, when the friendly atmosphere of the White House was sharply broken one day after Roosevelt had given his views on

[1] Woodrow Wyatt, *Distinguished for Talent*, Hutchinson, 1958.

India's future. There was a violent explosion, and we had Mr. Churchill's own word that the President did not venture again to raise the subject when they met. But in his correspondence Roosevelt did not exercise the same self-denying ordinance.

The P.M. looked with pride on the story of our Indian Empire— Henry Lawrence and Clive and Dalhousie were men after his own heart—whereas the President, whose feelings went back to the American War of Independence, saw only a subject people in the grip of a conqueror, a lamentable example of British imperialism.

The issue was simple. The Prime Minister was willing to summon a Constituent Assembly and ready to grant full independence to India if the Assembly should demand it, *after the war*. But any attempt, however well meant, to solve the problem during the war would, he feared, lead to unrest and bloodshed. With the Japanese at the gates of India, he dreaded the effect on the Indian Army of opening up an issue which must divide Moslem from Hindu.

The President, however, was not convinced. He could not understand why, if we were willing to allow India to secede from the Empire after the war, we should deny self-government to them during the war. He wanted to set up a nationalist government immediately.

In the light of events, Mr. Churchill has been proved right. He was prepared to resign if he could not get his way. What the President proposed was, Winston felt, an act of madness. He did not feel that it was an issue that could be left to public opinion in the United States; it was not for them to decide, and if his colleagues had thought otherwise, the P.M. makes it plain that he would not have hesitated to lay down a personal burden 'which at times seemed more than a man could bear.'

His views about the future of India were another matter. His India was the land he knew as a subaltern. He could not conceive of an India without the British. How often on our travels did he come back in his talk to the religious massacres which he felt must happen when we left the country. He was a prophet of woe:

'I prophesy that in our lifetime the "softy" English people at home will let India in for a war in which the casualties will exceed those in the present conflict up to now.'

He was speaking not long after Pearl Harbour.

It may be that at this time the Prime Minister was suffering from a kind of rebound after the excitement and exhilaration which he had felt when America came into the war. Certainly he had expected some easing of the tension, whereas when in March he looked glumly around, he could see nothing but a deterioration of the whole position.

Perhaps, even then, something of the old crusading fire had already left him. At least he was more ready to make concessions to expediency than he had been. In Washington, in January, the Prime Minister was roused by Stalin's demand for the Baltic States. 'If that were done,' he said hotly, 'it would dishonour our cause.' As time passed his spirit became more chastened. 'Under the pressure of events, I did not feel that this moral position could be physically maintained. In a deadly struggle it is not right to assume more burdens than those who are fighting for a great cause can bear.' And he told Stalin in March that he had urged President Roosevelt to support Russia's claim to the Baltic States at the Peace Conference.

And yet these irritants, each of which could drive him into a frenzy for a short time, hardly counted when set against the persistent erosion of the submarine threat. I find this note in my diary:

'The P.M. tells me that 640,000 tons of merchant shipping have been sunk in the last two months in what he calls "American waters." I have been finding out that wherever he goes he carries in his head the monthly figures of all sinkings, though he never talks about them. He is always careful to consume his own smoke; nothing he says could discourage anyone. When I say the P.M. never talks, I am not quite accurate. There are times—this does not happen very often—when I fancy I serve as a safety-valve. Occasionally, too, I may pick up by chance a stray hint of what is going on in his head. One day when things at sea were at their worst, I happened to go to the Map-room. There I found the P.M. He was standing with his back to me, staring at the huge chart with the little black beetles representing German submarines. "Terrible," he muttered. I was about to retreat when he whipped round and brushed past me with his head down. I am not sure he saw me. He knows that we may lose the war at sea in a few months and that he can do nothing about it. I wish to God I could put out the fires that seem to be consuming him.'

Chapter three

The American bid for a
second front

It was not, however, the Battle of the Atlantic, but the invasion of France which, in the spring of 1942, was growing in the Prime Minister's mind like a canker. When the Americans came into the war after Pearl Harbour they began to plan for the day when the Allied armies would land again upon the French shore. It was General Marshall's conviction that only in that way could the war be won. Mr. Churchill was as sure that only by the premature invasion of France could the war be lost. To postpone that evil day, all his arts, all his eloquence, all his great experience were spent.

Why did Winston so much dread this particular operation? He feared the casualties. It was the carnage on the first day of the Battle of the Somme which led the P.M. to invent a monster tank of his own. He told me this before we left London for Washington:

'The War Office,' Winston began, 'is always said to be preparing for the last war. I certainly entered this war with a mentality born in the last war. I had a waterproof suit made so that I might keep dry in the communication trenches. I wanted to be prepared for those visits to the front line which,' the P.M. added with a mischievous smirk, 'I felt my position as First Lord of the Admiralty entitled me to make. What I had learned in the last war was deeply rooted in my mind—the terrible losses in an assault on a prepared position. But I still believed that the Siegfried Line facing us could be broken with the increased fire power of this war without those losses.'

'This was the way I planned to do it. In the last war the tanks went overland. In this war they would have to plough through the surface of the ground. In the next war,' Winston added with a grin, 'they will be underground. So I evolved a plan in which a tank of great length,' and here the P.M.'s eyes dilated, 'weighing sixty or seventy-five tons, ploughed a way six feet deep by six feet wide, giving the troops cover to attack through this communication trench. There were to have been eighty or ninety of these tanks,' Winston added reflectively, 'but it all came to nothing.'

The whole episode was pure Winston. On the one hand, the never-failing fertility of ideas and the astonishing capacity to impose them on others:

'It passed the Cabinet,' he said. 'It was demonstrated to Gamelin and Georges. All were impressed.'

On the other hand, the unscientific approach to a problem. The P.M. admitted that he had not followed the development of tanks between the two wars. He did not know that the tank he invented was already obsolete. de Gaulle's conception of tank warfare, outlined in his book, *La France et son Armée*, published in 1938, and adopted by the Germans in the invasion of France, was quite new to Churchill in 1940.

Winston's service with a battalion in France in the First World War had not weaned him from the great game of playing at soldiers. But it must be his kind of war. He shrank back from the bloody immobility of Continental warfare. His imagination was staggered by the thought of what might happen if things went wrong in an invasion of France or Belgium.

President Roosevelt was impressed at that time by the P.M.'s knowledge of military matters; his dread of a frontal attack on the French coast appeared reasonable. Roosevelt was a humane man, and the P.M.'s picture of the probable fate of the cross-Channel operation appalled him. However, he had complete confidence in his Chief of Staff, and Marshall was convinced that there was only one way to shorten the war—to invade France. Full of that conviction, he set out to educate the President.

Early in April, Roosevelt, with the zeal of a convert, sent Hopkins and Marshall to London to say that his heart and mind were in this plan for landing on the French coast.

Brooke and Marshall, who now met, had a good deal in common. They both came of virile stock. Brooke's ancestors, the 'Fighting Brookes,' had taken part as soldiers in the settlement of Ulster in the reign of Queen Elizabeth, while a forebear of Marshall's, an Irish Captain of Horse, fought for Charles I against Cromwell.

However, the acquisitive instinct, common enough among full-blooded men, had no part in their lives. Their one ambition was to lead armies in the field, but they would not lift a finger to bring this about. They were both selfless men with a fine contempt for the pressures of the mob.

Brooke, who had a feeling for character, decided in Washington that Marshall was 'a great gentleman and a great administrator,' while Marshall, in his own slow and rather cautious manner, came to much the same conclusion about Brooke. When, however, the two men first met in London, neither impressed the other.

To Brooke it was inexplicable that Marshall would cross the Atlantic to advocate the early invasion of France without first priming himself by a prolonged study of all the relevant factors. And yet when he asked Marshall on the eighth day of the Conference, 'Do we go west, south or east after landing?' he found that the American had not begun to think of it. As for Marshall, he decided that Brooke 'lacked Dill's brains.'

Even if Brooke was not impressed by Marshall's ability, he could not help liking him; he felt he could trust him—and that went a long way with the C.I.G.S. In truth, it was impossible not to trust Marshall the moment you looked into his plain, home-spun countenance. It was indeed an unusual face. With his long upper lip and craggy features, Marshall looked more like a painting by Dobson than a modern staff officer. He was a man of simple faith, and yet we owe it to this man of God, as we shall see, that Stalin got his own way at Teheran, with all the mournful consequences that have followed in the world. In such fashion do we see the imp of history grinning at our impotence.

Marshall was a man of strong convictions; he did not find it easy to give way. It appeared inevitable that there would be a prolonged tussle between these two obstinate men, whereas, in fact, the mission from Washington seemed to get almost at once what they wanted, and it was decided that a force of forty-eight divisions should take part in the invasion of France.

I was puzzled at the time by the manner in which the P.M. agreed with Marshall, almost, as it were, without a fight. It was not like him. I made this note in my diary:

'The P.M. is an experienced and tenacious campaigner, and he may have decided that the time has not yet come to take the field as an out-and-out opponent of a Second Front in France. Anyway, 1943 seems a long way off, and a good deal may happen in the meanwhile.'

From what the P.M. said to me then, I know that he was still fearful that the President might be driven by public clamour to concentrate on the war with Japan. It was not a time for argument. Winston put it like this: 'I had to work by influence and diplomacy in order to secure agreed and harmonious action with our cherished ally.'

Whatever may be the truth, we know that the Americans left London in great heart; they were satisfied that there was complete agreement, and that the question of a Second Front had been settled once and for all. However, if the P.M. had yielded too quickly, he soon made amends. In the first days of June he sent a cable to the President impressing on him that we must never let TORCH (the invasion of North Africa) pass from our minds, while Mountbatten was sent to Washington to explain that certain difficulties had arisen in the planning of an invasion of France.

The P.M. did not doubt that he could convince the President of the folly of such an invasion at the present time, if only he could talk with him. He determined to make such an opportunity without more delay.

Chapter four

In which the full size of the Prime Minister is seen

That was how we came to leave London for Washington on June 17, travelling comfortably in a flying-boat for twenty-eight hours before we came down on the Potomac River.

June 18, 1942

The P.M. is always a little apprehensive in the air and our 'narrow squeak' flying back from Bermuda has not helped matters. He asked me whether I minded flying. But before I could answer, I saw that he was thinking of something else. Last night, when we were making our way along the quay at Stranraer to the launch which took us to the flying-boat, I heard him humming: 'We're here because we're here.' I wondered if he was whistling to keep up his spirits. All the same, he is in good shape.[1]

Once installed in the White House, the P.M. lost not a moment in beginning his campaign. It was not an easy task which he had set himself. Those whom the President trusted, Hopkins, Marshall and the rest, were of one mind: there was only one way to shorten the war, and that was to set up a Second Front in France. No one but Winston could have hoped for a hearing in such circumstances.

June 21, 1942

Went to the White House this afternoon when the P.M. sent for me. Found him pacing his room. He turned on me:

'Tobruk has fallen.'[2]

[1] The Prime Minister thought it necessary on this occasion to advise the King to send for the Foreign Secretary in the event of his death.

[2] After heavy defeats in the Gazala area (May 27–June 18), General Ritchie was intent on withdrawing his forces to the Egyptian frontier, and, in so doing, left only a weak garrison to hold the ruined defences of the Tobruk perimeter. Rommel's troops overwhelmed this force and Tobruk fell on June 20, 1942. The loss of Tobruk was the rallying point for those who had lost confidence in Churchill's leadership.

He said this as if I were responsible. With that, he began again striding up and down the room, glowering at the carpet:

'What matters is that it should happen when I am here.'

He went to the window.

'I am ashamed. I cannot understand why Tobruk gave in. More than 30,000 of our men put their hands up. If they won't fight——'
The P.M. stopped abruptly.

He forgot all about me, and kept crossing and recrossing the room with quick strides, lost in thought. After a little, he fell into a chair. He seemed to take a pull at himself.

'It was the President who told me; he was very kind. He only asked, "What can we do to help?" And then, although they were already allocated, the President promised me Sherman tanks. Some of them must be sent at once to Alexandria to reinforce the army.'

Only last week the Admiralty pressed that no ships should be sent through the Mediterranean, which is swarming with submarines and quite unsafe.

'I shall take the responsibility of sending them through the Mediterranean. If I give a direct order, they will carry it out.'

The P.M. got up; there was vigour in all his movements. He found comfort in action.

June 23, 1942

Winston's buoyant temperament is a tremendous asset. The fall of Tobruk, like the loss of the *Prince of Wales* and the *Repulse*,[1] has been a blow between the eyes. Not only Cairo and Alexandria, but the Suez Canal and all the oilfields of the Near East seem to be at the mercy of Rommel.[2] And yet, before I left his bedroom on Sunday, Winston had refused to take the count; he got up a little dazed, but full of fight. I sat up on the night of Tobruk and last night till he went to bed, thinking he might want me. But he isn't made like that. There is never any danger of his folding up in dirty weather. My heart goes out to him. I do like a really full-sized man. With our military prestige at zero here, he has dominated the discussions.

All day and half the night, they have gone on since the news of Tobruk came through. Winston has battled with the Americans; he has not allowed the facts, damaging as they are, to handicap him. At this game, there is no one here of his own weight. He has made

---

[1] The battleship *Prince of Wales* and the battle-cruiser *Repulse* were sunk off Malaya by Japanese air attack on December 10, 1941. They had no air cover. Admiral Sir Tom Phillips and more than eight hundred officers and men lost their lives.　　　　[2] General Rommel, Commander of the Afrika Korps.

use of the crisis as an argument for postponing the Second Front; without any help from anyone, he has sustained the theme that only an invasion of North Africa can relieve the crisis. Marshall and Hopkins have not accepted the postponement of the Second Front, but they have agreed to divert tanks and other supplies to the Nile Valley, which is perhaps the same thing, since it means a revision of the shipping.

Harry Hopkins tells me what is happening: the big man on the American side in this dismal time is apparently the President. He reminds me of Lloyd George. Discerning people grieve over flaws in his character; they say, for instance, that he is not truthful. But now, when day after day he has to take big decisions, and the people around him are conscious of a crisis, his brain goes on working as if it were packed in ice. The stuff surely is in him; he is built for great occasions.

And if he needs a prop, there is Marshall. He has seen the British collapse in the Middle East end in the success of the P.M.'s efforts to postpone a Second Front. A smaller man would have turned sour. When our army has taken a bad knock, when its fighting spirit is suspect, Marshall has been driven to try to reassure the P.M. that the American infantry is better than the P.M. thinks. Winston has promised before he returns to England that he will go to see this infantry for himself, and it has been arranged that we are to go tonight in the President's train to South Carolina. However, the coach in which the P.M. was to have slept has collided with some railway carriages, and a worthy substitute cannot be provided at a moment's notice. So we are to dine at the White House while they search for rolling stock.

June 24, 1942

During dinner last night, when my thoughts were a long way off, I heard my name. It was the President admonishing me:

'You, Sir Charles, do not know the South Carolina sun in June. Be careful of the Prime Minister tomorrow.'

His words soon went out of my head, but this morning, as I stood in a cloud of dust raised by an endless line of tanks, clattering and crunching past the saluting post, General Marshall came up and handed me an open telegram.

'Secret.

'To be delivered to General Marshall immediately upon his arrival at Camp Jackson stop. You and Sir Charles Wilson are in command stop enough said stop Roosevelt.'

39

It was the President's friendly way of reminding me of my duty to my patient, his friend. All the long morning, we stood in the open, enveloped in dust, sweating in the sun, which beat down on the sandy stretch, as devoid of shelter as Salisbury Plain. All afternoon, still standing, we watched a battle between two mechanized forces until my eyes watered with the glare and my feet seemed too big for my shoes.

I suppose, instead of recording the small change of a great friendship and telling how the President watched tenderly over the well-being of his guest, I ought to have told how 600 men with parachutes were dropped from aircraft and fell to earth in the wandering, indecisive way of flakes of snow, how four of them broke their legs, and how the guns and mortars fired live ammunition. But while Winston, so easily bored by most things, can spend hours, apparently with profit, inspecting troops, their evolutions are quite lost on me.

I certainly ought to record what the P.M. thought of this American army. He surely said the right things; he never says the wrong ones where America is concerned. But is he convinced that they can now stand up to the German hordes in open warfare on a grand scale? It is typical of Winston that I have never heard him answer that question; he will not listen to any criticism of America, her people or her army. Nor is it necessary. His attitude to a Second Front is his answer. He does not believe that these troops are, as yet, sufficiently hardened to be war-worthy on the battlefields of Europe.

All the same, he can see that they are wonderful material. Himself half-American, he seems to understand how they feel when faced by this new job of soldiering: they will certainly bring to it a kind of cold determination to succeed, so that they can get back home.

At last we were taken to the airfield. When I got back to the hotel in Washington about seven o'clock this evening I sat down in the lift; I was glad to turn in.

June 25, 1942

It was a quarter to four this morning, they tell me, when the P.M.'s light went out and his exhausted secretary slunk off to bed. I can hardly credit it.

There are some in the military hierarchy to whom war is an enthralling business. But it is not like that for everyone. We had seen in the First World War what it can mean, what in the end it must mean, to any man in the ranks who keeps on his feet for any length of time: the long-drawn-out struggle with fear. It was in that mood that I went to an Intercession Service in the Cathedral here.

I was brought up on the Bible and the Book of Common Prayer, and at times, often when my thoughts are quite mundane, those splendid utterances march through my mind, and I find myself repeating: 'Therefore with Angels and Archangels, and with all the company of heaven, we laud and magnify thy glorious Name.' Is it no more than a love of words? I have drifted away from churchgoing because the literal interpretation by the Church of what was surely meant only as symbols threatened to interfere with my own belief that scientific materialism does not explain everything.

When it was all done, I walked with Halifax to the Embassy and neither of us spoke. It was said of Lord Quickswood that he could not attend church twice in one day: the emotional strain was too great for his strength.

June 27, 1942

Our flying-boat landed on the water at Stranraer at five o'clock this morning. It happened that the sports at Geoffrey's[1] preparatory school were to be held at Sunningdale this afternoon, and my only chance of getting there in time was to return to London by the aeroplane which had brought the P.M.'s mail. When I had arranged this, I thought I ought to acquaint him with my plans. He was not at all pleased.

'Now why, Charles,' he demanded, 'do you want to break up the party like this?'

I gave him my reason. He thought it a very poor reason. He said so:

'You have taken enough risks.'

I did not argue the point. Nor did I change my plans. But Winston's words came into my head when something went wrong and we made a forced landing in long grass two miles from Worcester. But I forgot all about them when I arrived by another plane and saw the look of relief on the small, eager face of my son, who had been building on my coming.

'Hurry, Daddy. I am in the next race,' he said, pulling me along.

[1] Geoffrey Wilson, my younger son.

Chapter five

Another man made for
great occasions

July 2, 1942

When the P.M. boarded the train at Stranraer a week ago, he was told that the Government had lost the Maldon by-election. Their candidate had polled only 6,226 votes out of a total of nearly 20,000. Winston looked pretty glum, I hear, but all he said was: 'This is Tobruk.' He was not really surprised. Before leaving Washington, he knew that Sir John Wardlaw-Milne, Chairman of the All-Party Finance Committee, had put down a vote of censure on the Order Paper of the House of Commons. The only way to stop the rot, the P.M. said to me later, was to convince the House that no one could have done any better.

'I mean to do that,' he added, setting his jaw.

*

Winston had been out of the country only ten days, but he felt out of touch with affairs; he wanted to know what his critics were likely to say, so that he might be ready with an effective answer. Sir Stafford Cripps, the Leader of the House of Commons, was asked for a report. But when it came it was not at all what the P.M. had hoped for. There was not a single point in the whole paper that he could make in his speech.

Sir Stafford said bluntly that Maldon 'shows the profound disquiet and lack of confidence of the electors.' There was 'a general feeling of dissatisfaction that something is wrong and should be put right without delay.'[1]

The Prime Minister was inclined to dismiss these strictures as 'all theory.' 'You can't run a war as if you were in a laboratory,' he growled. Sir Stafford had spoken of lack of confidence; he, Winston, did not agree that there was any lack of confidence—except, of

[1] Winston Churchill, *The Hinge of Fate*, p. 354.

course, among a few cranks in the House of Commons, and they were well known to everyone. He had been a lifetime in politics, and he knew how to handle the House without anyone's help.

It was in this mood that he rose to wind up the two-day debate. Is it so surprising that he let himself go? 'Naturally, I made every point which occurred to me,' he said. But they were debating points; they were not those Sir Stafford had made. These remained unanswered. If the public wanted information on the succession of defeats, the P.M. did not give it to them. Instead, he gave them a superb demonstration of his skill in debate. One heard on all sides that 'his handling of the House was indeed masterly.'

And it must be said that those who led the attack went out of their way to make his task easy. Wardlaw-Milne argued that the Prime Minister interfered too much in the direction of the war, whereas Sir Roger Keyes,[1] in seconding, said he did not interfere enough. And when Wardlaw-Milne proposed that the Duke of Gloucester should be appointed Commander-in-Chief of the British Army, the House ceased to take him seriously. When Keyes had resumed his seat, a Member pointed out that if the motion was carried the Prime Minister would have to resign. Was that what Sir Roger thought desirable? Whereupon Sir Roger jumped to his feet.

'It would,' he exclaimed, 'be a deplorable disaster if he had to go.'

Members were frankly mystified. What were these critics of the Government trying to say? They wanted to put something right, but what was it? The House had been unhappy about things for some time, but would they be any better if these people had their way? The figures that the Prime Minister produced were positively devastating. The House was now becoming restless; all interest had gone out of the debate. And when a division was taken, only twenty-five members voted for the motion, while 475 were against it.

The P.M. sat back; he was well content. The noisy minority had had their noses rubbed in the mud. Perhaps it would be a lesson to them. Walter Elliot had reminded the House that after eight years of ignominious defeat in the field only twenty-five members had gone into the opposition Lobby against Pitt. The P.M. was deeply interested. It was certainly curious that the number should be repeated like that. Macaulay had recorded that every disaster that happened without the walls of Parliament was regularly followed by triumph within them. And that, too, was happening again. The Prime Minister's mind went back to Pitt's problems,

[1] Sir Roger Keyes, Admiral of the Fleet, Director of Combined Operations 1940–1.

and when I saw him after the debate he compared them with his own. As for Sir Stafford's analysis of the causes of discontent which had led to the vote of censure, he did not think there could have been much in it after all, for the House was nearly solid. Anyway, he had other things to think of.

The P.M. had gone to Washington in June to persuade the President to agree to the invasion of North Africa as an alternative to landing in Normandy. He had failed—at least that was his impression—because of the loss of prestige of the British after the fall of Tobruk.

Roosevelt's advisers took a rather different view. In their eyes, the Prime Minister had been only too successful. He had got what he wanted indirectly; he was altogether too clever for them. They spoke of his influence with the President as a positive menace, and when Mr. Churchill went off to meet the House of Commons, he left behind him in Washington a sense of uneasiness, and even alarm. It did not appear that there would be a Second Front in 1942, or 1943 either. Even the steadiest minds around the President seem to have been affected by the feeling of disappointment and frustration. Marshall himself, at a meeting with the President on July 15, supported Admiral King[1] in his claim that the war in the Pacific should have priority.

The President took this clash of opinion very much to heart. For the first time in the war he found himself at variance with his Chiefs of Staff. But he did not hesitate. Flouting the sentiments of his countrymen, he made it clear, once and for all, that there could be no question of transferring to the Pacific the full weight of American effort. He determined to send Hopkins, Marshall and King to London, and with them he sent written instructions. They were to press as strongly as they could the case for invading France in 1942. If they failed to get this, they were to report to him, but, he added, in that event they must find another place for American troops to fight the Germans in the autumn. He wanted an agreed plan now.

In London, Marshall found that the British had quietly made up their minds that an invasion of France that autumn must end in disaster. In vain, with Hopkins's able help, he argued his case. Nothing that they said appeared to make the slightest impression on General Brooke's settled convictions. As Hopkins put it, he kept looking into the distance.

'I feel damn' depressed,' Harry wrote.[2]

At the second meeting on July 22 it was apparent that a complete

[1] Admiral King, Chief of American Naval Operations.
[2] Robert E. Sherwood, *The White House Papers of Harry L. Hopkins*, Vol. II, p. 610.

deadlock had been reached, and Marshall said he would have to report to the President that the British were not prepared to go ahead with the invasion that year. The President's reply was prompt and even categorical. If they could not get agreement about France, they must search for an alternative—perhaps the invasion of North Africa. To Marshall, as a soldier, these were orders from his Commander-in-Chief, and with a heavy heart he accepted TORCH, the plan to land in North Africa.

Marshall could see many good points in the African plan. It was strategically sound, certainly, but to land at Algiers, Oran and Casablanca in the autumn of 1942 would take up so much shipping that it meant inevitably the postponement of the invasion of France until 1944. That was why Lewis Douglas [1] said that TORCH was the most important decision taken during the war: why it was in the President's judgment a turning-point in the whole war.

This brings me to the Prime Minister's part in these proceedings. Winston had used the fall of Tobruk to persuade the Americans to divert to the Nile Valley material set apart for the invasion of France. He thus set in train a series of events which led to TORCH, and so to the postponement of the invasion of France until 1944. Did he, by his sagacity and wisdom, save the Allies from a disaster of the first magnitude that might have led to the loss of the war, or was he responsible, by what the Americans call his pigheadedness, for dragging out the war into the sixth year? Was Winston himself sure that this postponement was in England's best interest? Anyway, as far as I know, he has never claimed credit for postponing the invasion of France, though the Secretary of the Cabinet held it to be his most solid achievement after what he did in 1940. Was his silence a kind of escape clause or insurance in case posterity held him responsible for prolonging the war?

Nor, perhaps, was that the end of the train of consequences of this signal decision. It may well be that the failure of Britain to bring the First World War to a victorious conclusion in 1916, combined with our inability to win the Second World War in 1942, imposed a drain on the resources of a small country, in men and in material, from which it has never completely recovered. It was not enough to win a war; it must be won quickly, or victory might be as disastrous as defeat.

[1] Lewis Douglas, U.S. Ambassador to the Court of St. James's 1947–50.

45

Chapter six

A sad business

My diary for 1942 has the same backcloth to every scene: Winston's conviction that his life as Prime Minister could be saved only by a victory in the field. It accounts for the sharp exchanges he had at this time with General Auchinleck.[1]

I find a pencilled note with February scrawled in the margin:

'Found the P.M. in an explosive mood today. Auchinleck will not be ready to take the offensive in the Desert till June. "The bloody man does not seem to care about the fate of Malta. Anyway," said Winston, setting his jaw, "we can't settle this by writing letters." '

It appears that on March 8 he sent a telegram to Auchinleck telling him that he would be glad if he would come home for consultations. The General replied that he could not leave Cairo at that juncture.

*

March 14, 1942

The P.M. is furious with the Auk. He wants to relieve him of his command and talks of Gort[2] taking over. My informant spoke darkly of the Ides of March. 'In your jargon,' he said to me, 'I would not call the Auk a good life.'

*

Alan Brooke in his diaries put this in a different light. He spoke of the Prime Minister's persistent attempts to prod Auchinleck into a premature offensive when the P.M. himself was not familiar with all the aspects of the situation, and when he knew that the Chiefs of Staff were against an offensive at that time. Brooke wrote on

[1] Sir Claude Auchinleck, Commander-in-Chief, Middle East 1941-2.
[2] Lord Gort, Governor of Malta 1942-4.

Fayer

FIELD–MARSHAL SMUTS

SIR JOHN ANDERSON

March 24: 'It is very exhausting, this continual protecting of Auchinleck.'

It was not only the political situation that was worrying the P.M. The plight of Malta had become an obsession with him. He was anxious to help the island by an attack in force on Rommel, but Auchinleck persisted that he was not ready to give battle. And then early in May he offered to send strong forces to India. This was the last straw. It was decided to send him definite orders for an early offensive, which he must obey, or in default be relieved of his command. 'This was,' the P.M. writes,[1] 'a most unusual procedure on our part towards a high military commander. There was,' he continues, 'a considerable pause, during which we did not know whether he would accept or resign.' At length the General intimated that he would carry out the P.M.'s instructions. The P.M. urged him to take personal command of the army, but the General replied that he was very reluctant to 'become immersed in tactical problems in Libya.' This unfortunate phrase stuck in the Prime Minister's gullet. Twice he spat it out with great scorn.

The battle that began at the end of May seemed to bear out Auchinleck's fears. Rommel attacked on May 26, and by the end of June our army had been thrown back to Alamein. I think that it was at this time that the P.M. made up his mind that Auchinleck must go. My diary takes up the story at this point.

July 28, 1942

I was summoned this morning to No. 10 Downing Street, where I heard that we should soon be on the move. The P.M. has decided to fly to Cairo. From Gibraltar he will fly south to Takoradi on the Gold Coast, and so across Central Africa to Cairo. It means about five days in the air, landing at places where malaria and yellow fever are rife. The P.M. wanted my advice about inoculations. I did not like the plan and gave my reasons.

As I was leaving I met John Anderson.[2] He said that certain members of the Cabinet were concerned about the Prime Minister's travels and the dangers he was running in flying over hostile territory in an unarmed bomber. He and Cripps had arranged to see the P.M. this afternoon, and, as health might come up, he would like me to be there.

At the appointed hour I joined them in the Cabinet Room. I was most concerned with the actual risk of the protective measures

---

[1] Winston Churchill, *The Hinge of Fate*, p. 275.
[2] Sir John Anderson, Lord President of the Council.

against yellow fever.[1] While we were discussing these problems, the door opened and the Prime Minister hurried in, beaming at us disarmingly—always a sign that he is up to mischief. He began to unfold a large map, spreading it on the table.

'Vanderkloot says it is quite unnecessary to fly so far south. He has explained to me that we can fly in one hop to Cairo. Come here and look.'

Sir John knelt on a chair to get nearer the map, while Cripps leant over his shoulder. The P.M., with a pencil, traced the route from Gibraltar across Spanish Morocco till he struck the Nile, where his pencil turned sharply to the north.

'This changes the whole picture,' the P.M. added confidently.

I ventured to ask who Vanderkloot was. It appeared that he had just crossed the Atlantic in a bomber, and it is in this machine that we are to fly to Cairo. I wondered why it was left to an American pilot to find a safe route to Cairo, but that did not seem a profitable line of speculation.

'You see, Charles, we need not bother about inoculations.'

Anderson and Cripps pored over the map like excited schoolboys, and the party broke up without a word of warning or remonstrance about the risks the P.M. was taking in flying over hostile territory in an unarmed bomber by daylight. The P.M. gets his own way with everyone with hardly a murmur.

August 1, 1942

Called at No. 10 to see if anything was wanted. The P.M. seemed abstracted.

'There's something very wrong there,' he muttered half to himself. 'I must clear things up.'

For a long time he has been worried by the reverses in the desert, and when he told me that he had asked Smuts[2] to join him in Cairo, I knew he meant to bring things to a head. As I was leaving, he put down a telegram the secretary had just brought in.

'We may go to see Stalin. He won't like what I have to say to him. I'm not looking forward to it.'

The P.M. is turning over in his head how he can break the news to Stalin. He has to tell him that there will not be a Second Front in France this year.

---

[1] That there was substance in my fears we learnt later when more than half of those inoculated against this fever developed an obstinate form of jaundice.

[2] Field-Marshal Smuts, Prime Minister of South Africa 1939–48.

August 3, 1942

It was after midnight when we left Lyneham in the unheated bomber. Two mattresses had been dumped in the after-cabin, and I passed the night in comfort. The P.M. was less happy; he dislikes draughts—and after all it is rather a feckless way of sending him over the world when he is approaching his seventieth year. However, he soon forgot his discomforts in sound sleep, and when we got to Gibraltar this morning he was ready for anything.

August 4, 1942

Vanderkloot has brought it off. We landed safely near the Pyramids and drove into Cairo. The Embassy is hot and steamy, but the P.M.'s bedroom is air-conditioned, and anyway he does not feel extremes of heat and cold like other people. He is in great heart. No longer is he compelled to deal with great events by correspondence; he is 'the man on the spot.' Twice he has said this to me. A great feeling of elation stokes the marvellous machine, which seems quite impervious to fatigue.

When I left the P.M., I found my hostess anxious to learn the habits of her formidable guest. Lady Lampson,[1] I have just discovered, is the daughter of the Italian physician, Castellani, who had enjoyed a considerable measure of success in practice in Mayfair before he went to Rome to help Mussolini with his medical arrangements. I found this interesting. A fortnight before we left London, Lord Dawson pestered me, as President of the Royal College of Physicians, to remove Castellani's name from the list of Fellows. He said that he was the Axel Munthe type of doctor, living in some comfort by his wits, and that he was now helping the enemy.

For my part, I have no liking for this witch-hunting. Besides, as an Italian he is doing the right thing. And there can be no doubt about his ability. After all, living by one's wits is an elastic term which might be stretched by some to include rather more conventional types.

After Lady Lampson had learnt that I held no recipe for the taming of Winston, I talked for a time with Smuts. His weather-beaten face is dominated by the penetrating gaze of the cold, measuring, grey-blue eyes, which are set deep above the prominent cheek-bones.

I do not feel that I have got to the bottom of him yet, any more than I can fathom Roosevelt. If Smuts had been born in Germany,

[1] Wife of Sir Miles Lampson, British Ambassador in Cairo.

he might have been one of the great captains of war. He collects his facts like a man of science—listening, sifting and rejecting what has not been proved. No other soldier I know has quite the same approach to evidence.

I am glad he is here. The P.M. hates the thought of removing one of his commanders. Smuts is more ruthless, and if the P.M. has to make changes in the higher command, even, it may be, to get rid of General Auchinleck, Smuts's presence and counsel will fortify and comfort him.

August 5, 1942

Very early this morning the P.M. drove with Auchinleck to his headquarters behind the Ruweisat Ridge. There, in a kind of wire cage, we breakfasted with some men burnt brown by the desert sun. There were flies everywhere. When they were disturbed they rose in a cloud with a buzzing sound. Wandering over the world with the Prime Minister, one meets new faces almost every day, until one hardly tries to put a name to them. From time to time, however, one encounters someone who refuses to be dismissed in this perfunctory fashion. Here was a face that interested me very much. There was nothing distinctive about the alert blue eyes set in a brick-red face, but there was about this man an air of authority. Those near him appeared to listen very attentively whenever he spoke. When I asked his name, they said, 'Straffer Gott,' and added that he had a way of turning up in the desert when things had gone wrong, and putting them right, so that he was much beloved by his men. After breakfast the P.M. took him off in his car to the airfield. He is clearly interested in him. It is said that Gott, after three years in the desert, is a tired man, but I fancy that the P.M. must have decided that he is not too tired to take over the Eighth Army.

At the airfield we took leave of Gott and were handed over to Tedder[1] and Arthur Coningham[2]—another personality. We flew with them to Coningham's headquarters in a tent in the desert. Here were all the heads of the Desert Air Force. A special luncheon, which Shepheard's Hotel had sent from Cairo by car, got lost, and while we waited I had time to look round. It is a new atmosphere. These men have not taken a bad knock; they are on top and know that they are on top. In an impersonal war of millions they remain individuals. These fellows were not groomed in a mess before the war. Their thoughts are not borrowed from others and their speech is forthright. They are critical of the Army, and they say what is in

[1] Arthur Tedder, Air Officer Commanding-in-Chief, R.A.F., Middle East.
[2] Arthur Coningham, Commanding Desert Air Force.

their minds without batting an eyelid. The P.M. is apt to be lost among his own species, but I think he caught the drift of their talk. Certainly the Army's shortcomings were set forth succinctly. It is not to them that one will look for a recommendation for mercy when the Commander-in-Chief stands in the dock.

And there is Tedder to speak for them if the P.M. is in doubt. Tedder's father, a rough diamond, fought his way from the bottom to become head of the Excise. In the son the facets have been polished, but the hard stone is left. I drove with him to the airfield. He seems quite unlike anyone in the service I have met—a quick mind and a sharp tongue. He admires Smuts, thinks he is a greater man than the Prime Minister, and says so. As we retraced our steps towards Cairo at the end of the day, the P.M. remained sunk in his own thoughts. He did not speak once, but I have a feeling that it is all settled.

August 6, 1942

All day the P.M. has shut himself up with Smuts and the C.I.G.S. —we have seen nothing of him, but tonight he came out to sit on the lawn under the stars, and as he talked it was possible to follow his thoughts. The Ambassador's son is here on leave. He is in the Guards and what he had to say about the morale of the troops in other units—though it leaked out in driblets—was disquieting. The P.M. said presently:

'There is something wrong somewhere. I am convinced there has been no leadership out here. What has happened is a disgrace. Ninety thousand men all over the place. Alex told me there are 2,000 officers in Cairo who wear a smart uniform called a gabardine, and that they are called the gabardine swine.' His voice rose: 'There must be no cozening. The Army must understand there are very serious penalties for not doing their duty.'

August 7, 1942

I have discovered that when the rest of the party go off to change for dinner, Smuts comes out on to the lawn and sits by himself for perhaps half an hour. Tonight I joined him, and when he quoted from *The Ring and the Book* and found that I could carry on where he left off, he began to speak about many things. I offered him my books, but he said he did not read fiction. The people in the house say that he takes his Greek Testament to his bedroom. When it slipped out that I had once passed an examination of sorts in botany, he began to talk of the different species of grass in South Africa. There were thousands of them. He carried his manual on botany about with him. Presently, when I had been talking to him of the value in war of the appraising, measuring mind, he began to show signs of impatience, drumming with his fingers on his chair. What I said he accepted, but he went on to speak of the supremacy of the man of ideas.

'That is why Winston is indispensable. He has ideas. If he goes, there is no one to take his place. Men of action,' he said, 'live on the surface of things; they do not create.' He rose at last. 'We must go in. They may be looking for us.'

During dinner there was a discussion on the profit motive; perhaps it would be more accurate to say that there was a dialogue between the P.M. and Smuts. I need hardly add that it was Smuts who raised the subject; the P.M. was plainly not interested. Smuts feels that big changes are coming.

P.M.: 'As I get older I begin to see a pattern in things.'

Smuts: 'There is a pattern in history, though it is not easy to see or follow.'

Smuts spoke of Gandhi: 'He is a man of God. You and I are mundane people. Gandhi has appealed to religious motives. You never have. That is where you have failed.'

P.M. (with a great grin): 'I have made more bishops than anyone since St. Augustine.'

But Smuts did not smile. His face was very grave.

While they talked I kept asking myself what kind of a man is Smuts. Is he the Henry James of South Africa? Does he think of his fellow Boers as James came to think of the American scene as perhaps a little primitive? A South African here speaks of him as 'remote'; even to his own people he is a stranger. No one really knows him. It appears that this solitary, austere Boer with his biblical background lives in a world of his own. It is as if he had been cut off from his kind.

He lives to get things done. Anyone who steps in his path is ruthlessly pushed aside. As for his colleagues in the Cabinet, they are kept at arm's length. The whole political apparatus is just a necessary nuisance. He is taken up with the war and with world events; social affairs in South Africa mean little to him: he is not interested in the slums of Johannesburg. Like Winston, he is sure that there is nothing in the world which he could not do as well as anyone. There is nothing that cannot be thought out. Certainly he has an extraordinary mind, thinking out everything for himself. And yet in the end, human nature being what it is, I am fearful that his arrogance will trip him up.

In my conversation on the lawn, I got an impression of a hard man—it is not to him that I should look for a reprieve for Auchinleck —a man interested only in ideas, and not much nearer the mark than the P.M. when it comes to summing up a man. He is one of the few men—I can think of only two—who have Winston's ear because he respects their mental processes; the other, of course, is the 'Prof'.[1] Winston is encouraged when he hears from Smuts that he is proceeding along the right lines.

As for Auchinleck, Brooke tells me that he is a man of splendid talents, a very able soldier, and a man, too, of great strength of character. He has come to grief, it would seem, because he could not pick the right subordinates. Those he appointed had so dispersed our forces in the desert that Rommel, with his more effective tanks and guns, had little difficulty in defeating the scattered fragments piecemeal. There is another reason: the Auk does not understand Winston.

As the P.M. went to his room after dinner, Jacob stopped him and told him that Gott had been shot down and killed flying to Cairo, on the same route which the P.M. had flown two days ago without an escort. He stood staring at the carpet, then very slowly he pulled himself up the stairs. It had been decided that Gott should be given the Eighth Army. I wonder what the P.M. will do now.

August 9, 1942

The end of the story came this morning. I had taken a book and was sitting under one of the two trees on the Embassy lawn. The soldiers were in conference, and I had the lawn all to myself, except for a sentry who passed up and down the raised path that separates the garden from the Nile. I was watching two hoopoes extracting worms from the grass with their long bills when Brooke appeared with Auchinleck; they took seats under the other tree. I could not hear what the C.I.G.S. was saying, nor could I see the expression on Auchinleck's face, but I did not need any help to follow what was happening. Auchinleck sat with his forearms resting on his thighs, his hands hanging down between his knees, his head drooping forward like a flower on a broken stalk. His long, lean limbs were relaxed; the whole attitude expressed grief: the man was completely undone. After a time they got up and went into the house. I tried to get on with my book, but I was somehow made miserable by what I had seen.

[1] Professor Lindemann, afterwards Lord Cherwell.

Chapter seven

Breaking the news
to Stalin

Moscow, August 12, 1942

It was five o'clock in the evening when our Liberator made a good landing at the Moscow airfield. A small crowd of officials, headed by Molotov,[1] met us, and a guard of honour goose-stepped past the P.M., while a band played the National Anthems of Britain, the United States and Russia. Then we got into cars and were driven at a great pace through Moscow to a house or dacha in a pine wood called 'State Villa No. 7.' The P.M. was preoccupied with the coming interview with Stalin; he was silent, abstracted and short-tempered.

The elderly concierge on the door mumbled something. As I was getting out of my greatcoat I heard loud shouts coming from upstairs. I went up them, two at a time, to find Winston sitting in a large bath, shivering and damning.

'The water is bloody cold and I don't know which is the hot tap.'

Their taps do not work like our taps, and the Russian lettering did not help. Sawyers had gone off to fetch something. I took a chance. There was a sudden big gush of icy water under terrific pressure. It caught the P.M. amidships. He gave a loud shriek and when he got his breath he cursed me for my incompetence. I flew to get help.

I am lodged in the nursery, a large room with a clever wallpaper and lined with cupboards full of ingenious toys.

The conference with Stalin, at which Molotov, Voroshilov,[2] Harriman and Archibald Clark Kerr, our Ambassador, were present, began at seven o'clock and lasted four hours.

The P.M. on his return was full of what had happened:

'The first two hours were bleak and sombre. I explained at

---

[1] V. Molotov, Soviet Commissar for Foreign Affairs.
[2] Marshal Voroshilov, Commissar for Defence.

54

length, with maps and arguments, why we could not do a Second Front. Stalin said he did not agree with our reasons. He argued the other way, and everyone was pretty glum. Finally, he said he did not accept our view, but that we had the right to decide. The only way to swallow a bitter mixture, as Charles will tell you, is to take it in a single gulp. At any rate, I did not attempt to sweeten it. I asked for plain speaking, and I certainly got it. But if Stalin was bitterly disappointed, he listened patiently to my explanation. He never once raised his voice, never once lost his temper. When I had told him the worst, we both sat in silence for a little. Then I spoke of the bombing of Germany, and he seemed a little more friendly. I thought that was the time to produce TORCH. Stalin was at last listening with both his ears. "May God prosper this undertaking," he said.'

'Did he really say that?' I asked.

'Oh, he brings in the Deity quite a lot. And before I had come to an end of my explanation of TORCH he astonished me by giving four reasons why this operation must help. First, it would surprise Rommel's troops in the rear; secondly, it would soon put Italy out of the war; thirdly, it would end in fighting between Germans and the French; fourthly, it would frighten Spain into staying neutral. I was astonished that he was able to master an intricate problem of this nature that was quite new to him in a few moments.

'It is typical of Stalin that the only reason he left out was the opening of the Mediterranean. He is a land animal. I put my cards on the table, and when I left we were good friends and shook hands cordially. I mean to forge a solid link with this man.'

If the P.M. was pleased, the Ambassador was delighted; he was obviously greatly relieved that the first meeting had gone so well. Harriman turned to me:

'You will be glad to know, Sir Charles, your fears were groundless.'

Clark Kerr took me aside.

'Things were pretty grim,' he said, 'until the Prime Minister described our bombing of Germany. Then Stalin, for the first time, became really interested. He said his information was that the bombing was upsetting the civilian population. He wanted to blast the German workmen out of their homes.'

'Did that break the ice?' I asked.

'Well,' the Ambassador went on, 'when Stalin began to thaw, the Prime Minister adroitly produced TORCH. He drew a crocodile— and explained to Stalin how we intended to rip open the soft underbelly.'

'That was what TORCH meant. Stalin had not taken his eyes

off the interpreter; he was following every word; and then he held up his hand'—here the Ambassador imitated his action—'to stop the Prime Minister. He wished to ask a question. At what date did Mr. Churchill plan to land in North Africa? When the Prime Minister said October, the Russians grinned with pleasure—though Molotov did ask if September was a possible date.' Clark Kerr chortled: 'There was one touch typical of Stalin. When the Prime Minister stressed the importance of secrecy, Stalin's face wrinkled with amusement. He said that he hoped nothing would appear in the British Press.'

It was now after midnight, and the P.M., who had had no dinner, proceeded to eat a huge meal; in between the courses he nursed his head in his hands and said nothing. At the end he yawned wearily.

'I will only do half a dozen telegrams and then go to bed,' he said rather petulantly.

Presently he put his half-finished cigar across the wine-glass, and got up and stretched himself; the telegrams, he decided, must wait till the morning. He was plainly very weary. After all, he had been on the aerodrome at Teheran this morning at six o'clock. I took him to bed, and while he was undressing I asked him what he thought of Stalin:

'Was he quick at getting on to your points?'

'Extraordinarily quick,' the P.M. replied. 'This alone was worth the journey. My strategy was sound,' he went on. 'For an hour and a half I told him bluntly what we could *not* do. At the end Stalin said he was, of course, very disappointed, but he thanked me for my very frank statement. He had not expected very much. Then I told him what we could do. He ended enthusiastic—in a glow.'

August 13, 1942

After luncheon the P.M., who was looking through the window at the blue sky, said he would like to walk in the wood—which surprised me a good deal, because he hardly ever walks for the sake of exercise. As we wandered among the trees he said:

'Now I have broken the news to Stalin I have a feeling the rest should be plain sailing. I spoke very plainly to Molotov this morning. I thought he ought to know that Stalin would not be wise to be rude to us when we had come all this distance to help him.'

'What did Molotov say?' I asked.

'Oh, he promised to tell Stalin what I had said, and from the way he said it I think he will. "Stalin is wise, and he will know how you feel, even if he argues." Those were Molotov's words.

Of course, I don't know how much the interpreter altered what he actually said. But if he really did say that—well, it's very interesting.'

The P.M. stopped at a great glass tank full of goldfish of different kinds. He sat down on the edge of the tank and proceeded to demonstrate to me the various kinds. Could we get any food for them? he wondered. When I went off to look for a Russian who spoke English, I discovered that the wood was surrounded by a green palisade about twice the height of a man. There were four or five green gates at intervals. Finding one without a guard, I came nearer until I could see a kind of peephole, the size of a brick; looking through this, I saw police and soldiers and barbed wire. They are plainly prepared for trouble with their own people.

When I returned to the P.M. he was with one of the Russians. This man wanted to know if Mr. Churchill would like to see the air-raid shelter. He directed us to a place in the wood, some distance from the house, where an electric lift took us down to a long passage lined with coloured marbles and wooden panelling. There were perhaps ten or eleven elaborately furnished rooms, with heavy, swinging doors, offices, a completely equipped kitchen with refrigerators and servants' quarters—like a section of the Strand Palace Hotel gone underground. In all the rooms there were candles in heavy silver candelabra, in case the electricity failed. The P.M. isn't interested in that kind of thing. His mind is with Stalin in the Kremlin, and when he could he thanked the Russians and went off to his room.

He saw Stalin at eleven o'clock this evening at the Kremlin. The meeting was a flop. It was as if yesterday's meeting, with its good humour and apparent agreement, had never taken place.

'I am downhearted and dispirited,' the P.M. complained on his return. 'I have come a long way and made a great effort. Stalin lay back puffing at his pipe, with his eyes half closed, emitting streams of insults. He said the Russians were losing 10,000 men a day. He said that if the British Army had been fighting the Germans as much as the Red Army had, it would not be so frightened of them. He was most uncomplimentary to our Army. He said we had broken our word about a Second Front.'

The P.M.'s lips were pressed together.

'I can harden too. I am not sure it wouldn't be better to leave him to fight his own battles,' he muttered. 'Losing all these British ships; only three out of fourteen got through in the last convoy. . . . I am sure that Stalin knows that we are right. His judgment is too sound not to know.'

At this point Sir Alexander Cadogan,[1] who isn't exactly pro-Russian, interjected:

'Should I tell Stalin in confidence that you are hesitating whether to accept his invitation to dinner tomorrow after what has happened?'

The P.M.: 'No; that is going too far, I think.'

When Cadogan had gone, the P.M. said half to himself:

'We're a long way from home—four days' flight.' He looked up at me. 'And the journey is not without danger.'

While the P.M. was undressing he kept repeating what Stalin had said to him at yesterday's meeting. He used exactly the same words he had used on his return from the Kremlin. He repeated the four reasons Stalin gave why TORCH would help, and told me again how he had invoked the blessing of the Deity on the undertaking. What Stalin said to him had lodged in his mind.

August 14, 1942

The Ambassador told me that Cadogan called on Molotov this afternoon, bearing a written reply to Stalin's memorandum; at the same time he told Molotov frankly that the P.M. felt 'puzzled and disheartened.' It seems that the tone of this outspoken document was not lost on Stalin. He has had time to turn over in his mind what might happen if the P.M. left Moscow in his present mood. It would be awkward if the democracies left him to his own devices. At any rate, by nine o'clock, when we dined at the Kremlin, it was obvious that Stalin had thought better of his truculent attitude and was anxious to make amends. He went out of his way to be agreeable to the P.M. I was too far away during dinner to hear what they were saying, but Clark Kerr told me later that it went all right for a time, though the P.M. had not yet forgiven Stalin for the things he had said about our soldiers. They talked about Lloyd George and Lady Astor. Stalin told how he had asked Lady Astor about politicians in England. ' "Chamberlain," she said, "is the coming man." 'What about Winston?'

' "Oh, he's finished," she replied.'

Stalin had retorted: 'If your country is ever in trouble, he will come back.'

During dinner Winston said: 'When the Germans declared war on you, I consulted nobody, but made my broadcast speech.' That went straight home, Clark Kerr told me.

At another time Stalin said: 'I am a rough man, not an ex-

---

[1] Sir Alexander Cadogan, Permanent Under-Secretary of State for Foreign Affairs 1938–46.

perienced one like you.' He begged that his roughness should not be misunderstood.

The dinner dragged on; the list of toasts appeared interminable. John Reed, acting Head of Chancery at the Embassy, said to me: 'Voroshilov challenged me to a competition in pepper-vodkas, and when I declined he refused all further conversation.'

At length Molotov got up and proposed the health of Sir Alexander Cadogan. Cadogan, who had noticed that the P.M. was not enjoying himself and was indeed beginning to betray some impatience, seized the opportunity to break up the banquet. When Molotov sat down he said quietly that with Stalin's permission he would himself propose a toast. 'I gave them: death and damnation to the Germans.' That did the trick. There was no one present to reply, and after a brief pause Stalin got up and left the table.

When Stalin had gone, Mikoyan[1] staggered out with his arm round a colleague's neck.

After dinner Stalin and the P.M. were photographed together; Stalin seemed to take the initiative in this and made it plain that it gave him pleasure. Then something went wrong. The P.M., Harriman and Molotov went over and sat at a table, where Stalin joined them, taking a chair next to the P.M., who, however, went on reading some document, and hardly spoke to Stalin. I received the impression that Stalin wanted to be friendly, but that the P.M. would not meet him halfway. At last the P.M. got up and said 'Goodbye' and moved off. He walked very quickly, with countenance overcast. His face was set and resolute. Stalin accompanied him through the vast and empty halls which separated the dining-room from the door by which we had come into the Kremlin. I had never seen Stalin move except in a slow and measured fashion. Now to keep up with the P.M. he had almost to trot. Watching him, I thought of the importunity of the small boy who is asking for a cigarette card and will not take 'No' for an answer. Perhaps Stalin realized that he had gone too far, and that this might be the end; he saw what that would mean.

The P.M. strode into the waiting car. He asked Alex Cadogan to drive with him. Cadogan told me in his dry, factual way of the P.M.'s mood when they left the Kremlin:

'I was surprised in the car to find the violence and depth of the resentment that he had worked up. I don't know what would have happened at the Kremlin if the party had gone on much longer. Nor was I able to discover the exact cause of the P.M.'s mood.

[1] A. Mikoyan, People's Commissar of Foreign Trade.

Anyhow, he was like a bull in the ring maddened by the pricks of the picadors. He declared that he really did not know what he was supposed to be doing here. He would return to London without seeing Stalin again.'

I followed in another car. On alighting at the villa, I was told the P.M. wanted me. I found him with Cadogan and Rowan,[1] sitting at a long table. They took no notice of me, but went on talking. There was a long dispute whether the proposed communiqué describing the results of the P.M.'s visit should be worded as the Russians proposed. The matter under discussion was so plainly secret that I rose to leave.

'Don't go, Charles,' the P.M. interjected, and went on talking.

He said the communiqué would be 'disastrous,' because it would be interpreted everywhere as meaning that the Russians and British had disagreed and that there was to be no Second Front. Cadogan said he could not see how it could be disastrous. It was, like all communiqués, bosh, but he could not see why it should be interpreted as meaning no Second Front.

The P.M. replied that there was no reference to any offensive action. Cadogan kept repeating that he could not see how it could be disastrous. I had never seen anyone talk to the P.M. like this. At last the P.M. said:

'Well, you have been in the Foreign Office all this time. Do as you think. But I want it recorded that I thought it would be disastrous.'

Cadogan retorted: 'Molotov, when I see him, will ask me how it is disastrous, and I must be able to answer.'

P.M.: 'I will authorize you to take the line you want.'

Whereupon Cadogan said he could not take a line if the P.M. thought it would be disastrous. There was a silence. The P.M. rose to go to bed. Cadogan got up, said 'Good night,' and left the room. Rowan followed him. I went after the P.M. to his bedroom. He had flopped into an armchair and sat staring at the carpet. When he noticed me he said:

'Stalin didn't want to talk to me. I closed the proceedings down. I had had enough. The food was filthy. I ought not to have come.'

The P.M. got up, pacing the room in nothing but his silk undervest, mumbling to himself. At last he pulled up before me:

'I still feel I could work with that man if I could break down the language barrier. That is a terrible difficulty.'

He wondered whether he should make another attempt. He might be snubbed. I said he must risk that. It wasn't a question of

[1] Leslie Rowan, Assistant private secretary to the Prime Minister.

whether Stalin was a brigand or not, but if we did not work in with him it would mean at least a longer war and more casualties. But the P.M. wasn't listening. He said he wouldn't go near Stalin again. He had deliberately said 'Goodbye' and not 'Good night.' If there was any fresh move, Stalin must make it. He wouldn't. He got into bed, put on his black eye-shade and settled his head in the pillow. I turned out the light. When I left the room I looked at my watch. It was a quarter to four. The night was nearly over. I could not sleep; the consequences of leaving Moscow like this with Stalin and the P.M. at loggerheads frightened me.

August 15, 1942

After breakfast I ran into Reed on the drive. I said to him that I would like to see the Ambassador, but hesitated to ring him up. Reed said: 'He is with Alec Cadogan now.'

As he spoke they came up the drive, the Ambassador puffing at his pipe, and passed us by. When I saw there was no chance of getting Clark Kerr away from Cadogan, I went into the house and wrote to him. I confessed my fears, prayed him to forgive my butting in, but I wondered if it would be possible to put into Stalin's ear:

(i) That the P.M. must not leave Moscow without seeing Stalin.

(ii) That the P.M. had said, 'I feel I could work with that man if I could break down the barrier of language.'

(iii) That Stalin must be made to understand that the P.M.'s success or failure in Moscow with the Russians would not influence the electorate in the United Kingdom; only continued defeats could weaken Winston's position.

(iv) That the P.M.'s only interest was to defeat Hitler; that was an obsession with him.

At the same time it would help if the P.M. could be persuaded:

(i) That a quarrel with Stalin meant more British casualties.

(ii) That Stalin coming to the door to see the P.M. off was, according to Molotov, without any precedent in the history of the Soviet Union.

(iii) That they both wanted to come together, but something was keeping them apart.

(iv) That it was up to the P.M., with his vast experience, to handle the situation so that this was brought about.

When I had finished the note, I was on the point of tearing it up. It seemed impertinent. At that moment Reed passed through the room, and that settled the matter. I gave my letter to him and through the window I watched him hand it to the Ambassador. About an hour afterwards Clark Kerr came up to me:

'I'm more hopeful,' he said. 'The P.M. listened and said to me at the end, "It was my fault." '

Winston was thinking of his mood at the dinner. I, too, was hopeful as the hours passed, because there is no word yet of our leaving Moscow.

The P.M. must have made up his mind to see Stalin before he goes, or we should by now be packing up.

While we were waiting for tea they brought me a letter from the Embassy. It was from John Reed. I read:

'From all that H.E. told me on the drive back to Moscow from the dacha after his interview with the Prime Minister I was left in no doubt at all that the P.M. intended to leave this afternoon. The Ambassador was cock-a-hoop because he had dissuaded him from doing so. The P.M. told him he could hardly bring himself to shake Stalin's hand. "Did he not realize who he was speaking to? The representative of the most powerful empire the world has ever seen." The Ambassador had a very difficult task talking the P.M. round; he considered it his greatest diplomatic triumph.'

As I put Reed's letter into my pocket Cadogan came into the room. He had been ringing up the Kremlin at intervals to arrange a call on Stalin by the P.M. He was told that 'Mr. Stalin is out walking.' As the hours passed he kept on telephoning the Kremlin and the reply was always the same—Stalin was still out walking. Cadogan did not dare to pass this on to the P.M. for fear it might bring on another crisis. At last—it must have been about six o'clock—when Cadogan had given up hope, the news came that Stalin would see the P.M. at seven o'clock.

The P.M. was resolved to make one final effort to break down the wall of misunderstanding which separated him from Marshal Stalin. He said he would be back at half-past eight, and ordered dinner for that hour. A good deal seemed to hang on this final interview and when 8.30 came and there was no sign of the P.M., I found myself pacing up and down the passage by the front door. Then nine o'clock, then ten o'clock, eleven, twelve, and still no sign. Was it a good or a bad omen, this prolonged interview? What did it mean? General Anders, the Commander-in-Chief of the Polish Army, had been asked to come at eight o'clock. As the hours went by, he seemed never to stop abusing the Russians. We were rather embarrassed, wondering if the Russian servants understood English. About midnight I decided to have something to eat.

MARSHAL STALIN

As the night wore on, the rest of the party slept in their chairs or read; one of the secretaries put his feet up on a chair and was soon fast asleep. His deep breathing and Anders's voice were the only sounds that broke the silence. At half-past three in the morning the P.M. burst in. A glance at his face told me things had gone well. He spoke a word to Anders and then went to his room, where I followed him. He was full of the interview.

'During the first hour,' he said, 'I was very cordial, but there was no response from this hard-boiled egg of a man. About eight o'clock I prepared to take my leave. Stalin asked when we were to meet next. I replied I was leaving at dawn. He then said: "Are you pre-occupied?" He meant engaged. I answered, "Not at all." He invited me to come to his apartments and to have some drinks. We walked about a hundred yards to his simple rooms, a dining-room and work-room and a bedroom. Then on the spur of the moment he asked me to dine with him and sent for Molotov to join us.

'Dinner began simply with a few radishes, and grew into a banquet —a sucking pig, two chickens, beef, mutton, every kind of fish. There was enough to feed thirty people. Stalin spoilt a few dishes, a potato here, an oddment there. After four hours of sitting at the table, he suddenly began to make a hearty meal. He offered me the head of a pig, and when I refused, he himself tackled it with relish. With a knife he cleaned out the head, putting it into his mouth with his knife. He then cut pieces of flesh from the cheeks of the pig and ate them with his fingers. Stalin's daughter, a red-headed, well-favoured girl, came in and kissed him, but was not allowed to stay. An old woman appeared, rather frightened; otherwise we waited on ourselves.

'Stalin is as keen as I am on a landing in Norway. He said if this fell through he might have difficulty in keeping his vast armies supplied. He wants lorries. He is making his own tanks. Stalin seems sure he can hang on till the weather breaks.

'When I raised the question of the collective farms and the struggle with the *kulaks*, Stalin became very serious. I asked him if it was as bad as the war. "Oh, yes," he answered. "Worse. Much worse. It went on for years. Most of them were liquidated by the peasants, who hated them. Ten millions of them. But we had to do it to mechanize our agriculture. In the end, production from the land was doubled. What is one generation?" Stalin demanded as he paced up and down the length of the table.'

Sawyers came in and out of the bedroom: 'We shall be late, sir, at the aerodrome.'

The P.M. took no notice.

'I was taken into the family,' he continued. 'We ended friends. It was true that argument broke out later, but it was very friendly argument. I said to Molotov when I was leaving: "I will not trouble you to come to the airfield. I will say goodbye to you here." "Oh, no," said Stalin. "He is a younger man. He will see you off!" '

And at 4.30, as dawn was breaking, Molotov arrived at the villa to accompany the Prime Minister to the airfield.

*

My diary of the four days in Moscow was taken down at the time; it sets out in some detail what happened in the seventeen hours that intervened between Winston leaving the dinner table in the Kremlin at half-past one in the morning of August 15, and his arrival at the Kremlin to say goodbye to Stalin at seven o'clock in the evening of the same day.

The P.M., incensed by Stalin's insults, resolved not to see him again. Cadogan underlined the depths of his resentment; the P.M. had told him that he meant to return to London without seeing Stalin. The Ambassador was satisfied that he intended to leave Moscow that afternoon. The following morning, after a night spent in turning over the incalculable consequences of a quarrel between Winston and Stalin, I sent a message to Clark Kerr in the hope that he might be able to persuade the P.M. to change his mind. The Ambassador found Winston in a difficult mood and he was cock-a-hoop when he at last persuaded the P.M. to see Stalin before leaving Moscow.

There is a discrepancy between this account of the conference and that of Winston in *The Hinge of Fate*. The Prime Minister, back in Cairo after the conference, reported to Mr. Attlee that the dinner had passed off in a very friendly atmosphere. He can hardly have forgotten the events of the night of the 14th. It is more probable that he saw little point in perpetuating in detail his own stormy reaction to Stalin's insults and generally provocative attitude in the course of their meeting on August 13, particularly now that the conference could be acclaimed as a complete success.

As one reads of these now-distant days, they seemed to be smoothed out, and as it were edited; the terrifically alive, pugnacious, impatient and impulsive Winston Churchill has been dressed up as a sagacious, tolerant elder statesman, pondering good-humouredly on the frailty of men and the part chance plays in their fluctuating fortunes. He himself once said that he was not designed by nature for that particular role.

This brings me to Winston's memory. I recall that he declaimed to me 'King Robert of Sicily', a poem of eighty-six lines, five days after his stroke in 1953, with only a few mistakes. He then asked me what part of the brain stores memories, and went on to tell me that he could recall in detail many incidents in his trench life at Plug Street in the First World War, whereas in the Second War one great event toppling over another seemed to wipe out the last, so that in writing his book he came to depend on what had been committed to paper. There were, however, times when everything was at stake which were stamped indelibly on his mind. I have heard him describe the scene in a deep shelter at Uxbridge on September 15, during the Battle of Britain, perhaps half a dozen times, and on each occasion in almost the same words.

Winston's first meeting with Stalin was another instance. He was keyed up to what was even in his life an unusual experience. He came back from his talks with Stalin in a state of suppressed excitement; he wanted to tell us what Stalin had said. I took it down at the time. Next day, while he was undressing, he repeated what Stalin had said to him in exactly the same words. We know now that they were Stalin's actual words, because Winston's account of these talks in *The Hinge of Fate* was taken from the interpreter's script.

Chapter eight

A soldier uninhibited

Cairo, August, 1942

Cairo feels airless after Moscow, and the news from home is not exhilarating. The Dieppe raid was, it appears, a fiasco; three-fifths of the Canadians—about 3,000 men—were either killed or taken prisoner. But the P.M. will not hear of the word 'failure.' The casualties were heavy, but the results were important. We had learnt a lot.

'You ought to remember, Charles, that in the air it pays us to lose machine for machine.'

I seemed to be back in the First World War, listening to the Brigade people explaining away an unsuccessful raid.

'It is a lesson,' the C.I.G.S. grunted, 'to the people who are clamouring for the invasion of France.'

August 19, 1942

I heard the P.M. singing in his bath this morning, and he was in high spirits when Alex [1] arrived at the Embassy to drive him into the desert. All day we bumped and jolted, through the blinding heat, until towards evening we came to a caravan tucked away among the sand-dunes by the sea. Monty [2] appeared in battle-dress and beret, and then we bathed. A little way off a lot of our men were shouting and splashing in the waves. Then Monty took the P.M. away to explain the battle, and we saw no more of him; Alex may be in supreme command, but I get the impression that it is Monty and his Eighth Army who have taken charge of this business. Which is all to the good, for this man clearly knows his job.

[1] General Alexander, who succeeded General Auchinleck as Commander-in-Chief Middle East on August 12, 1942.

[2] General Montgomery, Commander Eighth Army in North Africa, August 12, 1942.

66

August 20, 1942

The P.M. set out early to examine the ground near the Ridge, where the battle will be fought. On our way, we kept passing bunches of grinning, cheering soldiers, naked except for a loin-cloth, and burnt brown by months under the African sun. When we got out of our cars, the P.M. came up to me.

'Can you explain this, Charles? When I was at Omdurman forty-four years ago, it was a military offence to appear without a pith helmet, and we were clad so that our skins were shielded from the sun. Why don't these fellows here get sunstroke and heatstroke?' he demanded.

About noon we came to Freyberg's[1] canvas oven, where we were to lunch.

'Monty has worked a miracle; the atmosphere is completely changed.'

Everywhere the P.M. went he sensed quiet confidence and a good spirit. He was, indeed, well content.

'Where is Monty?' he asked cheerfully when we were about to begin luncheon.

We found him in his car eating sandwiches. He explained that he made a point of never lunching with a unit under his command.

The P.M. was full of all that he had seen. He talked on many things late into the night, while his little audience, revelling in this new experience, marvelled at the man—his boyish enthusiasm, his consuming vitality, his terrific vocabulary. As for our host, Monty had withdrawn to his caravan, according to his habit, at ten o'clock sharp.

*

I find this note on Monty written later in my diary:

The average Army officer tends to conform to a type; it is dinned into him at school that he must not be different from other boys until the approval of his little community becomes essential to his peace of mind. For my part, I can own to a liking for these inhibitions, which are a small part of good manners, even if they mean no more than a concern for the convenience of others. Ernest Bevin, for instance, talked about himself—non-stop, as they say—while Anthony Eden, a vainer man, has learnt reticence. To remain gentle and self-effacing after climbing to the top of a profession, as Wavell and Marshall have done, is to me an endearing trait.

[1] Sir Bernard Freyberg, Commander of New Zealand troops in North Africa.

There is, of course, none of this nonsense about Monty; he wanted it made plain at the very beginning that he is not at all like other people; he appears to be intent on creating a particular image in the public mind. Nor would you expect Winston to submit to inhibitions of any kind. After all, they imply a desire to placate, and Winston is singularly free from that urge; they call, too, for a measure of control and he has 'devoted more time to self-expression than self-discipline.'

Monty's boastfulness has been held against him as a breach of good manners, but it is, of course, largely irrelevant when sizing him up as a soldier. On the other hand, there was nothing new in his training methods. He has told us at some length how he made it his business to go among his men, how he deliberately set out to make the Eighth Army a *corps d'élite*, and every man in it cocksure of victory. This is the pride in arms of the Brigade of Guards, or, for that matter, of the Roman Legion. At least it was all to the good to have nothing to do with the impersonal leadership of the First World War. In my time in the trenches I saw the Divisional General once—at a horse show.

The P.M. spoke of it as an astonishing transformation; he said it was plain already that Monty knew the secret of preparing his men for battle. I ventured to argue that there were others—Straffer Gott and Alex himself—who had won the hearts of their men while shunning publicity. Winston gave a great snort. It is foolish, of course, to argue with him.

*

August 21, 1942

Brooke is sure that Monty is big enough for the job. When he talks to me about the retreat to Dunkirk, I notice that he picks out the generals who were imperturbable in adversity. A note of affectionate pride crept into his matter-of-fact speech as he explained how, when the position looked quite desperate, Monty was still cocky and full of confidence that he could carry out the orders given to him. His quick brain took in the situation almost at a glance; it was a great comfort to Brooke to have a lieutenant like that at such a crisis. And it was Brooke who brought him here; the P.M. took a lot of persuading. Knowing what the C.I.G.S. thought of Monty, I asked him how he had settled down in the Eighth Army. Brooke is usually pretty thrifty in praise, but to my surprise he then let himself go. He was astounded by what Monty had done.

'Why, he's only been here a few days, but he has got about and

sized up the position. And he has placed pretty accurately, I think, those under him. Why, he even told me what Rommel will do!'
  Brooke smiled.
  'I believe he is right, too.'

*

I shall leave my diary here to record a conversation with General Eisenhower in the White House in the summer of 1954. Ike had been talking to the Prof. and me of the importance of faith. And then he rather abruptly changed the subject: Patton[1] was an unusual general; he was not much good at fighting a battle, but he was the best pursuit general of recent years. If Monty had been as good in pursuit as he was in fighting a battle, then he would have been one of the great captains.

*

August 22, 1942
  While we were in Moscow the siege of Malta was raised. Five ships out of a convoy of fourteen successfully ran the gauntlet of submarine and bomber, and made it possible for the Governor, Lord Gort, to fly to Cairo to report to the Prime Minister. The P.M.'s relief is a joyful sight. The plight of the island—short of food and ammunition—has been distracting him. We found Gort at the Embassy on our return from the desert. He is hardly recognizable— stones lighter. The fat boy, as he was called, has disappeared, and in his place is a man years older, with sunken cheeks and tired eyes. The island has been on short commons, and the Governor has been setting an example in rationing.
  Gort has sustained without bitterness the cruellest disappointment that can befall a soldier, in that he was dislodged from the supreme command in the midst of a world war. But he tackles his present job, so unimportant in comparison with his responsibilities in France, with all his might. He simply hadn't enough wits for a really big post, but he has character enough for anything.
  The P.M. dabbed his eyes with a handkerchief as he listened to Malta's story. This morning the King has sent his congratulations on the success of the Moscow visit. There was a message, too, from Smuts. He showed it to me.
  'Your handling of a critical psychological situation was,' I read, 'masterly. You have firmly and finally bound Russia to us for this war at least.'

[1] General George Patton, Commander (successively), U.S. 7th and 3rd Armies.

69

It is at these moments that the P.M. is inclined to take the bit into his teeth and, kicking up his heels, gallop about for the fun of the thing. I thought it would do him no harm to show him a telegram I had just received from General Smuts. It was handed in at Pretoria and deciphered here:

'Following is personal message for Sir Charles Wilson from General Smuts:

'Please continue your efforts for Prime Minister's health. I feel convinced he cannot continue at the present pace without a breakdown. Grave national responsibility rests on you for Leader's health. All good wishes.'

'I am very well,' the P.M. pouted. 'Come. Let us go and see if anything has come in. We have clapped Gandhi into gaol.'

Chapter nine

Turning-point

In 1953 I asked Winston to pick out the two most anxious months of the war. He did not hesitate: 'September and October, yes, 1942.' And yet, if I can trust my diary, I was not unduly worried about him then. It is true that whenever I appeared at No. 10, there seemed to be some fresh burden on his mind, but he met these calls with such abounding energy that I felt his reserves had hardly been touched.

On our return from Cairo on August 24, 1942, the P.M. received from Washington what he calls in his book a 'bombshell,' though the epithet he used at the time was even more descriptive. The Chiefs of Staff of the two countries had come to a complete deadlock. The Americans wished to reduce the scope of TORCH; they wanted to confine it to attacks on Casablanca and Oran, abandoning altogether the plan for a landing at Algiers. The Prime Minister was shocked. Algiers, he felt, was the key to the whole operation. Why, he wondered, were the Americans tearing the agreed plan to pieces in this fashion at the eleventh hour? Were they afraid to commit their forces to a major operation in an inland sea because their lines of communication ran through the Straits of Gibraltar? Perhaps Lewis Douglas, years later, gave me the explanation when he said:

'Asquith,[1] I am told, in his day hardly made a major decision without seeking a parallel in the past. Winston isn't like that. But in the case of the Mediterranean the long history of the inland sea was always present in his mind. The control of the Mediterranean meant in his eyes the control of the Western world. We owe a good deal to Winston for keeping the historic importance of the Mediterranean in men's minds during the war.'

Did Marshall fail to understand the importance of the Mediterranean? He had always been opposed to TORCH, but the Prime

[1] Herbert Asquith, Prime Minister 1908–16.

71

Minister did not believe that he would allow a personal judgment to weigh with him once agreement had been reached. This correspondence with the President distressed the P.M. He was never so unhappy as when he was at odds with his military advisers or his American allies. Besides, he had promised Stalin TORCH, and he felt that to fob him off with a simplified version was to break his word. One day, when I called on him, he said:

'If the Americans are obstinate, the whole plan for invading North Africa may fall. Ike [1] and Mark Clark [2] are very much upset about it. They cannot understand what is happening in Washington.'

And then, on September 5, the President gave way. The pent-up feelings of the two men flashed across the Atlantic:

President Roosevelt to Prime Minister—5 Sept., '42: 'Hurrah!'

Former Naval Person to President Roosevelt—6 Sept., '42: 'O.K. Full blast.'

These events, though disturbing to the P.M., could be matched by the disasters of any similar period in the past two years. What made these months so crucial to him was not the number or severity of the reverses, but the steady deterioration in the political situation at home.

One day Brendan Bracken [3] sent for me.

'I want you, my dear Doctor, to keep an eye on your patient. There may be trouble ahead. The Prime Minister must win his battle in the desert or get out.'

I thought Brendan was fussing.

Wilson: 'I fancy the P.M. has too much on his hands to mope over things. You know, when the going is rough, he seems to find distraction in doing things.'

Brendan: 'Don't be too sure. There is a good deal going on under the surface. I'm afraid of that fellow Cripps. I think he means business. If he pulls out, there'll be the hell of a row.'

Wilson: 'I thought it was Trenchard who was making trouble.'

Brendan: 'Oh, he will make a bit of a stink, but he can't bring the Prime Minister down.'

There was something very wrong somewhere, and Aneurin Bevan made it his business to find out who was at fault. He was in the mood to make trouble. In the first months of the war, Winston and

---

[1] General Dwight D. Eisenhower, Commanding General of the U.S. forces, European theatre of operations.

[2] General Mark Clark, deputy to General Eisenhower.

[3] Brendan Bracken, Minister of Information, formerly Parliamentary private secretary to Mr. Churchill.

he had been good friends. The two men met at Cherkley, Lord Beaverbrook's house at Leatherhead, where, egged on by Max, they drank and argued through the night. But when in the spring of 1940 Bevan was left out of the Churchill Government, it was inevitable that he would soon become restive under the arbitrary reign of the Prime Minister.

The country was uneasy about the course of events, and Bevan made his paper, *Tribune*, the medium for ventilating this frustration. The climax came on May 1, when an article appeared in *Tribune* entitled: 'Why Churchill?' It was a devastating onslaught on the Prime Minister's conduct of the war.

Winston, himself, was disposed to dismiss Bevan as 'a squalid nuisance.' Attlee told me that Bevan's campaign was no more than an irritant. But it was another story when Lord Trenchard [1] and Sir Stafford Cripps, the Leader of the House of Commons, put themselves at the head of the insurgents.

'Boom' Trenchard, as he was known to his friends, was a legendary figure to the pilots of this war—the man who created our Air Force in the First World War. He appeared to be a block of granite. He told me once that the chief reason why men fight is because they fear what others may say of them; that an empty seat at the breakfast table in the mess is very bad for the morale of pilots; that if there are five seats vacant after a raid, they should be filled at once. His mind went back to the days before the war, when he set out to recruit the pilots who were to win the Battle of Britain. He did not attempt to compete with safer and more lucrative callings; an ace did not bother his head about getting on in life. The kind of fighting you get in the air will never be very attractive to the worldly-minded.

All this came out in instalments, for Trenchard was barely articulate and took some time to see a point. He was, I suppose, a kind of modern edition of the bearded Duke of Devonshire of my youth—the Lord Hartington of Gladstone's day—who eventually arrived at the right decisions, though by nature he was incapable of explaining how he had reached them. Trenchard had been so often right in the past. Who could say with certainty that he was wrong now?

Lord Trenchard himself had no doubts. 'We must avoid the stupendous drain on manpower of an attempt to win victory by land warfare. You must get this into the Prime Minister's head. If he puts his faith in bombers, it will save millions of lives.' I explained that the P.M. did not rely on his doctor for his strategy. I do not think he heard. 'If only I could get sense into their heads!' he went

[1] 'Boom' Trenchard, formerly Chief of Air Staff.

on. 'I want to help, but when I get on to my feet to speak, I cannot make what I want to say as clear to them as it is to me. I get no better,' he said to me sadly. 'In fact, I get worse. They don't seem able to follow what I am trying to say.'

Trenchard had said that if we put our faith in bombers, it would save millions of lives. 'He might be right,' the P.M. said, half to me and half to himself—Winston's imagination is not always a good friend. From what he then said, I believe that he, too, had doubts about the verdict of history on the way that England had 'got mixed up in land warfare in the two World Wars.'

But it was not the occasion for musing on the past. He was being attacked. There might, he said, be repercussions in the House and in the country. Lord Trenchard's personality and record certainly lent weight to his views in the Services and in the inner circle of Government, but the Prime Minister knew that, in time of war, his criticism would not rock a Coalition Government. He was pained, but he was not perturbed.

While this correspondence was passing between them, a more formidable critic had taken the field. Sir Stafford Cripps had long been dissatisfied with the direction of the war. In September he felt so out of tune with the Prime Minister that he felt he could no longer postpone his resignation. The two men were not designed by nature to run in double harness. Cripps's subtle intelligence, trained in the law, made him impatient of short-cuts, but when he went to the Prime Minister to get from him an important decision, he came away grumbling:

'The man simply will not listen to evidence.'

Cripps's case had rested, perhaps, on half a dozen premises, and he would have liked to examine each in turn, but when he was in the act of developing the second something he said sent the P.M.'s mind off at a tangent. He had started an idea, and it went ricocheting in Winston's head until it became plain to Cripps that the Prime Minister was no longer listening to what he said. The P.M. seemed to arrive at his conclusions by what I can only call a *saltus empiricus*. It was all very trying to the precise Sir Stafford.

The austerity of Cripps's nature, combined with his mental processes, were equally unintelligible to the P.M. One night he described Cripps to Stalin. He began by dilating on his virtues, then after a pause he went on:

'The trouble is, his chest is a cage in which two squirrels are at war, his conscience and his career.'

Sir Stafford's indictment of the direction of the war fell under three heads.

74

In the first place, he complained that, in a war which would be won by the scientists, effective use had not been made of our pre-eminence in science. He saw that the trouble began at the top—that the Prime Minister's mind was ingenious rather than scientific. Portal long afterwards said to me:

'The P.M. never really understood the air.'

Tedder said the same thing. It was true that he would always welcome any new idea; even if it did not sound plausible, he would insist that it be given a fair trial. He played, too, a considerable part in initiating some of our more fruitful inventions—such as the Mulberry Harbours used in the invasion of France in 1944—but the scientific habit of mind was wholly foreign to his mental processes.

Our equipment suffered in consequence. We met reverses in the desert because our tanks were inferior to those of the Germans and, in particular, because the guns in our tanks were outranged by the guns in their tanks. In this connection, I recall a conversation with a prominent Fellow of the Royal Society during the late summer of 1942. If, he said, we had been as inefficient in providing aircraft as we have been in turning out tanks, the war would have been lost already. It seemed to him incredible that the Prime Minister received scientific advice from one source only—Lord Cherwell.

In the second place, Cripps wanted more time to be devoted to the broad strategy of the war. The Chiefs of Staff were engulfed in routine.

Finally, Cripps doubted whether some of our generals had any aptitude for handling mechanized forces on a large scale. Their ideas and methods were obsolete.

In the correspondence that followed Cripps's paper, the Prime Minister challenged him to name those in whom he had no confidence. Cripps bluntly replied that the Chief of the Naval Staff, Sir Dudley Pound, was past his work. The P.M. was pained by this attack on Pound, to whom he had long been deeply attached.

The Prime Minister was still living on his balance at the bank that had accumulated in 1940. Broadly speaking, he got his way in everything. Lord Beaverbrook explained the position to me: 'The Prime Minister, Brendan and I used to meet every evening. We settled most things.' But the P.M. knew how far he could go. He knew that the resignation of the Leader of the House on such an issue as the conduct of the war must lead to a political crisis of the first magnitude. 'Anything might happen,' he said. During September the P.M. used all his powers of persuasion to convert Cripps, and in the end Cripps, whose high sense of duty had never been in

75

question, was persuaded to postpone his resignation until after the battle in the desert.

It was with a sense of relief that the P.M. turned to the preparations for the impending battle. But it was no more than a respite.

*

September 30, 1942

Brendan Bracken came to see me today. He says that if Rommel is victorious the position of the Prime Minister will become very difficult. 'You see, Charles, important changes in the direction of the war would then be inevitable, and Winston will never submit to any curtailment of his powers. If we are beaten in this battle, it's the end of Winston. Is he sleeping all right? You see, he is going through a very bad time.' So far as I can tell, Brendan is alarming himself unnecessarily. Of course, these thoughts may be passing through the P.M.'s head, but his confident nature is able to dismiss them from his mind. Why should he waste his time picturing what might happen if Rommel won? He does not for a moment believe he can win.

*

I can see now that I was completely taken in by the bold front the P.M. put up during those two critical months. This man, who is, after all, my patient, had been distracted by his cares. He knew what defeat would mean. Brendan did not exaggerate the turmoil in his mind when he said: 'Winston is finding the suspense almost unbearable.' Greedily he devoured the reports from the desert. It appeared that everyone in the Eighth Army was cock-a-hoop when the battle began on October 23.

The Prime Minister and his colleagues in the Cabinet were therefore both surprised and shocked when, after a week's hard slogging, there was nothing to show for 10,000 casualties. The offensive seemed little nearer its goal than at the beginning. When I had to see the P.M. about a sleeping pill, they warned me that he was in an explosive mood. I was with him only a few moments, but as I left he grunted half under his breath: 'If this goes on, anything may happen.' I found Brooke waiting for me. 'Is the P.M. all right, Charles? I thought he was going to hit me when he demanded: "Haven't we got a single general who can even win one battle?"'

Three more difficult days went by. All day and all night the devastating fire of 1,000 guns was supported by incessant bombing from the air, where we were dominant. I did not see the P.M. during that time, but it appears that he waited for news with mounting apprehension. And then Monty attacked. The P.M. breathed again. He was in a state of great excitement when he heard that Rommel was in full retreat. I find this note in my diary:

'The victory in the desert has brought great joy to the P.M. He talks of ringing the church bells all over Britain. But he won't do anything till the prisoners number at least 20,000. He will take none of the credit, though the changes he has made in the desert command have been triumphantly vindicated. He is lyrical about Monty and Alex. This victory will silence criticism, and it seems that for the moment all his troubles are at an end.'

Four days later there was more good news: the first British and American troops landed at Algiers on November 8. The invasion of North Africa had begun. The details of this vast operation had been carefully thought out. Six hundred and fifty ships passed through waters infested with submarines without loss; the actual landings at Algiers and Casablanca were made without heavy fighting; even at Oran the opposition was soon overcome. Coming on top of the victory at Alamein, the imagination, foresight and careful attention to detail shown in this brilliant operation left the country with a feeling that there could not be much wrong after all. Perhaps the worst was over.

Looking back, we can see that the battle was a turning-point in Churchill's fortunes during the war. He himself has told us that in September, 1942, his position was more vulnerable than at any other period in the war. After El Alamein, he was never again in danger of losing his job as long as the war lasted.

Chapter ten

A great friendship

January 13, 1943

I left my cottage at Harefield at nine o'clock after listening to a recording of the Brains Trust in which I had taken part, and kicked myself for the things I ought to have said if I had thought of them in time. It was raining as, with the help of a torch, I picked my steps through the pools on the garden path to the gate, where an Army car was waiting to take me to the Annexe at Storey's Gate.[1] I found the P.M. in high spirits, elated to be once more on the move. The airfield near Oxford was wintry, damp and dismal, but after ten hours in the air we breakfasted in a bungalow outside Casablanca, with the sun streaming in from a blue sky and oranges, with their leaves, on our plates.

The P.M. is full of zest, though the night was not a success. In the stern of the bomber there were two mattresses, stretched side by side, one for the P.M. and one for me. The rest of the party slept in their chairs. I woke with a start to find the P.M. crawling down into the well beneath, where Portal was asleep. When he shook him vigorously by the shoulder, I thought it would be well to find out what was wrong. Winston said he had burnt his toes against some metal connections of the improvised heating arrangements at the foot of the mattress. 'They are red hot,' he explained. 'We shall have the petrol fumes bursting into flames. There'll be an explosion soon.'

Winston was thoroughly worked up about the business; the

[1] The cellars underneath the Office of Works in Storey's Gate were converted into a fortress, with a concrete roof 15 feet thick and steel doors. There was a Cabinet room and a Map room and bedrooms for the Prime Minister and his Ministers. It was from his room here that Churchill made some of his famous broadcasts. Over the cellars a flat was prepared for Churchill and his family, and was known as the Annexe. They moved there when a bomb demolished part of 10, Downing Street.

FIELD–MARSHAL MONTGOMERY

MR. HARRY HOPKINS

simplest thing seemed to be to turn off the heating. How long I slept after we had settled again I cannot say, but I awoke to discover the P.M. on his knees, trying to keep out the draught by putting a blanket against the side of the plane. He was shivering: we were flying at 7,000 feet in an unheated bomber in mid-winter. I got up, and we struggled, not with much success, to cut off the blast. An hour or two later he woke me and we returned to the attack. The P.M. is at a disadvantage in this kind of travel, since he never wears anything at night but a silk vest. On his hands and knees, he cut a quaint figure with his big, bare, white bottom.

Anfa, Casablanca, January 16, 1943

This afternoon I went for a walk. The same idea had occurred to the Chiefs of Staff, and I found them talking at the water's edge. Dill, who was with them, gazing at the white breakers, said they had been very lucky in the weather for the invasion of North Africa: if the sea had been as rough as it is now, the landings would not have been possible. War is a game of chance, and luck had given them the one day in fifty when we could land. We walked slowly back. Portal, who is full of odd scraps of information, which he usually keeps to himself, explained to Dill how the sap travels in a cactus plant.

When I got back I found that there had been a great hunt for the P.M., who had been missing. Anfa Camp, the name given to the hotel and the villas surrounding it in which we live, is encircled by a wire fence in which there are only two entrances, guarded by sentries, but the P.M. had somehow slipped out and had gone for a walk. The Sappers are putting a wooden covering over the steps to our front door so that the President's chair can be wheeled up the ramp into the house when he dines with us tonight.

January 19, 1943

I asked Harry Hopkins today whether he thought these conferences are worth while. He grinned broadly:

'The President came here because he wanted to make the trip; he is tired of sending me to London and Moscow. He loves the drama of a journey like this. They are always telling him that the President must not fly; it is too dangerous. This is his answer.'

As for the P.M., when he gets away from his red boxes and leaves London, he puts his cares behind him. It's not only that he loves adventure; he feels, too, at times that he must 'let up'; even a week or two away from the unending grind helps. He wants to shed for a little the feeling that there are more things to do in the twenty-four hours than can possibly be squeezed in. Perhaps Roosevelt has that feeling too. It's the instinct to escape, to take a long breath. Besides neither of them, in a way, has ever grown up.

However this may be, they both came to Casablanca for one purpose: to decide where to fight next, when there are no Germans left in Africa. The Chiefs of Staff have been hammering away at the alternatives for a week. Yesterday it was finally agreed to attack Sicily. Harry doesn't seem very happy about this decision; as he puts it, he is 100 per cent. with Marshall in wanting to get on with the invasion of France.

January 22, 1943

The President, Harry told me, cannot return to Washington without patching up this de Gaulle–Giraud [1] feud. It will not be easy. de Gaulle positively goes out of his way to be difficult. He seems as sure about everything as when I first met him in the hall at Chequers, just as he was about to leave for London: an improbable creature, like a human giraffe, sniffing down his nostrils at mortals beneath his gaze. When I questioned him about his book on the use of the tank in wars of the future, he began speaking very rapidly in French, leaving me staring up at him like an urchin gazing in awe at a Palace guardsman.

Since then he has popped in and out of the pages of my diary, and whenever he appears he has a crack at the P.M. The P.M. is a bad hater, but in these days, when he is stretched taut, certain people seem to get on his nerves: de Gaulle is one of them. He is so stuffed with principles that there is no room left for a little Christian tolerance; in his rigidity, there is no give. Besides, men of his race do not find it easy to accept any foreigner as a superior being, and Winston does not like that kind of agnosticism.

However, it is plain that the President has set his mind on making peace between the two generals; they must be friends. And time is running short. So Anthony Eden has been given the job in London of getting de Gaulle out here—a pretty stiff task, for the General is a haughty fellow and crammed full of grievances.

At first, apparently, Anthony made no progress at all. Indeed, de Gaulle's curt refusal seemed final. It was only when the P.M. despatched a sharp message, intimating that if the General could not be more helpful the Allies would have, in the future, to get on without him, that de Gaulle at last thought it prudent to come here. He came with no good grace this morning, and even now half the day has been spent in persuading him to meet Giraud; it was like

[1] General Giraud, High Commissioner, French North Africa.

entraining a difficult horse. Nor was his interview with the Prime Minister more successful. When at last they emerged from the little sitting-room in our villa, the P.M. stood in the hall watching the Frenchman stalk down the garden path with his head in the air. Winston turned to us with a whimsical smile:

'His country has given up fighting, he himself is a refugee, and if we turn him down he's finished. Well, just look at him! Look at him!' he repeated. 'He might be Stalin, with 200 divisions behind his words. I was pretty rough with him. I made it quite plain that if he could not be more helpful we were done with him.'

'How,' I asked, 'did he like that?'

'Oh,' the P.M. replied, 'he hardly seemed interested. My advances and my threats met with no response.'

Harry Hopkins had told me of the President's quip that de Gaulle claimed to be the lineal descendant of Joan of Arc. I repeated this to the P.M. He was not amused. It did not seem at all absurd to him.

'France without an Army is not France. De Gaulle is the spirit of that Army. Perhaps,' he said sadly, 'the last survivor of a warrior race.'

If this Frenchman's arrogance, his defiance of everyone and everything, do at times get on the P.M.'s nerves, there are days when he cannot withhold his admiration. He was in tears when he said:

'England's grievous offence in de Gaulle's eyes is that she has helped France. He cannot bear to think that she needed help. He will not relax his vigilance in guarding her honour for a single instant.'

I wonder what will happen tonight when de Gaulle sees the President. Roosevelt is in no mood, if Harry can be trusted, to make allowances for Gallic pride. And, as Winston said, de Gaulle is the quintessence of an inferiority complex.

January 23, 1943

It appears that when the President met de Gaulle things went better than any of us had anticipated. The President was attracted by 'a spiritual look' in his eyes, which the P.M. had somehow missed.

January 24, 1943

The President and the P.M. were with de Gaulle before the Press Conference, when, to everyone's astonishment, Hopkins walked in with Giraud. I am sure Harry had planned this bringing together in public of the two French generals. Roosevelt, though he was taken aback, seized the opportunity. Before they could recover from their surprise, he had arranged that this historic moment—for such both the President and the P.M. deemed it—should be recorded for posterity by the camera. There were plenty of volunteers to take the picture, for a flock of photographers were waiting for the Conference, and the President decided that the lawn behind his bungalow should be the site of this interesting ceremony. The picture which the photographer obtained may be stuff for the historian. He will see the long, stiff-necked de Gaulle gingerly proffering his hand, though his face is without a flicker of a smile. Behind the outstretched arms he will detect the seated President, his head thrown back in hilarious enjoyment of the moment, while Winston sits demurely on the edge of his chair, his face wearing the expression of a child who has the sixpence in his hand, and is anxiously waiting for the opposite side to call, 'Up, Jenkins.'

The Conference has lasted ten days. The soldiers and sailors are returning by air to England, while the P.M. goes by road to Marrakesh for twenty-four hours; after which the President will go home and we shall go to Cairo.

We set off in a fleet of cars, taking a picnic lunch with us. All the way to Marrakesh, 150 miles across the desert, there was an American soldier stationed every hundred yards, and when we paused by the roadside for luncheon fighter planes hovered protectingly over us. We were about to take the road again when Randolph went back to find the President's car to read him an extract from Machiavelli, which he thought appropriate.

While yet a long way from Marrakesh, we saw on the horizon the foothills, with the snow-capped Atlas Mountains behind them. And so we came to a house on the fringe of the town that had been set apart for us.

It was the hour when the sun was setting. To see the colours changing over the snow-capped mountains, Winston climbed on to the roof. It was so lovely that he insisted the President must see it. Two of his servants, by holding hands, made a chair with their arms, and in this fashion he was carried up the winding stairs to the roof-top, his paralysed legs dangling like the limbs of a ventriloquist's dummy, limp and flaccid. We stood gazing at the purple hills, where the light was changing every minute.

'It's the most lovely spot in the whole world,' the P.M. murmured.

When the President had been carried back to his room, I walked with Winston in the garden among the orange trees.

'I love these Americans,' the P.M. said. 'They have behaved so generously.'

82

At night there was a family dinner party, when the President and the P.M. made little, affectionate speeches to each other, and Winston sang. There were choruses, which grew in gusto as the night went on. The President proposed the health of one who would very much like to have been here—the King.

In the morning the P.M., who intended to see the President off at the airfield, kept putting off, as usual, the moment when he must get out of bed, until he made himself late. Then we heard his bedroom slippers flopping on the stone floor, and he appeared at the door in his most flamboyant dressing-gown, covered with red dragons. He got into the President's car in this gay garment and drove with him to the airfield.

The P.M. tells me that the War Cabinet are being very obstinate about Turkey. 'They don't want me to go to see Inönü,' he said. As far as I can make out, Anthony has made a stand for once. He is cautious, and feels that nothing will come of it. Besides, he must dislike the negotiations being taken out of his hands. But in the end the P.M. has had his way, of course, and expects that an answer from Inönü will be awaiting him in Cairo. He seems to be convinced he will be able to bring Turkey into the war, and is in great heart about it all.

About noon the P.M. got out his paints, which I have not seen before,[1] and, climbing the tower, gazed for a long time in silence at the Atlas Mountains. He seemed reluctant to break the illusion of a holiday, which for a few hours has given him a chance to get his breath.

[1] This was the only picture the Prime Minister painted during the war.

Chapter eleven

Faith abounding

January 30, 1943

Ever since the collapse of France and the appearance of the Germans in the Caucasus, Turkey has been kept on tenterhooks; her army has been permanently mobilized to resist invasion. The Turks have been so circumspect in their dealings with Germany that it was a milestone when the wise and prudent President of Turkey agreed to meet the P.M. on Turkish soil. It means that our stock has risen as the German military position has deteriorated.

As we climbed into the aeroplane at Cairo, bound for somewhere in Turkey, we had a feeling that this particular trip was a little off the beaten track. Landing at Adana, where a number of cars met us, we drove through narrow, flat, muddy roads to a train in a siding. There was no platform, but we heaved the P.M. up into his compartment, and the train proceeded to meander along, at about eight miles an hour, under the shadow of the Taurus Mountains, until out of the snow-capped hills there crawled, 'like an enamel caterpillar,' the President's train: I have borrowed this image from the P.M.; he likes it and has repeated it several times.

Our train pulled up with a great clanking of carriages in a siding. The President of Turkey [1] descended from a compartment and climbed into our saloon, which had been prepared for luncheon. The President, his Prime Minister and his Foreign Minister are all deaf, and the Marshal who commands the Turkish Army, dour and aloof, may have been deaf too: he took so little part in the exchanges. On our side the P.M., the C.I.G.S. and Alex shouted cheerfully. Jumbo Wilson [2] paired off with the Turkish Marshal, and no one feared that either would be guilty of any light indiscretions.

The President, in spite of his deafness, has an air of great alertness

[1] Ismet Inönü.

[2] General Sir Henry Maitland Wilson, Commander-in-Chief, Middle East.

and was all smiles; he speaks English and made a good impression on the P.M. I was on the point of mobilizing my halting French for the benefit of the President's secretary when he informed me in fluent English that he listened every week to the Brains Trust.

There were more conferences in the afternoon, but the train was stuffy, and I jumped down and went for a walk along the sleepers. Before dinner I found the P.M. in his bedroom at the back of the train. He was pleased with the talks.

'This is about the best day's work I have ever done,' he said to me. 'The President put both hands on mine. I now understand how he seduces people. I'm sure I have completely won him over. But I don't want the Turks to come in until they are ready. I don't want them massacred. Let them be armed, and then, if it is in their interest, they will come in. I only pressed that this rearmament business should be thoroughly organized.'

To an onlooker there does not seem to be any danger of precipitate action on the part of the Turks. They will not do anything rash. They are much too scared of the Russians and of what may happen when peace comes.

The American Ambassador, Steinhardt, however, was as optimistic as Winston: 'Let them take their own time. Don't hurry them. You'll see events will bring them in.' The British Ambassador, Sir Hughe Knatchbull-Hugessen, seemed to agree with his colleague's point of view. He had, I think, borrowed it from him. Both of them appeared apprehensive that the P.M. would go too quickly. It seems that the Turkish Prime Minister told the P.M. that Russia would be very powerful after the war, and that Turkey must be prudent. The P.M. retorted that there would be an international organization to see that Russia was kept in her place. The Turk complained that he was looking for something more 'real.'

'I don't know what he means by "real," ' the P.M. grumbled when he got back to his compartment. 'I should have thought an organization of this nature is real enough for anyone.' The Turk made it plain that he feared a Russian occupation of the Dardanelles and not German bombing. But neither Winston nor the Ambassadors would listen.

At night there was a great feast and much liquor was drunk in toasts. The P.M., becoming quite hilarious, did all the talking. He was entirely taken up with the task of converting some of his stories into his own brand of French. It isn't French, and it isn't English, but something in between. When he quotes poetry, he gabbles it like a self-conscious schoolboy, but now he was too busy with his speech to bother about us. Before we arrived, the Turks may have wondered how things would go, and no doubt there was a sense of relief at the turn of events. Anyway, when they found the P.M. in tearing spirits they, too, laughed immoderately. At times there was so much uproar that I could not hear what Ismet Inönü's A.D.C., who was sitting on my right, was saying. However, after his tongue had been loosened by many drinks, I had less difficulty in following his talk. He said that the 'high-ups' in Turkey give Germany four months before she collapses.

January 31, 1943

We slept in the train, and today the Turks came to lunch. Then the train returned as it came, at the same cautious pace, and the same cars took us to the same aerodrome, where the Turks had assembled in force to see us off. We bade friendly farewells and climbed into the big bomber. The engines roared, we began to move, and at that moment the pilot carelessly allowed the right wheel to leave the runway, whereupon the big tyre at once sank a foot into the mud. The engines raced, but nothing happened. We were bogged. The Turks looked sympathetic. I was afraid that the P.M. might be upset by the delay, but when I looked round he was nowhere to be seen. I found him surrounded by Turks, who were all talking at once. Winston had taken charge in his best Sidney Street[1] manner, and kept pointing to the wheel and gesticulating to the Turks. If only he could make them understand his plan. . . . Lorries with chains appeared, but all were of no avail. The Turks crept away. Spades were produced and men dug round the sunken wheel. The P.M. removed his hat and mopped his head. At last it was decided that we must change aeroplanes. The afternoon had slipped away; it would be dark before we landed at Cairo.

Brooke was fretting because the P.M. kept changing his mind. First he wanted to stay another night in Turkey. The negotiations with Inönü were of vital importance; they must on no account be scamped. Then, when he had talked to the C.I.G.S., he decided that no time must be lost in getting back to Cairo, where a pile of work had accumulated. The engines began warming up, and suddenly the P.M. decided that he would not go to Cairo after all. He would spend a night in Cyprus.

---

[1] The siege of Sidney Street took place in 1911. Foreign anarchists murdered a policeman in the course of burglary and then barricaded themselves in a house in Sidney Street, East London. Churchill was Home Secretary at the time, and when the police asked for his permission to bring in armed soldiers he clambered out of his bath and went to the scene of the fighting to take charge of operations himself.

After a flight of less than an hour, we landed and drove to Government House, a comfortable mansion that had been built at the expense of the islanders in expiation of their crime in burning the old residency to the ground. Across the middle of the main reception-room is a wooden partition, which, on pressing a button, rises slowly like a curtain and finally disappears into the ceiling. This new toy greatly intrigued Winston. Three times the performance had to be repeated, up and down. Tomorrow our bomber will take us back to Cairo.

February 3, 1943

To Tripoli by air. The military situation here is full of problems. The C.I.G.S. sitting opposite me is, however, serenely indifferent to everything but Lansborough Thomson's *The Migration of Birds*, in which he has been immersed since we left the airfield at Cairo. The P.M., removing his cigar from his mouth, began advising Randolph to give up smoking. It made him cough for an hour every morning, leaving his voice husky, and as a politician his voice was part of his stock-in-trade; he was prejudicing his career for these wretched cigarettes. The plane was noisy and they were still bawling at each other as I fell asleep in my chair.

When our bomber landed at Castel Benito, a lot of figures in khaki, fringing the airfield, rushed forward to greet the P.M. as he emerged in his Air Commodore's uniform. The P.M. advanced towards Monty and clasped his hand in both of his own. The Eighth Army had fought their way here hardly a fortnight ago, and now, in a grassy space, bounded by eucalyptus trees, the P.M. was in his element when he addressed the troops. No one can do this sort of thing so well.

A few miles outside the town of Tripoli, a little off the main road, we came to three caravans, outspanned like gipsies on a heath. One is for the P.M., a second for Alex and the third is mine. Commanders-in-Chief no longer live in comfort, as they did in châteaux in France in the First World War. It is not that they fear attacks from the air, but rather that they dread democracy. They want to persuade the soldiery that their leaders are not lounging in luxury while they grovel in discomfort.

Haig[1] would have been shocked by this modern, thought-out approach to democracy, of which Monty is a master and the others eager disciples. Alex's caravan is a one-room affair with a bed, a small table, a chair and a washstand.

*

[1] Field-Marshal Earl Haig, C.-in-C., British Expeditionary Force, 1915–19.

A week after our return to London from Algiers, the P.M. started a cold in the head. He kept to his room, but during the evening of February 16 his temperature shot up, and, after examining his chest, I had to tell him that he had a patch at the base of the left lung. 'What do you mean by a patch?' he demanded impatiently. 'Have I got pneumonia?'

Next day an X-ray showed a small shadow, and bulletins became inevitable; I therefore called in consultation Dr. Geoffrey Marshall of Guy's Hospital. It was not until the 24th that the temperature fell, but we were at no time concerned about his condition. When a man approaching his seventieth year gets pneumonia it is, broadly speaking, the heart and not the lungs that decides the issue. Winston's heart, which nine months later was to cause us anxiety at Carthage, did not worry us then.

The patient himself took a more serious view of his illness. Apart from his appendix, he had never been seriously ill, and his attention was caught now by the high fever; his imagination did the rest. He tells us that it was 'a very disagreeable experience,' and that he 'sometimes felt very ill.' To Harry Hopkins he wrote that he 'had had a bad time and might easily have been worse.' To the President he spoke of the fever as 'heavy and long.' While his mind was busy conjuring up possible complications of his illness, Marshall, a genial but offhand physician, told him that he called pneumonia 'the old man's friend.'

'Pray explain,' said Winston.

'Oh, because it takes them off so quickly,' Marshall answered unabashed. He was soon established high in the P.M.'s favour.

It is one of Winston's foibles to pretend that he never allowed any of his illnesses to interfere with his work, though he admits on this occasion that the flow of his minutes dried up for a week. President Roosevelt, who was also on a sick-bed, sent a cable claiming that he had been dubbed a thoroughly model patient. He exhorted Winston to live down the reputation he had won in the American Press of being 'the world's worst patient.' He is, of course, nothing of the kind. I keep my chiding for him who turns his face to the wall, whereas Winston has no intention whatever of dying if sheer will-power will keep him going. Besides, no intelligent man, properly handled, can ever be a bad patient. On the contrary, when Winston is sick he does what he is told, provided, of course, that he is given a good reason.

In fact, he positively beseeches his physician to try fresh remedies. He does not believe in leaving things to Nature. 'Can't you do anything else?' he will ask reproachfully.

88

If there is a blot on the certificate I have given him, it is that, alas, he takes instinctively to a quack, gulping down his patter and his nostrums indiscriminately. During the twenty-five years he was in my care, I had to call in a number of doctors for various parts of his body, and it is, I think, substantially correct to affirm that he took to them in inverse ratio to their scientific attainments.

Part two

The President digs in

Chapter twelve

Their minds made up

When the P.M. got about after his illness at the end of February, I tried to keep an eye on him—a pretty thankless task—though there are no entries in my diary until late in April, when he told me that he was going to Washington.

Before Winston crossed the Atlantic he appeared to go through a period of indecision: one day he would decide to go by sea and the next he was sure that he could not spare the time and must go by air. If he travelled by sea he had a feeling of being out of touch with things; something might happen and he would hear of it too late to do anything. Furthermore, he had always had a horror of time wasted; during the war this became an obsession with him and in mid-Atlantic he would say, 'If we had flown as I wanted we should be in London now and could do business.' On the other hand, he disliked flying. I think this may date back to the time when he was piloting a small plane and crashed. His passenger was dreadfully mauled, breaking both legs. Winston, however, was so made that he would not give way to fears of that kind; because he disliked the air, he was more likely to fly. On this occasion he credits me with the decision to go by sea, affirming that I did not want him after his pneumonia to fly in a bomber at perhaps ten thousand feet.[1] It may be so, but I had little say in matters of this kind. It was the P.M. himself who weighed the pros and cons; I was never allowed to touch the scales.

His purpose was to persuade the President that the only fitting sequel to the victory in North Africa was to drive Italy out of the war and to bring Turkey in as our ally. He did not believe that an easy task lay in front of him, and throughout the voyage he remained engrossed in the preparation of his case. It was the business of a large party of experts to provide chapter and verse for his arguments,

[1] Winston Churchill, *The Hinge of Fate*, p. 700.

and here they were at his beck and call at any hour of the day or night.

The P.M. was interested in the *Queen Mary* as a troopship. She repeatedly carried a whole division, about 15,000 men, eastbound from New York to the Clyde. At first the Americans were reluctant to put too many eggs in one basket. Then one day General Marshall said bluntly to the Prime Minister: 'If you had to give the order, would you take a risk and send a division on this ship, knowing that if it were torpedoed there would only be boats for a fraction of that number?' That is the kind of awkward, sleep-disturbing decision which the men at the top were always taking. The P.M. did not hesitate; he would accept the risk.

The third day out Sir William Beveridge,[1] who happened to be a passenger, came to luncheon. In my diary the occasion was dismissed with the laconic statement: 'The atmosphere was correct without being unduly cordial.' It generally happened like that when the P.M. summoned to his table an acquaintance in whom he had little interest. Then, as if exhausted by his act of civility, he would make no further attempt at conversation, sitting all hunched up and scowling at his plate, with his thoughts a long way off. Besides, his guest on this occasion was not particularly congenial. Sir William, no doubt, was conscious that he, too, had done a good job of work for the country. The trouble was that this did not occur to the P.M.; at any rate, if it did he kept it to himself, and at about half-past two the bleak little function just petered out.

When I went back to my cabin after Beveridge had taken his leave I felt hot, and taking my temperature, found it was 103°. It was soon plain that a microbe, the *Colon Bacillus*, which had bothered me before, had come back, and I spent the next forty-eight hours in a somnolent condition. Winston was always uncomfortable and put out when anybody about him was sick; he would have liked to do something, but did not know what to do. He hated doing nothing. The ship's doctor told me how upset the P.M. had been when he heard I had taken to my bed. 'Damn it,' he growled. 'Have you seen him? Well, what is the matter? I trust it's not serious?' I must have been half asleep as he marched in. But I remember him, rather vaguely, standing in the middle of the cabin, as if I were infectious, and demanding: 'Are you taking care of yourself? Is there anything I can do? Anything I can get?' There was a short silence, and then he turned to the doctor: 'I shall want to know all about the temperature. Pray keep me posted.' And with that he turned on his heel and marched out.

[1] Sir William Beveridge, Economist and author of the Beveridge Report on the Social Services.

However, if Winston's bedside manner was poor, his heart was kind, and when the *Queen Mary* docked at New York on May 11 I found he had been busy. Though no one was to be allowed to land before morning, it had been arranged that I should be taken at once on a stretcher to the Presbyterian Hospital, where Harriman had arranged accommodation in the Harkness Pavilion. Looking round the spacious room assigned to me, I began to be concerned about the economic consequences of my illness. When my surgeon appeared I was reassured to find that I was in the hands of a man who knew his job and did not depend on his personality for practice. When he went the pathologist came; he pricked my finger and said presently, 'What have they been doing to you?' I learnt that the white cells in my blood which normally number 8,000 per cubic millimetre had fallen to 2,000. These cells are there to wage war with invading microbes, and it appeared that the mechanism on which my immunity depended had been put out of action by a surfeit of sulpha tablets.

When I caught up with the P.M. in Washington a few days later I had to explain it all to him. He seems fascinated by nature's processes. 'Some day, when I have time, I shall write a thriller,' he said. 'The villain, a doctor, will destroy his victims by breaking down their immunity.'

The P.M. was looking for work after his week-end at Shangri-La, the President's mountain refuge in the Catoctin Hills in Maryland; Harry Hopkins had come back full of stories about Winston's 'marvellous memory.' The President, too, was in good fettle, and Harry told me how he began quoting poetry: two lines from some verses about Barbara Frietchie, a semi-legendary character of the Civil War. 'Then when he was stuck and could not go on Winston came to the rescue and gabbled the whole poem. While we were still asking ourselves how he could do this when he hadn't read the darned thing for thirty years, his eye caught a sign pointing to Gettysburg. That really started him off.' No doubt encouraged by their interest in his feat, the P.M. went on to give a masterly review of the battle, ending with a lengthy disquisition on the characters of Stonewall Jackson and Robert E. Lee, two of his heroes.

Hopkins was a good deal less flattering about the P.M.'s contribution to the discussions, which had begun on May 12 in the oval study of the White House. Indeed, he looked pretty glum as he assured me that I had not missed anything. Winston, he said with a sour grin, recalled the last time they had met in that room, a year ago, when they learnt that Tobruk had fallen. It was not a very happy beginning. The Americans had not forgotten the occasion. They

95

had gone to the White House to clinch the plan for the invasion of France, when news had been brought to them of the disaster. Then in some manner—they were even now not quite clear how—they found themselves agreeing to the diversion of ships and troops to North Africa that were meant for the invasion of France. They could not help admiring the P.M.'s gift of dialectic, but they had made up their minds that it was not going to happen again. And here, damn it all, was the old story once more, shamelessly trotted out and brought up to date.

Harry was in one of his sardonic moods; imitating Winston, he said: 'The great prize when Sicily falls is to get Italy out of the war. Bulgaria's defeatism in 1918 brought about the collapse of Germany; might not Italy's surrender now have similar consequences? It will surely cause a chill of loneliness to settle on the German people and might very well be the beginning of the end.' The words were the P.M.'s, but somehow they sounded less convincing when put by Harry like this. I asked him what the President made of all this. 'Not much,' he answered. 'This fighting in Italy does not make sense to him. He wants the twenty divisions, which will be set free when Sicily has been won, to be used in building up the force that is to invade France in 1944.'

I enquired of Hopkins what was the effect of the President's attitude on the P.M. 'I thought he was a little subdued—for Winston, that is,' and Harry grinned broadly. For my part I was sorry for the P.M. He had been so sure in London that when they got together after dinner in the White House he would be able to bring the President over to his view. Since those disasters of a year ago, which the Prime Minister had so rashly recalled, a good deal had happened that was not known to him. The Americans had done some very hard thinking, and Marshall was at the President's elbow to keep in his mind the high urgency of a second front. The results, according to Hopkins, were very satisfactory. The President could now, Harry felt, be safely left alone with the Prime Minister. The P.M. is, I think, puzzled; he had not expected the President to lay down the law like this, but I don't believe he is really depressed. He still feels it can all be put right. There had been so much to settle during this visit, but if he could get Marshall to himself, perhaps in Algiers, he is certain it would all be plain sailing. Marshall would agree with him about the invasion of Italy. I own I am rather worried about the P.M.'s optimism. It seems to be interfering with the cold functioning of his judgment.

*

May 18, 1943

I am still bothered by a smouldering fever and my notes are thin.

Washington is hot and humid, but it does not seem to affect Winston. Today he spoke to Congress for fifty minutes and though he said nothing new it went down well. At least Harry Hopkins was sure that it had made a very good impression. 'They're saying,' he grinned broadly, 'that the only time they're told anything is when Winston addresses Congress.' The P.M. was a good deal worked up beforehand, saying: 'It was a great responsibility; a much more difficult speech than the first time I talked to Congress after Pearl Harbour.' I asked him why. He replied that he feared what he had to say would be 'inadequate,' and that he 'regretted taking it on.'

I was in the diplomatic gallery with Mackenzie King and the Duke and Duchess of Windsor. As the Duke descended to his seat in the front row, he got as much clapping as Winston, or more, by which we were surprised. He has lost his boyish good looks, and does not somehow fit into middle age. Winston was loyal to his King to the very last, but, I think, he learnt a long time ago that he had been wrong about the abdication. It is not Winston's habit to live long with his mistakes. He is a very loyal servant of King George and is no longer—it must be said—interested in the Duke; when they tell him that the Duke has asked for an appointment, the P.M. sighs and arranges the day and hour.

May 25, 1943

Found the P.M. pacing his room. There was no welcoming smile. When I asked him how he had been he did not answer. He had other things to think about besides his health. He stopped and said abruptly, 'Have you noticed that the President is a very tired man? His mind seems closed; he seems to have lost his wonderful elasticity.' I could not follow all that was in the P.M.'s mind, and when he saw that I was not going to help him he seemed to forget about me.

For a long time he went up and down his room, scowling at the floor. I could see that he did not want to talk, that he had work to do. I felt I was in the way, and left him. Perhaps he thought that he had been rather abrupt. At any rate, later he sent for me on some pretext. He seemed less worried and then the mood came back.

'The President,' he said, 'is not willing to put pressure on Marshall.

97

He is not in favour of landing in Italy. It is most discouraging. I only crossed the Atlantic for this purpose. I cannot let the matter rest where it is.'

There were forty-eight men lunching today at the White House. I sat next to General Stilwell, a sour, dried-up little man whom they call Vinegar Joe. He complained bitterly that Winston wasn't interested in the Pacific, implying that, if he were, the President would pay more attention to their needs in those parts. He is pretty critical of the British.

As the Conference unfolded (to use Winston's word) it was plain enough that the Americans had made up their minds. The P.M. was concerned because no definite recommendations had been made by the Combined Chiefs of Staff to follow up the conquest of Sicily by the invasion of Italy. Why, these Combined Chiefs of Staff would apparently be content with the capture of Sardinia; that was to be the proud objective for the rest of 1943 for all the mighty forces gathered in the Mediterranean. The P.M. deplored the prospect. The invasion of France had been fixed for May 1944. Was it conceivable that a million and a half of our best troops should be kept idle for nearly a year?

I hear tonight that he made a final appeal to the President to let General Marshall come with us to Algiers, and perhaps to his surprise, and certainly to his great satisfaction, Roosevelt has agreed.

May 26, 1943

This morning we took off from the Potomac River in a flying-boat. I wish we were bound for London. It is not easy to do my job with these bouts of high fever.

May 27, 1943

I was awake when there was a small 'pop' accompanied by a little flash of light like a small bulb fusing. I wondered what it was, and then I must have gone to sleep. This morning I learnt that in a storm the flying-boat had been hit by lightning.

May 28, 1943

I am back in London, when I ought to be in Algiers with the Prime Minister, and in pretty poor heart about it all. When we landed at Gibraltar yesterday my fever still hung about. I might be a nuisance, travelling round Tunis like this; it would be better, I thought, if I cut out North Africa altogether and flew direct to England. When I broached this to Winston he vigorously insisted that I must get fit. 'I am very well,' he said, 'and if anything went

98

wrong you could fly out in a few hours.' So I spent the afternoon in a quiet corner of the Convent[1] wondering if it would have been better to have gone to Algiers without bothering the P.M. about my ailments.

The light had nearly gone when they brought me to the small aircraft in which I was to travel to England. Its floor, as far as I could see by torchlight, was almost entirely taken up by a stretcher bearing a young soldier with a brain tumour, who was being sent home. The night in the air seemed to stretch out interminably. Would that loud, stertorous breathing never stop? I could not help listening to it as it rose noisily to a climax; then there was a pause that made me wonder if he had died, and then it began all over again. There was plenty of time to ruminate. I ruminated.

For three years the Prime Minister has been doing everyone else's job as well as his own, wallowing in detail; and there is no end to it in sight. It is easy to get into the way of thinking of him as different from other people, someone unique, a law to himself. But I know better. There will be trouble one day. I wonder in what shape it will come.

If in the end he is defeated I feel sure it will not be by a breakdown in body or mind, but rather by a gradual waning of his powers, brought on by his own improvidence, by his contempt for common sense and by the way he has been doing the work of three men. There is no hour of the night when I can be certain that he is in his bed and asleep. Of course, this cannot go on for ever.

However, it takes a lot of hard work to leave its mark on a robust constitution. I would go further. I doubt whether men at the top often go to bits through overwork by itself. There are generally other and less obvious factors dragging them down.

*

In the P.M.'s case it took me some time to find out what they were. They are recorded in some notes that I found in my diary; they bear no date but they must have been written a long time after this. I print them here because they may help the reader to understand how the Prime Minister's strength was gradually undermined: '. . . Is there something else sapping his strength? Is Winston's impressionable nature itself a source of weakness in war? The idea is, of course, far from novel. That a man's imagination may run riot in battle is indeed as old as the literature of war. "More life," wrote Thomas Hardy, "may trickle out of a man through thought than

[1] The Residence of the Governor of Gibraltar is called the Convent, though the nuns left it two centuries ago.

through a gaping wound." But does Winston Churchill suffer from that handicap? And if so, how does he show it? I learnt in the First World War what to look for; the danger signals I used to call them. They told me when a man was in distress. Often this waverer was most fearful when there was no danger; it was his own thoughts that festered in the mind and in the end brought defeat. Because there was no danger, his apprehension, fear in its infancy, was labelled imaginative fear, but it had its roots in reason, it fed on the memory of things.'

Once more it was my business to pick up these signals. In mid-Atlantic, as I have told, Winston touched me on the knee, 'Do you realize we are fifteen hundred miles from anywhere?' That is the kind of confession that I find, not very often of course, in my diary when we were on the high seas or in the air, and it was these signs of apprehension in Winston that first caught my ear.

When I found out for myself that Winston was by nature very apprehensive I was slow to credit my own evidence. Very gradually, however, it came to me that he was completely without the self-protective mechanism which is the only gift, as far as I can tell, common to men who last in war: a way of looking at things which alone makes it possible to carry on. In the First World War we spoke of men 'sticking it,' and I wrote then of the 'sticker' that he 'is just one who has contrived to cut off those messages from the outer world that reach the brain at times like these and threaten its balance. His business is to become insensitive, to give up thinking. The wise man lives only for the hour.'

Winston Churchill was less fortunate. And I had him in my head when I scribbled in pencil in the margin of my diary:

'If it should happen that a man of action, exercising supreme power, is also an artist, then God help him. He will have to change his nature to survive.'

Winston could not change his nature. As First Minister of the Crown in time of war he was bound to receive in the course of his lonely mission wounds deeper and more lasting than any weapon can inflict; it was vital to him that he should be able to shed the kind of thought that might distract or distress his mind; forget, if he could, for a short space at any rate, the anguish of the hour. He could not do it.

I find this note in my diary of December 11, 1941:

'Paid a routine visit to the Annexe. I ran into Mrs. Hill leaving his room. "He has just heard some very bad news." I said I would not bother him. "I think he would like to see you," she

100

said. I found him with his head in his hands. After a time he looked up; he seemed dazed.

' "You know what has happened?"

'I had not heard of the sinking of the *Prince of Wales* and the *Repulse*.'[1]

As I put down the diary, the whole sad business came back to me. He had sent those ships to Singapore without air cover, and against the advice of the First Sea Lord. And Smuts was not the only one who had sensed disaster. After his stroke in 1953, when it appeared that he might die, Winston told me that he had had a very bad dream. I asked him what he had dreamed. But he could not bring himself to talk about it. He did not speak for a long time, and then he turned to me: 'Do you know anything about dreams? Can doctors tell what they mean?' When I answered, 'Only up to a point,' there was another long pause. 'You know when the *Prince of Wales* and the *Repulse* were sunk?' He could not go on; he seemed to be so upset that I was frightened he might have another stroke.

[1] Captain Roskill writes to me: 'It is beyond doubt that Churchill initiated the idea of the two ships going East, and that the First Lord and the First Sea Lord, Mr. Alexander and Admiral Pound, strongly opposed it at many meetings of the Defence Committee and Chiefs of Staff Committee. . . . Smuts telegraphed a prophetic warning of the disaster which was likely to ensue from the despatch of those two ships. . . . In the end Alexander and Pound gave way.' Cf. *The War at Sea*, by Captain S. W. Roskill, R.N., Vol. I, pp. 553-9.

Chapter thirteen

The conversion of Marshall

In my diary there is a break in the narrative after I had parted from Winston at Gibraltar. I could not tell the story of his visit to Tunis and Algiers, because I was not there. The gap is bridged by two brief entries.

May 31, 1943

The news from Algiers is reassuring; my misgivings are set at rest. The P.M., they tell me, is in great shape. I keep wondering if he has persuaded Marshall that his plan is sound. I cannot make out why nobody mentions this; after all, that was the purpose of Winston's visit.

June, 1943

Winston is back in London. This morning he said to me: 'I am more happy about the conduct of the war than I have been for some time. Things are coming out as I want them.' 'What about Marshall?' I asked. 'Has he come over to your view?' 'He doesn't, for the moment, want to make up his mind what we ought to do when Sicily is taken. But he is ready to accept my plan. He is not opposed to the invasion of Italy now.'

The P.M. seemed to have no doubts at all on this score; he was quite sure that he would get his way. I did ask him why he thought Marshall had changed his mind. For a moment he appeared taken aback. 'The merits of the case,' he said half to himself, 'are surely beyond any question.'

*

Two months later at Quebec I discovered that my doubts had substance. There Marshall gave me his own version of the conversations with Winston.

'I did not think that the moment had come for a decision. It would be better, I said to the Prime Minister, to decide what to do when the attack on Sicily was well under way. I wanted to know whether Germany meant to put up a stiff resistance in southern Italy or whether she would decide to retire to the Po as Winston suggested. I wanted more facts. I wanted to ask Winston a dozen questions, but he gave me no chance. He kept telling me what was going to happen. All wishing and guessing. When I did get a question in, the Prime Minister brushed it aside. I tried to set forth some of the factors which ought to govern our decision. I tried to argue that we must exercise great discretion in choosing what to do after the conquest of Sicily. I said to the Prime Minister that I would be content if Sardinia were taken before the invasion of France. He replied that the difference between taking southern Italy and Sardinia was the difference between a glorious campaign and a mere convenience.'

Marshall's long upper lip stretched in amusement as he told this. It appeared that this monologue went on for a week, all day and often well into the night, when he wanted to go to his bed. Winston seems to have gone on and on, talking at the American, who for his part, as far as I could tell, listened and said but little. 'I have never,' Marshall went on, 'heard anyone talk like this before.'

I told the General how my mother, when she was very old, and everyone would talk at once, used to say that 'it made her legs ache.' 'Exactly; I felt like that,' and he smiled. 'I'd never met anyone like Winston,' he continued. 'He is a very wonderful man, but he won't look at things like a man who has been all his life a soldier. I must have facts.'

Looking back, where had Winston gone wrong? When he went to North Africa he was bent on converting Marshall to his plan for the invasion of Italy, and yet he did not attempt to follow what was passing through Marshall's head. Why, for instance, did Marshall remain, up till almost the last moment, silent and cryptic? He was, after all, a straightforward soldier; his affection for Winston was undoubted, and he must have longed to discuss with him differences in strategy, to make him see the American point of view. But as Harry Hopkins explained to me: 'We have come to avoid controversy with Winston; we find he is too much for us.' Clemmie once made the same point: 'I don't argue with Winston, he shouts me down. So when I have anything important to say I write a note to him.' That was how Marshall felt. 'Oh, no, Winston heard all right, but he kept telling me what was going to happen.' That is the trouble. Winston is so taken up with his own ideas that he is not

interested in what other people think. It is as if he had lived for
years in a foreign country without picking up the language. He must
lose a chunk of life in this way, and must often be lonely, cut off
from people.

I suppose that is why the pages of his great testament so often silt
up with military detail, while he apparently cannot remember—
more probably has never noticed—those little personal idiosyn-
crasies which might have brought to life the soldiers around him.

One morning, in the autumn of 1950, I found Winston sitting up
in bed in his room at Chartwell, dictating. 'Don't go far away,' he
said to his secretary as she got up to withdraw. I asked him how
far he had got in the book. 'You missed Algiers, Charles. I have
just finished the ten days I spent there visiting the troops. When you
have taken my pulse you shall read it.'

I was agape to find out how far the historian would be given the
facts. I was sure Winston must have learnt at Quebec that Marshall
had not changed his mind about the Italian campaign and would
correct in his book the error he made at the time. Would he chuckle
at the enormity of his mistake? It is, after all, from our mistakes
that we learn, though it has never been a form of instruction that
Winston found particularly congenial. This was, of course, rather
obtuse on my part. Men who do things in the world are not in the
habit of laughing at their mistakes.

Winston's own account begins:

'I have no more pleasant memories of the war than the ten days
in Algiers and Tunis. . . . The sense of victory was in the air. The
whole of North Africa was cleared of the enemy. A quarter of a
million prisoners were cooped in our cages. Everyone was very
proud and delighted. There is no doubt that people like winning
very much.'

And then he goes on to tell us in some detail what he said, what
Cunningham said, what Alex said, what Monty said; the divisions
available to Alex, on the one hand, and the distribution of the
Italian Army, on the other—twelve pages in all and not as many
lines about Marshall.

As I read this chapter sitting by his bed, I marvelled that Winston
did not sense the atmosphere even if he did not get much help from
Marshall. And then, on the impulse of the moment, I got up and
put my hand on Winston's shoulder. 'You old dear. I'd not like
you half as much if you had antennae.' He stared at me. 'What do
you mean by antennae?' he asked. And when I did not answer he
went on: 'You do say some strange things. Some of you doctors get

queer ideas about what is in people's heads. You think too much about these things. It isn't healthy. I don't know where all this psychological nonsense is going to take you.'

Perhaps he felt that he had been a little hard on me. He put his hand on my arm with a benevolent gesture. 'You have not let me down yet. I haven't found you out once. How many years is it? You know, Charles, I have come to feel very safe with you at my elbow.' Winston was not often in a mood like this, when you could say anything to him. He held out his hand for the typescript.

'You've finished it?'

'I've read it twice.'

'I thought you'd like it.'

'I keep trying to fathom how your mind works.'

Winston looked blankly at me. I fancy when I said that he had no antennae that he felt there must be something wrong with his account. He went on reading and I was left to my own thoughts. Could it be that he had come to believe what he wanted to believe?

Chapter fourteen

The end of an argument

Strange stories of a young brigadier in the jungle called Wingate had recently been filtering through to the P.M. He began to wonder if this leader of the Chindits in Burma was another Lawrence of Arabia; to him that was a quickening thought.

For Lawrence made a great dent in Winston's imagination, and the impression had remained. Winston writes that he felt himself in the presence of an extraordinary being, someone outside the jurisdiction of the world, someone strangely untamed and untrammelled by convention.[1] ... The exploits of this paladin in those sun-scorched, blasted lands, which seemed to forbid human existence, was an epic. And this epic had been marvellously told in *The Seven Pillars of Wisdom*, which Winston once told me in his judgment ranked with the greatest books ever written in the English language, with *The Pilgrim's Progress*, *Robinson Crusoe* and *Gulliver's Travels*.

There was enough in this to excite anyone's imagination. And yet we must dig deeper to unearth the roots of his affinity with Lawrence. He tells us that Lawrence had never been, in time of peace, 'in complete harmony with the normal.' Winston knew what that meant. He knew more than most what happens to a man who is different from other people; the penalty exacted from those who do not conform. In the years before the war he had come to realize that he had no real friends in any of the three parties; he could not remember a time when he was sure of his own reception in the country. He felt his isolation.

On July 24, 1943, ten days before we left the Clyde for Quebec, he wrote a directive to the Chiefs of Staff, in which he spoke of Wingate as 'a man of genius and audacity.' No mere question of seniority must be allowed to obstruct his advancement. The P.M. considered that Brigadier Wingate should command the Army in

[1] Winston Churchill, *Great Contemporaries*, pp. 164–5.

Burma, and gave instructions that he should come home. 'I want to have a look at him,' he said, 'before I leave for Quebec.'

Wingate arrived at the Annexe an hour before our train left London for the Clyde. When the P.M. heard that he was in the building he said he would like to talk to him about war in the jungle; he was greatly interested in the view that the Japanese could be beaten by landing men behind their lines. But there was no time then. It occurred to the P.M. on the spur of the moment to take Wingate with him on the ship. Wingate protested: 'I have no clothes. I have nothing but my tropical kit.' The P.M. brushed this aside: 'Oh, don't bother about that. I'll lend you some. I've plenty.' Wingate: 'But, sir, I've not seen my wife for a long time.' P.M.: 'Of course, you must bring her too.' So the Wingates were carried off, as you pick up a couple of books at the station bookstall to beguile the tedium of the journey.

Winston, in *Closing the Ring*, has given his first impressions of his guest. 'We had not talked for half an hour before I felt myself in the presence of a man of the highest quality.' I did not realize at the time that the P.M. had taken Wingate quite so seriously, and I only noted in my diary that he seemed to be rather unbalanced, and talked like a man full of undigested ideas.

*

R.M.S. Queen Mary, *August 8, 1943*

Wingate is only a gifted eccentric. He is not another Lawrence. When this became plain to the P.M. he lost interest in him, and presently forgot all about his presence on the ship, leaving him to his own resources. The second day out he came to my cabin because he wanted my help to get rid of some microbes he had picked up in the jungle. After that I saw a good deal of him. One day I had taken my seat for luncheon when he came across the saloon and asked me to join him at his table. When we had decided what to eat, Wingate put down the menu, and without any kind of introduction said he thought it was a pity that boys at our public schools were taught by men who had done nothing in the world, and indeed had usually no experience of its ways. They went straight from school to the University, and after three or four years there they returned as masters, where they remained for the rest of their working life. Wingate wanted men who had done things to be seconded to teach; the boys would feel then that their teachers were talking to them from experience and not out of books. I asked him what was his school, and he answered Charterhouse. He went on: 'There were two masters there who had a permanent influence on my life.'

He did not seem to see any discrepancy between this remark and his original thesis.

Wingate soon started another theme: 'All the things in the world that matter have been achieved,' he asserted, 'by the spoken and not by the written word.' I gave him Mahomet; however, the argument soon wilted through its own inherent weakness.

It would be easy to dismiss the mental processes of those who give way to impulsive outbursts of this kind, but I must be fair and admit that this was not the whole story. Some years later when I was talking to the Staff College at Camberley about leadership, I remember speaking in a critical vein of Wingate. When I had done, a soldier who had served under him in Burma got up and refuted what I had said. Speaking very earnestly, he defended his leader. 'We all swore by him. Of course he was a fanatic, but he believed so absolutely that there was nothing he couldn't do, that he succeeded in persuading other people he was infallible. Mind you, sir, that's not why his men would follow him anywhere. He was efficient, and they knew it. If he took them through the jungle behind the Japanese lines he would always bring them back safely.' Wingate had two bars to his D.S.O. And as your eye wandered to his face you might have noticed a scar across his throat—where he once tried to take his own life. He seemed to me hardly sane—in medical jargon a borderline case.

My own view of Wingate was no more than a surface impression, but one of his seniors in the Army in Burma damned the man beyond salvation: 'I did not think that he was quite sane. He was quite unscrupulous and lied for his own purposes.' General Slim told me some years later that Wingate had served under him: 'He came to me and asked for another division to turn into his irregulars. When I refused, he said that he had higher loyalties than the Commander-in-Chief. "What are they?" I asked. "To the President of the United States and the Prime Minister," he answered. "What do you mean by that?" I persisted. "I have been told to report direct to them if any General interferes with my plans. I have always got on with you, but I should have to report to them." When he said this I wrote down my orders and told him to go away and read them. The next day he was to come back at ten o'clock. I told him no one had yet disobeyed my command. If they did I should know what to do.' Slim smiled grimly, 'The next day he turned up with a sickly smile, saluted and carried out my orders. Attempted blackmail,' Slim grunted. He summed up: 'Wingate had strategical but not tactical ability. His first campaign in the jungle was a flop, his troops came out after heavy losses, disorganized. He had achieved little or nothing and used up a lot of resources in the material sense, but the psychological rewards were considerable.'

What does this all add up to? That Wingate was a size larger than I thought and several sizes smaller than the P.M.'s first impulsive appraisement.

The P.M. is not at all conventional, and his open mind has been a valuable asset in the war; no idea was too improbable, too absurd to be given a trial. But when he came to select men he was somehow less successful—the incipient genius rescued from obscurity was apt to prove a disappointment.

The P.M. has been kept in good humour by his preparations for the meeting with the President that have filled every minute of his working day on board. He has gone over in his mind, a good many times, Franklin Roosevelt's words at the White House in May. Even then there had been a sense of urgency that was new to the P.M., a touch of impatience, as the President set out his views on the invasion of France. Nothing must interfere with that. For all his obstinacy, Winston generally knows when the time has come to give way. Now two months have gone and a plan for the invasion of Normandy is taking shape. The P.M. cannot help being impressed by the numbers that will be engaged, the tonnage involved. More than once he has spoken to me of the plan as 'majestic.' Maybe his fears of a landing on strongly held beaches are exaggerated. Anyway, he feels the need of talks with the President. After all, there are some things, as he puts it, which can only be decided at the highest level.

Quebec, August 18, 1943

The Canadian Prime Minister was our host at a Citadel dinner. There was apparently a proposal that Canada should take part in the Conference, but this came to nothing. As it is, Mackenzie King seems rather like a man who has lent his house for a party. The guests take hardly any notice of him, but just before leaving they remember he is their host and say pleasant things. I wonder if he is as enamoured of his role at this Conference as the P.M. imagines.[1]

---

[1] 'There is no doubt,' the Prime Minister said in a telegram to the War Cabinet, dated August 25, 1943, 'that Mackenzie King and the Canadian Government are delighted and feel themselves thoroughly "on the map."' King, who had been my patient, wrote to me on June 9, 1950: 'I am afraid my notes of the two Quebec Conferences are even more meagre than your own. I was, as you recall, not so much a participant in any of the discussions as a sort of general host, whose task at the Citadel was similar to that of the General Manager of the Château Frontenac.'

August 20, 1943

Harry Hopkins was in a curious mood this morning. He told me that at yesterday's session Winston 'came clean' about a Second Front, that he 'threw in his hand.' Hopkins said this in rather an aggressive way, as if I were in the P.M.'s camp.

'Winston is no longer against Marshall's plan for landing on the coast of France. At least, so he says.'

Harry grinned.

'But he might change his mind again, as he did last year. I don't believe he is really converted.[1]

'Why,' Hopkins went on, 'before he said he agreed we had the most solemn warning of what might happen. The old, old story of enormous casualties and the terrific strength of the German fortifications.'

Why is this man so bitter? Harry is sure that Winston's obstinacy, his drawn-out struggle to postpone a second front in France, has, in fact, prolonged the war; that if he had been reasonable earlier we might now be in sight of peace. Is Hopkins right? That must remain the riddle of the war.

It is indeed a momentous change of front on the part of the Prime Minister; the end of an argument that has gone on since the Americans came into the war. I want time to think it over and to get my bearings.

When Hopkins questioned whether the P.M. meant what he said, I wonder if he is speaking for anybody but himself. I must not, of course, make the mistake of taking him for a typical American, any more than I would argue that Max Beaverbrook is a fair sample of our countrymen. But there are Americans in high places who, though they like and admire Winston, do feel that he has been rather disingenuous about the Second Front. Before their country came into the war there was no strategy to speak of. It was just a struggle for survival. Winston Churchill became a symbol of the English will to fight to a finish; his authority was not questioned. But after Pearl Harbour America began to think of a landing in France, and the timing of this expedition became a bone of contention between us. The Americans are not in doubt that Marshall was right in resisting the postponement of the landing in France. It appears that

[1] Prime Minister to Field-Marshal Smuts, September 11, 1943: 'There can be no question whatever of breaking arrangements we have made with United States for "Overlord" [the code name for the invasion of Northern France]. . . . I hope you will realize that British loyalty to Overlord is keystone of arch of Anglo-American co-operation.' This message was in response to a suggestion by Smuts that 'preparations for Channel plan should be slowed down.'

Imperial War Museum

BRIGADIER ORDE WINGATE

Press Association Inc.

GENERAL GEORGE MARSHALL

the President and Hopkins are no longer prepared to acknowledge Winston as an infallible guide in military matters.

For that matter, it is not only the President and Marshall who are uneasy about the P.M.'s judgment. Brooke is worried by his inability to finish one subject before taking up another, by the darting processes of his mind and by the general instability of his judgment. But are his critics measuring the Prime Minister by the right yardstick? His claim to a place in history does not rest on his strategy. His gifts are of a rarer kind.

What his critics are apt to forget is that you cannot measure inspiration. That is why it is not easy to bring home to the military hierarchy the list of assets which easily tilt the balance in his favour: the strength of will that has bent all manner of men to his purpose; the extraordinary tenacity—the Americans call it obstinacy—with which he clings for months, and if need be for years, to his own plans; the terrific force of personality that can brush aside all doubts and hesitations, and sweep away inertia, refusing to listen when weaker men begin to whine about difficulties; above all else, the superb confidence he exuded in 1940. When the Prime Minister set out to inspire the country with his will to win he made up his mind that it must begin in his own bedroom. I have been with him there at all hours, I have seen him take a lot of punishment, and not once did he look like a loser. Not once did he give me the feeling that he was in any way worried or anxious as to the outcome of the fight. Gradually I have come to think of him as invincible.

August 21, 1943

Some of us are going up the St. Lawrence on a twenty-four hours' trip. Marshall is on board, and he began asking my views about morale. He went on to tell me that he is troubled from time to time with fibrillation of the heart. I hope that he will keep on his feet, for in the difficult task of training the American Army he is indispensable; he is, too, a real friend of England. I talked to him for a long time and was comforted by his wisdom.

As the light failed, a blanket of white fog enveloped the little ship, and the hooting of our siren came echoing back from the hills flanking the great river. When Marshall went to his bed my thoughts took a sombre turn, the questioning mood of the First World War came back.

Yesterday, while the P.M. was arguing that it pays us to exchange plane for plane with the Germans, they handed me a letter from home. Two young pilots in the Air Force, who, if they had lived, would have done something in the world, had been shot down. War is a hellish business when you are not right in it. I cannot get used to being a distant spectator.

*

This is from my diary of the First World War:[1]

'If the medical officer with a Battalion escaped the responsibility for military decisions which gamble in human life, nevertheless he, too, has his own distresses. It is not the wounds he binds which matter, it is when something has been destroyed in the make-up of a man that the bloody business of war comes home to him. With a background of casualties in his mind, he is prone to think that the men are being treated as pawns in the game; he may question if all this loss of life is necessary. He begins to ask himself, Who is responsible?'

That black mood came back with the loss of the two pilots. It is generally agreed that our leaders in this war are better than the 'heavy blockhead type' (it is Winston's epithet) of the First World War. But is there not the same terrifying disparity between the size and scope of the great problems of war and the capacity of those who have to deal with them? Are Marshall's brains, for instance, first-rate? I think they are, but they are not, perhaps, of the creative kind. How can one tell a soldier's quality when he has not been in action?

Marshall told me that the problem of this war was the disciplining of the citizen soldier. Anyway, that has been his task. And it has not been easy. For the American youth is self-confident; he is quite certain that he knows a better way of doing things than those who are ordering him about. Marshall had had to begin at the beginning: to plan a three months' basic training, the sole purpose of which was to get the recruit to see that he must do what he was told. And, of course, in that fashion Marshall has done a magnificent job for his country; he has shown to the full that remarkable gift for organization which is everywhere behind American production. But I would not call it a work of genius. Can we ask as much of a soldier? Is it reasonable to look for the creative spirit in one of our generals? In science the sterile worker soon loses caste, and even in my own calling, that is half a science and half an art, we have no patience with empty vessels. It may be that we are rather harsh, a little arbitrary perhaps, in our assessment of capacity. If a doctor adds something to knowledge—describes, perhaps, a new disease, or discovers penicillin—we count him as having a creative mind. Short of that he is bundled unceremoniously into the second category. He

[1] Lord Moran, *The Anatomy of Courage*, p. 44.

may be a great clinician, who notices things in a patient that others miss, but if he is not productive he remains a secondary figure. But are the soldier and the scientist truly comparable?

They are surely very different. And the crucial point of difference is this: that the soldier must go on doing his job however grim the conditions. He must not quit. If he falters he is at once thrown aside. Whereas there is no certainty that the creative spirits who add to knowledge would prove as staunch. Would they keep cool heads amid the blind fury of modern war?

Winston at any rate had no doubt of the answer. In *The World Crisis* he was driven to an indictment of the General Staff. Their ideas were elementary, their scientific vision narrow, their minds rigid. They were slow to master a new mechanical idea. In short, he writes of men 'whose nerves were much stronger than their imaginations,' whom nothing could upset. Still, they were all we had; it was necessary to make the best of them. And Winston gives his reasons. 'No doubt more highly-strung men could not stand the wear and tear of high command in modern warfare.' They were necessarily eliminated in favour of those who, in his words, could preserve their sang-froid amidst disastrous surprises, 'to an extent almost indistinguishable from insensitivity.'

In war we must often be content with a modicum of brains, because other things are even more important and, on the whole, it is a better bargain than it seems. When things go wrong and there are heavy casualties, I ask sometimes: 'Would these men have got to the top in any other profession?' And it always seems to me a good enough answer that I do not know where to go to match them in strength of character.

In time to come some historian, another Trevelyan, may wonder how human nature stood up to the ordeal of the last of the Great Wars. Turning to his shelves he may find in the diaries of those days enough to piece together four unusual characters, Marshall and Eisenhower, Wavell and Brooke. Had they had their way they would have spent quiet lives in the country stillness, near some tree-reflecting stream, but that was not to be their lot. They loathed war. 'Every month,' Brooke told me, 'is a year off my life.' Yet he gave all he had to his work: a simple, gentle, selfless soul—a warning to us all not to give up hope about mankind. Taking a long view, it does not seem to matter whether soldiers win battles. What is important is that the world should go on producing men built on that pattern.

August 23, 1943

When the P.M. made a tour of Quebec this morning, attired in what the local papers call 'an unbleached linen suit,' the crowds gave him a noisy greeting, and he returned in very good spirits. A diet of that kind is much to his liking. By the afternoon the people had gone back to work and I had the ramparts to myself. They are still armed with the old sixteen-pounders which once guarded the St. Lawrence, and my head was full of the people who first came here. I got up at last and began to mount one of the narrow cobbled streets which climb abruptly from the ramparts to the old French town. There was no one about save for a single black figure, a priest, halfway up the street, like a fly crawling up a window-pane.

The hall of the hotel was full of soldiers, Pug Ismay [1] among them. Ismay is a perfect oil-can. It appears that he serves as a kind of filter between the Prime Minister and the Chiefs of Staff, only letting through, as far as he can, what is helpful and unprovocative. In the short passage between the two parties he is said to forget everything that could only ruffle and anger his masters. A useful role beyond question, and certainly Pug is the very man to play it.

August 25, 1943

The P.M. likes comfort, and Colonel Clarke, our host, who owns vast forests which nourish his paper mills, is able to provide it. Even here, in a clearing in a primeval forest on the banks of the Montmorency River, our two-storeyed house, built of rudely-hewn logs, has electric light and a bathroom, while the food and drink are up to Winston's requirements. To remind us that there were wolves and moose and bear in the forest until the lumber-men came, there is a huge black bearskin rug in front of the fire—a fire in August sounds strange, but we are sixteen hundred feet above the sea.

August 26, 1943

We made an early start climbing over rough roads to Snow Lake, the highest point in the Laurentian Mountains, four thousand feet above the sea. This morning each one of our little party sallied forth in a canoe, with a French Canadian paddling, and fished with a wet fly. The trout in this lake are big, and if a man is a fisherman he is often rewarded by big catches; Brooke and Portal, when they came here not long ago, took 151 trout, averaging one pound, in a single

---

[1] General Sir Hastings Ismay, Chief of Staff to the Minister of Defence (Winston Churchill).

day. When it was learnt that I was the only one to draw a blank the P.M. became much concerned. 'Nothing,' he repeated. 'Clemmie,[1] Charles has got nothing.' 'Where is my fishing rod?' he demanded, and when it was brought he proceeded to initiate me into the art of casting a fly. When he had done, he sent for the chief guide, and, after a spirited little speech, I was committed to his care. I was paddled to a little bay, reputed to be prolific in fish, but still nothing happened. My guide, in desperation, set off for another part of the lake. Only the lapping of the water broke the silence; I sat watching the changing lights on the wooded hills which guard the lake, while my thoughts kept wandering back to Fenimore Cooper's Red Indians. I suppose I had been trailing my line in the water for, all at once, I felt a tug, and to my joy I landed a trout—a three and a half pounder. I was relieved that honour was satisfied. As for the P.M., he became almost hilarious at my achievement. Already he is full of theories and laying down the law about the fisherman's art. This mountain air should bring new life to him. Even the Marine Orderly is stirred, and became so excited in a struggle with a big fish that he fell into the lake. While we were rescuing him, a loon flew over the water, making an unfamiliar cry. When night fell, Winston came out on the wooden pier, gazing up at the Aurora Borealis. This quiet life is doing him good, but he feels he is playing truant.

September 1, 1943

Last night, before we left Wolfe's Cove, on the outskirts of Quebec, at seven o'clock, I made this note: 'The P.M. stood for some time at the window of his car giving the victory sign to odd workmen in the fields, who could see nothing but a train rushing through the countryside.'

Washington, September 2, 1943

I went this morning with Clemmie to see the Lincoln Memorial. There he sits, an immense figure of a man, grasping the sides of the chair with his bony, gnarled hands. You feel that the sculptor understood the elemental grandeur and the spiritual force of the man. That is what we have missed in two world wars. The earnest goodness of the leaders.

[1] Mrs. Churchill.

Chapter fifteen

How Churchill learnt
his craft

September 6, 1943

On the train to Boston I found I was running a temperature again. One might think, from his irritability, that the P.M. had the bug. For some reason, which I have not yet fathomed, he is taking the speech he is to make at Harvard very seriously. The President, too, is interested. He was at Harvard in 1904, and he wants the ceremony at his old University to be up to English standards in pomp and colour. I think he has been sticking pins into Conant, the President of Harvard. At any rate, there has been a to-do about the P.M.'s robe. Conant wants him to wear his Oxford D.C.L. It is a scarlet affair, and certainly more impressive than the austere American gown, but it is too late to get a robe from England; however, they have unearthed one at Princeton and have borrowed it for the occasion.

When the P.M. came on to the stage of the Sanders Theatre at Harvard, it was plain that he had tried to make his own contribution to an academic event. He was attired in a black coat and a bow tie. But Winston would not be Winston if he was strictly conventional. Beneath the gorgeous scarlet robe appeared a pair of rather inadequate grey flannel trousers. Holding his quaint black velvet hat in his extended arm, he beamed on his audience as they welcomed him.

He began by reminding them in a few sentences of the bombed cities of Britain, recalling the last time he had worn academic robes. It was at Bristol, which had been heavily bombed during the night; indeed, 'many of the University authorities had pulled on their robes over uniforms begrimed and drenched.'

'Here now today, I am once again,' the P.M. paused, and there was a twinkle in his eye, 'in academic groves—groves is, I believe, the right word—where knowledge is garnered, where learning is stimulated, where virtues are inculcated and thought encouraged.'

It was a very mild quip, but his audience were in an indulgent mood as they thought of the bombing of Britain. Then, very gently, he told them of the price of greatness:

'One cannot rise to be in many ways the leading community in the civilized world without being involved in its problems, without being convulsed by its agonies and inspired by its causes.'

The subtle flattery of this passage was well designed to pave the way for what was to come. He could now lay bare the full scope of the workings of his mind:

'The most potent factor in human society at the end of the nineteenth century, Bismarck said, was the fact that the British and American people spoke the same language—this gift of a common tongue is a priceless inheritance and it may well some day become the foundation of a common citizenship.'

There, the cat was out of the bag, but how gently, how patiently, how prudently, were the audience prepared for its appearance!

With the end in sight, the main motif of his speech was allowed to peep out once more:

'I am here to tell you that nothing will work soundly or for long without the united effort of the British and American people. If we are together, nothing is impossible. If we are divided, all will fail. I therefore preach continually the doctrine of the fraternal association of our peoples, not for any purpose of gaining invidious material advantages for either of them, not for territorial aggrandisement or the vain pomp of earthly domination, but for the sake of service to mankind and for the honour that comes to those who faithfully serve great causes.'

That was as near as he dared go to proposing a closer union after the war. Winston told me on our way back to Washington that a little time ago he could not have gone so far. I do not doubt that he tried 'common citizenship' on the President before he launched it at Boston.

The speech ended on a typical Churchill note:

'And here let me say how proud we ought to be, young and old, to live in this tremendous, thrilling, formative epoch in the human story.'

'Now, God be thanked Who has matched us with His hour,' sang Rupert Brooke at the Dardanelles, and this old tough, so near to seventy years of age, throws up his hat that he is alive to play a part.

*

Neville Cardus wrote of the bowling of Wilfred Rhodes:

'Flight was his secret, flight and the curving line, now higher, now lower, tempting, inimical; every ball like every other ball, yet somehow unlike; each over in collusion with the others, part of a plot. Every ball a decoy, a spy sent out to get the lie of the land; some balls simple, some complex, some easy, some difficult; and one of them—ah, which?—the master ball.'

It would serve as a description of this speech of Winston Churchill. Each sentence is a spy sent out to get the lie of the land, and one of them is the master sentence.

*

September 7, 1943

When the P.M. has a speech on the stocks, it takes possession of him, and he usually banishes from his mind everything that is not connected with his script. But when he spoke at Harvard, I found that his thoughts kept wandering to the coming landing at Salerno.[1] That is where his heart is. As the appointed day draws near, the P.M. can think of nothing else. On this landing he has been building all his hopes. There are no doubts of any kind in his mind; anyway he admits none. It *must* succeed, and then Naples will fall into our hands. Last night, when the stream of his conversation was in spate, he talked of meeting Alex in Rome before long—the capture of Rome has fired his imagination; more than once he has spoken about Napoleon's Italian campaign.

Washington, September 9, 1943

For some time stories have been going about that Dudley Pound drops off to sleep in important committees, even at meetings with the Cabinet, but people add, with a knowing air, that he always wakes up when the Navy is mentioned. They would have me believe that he gets bored with anything that does not affect the Navy, and cannot be bothered to keep awake. But it does not seem much of a compliment to this sailor if they can detect no difference between his mental process now, when he is a very sick man, and the time when he was fit and well.

I first noticed this at the Guildhall one morning during a Freedom ceremony when I happened to be seated on the platform next to Pound, and I noticed that he had fallen asleep; his head had sunk until it almost touched my shoulder.

[1] On September 9, 1943, the U.S. 5th Army and the British Xth Corps landed at Salerno with the object of outflanking the Axis armies in Southern Italy, following the 8th Army's invasion of the toe of the peninsula.

As for the P.M., he does not notice this kind of thing until it hits him. And here at Washington it has hit him pretty hard. Today a message came from the White House. The Prime Minister would like to see me.

'I'm worried about Pound,' he began. 'I thought things weren't right when he got out of coming to Snow Lake. You know he is a keen fisherman. Last night after dinner he came to see us. The President asked him some very ordinary questions, and I was very surprised when he answered wide of the mark. I said to him: "But, Admiral, you don't really mean that?" He sat up straight and said he would let me have a full report in the morning. After that he rose, saying that he felt tired and would go to bed. After he had gone the President said that he had noticed at some of the meetings that Pound was torpid, and had decided that he was finished. 'This morning,' the P.M. went on, 'Pound asked to see me. In view of what had happened last night I felt he was going to say something very important to me. It did not seem right to receive him in bed. I got up and sat at a table in my dressing-gown. When he appeared I asked him to sit down. He said at once: "Prime Minister, I have to tell you that I am no longer able to carry out my duties and must ask to be relieved of them. I have had a slight stroke, my right foot does not work properly and my hand is affected so that I cannot write my name properly. My general activities are affected." I told him that in saying this he had behaved like a man and a gentleman, and that arrangements would be made forthwith to relieve him of his duties. I asked him to return with us in *Renown*. Can nothing be done, Charles? Will he get better?'

September 12, 1943

When our troops landed on the Salerno beaches it did not prove to be at all a walk-over. On the contrary, the news that filtered into Hyde Park, where we had followed the President, was disquieting: the Germans had launched a strong counter-attack and the situation was very uncertain. 'These things always seem to happen,' grumbled the P.M., 'when I am with the President.' Poor Winston, he had been so anxious to convince Roosevelt that the invasion of Italy would yield a bountiful harvest at no great cost. When we left Hyde Park tonight, on the long train journey to Halifax, the situation was still very obscure.

September 13, 1943

This morning things are no better. The P.M. is as irritable as if he had a big speech hanging over him. I have never seen him more on edge during a battle. Three 'bloodys' bespattered his conversation, and twice, while I was with him, he lost his temper with his servant, shouting at him in a painful way. He got up and walked down the train. He was sure that Alexander was doing the right thing, but he could not help wondering what he was doing and whether he was on the spot. He did hope Alex would keep him posted. 'Has any news come in?' he kept demanding. In truth, the reports that are reaching him only leave him more anxious. There is a dreadful hint, though it is carefully covered up, that we might be driven into the sea. It appears, as far as I can tell, that the P.M. is largely responsible for this particular operation; if anyone is to blame, he is the man; and, from the way things seem to be going, I suppose he is beginning to think that there might be a good deal to explain. None of the generals in command, he tells me, has fought a battle before. Could he do anything to help, he wondered. He cannot stay still for long; twice in the last hour he has gone off wandering down the train as if he were looking for someone. At last he decided to send a message to Alex.

September 16, 1943

On board *Renown* the P.M. has become a little less abstracted. It is with a real sense of relief that he counts the days before the ship will drop anchor. He told me that he was anxious to get back to London to pick up the threads again. All the same, he has not found it easy, while the telegrams kept coming in, to settle down to his speech for the House of Commons. His habits in a ship don't help. Instead of coming on deck for a little exercise, he remains immured in his cabin. Today, when he had been brooding over his plate, he looked up, and, addressing no one in particular, said: 'My feeling is we are going to win.' He admits now that it has been touch and go, that for three days the issue hung in the balance. Anyway, he is pretty sure that we are out of the wood now. When he rose from the table to go to his cabin, I think we were all a little surprised —though we are accustomed to his moods—at this sudden revulsion of feeling: his spirits have come back, his dark fears are exorcised.

September 21, 1943

Back in London, the anxious days, when it seemed we might be driven back into the sea, are forgotten. The P.M. is in high spirits; he knows he has the country solidly behind him. Even the small group of members of the House of Commons, who had set themselves up as his mentors, held their peace on this occasion.

September 22, 1943

When the P.M. woke, and rang his bell for the newspapers, he was shocked to read of the sudden death of the Chancellor of the Exchequer, Sir Kingsley Wood, with whom he had been on very friendly terms. Sir John Anderson, the Lord President of the Council, who is now to become Chancellor, is a very different man. There has indeed been nothing quite like him in the Civil Service. His astonishing efficiency depends on an unusual combination of qualities. In the first place, he has an appetite for facts, which he has indulged freely for many years, so that it is almost impossible to catch him out in anything. This grip of detail is reinforced by what Maynard Keynes termed 'the gift of instinctive judgment.' Anderson only speaks as from the Bench. To this catalogue of virtues I must add his immense experience of administration and his shining moral courage, what Winston calls 'Sir John's firm spirit.' The Prime Minister has great need of such a man. Absorbed himself in the conduct of operations, he has been happy to leave the Home Front to Anderson; he knew nothing would go wrong. A special committee —the most important of all the Cabinet Committees, the P.M. used to call it—was set up to supervise all matters on this front, with Anderson as Chairman.

Sir John was thought by some to be censorious, but he felt he had the right to be critical. The world, after all, had accepted him as a great man, and he saw no reason to demur. It is said that he was pompous as an Edinburgh student, and in the days of his fulfilment they called him Jehovah. I remember once saying to him: 'Winston is hopeless with strangers.' He agreed, but added, in his pontifical manner: 'Winston must not only get to know a man, he must also find him congenial,' and Sir John permitted himself a slight smirk. He would indeed have been pained if he had known that his own solid gifts were not those to set the P.M.'s mind on fire. Winston trusted him, he respected his judgment, but he did not always find him congenial.

October 24, 1943

The P.M. told me that he saw Pound the day before he died.[1]

'His face was set,' and here the P.M. imitated Pound's expressionless countenance: 'He could not speak. But he took my hand, and when I said things that might be agreeable to him, he gripped it hard. His mind was all right; he knew what I was saying. He died

[1] October 21, 1943.

on Trafalgar Day,' the P.M. mused. 'Death is the greatest gift God has made to us.'

October 26, 1943

The P.M. is already beginning to have his own doubts and hesitations, a good deal of his optimism after Salerno has oozed away. But on one point his mind is made up. He is resolved not to let Alex down. When I called at No. 10 this morning I found the P.M. glowering over a telegram from Eden. His face was glum, his jaw set, misgivings filled his mind.

'Stalin seems obsessed by this bloody Second Front,' he muttered angrily. 'I can be obstinate too.'

He jumped out of bed and began pacing up and down.

'Damn the fellow,' he said under his breath. And then he rang for a secretary. When he began dictating a telegram to the Foreign Secretary I got up to leave the room.

'No, Charles, don't go. This,' grumbled the P.M., 'is what comes of a lawyer's agreement to attack on a fixed date without regard to the ever-changing fortunes of war.'

Alex's fears had upset the P.M. His mind was now made up. He turned to the secretary, who held her pencil ready.

'I will not allow the great and fruitful campaign in Italy to be cast away and end in a frightful disaster, for the sake of crossing the Channel in May. The battle must be nourished and fought out until it is won. Molotov must be warned,' the P.M. continued striding to the door and back, 'that the assurances I gave to Stalin about OVERLORD in May are subject to the exigencies of the battle in Italy. Eisenhower and Alex must have what they need to win the battle, no matter what effect is produced on subsequent operations. Stalin ought to be told bluntly that OVERLORD might have to be postponed.'

The P.M. seemed preoccupied and short-tempered today.

October 29, 1943

Went to the House of Commons yesterday to hear the P.M. speak on what he calls 'the physical aspect of the new House.'

'If,' he said, 'the House is big enough to contain all its members, nine-tenths of its debates will be conducted in the depressing atmosphere of an almost empty, or half-empty, Chamber. The essence of good House of Commons speaking is the conversational style, the facility for quick, informal interruptions and interchanges. Harangues from a rostrum would be a bad substitute for the conversational style in which so much of our business is done. But the conversational style requires a fairly small space, and there should be, on great occasions, a sense of the importance of much that is said, and a sense that great matters are being decided, there and then, by the House.'

This morning when he talked to me of his beloved workshop, the old House of Commons, his voice broke:

'There I learnt my craft, and there it is now, a heap of rubble.[1] I am glad that it is in my power, when it is rebuilt, to keep it as it was.'

His mind travelled back over the long and painful apprenticeship that he had served. For some time he went lovingly over the past, and, as he tried to tell me the tale, the tears ran down his cheeks. For my part, though I had heard it all before, when he asked me a question, I could not speak to him.

Winston seemed concerned chiefly with his early struggle to win the confidence of the House. He spoke as it were of a vocation, and, in fact, few men have stuck so religiously to one craft—the handling of words. In peace it made his political fortune, in war it has won all men's hearts. Without that feeling for words he might have made little enough of life. For in judgment, in skill in administration, in knowledge of human nature, he does not at all excel.

Winston found that out for himself quite early. 'You see, Charles, it all began at Harrow.' Sitting at the bottom of the school, under something of a cloud, he discovered that he could do what other boys could not do—he could write. And when, as a subaltern in India, he began to read Gibbon, already he knew what he wanted to do in life. He confessed that from the beginning 'personal distinction' was his goal, and he knew, too, that it could only be achieved by cultivating this inborn aptitude; if he had always done what he liked in life, that did not mean that he was afraid of hard work. Above all, he had set his heart on one thing: he wanted to be an orator. He read everything he could get hold of about Chatham; he studied his father's speeches; he practised his own before the looking-glass. Even then he dreamed of the day when he would dominate the House of Commons, when they would have to listen to him.

He told me this very simply, stopping when his voice threatened to get out of control, while I marvelled at his will and purpose. The wonder to me was that he had not lost heart. For, in truth, he did not seem to be designed by nature for his part. Small, tongue-tied, with an impediment in his speech, when he rose in the House, he was always fearful that he might blurt out something that would get

[1] During the night of May 10, 1941, a German bomb severely damaged the Parliament buildings at Westminster.

him into trouble, and that he would wake in the morning to find that he had blighted his prospects. When he told me this he hesitated and then went on: 'I did not get completely rid of that until the war.'

'Without the most careful preparation,' he continued, 'I could not speak at all in those days. And even then I always kept strictly to my notes.' Moreover, in spite of all the pains he took, he was always in danger of breaking down in the course of a speech. Once he had found himself on his feet, with his mind a complete blank, while the awful silence was broken only by friendly, encouraging noises; he stood his ground until at last he could bear it no longer; back in his seat, he could only bury his head in his hands.

After his breakdown in the House of Commons he dreaded getting up to speak more than ever. Sometimes he would persuade himself that what he was about to say had already been said, or that the time to say it was past. Any excuse served to keep him in his seat. But he obstinately refused to give in. He would not admit defeat.

Perhaps at this point it occurred to him that he had already told me too much. Anyway, when he had solemnly warned me against my practice of speaking without notes, he began to ask me about medicines, and I knew that the conversation was at an end.

November 7, 1943

The P.M. seemed in a better mood today. He had heard from the President that no more landing-craft would be withdrawn until December 15. Looking at me over his spectacles, he said, 'We need not take that date too seriously.' He needs a fillip, for October was a bad month, and now there is a good deal of grumbling over the inoculations.

Chapter sixteen

On the way to Teheran

H.M.S. Renown, *November 16, 1943*

The P.M. is in the doldrums. He came on board with a heavy cold, and inoculations against typhoid have left him with some fever. I had been looking forward to the sea voyage to get him into good fettle for the strenuous days that lie ahead. I pictured him ticking over for a time, cut off from things. But Winston is upsetting all my plans. For four hours yesterday he and Randolph sat in his cabin hunched over their cards, and then after a break for dinner, Winston said to Randolph: 'What about another cut of the cards?' It was after five o'clock in the morning when they went to bed.

Gil Winant[1] breaks pleasantly our ordered lives. Other men have to win the confidence of those they meet; Winant is allowed to skip that stage. Before he utters a syllable people want to see more of him. He has the rapt gaze of a monk; the big dark eyes, buried in his head, look beyond you—I do not wonder that Epstein wants to do a bust of him. I have heard some say of Winant that he is just an impressive façade, that there is nothing behind that prophetic presence. They say that a man's face is sometimes his fortune. Yet to me he seems a discerning man. When I said to him that Winston had no informed likes, meaning that he likes people in a superficial way without really knowing what there is in them—a kind of surface impression as it were—he nodded eagerly, saying that he had not heard it put that way. How typical of Gil when I try to bring him to life that I cannot call to mind anything that he said, but have to fall back instead on something I said.

Winant holds men, but that is as far as they get. He has wrestled with the world and has hidden, like Brooke, behind a curtain of his own making. It appeared to lift a little when the two men came

---

[1] J. G. (Gil) Winant, U.S. Ambassador to the Court of St. James's, 1941–3.

together. There was Winant talking eagerly about *Fallodon Papers* and Brooke—a new Brooke to me—hardly able to wait his turn as he thought of some lines from *The Prelude*. When Winant had done, how his words cascaded!

Winant worries about the P.M.; he thinks that he is wearing out and that there is no one to take his place. Winant is concerned to build a better world after the war, and he has Winston in mind as the architect. 'Tell me, Charles, do you think he is interested?' Winant came closer to me in his excitement. I had to own that Winston has come to look askance at change.

The P.M., of course, is not blind to Winant's quality. There was talk tonight of the possibility of putting France on her feet again, and of the great difficulty of doing this because so many Frenchmen were quarrelling among themselves. Winant would not accept this; those who were helping in France and working for us stood, in his sight, for a sounder France. The P.M. intervened: 'The ambassador always stands out for the larger view, and he is, of course, right.' The P.M. is attracted by Winant's optimism, but it is not to him that he turns for advice. He prefers the tart cleverness of Harry Hopkins, for the same reason that he is drawn to Max Beaverbrook.

When there was a break in the conversation, Winant rose to go on deck—the temperature of Winston's saloon is kept at 73 degrees Fahrenheit. 'These great men,' he said, as he took a long breath of the cool night air, 'are very thrifty in the expenditure of their time.' It did not seem a particularly appropriate observation at that moment, when we had been at the dinner table for more than two hours. 'Roosevelt,' he went on, 'has many interviews, timed to last from ten to fifteen minutes; when he does not want to be asked questions, he just goes on talking till his secretary appears, saying he is very sorry, but Senator So-and-So has been waiting a long time. Whereupon the President's visitor takes his leave. This is the point, Charles. He goes away not at all dissatisfied, though he may not have succeeded in asking the President a single question. Tell me, is Winston clever, like the President, in getting rid of people?'

I sensed that Winant wanted to know more about Winston, but I dodged the question. For Winston is not at all clever at that sort of thing. We do not think of him as in any way subtle; if he talks, it is because he likes talking and is, at best, but an indifferent listener; and, if he dreads being left alone with a stranger, it may be because he can find nothing to say which will bridge the silences. His dislike of strangers, never very well disguised, often flusters the unfortunate intruder, who arrives full of what he is going to say, the arguments tidily and carefully arranged. And then somehow there is no time, or so it seems, to say it in an orderly manner as he had planned; sometimes he even wonders if Winston is attending to what he is telling him. It is all very awkward and unexpected. After a little the Prime Minister holds out a limp hand with a rather unconvincing smile, and it is with a feeling of disappointment but also a sense of relief that the caller finds himself on the stairs.

If Winston is not interested in the strangers he meets, he does not, to be sure, know much about those with whom he works. I said to him the other night that Leslie Rowan might one day be head of the Civil Service. He stared at me in bewilderment. 'Now why did you say that?' seemed on his tongue. It would never occur to Winston to wonder about Leslie's future. I suppose that is because he is not interested in people and cannot follow their thoughts—he speaks with scorn of anyone who pretends he can. I am on the black list. It happened like this. War has always fascinated him; he knows in surprising detail about the campaigns of the great captains; he has visited nearly all the battlefields and he can pick out, in a particular battle, the decisive move that turned the day. But he has never given a thought to what was happening in the soldier's mind, he has not tried to share his fears. If a soldier does not do his duty, the P.M. says that he ought to be shot. It is as simple as that. When he dipped into the manuscript of my little book, *The Anatomy of Courage*, he said that the picture of what goes on in a soldier's head, as I had painted it, would discourage the young soldier; it might affect recruiting. I had tried to unravel the behaviour of men in war, to discover what was happening in their minds. In those years in the trenches in the First World War we had lived on our will-power. It was our capital, and when it was spent we were finished. We had learnt painfully how it could be eked out for a little longer, and I was disappointed that Winston did not think it would help if I put this on paper.

Malta, November 17, 1943

There is nothing new in the P.M.'s impatience with 'all this psychological nonsense.' In fact, I gave it so little thought that I was not prepared for a letter from Dorothy which I found awaiting me at Malta telling me that Macmillans had refused to publish the book. They took the same line as Winston. I replied:

'My dear Dorothy,

'I have just got your letter. It is, of course, a blow. I cannot reconcile it with Desmond's[1] opinion. Though it is a little disturbing that Winston seems to agree with Macmillan. It would not be fair

[1] Desmond MacCarthy, literary and dramatic critic.

to hold him to his promise to write a preface to the book when he feels like this. I shall just forget about it. Now I feel more determined than ever to get it published. The next publisher to try is, I think, Constable. I have not yet decided how to approach them. The delay is the main bother. Don't worry about me. These things stir in me some primal fighting instinct, and I will not let them beat me. I am going straight on with my three articles for the *Sunday Times* when I have finished this letter.

'My dear Child, I sometimes long for a more peaceful way of life without all these setbacks, but I see clearly I was so made that these things will pursue me to the end. What I do most regret is that you with your very different temperament should have to share in these blows. I see that you and the boys and this book have become what I value in life, and that the rest is nothing. This book has become part of me, my apologia. It was a declaration that the little administrative, competitive life in which I have been caught up was not really me, but it was more, much more than this, for in a way it was inspired by the constant feeling (which never leaves me) of the loss in war of all these boys. I have scribbled this hastily that you may not sorrow about the effect of this news on me. The time is gone when anything can really get me down as long as John is all right.'

I decided to ask Winant's advice. Winant was a pilot in the first war; he has read *The Anatomy of Courage* in typescript twice, and understands what I am trying to say. The following conversation took place:

Moran: 'Macmillans have refused my book.'

Winant: 'Good God! Well, you'll have no difficulty in finding an American publisher.'

Moran: 'I wonder.'

Winant: 'You are bound to be down about it for the moment.'

Moran: 'I am not sure you understand. When I began to write about courage I soon found I was writing about fear. My book is all about how courage is spent; it is the story of man's failure to control his animal instincts. You see, Gil, I don't know enough Americans to hazard a generalization, but I have got it into my head that as a race you are not really interested in failure.'

Winant (nodding vigorously): 'That might be true.'

Moran: 'Whereas we English rather like a man who hasn't come off, anyway if he is staunch and uncomplaining in adversity. You see, it's a man's character that counts with us, not his achievements. Ask anyone who matters to put our soldiers in some order of merit and

128

at once he begins talking about Wavell. But it was Wavell who said to me, "I have had a bad war." '

Winant: 'Yes, I agree. It's not failure you like, but the fact that some men grow in adversity. I think it is because you people are so interested in character and put it before anything else that you find failure not unattractive.'

Moran: 'There were times before the war when I have come home sick at heart with the ugly ways of the little competitive world and have said to myself: Is success after all pathological?'

Winant (smiling): 'Well, I guess my countrymen would not have much sympathy with that line of thought.'

Moran: 'Winston seems to me a hundred per cent American in his feelings about failure.'

Unless a man has done something in life, something really worth doing, he does not interest Winston. The fact that he has not come off and is a bit of a failure merely depresses him. It is what a man does, not what he is, that counts. I suppose the trouble is that Winston has no nose for character; he is not very good at spotting a wrong 'un. You will find him rigidly adhering to his own almost finicky standards of rectitude and at the same time quite oblivious that some of his friends have fallen short of his own standards. It is, Winant argued, what you would expect in a man of action.

Malta, November 18, 1943

It seems that, for security reasons, the authorities do not wish the P.M.'s presence on the Island to be known, so he was driven last night by a devious route to the Governor's Palace. Lord Gort has placed his own bedroom at the disposal of his guest; this room on the second floor overlooks a street which is a favourite promenade of the Maltese. The P.M. was resting when I paid him a visit. From the street below came a great hubbub of voices. His brow darkened. He threw his legs out of bed, and striding across the room thrust his familiar head through the open window, bawling:

'Go away, will you? Please go away and do not make so much noise.'

The P.M. is still mouldy; a cold in the head has dragged on; he will not take any precautions, but expects me, when summoned, to appear with a magic cure. Meanwhile he has relieved his feelings by drawing up an indictment of our operations in the East Mediterranean since the army landed in Italy.

Cairo, November 23, 1943

I was asked yesterday to see Madame Chiang Kai-shek, who is living in a well-guarded villa near Mena House. I waited in a room on the ground floor, while they brought her doctor, a middle-aged Chinese, who seemed intelligent and apprehensive. I am not sure that his expectation of life was as good as that of his patient. At any rate, what I said to Madame might have a decisive influence on his future. 'You know the history of Madame?' I explained that I knew nothing about Madame. He gave it to me shortly and coherently. Madame had been to many doctors in America for diverse maladies. She got nettle-rash at times of mental stress; it first appeared after the death of a relative. It was this which was troubling her now. She was sensitive to many things, such as shell-fish. Every conceivable investigation seemed to have been done in America; some of them had led to active measures. Indeed, every form of treatment seemed at one time or another to have been confidently advised.

I suggested that Madame, who had been told that I had come, might wonder what plot we were concocting. Would it not be well to see her? Her doctor nervously agreed. I followed him upstairs to a room where I found Madame in bed. She is no longer young, but there is about her an air of distinction; there is still left a certain cadaverous charm. She speaks English, so that I soon discovered that she was very intelligent. She was always tired, as the nettle-rash interfered with her sleep. She wanted to get well quickly, so she was willing to try anything new which might be suggested. At that point the door opened and a man stood with his hand on the doorknob. Madame spoke to him in Chinese, and he advanced towards me. He was a formidable-looking ruffian, with a square jaw, carelessly shaven, dressed in a black robe like a monk. Madame explained that it was Chiang Kai-shek; he shook hands and withdrew. When I had finished my examination she fixed me with a searching look.

'Well, what is wrong?' she demanded.

'Nothing,' I answered.

'Nothing?' she repeated.

A slight smile played round her lips. She looked at me with more interest than she had so far shown.

'I shall soon get well, you think?'

'Madame, you will only get better when the strain of your life is relaxed.'

She scrutinized me intently.

'I have seen many doctors in the States; they have all told me stories saying that if I did something I should soon get well. You are about the first honest doctor I have seen.'

She rang a bell and said something to a Chinese servant, who reappeared in a few moments with a parcel, which Madame handed to me with a pleasant smile and suitable expressions of her gratitude. It contained an ivory tablet, exquisitely carved. I saw that the audience had come to an end.

November 24, 1943

Madame brought Chiang Kai-shek to dine with the P.M. She acted as interpreter; without her, things would have dragged. The P.M. is always attracted to a soldier who has done something in the field, but he is sceptical of China as a great power and grudges all the time that Roosevelt has given to her affairs. To the President, China means four hundred million people who are going to count in the world of tomorrow, but Winston thinks only of the colour of their skin; it is when he talks of India or China that you remember he is a Victorian.

November 25, 1943

Ran into Harry Hopkins, and found him full of sneers and jibes. He had just come from a meeting of the Combined Chiefs of Staff, who were framing a plan of campaign to put before Stalin at Teheran. According to Harry, Winston hardly stopped talking, and most of it was about 'his bloody Italian war.' Harry went on in his dry, aggressive way:

'Winston said he was a hundred per cent for OVERLORD. But it was very important to capture Rome, and then we ought to take Rhodes.'

Harry made it clear that if the P.M. takes this line at Teheran and tries again to postpone OVERLORD the Americans will support the Russians.

All Hopkins's views on strategy come, of course, from Marshall, but in changing hands they seem to go sour, as a microbe gains in virulence when it passes from one host to another. However, making allowance for the fact that Harry is a born partisan, I have noticed lately a certain hardening of purpose in the American camp. They left Quebec in great heart, assured that everything was settled for good. And here is the British Prime Minister at his old game again. There is an ominous sharpness in their speech when they say that they are not going to allow things to be messed about in this way indefinitely. 'Some of us,' Hopkins snarled, 'are beginning to wonder whether the invasion will ever come off.'

Harry thinks that the P.M. is trying to get out of his commitments.

When I argued with him he got up impatiently: 'Sure, you're not going to tell me that Winston has cold feet.' That, in fact, is the explanation of all this havering. The P.M. has always dreaded an unsuccessful attempt to land in France; it might, he feels, turn the issue of the war. He left Quebec committed, but far from happy. And the long, anxious days that followed, while the fate of the landing at Salerno hung in the balance, only confirmed his forebodings. On the way here it became plain that he is brooding on the extraordinary difficulties of this 'prodigious undertaking.' He has grown more and more certain that an invasion of France as planned must fail.

It is in that mood that the P.M. has come to Cairo. Only a spark was needed to cause him to blow up. It has not been long in coming. The twenty-five per cent increase in landing craft, which was promised at Quebec to strengthen OVERLORD, is to be used instead in the Indian Ocean. Winston was flabbergasted. Throwing aside all tact and common prudence, he argued vehemently that OVERLORD must be postponed or reinforced. The British Prime Minister, according to Hopkins's words to me, was 'explosive and obstreperous'; and the President, torn between Winston's shrill protest and the forceful arguments of his advisers, sought peace in compromise. If the forces assigned for the invasion of France are not sufficient, he is in favour of more operations in the Mediterranean in order to weaken the Germans until the time comes when OVERLORD can safely be undertaken. The P.M. thinks this is a very wise provision. The President, he tells me, is the most skilful strategist of them all. 'Better than Marshall?' I queried. 'Yes, better than Marshall.'

The effect of the President's intervention on Marshall had been rather different. He can never be sure what will happen when Winston and the President get together. With the President wobbling, he and Admiral King fear that the Prime Minister may, after all, get his own way. Harry became quite fierce as he told me this story.

'Sure, we are preparing for a battle at Teheran. You will find us lining up with the Russians,' he threatened.

What I find so shocking is that to the Americans the P.M. is the villain of the piece; they are far more sceptical of him than they are of Stalin. Anyway, whoever is to blame, it is clear that we are going to Teheran without a common plan.

Chapter seventeen

How Stalin found an ally

Teheran, November 28, 1943

The P.M. loves to be on the move once more; the thrust and parry of these conferences are much to his liking; he feels he is getting on with the war. But as he flew over the dark, jagged crags which guard the approach to Teheran, his mind was full of misgivings. When we were losing height he looked up at me and said:

'I could not justify to the House of Commons the last two months in the Mediterranean. Ever since Salerno there have been divided counsels, and the campaign in Italy has been put in jeopardy by sending landing craft home. The Germans have been allowed to get their breath after Mussolini's collapse.'

Suddenly he said with great vehemence:

'Because the Americans want to invade France in six months' time, that is no reason why we should throw away these shining, gleaming opportunities in the Mediterranean.'

The P.M. cannot get Anthony's warning out of his head. He said that when the Foreign Ministers met at Moscow last month Stalin appeared so anxious for a Second Front that our people began to wonder if all was well with the Red Army. Stalin, Eden reported, could talk of nothing else.

Roosevelt cannot understand why both men take this question of a second front so much to heart. Harry tells me the President is convinced that even if he cannot convert Stalin into a good democrat, he will be able to come to a working agreement with him. After all, he had spent his life managing men, and Stalin at bottom could not be so very different from other people. Anyway, he has come to Teheran determined, if I can trust Hopkins, to come to terms with Stalin, and he is not going to allow anything to interfere with that purpose. The mathematics of this is two to one, and before the first day was spent Brooke said to me: 'This Conference is over when it has only just begun. Stalin has got the President in his pocket.'

Hopkins tells me that when Davies[1] saw Stalin in Moscow in May he found him full of distrust. If the President wanted to see him alone, without the British Prime Minister, it could only be part of a deep-laid scheme designed to thwart his plans. It appears that Davies has not been able to dispel Stalin's suspicions. It happens that the American Legation, where the President was to stay, is some distance from the British and Russian Embassies, which are cheek by jowl, so that he would have to pass through the streets every day to the meetings. After Molotov, Harry says, had spoken about the possibility of a plot to take the President's life, Stalin invited Roosevelt to move into a villa in the Russian Embassy compound for greater security; the President at once acknowledged the Marshal's kindly thought and moved this afternoon. He will be well looked after, for his servants are all members of the NKVD, the Soviet secret police.

The P.M., too, was touched by Stalin's solicitude, and, when someone professed to be sceptical of his motives, he spoke in anger of our unhelpful attitude. All the same, no one in our party, except Winston, believes in Stalin's concern for the President's safety. Plainly it is convenient to him to have the President under his eye, where he cannot spend his time plotting with the British Prime Minister.

When the President was safely ensconced in his new quarters, Stalin lost no time in calling on him. When I heard this, I expressed my misgivings to Harry. If Winston was not invited, would it not encourage Stalin to think that the Democracies were divided in their aims? At this, to my consternation, he blew up. 'What possible objection,' he demanded hotly, 'could there be to the President meeting Stalin by himself for a heart-to-heart talk?' Things had gone well and Harry was full of it. There was absolutely nothing to hide. And then, as if he wanted to convince me that there was no guile behind this secret conclave, he poured out the whole story. The President, Hopkins said, made it clear that he was anxious to relieve the pressure on the Russian front by invading France. Stalin expressed his gratification, and when the President went on to say that he hoped Malaya, Burma and other British colonies would soon be 'educated in the arts of self-government' the talk became quite intimate. The President felt encouraged by Stalin's grasp of the democratic issue at stake, but he warned him not to discuss India with the Prime Minister. Stalin's slits of eyes do not miss much; he must have taken it all in.

[1] Joseph E. Davies, Roosevelt's special envoy to Moscow, 1943; former Ambassador to U.S.S.R.

As I listened to Harry, I felt that the President's attitude will encourage Stalin to take a stiff line in the conference. But Harry is not worried. Things are going fine, he said.

When I saw the P.M. after the first Plenary Session, which began at four o'clock, he seemed so dispirited that I departed from my prudent habit and asked him outright whether anything had gone wrong. He answered shortly: 'A bloody lot has gone wrong.' He did not wish to talk about it, and I soon left him.

The session began, according to Brooke, with a lot of blah-flum. As he quoted these exaggerated sentiments, buttering up the Russians, his face hardened until it became stern and uncompromising; in this mood his features recall those of the Iron Duke. I asked him what part Stalin had played in this exchange of compliments. I was told that he had sat silent and watchful. He is always thrifty of gush. Before long the session developed into a wrangle between the Prime Minister and Stalin. Stalin said that the campaign in Italy had been useful in opening up the Mediterranean to Allied shipping, but he could see no point in the British fighting their way up Italy, foot by foot. The capture of Rome did not matter to them. General Suvorov,[1] in his day, had barked his shins against the Alps.

The P.M. said at once that they were all agreed that the invasion of France must come first, but we were short of landing craft and there might be delays. If there were it was 'to Russia's advantage that we should not remain idle.' He wanted to get Turkey into the war. Stalin interposed quietly that Turkey had no intention of coming in. He said this as if he knew. But the P.M. said he could not believe Turkey would be so mad as to stay out.

It was the 'mixture as before,' in Harry's mockery of doctors' jargon, and I cannot help noticing that every time he has to swallow the medicine he pulls a longer face. It appears that the Americans welcomed Stalin's suggestion that we ought to abandon the campaign in Italy. As far as I can make out, the President supported Stalin. At any rate, it is plain that Stalin was pleased.

He certainly gave as good as he got. When Germany was defeated, Stalin promised that Russia would join in the war against Japan. Hopkins told me that he made this important announcement in a casual way, and without raising his voice, so that it was only audible to the interpreter, Pavlov, sitting by his side. Then he went on doodling as if nothing had happened. 'I thought we were going to be late for dinner,' Harry continued, 'when the President suggested an adjournment.'

[1] The Russian Field-Marshal who led the Russian armies in Italy (1799–1800) during the French Revolutionary Wars.

November 29, 1943

When I saw the P.M. this morning he was plainly put out. It seems that he had sent a note to the President suggesting they should lunch together, but the President's answer was a polite 'No.' 'It is not like him,' the P.M. murmured. He does not, Harry explained, want an impression to get abroad that he and Winston are putting their heads together in order to plan Stalin's discomfiture.

This, however, did not prevent the President seeing Stalin alone after lunch. Harry made little of the occasion. He told me with his broadest grin how the President asked Stalin 'whether he would like to discuss the future peace of the world.' There was nothing, Stalin answered, to prevent them from discussing anything they pleased. Roosevelt then poured out to Stalin his own idea of a new League of Nations. Stalin listened patiently, but when the conversation turned to the future of Germany he became animated.

About a quarter to four this *séance* broke up and Stalin and Roosevelt went together to the large conference room of the Russian Embassy. There the P.M., who twice repeated that he was acting for the King, presented to Stalin the Sword of Stalingrad. Stalin seemed to be moved by this simple act of friendship; he bent and kissed the sword. Roosevelt said that there were tears in his eyes as he took the sword. For the first time in my dealings with the U.S.S.R. the Russians have shown themselves human beings. This afternoon this hard-boiled Asiatic thawed and seemed to feel the emotions of ordinary people. For a moment it seemed that we were meeting as friends.

Stalin has discarded his workaday clothes—the grey-brown cloth tunic buttoned to the chin and the trousers of the same material, tucked into knee-boots, which became him well in Moscow last year —and has blossomed out into a mustard-coloured uniform that looks as if it has not been worn before, and gives one the impression that it has been specially designed for the occasion. It looks, too, as if the tailor has put a shelf on each shoulder, and on it has dumped a lot of gold lace with white stars. And there is a broad red stripe down the trousers, which are immaculately creased. All this is crowned by a dreadful hat, smothered with gold braid. His old rig fitted his blunt contempt for appearances; it seemed to scoff at all the uniforms around him, with their five or six rows of meaningless decorations. Has Stalin to make up and play a role like other people? I wish I could follow how his mind works. Why, for instance, did he get into uniform?

When the ceremony was over the members of the Conference took

their seats around the table and the second Plenary Session began—
and from what Harry told me it began on the wrong foot: 'Who,'
Stalin demanded, 'will command OVERLORD?' Roosevelt appeared
to be taken aback; he had to tell Stalin this was still not settled.
Whereupon Stalin said abruptly he would not believe we meant
business until we had decided on the man to command the operation.

Then the P.M. said his piece, and this took some time. They all
wanted to help Russia, he said, and they were of one mind about
OVERLORD, but . . . With this preface he proceeded to traverse
systematically the northern coast of the Mediterranean. Stalin never
betrays impatience; he doodled and smoked cigarettes, which looked
as if he had rolled them himself and stuffed them loose in his pocket.

(Harry notices these things; he tells a story like Max. Sometimes
I fancy that like him he improves upon the original text.)

When Winston had done, Stalin came to the point at once.

'If we are here in order to discuss military matters, then Russia is
only interested in OVERLORD.'

He demanded that a date be fixed and that we should keep to it.
The President not only forgives Stalin his impatience, he shares his
feelings. When the P.M. began once more to stress the strategic
importance of Turkey and Rhodes no one was surprised when the
President intervened.

'We are all agreed,' he said, 'that OVERLORD is the dominating
operation, and that any operation which might delay OVERLORD cannot be considered by us.'

'Sure, there was no God-damn alternative left,' Hopkins snapped.
This was final. I asked Harry how Winston had taken it. He grinned
broadly. 'Stalin looked at Winston as much as to say: "Well, what
about that?"'

Stalin, who does not bother about the graces of intercourse, was
bent on rubbing it in. When Roosevelt had finished he turned on
Mr. Churchill and said he would like to ask him a simple question:

'Do the English believe in OVERLORD, or do they not?'

About eight o'clock Sawyers put his head into my room.

'Can you come at once, sir, to syringe the Prime Minister's throat?
He is due to dine with Marshal Stalin in an hour's time.'

I followed him to the P.M.'s room in the Legation. Winston was
pacing the room, mumbling to himself: 'Nothing more can be done
here,' he muttered. But once before in exactly similar circumstances
the fall of Tobruk came to his rescue. In a man of Winston's
temperament, defeat is never final. If Turkey can be induced to
enter the war it will be reasonable to propose delay in the date for
OVERLORD. From what the P.M. said to me it seems that he is turning

over the next step in his mind, and that he is now looking forward impatiently to his meeting with the Turkish President at Cairo.

'You are late, Sir,' Sawyers interposed.

'Bloody,' the P.M. ejaculated as he stumped out.

I went back to Holman's[1] house, where I was staying, and found that they were waiting for me to begin dinner. The three Chiefs of Staff were the guests. They are always the same, quiet and equable, but tonight they seemed put out. It has been a bad day for our people.

I can make nothing of Portal. He is a plain man. His head is unduly small and shaped like a sugar-loaf, with a bald circle at the summit; his great beaked nose is always in some book or paper. He has a quiet, serene way with him, and that is as far as you get. His aspect checks curiosity; it seems to say, 'All trespassers will be prosecuted.' He smokes a pipe most of the day and often, after dinner on our travels, a cigar. But he has not established a tolerance of nicotine. Once, in Canada, in the train, I was sitting opposite to him, when he turned quite green. He put down his cigar, rose and left the compartment. I could see him in the corridor standing by an open window. Presently he came back, picked up his book and relit his cigar. He is not a man to be defeated easily. Trenchard once told me that Portal is equally outstanding as a pilot and as a Staff Officer—and that is not common.

Portal: 'What would happen if we went off to Cairo, saying that no useful purpose is served by our being here, and that we had work to do in Cairo?' After a pause he added: 'I think it would be all right.'

First Sea Lord[2]: 'What a waste of time this is.'

Portal: 'It is the first time at a Conference I have felt I was completely wasting my time.'

The C.I.G.S. turned away and came across to me:

'I shall come to you to send me to a lunatic asylum. I cannot stand much more of this. Seven hours' conference today, and we are not an inch further.'

We sat down to dinner, and presently Holman, perhaps to get a better atmosphere, said:

'How will Germany break, at the top or the bottom? Let us vote on it.'

Portal: 'At the top.'

Cunningham: 'No, at the bottom.'

In turn they gave their views. Portal said at the end:

'The Doctor shall be the judge.'

[1] Adrian Holman, First Secretary British Embassy.
[2] Admiral Sir Andrew Cunningham.

There was no escape.

'Take Ludendorff,' I began. 'Was his action in saying Germany could not go on fighting the cause or the effect of her collapse? Did he take action because he knew that the home front had collapsed, or did he himself crumble under the strain? That is the question which has not been answered. I rule that the crack may appear at the top, but all the time it may be really the bottom that has collapsed.'

Chorus: 'Very clever, but what hedging!'

About midnight I went to the Legation to the P.M.'s room to see if he needed anything. I found Clark Kerr and Anthony Eden with him, glasses of whisky in their hands. The P.M. was talking in a tired, slow voice, with his eyes closed.

'There might be a more bloody war. I shall not be there. I shall be asleep. I want to sleep for billions of years. But you will be there.' He stopped. 'Charles hasn't a drink—— When I consider the vast issues,' he went on, 'I realize how inadequate we are.'

'You mean a war with Russia?'

I do not think he heard. Then he appeared to make a great effort to cast off the black depression that had settled on him.

'Stalin said we ought to take Turkey by the scruff of the neck. I said: "I think we ought to say to them: You are missing the chance of a lifetime if you do not accept Russia's invitation to be one of the victorious powers at the peace conference. If you don't, Russia has several things to settle with you. And we shall take no further interest in Turkey. If Russia has views about the Straits, that will not affect us." ' The P.M. was silent for some time. 'But Russia has not worked out a role for Turkey if she does declare war. That is obvious.' Winston re-lit his cigar; then he went on: 'The President said to me: "You may go at the Election, but I shan't." I said, "Anthony will have to wait."

Anthony: 'I'm not discontented.'

P.M. (smiling affectionately): 'No, I know. I told Stalin we wanted nothing. We desired no new territory. Stalin didn't agree with me. He rather pressed the point. You see, it would make it easier for Russia if we took something. When I asked what Russia wanted, Stalin said: "When the time comes we will speak." '

Anthony: 'It will be a poor job at the Peace Conference.'

P.M.: 'I would give them the Italian Fleet.'

Clark Kerr: 'That would be a stupendous issue. Cunningham is against.'

Anthony: 'Admirals are a Trade Union.'

P.M.: 'We must be supreme in the air, not merely in numbers, but we must lead in everything. The figures will be Air 6, Navy 3, Army 1. After the war we must have the Swiss military system. If we are strong in the air, other countries, remembering this war, will hesitate to attack us. Moscow will be as near to us as Berlin is now. I don't believe in battleships after the war.'

The P.M., who had been pacing the room, slumped into a chair.

'Stalin was ready to talk about the frontiers of Poland, but I said I had no mandate from the Cabinet nor the President's agreement. So it was left. If present ideas go, there will be a stronger Poland than before the war.'

I asked the P.M. if the President had taken an active part in the conversation. He hesitated; then he answered:

'Harry Hopkins said the President was inept. He was asked a lot of questions and gave the wrong answers.'

When the P.M. said that Roosevelt went a green colour during the first course I wondered if he was well. The strain at the top must be prodigious. Stalin himself, though he comes of tough peasant stock, is thinner and greyer than when I first saw him two years ago.

When the others had gone I took the P.M.'s pulse. It was 100. I told him that it was due to all the stuff he drank and that he ought not to go on at this rate.

'It will soon fall,' he retorted cheerfully.

When we went to his room his mood changed. He could not rid himself of that glimpse of impending catastrophe. Blurred and ill-defined as it was, it stuck in his mind. He pulled up abruptly, so that he stood looking down at me, his eyes popping.

'I believe man might destroy man and wipe out civilization. Europe would be desolate and I may be held responsible.'

He turned away with a gesture of impatience:

'Why do I plague my mind with these things? I never used to worry about anything.'

His face became very grave.

'Stupendous issues are unfolding before our eyes, and we are only specks of dust, that have settled in the night on the map of the world. Do you think,' he demanded abruptly, 'my strength will last out the war? I fancy sometimes that I am nearly spent.'

He said no more as he got into bed. I hung about for a few minutes and then asked him whether he wanted his light put out. He did not answer. He was already asleep.

I lay awake for a long time, frightened by his presentiment of evil. I own that I fear the days that lie ahead. Until he came here, the P.M. could not bring himself to believe that, face to face with Stalin, the democracies would take different courses. Now he sees he cannot rely on the President's support. What matters more, he realizes that the Russians see this too. It would be useless to try to take a firm line with Stalin. He will be able to do as he pleases. Will he become a menace to the free world, another Hitler? The P.M. is appalled by his own impotence.

November 30, 1943

I expected to find Winston in poor fettle this morning, but he seems to have dismissed the night's happenings as if they were only a bad dream. His fears, I fancy, are too vague and intangible to be translated into action. I may be wrong. If he has thought out any plan for meeting the threat he would keep it to himself.

After we had breakfasted, Clark Kerr gave me his version of what happened at Stalin's dinner party last night. At first, while they discussed the treatment of Germany, Stalin was grim and serious. Winston was optimistic, magnanimous and tender-hearted; he did not fear that Germany would rise again as a menace to Europe. Stalin's precarious life has left him a realist, his lessons have not been learnt from books. And what he has seen of human nature has taught him not to expect too much of it. He did not believe the German people would turn over a new leaf; obedience was in their bones.

When they had disposed of Germany, Stalin threw off care; he was, the Ambassador said, in superb form, pulling the P.M.'s leg all the evening. I asked the Ambassador:

'Was Stalin's ragging a cat-like instinct to play with a mouse, or was he just in great spirits now that he had gained his end?'

He did not answer. The P.M. had not, he said, tumbled to Stalin's game. The Ambassador was full of Stalin's talk.

Stalin: 'Fifty thousand Germans must be killed. Their General Staff must go.'

P.M. (rising and pacing the room): 'I will not be a party to any butchery in cold blood. What happens in hot blood is another matter.'

Stalin: 'Fifty thousand must be shot.'

The P.M. got very red in the face.

P.M.: 'I would rather be taken out now and shot than so disgrace my country.'

The President, said the Ambassador, then joined in the fun.

Roosevelt: 'I have a compromise to propose. Not fifty thousand, but only forty-nine thousand should be shot.'

The Prime Minister got up and left the room. Stalin followed him, telling him he was only joking. They came back together, Stalin with a broad grin on his face.

Stalin: 'You are pro-German. The devil is a communist, and my friend God a conservative.'

P.M.: 'I'd like to go to your front'—Stalin received this with pleasure—'I'm in my seventieth year.'

Stalin: 'You need not boast about that. I'm only four years younger.'

The P.M. admitted today that he was 'pretty nearly all-in.' I daresay Stalin is in no better shape. Now they could relax, and even let themselves go.

'The conversation ended in a convivial embrace. The P.M. and Stalin stood with their hands on each other's shoulders, looking into each other's eyes. The last thing I saw of them was Stalin with his arm round the P.M. I wish,' the Ambassador went on, 'we had a record of what was said, that people might know what piffle great men sometimes talk.'

I was about to question whether it was fair to sit in judgment on this man, with all his cares, when a marine broke in on the Ambassador's story. He came to tell us that Stalin had arrived. Afterwards the Ambassador told me what had happened. The President asked the P.M. to tell Stalin the verdict of the staff meeting. The P.M. proceeded to read these decisions, which he had opposed to the very last, as if they were his own chosen strategy. There was not a trace of bitterness in his voice. It is at such moments that you get a whiff of greatness from this strange creature. I asked Winston about Stalin. 'Oh, he was reasonably affable.' His eyes twinkled. 'He can be quite friendly when he gets what he wants.' The smile vanished. 'When we were alone Stalin told me that the Red Army was war-weary.' 'Is that why he wants the invasion in May?' I asked. The P.M. nodded. The President, if Hopkins is right, does not seem to have a care in the world.

'Tell me, Harry, is the President quite certain about Moscow?'

'Why, sure,' answered Hopkins. 'The President knows now that Stalin is "get-atable" and that we are going to get along fine in the future.'

Harry kept repeating the word 'get-atable'.

During luncheon, which followed this interview, the P.M. made a gesture to Stalin which, in all the circumstances, was a patent of nobility. He spoke of Russia's need for warm-water ports; he said they ought to meet the need, and, speaking for his Government, he hoped to see Russian ships on all the seas. There you have the measure of the man in defeat.

All day Stalin has been as amiable as he can be, and it was in this mood that he came to the dinner party at the Legation, to celebrate

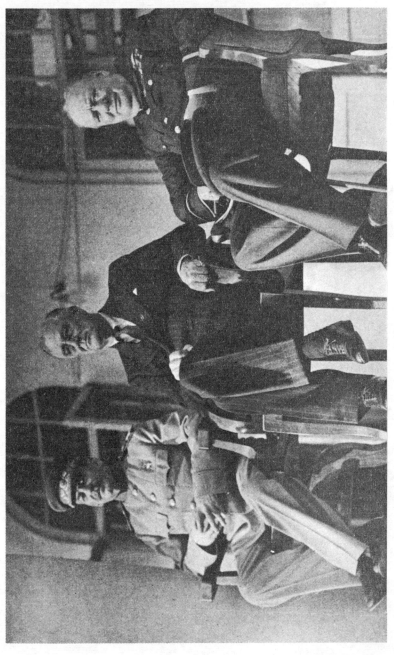

TEHERAN

Winston's sixty-ninth birthday. The atmosphere was genial; things seemed to go smoothly from the outset. It is true that there was one discordant note. The President made a speech proposing the health of Brooke. Just as he was ending his speech, Stalin rose and said he would finish the toast. Looking across the table at the C.I.G.S., Stalin said:

'General Brooke has not been very friendly to the Red Army and has been critical of us. Let him come to Moscow, and I'll show him that Russians aren't bad chaps. It will pay him to be friends.'

While Stalin was saying this the C.I.G.S. sat very quiet and grim. Like Cunningham, he does not pretend to like Stalin; he is indeed repelled by the man's bloody record. His reply was a little involved, but when translated by Pavlov it seemed to please Stalin. At any rate, when he sat down Stalin said: 'I like that man. He rings true.'

And when we left the table and the C.I.G.S. bearded Stalin in his downright way, Pavlov said:

'The Marshal says that the best friendships are those founded on misunderstandings.'

Whereupon they shook hands as if the incident was at an end.

After dinner, when the President and most of the guests had left, Stalin lingered. Those still present were standing and talking in little groups. Randolph went over to Stalin, who was almost boisterous. Winston, coming across, said:

'England is becoming a shade pinker.'

When this was translated to Stalin he immediately said:

'That is a sign of good health. I want,' said Stalin, 'to call Mr. Churchill my friend.'

P.M.: 'Call me Winston. I call you Joe behind your back.'

'No,' said Stalin, 'I want to call you my friend. I'd like to be allowed to call you my good friend.'

P.M.: 'I drink to the Proletarian masses.'

Stalin: 'I drink to the Conservative Party.'

Two of Stalin's observations have stuck. 'Without America we should already have lost the war,' and 'In Russia it is dangerous to be a coward.'

When they were all gone I followed the P.M. to his room in case he was the worse for wear. Though five minutes previously, talking to Stalin, he had been all smiles, a storm was coming up. He was pacing up and down the bedroom with quick strides. He turned to me: 'Read that.' It was a telegram from Attlee.[1]

[1] Clement Attlee, Deputy Prime Minister.

P.M.: 'The Government may go out over Mosley.[1] Bevin is kicking.'

There followed a great diatribe over Labour's folly and stupidity. Much about Habeas Corpus.

'Where is Eden?' he said with great impatience. 'I want Eden.'

I had seen him talking in the banqueting room, so Kinnear[2] was sent to tell him that the P.M. wanted to see him. He delayed coming upstairs for a few minutes.

'Where is Mr. Eden?' the P.M. shouted. 'Tell him I want to see him at once on most urgent business, and less talking there,' he said sharply to a little group at the end of the stairs. I am beginning to be worried about the P.M. He has been profligate of his resources on this trip. I don't know where this will end.

I looked at my watch. It was twelve-thirty. I went to my room.

December 2, 1943

As the Skymaster took us through the clouds towards Cairo, Clark Kerr remained absorbed in David Cecil's *Hardy the Novelist*. The P.M. seemed too weary even to read. He sat with his head in his hands; his cigar had gone out; he was not asleep; he appeared to be lost in thought.

Cairo, December, 1943

When we got here on our return from Teheran I knew that we were in for trouble. Winston seems to be sickening for some malady. His exhaustion is very disturbing. But he keeps insisting that he must go to Italy without delay to see Alex. I can't make out why he is so stubborn. This morning I decided that I must not beat about the bush any longer. I told him that it was madness to set off on a journey when he was under the weather like this. At that he lost his temper. 'You don't understand. You know nothing about these things. I am not going to see Alex for fun. He may be our last hope. We've got to do something with these bloody Russians.'[3]

---

[1] Sir Oswald Mosley was arrested after the suspension of Habeas Corpus at the beginning of the war. He was released on the orders of Herbert Morrison, the Home Secretary, in November 1943, following medical reports which showed a serious deterioration of his health. There was considerable opposition to this in the Commons, but Morrison, backed by Churchill, stood by his decision on grounds of humanity.

[2] A sergeant on Churchill's staff.

[3] This meant nothing to me at the time. I put it down to his 'cussedness,' but I wonder now whether it was the first indication that Winston had arrived at the conclusion that if he wanted to help the countries of Eastern Europe he must get there before the Red Army. He looked to Alex to help.

Chapter eighteen

Touch and go

Casey Villa, Cairo, December 5, 1943

There has been a final attempt to bring Turkey into the war. Yesterday Collins, the P.M.'s pilot, went to Adana to ferry President Inönü to Cairo for a conference. It is only a month since Eden met Numan Menemençioğlu, the Turkish Foreign Minister, at Cairo, and nothing came of their talk. Further, the Americans are not going to help. Their Chiefs of Staff believe—and they have converted the President—that the re-armament of Turkey will mean postponing the date of the invasion of France; indeed, they make no secret of their aim to hinder any move to persuade Turkey to enter the war.

The P.M., however, is full of hope. He has persuaded himself that he can bring Turkey into the war and keeps turning over in his mind the consequences, just as if it had already happened. He does not stop to ask what the Turks themselves are thinking.

Tonight Casey[1] gave a dinner to President Inönü and his Foreign Minister before they return to Ankara. I sat opposite the Turkish President. If a man's thoughts are ever truly reflected by the expression of his features, here was a soul in torment. His face wore a distracted look; then someone would address him and he would force an agreeable smile, only to relapse once more into his own sombre thoughts. He knew he was being pressed to bring his country into the war, and he was alive to the possible consequences if she stayed out. He was even more conscious of the certain consequences if she came in. His intelligent face mirrored his pitiful predicament.

Speaking in French, he said that when he commanded an army, before he took to politics, every soldier in Turkey was his son, but he had had to make decisions which cost thousands of their lives.

[1] R. G. Casey, Minister of State resident in the Middle East, and a member of the War Cabinet.

He was not frightened of possible bombardment. Once it was decided that war was the best thing for his country, he would not hesitate. And his record before the war should satisfy us that this is no idle boast. Inönü went on to tell us—if only the P.M. would listen—in plain terms what would influence him when he had to decide between war and peace.

'It is for these Ambassadors, with their knowledge of Turkey, to tell us whether we can argue with truth that it will be to her advantage to enter the war.'

Inönü had made it clear at Adana that it is Russia and not Germany that the Turks fear. They fear that if the Russians come to their assistance they will remain; once the Kremlin has her troops in command of the Straits, only force will displace them.

Eden turned to me. "What do you make of this?"

And when I replied, 'The President, I think, means what he says,' he said shortly, 'If they don't come in I have no interest in them, and I shall not lift a finger if the Straits are threatened by Russia.'

*

The P.M. believes that it is difficult to exaggerate the benefits to the Allies if Turkey comes into the war: he knows that this alone can delay a second front in France. He feels that it is now or never. He is very tired, but he will not accept defeat. He is resolved to make one last effort to persuade the Turks. He will see President Inönü alone; surely they cannot let such an opportunity pass. They came at his bidding and listened in silence as, forgetful of time, he proceeded to admonish them on Turkey's future, speaking in eloquent terms of her glorious hour of destiny.

The P.M. appears almost as distracted as Inönü himself. He has become very irritable and impatient; at times he seems almost played out. I went to his bedroom tonight and found him sitting with his head in his hands.

'I have never felt like this before,' he said. 'Can't you give me something so that I won't feel so exhausted?'

Nevertheless, he still talks of going to Italy when he leaves here. At this time of the year the climate there is vile, and Alex's tent is no proper resting-place for a man who is tired out. I feel so certain that he will get harm if we go to Italy when he is like this that I've written to Smuts in the strongest terms. He is the only man who has any influence with the P.M.; indeed, he is the only ally I have in pressing counsels of common sense on the P.M. Smuts sees so clearly that Winston is irreplaceable that he may make an effort to persuade him to be sensible. But I doubt whether even Smuts can alter his plans.

Whatever the strain, it is still broken by convivial nights, when for a few hours the P.M. seems to recover his old good spirits as if there has been a new gush of vitality pumped into his veins. Last night at the Embassy we sat at the dinner table from 8 p.m. till 11.50 p.m. Mountbatten's[1] eyes closed and opened spasmodically. I looked down the long table at the faces of the soldiers and sailors. They seemed only half awake. I was sorry for Winston: surely someone ought to show some interest in the drawn-out monologue. On the spur of the moment I blurted out: 'Do you remember Landor's lovely lines?' Winston glared at me. He hates being interrupted. 'What are they?' he snorted. I wanted to get under the table. 'What are they?' Winston shouted with growing impatience. I could think of no way of escape.

' "There are no fields of amaranth on this side of the grave; there are no voices, O Rhodopé, that are not soon mute, however tuneful; there is no name, with whatever emphasis of passionate love repeated, of which the echo is not faint at last." '[2]

I scampered over the lovely vowel sounds.

Winston (*with great contempt*): 'I call that pure defeatist stuff.'

I would not give in. I tried Milton:

' "While the still morn went out with sandals grey." '[3]

'He was on the wrong side in the Civil War,' Winston growled.

I gave it up.

After leaving the table we spent another hour and a half in the drawing-room. The servants talked in whispers. No one kept quite awake. At last, in a lull in the conversation, the P.M. was heard to make the same remark he had made three hours before. We were where we began.

*

December 10, 1943

Better news this morning. Italy, thank God, is off, at any rate for the present. Tonight we go by air to Tunis and then on by car to Carthage, to stay with General Eisenhower. I have never before been so blunt with the P.M., rating him for his folly, but I take no credit for the change in plans. He knows without my help that he is at the end of his tether. Teheran seems to have got him down. It is plain that he is riding for a fall.

[1] Supreme Allied Commander, South East Asia.
[2] Walter Savage Landor, *Imaginary Conversations*, Vol. I, p. 17.
[3] *Lycidas.*

Eisenhower's Villa, December 11, 1943

Our luck is out. Soon after daybreak we came down near Tunis. A cold wind blew across the deserted aerodrome, there was no one about, no car, nothing. The P.M. got wearily out of the hot aircraft, looked around blankly and then, in spite of our protests, he sat down on a box, took off his hat and gloomily surveyed the sandy ground. The wind blew a wisp of hair this way and that, his face shone with perspiration. I pressed him to get back into the Skymaster; he only scowled. I went off to find out what had gone wrong, and learned that the airfield where we were expected was fifteen miles from this spot. There was nothing for it but to re-embark. As the P.M. walked very slowly to the aircraft there was a grey look on his face that I did not like, and when he came at last to this house he collapsed wearily into the first chair. All day he has done nothing; he does not seem to have the energy even to read the usual telegrams. I feel much disturbed.

I went to bed early and woke to find the P.M. in his dressing-gown standing at the foot of my bed.

'I've got a pain in my throat, here.'

He put his finger just above his collar bone. I rubbed my eyes and got up.

'It's pretty bad. Do you think it's anything? What can it be due to?' he demanded in one breath.

I reassured him, and indeed I am not unduly perturbed. For a man with his strong constitution he never seems to be long without some minor ailment. Probably in the morning I shall hear no more of this pain.

December 12, 1943

I went, on waking, to the P.M.'s room. The pain had gone, he complained of nothing, but his skin was hot, and on taking his temperature I found it was 101. I could find no signs on examining his chest. We have had alarms like this before that have come to nothing, and in his position you cannot prepare for an illness without letting it be known everywhere. On the other hand, if he is going to be ill we have nothing here in this God-forsaken spot—no nurses, no milk, not even a chemist. He is, too, in poor shape to face an infection. In Cairo he had a severe bout of diarrhoea following a troublesome cold in the head. And he is, after all, in his seventieth year. It is up to me to make a decision; there is no one here whose opinion in a matter of this kind is worth having. I telegraphed to Cairo to send two nurses and a pathologist. Immediately Martin

148

wanted to know how much we ought to tell Mrs. Churchill and the Cabinet.

'Tell the Cabinet the truth,' I said.

With that he left me. Of course, if this all turns out to be nothing, and the temperature in the morning is normal, the P.M.'s faith in my good sense will be shaken, particularly when he finds the Cabinet in a flap and the Press busy. Tonight his temperature is still up. There is no bell in his room, so I left Inspector Thomson sitting outside his door when I turned in about one o'clock. He knocked at my door an hour later and said the P.M. wanted me. I found him restless and concerned about himself. He felt poorly and his pulse was shabby. Once I put the light out, thinking he was asleep, but he said:

'Don't go away, Charles. Is my pulse all right?'

December 13, 1943

At eleven o'clock this morning the P.M.'s temperature was only 99. He felt better; indeed, he was quite perky. He always goes entirely by the thermometer, and now he had made up his mind it was all over. At that moment Sawyers came into the room and blurted out that Dr. Pulvertaft and the nurses had arrived.

'Now, Charles,' the P.M. expostulated, 'what have you been up to? I'm not ill, and anyway what's wrong with me?'

I had no ready-made diagnosis to offer him. All I could say was:

'I'll tell you that later in the day when I know the answer.'

Pulvertaft, the pathologist, did a blood count. It was normal; there was no leucocytosis. But the P.M. did not blow up as I expected, he became interested in the enumeration of the white cells in the blood. He listened to the tale of how these cells are mobilized in an infection to fight the invading organisms, of the battle that takes place between them and the microbes, how the cells which die in the conflict are called pus cells.

'If I pricked your finger,' he said to the pathologist, 'how many white cells should I find when I examined the drop of blood under the microscope?'

'Oh, between six and ten thousand per cubic millimetre.'

'And how many have I?'

'Nine thousand nine hundred,' Pulvertaft replied, entering into the spirit of the occasion.

'Well, then,' the P.M. said, 'I'm quite normal.'

The P.M. made no objection to the arrival of a man from Tunis with a portable X-ray apparatus. But, when there was a little delay in getting the instrument to work, he grew fretful and a little petulant.

'Oh, now, damn it, come along, get this business done,' he said to the operator. 'When will you get the result?' he demanded.

'Now, sir, in half an hour.'

'Good,' he grunted.

Sawyers came in presently. The operator, he said, had developed the plates and wanted to show them to me.

'Oh, bring them in,' interrupted the P.M., 'I want to know all about this.'

I took the films from the operator and held them to the light. There was a considerable opaque area at the base of the left lung. I showed them to him.

'Well, what does that signify?' the P.M. asked.

'You've got a small patch of congestion.'

'Do you mean I've got pneumonia again?' he demanded impatiently.

At least I know where I am now. It is something to know the diagnosis within twenty-four hours of the first rise in the temperature. It means we can begin giving him M. & B.[1] straight away.

December 14, 1943

The temperature, pulse and respiration are all rising, the blood count is up, and there are now signs of pneumonia at the base of the left lung. Martin has sent a cable to Attlee that a signed bulletin will be telegraphed to him.

'Meanwhile, in Lord Moran's opinion, it is undesirable to delay any longer some intimation of the position to the public; he suggests something to the following effect: "The Prime Minister, who is on his way back to London from the Middle East, has contracted pneumonia and is confined to bed. A further bulletin will be issued tomorrow." '

Harold Macmillan[2] is inclined to fuss. As the only Cabinet Minister here, he claims that all decisions ought to be submitted to him. But this is a medical matter; and any decisions that have to be made are going to be made by me and no one else. Bedford[3] has just arrived from Cairo. The diagnosis has already been made and he has not suggested any change in the treatment, but his presence will keep the people at home quiet.

[1] An antibiotic sulphonamide made by May & Baker.

[2] Mr. Harold Macmillan, the Minister resident at Allied Headquarters, North-West Africa.

[3] Dr. D. E. Bedford, Consultant for Heart Diseases, Middlesex Hospital.

At six o'clock this evening the nurse came to me—would I come at once to the Prime Minister?

'I don't feel well,' he said to me. 'My heart is doing something funny—it feels to be bumping all over the place.'

He was very breathless and anxious-looking. I felt his pulse: it was racing and very irregular. The bases of his lungs were congested and the edge of his liver could be felt below the ribs. I had taken the precaution this morning to send to Tunis for digitalis, and now I gave it to him. As I sat by his bedside listening to his quick breathing, I knew that we were at last right up against things. It was four hours before the heart resumed its normal rhythm, and I was relieved to count a regular pulse of 120. A man feels pretty rotten, I imagine, when he fibrillates during pneumonia, but the P.M. was very good about it. I told him it was a temporary change of the rhythm of the heart which occurred in pneumonia; that it might become regular again at any moment. Once he asked me:

'Can't you do anything to stop this?'

But when I told him that digitalis was a specific for this condition, like quinine for malaria, and that when he was under its influence the fibrillation would probably stop, he seemed comforted. Later, when it suddenly vanished, he remembered my words that this would happen. In medical matters he always remembers exactly what I say. If it is borne out by events all is well; my stock rises. If it isn't, well, I fancy I should soon cease to be his doctor. I am often astonished by the way he will reproduce verbatim something I have said months earlier.

It was half-past ten, and now that he was comfortable and drowsy, I decided to get something to eat while the going was good—it was nine and a half hours since we lunched.

December 15, 1943

No signs of improvement yet. There are plenty of people about, but they do not add to my troubles by asking useless questions. No one greets me with, 'How is the P.M. this morning?' or 'I hope you are pleased with things.' They have learnt in these war years—probably most of them acquired the habit long ago in their self-disciplined lives—not to be curious about things which they don't know, and to bridle their tongues when they do know. At home things are different. Some of the Cabinet have been getting agitated—they seem to be in a complete dither. They have persuaded themselves that the Prime Minister is not going to come through this attack, and have been sending telegrams to Martin, urging me to agree that they should send out from England any specialists I care to name.

They want to feel, bless their hearts, that they are doing something.

I went out alone, wandering among the rubble, which is all that is left of Carthage. Was all that could be done being done? I could not see that anyone, even a Prime Minister, could be properly treated by a committee. I hardened my heart and went my way. I told Martin to thank them and to say that it was not necessary to send out any doctors. I could see he did not think that I was wise. And of course if I arrive back in England without my patient they will remember this against me. I shall be another Morell Mackenzie.[1] Even now, after sixty years, the way he mishandled the illness of the Crown Prince Frederick makes a best-seller in which his infirmities, moral and intellectual, are all carefully set forth. And if there was all this fuss because a foreign Prince did not get well, what will they say if Winston slips through our hands before his job is finished? Well, if I'm going to be shot at if things go wrong, I am going to use my own judgment to prevent them going wrong.

It was left to me to compose a bulletin, which I gave to Martin when Bedford and Pulvertaft had signed it.

'The Prime Minister has been in bed for some days with a cold. A patch of pneumonia has now developed in the left lung. His general condition is as satisfactory as can be expected.'

Mrs. Churchill arrived by air today. The P.M. received the news of her arrival with considerable emotion, but when I told her later how pleased he had been, she smiled whimsically.

'Oh, yes,' she said, 'he's very glad I've come, but in five minutes he'll forget I'm here.'

December 16, 1943

I think we have turned the corner. The temperature is still 101, but the signs in the chest are clearing up. Though this is the fifth day, Martin told me this morning that the public still do not know the P.M. is ill. Mr. Attlee will tell the House at the end of Questions, and the news will be broadcast at one o'clock, just when we are no longer anxious about him.

We gave Martin another bulletin, which will appear in tomorrow's papers:

---

[1] Sir Morell Mackenzie (1837–92), specialist in throat diseases. In 1887 he was summoned to attend Crown Prince Frederick William of Germany. The Crown Prince, who became Emperor Frederick William III in the same year, died of cancer in 1888. Mackenzie had ruled out this diagnosis when he was called in.

'The Prime Minister has had a good night. There is some improvement in his general condition.'

Scadding[1] arrives tonight. To placate the Cabinet, I had asked the people at Cairo to send him.

December 17, 1943

The temperature is settling, and I have stopped the M. & B. We were able to give a more cheerful bulletin:

'There has been no spread of the pneumonia, and the improvement in the Prime Minister's general condition has been maintained.'

The P.M. fibrillated for an hour and a half this afternoon, but it did not distress him as it did the first time.

December 18, 1943

After six days' fever the temperature is normal, but when I suggested to the P.M. that there was no longer any necessity for a daily blood-count he demurred; he had been fascinated by the battle between the white cells and the pneumococci, and has insisted every day that he be told not only the total number of white cells but the percentage of the various kinds. And now he is determined to follow the demobilization of the forces which came to his rescue when he was so hard pressed.

So far the heart has not been mentioned in the bulletins, but it seems safe now to make a reference to the gravity of the illness. The public ought to know that it will be a little time before he can get between the shafts again:

'There has been some irregularity of the pulse, but the temperature is subsiding and the pneumonia resolving.'

December 19, 1943

'The Prime Minister's temperature is normal, and the signs of pneumonia are disappearing.'

December 20, 1943

'The temperature remains normal and the Prime Minister is making satisfactory progress.'

Now that the P.M. is beginning to be convalescent he is very difficult—on two occasions he got quite out of hand. He is tiring

[1] Professor John Scadding, Physician for chest diseases at the Brompton Hospital.

himself with his ebullitions. It is time he took a pull at himself. He has been savaging Bedford and Scadding, who know their job and have been helpful. Perhaps they made rather a song about the necessity for taking things very slowly. They kept saying that he had fibrillated and that this was his second attack of pneumonia in one year, and that he was nearly seventy. They want to lay down that he should not attempt to leave his bed for another fortnight. I said that if they specified an exact time he would immediately demand their reasons. It was better, I argued, to gain time and to fight a rearguard action from day to day. While it mattered I have gone my own way, and have made my own decisions, so I was particularly anxious to meet them in anything which was of less consequence. At last, against my better judgment, I agreed that they should put their point to the P.M. But when Bedford, speaking impressively, advised him to rest for a fortnight, Winston suddenly became red in the face with rage.

'Why,' he growled, 'a fortnight?'

They replied vaguely that he might get a relapse.

'Have you,' he said angrily, 'in the course of your long experience ever seen a patient get a second attack of pneumonia through getting about too early?'

Rather cowed by his violence, they admitted that they had not.

'If, Prime Minister,' they went on, 'you get up too early, you may fibrillate again.'

Once more he demanded if this warning was based on their personal experience and once again they owned that it was not. I was upset by Winston's rough handling of my colleagues, and when he turned on me with some asperity, without any warning my patience gave out. Perhaps I was a bit short of sleep. Anyway, I told him that he must not shout at me; that he was behaving foolishly. I left him before I said more.

December 21, 1943

'The Prime Minister continues to improve. The condition of the circulation is more satisfactory. The P.M. sat by his bed for an hour today.'

December 22, 1943

The P.M. said to me yesterday:

'Your arrangements at home must be in a mess. It looks as if this trip will keep us nearer two months out of England than the three weeks I planned.'

I answered without thinking, that the only thing that worried me at all was that I should miss John's[1] leave.

When I went to his room this morning he looked up from his book with a friendly smile.

'Charles, I don't want you to miss your boy's leave because of all this. I will arrange with the Admiralty for John to come out here by air for a few days. He could come with the courier.'

I am thrilled, but I am perturbed. I do not know the exact date of John's leave, and I am sure he ought to wait till he gets it in the ordinary way. I am worried that the Admiralty may take some action to please the P.M. I don't want anything done which will lead his mates on the lower deck to feel he is being pampered or favoured.

Christmas Morning, 1943

To Early Service with Mrs. Churchill. It was held in a barn with a few officers and men of the Coldstream Guards as communicants. During the service a dove flew in and perched on a rafter. The men said it meant that there would soon be peace.

An officer asked me, a little wistfully, how long the war would last. They are out of it all for a week or two guarding the Prime Minister, but they must know that when they go back the odds are against them; that it is just a matter of time. These highly civilized young men, who are so meticulous in the discharge of their duty, feel the utter beastliness of war, though they never speak of it. They have been brought up by their fathers to think that there is no sense in war, that it brings the solution of nothing.

December 27, 1943

We flew to Marrakesh this morning. I wondered a little if the P.M. would find himself short of breath in the air after his illness, but the pilot assured me we need not go higher than five thousand feet. I waited for Winston in the hall. When he appeared he was beaming. He called out to me:

'The *Scharnhorst* has been sunk by the *Duke of York* and three cruisers. One of them was hit.'

He wasn't sure which. It might have been the *Norfolk*. No, he couldn't be certain that it was not the *Sheffield* or the *Belfast*. I knew John was in the *Belfast*. Dorothy might hear it on the wireless.

'You are quiet, Charles. Why, we're beginning our holiday with good news.'

[1] My elder son John was at this time an ordinary seaman in H.M.S. *Belfast* with the 10th Cruiser Squadron in the Arctic.

He had got back into his uniform and had a feeling that he was leaving behind him the bad luck which had dogged his steps since leaving England. But he is still feeble, and when he stepped out of the house and found a guard of the Coldstream standing to attention it was only very slowly and rather hesitatingly that he passed along the ranks. I was relieved when they helped him into his car. When we had been some time in the air the P.M. said to me:

'I don't like flying through these clouds, they may contain mountains.'

I looked out, but could see nothing but a white mist scudding past me. Presently he sent for the pilot and asked him what was the highest mountain anywhere near our course, and told him to fly two thousand feet above that level. I knew there was nothing for it but to await developments. However, none came, and when I saw that the P.M. was quite happy playing with his oxygen apparatus I fell asleep in my chair.

*

Marrakesh

The P.M. is gaining strength every day and seems well content with life here. Clemmie invited Max to come to Marrakesh to amuse him. She used to dread his influence on Winston, but when Winston became Prime Minister she resolved to bury the past. It was a wise choice for a difficult task.

Every day we picnic in the valleys at the foot of the Atlas Mountains. About noon cars appear, Winston leads with Max, and we tear after him over the red plain in clouds of red dust. I call it a picnic, but it is simply luncheon out of doors. Deck-chairs and hampers are piled on top of the cars, and the fare is adequate even for Winston's demands. Half a dozen Arab children gather round like sparrows waiting for crumbs, and when we are done, they greedily accept in their lean brown fingers what is left. But they do not eat it themselves, they put it in the hoods or pouches of their shapeless garments. Then, after luncheon, Winston, wearing an immense sombrero, slumps in a deck-chair and decides with Max that the Marconi case[1] was a squalid business. They go over once again how F.E.[2] and Carson[3] rescued Lloyd George, or Winston gets

---

[1] A complicated politico-financial imbroglio in 1912–13. It involved allegations, partly substantiated, of speculation in Marconi Company shares by some members of Asquith's Government, at a time when a government contract with the Company was under consideration. Churchill was completely cleared of any personal complicity.

[2] F. E. Smith, 1st Lord Birkenhead.

[3] Sir Edward Carson, later Attorney-General.

absorbed in *Emma*; so that when the sun has gone and the evening air chills, he becomes quite petulant when we press that it is time to go home.

One day we climbed into the mountains by a road which binds the side of a precipice like a rope. Duff Cooper,[1] who has no head for heights, became so uncomfortable that at last he got out and walked. Presently we came to our destination by a deep gorge, at the bottom of which there was a mountain stream. The P.M. insisted on descending this by a steep and rocky path. But when he came to the bottom he had no heart left for the climb back. At last, led by Diana,[2] we took the white tablecloth, folded it like a rope and put it round his middle. John[3] taking one end and the detective the other, they tugged him up while two of us pushed from behind, and a third carried his cigar.

Another day I left the house to walk in the garden and found Max and Monty sitting in the sun. Max called me to join them. He was in a mischievous mood. He took Monty up into an exceeding high mountain and showed him all the kingdoms of the world and the glory of them. And the rarefied air that he breathed on the mountain-top so suited Monty that he found nothing inherently improbable in all that Lord Beaverbrook said to him.

'Of all the soldiers, sailors and airmen in this war, you,' Max said, addressing Monty, 'are the only one the public knows.'

Monty faintly demurred.

'Oh, yaas, I tell you, it is so,' Max went on. 'The only one. There's nobody else who counts. After the war you can have a great political future if you like. You will appeal to all parties. You have no political past, only the glory of your victories, which has taken your name into every cottage.'

Monty sipped the heady wine. He made a few rather feeble, deprecating interjections.

'Isn't it so, Charles?' Max appealed to me.

I did not quite rise to the occasion, murmuring something about Cromwell. The introduction of Cromwell seemed to have a damping effect. The conversation languished.

As the P.M. grows in strength, his old appetite for the war comes back. The C.I.G.S. is in England, but the P.M. has a bright idea. He is organizing an operation all on his own. He has decided that it should be a landing behind the lines at Anzio. If the Chiefs of Staff are not available, there are plenty of lesser fry to work out the

[1] Duff Cooper, British Representative with the French Committee of National Liberation. [2] Lady Diana Duff Cooper.
[3] John, my elder son, was on leave after the *Scharnhorst* battle.

details. Hollis[1] is here to guarantee that they have been properly thought out, and there is Pug; he murmurs that it is the most important operation in which he has been concerned. Alex, too, is sympathetic. He sees that the Italian campaign may receive a great fillip. Why, it may even shorten the whole war. The P.M. has become absorbed in his plans; twice the picnics have had to be sacrificed to stern duty. Councils of war have been held in Mrs. Moses Taylor's pleasant villa. Hitler, I said to the P.M., seems not only to direct the policy of war, he even plans the details. 'Yes,' the P.M. answered with a smile, 'that's just what I do.'

[1] General Sir Leslie Hollis, assistant to General Ismay.

Part three

Under the Shadow of Stalin

Chapter nineteen

Alex

Seven months have gone by since the last entry in my diary. The Allies invaded France on June 6, 1944, and the Russians have advanced into Poland and the Baltic states.

August 4, 1944

This morning, when I went to the P.M.'s bedroom, he did not bother to hide his cares. The fact is that he is no longer in good heart about the general situation, though he can still put up a bold show to the world. I tried to comfort him: I said that victory was following victory—the Third Army had crossed the Seine—and that some of the Americans were talking already as if the war were over. He merely grunted, as if I did not understand. In truth he is less certain of things now than he was in 1940, when the world was tumbling around his ears. It would have been wiser if I had kept my peace. He burst out:

'Good God, can't you see that the Russians are spreading across Europe like a tide; they have invaded Poland, and there is nothing to prevent them marching into Turkey and Greece!'

And then he made an impatient gesture: it was as if he said, What is the use of talking like this? How could I tell him where it would all end?

The American landings in the south of France[1] are the last straw. He can see 'no earthly purpose' in them: 'Sheer folly,' he calls them. He had fought tooth and nail, he said, to prevent them. If only those ten divisions could have been landed in the Balkans . . . but the Americans would not listen to him: it was all settled, they said.

The Prime Minister is distraught, but you cannot get him down for long. He has got it into his head that Alex might be able to solve

[1] Operation 'Dragoon' was launched on August 15, 1944, when American troops landed near Toulon.

this problem by breaking into the Balkans. Our troops are already in the outskirts of Florence. They would soon be in the valley of the Po. As he said this, his speech quickened, he sat upright in bed. He seemed to forget all about me. Perhaps, after all, the position was not as desperate as it seemed. He must see Alex without any delay. So we're off to Italy next week.

I dread the way he's banking everything on Alex. For four years Winston has kept his own counsel, sharing his secret thoughts with no man. The President seems to need a Harry Hopkins, someone in whom he can confide; the P.M., as far as I can tell, has never felt like that. In England, at any rate, there is no one to whom he opens his heart. Brooke is too cold and critical; he always seems to be doubtful of the P.M.'s facts and often throws cold water on his pet projects. There is Monty, of course; Winston admires him as a professional soldier, but he is put off by his boastfulness. Besides, Monty wants to be a king in his own right. But now something must be done, and Winston has a feeling at long last that he must unburden his soul to someone. Of course, he did not say as much, but when he mentioned Alex, he did murmur: 'Two heads are better than one at a time like this.' It is not at all like him, and, for the first time since he became Prime Minister, I believe that he feels a sense of isolation.

August 6, 1944

Now that we are going to Italy in August, there is the question of malaria. I had a presentiment that the battle for mepacrine[1] would have to be fought all over again.

I determined to get my facts right—it avoids a massacre. I went for them to Millbank.[2]

'Whatever else he does in Italy,' they said, 'he must take mepacrine as a safeguard against malaria.'

As I made my way along the Embankment I could find no flaw in their arguments. I wanted to avoid, if I could, a pitched battle with the P.M. After all, he has enough trouble, without my adding to it. He will always listen to advice if the reasoning seems to him sound—it is futile, of course, to lay down the law—though I am careful to administer it in small doses and—this is important—I only give him the draught when we are alone.

So next morning I went to the Annexe soon after nine o'clock,

[1] Mepacrine or hydrochloride atebrin is a synthetic anti-malarial drug, which was widely used for prophylaxis and treatment during the Second World War, when there was a shortage of quinine.

[2] Army Medical College, Millbank, London.

knowing by experience that I was likely to find him alone at that hour. When I had said my piece, he glowered at me. Mepacrine, he was told, made people quite ill. And, anyway, he thought it was quite unnecessary. I stuck to my point, leaving him to think it over. When I had gone he telephoned Buckingham Palace, and the answer came back, 'The King knows nothing about mepacrine.' He hadn't taken anything at all when in Italy. Winston is just incorrigible. He has only to press a bell to bring into the room the greatest malarial experts in the world; instead, he turns his back on science and asks the King whether he ought to take mepacrine when he visits Italy. When the P.M.'s doubts were confirmed in this fashion he sent a telegram to Alex in Italy to elicit his views. I first heard of this when the P.M. sent me Alex's reply:

'Top Secret.

'Special Unnumbered Signal.
'7.0.0. 1025. 4th August.

'Top Secret and personal for Prime Minister from General Alexander.

'My doctors tell me that these yellow pills do not prevent malaria but only suppress it temporarily. They upset some people considerably. Whilst I cannot guarantee you immunity from malaria, I think you may regard the risk as slight. Neither I nor my staff take pills and we have virtually no malaria at my headquarters. I suggest you tell the doctors to keep their pills. If you have Mess wellingtons or mosquito boots, bring them with you for evening wear.'

When I had collected ammunition I fired my gun at the Prime Minister. I began with figures. I explained that during the first two months of the Sicilian campaign last year we lost the effective strength of two infantry divisions from malaria. In the campaign in New Guinea half the force were evacuated sick in six months— 47,534 of 95,050 men, whereas there were only 3,140 battle casualties. Those in command agreed that this wastage from malaria could have been avoided, for if mepacrine were taken regularly there was little or no malaria. It was simply a question of discipline, of a drill for the administration of mepacrine. The principle was laid down that commanders would be held personally responsible for malarial wastage. As for Alex, when he proclaimed to the Prime Minister that neither he nor any of his staff set an example to their men by taking the pills themselves, he may not have known that it was a court-martial offence in the Army in Italy under his command to omit mepacrine drill.

The instruction of Winston is not without its own hazards, and I thought it prudent to close on a lighter note. The postscript to my letter read: 'General Alexander suggests the doctors keep their pills. I venture to wonder if General Alexander's views on medical matters have the same value as mine on military affairs.'

The P.M. lost no time in replying to this blast:

'Most Immediate.
'Secret.

'Telephone Message 6th August 1944 from the Prime Minister to Lord Moran.

'In view of your salvo, all surrender unconditionally and hoist the yellow flag.'

After that sally, how could anyone be out of temper?

August 10, 1944

Dorothy had been standing under a poplar tree for a long time. I went over to her to see what she was doing. 'Listen to the sound these leaves make in the wind. I'm trying to think what it is like. It is quite different from the sound other leaves make.' I wish in these harsh times that she had been built on coarser lines. One day, when John[1] was in her mind, she said: 'When a destroyer in an Arctic convoy is sunk, how long does one keep alive in the water?'

Dorothy drove me to the airfield at Northolt. We were stopped at the entrance, but the man on duty spotted me. We drove through two great hangars to the edge of the runway where the Skymaster was warming her engines. 'I don't think I'll wait for the P.M.,' said Dorothy. She did not want to be in the way. I knew she would stop the car on Western Avenue and wait until our great plane had gone over her head, roaring as it gathered speed and height.

August 11, 1944

After ten hours in the air we landed this morning at Algiers. Duff Cooper met us, and we drove straight to his house. Diana looks tired. Her bedroom, she told me, was 95° last night, so she slept on a balcony.

When a beautiful woman begins to lose her looks she needs something else to keep her afloat. Once I was called to the bedside of a woman whose beauty had been on many tongues. When it dawned

---

[1] John was now serving in a destroyer, H.M.S. *Oribi.*

upon her that her day was over and her reign had come to an end, she took to her bed, and, turning her face to the wall, presently snuffed out. The pathology of the business remained obscure, and for that matter no surgeon can tell me why he dreads to operate on a man who does not wish to live. When the time comes, Diana, who is still beautiful, will, I think, be saved by her character. Meanwhile she is one of the few women who are not intimidated by Winston.

After a pleasant break of a few hours we flew to Naples. The Villa Rivalta hangs over the Bay. I sat for a time looking across the water, turning things over in my mind. I had been talking to a young subaltern, who had been sent here for a rest. His three brothers have been killed, and he himself has been badly knocked about. He said, with a cheerful grin, that he liked his 'home comforts' and was in no hurry to go back to the line. He is not broken yet, but thank God it is not my job to return the poor devil to his unit. That was what the First War meant to me.

August 12, 1944

Tito[1] has been here all day. Winston is amused by a couple of fierce-looking bandits, bulging with pistols, who came as a bodyguard. Tito wanted to station them behind his chair during luncheon, presumably in case of treachery, but agreed as a compromise that they should be planted outside the door, where they looked like two Ruritanian figures out of a musical comedy. Winston makes great fun of Tito's gorgeous uniform, imitating the way in which from time to time he puts his finger between his collar and his neck to relieve the pressure of his blue-and-gold tunic. While Winston had readily accepted Wingate as a man of genius, he is only mildly entertained by Tito, who is, after all, playing for very high stakes. Surely the only excuse for these irregular practitioners of violence is that they should bring off their coups. Winston urged Tito not to let King Peter[2] down and expressed his conviction that Yugoslavia's international position would be stronger under a king than as a republic. One can but hope that Tito derived some benefit from Winston's homily on the blessings of a constitutional monarchy.

[1] Marshal Tito, Yugoslav Resistance leader.
[2] King of Yugoslavia. During the German invasion in April, 1941, King Peter had become a national hero, because of his courageous defiance of the Nazis.

August 13, 1944

This morning I found ants in my bed; they were in great numbers on the floor, but my batman, a handy fellow, got four cigarette tins and raised the bed on these canisters so that the ants were defeated.

While the P.M. bathed at Capri this morning, I climbed up to Axel Munthe's house. He was, I suppose, one of those doctors who trade on their personality and on drugs, though I am told that he had a strange gift of sympathy. The great charlatans—they are not all in medicine—have always fascinated me. When it falls to my lot to give the Harveian Oration at The Royal College of Physicians I shall choose as my subject 'Human Credulity.' It will be the story of the war with the quacks, which has gone on for more than four centuries. I shall give the P.M. some specimens of my script: I think it might be good for his education. Munthe claimed that *The Story of San Michele* was his autobiography; it was in fact a work of fiction that became a best-seller. Now I hear that he is staying with the aged King of Sweden; very nearly blind, he spends his days in a kind of helpless horror at the approach of death. A pathetic, decrepit figure, he cannot understand why the King does not seem to fear death and is not always thinking of it.

In the late afternoon I went with Attlee to see the Blue Grotto; It was pleasantly fresh crossing the Bay. Most of these politicians are cool customers, who have spent their lives dealing with human nature, but Attlee does not seem to have any self-confidence. He answered my questions in a quick, nervous manner, though he told me that he never worried about anything, he just did his best. I have a feeling, however, that there is a good deal more to him than this. Winston, I am pretty sure, underrates him. Anyway, I have made up my mind to find out more about him.

On our return to the Admiral's barge, we picked up Winston and then ran into a big convoy, which was on the point of setting out for the landing in the South of France. The P.M. directed our barge to go round the ships, while he stood in the stern waving and giving the V sign. Some of the men gathered on deck cheered, a few waved their caps. Twenty-nine years ago another armada left the harbour of Mudros for Gallipoli, and Masefield in a famous passage has given us the mood and temper of the men:

'All that they felt was a gladness of exultation that their young courage was to be used. They went like kings in a pageant to the imminent death. As they passed from moorings to the man-of-war anchorage on their way to the sea, their feeling that they had done with life and were going out to something new welled up in those battalions; they cheered and cheered and the harbour rang with cheering. . . . They left the harbour very, very slowly; this tumult of cheering lasted a long time; no one who heard it will ever forget it or think of it unshaken.'[1]

I wanted to say to Winston that it made me sad to see these boys going to the war—many of them to their death—with but one thought in their heads, the futility of war. But I knew he would not see things like that.

August 14, 1944

The P.M. was in a speculative mood today.

'When I was young,' he ruminated, 'for two or three years the light faded out of the picture. I did my work. I sat in the House of Commons, but black depression settled on me. It helped me to talk to Clemmie about it. I don't like standing near the edge of a platform when an express train is passing through. I like to stand right back and if possible to get a pillar between me and the train. I don't like to stand by the side of a ship and look down into the water. A second's action would end everything. A few drops of desperation. And yet I don't want to go out of the world at all in such moments. Is much known about worry, Charles? It helps to write down half a dozen things which are worrying me. Two of them, say, disappear; about two nothing can be done, so it's no use worrying, and two perhaps can be settled. I read an American book on the nerves, *The Philosophy of Fate*; it interested me a great deal.'

I said: 'Your trouble—I mean the Black Dog[2] business—you got from your forebears. You have fought against it all your life. That is why you dislike visiting hospitals. You always avoid anything that is depressing.'

Winston stared at me as if I knew too much. He went on to talk about the folly of repression. And then he spoke of asepsis and antisepsis. Turning to John Martin, who had come into the room with some papers, he said: 'You don't know the difference.' If John did, he held his peace, while the P.M. began to speak of the wonder of all the mind's activities being contained in a bit of brain the size of a hazel nut—'the memories of a lifetime all in that little bit,' and his eyes dilated. He has a working idea of immunity, as of so many

[1] John Masefield, *Gallipoli*, p. 35.
[2] Black Dog: Winston's name for the prolonged fits of depression from which he suffered.

other things, and he asked all sorts of questions. Some of them made me think.

Watching the wear and tear of his life is, of course, part of my job. Is it because he is intensely interested about medical problems and wants to hear more about them that we go through this catechism? Is he aching to explore new ground? Or is he, perhaps, holding out signals of distress? Perhaps he is picking my brains and asking for help.

This afternoon Winston flew in Jumbo Wilson's Dakota to Corsica. There he will board a destroyer to see what he can of the American landing on the beaches somewhere near Cannes.

August 16, 1944

The P.M. came back from his trip in a querulous mood. He had only got within seven thousand yards of the beaches. He had not heard a shot fired. When I asked him what he had done, cooped up in a ship and cut off from everything, he answered that he had found a novel in the captain's cabin. Probably he did not mean this to be taken literally, for he rarely gets his nose into a book on our travels. I think he feels that it is wasting time.

August 17, 1944

We drove this morning, in great clouds of yellow dust, from Naples along 'Highway 6' to Monte Cassino. Winston dislikes other people's stories, and up to now I have respected his feelings. But as we stood in silence by the rubble of the old building I blurted out, on the impulse of the moment, how I had come to the monastery more than thirty years ago. Winston's attention was caught.

'You must tell me, Charles, why you became a monk.'

'Oh, it's a long story. It would only bore you. I was in a state of youthful rebellion against the wickedness of the world.'

Just then Alex came up and I moved away. It was soon plain to me that the minds of the soldiers were occupied by rather different thoughts, as with trained eyes they took in the scene. And even to a civilian intelligence a glance at the heights, which our men had been ordered to storm, brought home the cruel demands that were made on them. We seem indeed to have sunk back into the blind, un-thinking warfare of the First War. Perhaps the men are stale.

After a picnic lunch we flew with Alex to his headquarters near Siena. The narrow streets of the old town were blocked by American cars, but we are quartered in a villa, in a peaceful spot, a few miles to the west. Tonight, when I was alone with Winston, to my consternation he said: 'I want you to tell me your story about the monastery. No. I'd like to hear it. I have always tried to understand the point of austerity'—a broad grin appeared—'though I cannot claim that I have seriously practised it.'

This is the story I told him. It was before the First War, when I held the coveted office of Medical Registrar at St. Mary's Hospital. There was then only one registrar, and the occupant of the post was, as it were, on approval for two years. If he passed the scrutiny, he was generally elected to the next vacancy on the staff and became a physician to the hospital, a full-blooded consultant. But, after a year in the office, I got it into my head—I was very young then—that some of my seniors were more concerned with their practices than with the students' training. It appeared a stuffy, material, and not very attractive existence, and I decided to send in my resignation. I did not give my reasons. It would sound priggish, I thought, if I tried to explain how I came to take such a suicidal step after all those years of apprenticeship.

As far as I can remember, I was not at all disconsolate that I had burnt my boats, irrevocably it seemed then. For some years my days had passed in the underground outpatient department of the hospital, lit even at noon by artificial light. I worked in a small room, like the inside cabin of a ship; it had no windows, and got very hot, and was full of microbes and of the sour smell of the human body. Then in the late afternoon, exchanging my white overall for a morning coat, I would don my top-hat and wind my way in and out of the vehicles and vans crowding the goods yard of the Great Western Railway, which then separated the hospital from the Harrow Road. For it was in that dreary street that I rented a single, shabby little room.

By coaching students for their final examinations I had been able to save a small sum of money, and this I planned to spend in travel—my resources would come to an end, I reckoned, in about a year.

It was in these circumstances that, in the spring of 1911, I found myself in Rome ready for adventure. One day I met a professor from Yale University, who told me he was going to Monte Cassino that afternoon. Whereupon I asked if I could go with him. From the wayside station we climbed in a creaking phaeton drawn by a dilapidated horse up what seemed like the side of a mountain. At length the driver, who had been encouraging his exhausted beast with curses and cracks of his whip, stopped at the gate of the monastery and rang a bell so violently that I felt abashed. A monk opened the door and spoke in Italian to the professor. He led us to a

cell on the other side of the great stone building. That night I slept
fitfully in my cell. Leaving my bed in the small hours, I wandered
out into the long, deserted passages, until I found myself in a chapel
where a monk was at prayer. I do not suppose that I was a very
serious youth, but I got down on my knees and prayed. I waited
for a long time until he rose to his feet. He left the chapel, and I
followed him. He led me to a great terrace or battlement which
looked down a wooded precipice into a valley far below. He had
come to the monastery from Belgium to carve the screen in the
chapel. Quite simply he told me, when I asked him, why he had
given up the world. And then we stood in silence drinking in the
utter peace of the place as the night left us.

When I had come to the end of my story Winston seemed abstracted. At length he said:

'I suppose you believe in another life when we die?'

When I did not answer he pressed me:

'You have been trained in logic. Tell me why you believe such
things.'

I had a feeling that he, too, wanted desperately to believe in
something, but from what he said he did not find it easy.

'You would have made a good monk,' he mused. There was a
knock at the door. With an effort, Winston seemed to collect his
thoughts. 'Tell me, Charles, did you never drink anything when you
were with your battalion in France?'

August 20, 1944

I think I am beginning to get the hang of things here. If Winston
came to Italy eager to see Alex, Alex is even more eager to see
Winston. He has found that the preoccupation of the Americans
with the invasion of France and their indifference towards the
Italian campaign is wrecking his command. He knows that only
Winston can stop the rot. When we landed at Naples, it did not need
much acumen to see that the word had gone forth that the P.M.'s
stay was to be made as pleasant as it could be made by taking
thought and by remembering what he liked.

While I have been busy exploring the side streets of Siena, Winston
has spent the sunny days working in bed. But at night Alex comes
into the picture. If he has a grievance he is remarkably cheerful
about it. Mark Clark may complain that a great chunk has been
carved out of his Army and sent to France, but Alex says he is sure
that there is a good reason for weakening his front. He knows that if
the P.M. gets depressed nothing will happen. Only the timing, he
thinks, is perhaps not very happy. Alex turned to me:

'The Prime Minister knows so much about our job that he was the first to see that we should soon be well on our way to Vienna if only the Americans would be sensible.'

P.M.: 'Glittering possibilities are opening up'

Alex: 'There is still time to set things right. I am not at all pessimistic.'

A clock struck two, but the P.M. had no intention of going to bed.

It is not what Alex says that wins the day. He is not so foolish as to suppose that anyone has ever got his way with Winston by argument. Winston likes a good listener; he is always ready to do the talking. And Alex seems to wait on his words. He will listen attentively until half the night is over. Like a woman, he knows intuitively that listening is not just a question of keeping silent; it can be a means of communication of a more subtle kind. Besides, when Alex does open his mouth he is always so reassuring, always so sure that the P.M.'s plans are right, and that there will be no difficulty at all in carrying them out. That is what Winston wants; he dislikes people who are for ever making trouble. 'Anyone can do that,' he snorts impatiently. Soon he found himself confiding to Alex his most intimate thoughts.

'I envy you,' he said, 'the command of armies in the field. That is what I should have liked.'

When Alex told me of the P.M.'s confession I asked him whether Winston would have made a good general. At first I thought he was going to say 'Yes.' But he remained silent for so long that I added:

'Winston is a gambler. Marshall would make a big decision, but only after he had carefully removed every possible source of error.'

Then Alex, half to himself it seemed: 'Yes that's true. Winston is a gambler.'

The wooing of Winston has been deftly planned. Alex has promised to take him right up to the front line in the Adriatic sector, where he will receive the stimulus which danger always gives him. When Winston told me this he said: 'Before things happen I have a feeling of apprehension. But when things begin I feel almost gay. I get the same feeling at the tables at Monte Carlo.' And then, as if I were rebuking him for the risks he ran, he added: 'I cannot understand what is afoot unless I see for myself.' Yesterday Alex whisked him off to an American battery with a new nine-inch gun, where he was invited to fire the first shot—a very noisy performance which, however, gave him great satisfaction.

Alex not only thinks of the things the P.M. likes doing, he brings along the people Winston wants to meet. It was a happy touch to throw in General Mark Clark as a luncheon host. When Winston does notice anyone, he is usually attracted by male good looks and by a cheerful demeanour. Mark has both. After their first meeting the P.M. christened him the 'American Eagle': they were old friends. But there was a hitch in Alex's plans. Clark could not conceal his bitterness as he told his story: how a splendid instrument had been forged and then, when he was about to strike a shattering blow at the enemy, had been taken away from him and deliberately thrown into the sea. The P.M. was deeply affected by these words. He appeared to brood on them and went to bed last night grieved and forlorn.

When Alex learnt in the morning what had happened, he seemed to be put out. There was no purpose in sending the P.M. to bed in a bad temper, and he lost no time in taking steps to ease the tension. We got into a jeep, and for one and a half hours bumped down the very road up which the Fifth Army had painfully fought its way, foot by foot, crossing gorge after gorge on wooden planks because the enemy had destroyed the bridges. Alex knows his man. The P.M. never tires of playing at soldiers—the nearer to the real thing, the better. This grim expedition, he said, had helped him to grasp more clearly how we were winning the war. All day, whenever we passed Italian peasants by the roadside, they cheered and the P.M. gave them the V-sign. Tonight he remarked how friendly they were and that he must go again into the possibilities of more ships to bring them food.

Alex's little plot has been laid with great care, but in any case it was bound to succeed. The P.M. can never say no to Alex, whatever he asks; he keeps a place for him in his heart, apart from the others. Besides, both the P.M. and Alex have the same idea in their heads—they want to strengthen the Army in Italy. Already Winston stoutly affirms that he will not agree to any more divisions being withdrawn from the front.

Rome, August 21, 1944

The P.M. is sorely perturbed about Greece. His mind is full of forebodings about what will happen when the Germans leave Athens. The Communists will seize power, and he is resolved to thwart their purpose. That is why we are here.

When the P.M. saw Papandreou, the head of the Greek Government, this morning he made no promises. Indeed, I gather that the Greek got little out of him beyond one of Winston's homilies on the advantages of constitutional government. But I fancy that the P.M.'s mind is made up, and from what he said today it appears that he is thinking of landing a small force in Athens, to strengthen the Greek Government.

Winston never talks of Hitler these days; he is always harping on the dangers of Communism. He dreams of the Red Army spreading like a cancer from one country to another. It has become an obsession, and he seems to think of little else.

August 23, 1944

Winston was today received in audience by the Pope. When we left the Vatican, I asked him what had been the subject of their discourse. He replied that they had talked about the danger of Communism. Winston grinned. 'I talked about that with his predecessor eighteen years ago.' His eyes dilated as he declaimed a fine passage from Macaulay's essay on Ranke's *History of the Papacy*, setting forth how the Roman Church in the course of two thousand years had outlived all other institutions.[1] He felt that there must be something in a faith that could survive so many centuries and had held captive so many men. After his illness at Carthage he asked me rather abruptly: 'Do you believe that when you die it is the end of everything? Is there nothing beyond?'

*

Winston was not given to hero-worship of his contemporaries, and I was puzzled at the time by his affectionate admiration for Alex. It seems that Alex had been able to confirm what Winston had always felt about war. It is fashionable, of course, to subscribe to the belief that war is uncivilized, and Winston, like other politicians, had to make concessions to this popular sentiment. But he has an honest mind, and he knows that from the tremendous moment when he escaped from the Boers to the wonderful years of 1940 and 1941 the greatest thrills that he can recall have all been bound up with war.

To him it was a romantic calling, the highest man could embrace, but it was a game for gentlemen, which had to be played according to the rules. What he loved in Alex was that he had justified his own feelings about war, tried them out in the field and made sense of them. Alex had redeemed what was brutal in war, touching the grim business lightly with his glove. In his hands it was still a game for people of quality. He had shown that war could still be made respectable.

There were, of course, plenty of toughs in the Army, whose peace of mind came from a certain vacancy which had always passed for courage; in them freedom from fear was the outcome of the slow working of their minds, the torpor of their imagination. But Winston

[1] On three different occasions Winston declaimed this passage to me.

drew a clear line between Alex's gallant bearing and the blind courage of a man like Gort. 'Dainty,' 'jaunty' and 'gay' were the terms he chose for his knight errant as he flitted across the sombre scene. Here Winston's instinct was sound.

For my part I had come to think of Alex as a man without fear, until one day, when the war was over, I noticed that he had developed a facial tic or twitch, the certain badge of nervous tension. So he, too, was playing a part like the rest of us, only he was in more perfect control of his primitive instincts.

Winston loved to recount how Alex, when serving with a battalion of the Irish Guards in the First War, was reputed to bear a charmed life; his men, it was said, liked to tread in his footsteps when crossing no-man's-land, believing that they would share his good fortune.

*

The years that have gone since this was written have done little to settle finally the wisdom of the Italian campaign. Was the war in Italy a fiasco, as General Fuller thought, or was it a missed opportunity, a second Gallipoli? If the Americans had put their heart—and their landing craft—into the campaign, our first landing might have been in the North, perhaps in the Gulf of Genoa, as Smuts had pleaded. It might have changed the fate of Europe. At any rate, that is what Winston thought. He had no doubts about the merits of the high command. Once I asked him rather daringly: 'Was Alex a good general?' 'The best we had,' he answered at once, 'better than Monty.' Some of the serious people around the P.M. took a rather different view. They questioned the wisdom of the Italian campaign and Alex's handling of his army.

If Wavell is right, and there is not much in generalship beyond the knowledge of supply—logistics—then we may as well admit at once that Alex cannot claim a place among the great captains. But was Wavell's dictum meant to be more than a half-truth? Alex proved completely imperturbable in desperate circumstances—he brought up the rear in the retreat from Burma, and he was the last to leave the beaches at Dunkirk. There was indeed a singular serenity about the bearing of this man in battle. Is it surprising that he could implant in his men the will to fight—and in this war that will depended more on leadership than sometimes in the past. It is absurd to say that these things do not count in the mixed business of war. To be clever is not everything.

FIELD–MARSHAL ALEXANDER

Chapter twenty

Off the rails

September 5, 1944

Dorothy had arranged to take Geoffrey[1] to Scotland to show him
the mountains (a job I'd like) before he goes back to school, but our
early return from Italy upset her plans, and she had to cancel
sleepers and rooms. Then she learnt that we were off to Quebec
and she could go to Scotland after all. However, the P.M. came
to the rescue and suggested that they should travel on his train as
far as Greenock. Geoffrey was thrilled. Early this morning I took
them to Addison Road, which looked less like a station than usual; no
one seemed to be about save two tramp-like figures in battered soft
hats and Burberries, who turned out to be detectives. Winston
arrived at the last moment and the train moved off immediately.

After about twenty minutes we slowed down and then stopped.
It appeared that the P.M.'s spectacles had been left behind, and a
message was sent back to retrieve them. At one o'clock we were
summoned to luncheon with the P.M. After a little I peered down
the table to see how Geoffrey was faring. I was reassured when I
saw him engaged in earnest conversation with Peter Portal. Portal
told me later that they had been discussing the efficacy of the Eton
air-raid shelters.

At Carlisle we stopped. Apparently a message had been received
that Hitler was rumoured to be suing for peace. So the P.M. had
to speak on the telephone to Anthony Eden. 'I shouldn't be at all
surprised,' someone said, 'if we all turned round and went home
again.' Though no one was allowed on the platform at Carlisle, we
could see eager and inquisitive crowds behind the iron barriers, to
whom the P.M., who had been asked by the security people not to
show himself, gave the V-sign.

It was after seven o'clock when we arrived at Greenock. The P.M.

[1] My younger son.

descended in the gathering dusk and began inspecting the guard of honour, drawn up on the platform, while Tommy[1] told Dorothy to wait for word from the Admiral of the Western Approaches. From the tender I could see them, a little forlorn now, on the deserted platform; then the Admiral's Flag Lieutenant, splendid in his golden ropes, appeared and took charge of them and their rather inadequate luggage and the two disreputable bicycles.

R.M.S. Queen Mary, *September 8, 1944*

It is just ten days since the P.M. landed at Northholt with a temperature of 103; for some days after that he was chesty, and the X-rays revealed a shadow at the base of the lung, a third dose, though a very mild one, of pneumonia.[2] There had been some doubt whether he would be fit to set off on another trip so soon. I decided at the last moment to ask Lionel Whitby[3] and a nurse to come with us. Winston has got it into his head that a pathologist is an essential part of the team to deal with an attack of pneumonia, and I thought it would comfort him to have one on board.

It was a happy thought. This morning when the P.M.'s temperature went up again he became thoroughly rattled and bad-tempered, until Whitby restored morale by finding that he had a normal blood count. The trouble is that Winston always has pneumonia at the back of his mind. Now the temperature has subsided and he is quite himself again.

September 12, 1944

I am stopping the mepacrine, though we were advised to take it for a month after leaving Italy in order to ward off malaria. The P.M. makes very heavy weather about the tablets; he ascribes to them his bad turn on the ship. Besides, mepacrine gives you a yellow cachectic look, as if you had cancer, and people like Brendan say to him: 'You ought to stop that stuff; it's making you ill.'

Dill came to me today. He is a sick man with a refractory anaemia; he asked me if I would come to his rescue if he needed me in Quebec. He then took out of his pocket a crumpled bit of paper and gave it to me. It was a report on the last two examinations of his blood. I

[1] Commander C. R. Thompson, R.N., Personal Assistant to Churchill.

[2] On September 1, 1944, Winant wrote from London to Hopkins: 'His (Churchill's) message to the President will have told you of his illness on arrival, which is only known to a dozen people here. Tonight his temperature is back to normal and he seems on the way to a quick recovery. But each journey has taken its toll and the interval between illnesses has been constantly shortened' (*The White House Papers*, Vol. II, p. 806).

[3] Sir Lionel Whitby, bacteriologist to the Middlesex Hospital.

saw at a glance that he was not reacting to treatment, and I doubt if he will last long. I wonder if he knows?

September 13, 1944

There was a men's dinner at the Citadel tonight; the President, the P.M., Morgenthau,[1] the Prof., Admiral Leahy,[2] Leathers,[3] Ross McIntire[4] and I were all seated at a round table. How to prevent another war with Germany was the only subject of conversation. The Americans were all for drastic action, maintaining that Germany should not be allowed ships or the yards in which to build them; what they needed could be carried in our ships. Morgenthau wanted to close down the Ruhr to help British exports, especially steel. The P.M. was against this. He did not seem happy about all this toughness.

'I'm all for disarming Germany,' he said, 'but we ought not to prevent her living decently. There are bonds between the working classes of all countries, and the English people will not stand for the policy you are advocating.'

I thought he had done when he growled:

'I agree with Burke. You cannot indict a whole nation.'

If the P.M. was vague about what ought to be done with Germany, he was at least quite clear what should *not* be done. He kept saying:

'At any rate, what is to be done should be done quickly. Kill the criminals, but don't carry on the business for years.'

Morgenthau asked the P.M. how he could prevent Britain starving when her exports had fallen so low that she would be unable to pay for imports. The P.M. had no satisfactory answer. His thoughts seemed to go back to the House of Commons and what he knew of the English people. In five years' time, when passions would have died down, people, he said, would not stand for repressive measures. He harped on the necessity for disarmament. At that point one of the Americans intervened: he thought that Germany should be made to return to a pastoral state, she ought to have a lower standard of living. During all this wild talk only the P.M. seemed to have his feet on the ground. The President mostly listened; once he remarked that a factory which made steel furniture could be turned overnight to war production.

After three hours' discussion there seemed to be an absolute cleavage between the American point of view and that of the Prime

---

[1] Henry Morgenthau, U.S. Secretary of the Treasury.
[2] Fleet-Admiral William Leahy, U.S. Chief of Staff to C.-in-C. (the President).
[3] Lord Leathers, Minister of War Transport.
[4] Admiral Ross McIntire, Personal Physician to President Roosevelt.

Minister. The Prof., however, sided with the Americans. At last Roosevelt said: 'Let the Prof. go into our plans with Morgenthau.'

*

My notes of the conversation at this dinner party bring out Winston's instinctive revulsion to Morgenthau's scheme. He hates cruelty, and the thought of a great nation starving shocked him. Plainly it was an emotional response. Within forty-eight hours I was bewildered by a sharp right-about-turn. Someone had said that the plan would not work. At this Winston lost his temper.

'Why shouldn't it work?' he demanded. 'I've no patience with people who are always raising difficulties.'

It was plain that the Prof. had got hold of him. Winston had changed sides.

Lord Cherwell was a very clever man, and he had learnt a good deal about Winston's mental processes during their long friendship. Later I bluntly saddled the Prof. with the responsibility for this particular decision. I asked him how he had managed to make the P.M. sign the plan. At first he tried to dodge my question, but when I pressed him he began to justify his action. 'I explained to Winston,' he said, 'that the plan would save Britain from bankruptcy by eliminating a dangerous competitor. Somebody must suffer for the war, and it was surely right that Germany and not Britain should foot the bill. Winston had not thought of it in that way, and he said no more about a cruel threat to the German people.'

As Lord Cherwell spoke, I could see him producing from his pocket one of his graphs, with that quiet, confident air that he was right. He explains the peaks to the P.M. At first Winston regards them rather blankly, and then he begins to ask questions and soon he is convinced. It is after all so obvious: if Germany were left without industries Britain must step into her shoes and take over her trade.

'They brought it on themselves,' he grunted.

The Prof. did not invent the plan. He borrowed it from Morgenthau, who was bursting with a scheme that would convert Germany from an industrial into a pastoral country. Morgenthau had no patience with half measures. He wanted to strip the Ruhr so that it could not in the foreseeable future again become an industrial area. He wanted to wreck the mines. The vanquished must be left without industries. The German people must, in future, live on the land.

As it happened, Roosevelt, like Winston, was in the mood to listen to Morgenthau. He had felt for some time before the Conference that the Germans ought to be given a lesson that they would remember. His feelings, deeply stirred by their wanton conduct, were, too, fortified by a more practical line of thought.

'The real nub of the situation is to keep Britain from going into complete bankruptcy at the end of the war.'

For my part, I wonder how far Roosevelt's health impaired his judgment and sapped his resolve to get to the bottom of each problem before it came up for discussion. At Quebec he seemed to me to have lost a couple of stone in weight—you could have put your fist between his neck and his collar—and I said to myself then that men at his time of life do not go thin all of a sudden just for nothing.

Eden, arriving in Quebec the day after the President and the Prime Minister had signed the plan, flew into a rage when he learnt of the agreement. He had a heated discussion with the P.M. He asked him if he had forgotten that the Foreign Office had been working for many months on a plan which was to come into force when Germany surrendered. He reminded the P.M. that this plan had the backing of Molotov and that it had been sanctioned by the President himself. The P.M., however, was unrepentant; he instructed Eden not to take up the matter with the War Cabinet until he himself returned to London. He said that he was bent on pushing it through.

Morgenthau returned to Washington elated with his achievements. Mr. Churchill, he said, had at first been violently opposed to the plan. The P.M. had bluntly demanded whether he had been brought to Quebec to discuss a scheme that would mean 'England being chained to a dead body.' But he was won over by the Prof., and in the end, according to Morgenthau, the plan was drafted entirely by Mr. Churchill.

By the time that Roosevelt returned from Quebec to Washington, the mind of the Secretary of State had hardened against the course the President had taken. Cordell Hull lost no time in seeking an interview with Roosevelt, and told him that it was 'out of all reason' to condemn thirty million Germans to starvation. It was noticed that the President took little part in this conversation. He was plainly shaken, and when Henry Stimson[1] saw him alone on October 3 Roosevelt said that he had no intention of turning Germany into an agrarian state. Whereupon Stimson read out to him some of the memoranda of September 15, concluding with the words:

'Looking forward to converting Germany into a country primarily agricultural and pastoral in character.'

[1] Henry Stimson, Roosevelt's Secretary for War.

Stimson tells us that the President was staggered when he listened to this sentence. He had no idea, he said, that he could have initialled such language and confessed that it must have been done without much reflection. Those who were close to the President knew that the Morgenthau plan was dead.

We may well ask at this point how the Prime Minister came to Quebec without any thought out views on the future of Germany, although she seemed to be on the point of surrender. The answer is hardly in doubt. He had become so engrossed in the conduct of the war that little time was left to plan for the future.

In a long life, Winston had always done as he pleased. Military detail had long fascinated him, while he was frankly bored by the kind of problem which might take up the time of the Peace Conference. 'There will be plenty of time to go into that when we have won the war,' he would snap. The P.M. was frittering away his waning strength on matters which rightly belonged to soldiers.

My diary in the autumn of 1942 tells how I talked to Sir Stafford Cripps and found that he shared my cares. He wanted the P.M. to concentrate on the broad strategy of the war and on high policy. The P.M. played for time; he knew that a victory in the desert would silence his critics. No one could make him see his error. After El Alamein no one tried. The House of Commons and the country were reassured at the course of events, the crisis had passed and the P.M. was allowed to go his own way thereafter.

It seems that no one could stand up to him, either in the Cabinet or in the House of Commons. Once he had made up his mind, nobody could make him change it. That was Norman Brook's[1] considered verdict after the war. When Chatham was in one of his paroxysms of gouty fury, it is said, no man could look him in the face. I could believe this when I saw the effect of Winston's overpowering personality on those around him. Mackenzie King told me that Winston bullied Attlee, and he likened the other members of the Cabinet to a lot of schoolboys frightened by the headmaster.

Nature, however, is not so easily stared out of countenance, and Winston was beginning to realize that he was the worse for wear. For the moment we were able to patch him up, but as time passed, and the war dragged on, his work began to suffer, so that those around him came to invoke my help. The office had been complaining for some time that the tin boxes by his bed were never empty. For hours, or so it seemed to him, he would devour the indigestible mass, but all the time a secretary kept coming into the room with an armful of papers to replenish the pile. Winston

[1] Norman Brook, succeeded Bridges as Secretary to the Cabinet in 1947.

was conscious of a sense of oppression that he had not felt before.

This brings me to the Prof.'s graphs. They seemed to provide a short-cut to the mastery of a problem by peptonizing the facts. Almost at a glance, the P.M. could size up not only the problem but also the lines on which it might be solved. Sometimes these graphs appeared to serve a useful purpose, by fixing the P.M.'s attention on some pressing problem. More often they led him astray by over-simplifying the issue. One day Jock Colville[1] said to me:

'The P.M. is very tired. He insists on everything being boiled down to half a sheet of notepaper. It simply can't be done. He misses half the argument.'

Jock, of course, was right. As, year after year, I watched the P.M. doing the work of three men, I kept saying to myself that this could not go on for ever. 'Can't you do anything for this horrible feeling of exhaustion?' he demanded at Cairo. And then came his illness at Carthage. He never seemed to me to be the same man again.

Roosevelt soon woke to the fact that in signing the Morgenthau document he had done something that was foolish and even inexplicable, that might well have led to incalculable consequences. He was very penitent and much put out. Winston, on the other hand, was, as far as I could tell, not at all penitent. Anyway in Moscow he engaged in a serious discussion with Stalin about the future of the plan, a fortnight after the President had consigned it to the rubbish heap. Plainly Winston felt that it was still practical politics.

Why did Winston not admit that he had made a blunder? We shall have to turn back to the story of his early manhood for an explanation. Winston has never been at all like other people. No Churchill is. In his early days, as I have already recounted, he was afflicted by fits of depression that might last for months. He called them the 'Black Dog.' He dreaded these bouts and instinctively kept away from anyone or anything that seemed to bring them on.

Winston told me that when he was a young Member of Parliament 'a mistake would get him down.' It seemed to prey on his mind. The mere thought that he might trip up filled him with apprehension. When, for example, he made a speech in the House of Commons he would wake next morning oppressed with the fear that he had committed an irreparable error which might prejudice his political future. He had to school himself not to think about things when they had gone wrong, for he found that he could not live with his mistakes and keep his balance. This urge to obliterate had, in

[1] John (Jock) Colville, assistant private secretary to the Prime Minister, on secondment from the Foreign Office.

course of time, grown into a cast of mind in which he seemed incapable of seeing that he had been at fault. Of course, nothing of that kind could be absolute, and it is a fact that after his stroke in 1953, when death was round the corner, he did confide to me, not, however, without many qualifications, that he had been wrong about India. But the circumstances were exceptional, for his confessional was a sick bed. Of this need to forget, the Morgenthau plan is an apt illustration.

When, nine years later, the P.M. came to write the history of the Quebec Conference, he had to say something about the Morgenthau plan, and this is what he said:

'The so-called Morgenthau plan, which I had not time to examine in detail, seems to have carried these ideas to an ultra-logical conclusion. Even if it had been practicable I do not think it would have been right to depress Germany's standard of life in such a way; but at that time, when German militarism based on German industry had done such appalling damage to Europe, it did not seem unfair to agree that her manufacturing capacity need not be revived beyond what was required to give her the same standards of life as her neighbours.'[1]

It was, of course, no part of the Morgenthau plan, as Winston himself had drafted it, to give Germany the same standards of life as her neighbours. And the whole passage appears at first sight to be a little wanting in candour. Winston disposes of the plan in less than a page. It would be possible, I suppose, to dismiss the somewhat ambiguous sentences as no more than a good example of the political art of presenting a bad case in its least damaging form. I doubt, however, if this is the whole truth. So insidiously had this refusal to recognize a mistake grown on Winston, that it had become a habit of which he himself was probably not conscious, until it had affected not only his speech but actually his way of thinking. I am disposed to believe that his reluctance on this occasion to open up old wounds was but another instance of his drawn-out battle with the 'Black Dog.'

[1] Winston Churchill, *Triumph and Tragedy*, pp. 138-9.

Chapter twenty-one

At sea

R.M.S. Queen Mary, *September 20, 1944*

After a train trip from Quebec, we left New York yesterday, shortly before midnight, and the P.M. will have nearly a week at sea to turn over in his mind what happened at Quebec. On these voyages he really gets going and talks himself out, but he has been taking stock in a sober mood. Looking forward, he sees the future in grey tones; the old familiar buoyant note is wanting.

Moran: 'Did you find this conference less tiring than the Cairo meeting?'

P.M.: 'What is this conference? Two talks with the Chiefs of Staff; the rest was waiting for the chance to put in a word with the President. One has to seize the occasion. There was nothing to tire me. I don't have to work out things. And if they are not in my head I'm very good at handing them on to someone who squeezes the guts out of them for me. But I'm older, Charles. I don't think I shall live long.'

Moran: 'You haven't lost your grip on things.'

P.M.: 'Oh, my head's all right. But I'm very tired. Can't you give me something to pick me up? I wish I could go to the South of France for two or three weeks at Christmas and get the sunshine. You, Charles, could send me. I'd tell them you ordered me a rest. I have a very strong feeling that my work is done. I have no message. I had a message. Now I only say "fight the damned socialists." I do not believe in this brave new world. Why, Charles, tell me any good in any new thing. That is'—and here he put his hand on my arm in a kindly way—'excepting medicine.'

For a time the P.M. sat moodily surveying the papers on his bed-rest. His cigar had gone out and lay beside his glass.

Tonight, after dinner, somebody said: 'Does the size and shape of your head tell whether you have any brains?'

Whitby: 'No.'

P.M.: 'Oh, yes. Take a line through my eyes; there's as much above them as below them. Look at Charles.' And then with a little chuckle, 'Of course it is exaggerated in his case by the loss of hair.'

September 21, 1944

The P.M. told how Theodore Roosevelt, on the outbreak of the First War, asked to see Woodrow Wilson. Wilson gave him an appointment, but received him very coolly. Roosevelt wanted to command something in the field. On going out, he met Colonel House and said to him: 'Wilson was very rough with me. After all, all I asked was to be allowed to die.' House (*in his silkiest tones*): 'Did you make that last point clear to the President?'

Winston made some gurgling sounds in his throat. 'Do you know the yarn of the man who was castrated?' More gurgling. 'A man called Thomson went to a surgeon and asked him to castrate him. The surgeon demurred, but when the man persisted and argued he eventually agreed, and took him into hospital. The morning after the operation Thomson woke up in great discomfort. He noticed that the man in the next bed was in pain and was groaning. He leant towards him over the side of the bed. "What did they do to you," he called. The man replied: "I've been circumcised." "Good Lord," Thomson exclaimed, "that's the word I couldn't remember when the surgeon asked me what I wanted done."'

The P.M.'s face screwed up into creases and he made some crowing, expiratory sounds in his throat as he did when really amused.

'I shall use that story,' he said, 'when they give me my degree. I'll bring it in by urging the importance of precision of language. Oh, they'll never report it. They couldn't.'

His stories are borrowed from the smoke-room, and are richly flavoured. Nevertheless, it is not, I think, unfair to Winston to say that he has more wit than humour. He has never been a detached spectator of life; he cannot laugh at the foibles of others. Nor, when things go wrong, does he find relief in that particular brand of self-mockery to which the English soldier turns in adversity. Humour has never protected him from the bruises of political life.

The P.M. has a good deal to say about the great figures of the past, but he does not often get under their skins. There is, of course, a good deal of repetition; the same actors are always appearing on the stage.

September 22, 1944

After breakfasting today on an omelette, grouse, melon, toast and marmalade, Winston ought to have been at peace with the world. But I found him militant.

'I'm distressed about France. I must not let de Gaulle come between me and the French nation. He is an enemy of the English people. I must not let him have the revenge of putting me wrong with France.'

And if de Gaulle is often on his tongue, Max is not far from his thoughts.

'Max is a good friend in foul weather. Then, when things are going well, he will have a bloody row with you over nothing. When he was most useful to me about supply, and was very bad with asthma, I wanted him to go up in an aeroplane and work there. It would have been worth the petrol.'

Tonight he began about Kipling.

'I liked him. He had a great influence on my life. But for years he would not speak to me.'

I asked why.

'Oh,' Winston answered, 'something I had said offended him, or he felt I was bitterly opposed to everything he believed in. Then we came together over the war graves in France. Somebody had spoken lightly of the wooden crosses, under one of which his son was buried, and Kipling was furious. I'm bound to say I agreed with him. Later India brought us together.'

He turned to Turkey. Why had she taken sides with Germany in the First World War? Commonly he addressed his monologue to no one in particular, but this question was plainly put to the First Sea Lord, who thought that the seizure of the *Agincourt*,[1] which was being built in England for the Turks, did a lot to put the Turks against us.

P.M.: 'Well the ratio in Dreadnoughts was only sixteen to ten, and two of these were in dock. I wasn't going to let a first-class ship be lost to England. I don't mind making decisions in a crisis and I said: Not a ship shall leave this country now war is declared. Besides, Enver[2] had already decided to join the Germans.'

Then Cunningham got into trouble.

---

[1] Just before the outbreak of the First World War Churchill, then First Lord of the Admiralty, was responsible for the requisitioning of two powerful cruisers which were being built in British dockyards for the Turkish Navy. One of these was later renamed *Agincourt*.

[2] Enver Pasha, leader of the 'Young Turks' and ruler of Turkey in 1914.

'The United Nations will never be any use to anyone,' he said.

P.M.: 'I don't know why you say that; it is the only hope of the world.'

First Sea Lord, a little abashed: 'The idea is all right, but it will never work.'

The P.M., without further words, dismissed the subject as only he can, indicating by his attitude that it hardly came within the province of the Admiralty. But when all the others had gone and Winston was undressing he said to me:

'I like Cunningham very much. I'm very lucky to get such a successor to dear old Pound.'

As he settled into his pillow, he said:

'Well, you'd better get your bathing suit out. Good night, my dear.'

September 23, 1944

When he stands in the Map Room, gazing at the enemy submarines on the vast chart, I'm sure he sees the great ship torpedoed. He has too much imagination for these times. But the only thing he seems to dread is being taken prisoner. He'd much rather die, and he says so. On the last voyage he arranged that a machine-gun should be kept in the boat detailed to take him off if anything happened. This voyage the same arrangement has been made.

'How long,' he asked the First Sea Lord, 'would the *Queen Mary* take to sink after she was torpedoed; would it be a few minutes?'

First Sea Lord: 'More likely a few hours; she is well divided into watertight compartments.'

*

I remember Camrose[1] saying that he thought Winston had been a little in awe of Asquith. 'Asquith, you see, kept conversation strictly within certain limits; he had a sense of what was proper and relevant.' I thought of this when in the course of conversation during luncheon I referred to Asquith's fine intelligence. I wondered what the P.M. might say.

P.M.: 'Oh, he was more than a great brain. More than anyone I can think of, he knew exactly where he stood in relation to things. You could predict what he would do in certain situations, and you would be right—more often than not. Margot[2] was a great woman,

---

[1] Lord Camrose, Chairman of the *Daily Telegraph* and a personal friend of Churchill.

[2] Margot Tennant, wife of Prime Minister Asquith.

impudent, audacious, a flaming creature. Asquith counted it his greatest achievement when he pulled down this glittering bird on the wing. Besides, she took him into a world different from the bourgeois world he had known, and that counted for something in those days.'

I was under the impression that Margot married Asquith and that he was just a passive victim of her arts, until Desmond MacCarthy assured me that Asquith was passionately in love with her. And, now I think of it, this is the only time that I have heard Winston refer in his conversation to women. He is not interested in them. Besides, his chivalry forbids any dissection of them in public.

We hear very little of politics, and then Winston speaks darkly of the future. He dreads the financial consequences of the war. Even the housing problem depresses him.

'I am alarmed,' he said, 'at what would happen if peace was declared now. Some people—aesthetes,' he spoke with contempt, 'say the Portal house would deface the countryside.[1] As if the countryside isn't meant to live in. Nothing is more beautiful than smoke curling up above the houses, while'—with a grin—'brats are made below. We may have to have Nissen huts. There must be somewhere for two hundred to three hundred thousand returned soldiers to live and get married. Builders can't do it in time. I have asked the Beaver, Brendan and Portal to prepare a plan by the time I get back. Portal told me he wasn't afraid the houses would not be ready, but what he did fear was, would roads be built, drainage and lighting turned on? I don't think there is much in this.'

He turned to me:

'Now, Charles, on which side are you about the Health Bill, the doctors' or the Government's?'[2]

Moran: 'The doctors'.'

P.M.: 'It's a free country and this ought to be debated out.'

Laski had written to him suggesting a monster subscription Churchill Memorial Fund to buy a million books.

'A very nice letter, fulsome even. If anything of the kind is to happen I'd like the houses of the poor people south of the River rebuilt and a great park, like Battersea Park, prepared for the kiddies, with lots of ponds full of sticklebacks and many fountains.'

[1] June, 1943, Lord Portal, Minister of Works and Buildings, put forward a proposal to build 3,000 prefabricated cottages for agricultural workers.

[2] An early attempt in 1944 to put proposals for a National Health Service into statutory form. It was shelved and superseded after the war by the National Health Act, 1946.

Somebody criticized a Labour member of the Cabinet because he had once been a Liberal.

'A man who doesn't change his mind with new evidence is no use,' was Winston's verdict.

From time to time he spoke of the war, but when he did so he did not seem so much to be talking to us as arguing things out for himself. He seemed to want to clear his mind and straighten it all out for posterity.

I asked him about Lend-Lease and how it all began.

P.M.: 'I wrote a ten-page letter to the President putting our case. It was delivered to him on his yacht. I think it was among the Caribbean Islands. He sat on deck all day over the letter, and next day he saw no one. Then he came out with Lend-Lease.'

He mused. Then he began to talk of the First War.

'Stettinius Senior came to see me. I rang a bell and three attendants came in, each bearing a big volume with details of all the alterations in factories, etc., so that I could go through the accounts week by week. Stettinius said: "What does it amount to?" I said, "Sixty millions." "Very well," he said. "But don't you want to go through the accounts? They're all here." "Oh, no," he answered; "if you say that's what we owe, that's quite all right."

'Sometime later I ventured to ask him if he had treated the French in the same manner. "Good Lord, no," he replied.'

At times—but not very often—Winston drew aside the curtain that had hidden his feelings at the time of some reverse.

'Anzio was my worst moment in the war. I had most to do with it. I didn't want two Suvla Bays[1] in one lifetime. I felt if we went back their field guns would command the beach and nothing could be landed. The heavier guns didn't matter.'

September 24, 1944

This is our last night at sea. Winston seems in better heart—no doubt the rest has done him good—and we were soon back in the Boer War. Lord Roberts[2] had three Dukes on his staff, and this had led to talk.

'If I were Commander-in-Chief,' Winston said, 'I'd do what I damn' well liked, but Roberts was sensitive in such things. His A.D.C. said to Marlborough: "I fear you can't come up with us;

---

[1] The landing at Anzio on January 22, 1944, was intended by Churchill to outflank the Germans and secure Rome. It was not a success, and Churchill was criticized for his interference, which was compared with his conduct over the landings at Suvla Bay in August, 1915, during the Gallipoli campaign.

[2] Lord Roberts, Commander-in-Chief during the Boer War.

we are going to leave you behind." Sunny was much upset and came to me. I said: "I am going off in another direction. Why not come with me?" We had an ox-wagon with four oxen and two good horses (the kind of animal that costs two hundred pounds). The whole outfit cost the *Morning Post* a thousand pounds. The wagon was full of Fortnum and Mason groceries and of course' (with a grin) 'liquor. We nearly lost the precious wagon fording a river, it just got across. One night we found a lot of geese on a pond. I threw stones at them and Sunny shepherded them my way. But they took fright and, half flying, half scurrying, rushed past me. I took a flying kick and winded one, and before it could recover I was on it.

'I loved it all: all movement and riding. I took a message from Ian Hamilton[1] to Roberts through Ladysmith, which the Boers were evacuating. I bicycled in plain clothes through the streets. There were odd Boers about, but I got through and met Roberts's column. It was explained to him that Winston Churchill had a message for him. Roberts had taken very little notice of me, though my father had got him his Indian appointment, which was his heart's desire, but now he sent for me and was very affable. I gave him a full account, while they brought me food and drink. I felt relieved I had got through. I had been a prisoner once, and I didn't want to be taken a second time. If you do a thing at once, when it's not expected, it's surprising what you can bring off.'

[1] Later General Sir Ian Hamilton.

Chapter twenty-two

Poles apart

The P.M. had left **Italy** before Alex's summer offensive. I saw little of him during the few days that we were in London, but he was in good heart when we set out for Quebec early in September, and in his conversations at the Citadel[1] he made no bones about his plans: he wanted to forestall the Russians in central Europe.

On our return to London, towards the end of the month, I noticed that Italy had dropped out of the P.M.'s conversation. One day he owned to me that he was not so sure that Alex would be able to bring it off. He spoke his mind as he was getting into bed.

'Stalin will get what he wants. The Americans have seen to that. They haven't given Alex a dog's chance. He will do his best, but the cream of his army has been skimmed off.'

The P.M. got out of bed and began pacing the room. The advance of the Red Army has taken possession of his mind. Once they got into a country, it would not be easy to get them out. Our army in Italy was too weak to keep them in check. He might have to get his way with Stalin by other means.

All might yet be well if he could win Stalin's friendship. After all, it was stupid of the President to suppose that he was the only person who could manage Stalin. Winston told me that he had found he could talk to Stalin as one human being to another. Stalin, he was sure, would be sensible. He went on to speak of this proffer of friendship to Stalin as if it were an ingenious idea that had just occurred to him, and while he spoke his eyes popped and his words tumbled over each other in his excitement. He could think of nothing else. It had ceased to be a means to an end; it had become an end in itself. He sat up in bed.

[1] The Citadel in the enclosed city of Quebec was used during the Second Quebec Conference.

LORD BEAVERBROOK
portrait by Graham Sutherland

PRESIDENT ROOSEVELT

'If we three come together,' he said, 'everything is possible—absolutely anything.'

He appealed to the President to arrange a meeting with Stalin. The President's reply was brief and not at all helpful; he could do nothing before the Presidential election in November. The P.M. was unable to hide his irritation. The Red Army, he said scornfully, would not stand still awaiting the result of the election.

The P.M. decided at last that if the President would not play, he must 'go it alone.' One morning I found him in a rough mood. Without waiting for me to sit down he blurted out: 'I am going to Moscow.'

He said this as if he expected me to argue with him. When I said nothing he went on:

'The atmosphere there is quite different since we brought off the landings in Normandy. I shall take advantage of it to come to an amicable settlement with Stalin about Poland. That is why I am going.'

October 8, 1944

We left Northolt before midnight and landed near Naples at seven this morning. The 'York' is cold, and I was ready to get up when the P.M. sent for me half an hour before we landed. The man who called me had been put in charge of the oxygen cylinder. He said that the P.M. had been having oxygen throughout the night, although we had been flying no higher than 3,000 feet, adding that the P.M. had asked him to take his pulse. I found Winston dozing. The mask had fallen off his face into the bed, the oxygen was hissing out while he held his cigar, which was still alight, in his hand. One day we shall all go up in flames. I was about to turn off the oxygen when the hissing stopped. He woke suddenly and lifted the mask to his face.

'What's happened to the oxygen?' he demanded.

'There is none left,' I said.

'What would have happened,' he asked, 'if others had wanted it?'

'They would have been told,' I said shortly, 'that they did not need oxygen flying at that height.'

When the P.M. teaches his soldiers and sailors how to do their own job it's their affair, but when he sets up as an apothecary it's time to take a stand. I took it. He accepted it meekly.

While the others held a conference at Harold Macmillan's house on the outskirts of Naples, I had a short talk with Alex and asked him how things had gone.

'Well, I must confess they might be better,' was his rather unexpected reply. 'We took some prisoners from the 90th Panzer

Division. They were asked why they went on fighting when it was obvious that the game was up. They said: "You don't understand, or you wouldn't ask such a question. We belong to the 90th Division. As long as it is in the field we fight." '

Alex was determined that I should not miss the point. He wanted me to see what we are up against.

'They used to be a good division before they were mopped up in Africa. These fellows took on the old name, which was about all that was left. Now they in their turn have had an awful bashing, but they go on fighting. Pretty good, I call it.'

Alex is like Winston; his heart goes out to a good fighter.

The conference had broken up, the P.M. was in his bath, and Harold Macmillan as host kept the conversation going.

'The P.M.,' he began, 'has been told to keep off the grass as far as the King of Greece is concerned. We don't want him to commit himself to the Greek Prime Minister. Oh, he will, of course, whatever we do. He'll say: "You are the First Minister of the Crown. It is your duty to bring back the king." To Winston any king is better than no king.'

Macmillan smiled as he spoke of the P.M.'s wilfulness and of his romantic attitude to royal personages, to kings as kings, however impermanent their dynasties. At that moment Winston appeared. 'We are talking about kings, Winston.' The P.M.'s face brightened. He began to tell us about Edward VIII.

'Make no mistake, he had very engaging, crowd-compelling qualities, like his gaiety. He and Queen Mary exchanged very nice letters, but King George VI, when asked if he had a message for Edward, said: "I hope he is well and will make a permanent home in the U.S.A." The U.S.A.,' Winston repeated reflectively. 'Edward said: "England need not fear I am going to be a nuisance and settle in England." '

Eden: 'He was a wonderful host.'

It is the only time in four years that I have heard the P.M. refer to the Abdication. King and country, in that order, that's about all the religion Winston has. But it means a lot to him.

When we were alone the P.M.'s mood changed. Something had gone wrong. Before he saw Alex he had not given up hope that the army in Italy might be able to help. He was not prepared for Alex's doleful story. It appeared that our army was bogged down and that nothing could be done until the spring. 'Then,' the P.M. grunted, 'it will be too late.'

It was noon before we left Naples. The 'York' is very noisy; the P.M. addressed half a dozen observations to me during lunch, and

I did not hear one of them. When I asked Eden, who was sitting next to him, to repeat a remark he told me that the P.M. had said: 'A good many people are abusing Charles, but I feel very well.' Eden added: 'More will abuse you when the news comes out at noon.' I took this to mean that I have been criticized in the Cabinet for allowing the P.M. to make these journeys.

Moscow, October 9, 1944

This morning the first thing I heard was Winston's voice above the noise of the plane.

'What do you take, Anthony?'

Eden: 'I always take a red. I think it's good stuff if you want to sleep on these trips.'

P.M.: 'I took two. I'm a hardened case.'

This house in the heart of Moscow, that has been set apart for the P.M., has been well chosen. Winston likes comfort, and he was in a cheerful frame of mind when Anthony came to talk things over. The Foreign Secretary could be obstinate, he must be told that there is only one course open to us—to make friends with Stalin. When the P.M. had said this he thrust out his chin.

Eden: 'How are you going to begin with Uncle Joe?'

P.M.: 'I shall say that the President and I have been like brothers, but I don't want the U.S.S.R. to feel it is just an Anglo-Saxon affair. I want them to know it's the three of us. That's why I've come. We can settle everything, we three, if we come together. If we don't there'll be years of diplomatic wrangling and suspicion. The President has illusions about China, and France is not on the same level as the three of us. Then I'll say there are some small matters to settle, but that will be easy if we work together.'

Eden: 'But, Winston, Poland is a big, not a small thing. It may spoil Anglo-Russian relations. If people feel that Russia is putting in puppets and that everybody who doesn't agree with her is an enemy of Poland they will be uneasy. Poland must be allowed to settle her own affairs.'

P.M.: 'We've agreed to the Baltic States[1] and the Curzon Line.'[2]

---

[1] Lithuania, Latvia and Estonia—these small states changed hands many times, and eventually in the spring of 1942 the Allies reluctantly agreed to the Russian claims.

[2] The much-disputed eastern frontier for Poland, proposed by Lord Curzon, the British Foreign Secretary, at the Paris Peace Conference, 1919–20. Following the Teheran Conference, it was agreed that the post-war frontier should follow this Line, despite the bitter objections of the exiled Polish Government in London. In July, 1944 the Russians set up a rival administrative body in Lublin which agreed to the adoption of the Curzon Line.

Eden: 'We've got to bring up this Polish question at once and tell Joe that Russia has enemies and they could make out quite a case against her in the last few weeks.'

Clark Kerr: 'They fear here that England will be soft over Germany.'

P.M.: 'I'm not a bit soft, but I can't stand for killing in mass. You need not accept a man's surrender, but if you do you mustn't kill him. The Russians would blot out their prisoners-of-war without a moment's hesitation.'

Eden: 'I'd like the Ruhr and Saar[1] to be permanently internationalized.'

P.M.: 'I would not give them to France. Of course, if the Ruhr were grassed over, our trade would benefit. I'm changing my mind about a list of war-criminals; we'd not carry it out. I'd like sixty or seventy of the people round Hitler shot without any trial, but I am against shooting all the German General Staff. Of course, Russia can do what she likes by force, but she would like sanction at the Peace Conference that her action was just and correct.'

Eden: 'Russia thinks England is hard on Bulgaria.'

Clark Kerr: 'He means praise by that.'

P.M.: 'Rotten people. They flogged our prisoners over barrels and left them in the sun to blister.'

The P.M.'s interest in the conversation was flagging. He got up and left the room.

October 10, 1944

The P.M. does not intend to allow anything to interfere with his plans, and anyone who raises difficulties gets short shrift.

P.M.: 'I must say I greatly covet that man's goodwill. How did things go, Anthony?'

Eden: 'Pretty sticky.'

P.M.: 'You really had a rough time?'

Eden: 'Not as bad as that. They were jocular. It was all in good temper. They don't want us to have any finger in Bulgaria. Why were we interested? It's a big issue for us. We might as well know where we stand.'

Clark Kerr: 'You were tough as well as charming, Anthony.'

P.M.: 'I don't want you two to go after sticklebacks. If you get on to a bad patch I'd move on to another. There are a lot of things which don't matter.'

---

[1] At Teheran Roosevelt had proposed the partitioning of Germany into five sections. In addition the Kiel Canal area and Hamburg and the Ruhr and Saar would become two separate areas under the control of the United Nations.

Eden: 'Bulgaria isn't one of them.'

The P.M. can say this sort of thing so that it is plain that he has exhausted the possibilities of the argument. He turned to me:

'Stalin looks much older. He wasn't a good colour. Ashen, yes, that's it. When he came to Teheran he came in a ship across the Caspian Sea and then by car. He didn't fly. You mustn't tell anyone that.'

Moran: 'If anything happened to him it would be a disaster.'

P.M.: 'God, yes. A catastrophe.'

The party broke up and I went with the P.M. to his room.

I asked him if the luncheon had gone well, and he repeated some of Stalin's conversation.

Stalin: 'Fear is a psychological factor. But it has very practical results. It was the fear of invasion that prevented the Germans transferring fifty divisions to the Russian Front in 1942. Those fifty divisions might have made the difference. . . . I do not speak much, but drinking eases the tongue. . . . I am a rough man and not much good at compliments.'

P.M.: 'But, after all, as I always tell the House of Commons, it's you Russians who have torn the guts out of the foul Hun.'

Stalin: 'Guts is the word.'

The P.M. went on to tell me that there had been a lot of talk of unpreparedness, but that Stalin had brought it to a head by asking: 'What is the moral? Only the aggressors can be prepared. Are all of us to be aggressors?' I thought the P.M. was going to bed, when Harriman knocked at the door; presently they settled down to play bezique and went on playing till three in the morning.

October 11, 1944

An enchanting morning, quite a hot sun in a blue sky. We feed at all kinds of hours. The P.M. breakfasted at eleven. But the food when it comes is excellent, though one meal is like the rest. Caviare with bread and butter; then smoked salmon on a long plate; then sucking pig. Even breakfast begins with those three courses; but at luncheon and dinner it is only a beginning; there follows soup, fish, some kind of meat, chicken or game, ice-cream with stewed fruit, and coffee. It sounds terrific to the underfed Briton, but it soon becomes a long-drawn-out, tiresome ritual, lasting two to three hours. You get tired of the plethora and long for an underdone steak.

I hear that Mikolayczyk[1] has been peremptorily summoned to Moscow. It appears that he gets savage when Stalin's name is mentioned. There is bound to be a row, for the P.M. is in no

[1] Stanislav Mikolayczyk, Leader of the Polish Government in exile.

mood to listen to the Poles' strictures. I wish the meeting was over.

I would be quite happy here if I did not feel all the time that things at the College were going to pieces while I am away. The Abrahams and Miss Johnson of the Red Cross came to luncheon. I am sure that Clemmie had instructed Winston to be agreeable to them, but he is the poorest hand imaginable at small talk, or even at being polite to people who do not interest him.

The dinner at the Embassy tonight was rather tedious. People kept jumping up to propose toasts with turgid compliments (on our side), which all had to be translated. Winston's party manners were not at their best. The members of the English colony in Moscow, who were not asked to dinner, had been invited to a reception at the Embassy at eleven o'clock to meet the P.M. Poor things, marooned here, exiled in Moscow, they must be in sad need of a little excitement. At twelve forty-five we rose from the dinner-table and passed out into a great room, where those bidden to the reception awaited, with lively anticipation, the meeting with the legendary Churchill. The P.M. gave one uncomprehending glance at the assembled guests, sent for a glass of champagne and then, without further ado, went into a side-room to confer with Stalin. He had forgotten all about the reception. The guests did not like to leave and stayed until nearly three o'clock in the morning.

Before the dinner I contrived to put in an hour at the ballet; a light to lighten the Muscovites in their grim, grey city.

October 13, 1944

As Maisky,[1] at the last moment, failed to produce the aeroplane he promised, I decided to go to Leningrad by a plane that was due to leave at nine o'clock in the morning. However, it was after one o'clock before I took my seat—a hard bench—in a small craft, with a drunken soldier, a woman and her baby. I was cold, for the derelict waiting-room was dirty and draughty, and most of the glass was missing from the windows. It was half-past four when we landed near Leningrad; a young woman who met me suggested that we should drive to the hotel, but I was bent on seeing the city while the light lasted. My guide, who had evidently determined to improve the occasion by adding to her stock of English and her knowledge of English ways, bombarded me with questions.

'*Lord* Moran. . . . I do not understand. Then why *Mr.* Churchill?'

At last I decided on a small counter-offensive.

'What will you do when Stalin dies?' I enquired.

[1] Ivan Maisky, Soviet Ambassador in London, 1932–43.

She thought for a moment. 'Oh, I hope I shall die before dear Marshal Stalin.'

When I was ready to go to the Astoria, a palatial hotel, I found that they had reserved a suite of three sitting-rooms and a big bed-room, but the bath did not appear to have been used for months. The usual meal was brought, after the usual wait, but at five minutes to seven I proposed to my guide that we should abandon the rest of the banquet, as the ballet began at seven o'clock. She replied airily:

'Oh, they will not start till we get there. We need not hurry.'

I found the great audience waiting patiently in their seats. If their drab poverty was in sharp contrast with the lovely scene on the stage when the curtain went up, they seemed to follow the technique of the ballet with the same understanding, the same approval, as our crowds follow the fortunes of the Arsenal or Chelsea football teams.

October 14, 1944

Back in Moscow, I found a rather disquieting mail from London. While I have been away a special Comitia at the College has discussed the White Paper on the new Health Bill, and the motion which the College officers put forward was lost. That means that, in my absence, my Government at the College has been defeated. There can be no doubt that my frequent absences from England, at a time when the medical services are being transformed, are exciting more and more criticism. Many Fellows of the College feel that I am so much away that the College has not taken a proper part in counter-ing Willink's proposals.[1] I am always abroad, they say, when it is being discussed at the Ministry. There is a feeling, too, that I might be behind the White Paper and that I may indeed have inspired it. It is natural that this should be said, because I am always travelling with the P.M. We are bound to talk it over, people say, and it is inevitable, since the White Paper is anathema to most of the profession, that I am the target for adverse criticism. While many doctors are saying these things, a good many laymen are beginning to blame me because I allow the P.M. to go on these journeys. If I took a stronger line, they say, he would stay at home.

[1] The White Paper presented to the Commons in October, 1944, by Henry Willink, Coalition Health Minister. It was entitled 'A National Health Service' and envisaged a plan hardly less ambitious than that which Aneurin Bevan later introduced. Churchill supported the proposals with the words: 'Disease must be attacked in the same way that a fire brigade will give its assistance to the humble cottage as readily as it will to the most important mansion.'

197

It is rather distracting, steering a course between my two conflicting loyalties, but it is plain that I must not abandon Winston,
whatever happens at the College. After all, it is my job; the P.M.
has enough on his plate without my adding my little worries. I am
only sorry for Dorothy. She has to sit at home and watch the storm
gathering. She asks: 'Can anything be done?' And the answer is,
'Nothing.'

If the P.M. really came here to make one final attempt to break
down the deadlock between Stalin and the Poles the outlook is not
very promising. It seems that Mikolayczyk, who arrived here two
days ago, is agitated by the proposal to hand over half his country to
Russia. This came out in the P.M.'s conversation. Good relations
with Russia, he said testily, were more important than mapping
frontiers. He is apt to lose his temper when Mikolayczyk thinks
differently and cannot be persuaded that Stalin's intentions are
honourable. The Warsaw underground,[1] Mikolayczyk declared, were
deliberately incited to rise by the call to arms of Moscow Radio in
July, and were then left to be annihilated by the Germans while the
Russian Army stood by peacefully watching events. To Mikolayczyk the Russians' perfidy has been proven and he is impatient when
he hears references to 'our great Eastern ally.' The P.M. sees, of
course, that this kind of approach to Stalin leads nowhere. Squab-
bling between Stalin and Mikolayczyk will not help the Poles: it
will only make Stalin more obstinate. They must be patient and
leave it to him. The momentous meeting took place yesterday when
I was in Leningrad, but from what I hear no good came of it.

*

In that bald sentence the meeting is dismissed in my diary. It
was not till after the war, when I came across Mikolayczyk's own
account, that I grasped the full significance of this encounter as a
key to Winston's attitude to the Poles at that time. I give it in
Mikolayczyk's own words.[2]

[1] As the Russians neared Warsaw, the inhabitants rose up to help evict the
Germans from the city. The uprising began on August 1, 1944, and continued for
two months, but the Russian forces did not relieve the city. Some 200,000 inhabitants, mostly young boys and girls, were killed by the S.S. troops during the
fighting and on October 2 General Tadeuz Bor-Komorowski, the Polish commander, was forced to surrender. Thousands more were transported to Germany
or expelled from their homes, and in order to wreak more revenge, the Germans
began methodically to destroy the city. Warsaw was not liberated fully by the
Russians until January 17, 1945.

[2] Stanislav Mikolayczyk, *The Pattern of Soviet Domination* (Sampson Low, Mar-
ston, 1948), pp. 104–13.

Molotov invited Mikolayczyk to speak first. The Pole did nothing to placate the Russians. He ignored the Lublin Poles, whom he regarded as Stalin's stooges. The P.M. spoke next. He supported Stalin.

P.M.: 'The Lublin Government should have a bigger share in the post-war Polish Government—the Curzon Line must be your eastern frontier.'

Mikolayczyk: 'I cannot accept the Curzon Line. I have no authority to leave half my countrymen to their fate.'

Molotov (*abruptly interrupting*): 'But all this was settled at Teheran.'

Mikolayczyk looked from Churchill to Harriman. They were silent. Harriman gazed at his feet, but the P.M. looked Mikolayczyk in the face.

'I confirm this,' he said quietly.

Mikolayczyk was shocked.

The revelation of what had happened at Teheran, in the absence of the Poles, only seemed to make the Prime Minister angry, as if he wanted to persuade himself that he was the aggrieved person and not Mikolayczyk. He demanded that Mikolayczyk should agree there and then to the Russian demands. The Pole would not give way.

P.M.: 'You can at least agree that the Curzon Line is the temporary frontier.'

At this, Stalin rose in his place. 'I want no argument. We will not change our frontiers from time to time. That's all.'

Churchill held out his hands, looked up to the ceiling in despair and wheezed. They filed out silently.

When later the P.M. saw Mikolayczyk with Eden the harm already done was not undone. The P.M.'s argument was sound enough. It was the manner in which it was advanced that gave hurt. He could have said with some reason to the outraged Poles: you cannot expect to carry us with you in a policy which threatens the unity of the three Allies by its unfriendly attitude to Russia. What he did say was quite different. Anders had said to the P.M. that he hoped the Allies when they had finished with Germany would defeat and destroy the Russians.

The controversialist in Winston seized on Anders' admission as the central theme of his attack on Mikolayczyk. It was as if a boxer, dancing round the ring, had seen a small cut above his adversary's eye and had rained his blows to keep it open. You would have thought that Poland was on the brink of war with Russia.

'If,' the P.M. shouted, 'you think you can conquer Russia, well, you are crazy, you ought to be in a lunatic asylum. You would involve us in a war in which twenty-five million lives might be lost.

You would be liquidated. You hate the Russians. I know you hate them. We are very friendly with them, more friendly than we have ever been. I mean to keep things like that. I tell you, we'll become sick and tired if you continue arguing. We shall tell the world how unreasonable you are. We shall not part friends.'

This was not diplomacy. Nor did it intimidate Mikolayczyk. He was not going to be shouted down by anyone. He was furious and made no attempt to hide his feelings.

Winston told me the sequel with tears in his eyes. Mikolayczyk asked to be dropped into Poland, where he could rejoin the Underground Army. Winston in one moment forgot the obstinate peasant who had threatened our relations with Russia in his warm-hearted admiration for a soldier who is without fear.

Was Mikolayczyk a reliable witness? When Winston was recovering from his stroke in 1953 he was, for a short time, in the mood to listen to anything that I had to say, and I asked him if I might read to him Mikolayczyk's own account of his meeting with Stalin. When I had done, to my surprise he asked me to read it again. He seemed very sad. 'Does he exaggerate?' I asked. Winston hesitated: 'You see we were both very angry.'

October 14, 1944

It is plain that the P.M. has got the Poles on his conscience.

'I was pretty rough with Mikolayczyk,' he said this morning. 'He was obstinate and I lost my temper.'

Perhaps the P.M. was thinking of his own indignation when Chamberlain pressed Czecho-Slovakia to surrender a great part of her country in the interests of peace.

'It's a tragedy about these Poles,' the P.M. said tonight. 'All about one town surrounded in any case by non-Poles. Everything was signed, then Mikolayczyk said: "I cannot agree." I shook my fist at him and lost my temper. You see what will happen: the advancing Russians will be helped by the Poles. Then these villains will have them completely in their power. Whereas if the Poles are sensible I shall be able to help while they are bargaining with the Russians.'

*

This evening there was a Command performance at the Bolshoi Theatre, first ballet and then opera, both in small doses. The Russians, according to Clark Kerr, had a suspicion that this was not exactly the P.M.'s native diet. In fact, Winston only came to life when Cossack dancers appeared on the stage and the Red Army

Choir sang soldiers' songs. 'Are they going to sing the Volga Boat Song?' he asked. As we waited for the curtain to go up, Litvinov said rather excitedly: 'Almost anybody might come here in a few moments.' And then in a whisper: 'It's Stalin.' He had come in late by a side entrance and was with Winston in a box. The audience was looking in our direction, cheering. At the end of the performance I looked round, but Stalin had gone; he had slipped away as secretly as he came. I said to Winston that the applause was very vigorous and that I was surprised that Stalin excites such enthusiasm. He corrected me. 'There was passion in that outburst,' he said.

October 15, 1944

After breakfast I called on the P.M. and found that he had diarrhoea. He was, however, in good spirits, and very hopeful about the way things are going. This afternoon his temperature went up to 101. He is quite certain now that he is beginning another attack of pneumonia.

'I am in your clutches once more, my friend. What about getting Bedford? I wouldn't wait. The Cabinet will be getting fussed. Clemmie would like to come out, I am sure.'

He buried his head in his hands and moaned. Then Sawyers did something wrong and the P.M. flew at him. I fancy that his temperature is associated with the diarrhoea, but he won't accept this, because the diarrhoea stopped at noon, and now, seven hours later, the temperature is still up. Nothing is gained in such circumstances by arguing. If, on our journeys, I were to send for specialists and nurses every time the P.M. runs a temperature we might as well add them to our travelling establishment. However, I sent a message to Cairo asking Pulvertaft and Scadding and two nurses to stand by; it would take them twelve hours to get here. Time enough tomorrow to send a telegram to Clemmie.

October 16, 1944

The P.M.'s temperature is normal this morning. He has quite recovered his spirits, and we are on a level keel again.

Martin came in with a telegram. The P.M. smiled as he read it:

'Ha-ha, the F.O. making a bold gesture. They have told Tito that they are unable to understand the action of one of his officers. As if Tito cares a damn whether the F.O. understand! He has gone in with the Russians.'

I do wish that the P.M. would give himself a chance. I found him telephoning to Stalin. He wanted to see him this afternoon in spite of my protestations that the Kremlin was not a convalescent home.

The P.M. went off at five o'clock, saying that he would be back in half an hour. He returned in two and a half hours in good form.

'You see, my half-hour became two and a half hours.'

'I had anticipated that,' I put in.

He smiled mischievously. 'Well, take my temperature. I don't think it's up.'

As he got out of his clothes he showed me a brooch with the flags of the two countries, and 'Liberty' underneath, in Russian, which Stalin's daughter was sending to Sarah. I said it was 'very nice.' 'Unique,' he corrected, a little excitedly. He was excited by this fresh proof of Stalin's friendship.

'I got nothing out of it,' he went on, but in a surprisingly good mood. 'There were two points only, and Stalin wouldn't give way over either. I am bound to say I think he is right in one of them; the Poles want to accept the Curzon Line only as the "demarcation line" between the two countries; the Russians say this means it isn't final; they want the Curzon Line as the frontier. The other point can easily be settled. It's the relations between the London and the Lublin Poles. Mikolayczyk says that if he goes any further he will be repudiated by his own countrymen.'

Whenever the P.M. sees Stalin he seems to come back in a good mood. He wound up:

'I said to Stalin: "Mikolayczyk is a peasant and very obstinate." Stalin replied: "I am a peasant too." I said, "You can be as obstinate as any of them." '

As far as I can tell, the P.M.'s plan is prospering. Stalin seems to meet him halfway. It may be that our stock has gone up or simply that Stalin is getting his own way in everything; at any rate, it is beyond question that the Bear, as Winston calls him, is more friendly, since we arrived in Moscow, than he has ever been. From time to time, too, Stalin strengthens the good impression left by his friendly advances by statements of an entirely reassuring character. Only yesterday he denied with great earnestness that Russia wished to convert the world to Communism, as many people feared.

'We could not, if we wanted,' he told the P.M. 'We Russians are not as clever as you think; we're simple, rather stupid. No one in Europe can be persuaded that England is either simple or stupid.'

Do these reassuring words mean anything to the P.M.? Does he trust Stalin? The trouble is that when the P.M. gets an idea into his head he lets his imagination play round it and will not bother to fit it in with the facts. At any rate he still makes his plans in the faith that Stalin's word is his bond.

There are relapses, to be sure, when the P.M. discovers that he is getting nothing out of Stalin.

'Of course,' he said today, 'it's all very one-sided. They get what they want by guile or flattery or force. But they've done a lot to get it. Seven or eight million soldiers killed, perhaps more. If they hadn't, we might have pulled through, but we could not have had a foot in Europe.'

Besides, he wants nothing except Stalin's friendship. I said to him this morning that Russia would have things all her own way in Europe after the war. He answered as if he were only half interested:

'Oh, I don't think so. When this fellow goes you don't know what will happen. There may be a lot of trouble.'

It seems incredible, but for the moment the red light has gone out.

While the P.M. was making friends with Stalin, I went over the Kremlin. An air of mystery hangs over the vast fortress. You feel it at once when the soldiers come out of the tower, which reinforced the defence of the wall in the old days, and one of them scrutinizes your pass pretty carefully—mistakes in Russia are expensive. The great wall, now that it has shed its camouflage, is like a lovely old garden wall, only three times the height. It's a bad simile, for the great wall *is* the Kremlin. There it stands for all that is secretive and sinister in the Russian character. Try to think of Moscow without the Kremlin, and what is left? Of the interior, the only part that comes to life is the old palace, built about 1400, where Ivan the Terrible and his kind lived in semi-darkness. Three or four rooms with low ceilings and hardly any windows lead to the Czar's sitting-room. Beyond, a bedroom with a four-poster, and beyond this, a small chapel, where Ivan lost his temper and killed his son. All these rooms, all small, dark and barbaric, were the living-quarters of the Czars until Peter the Great, wishing for a casement opening on Europe, migrated to St. Petersburg. My guide smoked as he led me round, as if he would detach himself from all aristocratic folly, or perhaps just because he loved smoking.

As I drove from the Red Square I noticed that they were repairing Lenin's tomb. He had been removed for fear he might be damaged by enemy action.

October 17, 1944

The P.M.'s temperature is still normal. 'You see, Charles, I did myself no harm. You oughtn't to fuss.' I asked him what were his plans for today. He replied:

'I shall not go out this morning. I've nothing till ten o'clock tonight, when I see Stalin.'

Moran: 'Couldn't 10 p.m. be altered to 6 p.m.?'

P.M.: 'No. Stalin specially said it would be more convenient for him at ten o'clock.'

Moran: 'You do all the travelling. Surely he could make this slight alteration?'

P.M. (*a little impatiently*): 'Stalin isn't as safe in his capital as I am in mine. When he came to the ballet it was all very secretive. I think we shall soon be on the move; the Poles' game is up; neither side will give way.'

October 18, 1944

Went to the P.M.'s room at ten o'clock this morning.

'Well,' he began, 'we got back at four-thirty this morning. But it was worth it; all very friendly. We went from the Kremlin to his private apartments. Stalin ate heartily, pork mainly. I picked at things. He dines at 1 a.m. as a rule, goes to bed at four and rises between noon and one o'clock, a relic of the days when it was safer for him to lie low during the day. Stalin is more friendly these days. The invasion and the number of prisoners taken by us have sent us up in his eyes. He talks freely to me.

'He told me stories of his exile in Siberia; he was a political prisoner with nothing to do in a forlorn place, with eight roubles a day to live on. He was there for four years before the 1914 war. Stalin told me how he caught a sturgeon. "With a rod and line?" I asked. "No," said Stalin, "I floated logs down the river with a hundred hooks on them, and with this contrivance I caught a big sturgeon; his length, from here to the end of the table where those seats are." I asked him what emotions it caused him: joy, elation? "Oh, no, I was alarmed how in a small boat I could tow the big sturgeon in." Stalin put the sturgeon in a pool in which he had several smaller sturgeons. The sturgeon was half-dead, but it revived and ate some of the smaller fish. The colonel of the police said to Stalin: "We've had you three times in our power, and can never find anything against you, but we shall, and then you will get twelve years." Stalin spoke of all this without any bitterness. Then he was called up into the army.'

'Did he,' I asked the P.M., 'do much soldiering in the war?'

'Oh, no, he revoluted.' The P.M. continued: 'Stalin's sense of humour is his strongest characteristic. He talked about my private war with Russia in 1919,[1] all in a friendly way. I said: "I'm glad now

---

[1] As Secretary for War in 1919, Churchill was vehement in his denunciation of the Bolsheviks and made no secret of his belief that the Allies should support the White Russian armies. The Allied Supreme Council, while sympathizing with

that I did not kill you. I hope you are glad that you did not kill me?" Stalin agreed readily, quoting a Russian proverb: "A man's eyes should be torn out if he can only see the past." We all made a move at three in the morning, but Stalin would not let us go and kept us till four. All the time he got more animated and expansive.'

---

the White Russians, agreed to withdraw their forces from Russia in May, 1919. Churchill supplied and organized a volunteer force of 8,000 men to cover this withdrawal. Stalin was one of the leaders of the Red Army at the time.

Chapter twenty-three

Athenian interlude

At Teheran in December the Prime Minister had obstinately affirmed: 'We want nothing'—an attitude of mind not perhaps altogether appropriate to the transaction of business with Stalin. Whereas at Quebec, in the autumn of 1944, we find him more belligerent; he had been driven to the conclusion that the only way to save a country from the Russians was to occupy it. A month later, when Alex could not help, he was not so sure that such a policy made sense. He became certain that the only way to help the Poles was to make friends with Stalin. On his return from Moscow, the P.M. seemed to realize that he had got nothing out of Stalin and that Poland had been left in the grip of Russia. He lost no time in reverting to a more realistic policy.

Though there is nothing in my diary to account for this change of heart, I had come to connect these abrupt switches with Winston's physical state. I suppose I was at that time unduly preoccupied with his dwindling resources. I find this note in my diary under the date October 30, 1944:

'All this havering, these conflicting and contradictory policies, are, I am sure, due to Winston's exhaustion. He seems torn between two lines of action: he cannot decide whether to make one last attempt to enlist Roosevelt's sympathy for a firmer line with Stalin, in the hope that he has learnt from the course of events, or whether to make his peace with Stalin and save what he can from the wreck of Allied hopes. At one moment he will plead with the President for a common front against Communism and the next he will make a bid for Stalin's friendship. Sometimes the two policies alternate with bewildering rapidity.'

Havering indeed! It reads to me now like the story of a fighting retreat that began in January, 1944, with Anzio, and only ended with

his flight to Athens at the turn of the year—his stand in Greece was a
kind of Battle of the Marne. If he appeared to haver it was because
he was not strong enough to act. He was ready to act when he could.

The P.M. made his stand in the face of mounting criticism, both
in America and in Britain. He seemed to be alone in his grasp of the
danger to the liberty of the Greeks. But the bleak atmosphere
created by this spate of criticism did not in any way deflect the P.M.
from his purpose. He paid no heed to the clamour; his mind was
sealed. He was grimly resolved that his timing on this occasion
should come up to Stalin's standard. He would hold on to Greece—
Stalin could have the rest of the Balkans. All his plans were made,
and the P.M. felt a sense of relief that the time had come to act.

When the Germans marched out of Athens on October 2, only a
few days passed before our troops, under General Scobie,[1] took possession of part of the city. The P.M. was ready, but the Communists,
who were known to us as ELAS,[2] were ready too. It was not, however,
until December 3 that civil war broke out.

When this was made known to the P.M. in London, he felt impelled to send a telegram to General Scobie in order to strengthen
his hand and, in Winston's own words, 'to ginger him up a bit.'
But before anything could be done, things must be put in their proper
order, for, even in his most arbitrary moods, the P.M. was careful to
conform to the usual procedure—that is, if it did not interfere with his
set purpose. It was only right, he felt, that the steps he was about to
take should be submitted to the Foreign Secretary, who surely ought
to agree that the time had come for our troops to intervene and, if
necessary, open fire. Winston resolved to see Eden at once. So he
was summoned to No. 10, where the P.M. set forth with unusual
vehemence the case for action in Athens. The Foreign Secretary
listened to this harangue in silence; he hated Winston's habit of
taking over his job.

Winston himself has told us the sequel. About two o'clock in the
morning of December 5, noticing that Eden was very weary, he said
to him: 'If you like to go to bed, leave it to me.' When Eden had
left the room, the P.M. began to draft a telegram to General Scobie,
but it was not until a quarter to five that it was ready to be sent. I
quote here only those words which the P.M. in his book put in italics
as the pith of his message:

'Do not, however, hesitate to act as if you were in a conquered
city where a local rebellion is in progress . . . we have to hold and

[1] Lieut.-General Sir Ronald Scobie, General Officer Commanding Greece.
[2] National Popular Liberation Army (military arm of EAM).

dominate Athens. It would be a great thing for you to succeed in this without bloodshed if possible, but also with bloodshed if necessary.'[1]

Of this order Winston wrote in 1953:

'I must admit that it was somewhat strident in tone . . . I had in my mind Arthur Balfour's celebrated telegram in the eighties to the British Authorities in Ireland: "Don't hesitate to shoot" . . . it hung in my mind as a prompter from those far-off days.'[2]

Opinion in the United States was rudely shaken by Churchill's weakness for kings and by his seemingly blatant disregard for the will of the Greek people. The P.M. was much incensed by this criticism. Without waiting to cool down, he despatched a cable to President Roosevelt which, according to *The White House Papers*, may well have been the most violent outburst of rage in all their historic correspondence. From the same source we learn that shortly afterwards 'relations between the White House and Downing Street were more strained than they had ever been before.'

At this point the P.M.'s order to General Scobie to act as if he were in a conquered city, which was in cypher and had been marked 'Personal and Top Secret,' was allowed by the State Department in Washington to leak out to the Press. The President felt the mounting public anger, and on December 13 he cabled the P.M. that he was unable to support his action in Greece.

The P.M.'s instinct was to press on with military operations until he could see light, but Alex, who was in Athens, was for once obdurate; he insisted on the necessity for a political solution. In this he had the backing of Leeper, the British Ambassador in Athens, who had revived the idea of appointing Archbishop Damaskinos[3] as Regent. This was the President's solution, and it found a strong advocate in Harold Macmillan. The P.M. still hesitated; he was not happy about entrusting absolute power to the Archbishop. Besides, the King of Greece was against this step, and it would therefore entail in the P.M.'s words 'an act of constitutional violence' to overrule the King's veto. Something had to be done, and done at once. The day before Christmas the P.M. decided to fly to Athens, to see for himself what could be done.

[1] Winston Churchill, *Triumph and Tragedy*, p. 252.

[2] Arthur James Balfour (1848–1938), Chief Secretary for Ireland (1887). He was an implacable opponent of Home Rule and earned the nickname 'Bloody Balfour,' because of his determined measures.

[3] Primate of Greece, 1938. Active leader of resistance movement.

Harefield, December 24, 1944

I was sitting over the fire in the cottage after tea, pondering how I could make Christmas amusing for Dorothy, who has had a dusty war, when the telephone rang. It was one of the secretaries at Chequers; he said that the P.M. wanted to speak to me. I held on, then the same voice said, 'Is Lord Moran there?'

'Charles?' the friendly voice was a little faint. 'I'm off to G. . . .'

'When?' I asked.

The P.M. irritably: 'I can't hear.' With angry resignation. 'I can't hear a word you say.'

I shouted: 'When?'

'Oh, tonight,' he answered.

When he had rung off I asked Dorothy where she thought G. might be. She suggested Gibraltar, 'but we must know because of clothes.' 'They won't tell us anything on the telephone; there's nothing for it but to drive over to Chequers and find out something definite.'

This morning the restriction on headlights was removed, so we joyfully stripped the black paper from the lamps of the car. We had forgotten what it felt like to sweep along a road thrown up by a searchlight instead of groping our way anxiously along the dark lanes around Harefield.

G. is Greece.

December 25, 1944

Our aircraft landed in the failing light at an airfield near Athens; from this we went in an armoured car by a coast road to a jetty, where a launch was waiting to bring us to H.M.S. *Ajax*,[1] a small cruiser which had been in the River Plate engagement. Eden told me with a wry smile that it was along that very road that he had passed through great crowds, wild with elation, only two months ago.

We dined on board with General Scobie, Harold Macmillan, Alex and the captain of the cruiser. The P.M. complained of the slow progress of Scobie's troops. Alex pointed out the difficulty of house-to-house fighting, of knowing, in such conditions, who was the enemy. He was soothing and cautiously optimistic. But the P.M. was not to be comforted. We were, he said, faced with two very forbidding alternatives: either to take on most of Greece with the growing disapprobation of the world, or to abandon our friends to be massacred.

[1] One of the four cruisers which were successful in forcing the German pocket battleship *Graf Spee* to scuttle herself at the mouth of the River Plate in December, 1939.

There had been a conference on the plane, and when the P.M. retired to his cabin Macmillan said that he had never seen him listen so patiently or so attentively.

'The truth is,' he said, 'he has no solution himself.'

Macmillan affirmed that help was coming from the North, from Russia.

The P.M. joined us again. He blew up about the attitude of *The Times*; it was very badly informed. He grew vehement about some of his critics in the House of Commons, and promised that he would expose them on his return. I don't know whether it is that he is getting more and more restive under criticism or simply that he has taken a strong line over Greece and is not certain whether he can stick to it; anyway his language is pretty violent.

December 26, 1944

We lunched on board and waited to go ashore for a conference with the Greeks at their Foreign Office. A shell or light mortar bomb fell somewhere near; we crossed the deck to see where it had fallen, perhaps sixty yards astern. As we stepped into a launch another shell came over, hitting a landing craft by the water's edge. At the jetty two armoured cars were waiting. The P.M. began to climb into the first, and I clambered into the other, where I found the Archbishop sitting patiently on a rough form. We had this car, which was like a furniture van, to ourselves, save for a security officer in the uniform of the 60th, who sat opposite me, fingering his tommy-gun. I could not talk to the Archbishop without an interpreter, so I stood looking through the one tiny peep-hole at the coast road. The great lumbering car swayed and turned clumsily around the sharp bends; suddenly we came round a corner on the top of some children. They scattered with a scream, all but one, and I was shocked that we did not pull up to see if the child was hurt. At last we stopped with a jerk, the door was drawn back and an officer appeared; he seemed a little fussed. He said that he wanted to get the P.M. into the Embassy as soon as he could. A woman had been shot dead a few yards down the street, just before we arrived. But the P.M. stood gazing up at the windows of the house opposite, giving the V sign to the Greeks looking out.

The great rooms of the Embassy were unheated, and in the dining-room the wife of the Ambassador, in a fur coat, was preparing tea for the typists, secretaries and cypher staff, who had been brought into the Embassy for safety. The back of the house was less safe from snipers than the front, and a small garden there was said to be particularly exposed. Into it the P.M. now went with the Archbishop, to pose before the photographers, whereupon an officer spoke to two soldiers, who proceeded to cover the upper windows of the adjoining buildings with their tommy-guns. The P.M. returned to the dining-room and made a graceful little speech to the staff around the long table, thanking them for their cheerfulness and fortitude.

We made the short journey to the Ministry of Foreign Affairs in our armoured car. I could not see if there was anybody in the streets. At the Ministry we were led by an old man with a haggard face to a room with an immense table and chairs; hurricane lamps flickered on the table, casting shadows in the dim light. Two soldiers drew down the shutters. The Archbishop took the centre seat; on his right sat the P.M. and beyond him Eden. On his left were placed Alex, and then Harold Macmillan and General Scobie. Opposite the Archbishop, M. Papandreou, the Prime Minister of Greece, and members of his Government sat uneasily. There was no sign of ELAS and it was decided to start without them. The Archbishop rose. His black head-dress added to his great height, and his flowing beard gave him a patriarchal aspect. His words of greeting were translated sentence by sentence by a young Englishman, as if it were his own speech. Then the P.M. rose:

'Your beatitude:

'Today Greece may march with the United Nations to victory, which is not far distant. But if all our efforts fail, we shall have to bend to our hard task, to secure the city of Athens from anarchy. We do not shrink from that task, but we hope for a happier issue. . . .'

There was a knock on the door. The Prime Minister stopped speaking. A soldier half opened the door and spoke to someone on the other side. He closed the door again and whispered to an officer who had approached him. The officer went and spoke to the P.M., who announced that the representatives of ELAS had arrived. Three men filed in, led by M. Partsalides.[1] He had a grey waterproof and brown muffler over his British battledress. In the dim light I could not see how the other two were dressed, but they were muffled to the ears, like pilots coming into the mess from a winter flight. Without further greeting they took the chairs nearest to the door.

I glanced involuntarily at the members of the Greek Government. M. Papandreou did not look at the Communists; even when their leader spoke he kept his eyes fixed on the other side of the room. He appeared ill at ease, while the Greek on his right had the aspect of a sick man. A long tendon stood out in his scraggy neck, and I noticed that he kept swallowing. These members of the Greek Government were lean cattle, who looked as if they had not been outside their

[1] Leader of ELAS.

houses for months and were now blinking at the pale light of the hurricane lamps. The Communists had the look of men who had spent their lives in the open air and were always making decisions on the spur of the moment. They sat very still and upright in their chairs, all keyed up, as if they were waiting for something to happen. The suppressed vitality of ELAS contrasted strangely with the gaunt, grey, weary faces of the Greek Government. Someone dropped his spectacle case on the floor. It made a clatter, very distinct in the silence that had fallen on everything.

The British Prime Minister began his speech again:

'I trust,' he said, 'that the representatives of ELAS will not feel that we misunderstand their point of view and their difficulties. We came here because we were invited by all parties in Greece. We cannot leave until we have brought this matter to a good conclusion. We want nothing from Greece, not an inch of her territory. We must, of course, ask acceptance of General Scobie's terms. But we hope this conference may restore Greece again to her place among the Allies.'

I was sitting a·little behind and to the right of the Communists and had scarcely taken my eyes off their faces, which were alert and yet expressionless. Nothing that the P.M. said was reflected in their looks. M. Partsalides was listening intently, but his intelligent face revealed only his concentration. Siantos' sharp, foxy features, preceded by a full moustache, were equally without expression. He had put on spectacles and was now busy making notes. I moved my chair that I might be able to see his face. He was stroking his moustache, and, as the P.M. continued, he shaded his eyes with his hand.

When the Prime Minister sat down, the Archbishop asked if there were any questions; Mr. Churchill, he said, was willing to answer them. At this ELAS began whispering among themselves. At last M. Partsalides rose. He spoke at first as if he was not certain of himself or of his audience, but after a little his right hand began to pound the air with a slow piston movement, and his voice grew more confident.

'I take this opportunity of expressing sentiments in common with the Archbishop. I am,' he said, 'expressing the feelings of the Greek people,'—here M. Papandreou made little restless movements with his hands,—'on behalf of EAM,[1] for the efforts of the Prime Minister of our great ally, England. Despite the fact that we find ourselves face to face with exceptionally tragic circumstances, we are convinced that the clashes between the Greek people, and between them and the British troops, will not shake the traditional relations of the Greek people with the British people. The Greeks rose as one man

---

[1] EAM, National Liberation Front.

because they believed in the destruction of Fascism, in the right to live free upon the basis laid down in the Atlantic Charter.'

The other two representatives of ELAS might have come from a camp in the mountains, with red hands, and this was their sleek-faced lawyer, with white hair brushed smoothly back from his delicate features.

'We thank Mr. Churchill,' he ended, 'for taking the initiative, but inasmuch as it is a conference of our political parties, we feel that the party of EAM should also have been called, EAM, which commands the living forces of the nation, which was the first to rise in support of the great struggle which the British people waged alone.'

Eden rose to point out that the conference could invite anybody they wished to attend the meeting.

'Winston said: "We would now like to go. We have begun the work; make sure you finish it." '

Everyone rose. The P.M. passed down the side of the long table, shaking hands with the members of the Greek Government, until he came to the Communists, when he paused. He had vowed that he would not shake hands with these villains. What was he going to do?

'Who,' he asked, 'will introduce these gentlemen to me?'

He then shook hands with each of them in turn. And now for the first time the expressionless features of ELAS came to life, and a look of pleasure crossed their faces. They wrung Mr. Churchill's hand with slight, stiff bows.

As we returned in the armoured car to the ship the P.M. said that the Communists did not seem as bad as they had been painted; they were a different lot of people from the Lublin Poles. They had wrung his hand on parting. This had impressed him. He felt that if the three Communists could be got to dine with us all difficulties might vanish.

After dinner the P.M. again argued that the fighting was very slow. Couldn't, say, twenty tanks go one way and twenty another, with say twenty in reserve? And then the area between the two lots of tanks could be cleaned up. Alex repeated that street fighting was a slow business. Men of ELAS in civilian clothes infiltrated behind the lines. He pleaded for patience. Of course, Germans or Russians would soon have liquidated the affair, blowing up houses and exterminating those who resisted, but we could not do that.

The P.M. said that he would not, of course, presume to give a military opinion, but he wanted them to know the political aspect of the matter. If the fighting dragged on, difficulties might arise with America and even with Stalin; the affair ought to be finished off as quickly as possible. Finally, he said that Parliament would be meeting on January 12, and he asked Alex if he thought the military situation could be cleared up by then. Alex thought it could. The P.M. then said:

'I don't want you to alter your plans to suit me or Parliament.'

December 27, 1944

As I was waiting for breakfast Eden passed through the cabin on his way to see the P.M., who had apparently sent him a message that he was going ashore forthwith to see the Archbishop.

Eden, a little wearily: 'I do wish he'd let me do my own job.'

Presently the P.M. came out of his cabin and, seeing Alex and Scobie talking to me, sat down.

'I'll stay two days here,' he began, 'but you must find something to amuse me. I'd like to go to some forward observation point and see the problem for myself. It helps me to see things. . . . I'm not doing this for amusement.'

He went out on to the deck.

'I hope,' said Scobie to me, 'he won't go ashore; it isn't safe. I simply can't compete if the P.M. will keep going ashore in the next two days.'

Last night the Admiral harped on the same theme.

'I was horrified,' he exclaimed, 'to hear that the P.M. is going ashore. These Communists have their duties and he has his—and his is to keep alive. It's as simple as that.'

The P.M. came into the cabin and sat down; the launch had not come back from the shore.

'I shan't see the Parthenon this time. The last time I was here before the war I spent eight days there with my paintbox; sandwiches were sent up to me. I didn't really paint. I just loved it. The faint pinks and blues. Have you been to the Acropolis, Charles? You haven't? Oh, we must remedy that.'

We were sitting at luncheon with the Ambassador and his wife when there was a knock at the door. It opened and a paratroop officer saluted and stood to attention.

'I have come,' he said, 'for Lord Moran.'

It was all like an incident in one of Sean O'Casey's plays, where some wretched man is taken for a ride and bumped off. Alex turned to me:

'Where are you going, Charles?'

'The Acropolis, I suppose.'

'Can I come with you?'

No armoured car was waiting, but a local touring car. We were apparently to see the Acropolis with an armed escort of two para-troop officers. When we got to the Parthenon Alex went to speak to a machine-gun section stationed in a position to command the entrance. One of the paratroop officers came up to me.

'It's a lovely spot,' he said. 'We have got all Athens in our arc of fire.'

As we left, Alex said: 'I propose we send the car away and walk. I want a little exercise. What about it, Charles?'

Halfway to the Embassy, Alex stopped. 'Do you see that little temple there?' pointing to a small building about a quarter of a mile from the road. 'I have never been there; let's go and have a look at it.'

We started off, but one of the paratroop men came up. 'I don't think, sir, you ought to go there. There was a man killed there this morning; there are some snipers overlooking it.'

'Oh, nonsense,' Alex broke in. 'If we go that way'—pointing to a short detour—'it's quite all right.'

Our guard made one more attempt a little further on to dissuade Alex, but to no purpose. We loitered in the little temple for some time.

*

To a man of my calling, the bald record in my diary of events in the weeks immediately preceding the P.M.'s arrival in Athens reads like a bulletin issued at the crisis of a protracted illness. It was in this parlous state of mind and body that the P.M. was confronting the growing hostility of public opinion in the United States, which found expression in a press campaign of some virulence. This was echoed in the British Press: even papers like *The Times* and the *Manchester Guardian* were, in their demure way, full of lamentations over the P.M.'s 'reactionary' policy. Intervention in Greece was his own idea, and he had to defend it practically single-handed.

It is one of Winston's engaging qualities that he will never say 'I told you so,' yet two years later the temptation must have been compelling, for his policy was taken over, lock, stock and barrel, by the United States.

'A Communist-dominated Government in Greece would be con-sidered dangerous to United States security.'

That was part of the evidence given on March 21, 1947, by Mr. Dean Acheson, the Acting Secretary of State, before the Foreign Affairs Committee of the House of Representatives.

Once again Winston had spoken before his time: he had given a lead to the English-speaking peoples, and before they had fallen into step he had saved Greece from the fate of Czecho-Slovakia, leaving it a free nation.

Chapter twenty-four

Yalta diary

London, January 29, 1945

Greece is, after all, only a fragment of the P.M.'s problem. What is to be the fate of the rest of Europe? What is to happen to Germany? Will Stalin help to knock out Japan? These are the issues to be settled at Yalta.

The P.M. has decided on the spur of the moment to fly to Malta tonight. There is bad weather coming in from the Atlantic, and snow is expected at Northolt. This might make taking off difficult, so we are to be in the air by nine o'clock. The idea is to fly before the gale.

January 30, 1945

I turned in soon after we were in the air to get some sleep, as we were to land at Malta between four and five in the morning; an hour later Sawyers pulled my curtain back and said that the P.M. had a temperature—a good beginning to a winter journey of three thousand miles. The P.M. blames my sulphaguanadine tablets, which he has been taking during the day. As they are not absorbed from the gut, they could not be responsible, but the P.M. has views on everything, and his views on medicine are not wanting in assurance.

He was restless, and I soon gave up any attempt to sleep. He asked me if I would like to send for Whitby, the pathologist, and what about Clemmie?—the Moscow performance over again. He has developed a bad habit of running a temperature on these journeys.

It is not the flesh only that is weaker. Martin tells me that his work has deteriorated a lot in the last few months; and that he has become very wordy, irritating his colleagues in the Cabinet by his verbosity. One subject will get in his mind to the exclusion of all others—Greece, for example.

Winston stayed in bed in the plane till noon, when he was taken to H.M.S. *Orion*. He rested until the evening, when Harriman came to dinner. Only this morning he was in the doldrums when, turning his face to the wall, he had called for Clemmie. Surely this bout of fever should put sense into his head. But Winston is a gambler, and gamblers do not count the coins in their pockets. He will not give a thought to nursing his waning powers. And now, when it was nearly midnight, he demanded cards and began to play bezique with Harriman. Damn the fellow, will he never give himself a chance?

H.M.S. Orion, *Malta, February 1, 1945*

When Sarah began talking about palmistry today I explained that there was a perfectly simple anatomical explanation of all the lines in the palm of the hand, which had been invested for commercial purposes with such portentous significance.

'You think there is nothing in it?' There was an air of disappointment as she traced the line of life and the heart line in my hand. I thought it wise to change the conversation to hands in general, telling her of a dinner-party given by Macready, the grandson of the actor, who is Major-General on the Q. side,[1] and his Polish wife, at their flat in Washington. I was tired and only ticking over when the woman on my right said without warning: 'Why are your hands so much younger than your face?' Winston looked up from his work; he had been listening. 'Let me see them,' he demanded, and went on: 'You must have watched complete strangers walk into your consulting-room one after the other, for how long? Forty years? Now, Charles, did you really look at their hands? Did you learn anything from them?' I had landed myself and had to say something. 'I think it was after I read what Gorky wrote about Tolstoy's hands that I got into the way of looking at people's hands.'

'What did he say?' Sarah broke in.

'He has wonderful hands—not beautiful, but knotted with swollen veins and yet full of the singular expression and power of creativeness. Probably Leonardo da Vinci had hands like that. With such hands one could do anything. Sometimes, when talking, he would move his fingers, and gradually close them into a fist, and then suddenly opening them, utter a good full-weight word.'

I wanted to tell Winston about Dudley Pound's hands, which were like a navvy's, very muscular and insensitive, but he had taken up his work. Winston has small, white hands—misleading hands; they give one the impression they have not been used.

---

[1] The Army administrative side.

February 2, 1945

This morning the *Quincey*, with the President on board, passed slowly by us. The President, in a cloth cap, sat scanning our ship for Winston, who was on the quarter-deck raising his hat in salutation.

After tea the P.M. appeared. He said that the President had been very friendly.

'He must have noticed the candle by my bed when we were at the White House, because there was a small lighted candle on the luncheon table by my place to light my cigar. The President's very friendly,' he repeated, half to himself.

Winston would normally never notice anything like that.

February 3, 1945

All night planes have been taking off from the large airfield to carry our party of seven hundred across the Aegean and the Black Sea to the Crimea, fourteen hundred miles away. There, after a flight of seven hours, we made a bumpy landing on Saki airfield, from which the snow had been swept, leaving an icy runway only just long enough for our craft to land on. Molotov, Litvinov,[1] Vyshinsky[2] and Pavlov[3]—the usual people—met us.

The P.M. walked over to the President's aircraft, the 'Sacred Cow', and stood while he was helped out by Mike Reilly, his bodyguard, and deposited in a jeep, which then proceeded to move slowly to another part of the airfield, where a guard of honour and a band were posted. The officer commanding the guard stood frozen to attention. He held his sword straight in front of him like a great icicle. The P.M. walked by the side of the President, as in her old age an Indian attendant accompanied Queen Victoria's phaeton. They were preceded by a crowd of camera-men, walking backwards as they took snapshots. The President looked old and thin and drawn; he had a cape or shawl over his shoulders and appeared shrunken; he sat looking straight ahead with his mouth open, as if he were not taking things in. Everyone was shocked by his appearance and gabbled about it afterwards. While this was happening, one of our party decided to explore the three big tents on the aerodrome. He was well rewarded for his curiosity. The Russians had done things well: caviare, smoked salmon and every kind of drink. But he was the only man in the tent.

[1] Maxim Litvinov, Soviet Vice-Minister for Foreign Affairs.
[2] Andrei Vyshinsky, Soviet Deputy Foreign Minister.
[3] Marshal Stalin's interpreter.

When the band had worked off the three national anthems we were packed into cars; the P.M. called me to his car. I could see that we were crossing a snow-covered moor before we began to climb into the mountains. All the way I caught glimpses of sturdy girls, dressed like Russian soldiers, and carrying tommy-guns, who stood rigidly to attention as each car passed. I must have dropped off to sleep, when we pulled up with a jerk at a house on the outskirts of a village, where luncheon was set out on great tables. It is always the same. Caviare, smoked salmon, sucking-pig and the rest, with their sweet champagne. I looked on this collation doubtfully, for we had already lunched on sandwiches, but the P.M. likes good food and he soon got into form, making some rather daring remarks.

'I don't think much of the Lublin Government,' he confessed, 'but I suppose they are the best you can get.'

The short winter day was closing in before he rose from the table. For a long time we went uphill and downhill, flanked as long as we could see by mountains. The light had gone when we stopped. As I got out of the car, I noticed how mild and balmy the air was after Saki. We followed the P.M. into the great hall of a palatial house. I went to his room after dinner to see how he had weathered the journey. I found him talking to Anthony and Sarah. He made me sit down, though it was nearly midnight and I was weary. He was in great form, protesting that he could easily make the same car journey now, and—raising his voice—make a speech at the end of it.

The P.M. began talking about the Poles—we were in for a late night. A message had come from Roosevelt suggesting a start at four o'clock tomorrow afternoon.

P.M.: 'If the President is only going to be here for five days, we mustn't waste time like this. We must begin with the political part of our programme, the Poles in particular. After all, I can't tell the Russians how to advance more quickly in the East. Stalin must realize that the people in England who are keenest on good relations with Russia are most worried over Poland. Our future good relations with our ally are at stake. We can't agree that Poland shall be a mere puppet state of Russia, where the people who don't agree with Stalin are bumped off. The Americans are profoundly ignorant of the Polish problem. At Malta I mentioned to them the independence of Poland and was met with the retort: "But surely that isn't at stake." '

When the P.M. begins to talk of the Poles, I know what is coming. I could prompt him if he faltered in his piece. I slipped off to bed.

February 4, 1945

Breakfasted with the C.I.G.S. I said jokingly he must hurry up and finish off the Germans, or I should have to make a separate peace. He replied quite solemnly:

'You cannot be more weary of the war than I am. It's becoming a damned nightmare.'

To get out of uniform, to turn his back on London streets and to return to a country life—this is the sum of his ambitions.

When I left the C.I.G.S., I went to find out where everybody was. At the end of the nineteenth century this part of the coast, which is blessed with the mildest climate in Russia, became a fashionable watering place. After the Revolution the palatial residences of the Czar and his Grand Dukes were converted into sanatoria or rest homes for Russian workers: the 'star' workers are given free railway tickets to Yalta, and lodge at the Government's expense, but they have to bring their own beds. When the Germans occupied the Crimea they looted everything and destroyed the buildings. But this immense castle where we are staying, which was built at some fabulous cost for a Prince Vorontsov, Ambassador to the Court of St. James's in 1837, was left undamaged because Hitler gave it to Mannstein [1] to be his summer home when peace came.

It is a curious mixture of Gothic and Moorish art. Passing through a great Moorish archway, I descended a wide flight of steps, flanked by six marble lions, to the garden, which falls in terraces to the Black Sea. There are two fine cypresses in the courtyard, and rare subtropical plants are scattered through the garden. The house is sheltered by mountains, which are clothed with vineyards on their lower slopes, and higher up there are dark pine trees. When I returned to the house I found that the reception rooms are what might be expected from the gentleman who was responsible for the lions, but the plumbing and sanitary arrangements are elementary.

Down a dozen stairs, there is a passage, off which perhaps a score of small bedrooms open, as in an hotel. These must once have been the servants' bedrooms; they are now full of Air Marshals, Generals and Admirals. This morning I found them hunting for a tin to wash in. If anyone had any success in the search he promptly secreted it in his own room so that he could get a wash without lining up for the two communal basins, which have no plug and where only the cold tap works. There are two baths in the castle, so I shall take a tub in the middle of the afternoon, when there is a lull in the demand.

[1] Field-Marshal Erich von Mannstein, Hitler's adviser on military affairs.

Nor is plumbing the only thing missing in our stately home. The Russians have done their best, but their task has not been easy; for, if the Germans spared the building, they removed everything in it. All the furniture and pictures and food and wine, even the waiters, have been brought for our entertainment from Moscow, which is nine hundred miles to the north of Yalta. These waiters are really the only people I recognize when I revisit Russia—apart from Stalin himself, Molotov, Litvinov and the immense fellow who is head of the Security Police—and all my Moscow friends seem to be here in their white coats; their faces are glum, and there is a furtive air about them, but they, at least, look the part and sometimes seem to be the only links with the old Russia of the Czars.

The Russians thought nothing of converting the eighty miles of snowbound mountain road which connects Saki with Yalta into a good surface for a car; they lined the road all the way with troops, but in the end they were defeated by the common bug. In this palace, with its gilt furniture, its lashings of caviare, its grand air of luxury, there is nothing left out but cleanliness. The P.M. sent for me this morning because he had been bitten on the feet. A more thorough assault had been made on Sawyers, while Dixon,[1] Eden's right-hand man, had been eaten up by bedbugs in the night. While thinking out a line of action, I was asked to go to one of the two sanatoria where the rest of our party are lodged, to see one of the Foreign Office people who was running a high temperature. I found seven officers in a room, with the most elementary bedding arrangements, spread out on the floor, and bugs in all the bedding. Give the Englishman real discomfort, and he becomes cheerful, but it was plain something must be done. I telephoned the Americans, and found they were in trouble too. They lent me a couple of their sanitary squads, and we began going round all the beds with an instrument which squirted D.D.T. But I haven't unpacked my suitcase, and I have no intention of doing so.

Stalin called after luncheon. He stayed only a short time, visiting the map-room before he went. I had a talk with Bridges[2] this afternoon. He does not exactly radiate geniality. His steady, appraising gaze behind thick spectacles seems to register disapproval; and when I used to run into him at No. 10 I thought he took unnecessary pains to frown on a stranger. Now I find this is only a mask. His uncompromising integrity, his dislike of intrigue of any kind and his rugged honesty are known to everyone. That is why he is Secretary of the Cabinet, and also head of the Civil Service. But what I've seen

---

[1] Mr. Pierson Dixon, Principal Private Secretary to the Foreign Secretary.
[2] Sir Edward Bridges, Secretary to the Cabinet.

since we left England is quite new to me: his eagerness and his un-spoilt pleasure in sightseeing—the Isles of Greece brought him out of his bunk in the 'Skymaster' at five o'clock in the morning. I have seen a good deal of him while we have been here, and I like what I have seen. He has a good headpiece and thinks for himself. He is very loyal to the P.M., but, evidently, thinks the present régime unusual in more than one respect. He feels that you can influence Winston up to a point, but that it is useless trying to do so beyond that. 'People,' he said, 'criticize me, I know, for not doing more, but I'm sure it's no good.' Of course, he is right. The P.M. will listen so far; after that he becomes antagonistic. Archie Sinclair [1] does not seem to realize this; he will go through his whole piece independent of the effect on the P.M. Portal tells me he feels sometimes he must nudge him but that he has not got as far as this yet. Bridges thinks very highly of the C.I.G.S. He feels that Brooke has shown great judgment in his dealings with the P.M., giving his own opinion firmly and independently, but without making it too assertive. In response to my doubts, Bridges admitted that he, too, is dubious about the next fifteen years.

Livadia Palace, where the President is housed, is about a mile from Yalta; it was the summer home of Nicholas II. The Czar had a number of bedrooms on the first floor, for it was his custom to sleep in a different room every night—sometimes he would even change his room during the night. Stalin said, with a grin, that the only place where one could be certain of finding the Czar was in the bathroom first thing every morning. Probably Stalin felt that the Imperial security technique was rather an amateur business.

Here, in the Grand Ballroom, at five o'clock today, the first formal meeting of the Conference was held, and developed into a three-hour discussion about the military position. Stalin expressed pleasure when he heard our main drive was planned to begin in a month's time. But what we do or do not do is no longer vital to the Russians.

Dined next to Portal. He led me on to talk of medical matters, cancer research, cerebral localization and the possibility of lengthening the span of life. Then I started him on the selection of men. He began:

'Someone maliciously said that the P.M. will fight to the last ditch but not in it. He does not like making decisions.'

Alex broke in: 'And he will not listen to evidence.' This remark, coming from Alex, surprised me. It was not in character. Alex went on: 'Winston is not really interested in those around him.'

I told Portal my impression of the President when we were in

[1] Sir Archibald Sinclair, Secretary of State for Air.

222

Washington after Pearl Harbour: that he doesn't like thinking things out, but waits for situations to develop and then adapts himself to them. His face brightened.

'That is the exact truth,' he said. 'I never thought of putting it like that.'

There was a good deal of talk after dinner about the conference at the President's house. Everyone seemed to agree that the President had gone to bits physically; they kept asking me what might be the cause. I first noticed his loss of weight at Quebec. It was not only his physical deterioration that had caught their attention. He intervened very little in the discussions, sitting with his mouth open.[1] If he has sometimes been short of facts about the subject under discussion his shrewdness has covered this up. Now, they say, the shrewdness has gone, and there is nothing left. I doubt, from what I have seen, whether he is fit for his job here.

Roosevelt blurted out to Stalin: 'We always call you Uncle Joe.' Stalin did not appear a bit amused; he said he ought to have been told this before or not told now. Byrnes attempted to pacify him by saying that Uncle Joe was no worse than Uncle Sam. But Stalin was not mollified. He demanded how much longer he must remain at the dinner, and Winston, on the other side of the table, said: 'Half an hour.' When the P.M. told us about this someone asked if Stalin has a sense of humour. Winston said at once that he had, but that he was not always as amused by our jokes as he was meant to be. You could not be certain how he would take things.

February 5, 1945

Winston was in great form at the President's dinner last night. He told me about it while he disposed of a substantial breakfast. 'In the White House, I'm taken for a Victorian Tory.' I broke in: 'It isn't fair. You never were a Tory.' He looked at me as if he would like to know what was behind my remark. When I was silent, he went on: 'Stalin and the President can do what they like, whereas, in a few months' time, I may find myself in the street.' Then he began trumpeting. He counted up on his fingers the number of elections he had fought. He likes them. They were fun. All the same, I fancy that it will irk him when he has to go to the country for orders.

[1] Was Roosevelt properly briefed for Yalta? J. F. Byrnes, Director of Office War Mobilization, writes: 'So far as I could see, the President had made little preparation for the Yalta Conference. . . . Not until the day before we landed at Malta did I learn that we had on board a very complete file of studies and recommendations prepared by the State Department. . . . I am sure the failure to study them while en route was due to the President's illness.' (From *Speaking Frankly*, p. 23.)

It is the first time that I have heard him mention the election, though he must know that it is bound to come when the Germans surrender.

All morning the P.M. has been losing things.

'Sawyers, Sawyers, where are my glasses?'

'There, sir,' said Sawyers, leaning over his shoulder as he sat, and tapping the P.M.'s pocket.

At last, when the P.M. was getting ready for his afternoon sleep, he cried out irritably:

'Sawyers, where is my hot-water bottle?'

'You are sitting on it, sir,' replied the faithful Sawyers. 'Not a very good idea,' he added.

'It's not an idea, it's a coincidence,' said the P.M., enjoying his own choice of words, and without a trace of resentment.

There was a sharp discussion today on whether France should be given a representative on the Allied Control Commission for Germany. For Stalin, France is a country without an army; he measures nations in his practical way, by the number of divisions they put into the field during the war and how they fought. By that test Poland and Yugoslavia have done more than France for the Allied cause. Stalin made no bones about the matter; he could not see the Prime Minister's point. Perhaps the P.M. did not say plainly what was in his mind. He was thinking of the future, when the Americans would have gone home and Britain would be left alone to contain the might of Russia. The President sides with Stalin; he likes France, but de Gaulle gets on his nerves. However, Hopkins is backing the P.M.; he has the good sense to see that a stable Europe is impossible without a strong and virile France. France, in Eden's words, is a geographical necessity.

Hopkins is, of course, a valuable ally, particularly now, when the President's opinions flutter in the wind. He knows the President's moods like a wife watching the domestic climate. He will sit patiently for hours, blinking like a cat, waiting for the right moment to put his point; and if it never comes, he is content to leave it to another time. The battle is not lost yet, but I wish Harry was in better fettle.

When the P.M. told me Stalin's words it was clear that he was puzzled.

'Do you suppose Stalin reads books? He talks of France as a country without a past. Does he not know her history?'

The P.M. did not expect an answer. He loves France like a woman. When Stalin said that he did not know what France had done for civilization he felt bewildered. In Winston's eyes France is civilization.

February 6, 1945

'The next war,' the P.M. said to me while breakfasting in bed, 'will be an ideological one.'

'Between whom?' I asked.

The P.M. shrugged his shoulders and made a gesture with both hands, but did not answer.

'I do not think that Russia will do anything while Stalin is alive. I don't believe he is unfriendly to us.'

That is as far as he would go.

The discussion on the United Nations Organization [1] today threw some light on the difference between the mental processes of Stalin and Roosevelt. In American eyes the first purpose of this Conference is to lay the foundation of an international peace organization. It appears that Byrnes was quite put out when he discovered that, two months after Washington had sent Stalin a proposal about voting in the Security Council, he had not even read it. As Hopkins puts it: 'That guy can't be much interested in this peace organization.'

Stalin can see no point in vague sentiments and misty aspirations for the freedom of certain small nations. He is only concerned with the borders of Poland, with reparations and with what he can pick up in the Far East. These are tangible things that he can get his teeth into. He said yesterday: 'We are interested in decisions and not in discussions.' Roosevelt would like to prescribe for the world, Stalin is content to make clear what the Soviet Union will swallow.

February 7, 1945

Drove with Jumbo Wilson, Alex and the Chiefs of Staff to Sebastopol. We got out of the cars after leaving Balaclava, when the C.I.G.S. pulled out a map, which he studied attentively for some time; then he gave it back to his A.D.C. and pointed to the valley below us.

'That's where the Light Brigade charged.' But I noticed that no one was paying any attention to his discourse; they were all looking intently at a skull, a thigh bone and some ribs scattered on the ground. One of them touched the skull with his foot.

'Can you,' he whispered, 'tell if it is a Russian or a German skull?'

[1] The Declaration of the United Nations was signed by twenty-six states on January 1, 1942, and set forth the aims of the Allied Powers. A United Nations' conference met at San Francisco on April 25, 1945, when the Charter was drafted, and signed on June 26, 1945.

To a doctor's eye, the President appears a very sick man. He has all the symptoms of hardening of the arteries of the brain in an advanced stage, so that I give him only a few months to live. But men shut their eyes when they do not want to see, and the Americans here cannot bring themselves to believe that he is finished. His daughter thinks he is not really ill, and his doctor backs her up.

The day before we left England, I received a letter from Dr. Roger Lee of Boston.[1] He wrote:

'Roosevelt had heart failure eight months ago. There are, of course, degrees of congestive failure, but Roosevelt had enlargement of his liver and was puffy. A post-mortem would have shown congestion of his organs. He was irascible and became very irritable if he had to concentrate his mind for long. If anything was brought up that wanted thinking out he would change the subject. He was, too, sleeping badly.'

Winston is puzzled and distressed. The President no longer seems to the P.M. to take an intelligent interest in the war; often he does not seem even to read the papers the P.M. gives him. Sometimes it appears as if he has no thought-out recipe for anything beyond his troubles with Congress. Nevertheless, though we have moved a long way since Winston, speaking of Roosevelt, said to me in the garden at Marrakesh, 'I love that man,' he is still very reticent in criticism. It seems to be dragged out of him against his will. And with half a chance he will tell over dinner how many divisions the Americans had in a particular show against our handful, and how their casualties in that engagement dwarfed ours, and things of that kind.

February 8, 1945

Drove with Alex to see Chekhov's house. The dining-room was a grim little apartment with a piano, a big photograph of the author, a print of Leighton, and a life-size painting by Chekhov's brother of a young woman sitting distractedly trailing a very shapeless hand. His sitting-room was less forbidding: the window looked down on a valley and the room looked as if it had been lived in; there was a small bronze figure of Tolstoy on the table, with paper-cutters, half a dozen pencils, some books, two small black elephants in ebony and Chekhov's small wooden stethoscope.

I went to see Hopkins, who is in a poor way. Physically he is only half in this world. He looked ghastly—his skin was a yellow-white membrane stretched tight over the bones—but he began to talk

---

[1] Dr. Lee had been President of the American College of Physicians and also of the American Medical Association.

with all his old verve. He was full of the Russian claim for two additional votes in the General Assembly, one for the Ukraine and one for Byelorussia. The President seems to have no mind of his own. He came to Yalta apparently determined to oppose any country having more than one vote, but when the P.M. came out strongly in favour of Stalin's proposal Roosevelt said he, too, would support Stalin at San Francisco.

February 9, 1945

Stalin's dinner-party did not break up till two o'clock this morning. The P.M. was sentimental and emotional. I asked Clark Kerr bluntly if he really thought much came out of the Conferences. Couldn't it all be done without the Big Three? The Russians were realists; they would toe the mark as long as it suited their purpose. The Ambassador had no need for reflection. He said at once:

'No, these meetings have helped, I think, quite a lot. Stalin has got an impression of the P.M. as a broth of a boy, full of guts and determination—what Stalin calls his "desperation." And that helps.'

Stalin's speech last night in proposing a toast to the P.M. had made a great impression on the Ambassador. He went on quoting it while I scribbled down his words:

'Without the Prime Minister's guts—the interpreter didn't say guts but that's what he meant—England could not have stood up to Hitler. She was alone; the rest of Europe was grovelling before Hitler. Do you know what Stalin said? He said that he could think of no other instance in history where the future of the world depended on the courage of one man.'

Clark Kerr is an earthy creature, with his feet planted firmly on the ground, and he has had opportunities in Moscow of sizing up Stalin. When he says Stalin respects the P.M.'s guts it rings true. Whereas it is plain that Stalin can make nothing of the working of the President's mind. But it is typical of Stalin that he does not let his feelings count if it does not suit his book. During the Conference he has been quite rough with the P.M. All the same, when I look through my diary I am left in no doubt about Winston's feelings of friendship and respect for Stalin. He is thinking already of Stalin's place in history.

At other times Winston's eloquence is less usefully employed. When the British Empire is mentioned he indulges in histrionics, which do no good. There was rather a sad scene this afternoon. It all began with a report by Stettinius on the appointment of trustees for colonies. I have not been able to check Hopkins's account and he, like the President, seems to lose his balance when colonies are discussed; they might be back in the War of Independence, fighting their English oppressors at Yorktown. It seems that Stettinius had hardly got under way when the P.M. shouted his disagreement. According to Harry, Winston spoke so rapidly that he could hardly follow what he said. He would not have the British Empire run by a lot of bunglers. He would refuse point-blank to countenance such folly. He spoke with heat. Stettinius, it appears, was a good deal rattled by the violence of this outburst, and hastened to explain that what he was saying did not apply to the British Empire. The P.M. appeared a little mollified. He would not argue if they were only thinking of enemy territory. After the P.M. sat down he kept mumbling: 'Never, never, never.'

There was a general feeling of relief when Mr. Churchill at last agreed to the American formula. This sort of thing does harm, of course. When Winston talks big about the British Empire the President gets very restive; he has a bee in his bonnet about our colonies. Besides, it is all so unnecessary, for the P.M. could, without all this diatribe, have found out from Stettinius that the principle did not apply to the British Empire. If only he would listen occasionally!

And yet, I wonder if I am fair to Winston. When the Prime Minister announced, 'I have not become the King's First Minister in order to preside over the liquidation of the British Empire,' it was not just bravado. He was affirming a faith for which he was prepared to give his life. The President knows this side of the P.M., but he cannot leave the Empire alone. It seems to upset him, though he never turns a hair when a great chunk of Europe falls into the clutches of the Soviet Union. I don't think he has ever grasped that Russia is a Police State in which freedom is more at a discount than in Hitler's Germany. He appears to be happy to seek the advice of his confidants, Stalin and Generalissimo Chiang Kai-shek, about how best he can secure the freedom of small states.

February 10, 1945

The President has changed his mind again. But nobody appears in the least surprised. He has now agreed with the P.M. that France should be a member of the Control Commission. Stalin made it plain at once that if this was the President's wish he would accept it. One cannot help noticing Stalin's deference to the President's opinions throughout the Conference. This frame of mind does not come naturally to Stalin. It must cost him a great effort. What is behind it all? As far as Stalin has a steady policy and as far as his actions are not governed by mere opportunism, I believe his one purpose is to drive a wedge between the two democracies. If this can be done, the rest must seem simple.

Whenever the future of Germany is discussed the Russians bring up the question of reparations. That is what interests them. It is, at any rate, something they can get hold of, and Maisky, their expert on reparations, has a firm grip on the facts. The little man, with his slanting eyes and pointed beard, asked for his pound of flesh as if he were addressing the students of the London School of Economics. I watched, once, a farmer being sold up. I remember the anguish of his wife, as, with tears rolling down her cheeks, she saw a hard-faced woman bearing away to her car as much as she could carry between her hands and her chin. The Russians have, of course, no reason to feel compassion for the Germans; they hate them with a cold ferocity for the savage scorching of their land, and this combination of greed and venom is frightening.

I tried to explain to Hopkins that the P.M.'s mind is full of what happened at the end of the First War. He thinks the Russian demands are madness. Who, he demanded angrily, is going to feed a starving Germany?

Then Stalin spoke. Harry brought it all to life. How Stalin rose and gripped the back of his chair with such force that his brown hands went white at the knuckles. How he spat out his words as if they burnt his mouth. Great stretches of his country had been laid waste, he said, and the peasants put to the sword. Reparations should be paid to the countries that had suffered most. While he was speaking no one moved.

When Harry had given me the story I made the mistake of arguing with him. He flared up and said bluntly that he had advised the President to support the Russian proposal, whatever course the British took. The Russians had given way a good deal at the Conference. It was our turn to give something. We could not expect them always to climb down. The President took Harry's advice. Once again, as over France, he changed his mind. The Reparations Commission, he said, should take, as a basis for discussion, the suggestion of the Soviet Government.

When Winston told me about the discussion he spoke as if he felt very sad about the greed and folly of the Russians. And I noticed a grey look about his gills which I haven't seen before. I never think of him as an old man who is past the span of life given to us in the Psalms.

February 11, 1945

Found the P.M. moody when I went to him after breakfast. He gave me a sour look.

'The President is behaving very badly,' he said. 'He won't take any interest in what we are trying to do.'

I interjected that I thought he had lost his grip on things. The P.M. replied that he thought he had. I suggested that the President had been a passenger at the Conference. I think the P.M. felt this was going too far. He spoke gloomily of reparations, and said he was worried about Poland. 'With the Red Army where it is, isn't it too late,' I ventured, 'to try to bargain? Wasn't the damage done at Teheran?' The P.M. did not seem to hear. He picked up a document rather wearily, and I left the room. Hopkins tells me that the President does not want to fall out with Stalin. He is quite sure that Russia will work with him after the war to build a better world. He does not see that he has invented a Russia which does not exist.

In the passage I ran into Clark Kerr.

He told me that the P.M. is obstinate about the President staying one more day. Winston had got on his sulky look and meant business.

P.M.: 'But Franklin, you cannot go. We have within reach a very great prize.'

President: 'Winston, I have made commitments and I must depart tomorrow as planned.'

Then Stalin said he thought they might have difficulty in completing the business without more time. Roosevelt answered that he had three kings waiting for him in the Near East. Stalin, however, stuck to his point, and the President, after a little, gave way.

'Why,' Clark Kerr exclaimed, 'they haven't yet got down to an agreed communiqué.'

Sarah came up. Yesterday, she said, had been a bad day. The P.M. had an appointment with the President, but he left the villa half an hour late and went and saw Stalin.

'Probably he forgot all about the President,' she said with a smile.

Anyhow, he was an hour late when he stalked into the President's room and found him sitting patiently. Left to himself, the President would not harbour resentment, but the little people around him work him up. Sarah dined with Roosevelt's daughter, who said the President had appointments which he must keep.

'As if,' said Sarah, 'the Conference isn't so much more important than anything else.'

This afternoon, at half-past four, as I was going for a walk, the P.M. swept into the house.

'We leave at five o'clock. Where's Tommy? Sawyers!' His voice rose, 'Sawyers! Where is everyone?'

Apparently there is bad weather approaching, and we must get off before it. It was half-past five when we left, and two hours later the car drew up on the jetty at Sebastopol. We were to dine and sleep in the *Franconia*. The P.M., who has been in a vile mood throughout the Conference, irritable and bad-tempered, is now in tearing spirits.

'I'm so relieved to get this bloody thing off.'

The bloody thing was the agreed communiqué.

'Anyway,' he growled, 'that's done with and out of the way.' He is trying to forget that he has achieved little. He is playful, smiling, mischievous.

'Charles,' he said, 'is silent, kindly and grave, but make no mistake, when the occasion comes, he lashes out like a horse.'

He put his hand affectionately on my knee.

'He demolished the President of the other College[1] in *The Times* without any mercy.'

Twice he sang (very flat) snatches of old songs, 'The Soldiers of the Queen' and some ditty I had not heard before. This during dinner. Then he gurgled:

'Grand to get back to English fare after the sucking-pig and the cold fatty approaches to all their meals.'

The P.M. moves among words as a friend. His precision in their use is helpful at these Conferences, where sloppy thinking may lead to recrimination later. When he had given his blessing to the revision of the Montreux Convention[2] about the Dardanelles, and Stalin was in a relaxed mood, he gravely enquired of the President what he meant by 'Freedom from want.'

'I suppose the word "want" means privation and not desire.'

And when there was agreement about the joint communiqué, and everyone was smiling happily, he persuaded the President to cut out 'joint':

'The word "joint,"' he said, 'means to me the Sunday family roast of mutton.'

The Americans pitch their song on a higher note. They are leaving Yalta with a sense of achievement, they feel they are on top of the

---

[1] Royal College of Surgeons.

[2] Signed July 20, 1936. It established a new international régime of the Turkish Straits, replacing that of the Lausanne conferences, 1922-3. At Montreux the International Commission of the Straits was abolished and its functions were handed over to the Turkish Government. The latter was also authorized to remilitarize the zone.

world and that while other conferences had been concerned with proposals of policy, Yalta has been the scene of important decisions that must influence the future of the world. Harry Hopkins, lying on his sick-bed, is firmly convinced that a new Utopia has dawned. He says the Russians have shown that they will listen to reason, and the President is certain that he 'can live at peace with them.'

I do not know what decisions they have in mind. It was plain at Moscow, last October, that Stalin means to make Poland a Cossack outpost of Russia, and I am sure he has not altered his intention here. He has, too, been given the additional votes he demanded, and he seems to have secured the President's support for a policy of greed in reparations which must bring plenty of trouble in the days to come. It is the story of Teheran over again. Stalin fights for and gets what he wants. Then, at the banquet, which brings the proceedings to a close, he thaws and is polite.

Only a solid understanding between the democracies could have kept Stalin's appetite under control. The P.M. has seen that for some time, but the President's eyes are closed. What is more remarkable—for Roosevelt is a sick man—the Americans round him do not seem to realize how the President has split the democracies and handcuffed the P.M. in his fight to stem Communism. They cannot see that he is playing Stalin's game. As at Teheran, he has been at some pains to see Stalin alone. Hopkins boasted this morning that the President had gone out of his way to inform Stalin that there had been disagreements between Winston and himself about the zones of occupation of Germany and the general policy to be followed where France was concerned. Roosevelt went further: he repeated to Stalin what he had said at Teheran: that Hong Kong should be given back by Great Britain to the Chinese. One can almost see the grim old gentleman from the Kremlin rubbing his hands with glee, in Hitler fashion, as we play his game. He purrs when anything like this happens.

The Americans are saying that the relations between Stalin, Roosevelt and Churchill have never been so close. Alas, it is far from the truth. Winston's emotional nature, to be sure, has been deeply touched by the faithful manner in which Stalin has discharged his undertaking not to interfere in Greece. He has stuck to his bargain to the letter. The P.M. put it like this tonight:

'Stalin has only referred to Greece once, when he asked me what was happening there. He said: "I don't want to criticize anything, nor to interfere. I'm quite content to leave it to you." '

When Winston had said this he seemed to go over the past in his thoughts, then he went on:

232

'Stalin isn't going to butt in in Greece. In return, he expects a free hand in Bulgaria and Rumania. The fifty–fifty plan[1] arranged at Moscow is working out in his favour. He'll let his people be beaten up in Greece for the sake of his larger plans. I find he does what he says he will do. It isn't easy to get him to say he will do it, but once he says something, he sticks to it.'

The P.M. spoke once more of the disaster it would be if anything happened to Stalin. His humour, understanding and moderation, on many occasions, had made a deep impression on him.

'When Stalin had a strong case—so strong that I was supporting him—he would say: "We attach importance to this, it means a good deal to us, but if the President feels it will conflict with his plans, I'll withdraw it." '

But, if Stalin and the P.M. are working together more smoothly than ever before, it is quite another story where the President and the P.M. are concerned. The storm of criticism in America for his actions in Greece had partly prepared the P.M. for what has happened here. The President's decrepitude has filled him with grief and dismay. All the same I do not think he realizes how ill he is. The P.M. has for some time been thinking of the outcome of the war; and he can see that the map of Europe will be redrawn in red ink. Far more than at Teheran he is conscious of his own impotence.

February 12, 1945

A parcel came to my cabin addressed to me in both English and Russian. When I opened it I found a big tin of caviare, and ten small boxes of Russian cigarettes—a present from Stalin.

In this ship of 20,000 tons, which had been acting as a troopship until at a moment's notice it was painted and furnished and reconditioned so that our delegates to the Conference might use it if the accommodation at Yalta proved to be inadequate, we are comfortable to the point of luxury and wonderfully over-fed. The chef of the *Queen Mary*, borrowed for the occasion, produces perfect food, and the white rolls take one back to times of peace.

For two hours this morning Alex and I wandered through the rubble of Sebastopol. This afternoon when we asked the Russian soldier sitting in front with the driver to take the P.M. to Balaclava he shook his head; he had never heard of the village. He did not know what we meant by the Crimean War. After a short drive we got out of the cars and walked through the streets of Balaclava. The P.M. pulled up short: 'I have been studying their faces, Charles.

[1] Stalin agreed with Churchill on the spheres of influence in the Balkan countries. See note on p. 452.

There is pride in their looks. They have a right,' he added, 'to feel proud.'

Sarah was giving chocolates to some children, when a Russian soldier waved the children away, and, turning to Sarah, said that their children did not need feeding.

The P.M. asked his guide if the Russians were short of glass, and he answered that they were, and used plywood in its place. Stalin had told Roosevelt that all they lacked in Russia was tin, rubber and pineapples. The P.M. explained that we, too, were short of glass: two million houses in England had been hit, ten per cent. were made uninhabitable.

On our return from Balaclava I said, without thinking, that a hill on our left was like the Berkshire downs. Bridges said he could not pass that remark: the contours of hills of stone and hills of chalk were quite different. But later, when someone said the Russians were not demonstrative, and I had interjected that if they were they would not fight as well as they do, he grunted: 'There speaks the expert.'

February 13, 1945

No one has any idea where we are going when we leave tomorrow. The plans have been changed half a dozen times, till even the mild Martin thinks our vacillations and inability to make up our minds must make a bad impression on the Americans, who are making the flying arrangements. First, the P.M. was to fly to Athens and go from there to Alexandria. Anthony did not like this plan; he wanted to go to Athens by himself. Last night, it was decided that the P.M. would fly to Alexandria, while Anthony would go to Athens. This morning, Athens is on again. Anthony is piqued and avoids the P.M.

Before dinner I found Pug waiting outside the P.M.'s cabin. Winston had promised to address the ship's company, and they had already been drawn up waiting for him for more than half an hour.

'It's very naughty of the P.M.,' Pug said in a low tone. 'It's this unbridled power. The heating throughout the ship has all been cut off because his room seemed too warm for a moment.'

I had dinner in the *Franconia* with the P.M., Eden, Clark Kerr and Pug Ismay. The P.M., as usual, did most of the talking. He spoke at great length of the Greek situation, arguing vehemently for firmness in dealing with ELAS. When he went to Athens at Christmas the situation at home was very uncertain, and the truce was made largely because of that feeling. It was a mistake. We ought to teach the Communists a lesson. They were getting quite cheeky again since the truce. He wouldn't shake hands with them again after the exposure of the atrocities they had committed. Leeper had been very weak. The P.M. wanted to visit Athens to ginger up the Greek Government and the Archbishop so that they might take a firmer line. Usually he is magnanimous to a fault, but the opposition to his policy and the way public opinion has been stirred have entered into his soul. Someone suggested he had had a great moral victory, but he was not satisfied with this. He would plainly like to beat up the Opposition at home, and he is prepared for more shooting in Greece.

No one had the temerity to change the subject. It was only when the P.M. had exhausted the topic of his crusade against Communism in Greece that he reverted to the natural conversation of old age, with its dislike of change. He bemoaned the passing of ritual. He had not really forgiven the King and his family for allowing the eight cream ceremonial horses to disappear. They could not be replaced now. The breed was extinct, or at any rate, since they came from Holland, and Holland was in a turmoil, their successors could not be bought. Black horses would draw the coach of state in future; they were well enough, but—well, they were not the same thing.

The P.M. had had a battle (including an acrimonious debate in the House of Commons) to get the Guards back into scarlet after the last war. Northcliffe had talked of the waste of money; he said that was why the income tax was so high. The P.M. had arranged with the King to put the sentries at Buckingham Palace into scarlet when this war came to an end. He wanted the bands of other regiments to resume their formal dress.

Then the inevitable Max came up. Leaning across the table to Eden, the P.M. said:

'Don't underrate Max. He is one of the most remarkable men, with all his faults, I've met in my long journey through this world. He made Bonar Law [1] Premier. Walter Long [2] was a mediocre man, but the Tories didn't want a Liberal Unionist, like Austen, [3] being elected Leader of the Party. The strength of both factions was about the same, there was nothing in it. Austen always played the game'— Winston smiled—'and always lost it. Austen said, if it helped towards the unity of the party, he would stand down, and Walter Long had to do the same.'

It all sounded to his audience, who, apart from Anthony, were politically unconscious, as if a voice out of the past was talking about

---

[1] Andrew Bonar Law, Prime Minister, 1922.
[2] Walter Long, Tory politician in running for leadership.
[3] Austen Chamberlain, Tory politician in running for leadership.

Peel and Stafford Northcote and the worthies of a bygone age. The talk, however, still stuck to politics.

Winston: 'I have not lost one night's rest in the war, but,' turning to Eden, 'when you resigned in 1937——'

Eden: 'It was early in 1938.'

Winston: 'Yes, in 1938, I didn't sleep from the time I put the light out till dawn. I was too excited. It was a grand thing to do, but I never felt it was done in the right way. More could have been made of it.'

The P.M. was kept awake when Anthony resigned because he could not help wondering if any advice he had given to Anthony had influenced his fateful decision. He is, of course, a little *naïf* when he preens himself on not losing a night's sleep in the war; he forgets that he takes precautions each night to prevent such a mishap, in the shape of a red tablet.

The difficulty in remembering the names of members of the House came up.

Eden: 'I think it's bad to say: the Member who has just spoken. One ought to say: the Member for Salford.'

P.M.: 'One ought to spend an hour a day in the smoke-room.'

Eden: 'But you only meet there the members whose names you already know.'

P.M.: 'Your P.P.S.[1] can bring other members along.'

Eden: 'I suppose so, but I don't like it.'

P.M.: 'Harold Macmillan has done very well. I like him very much. I had thought of him for the War Office.'

Eden: 'He wants the F.O.'

P.M. (*dryly*): 'There isn't a vacancy at the Foreign Office.'

The P.M. wandered on and the conversation became a monologue. There would be a general election at the end of the war. The P.M. said he would use the Greek business against those who had attacked him. His eyes became more prominent, his voice rose: 'I'll say: You went about maligning British troops in Greece, and what'— the voice became louder still—'were *you* doing at that time?'

The 'you' was almost spat out.

Then we went back to the Boer War—the P.M. always goes back to the Boer War when he is in a good humour. That was before war degenerated. It was great fun galloping about. Alex agreed. Modern war, he said, was not fun; he was the only officer in his battalion to come out of the Somme. To lose, say, two out of twenty, was a sporting risk, but after the Somme there was no mess and no mess servants. That wasn't really fun.

[1] Parliamentary Private Secretary.

The P.M. spoke of Monty. It was a great blow to him to have an Army taken away from him just before the great advance in Normandy.[1] The P.M. had made him—he corrected himself: recommended that he be made—a Field-Marshal as a solace. But when Monty was given back the Army, after the Germans had broken through in the Ardennes, he made such a cock-a-doodle about it all that the Americans said that their troops would never again be put under an English general. The P.M. made a fine, flamboyant gesture as he quoted Monty's words: 'I flung in the British Army.' The facts were, the P.M. added with a grin, that we had five hundred casualties and the Americans sixty thousand.

The P.M. contemplated his plate for some time. Then he told us about Esmond Harmsworth's two brothers, who were killed in the last war. The elder, who had blue eyes and fair hair, was a good fellow. Harold (Lord Rothermere) was eaten up with love of this boy, and one night, when the P.M. called at the Ritz, where Rothermere lived, he said the boy was on leave, and took the P.M. up to his room. They entered on tiptoe. It was very late, and when Harold opened the door he could see him sleeping like a child. Rothermere asked Sir John French[2] if his leave could be extended, and it was. But the boy got restive and wrote to his battalion in France to ask for him. He went. The P.M. thought he was gassed and died from the effects. He was a good fellow, the P.M. repeated, half to himself.

For three hours last night Anthony kept on saying he would not go to Athens if the P.M. did. The P.M. didn't trust him to finish off the business. It weakened his position. The trouble is that he doesn't like playing second fiddle to anyone.

As I was about to turn the light out in my cabin in the *Franconia*, Alexander Cadogan put his head in. He had finished his packing.

'I never bargained,' he said in his quiet, dry way, 'to take Tetrazzini and Melba round the world together in one party.'

February 14, 1945

We left the *Franconia* at nine o'clock this morning and, after bumping for three and a half hours on a bad road, arrived at Saki

---

[1] General Eisenhower, the Allied Supreme Commander in Europe, assumed the role of Ground Force Commander on September 1, 1944, in order to conduct personally his broad-front strategic policy in the military offensive against Germany. General Montgomery had held this role since the D-day landings and now returned to command his own Army Group. From then on he commanded British 21 Army Group and temporarily ceded all direction of American forces.

[2] Sir John French, Commander of the British Expeditionary Force in France, 1914–15.

237

airfield, which was covered with a thin layer of snow. A bitter wind blew across the open space, and I grew anxious as we stood shivering for twenty minutes while the band went on playing and the guard of honour marched past. There were some new ceremonial trumpeters, who greatly pleased the P.M. with their precision. He said their movements in bringing the trumpets to their mouths were heraldically correct. They might have stepped out of the Moscow ballet.

We crossed the Black Sea, flying over Turkey and past Lemnos, Samothrace, Mount Athos, names with long echoes. It was pleasant coming from the bleak, snowy Saki into the blue skies and sunshine over the Isles of Greece, and there was a feeling of security with an escort of six fighters.

On landing, we went in cars straight to the Royal Palace, through streets lined with cheering Greeks. In the vast square the crowd was packed so tightly that they could just throw up their hats without much chance of recovering them. The size of the crowd and its noisy enthusiasm impressed the P.M., who is apt to assign more significance to these mass demonstrations than should be given to them. At the Embassy he came eagerly up to me:

'Were you there, Charles? I have never seen a greater or more demonstrative crowd. If we'd been wrong that wouldn't have happened.'

I remember when we went in cars to Leghorn, how impressed the P.M. was by the plaudits of the Italians we passed by the roadside. At the end of the day he took quite a different view of the Italian people. Now it was the turn of the Greeks. Ought they, after all, to have more food sent to them? Perhaps we could spare the ships. I was glad when we got him safely into the Embassy; some of the crowd had the look of brigands.

The 'Mosquito' has brought the mail to Athens, and it was waiting for us at the Embassy. I found a small parcel addressed to me. It was my book, *The Anatomy of Courage*, bound and ready to be launched on its precarious voyage. The binding, print and paper are better than I had expected. How many years has it been on the stocks? I have wanted to do this job as well as I can—more, I think, than I have ever wished to bring off anything else in life, and now, when it is done, and I ought to be on tenterhooks how it will be received, it is hardly ever in my mind. The thing is done and it can't be undone. What fun it has been in the writing! What a constant source of comfort and interest when things were going badly in the competitive world in which I live. It has been my child, and now it has thrown off all parental control and must face the world on its merits, if it has any.

238

YALTA

Seated, Mr. Churchill, President Roosevelt, and Marshal Stalin. *Behind*, Field-Marshal Sir Harold Alexander, Field-Marshal Sir Henry Maitland Wilson, Field-Marshal Sir Alan Brooke, Admiral of the Fleet Sir Alan Cunningham, General Sir Hastings Ismay, Fleet Admiral E. J. King, Air Chief Marshal Sir Charles Portal, Admiral Leahy, General Marshall and Russian Delegates

GENERAL DE GAULLE

This evening, in failing light, I went to the Acropolis, and when I got back I found them still sitting at the dinner-table. The P.M. was still speaking of Greece. He told us what he had said in the House about *The Times*, which had attacked his policy.

'Never have I heard louder cheering, from all parts of the House, at any rate since the last war. Barrington Ward was in the gallery. Members looked up at him. The proprietor of *The Times* was also in the House.'

The P.M. said that Barrington Ward had done well in the last war; he had been given two decorations. It was a little like the judge saying the little he could for the prisoner in the dock before passing sentence.

'*The Times*,' the P.M. went on, 'had no policy between the two wars; it drifted.'

They spoke of E. H. Carr[1] and his influence. The P.M. said that during the debate the Speaker had been very weak, and his shuffling when one Member called another a liar was a sorry business.

Winston went on: 'His Beatitude said to me that he hoped the ancient claims of Greece to Constantinople might be remembered.' I retorted: 'Dismiss those dreams from your mind.'

Randolph broke in to ask what was the effect on the Archbishop of these words.

The P.M., with a smile: 'He dismissed them.'

Once more he spoke gloomily of England's financial position after the war, when half our food would have to be paid for by exports. The P.M. had sat down to dinner at a quarter to nine. It was now a quarter to one. For nearly four hours a figure out of history had talked to us without reserve, and yet those who heard him appeared half asleep.

February 15, 1945

Flew from Athens to Alexandria to take leave of the President before he departs for the United States. And so by air to Cairo. The dreary story of de Gaulle's gaucherie came to its melancholy climax today. He has sent a curt message to Roosevelt that he will not come to Algiers to meet him. It appears that the communiqué issued after Yalta contained no reference to him.

February 16, 1945

The P.M. has spent the day in a series of conferences, first with the Emperor of Ethiopia, then with the King of Egypt and after that with the President of the Syrian Republic.

[1] E. H. Carr, Assistant Editor of *The Times*.

February 17, 1945

This morning, shortly before noon, we set out across the desert for L'Auberge du Lac, fifty miles from Cairo, where the P.M. will act as host to the King of Saudi Arabia. Two jeeps, each with four military policemen in their red caps, followed by three policemen on motor bicycles, with white tin hats, like basins, escorted a string of cars, as they bumped in single file through the desert. Trees and a green field marked the oasis where the hotel had been built on the shores of the lake. The setting provided by the hotel was an inadequate background for the ten Sheiks with their brilliant robes and curved swords. The King, Ibn Saud, himself appeared, wearing ceremonial robes, gold and brick red; he has a fine face with brown, benevolent eyes, a high, hooked nose and expressive lips. The party included the King's sons and brothers; his Ministers; the King's physician; Magid Ibn Kalayella, Astrologer, Fortune-teller; Abdul Rachman Djuez, the chaplain who leads the Palace prayers; the Commander and Adjutant of the King's Guards; Mohamed Abdul Djither, Chief of Communications and Radio Officer; Mahsoel Effendi, Radio-supervisor of the Nejd; Siraq Dahran, official Food-taster and Caterer; Abdullah Al Hadrani, Royal Purse-bearer; with the Chief and Second Servers of Ceremonial Coffee. There were also ten guards, with sabres and daggers, who had been chosen from the principal tribes, three valets, and nine miscellaneous slaves, cooks, porters and scullions. During luncheon the Food-taster stood behind the King, holding a glass of water, a grim, dark-faced figure. On his left, the interpeter stood, leaning forward with animation to interpret what the P.M. said to the King and what the King said to the P.M. Behind the interpreter stood two armed guards, who looked the part. Their faces were unpleasant and contrasted with the open, intelligent countenances of many of the Sheiks. Before luncheon began, the P.M. retired for a conference with the King. It may well be that the exchanges were of some interest, for Ibn Saud is made after the pattern when kings were kings. He has led armies in the field with unfailing success and is the master of the Arab world; he was not in the least overawed now by his English visitor, whose Zionist sympathies were no doubt known to him. I do not suppose that either the King or the British Prime Minister had much success in persuading each other. But the gestures were not affected by this.

After luncheon presents were handed to our party, who had been graded into three classes: the first was confined to Mr. Churchill and Mr. Eden. The P.M.'s sword was inlaid with jewels and his dagger was also embellished in this fashion. There were two ropes

240

of pearls—no one present felt capable of valuing them—marvellous robes for Mrs. Churchill, one purple and gold, each more splendid than the last. Thrown casually into the box containing these was a small box containing a diamond, valued later at eight hundred and fifty pounds. I fell into the second class and received a parcel in a red cloth like a cushion, which proved to be an Arab's ceremonial robe with a dagger. The third class received wrist-watches. The choice of a present for the King had been left to Tommy, who is a little parsimonious in these matters. He produced some scent, concentrated essence of amber, musk, mimosa and jasmine. The P.M., with great presence of mind, sensing the munificence of the King's gifts, told him that, if he would accept it, he was sending him a motor car. The P.M. talked about returning the more valuable of the gifts, but was told this would cause offence. He is very punctilious in such matters, and they will all be reported to the appropriate quarters. The warning that no one may smoke or drink in the King's presence had induced in the P.M. a mood not particularly receptive to this visit, but he was favourably impressed by the King, and the story has a happy ending.

Book two

The withered garland

April 1945–January 1965

O wither'd is the garland of the war,
The soldier's pole is fallen: young boys and girls
Are level now with men: the odds is gone.
And there is nothing left remarkable
Beneath the visiting moon.

ANTONY AND CLEOPATRA

Part four

Fall from Power

Chapter twenty-five

The Prime Minister
loses his touch in politics

After Yalta there is a break in my diary until April, 1945, the month in which President Roosevelt died, when, with an election in sight, I began to take down again what Winston said to me. The entries for the next two months are a brief record of the lonely processes of his mind. The war had exaggerated the isolation in which he had dwelt apart during his political life.

'Winston,' Clemmie said to me, 'has always seen things in blinkers.'

She held up her open hands at the level of her eyes, so that they were a foot apart, to illustrate the cutting off of the field of vision.

'His eyes are focused on the point he is determined to attain. He sees nothing outside that beam. You probably don't realize, Charles, that he knows nothing of the life of ordinary people. He's never been in a bus, and only once on the Underground.' She smiled. 'That was during the General Strike, when I deposited him at South Kensington. He went round and round, not knowing where to get out, and had to be rescued eventually. Winston is selfish; he doesn't mean to be, he's just built that way. He's an egoist, I suppose, like Napoleon. You see, he has always had the ability and force to live his life exactly as he wanted.'

Clemmie went on: 'Winston is non-party; he makes up his mind on questions as they strike him. He said to me yesterday: "If I were ten years younger I might be the first President of the United States of Europe."'

If Winston did not at any time find it easy to follow what other people were thinking, when war came he appeared to give up the attempt altogether. As early as the autumn of 1944, Gil Winant, the American Ambassador in London, came to me because he was worried about Winston, who had become so engrossed in the war that he had lost touch with feeling in the country. Winant told me that there was a good deal of disquiet in the Labour Party, which would have been more vocal if Ernest Bevin had not exerted a moderating influence. Even as it was, some of the big trade unions had passed resolutions critical of the Prime Minister's handling of the troubles in Greece. That Winston might lose the election had never crossed my mind. After all, it could not be easy for an American to say how labour would vote. I had forgotten how close Winant was to the leaders of the Labour Party. He pressed the point. He asked me very earnestly whether anything could be done. I had to explain to him that the P.M. did not turn to his doctor for political guidance.

In the spring domestic politics could no longer be put on one side; the war was on its last legs, and an election was in the minds at any rate of the Labour members of the Government. Neither Max nor Brendan, his advisers, were wise counsellors, and the P.M.'s political judgment—it had never, perhaps, been his strongest suit—was always threatening to get him into trouble.

The P.M. did not even follow what his colleagues were thinking. One day, late in April, he spoke to me about Ernest Bevin,[1] who was 'rather putting his weight about.' Bevin had attacked the Tories in a speech at Leeds, and the P.M. could not understand why he had broken the Party truce. I confess that I was worried by this development, and I wondered if Bevin's health was making him difficult. He was already a very sick man, suffering from alarming attacks of heart-block, in which he would lose consciousness. But full of guts, he was determined to do his job and would not give in.

One evening at a sherry party at the Russian Embassy I was asked if I could stay until Bevin left the house. I was told that he had had a heart attack just before the party. When most of the guests had left the Embassy I found Bevin in a small room drinking with Molotov. Bevin was tossing back vodka, while Molotov sipped a red wine—an unequal contest. I sensed that things were not going well. I think that was why Molotov beckoned me over, for I hardly knew him. He called on me to propose a toast. When I stood with a blank face he appealed in his wooden way to Winant. Winant stood gazing vacantly over our heads for some time, but nothing happened. Bevin was rather the worse for wear, and when at last I got him away he told me that he was lunching with Reggie Purbrick[2] in the country next Sunday.

When Bevin entered the dining-room of Purbrick's house he stopped at the door to take in the lovely Georgian silver laid out on

---

[1] Ernest Bevin, Minister of Labour and National Service, 1940–5, Foreign Secretary, 1945–51.

[2] Reginald Purbrick, M.P., Australian industrialist.

an exquisite lace centrepiece. A great grin spread over his untidy features as he rubbed his hands together.

'I always like,' he said, 'to return to the atmosphere of the proletariat.'

During lunch Bevin drank a great deal and became very talkative. Beaming on the company, he rattled on, and soon began to talk about what he wanted for 'his people.' After the war seventeen million would get three weeks' holiday every year with pay. He had a plan with an architect to build a thousand flats at Hastings, where working people could go for their holidays and get a bath and a bed. He was going to have circular glass shelters on the Front so that they could sit by the sea, even in winter. Someone blurted out: 'What's wrong with the working classes?' Bevin gave a great guffaw. 'Well, they aren't here,' he snorted.

When we rose from the table I asked him about his speech at Leeds. Bevin answered very seriously:

'We have a political Rasputin (Max) who very thoroughly and scientifically has been putting it about that I was going to be another Ramsay MacDonald.[1] I was asked about this, even by a large trade union. I didn't want to do it. I hesitated for a long time, but when I had made the speech my stock went right up.'

Bevin held up his hand to illustrate the point.

Bevin had played a man's part in the war and supported Winston loyally, but that wasn't going to do him any good when the war was over and the Tories were once more the enemy. He knew that his position in the Party was at stake.

The P.M. did not follow the workings of Bevin's mind. In the Labour Party when a man falls out of favour he is politically dead; he cannot retire for a season to Chartwell to write the life of one of his forebears. He does not know, perhaps, who they are. Bevin broke the party truce to save his skin. In this sense Winston has led a sheltered life, and for all his prestige, this complete detachment from the tooth-and-claw business in politics has been a big handicap.

April 27, 1945

At the Annexe this morning I ran into Jock Colville, who informed me with a seraphic smile that he was in a Bolshie frame of mind; the P.M. had not gone to bed till 5 a.m. A bit of paper with 'Resting' on it was still pinned to his door. Sawyers said that he had been given orders not to call him until 10.30 a.m. When he was awake the R.N.V.R. sub-lieutenant from the Map Room took him the news

[1] Ramsay MacDonald, Prime Minister of the Coalition Government, 1931. See footnote 2, p. 347.

and a big map; then I went in with his breakfast. He made no attempt to tackle it, but, picking up a paper, read me a letter from Stalin, which he said had given him a lot of pleasure.

'Himmler'—he stopped and looked up at me—'this is very secret, has proposed surrendering to us, but going on fighting the Russians. I sent the whole correspondence to Stalin. I told him we should insist on unconditional surrender to all the three great powers. Stalin, though lately he has called us all the names under the sun, wrote, "Knowing you, it is what I should expect from you."'

The P.M. leant over to the table by the side of the bed and put down the papers.

'A more friendly letter than he has written yet,' he added. 'Their suspicions and their sense of inferiority have made things difficult up to now.'

The P.M. ruminated moodily. He read me some of his reply to Stalin. His heart is still in the war, and he cannot put his mind into the election.

May 7, 1945

When Winston woke this morning Pim[1] took him the news of the German surrender.

'For five years you've brought me bad news, sometimes worse than others. Now you have redeemed yourself.'

And yet the P.M. does not seem at all excited about the end of the war.

May 8, 1945

The Government's warning to housewives to lay in bread for VE day has not worked according to plan, and there were bread queues everywhere as I made my way to the House of Lords this morning to hear the P.M.'s broadcast on victory over the enemy. There was not a seat vacant in the Library; I found partial support against one of the ladders which served the upper shelves.

At three o'clock the loudspeaker gave us the Prime Minister's speech from Downing Street. It was a short, factual statement, arranged by a man of letters, though the ending had a tinny sound.

'Advance, Britannia. Long live the cause of Freedom. God Save the King.'

The peer next to me (I could not put a name to him, for all sorts of unfamiliar faces turned up for the occasion) thought it strange that

[1] Captain Richard Pim, R.N.V.R. In charge of the Prime Minister's map room.

there was no allusion in the speech to God. There was, however, no doubt in Winston's mind to whom the credit was due.

I asked John Masefield [1] what he thought. 'I'd rather,' he answered, 'have the honest utterance of Winston than the false rhetoric of a lesser man. Lloyd George might have gone in for this rhetoric.' Lincoln, I argued, would have struck a deeper note. Masefield agreed; but added that he was a man of deep piety.

May 20, 1945

Went to see the P.M. at a quarter to ten, but he was still sleeping. I returned at half-past ten and found that Sawyers had just called him. 'He's keeping dreadful hours, sir, these days.' Rowan, too, spoke to me about it and asked if I could do anything; on four of the last eight nights it had been between three and four o'clock in the morning before he went to bed. He seemed tired.

P.M.: 'I wrote a letter which Attlee took to Blackpool. He hoped to persuade the Party to let their Ministers stay in the Government until the war with Japan is finished. A.V.[2] was very keen on this and Bevin agreed. But they wouldn't look at it. Boiling with hate.'

So the election will be in July.

The P.M. has tried to keep the Government together. He has failed. His thoughts turned wearily to the election. To have had arbitrary powers for five years, to speak for Britain without anybody's leave or question, and then to wait, cap in hand, on the doorstep, irks him. 'There are two opposing ideas in the country,' I said to him. 'There's pretty universal gratitude to you, and there's a notion about that you aren't very keen on this brave-new-world business.'

Winston answered: 'The desire for a new world is nothing like universal; the gratitude is.'

I did not argue the point.

The P.M. seems too weary to think out a policy for the restoration of the country after the havoc of the war. This morning he sent me that part of the Conservative Election Manifesto which deals with the new Health Service. He asked for my comments, though it is printed and ready for circulation. I found the manifesto full of platitudes: 'Liberty is an essential condition of scientific progress,' and other resounding phrases of that kind. It is all politics. No attempt is made to face the facts. Poor people have come to dread the expense of illness. They want their doctoring for nothing, and the party which gives them this will be on a winner.

[1] John Masefield, Poet Laureate since 1930.
[2] A. V. Alexander, First Lord of the Admiralty.

Unhappily this is not the kind of thing that stirs Winston's imagination. As for the rest of the Party, they ought to come out of the smoking-room of the House of Commons and plot a little less and feel a little more. I sat down and wrote a short criticism of the manifesto, and after lunch I took it to the Annexe, where I found John Anderson and Ralph Assheton, the Chairman of the Conservative Party, closeted with the P.M. Anderson left, but Assheton remained. The P.M. read what I had written in grim silence. My quips did not seem to amuse him. He did not really want my help, he only wanted my blessing for his plans. He looked up and scowled.

'The doctors aren't going to dictate to the country; they tried to do that with Lloyd George.'

I did not answer. I wondered who had put these ideas into his head.

'It isn't bad really?' he demanded. I answered that the manifesto, where it dealt with health, was feeble stuff; like the coloured water some doctors prescribe for their patients, it would do no harm if it did no good. He asked sharply how I would alter it. I answered that Health Centres ought to be in the manifesto, not a few experimental centres, but a thought-out scheme. To my surprise he agreed. Then he went off into a little harangue, all about the great advances medicine had made; doctors could not make use of these working as individuals, they must come together in these centres and have the necessary means and equipment. He turned to Assheton, and in his arbitrary way said: 'Get them to put it in.'

As the British Medical Association has dug in against my zeal for health centres, I thought I ought to warn the P.M. what might happen, but it was plain that he had exhausted the possibilities of the centres and indeed of health generally. When I said that the health proposals in the manifesto would not bring many votes to the Party he said testily that he was not after votes; he wanted to do the thing properly. He was in a bad temper.

The P.M. told me that the B.B.C. had asked him to take twenty minutes only for his first election broadcast. 'I insisted on at least half an hour.' This is a sign of the times. While the German War lasted he could wander on as long as he liked. Now things are different. Presently he will be treated like other men. It is going to be a big drop to earth. It will hurt him. He will hate it.

June 4, 1945

I am staying at Professor Wynn's house in Birmingham, where I have come to examine students, and we were checking the marks in the papers when Wynn proposed that we should break off to listen to the Prime Minister's broadcast. 'It's the kick-off in the election campaign.'

When it was done I glanced round the room. It was plain that it had not gone down with anybody. Cloake thought it was all negative, just abuse of the Socialists; Wynn felt that it was out of tune with the forces that are trying to plan a better world: his daughter considered it 'cheap.' No one agreed with the line that Winston had taken. He scoffs at 'those foolish people' who want to rebuild the world, but beneath this bluster he is, I believe, less certain about things. He has a feeling that he is back in the thirties, alone in the world, speaking a foreign tongue.

And so he falls back on vituperation. He was brought up on that, and well it has served him in the Commons, where he could demolish the Stokeses and Shinwells. But now his blows seem to miss the mark. The war is over and the public are tired of strife, they do not want bickering. They want to get on with things.

June 5, 1945

Attlee, the 'poor Clem' of the war years, did his piece tonight, and did it well. Perhaps his years in Bermondsey have brought home to him that politics are more than a game. At any rate, as I listened, it became plain that one ounce of Gladstone's moral fervour was worth a ton of skilled invective. And this in spite of the handicap of Attlee's delivery. It is clear that the P.M. is on the wrong tack; Max and Brendan are his advisers, and he will not learn from anyone else. For the first time the thought went through my head that he may lose the election.

June 14, 1945

Told the P.M. about Eden's illness. I think he misses him. He glanced at me as he said: 'I expect you liked my second broadcast better than the first.' He looks on me indulgently as 'rather red.' He added that he was going to do two more. 'Everybody listens and you get your message home.' He does not realize that after each broadcast he has lost ground.

Miss Watson, one of the staff at No. 10, met me in the passage. She feels that neither of the two broadcasts is the true P.M.; there was no 'vim' in them. 'You know, Lord Moran, his heart isn't in this election.'

It appears that Winston is now resigned to the election. Only, if the play must come to an end there ought at least to be a curtain; but as he stands there in the wings, waiting for the call, the theatre

253

is emptying. I urged him to take a holiday in France. He is toying with the idea. He puts off a decision; he hates making decisions.

June 22, 1945

I am counting the weeks until I can take the P.M. away for a rest. It seems that he cannot make up his mind about anything. He is still sleeping at the Annexe, and had not breakfasted when I called this morning. I ran into him as he crossed the passage to his bathroom. He beamed, and was obviously in a very different mood. 'I shan't be a moment,' he said. 'Go to my room.'

When he rejoined me he began at once in a cheerful voice:

'I have been quite rattled. I showed my broadcast to Max and to Margesson.[1] They said it wasn't good. I don't like other people doing things better than I do.'

It was his old, very personal, way of looking at everything.

'There's usually something in the well which I can fish up at any time. It was very unlike me. I did ten thousand words before I got the eighteen hundred I wanted. With an audience I can tell how things are and what they will take. But speaking into a microphone, you don't know what's there. I stayed in bed for four days. They brought me papers and documents, but I sent them away. I didn't want to work on them with this damn' business hanging over my head.'

I asked him how he was. His face flickered into a smile. 'The appetite is good,' he replied with mock solemnity, surveying the substantial breakfast set out on the bed-rest. The smile vanished. 'I am worried about this damned election. I have no message for them now,' he said sadly. In the war, compared with other members of the Cabinet, he understood what his soldiers and sailors were after. Now, men who did not count then, Attlee and Morrison, are coming to the microphone and seem to know better than he does what people are thinking and what they want. The vision of a better world, at which he has so often jibed, seems the only thing that interests them. 'If things come out pretty level, they will think of another coalition,' he said, 'but without Max.'

He was now half talking to me and half reading the headings of the newspapers spread on the bed-sheet. On Monday he is setting off electioneering. He will sleep in his train. 'Oh, no, I can use it, because I shall get back to it in the evening and do my office work there.' And then, confidingly, as if he was at last addressing me and not just ruminating: 'I feel very lonely without a war. Do you feel like that?'

[1] Viscount Margesson, Secretary of State for War, 1940–2.

Chapter twenty-six

Suspense

When a man begins to grow old his future becomes guess-work. His faculties may be unimpaired, his health by all appearances sound, yet any day, without warning, a coronary thrombosis may strike him dead, or leave him an invalid, who remains a tenant of this world only by courtesy, well knowing that another arrow from the same quiver will get him in the end. Winston was in his sixty-sixth year when in the spring of 1940 I was first asked to see him. I could find no evidence in mind or body of the corroding effects of a long and arduous existence; it was not until the last years of the war that I began to notice intimations of mortality.

The Prime Minister was slow, even then, to heed any warning or remonstrance. He had taken on a job; he was determined to see it through. His whole being was in the struggle.

But now the General Election had brought home to him that his resources were nearly spent, and when I pressed him again to take a short holiday before the Conference at Potsdam he said quietly that he had made up his mind to go to the South of France for ten days.

Ten days' rest would not repair the hurt done by the prodigious strain of the last five years, but patchwork was better than nothing. Moreover, if peace of mind was the first necessity, Hendaye had been well chosen. He could get busy there with his paint-box, and there was good bathing, which he loved when the water was warm.

Hendaye, July 7, 1945

The château of Bordaberry is a white manor house on a tongue of land at the mouth of the Bidassoa River, which separates France from Spain. It stands in a place apart, about a mile from the sea, where the P.M. is not bothered by the curious; but he has only to go down into Hendaye to excite the friendly and indeed affectionate interest of the inhabitants. The P.M. is too most fortunate in his

255

host. General Brutinel is intelligent and contrives to interest the
P.M. That is an achievement at any time, but in his present mood
it is more: it is a certificate of the General's tact. He is not frightened
of his guest; he seems to know intuitively that Winston, though not
interested in other people's opinions, is curious about facts, and the
General serves these up with a wise economy of words. The P.M.
wished to know when the Germans first showed signs of clearing out
of these parts; he had wanted to attack Bordeaux when Normandy
was invaded, but expert opinion had been against any dispersal of
the forces available. Winston seemed pleased when the General
told him that in August, 1944, the Germans in these parts wished
to surrender, and overtures were made to our Military Attaché in
Madrid, who was then in France. But the officer commanding the
F.F.I.[1] intervened; the Germans were beaten, he said, and ought to
surrender to the F.F.I., and General de Gaulle backed him up. The
Germans, however, would not surrender to the F.F.I., and so possession of Bordeaux was denied to us for another nine months. The
P.M. listened to Brutinel closely, nodding his head from time to time
in agreement.

'Another example,' he grunted, 'of de Gaulle's folly.'

The General went on to tell him in detail how the Germans who
were billeted in his house had behaved. The P.M. confessed that he
liked detail, he wanted the picture filled in. If our host gives the
P.M. the facts he wants, he also displays sagacity in selecting subjects for conversation which are congenial to him. He spoke today
of the gratitude of humble folk to the P.M. Before the whisper went
round that the General was to be Mr. Churchill's host he could get
no one to do any work in the house, charwomen were unprocurable;
but when his agent was told that the P.M. was coming, four charwomen volunteered. His words only confirmed Winston's own convictions. As he drove up from St. Jean de Luz this morning, some
of the friendly inhabitants, mostly women and children, cheered.

'I believe,' the P.M. said, 'I could go to any country in the world
and be received with cheers from humble folk.'

If he loses the election he will miss this heady wine. Wherever he
goes, too, people say acceptable things, selecting what they think
will be most gratifying to him. The General, an astute man, goes one
further and brings him books which show him in a light he will like.

[1] Free French Interior forces. Admiral Meyer refused to surrender to Colonel
Adeline, commanding the Bordeaux Forces of the Interior in September, 1944, and
instead withdrew to entrenched positions at Royan and the Graves peninsula, on
either side of the Gironde estuary. Meyer was able to effect a partial blockade of
the port of Bordeaux until forced to surrender by the Americans six months later.

'This book,' Winston said, holding up *La Verité sur L'Armistice*, by Albert Kammerer, 'is very fair to me.'

And that, too, does not go on for ever.

July 8, 1945

'I'm very depressed,' said the P.M., walking into the room before luncheon and flopping into an armchair. 'I don't want to do anything. I have no energy. I wonder if it will come back.'

The election festers in his mind.

'Nothing,' he says, 'will be decided at the conference at Potsdam. I shall be only half a man until the result of the poll.[1] I shall keep in the background at the conference.'

He seemed very doubtful whether he had enough energy to paint. But after luncheon he got up suddenly as one gets out of bed.

'Come along, Charles, and watch my preparations.'

Clemmie was trying to sleep, but he stumped through her bedroom on to a balcony where the paints had been set out on a small table; his feet brushed the floor as if he were too tired to lift them off the ground.

'Where are the other paints?' he demanded impatiently of Sawyers as he surveyed those before him with displeasure. 'I've no reserves here'—his voice rose in anger—'you've left a lot behind. Why did you do that? Who told you to bring only these?'

Sawyers bluntly disclaimed responsibility for the paints.

'Where is the cobalt?' The P.M. spoke with great irritability and vehemence. 'You ought not to have left everything at home. Ah, here it is,' he murmured, in subdued tones. 'Get me a stool. I must sit.'

When he had done I followed him back to his bedroom.

'I'm going to relax completely. I'm not going to look at any papers. Only twice in my life have my knees shaken under me when speaking; at Edinburgh and on Richmond Common, when I was speaking for Harvie-Watt.[2] I imagine one is nearly all in when that happens. Take my pulse, Charles.'

During dinner the P.M.'s mind went back to Moscow. One night he was dining with Stalin and Molotov—they were alone save for the interpreters—when Molotov told of a visit to Berlin in the winter of 1940, before Germany attacked Russia, and how Ribbentrop had

---

[1] Polling had taken place on July 5th. In order to allow time for the collection of votes from the Services, three weeks were to elapse before the declaration of the result of the poll. The conference at Potsdam was due to open on July 17.

[2] Sir George Harvie-Watt, Parliamentary Private Secretary to Churchill, 1941–5.

taken him into a safe place during a heavy raid. Ribbentrop had suggested that after the war Germany and Russia should agree to share the spoils. Molotov had asked what about England, but Ribbentrop replied England didn't count. Molotov retorted: 'Why, if England doesn't count, are we where we are? Whose bombs are falling, anyway?'

The P.M. went on to speak of the Russian purges. Beneš[1] told him that he had warned Stalin of the plot of high Russian officers to make an alliance with Germany. The plans passed through the Russian Embassy at Prague. So Stalin acted, and four thousand or so officers in the Russian Army, whose rank was above that of Colonel, were liquidated.

'Stalin was thoroughly justified,' the P.M. added. 'These officers were acting against their country.'

When Clemmie and Mary had gone to bed the talk drifted to medicine. At last I said:

'We have been talking about the advances medicine has made in curing diseases of the body, but in the future the doctor must find out more about how the mind works.'

The P.M. said at once: 'As long as you keep this psychiatric stuff out of the Army I don't mind.'

I suppose I had forgotten that nothing could come of a discussion on morale with him. Anyway, I allowed his antiquated approach to the vagaries of the mind to irritate me into an argument. I was sufficiently ill-advised to quote Wilfred Trotter[2] on the herd instinct. He flew at me:

'You are ascribing to instinct the noblest motives of men. War broke out and people spoke to each other in buses. Well, that wasn't herd instinct. It was men coming together for a common purpose.'

His words followed each other with gathering speed, his voice rose. He ended with a great outburst against Herbert Morrison:

'He is a loathsome creature with a warped mind; he was a "conchy" in the last war, he would not let boys drill, and he even opposed conscription. I shall never speak to him again.'

In such a mood you cannot reason with him; you can only listen.

July 9, 1945

All morning the P.M. has been painting a sea piece with the hills beyond. As he left, a crowd of smiling women and children pressed into the open gateway to greet him, and a photographer dodged from one point to another. The P.M. called him and asked him to

[1] Dr. Eduard Beneš. Led exiled government of Czechoslovakia from London.
[2] Wilfred Trotter, author of *Instincts of the Herd in Peace and War*.

photograph the scene which he had been painting, that he might study the composition.

He is thinking a lot these days of the election. One moment he sees himself victorious; the next he pictures himself beaten. If he wins, he will work out plans which would make Communism unnecessary and distasteful; if he loses, well, that would release him from a crazy world. He would feel the British public had treated him ill, but that would pass. He would take long holidays, appearing from time to time in the House and intervening perhaps in debate.

He finds this state of suspense unpalatable, and turns for comfort to other thoughts. In three years, Winston told us, he had lunched more than two hundred times with the King. No servant was present; they waited on themselves. If the P.M. rose to get something for His Majesty, the King in turn got something for the P.M. No subject had ever been so honoured. He wanted no other reward.

Tonight he spoke of France: 'As long as there is a kick left in my carcass I shall support France's efforts to re-establish herself. She must have a great Army; France without an Army is a cock without a comb.'

He went on to talk of the destruction of the French Fleet—the best since the fleets under the Kings of France.

'It was a terrible decision, like taking the life of one's own child to save the State. Our admirals were very loath to act, they were very sad; it was necessary to give them the most precise orders. I accepted full responsibility. I was determined to prevent the French ships falling into German hands. If this had happened, then with the German, Italian and Japanese ships, a formidable challenge to democracy might have been thrown down.'

The P.M. told us of England's offer of common citizenship to France, when she was on her knees.[1] There was a Cabinet on a Sunday. All sorts of improbable people were there, Corbin,[2] de Gaulle, Margesson. Neville Chamberlain[3] put the suggestion to the P.M. Winston described the scene:

[1] Following the withdrawal of the British Expeditionary force from Dunkirk at the end of May, 1940, and the decision to reserve our fighter aircraft for the defence of Britain, the War Cabinet evolved a Declaration of Franco–British Unity, which included plans for common citizenship and joint organs for defence, foreign, financial and economic policy. It was hoped that this unprecedented offer would help Reynaud, the French Prime Minister, to carry a majority of his Cabinet for a move to Africa and the continuance of the war. The offer was rejected, and Reynaud resigned on June 16.

[2] André Charles Corbin, French Ambassador in London.

[3] Neville Chamberlain, Prime Minister, 1937–40; at this time Lord President of the Council.

'That rough Cabinet,' he said, turning to General Brutinel, 'to which men had come by so many different ways, was carried off its feet. It was like a religious revival. It was a *cri de cœur* from the rough heart of Britain.'

There were tears in the P.M.'s eyes. The recollection was to him profoundly moving.

He marvelled at America's disinterestedness. She had come into this war and 'cast away her wealth for an idea.' If his father as well as his mother had been an American he was not certain that he would have advised her to come into the war.

(This was an emotional outburst rather than a considered verdict. America came into the war because Japan attacked her.)

The P.M. had been speaking with great animation. The vast brow, which mounts straight above his eyes, was puckered, so that a deep line passed up vertically from his nose. The eyelids seemed pressed down on his eyes by the weight of his brow, the thin lips were pursed together, pouting. At the summit of his forehead two wisps of hair went their several ways, and gave an impression that he had more hair than was actually the case. He became silent and no one spoke. At last he looked up and laid bare where his thoughts were:

'I hear the women are for me, but that the men have turned against me.'

Clemmie reminded him how bitterly he had opposed the vote being given to women.

'Quite true,' he mused.

At that moment Jock came in and gave me a telegram. It was from Lübeck. There had been an accident and John had been shot through the knee.

July 10, 1945

The P.M., during luncheon, recalled 1918, when he was hard at work on his plans for the 1919 campaign.[1] He had an entirely new conception to break the enemy front. He talked it over with Foch,[2] and then came the 'bloody peace.'

There was a pause. I said that when we heard in Washington of the fall of Tobruk it was the worst moment of the war. The P.M. retorted at once:

'Oh, no, it was painful like a boil, but it was not a cancer. I was

---

[1] Churchill was Minister for Munitions during the period July, 1917–January, 1919, and was most concerned that we should break through on the Western Front by reason of our superior technical and mechanical equipment.

[2] Marshal Foch, Generalissimo of the Allied Armies on the Western Front, 1918.

miserable because thirty-three thousand men had laid down their arms; even now we don't know why. It was a muddle, but all war is a muddle. The two critical moments in the war, when everything was at stake, were the Battle of Britain and the submarine attack.'

Once more he told how the German submarines gripped us by the throat. When the Germans held Brest and could fly over Southern Ireland to the mouths of the Mersey and the Clyde they could report to their submarines and then go on to Norway.

'It was touch and go. Yes, it was life and death. Our food supply was balanced on a knife-edge.'

When Winston was First Lord he had told Neville Chamberlain that he would never ask him to use force against Southern Ireland unless the safety of England was at stake.

Once again he speculated on the chances of success if England had been invaded. It was as if he wanted to say: 'Do you quite realize how near you came to defeat? Has it gone home how narrow a squeak you have had?' He stopped abruptly:

'Mary,[1] you oughtn't to drink spirits at your age; it isn't becoming.'

Mary, demurely: 'I can't do anything right.'

The P.M., affectionately: 'You do very little wrong.'

After Clemmie, Mary, Jock and Tommy had left the luncheon table the P.M. talked till four o'clock struck. His mind wandered back to his boyhood.

'I think,' he said, 'I gained a lot by not overworking my brain when I was young. I never did anything I didn't like. I used to write essays for older boys. I would dictate to them. But presently the master became suspicious. The stupid Jones was raising quite interesting points. Jones was invited to elaborate the points he had made. But Jones had nothing to add to what he had said in his essay. I got kicked,' the P.M. added ruefully, 'for landing him in this position.

'Two things have disappeared in my lifetime. Men no longer study the classics. It was an advantage when there was one common discipline and every nation studied the doings of two states. Now,' with a sniff, 'they learn how to mend motor cars.'

'The other thing is—— Can you guess what I am thinking of?' he asked the General. 'No? Why, the horse. We have lost a good deal in these two things.'

[1] Mary Churchill, youngest daughter of the Prime Minister, serving in the A.T.S.

He did not know which he would hate more: leading the Government with a small majority in a sick world or guiding the Opposition. I thought he had done when he said:

'I don't want anything. I've had five years of continuous excitement.'

Of course, it is not true that he is satisfied. He keeps stamping into the Secretaries' room from habit. 'Any news come in?' And when Jock, for the sixth time, assured him that there was none he became petulant:

'I won't have it. Telegraph to Leslie that I must have more regular reports.' To Jock, severely: 'It's your business to keep me informed.'

July 11, 1945

The P.M. disclosed during luncheon that he had had reassuring reports both from Ralph Assheton,[1] and from Max, which confirmed Margesson's earlier estimate of a majority of a hundred. I said Max had set his heart on winning this election. The P.M. turned to me and said:

'Do you think his support is a liability or an asset?'

He described him as a remarkable man.

'There is no one like him. He has unmade several Governments in my lifetime. It's better to have his support than his opposition. The *Express* has a circulation of between three and four millions.'

I expressed doubts about whether those who read such papers necessarily voted as they were told. He looked unconvinced, but said nothing. He had put Max into the Cabinet when things were very bad and no one had liked to say anything. Then Max wanted to resign and pressed his point until the P.M. had to let him go. But when some time had passed and Max was ready to rejoin the Cabinet the P.M. sent his name to the King without a word to anyone. The King, according to the P.M., was very reluctant to accept his advice. Max didn't trouble to attend important Cabinet meetings. Then he would get hold of some idea and champion it fiercely.

I hummed something out of *The Mikado*; the P.M.'s eyes brightened, he began to sing refrain after refrain from that opera. He sang, with great gusto, 'A Wandering Minstrel I.' He loved the words and the tunes. And Mary in her eager way joined in. Then I asked him about some game they had played at Chartwell, and soon we were saying, 'I have a cat,' to be asked by one's neighbour, 'What kind of cat?' Whereupon one had to find adjectives beginning with the

---

[1] Ralph Assheton, Chairman of the Conservative Party.

letter chosen, a tame cat, a timid cat, a troublesome cat, a tabby cat
and so on until no more adjectives would come into your head and
you were counted out, and only those with a full vocabulary were left
in. Winston searched his store-house of words as earnestly as if he
were writing for posterity. This went on until ten minutes to four,
when the P.M. went off to the Nairns [1] to paint.

July 12, 1945

The P.M. woke with indigestion, which he confidently ascribed
to his painting.

'Where is the General?' he demanded angrily. 'Send for him at
once.' When he came, the P.M. wanted to know why Nairn was
fussing him to see de Gaulle. De Gaulle would love to hand out a
snub to him. Besides, the time could hardly be more unpropitious
for any advance to him; just before the Potsdam Conference, from
which de Gaulle was excluded. General Brutinel waited patiently for
a lull, then, when the P.M. had subsided, he explained that he only
wanted to approach de Gaulle to suggest he should come to see the
Prime Minister. Winston would have none of this; he complained
that de Gaulle had sent a telegram to Roosevelt asking for assistance.
He could trust America not to take France's colonies; he could not
trust Britain. And this, said Winston scornfully, at a time when we
were pouring men into France for her relief. No, he would not see
him. General Brutinel was puzzled. After all, it was the Prime
Minister who had begun the whole business; it was he who had suggested breaking his journey to Berlin at Paris in order to see de
Gaulle. Then, on second thoughts, it occurred to him that he might
be snubbed. If, the P.M. ruminated, it had been the other way
round, if, for instance, de Gaulle were in Scotland, he would have
sent him a telegram to welcome him and to ask if he could do anything for him. No such telegram had come from de Gaulle when the
P.M. came to France. So, after many hesitations and endless pre-
ambulations, he decided to do nothing till Duff Cooper [2] arrived
in the afternoon.

He got up, very grumpy, to go bathing, but returned completely
renovated and almost hilarious. No, he would not have a bath; he
would leave the salt on him. It did good.

Our pilot came to luncheon. The navigator of the Skymaster has
been offered a job in Washington; he wanted to go. It meant pro-
motion. The P.M., however, does not like changes. Had the pilot
anyone else in view? The pilot had. Was he a good navigator?

---

[1] Bryce Nairn, British Consul at Bordeaux, and his wife, an artist.
[2] Duff Cooper was at this time British Ambassador in Paris.

Was he as good as the man who was leaving us? He, the P.M., did not want to find himself over the Atlantic when he ought to be crossing the Pacific. He might be heading for the Pacific presently, he added reflectively.

The P.M. asked who was in the aeroplane that was taking Attlee to Berlin. His eyes twinkled; a smile hovered not far away.

'We don't know whether we are on speaking terms until we meet at Berlin.'

The General, overnight, had asked Tommy Thompson whether the P.M. could lunch early so that the servants might be able to attend the Basque games and dancing. Tommy promised to do something, but it was after three o'clock before he mildly suggested to the P.M. that they might make a move to let the servants clear the table. The P.M. said he must be allowed to drink his coffee. Clemmie brought him downstairs at a quarter to four. He squatted like a child who is a little out of temper.

'Why do they bring me down so early?' he complained petulantly. After a pause: 'Is there anything I can do in the meanwhile?'

Clemmie said that his boots, which were done up with a zip fastener, were very shabby.

'Are they your best?' she asked.

'No, but they are the most comfortable, and'—with a return to good humour—'I have reached a time of life when I allow that to count.'

The Mayors of Biarritz and St. Jean de Luz and other local potentates arrived and were presented to him. They gave Basque bowls and flowers and walking-sticks to him, to Clemmie and to Mary. Then we filed to the great court lined with French folk in their holiday clothes, where there was an awning to shield a few of the most important guests and spectators from the powerful sun. The proceedings opened with a Basque game, like fives. Soon after the game began the P.M. rose from his place in the front row and stalked out, followed by Tommy and myself. I thought for a moment he felt ill, but he was only bored. To Tommy he said impatiently:

'I don't know why they arranged this, they know I hate all games.'

Jock came into the sitting-room looking for the P.M. He found him in a very bad temper.

'I have come as an ambassador to ask you to return. They were very much upset by your leaving.'

'Go to Hell,' was the P.M.'s unpromising response.

Jock is not without courage, and is the only one of the secretaries to say this sort of thing. About three-quarters of an hour later Winston returned to the court with Duff Cooper, who had just arrived.

There was a lot of Basque dancing, and games. When it was all over the P.M. made a short speech in his most Churchillian French, and we dispersed.

The P.M. came up to me: 'It would have killed me if I had stayed all the time.'

I said it was pretty stuffy.

'Hot and boring,' he corrected me.

When Winston had gone to his bedroom he said to me that he thought that General Brutinel was a very agreeable man and very well informed. He asked me his age. I fancy he must be thinking of using him in some way. *La Verité sur L'Armistice* and his carefully selected remarks had done their work.

July 14, 1945

Went after breakfast to find out if the P.M.'s indigestion had gone.

'I've just thrown the reins on the horse's neck and let things rip,' he said. 'I've never done it before.'

This is true. He has hardly read a document or dictated a letter since we came here. Whether this is nature demanding a let up or the absence of any interesting news, I cannot say.

In all the P.M.'s ruminations about the election he has been concerned with how it would affect him, but this morning as we came back from bathing he said the election had done a lot of harm.

'You mean abroad?' I asked.

'No, they take my re-election for granted, but at home one section of the Liberal Party cannot say too poisonous things about the other section, and there has been a great stirring up of feeling and strife.'

Whether this point of view was present in his mind during the election campaign, when something might have been done by example to soften the discord, is open to doubt. Anyway, it is a little late for a death-bed repentance. Probably, once an election was unavoidable, much bitterness was inevitable. But many think things would have been different if the P.M. had said at the outset: 'I have worked with these men as colleagues, we have been through pretty tough times together, and whatever they do I cannot bring myself to exchange hard words with them. The German War is over. We have had a miraculous deliverance. The only fitting way to make a thank-offering for our escape is to turn our hands with the same single purpose to prepare our country as a proper habitation for a people which has endured so much. I mean, if you still trust me— and I have never promised you what I could not carry out—to get the houses which are needed, to see everyone has work and food, and to ask that all kinds of people, from every class, who have

265

worked together to save England, should continue to plan as one man for the betterment of all. I can say no more.'

When we were leaving the sands Jock sought out Monsieur to pay him for the tents and deck-chairs which we had hired from him, but he would not hear of it. Five times Jock tried, five times it was refused with growing emphasis. He would take nothing from the man to whom France owed so much. Last night at Hendaye when we arrived for the fireworks the crowd were so friendly and even affectionate that when the P.M. came to speak and said only, 'Vive la France,' it seemed just right. Mrs. Nairn, wife of the Consul, tells me that it is like this all through France.

She paints with the P.M.—she was a professional artist before she married—and advises him. A wise little woman, with a quiet, sympathetic manner, she has succeeded where so many have failed in breaking down the formidable ramparts of indifference which he presents to women generally, and to his hostess in particular. All the same, I doubt whether she could have done this without her paints.

The maid brought coffee and we sat round the table listening to the P.M., who had some difficulty in keeping awake. He nursed his head in his hands, and for a time seemed oblivious of the company. Then he looked up.

'Tommy, could you get me some brandy?'

They brought books and photographs, which he autographed, and some caricatures, which he refused to sign, as is his habit. Then he went to prepare his last attack from the land front on the house of the Black Prince, which he has been painting and repainting for three days. There is no light in the water, or on the house, or in the tree tops which surround the house, as he has painted it. But he has stuck to it. One day he painted for nearly four hours on end. It brought on an attack of indigestion. He would not be defeated. He had the house photographed and compared it with his picture. Mrs. Nairn, too, put on canvas her impression of the scene, and he stood for a long time in silent scrutiny of the two pictures. The P.M. is a determined man; if organization could have produced a painting all would have been well.

Chapter twenty-seven

Too late

Potsdam, July, 1945

In the autumn of 1914, when my hospital in London would not give
me leave to join the Army, I had fretted that I should miss the march
on Berlin; then I had gone without leave, and had crouched in a
waterlogged trench in front of Armentières all winter; there was a
milestone on the road, which cut through the trenches, marked 'Lille
8 kilometres.' And that was as near as we got to Berlin in my time
with a battalion. Now, thirty-one years later, the Army is in Berlin,
but youth has gone, and with it the illusions of youth; it is no longer
an adventure, but just a business appointment.

The sun blazed down, and members of the Conference, who had
been waiting for a long time on the airfield outside Berlin, looked
hot and uncomfortable buttoned up in their uniforms. There were
Russian soldiers everywhere, lining the road, behind bushes, knee
deep in the corn. We drove to where a substantial stone house, which
was said to have belonged to Schacht, the banker, had been reserved
for the Prime Minister. I followed him through two bleak rooms
with great chandeliers to the opposite side of the empty house,
where french windows, that had not been cleaned for a long time,
opened upon a balcony, and there, without removing his hat,
Winston flopped into a garden chair, flanked by two great tubs of
hydrangeas, blue, pink and white. He appeared too weary to move.
Presently he looked up:

'Where is Sawyers?' He turned to Tommy Thompson. 'Get me a
whisky.'

We sat in silence for a long time, looking at the lawn that sloped
to a lake, into which, so it was said, the Russians had thrown some
German soldiers who could not walk because of their wounds. Beyond the lake a field rose sharply to a wood. The only sign of life
that we could see was a Russian sentry, who came out of the wood,

looked round and disappeared again into the trees. When the light had gone a rifle shot, that seemed to come from the wood, broke the silence that had fallen on everything.

July 16, 1945

Alex called for me this morning; he wanted to see the sights of Berlin. The road was littered with German civilians; they all seemed to be looking at their feet as they trundled their belongings in box and barrow—anything on wheels. I wondered if they knew where they were going. The Russians had planted posts by the side of the road, bearing white placards, framed in a broad red band, with extracts from Stalin's speeches printed above his signature, which was engraved in large red letters. 'The teaching of history tells us that Hitlers come and go, but the German people and the German State remain.' The messages on the road to Berlin seem designed to persuade the German people that the Russians are really their friends, while the American and British are their enemies. Or perhaps the idea is that the Russian sector, though nominally independent, will presently become a puppet state of the Soviet Union. What are they up to? What are they thinking?

In Berlin itself we came across notices pitched in another key. Here the Russian authorities responsible for these posters have made no attempt to hide the primitive satisfaction they derive from frightening people. On one column of a great museum, that had been gutted, is printed: 'To forgive will never be possible. Don't go to Russia.' And on another pillar: 'For Stalingrad and Leningrad and all the ruined cities of Russia we bring back our hate to Germany.' A German, who was standing near, told us that the Russians had done a lot of damage deliberately.

On other boards the Russians have posted notices which, the interpreter explained, are to warn their own troops of the danger of loose talk: 'Remember when speaking on the telephone the enemy may be listening'; 'When moving from one sector to another don't stop and talk with anybody'; 'Don't talk to anyone, for it passes from ear to ear and is heard from one corner to another'; 'Whoever talks helps the enemy.' To the casual observer these restraints on the social proclivities of the Russians seem unnecessary. On another small board was written: 'Don't use captured food. It may be poisoned by the enemy.'

I stopped a German at the door of a ruined cathedral and asked him where he got his food. He produced his ration card. It is very difficult, the old man said. He came from the Rhine and wanted to get back there. With a gesture:

'There is nothing to do here.'

As we were leaving the porch three Russian officers came up the steps. We spoke to them. The Colonel, looking at the destruction before us, remarked:

'You sow a wind and reap a whirlwind.'

A number of Germans had gathered on the steps of the Reichstag and were busy bartering with Russian soldiers all kinds of articles for marks or cigarettes. I saw a Russian soldier carrying away what looked like a new pair of black boots. Some peddled their goods through the crowd, field-glasses for two thousand marks, fountain pens, a camera, a great mantelpiece clock, boots and slippers, dresses and handkerchiefs—every kind of garment; others sat on the wall with their particular possession in their laps, apparently waiting to be accosted.

As I watched this evisceration of their homes I felt a sense of nausea; it was like the first time I saw a surgeon open a belly and the intestines gushed out.

We climbed for a time about the rubble, but when we tried to enter the Chancellery a Russian sentry stopped us. Alex became very impatient.

'Do you know who I am?' he demanded, pausing for an answer, but the sentry's face remained impassive. 'I have not come all this way to be stopped like this.'

In the Chancellery the first room was carpeted a foot deep with papers and ribbons and Iron Crosses, and there was Hitler's up-turned desk. Alex was rather horrified, a little stunned by it all; he seemed to feel as if he was gazing on a corpse for the first time. He does not really like this brutal humiliation of a proud people, beaten to their knees.

In the Sieges-Allee there had been hard fighting, and some of the statues were chipped by bullets. In front of the effigy of Albrecht der Bär was a garden seat with a notice: '*Nicht für Juden.*' Near the end of the avenue a cross marked the grave of two Soviet soldiers, one born in 1926, the other in 1908; a Russian inscription recorded that they 'perished in battle for their Soviet motherland.' How long will the Germans tolerate that alien sepulchre, planted in their victory avenue?

As we mused, a frieze of old men and women and children kept passing; they did not look at us. It made me think of an incident in the summer of 1915, after the Battle of Hooge, when some German prisoners were coming down the village street in front of Ypres; the Colonel of my battalion saw them approaching and stepped back into a house until they had passed.

On our way back we stopped the car to look at a board that was propped against a wall; it was plastered with bits of paper such as you might see in the window of a registry office advertising for domestic servants; they were stuck down with bits of gummed paper or drawing-pins. They all bore some offer. One German was anxious to barter some clothes for food; another was trying to go to Hamburg in a few days and was willing in return for food to take messages for anyone who had relatives in that city. While I watched, an old woman walked up and pinned up her offer. When she had gone a man approached the board and, taking out a pen, amended his previous offer.

When I told the P.M. about it, I saw that he was not listening; he had not come to Berlin to see the sights. However, this afternoon he announced that he would visit Berlin at four o'clock. I decided to go with him, for I was curious to see how he would react to this grim sight. I wondered, too, how German civilians would behave when they saw him. As we drove to Berlin no one on the road seemed to recognize him, until we came to the centre of the city, where a workman looked hard at us and pointed after the car. I had forgotten that the press and the cinema, which have made his face as familiar to the Canadian lumberman as to the Russian peasant, have in Germany by neglect brought him to earth and made him anonymous. We found a good many people at the Reichstag. The P.M. got out of the car and walked round what was left of the building—it did not seem a very safe performance. Some of the crowd looked away, others glanced at him with expressionless faces, one old man shook his fist, a few smiled.

As for the P.M., he said nothing. He did not seem greatly interested. His guide, a Russian soldier, led him across the courtyard outside the Chancellery to the dug-out where Hitler, like a wounded animal taking to its hole, is supposed to have died; the P.M. followed him down a flight of steps, but hearing there were two more flights, he gave up the idea of exploring the depths and slowly remounted the stairs. At the top he sat down on a gilt chair, mopping his brow.

'Hitler,' he said, 'must have come out here to get some air, and heard the guns getting nearer and nearer.'

I went back to the dug-out. Breathing the damp, acrid, foetid air, I felt my way down a lot of steps to another cell, strewn, as far as I could see by the light of a torch, with clothes and gas masks and every kind of litter. I picked up a burnt glove.

When I rejoined the P.M. we drove back in silence past the unending saluting Russian soldiers. His thoughts were elsewhere, I

POTSDAM

PRESIDENT TRUMAN

think; at any rate, he did not comment on what he had seen. As for Alec Cadogan, he merely complained how badly the tour was organized.

I talked to Winston while he undressed for bed.

'The Socialists say I shall have a majority over all other parties of thirty-two.'

I asked him if that was a working majority.

He replied: 'If my Government keeps being defeated I could resign. I should do so and have another election in the spring.'

This is a completely different tune from his demands during the election campaign that he would not tolerate anything but a majority that gave him real power. The truth is he is much less confident and, I think, would be content to win with any majority.

Before I put out the light I asked him what he had thought of Berlin. He answered with a smile:

'There was a reasonable amount of destruction.'

He asked me what I made of it. When I said I had picked up two Iron Crosses he asked to see them. I went to my room and brought them to him. All he said was, 'Poor devils.' Berlin did not seem to touch his imagination. It was not like that at Carthage when the P.M. found himself among the soldiers of the Eighth Army in the ruin of the Roman amphitheatre. Then, when he was about to speak to them, the associations of the place suddenly gripped him and for some time he dared not trust himself to speak.

I told him of Alex's reaction.

'I don't feel like that at all,' he replied.

I spoke about the vast, grandiose rooms of the Chancellery. For the first time he appeared to be interested.

'It was from here that Hitler planned to govern the world,' he mused. 'A good many have tried that; all failed.' He smiled. 'That is why England is where she is. I'll tell Stalin about this.'

The P.M. said he had looked very carefully at the children for signs of malnutrition, but they appeared much better fed than those he had seen at Hendaye. He spoke of Germany as a decomposing carcass and told me that he looked with terror at the coming winter.

As an historian the P.M. has been interested in the latest attempt to grab world power—he does not believe it is the last. As a practical politician his long experience of government gives reality to the difficulties of providing food and work for the Germans.

Mary was excited about the first meeting with President Truman:[1]

[1] Harry Truman succeeded as President on April 12, 1945, on the death of President Roosevelt.

'Papa is relieved and confident. He likes the President immensely. He is sure he can work with him.'

July 17, 1945

The P.M. dined last night with General Marshall. Afterwards he said to me:

'That is the noblest Roman of them all. Congress always did what he advised. His work in training the American armies has been wonderful. I will pay tribute to it one day when occasion offers.'

He gave out that he would go and see Sans Souci[1] at twelve-thirty. At one o'clock he emerged from his room and strode into his car. The Russians were told that he had just a quarter of an hour to go round. With quick, impatient strides, he hurried through the rooms, looking neither to the right nor the left; his eyes were fixed on the floor; his look was abstracted. His thoughts were far away in the coming Conference—or was he once more counting the votes?

The first meeting of the Big Three took place at five o'clock. I talked to the P.M. on his return, when he was changing. He was in good form. It was obvious that things had gone well and he felt relieved.

'Stalin was very amiable,' the P.M. began, 'but he is opening his mouth very wide.'

The P.M. stopped opposite me:

'He has started cigars. He says he prefers them to cigarettes. If he is photographed smoking a cigar with me everybody will say it is my influence. I said so to him.'

'What had Stalin to say?' I asked.

'Oh,' the P.M. answered, 'he doesn't care a damn about that sort of thing. I pulled Vyshinsky's[2] leg. He looks so mild and benevolent. I said I could not believe he could be fierce. He replied that he was only fierce when it was necessary. The other day he banged the door on the King of Roumania so that some of the pictures came down, and the monarch was left to pick them up. Now the Russians have given the King their highest decoration. He is doing what they want.'

The P.M. palpated his tummy. With a mischievous smile:

'I had some caviare and champagne. Can I take some of your medicine? I feel rather acid.'

As Winston was in a good humour, I asked him about Truman. Had he real ability? The P.M. stood over me. The white of his eyes showed above his pupils, his lips pouted. Looking down at me as if he were saying something he did not want to be repeated:

---

[1] The royal palace, built by Frederick II, near Potsdam.
[2] Andrei Vyshinsky, Vice-Commissar for Foreign Affairs.

'I should think he has,' he said. 'At any rate, he is a man of immense determination. He takes no notice of delicate ground, he just plants his foot down firmly on it.'

And to illustrate this the P.M. jumped a little off the wooden floor and brought his bare feet down with a smack.

July 18, 1945

Truman came here to lunch with the P.M. Half an hour before, fifty men of the Scots Guards had taken up their position in the strip of garden in front of the house; from my bedroom window I watched them being dressed in line. The band of the Royal Marines arrived and, at last, Truman. His strong, friendly face gives everyone a feeling that he is going to play a big part.

We all shook hands with the President in the anteroom; then he lunched alone with the P.M. Some hours later Winston said, 'You might be interested in our conversation,' and told one of the secretaries to give me a summary that he had dictated after the President left.[1] 'You can take it away,' he said, when I began reading it.

'I dwelt on the tremendous cost in American life, and to a small extent in British life, which would be involved in enforcing unconditional surrender upon the Japanese. I had in mind saving their military honour and giving them some assurance of their national existence after they had complied with all the safeguards necessary for the conqueror. The President countered that the Japs had no longer any military honour after Pearl Harbour. He spoke of the terrible responsibility that rested on him in regard to the unlimited effusion of American blood. I left it at that. It was obviously in their minds, and they are thinking a good deal about it.'

Yet he has always refused to admit that the use of the words 'unconditional surrender' at Casablanca might have been a factor in prolonging German resistance. The President's kindly attention had led the P.M. frankly to unfold some of our difficulties.

'I spoke of the melancholy financial position of Great Britain. Half our foreign investments had been spent in the common cause when we stood alone. There is a great external debt of three thousand

---

[1] Mr. Churchill's account of this luncheon in *The Second World War*, Vol. VI, *Triumph and Tragedy*, is obviously taken from the same summary. Note what seems to him in retrospect worth quoting. He passes over the President's intention to 'Press with severity the need of the true independence of small States,' and his own concern at the time with the risks involved in enforcing unconditional surrender upon the Japanese, while he devoted a page to the advantages of American bases in England in time of peace.

million pounds. We should require time to get on our feet again. The President listened closely, attentively and sympathetically. He spoke of the immense debt the Allies owed to Britain for that period when she fought alone. "If you had gone like France," he added, "we might well be fighting the Germans on the American coast at the present time."'

The summary ends with a passage which brings out the warm friendship and trust that has sprung up between the two men:

'He was good enough to say that this had been the most enjoyable lunch he had had for many years, and how earnestly he hoped the relations I had had with President Roosevelt would be continued between him and me. He invited personal friendship and comradeship and used many expressions at intervals in our discussion which I could not easily hear unmoved. He seems a man of exceptional charm and ability, with an outlook exactly along the lines of Anglo-American relationships as they have developed. He has direct methods of speech and a great deal of self-confidence and resolution.'

Winston has fallen for the President. Truman's modesty and simple ways are certainly disarming. When he was on his way out, passing a piano in one of the rooms, he stopped and, pulling up a chair, played for a while.

Winston has twice spoken to me of the 'beginning of a fruitful partnership.' I would to God this had come earlier.

July 19, 1945

No doubt Stalin came here greedy to get what he could, but he is too shrewd to miss the change of heart in the American camp; he must see by now that Truman and the P.M. are going to act together. Things are not going to be as easy for him as they were in Roosevelt's time. Stalin has learnt to be cautious in a hard school, and it was plain yesterday that he is not going to take unnecessary chances. It appears that he set out to reassure the P.M. when they dined together last night, and from what Winston told me this morning he has lost none of his cunning. His opening remarks were well chosen to put the P.M. in a good humour.

'The Marshal was very amiable.' (The P.M. has used this word three times.) 'I gave him a box of my cigars, the big ones, you know. He smoked one of them for three hours. I touched on some delicate matters without any clouds appearing in the sky. He takes a very sensible line about the monarchy.'

'In what way?'

'Oh, he sees it binds the Empire together. He seemed surprised that the King had not come to Berlin.'

There was a long pause.

'I think Stalin wants me to win the election.'

From the P.M.'s comments it seems that Stalin deliberately set out to convince the P.M. that his intentions are entirely straight-forward. Up to a point I think he has succeeded. They talked together for five hours. Winston does not allow things to be drawn out like that unless they are going well and he is pleased with life.

'Stalin gave me his word there will be free elections in the countries set free by his armies. You are sceptical, Charles? I don't see why. We must listen to these Russians. They mobilized twelve million men, and nearly half of them were killed or are missing. I told Stalin Russia has been like a giant with his nostrils pinched. I was thinking of the narrows from the Baltic and the Black Sea. If they want to be a sea power, why not?'

When the P.M. coins a phrase that he finds pleasing he keeps repeating it.

Things must have been going pretty well when the P.M. agreed with Stalin that the Germans have no mind of their own.

'When I said they were like sheep Stalin told me a story of two hundred German Communists who remained rooted to a station platform for two hours because there was no one at the barrier to take their tickets.' The P.M. grinned. 'They never got to their meeting.'

'Stalin said that people in the West wondered what would happen when he died. It had all been arranged; he had brought up good people, ready to step into his shoes. Russian policy would not be changed if he died.'

The P.M. gazed at the carpet for a time.

'I think,' he said, 'that Stalin is trying to be as helpful as it is in him to be.'

After the second conference at five o'clock this afternoon the P.M. said:

'We had a good wrangle for three hours. I don't think Stalin was offended at what I said. He doesn't mind straight speaking. I felt reassured. Stalin, at the end of the meeting, said he saw our difficulties.

'He pressed the case against Franco. When,' said Winston, 'you come to a stony place, you adjourn. You have a conversation, carry it a certain distance, and then drop it. Because we don't like the ways of a particular country, it is no reason for interfering in its internal affairs. Otherwise you get into no end of difficulties; how can you condemn a state in its absence? We didn't want to hold a court of enquiry.'

The P.M. rose and went to his room. Peck[1] turned to Rowan: 'Was Joe impressive at the Conference?'

Rowan: 'Yes, he speaks in a very low voice, but he is very certain of himself. On the whole, he is probably better briefed than we are. There was a spot of trouble over Austria. Joe ascribed the delay in working out zones for the Allies to the fact that General Alexander put his oar in: he was not in command of the Russians. The P.M. replied warmly that no complaint had ever been made of the general. He would like any complaint in writing, when it would receive consideration. Stalin interposed that he was not speaking as a public prosecutor. All this time the Americans remained silent, taking no part. The P.M. said later that he had the distinct impression that Stalin was in retreat and was sorry that he had brought up the matter.

'The P.M. rebuked the President for not supporting him. America and Britain are in the same boat. Truman said he was not quick and apologized to the P.M. Afterwards the P.M. said that the President was all right if he had had time to consider a question, but when something came up which he had not thought about he was rather at a loss. After all, he had little experience of these conferences. He was very conscientious, and, when he thought he had not dealt properly with something, he could not sleep.'

Truman was not the only one to come under criticism today. Stalin rose at the banquet given by the President, and said: 'There is one toast in particular I wish to propose. I drink to the American Navy.' This little pinprick evidently stung the P.M. He said that of the six hundred U-boats sunk in the German war, the British had accounted for a far larger number than the American Navy; the proportion was four or five to one.

July 20, 1945

When I went to the P.M. this morning he began at once:

'The Russians are being very difficult. They talk about the same things as we do, freedom and justice and that sort of thing, but prominent people are removed and are not seen again. We are not even allowed to enter Vienna.'

Last night about eighty of their security people took possession of the President's house before Stalin arrived for dinner, and surrounded it almost shoulder to shoulder. Two fat Security Generals came, not to dine but to see that the watch over Stalin's life was not relaxed for one second.

[1] John Peck, Assistant Private Secretary to the Prime Minister.

In Stalin's brute cunning there is not a tincture of the sagacity that is nurtured on the lessons of the past. He has been at pains to still Winston's suspicions, and then, like a mule, with one vicious kick, he has demolished the structure so carefully built up, brick by brick. Perhaps he does not care. He must know that he holds all the trump cards.

The P.M. stretched himself wearily.

'I shall be glad when this election business is over. It hovers over me like a vulture of uncertainty in the sky.'

For three days the P.M. has been certain that Truman's firmness has changed everything. Stalin has been very fair and reasonable. Now Winston is less certain about things.

On leaving the P.M. I drove with Colonel Peter Wilson, who is in the map room, to visit the 11th Hussars at Spandau. They have taken over a German military barracks. They found the Russians had been in it. They had been there for four or five weeks with no water, and everything was filthy. Their men had reared wherever the spirit moved them; there were no latrines. The stink of the place made some of our men vomit. Before the Russians left they had stripped the place of everything, and what they didn't take away they smashed. The Colonel told me that the voting papers of the 11th Hussars had been lost in some inexplicable way. When this was explained to them, they said they wanted to vote again. In the first instance they had voted for the Socialists, but since they had met the Russians and seen what they had done, they wanted to vote Conservative. Another regiment did not vote at all. When asked why, they said that now that they knew something about the Russians, their views had altered.

The P.M. asked me to dine with him and the Edens. He warned me that Anthony had just had a telegram to say that his boy, who was missing, had been found dead by the wreckage of his plane. During dinner nothing was said of this. They talked until nearly midnight as if nothing had happened. I wondered if I could have behaved with the same quiet dignity immediately after hearing that my John had been killed.

July 21, 1945

I had gone to bed when a messenger knocked at the door: the P.M. would like to see me. I went down in a dressing-gown and found him with Anthony; they were standing with glasses of whisky in their hands, conducting a post-mortem into Stalin's dinner-party.

Winston: 'I thought the Russians were silent and not very forthcoming.'

277

Anthony: 'Oh, it went well, considering the row in the afternoon.[1] Anyway, I'm sure they were making an effort to be agreeable. This has been the President's best day so far.'

Winston, muttering: 'I thought the evening interminable.'

Last Wednesday Winston, dining alone with Stalin, was reluctant, after a five-hour sitting, to break up. 'Things,' he said, 'were really moving.' Tonight, however, was just part of the ritual; ceremony bores Winston, and unfortunately he shows it.

July 22, 1945

The P.M. woke in better form; his indigestion had gone. There was one moment when he complained that 'this bloody election' hung like a veil over the future. I didn't exactly help matters by asking if all these estimates of the majority had any substance.

'They are not guesses, Charles, but the most careful estimates which come from each constituency—and,' he added irritably, 'you ought to know it doesn't help to tell me I can't attach any weight to these people's advice. Besides, they all agree I shall have a majority, Conservatives and Labour people alike.'

Later he said: 'I had a most fruitful hour with the President. We not only talk the same language, we think the same thoughts.'

He turned to Anthony and asked him how the meeting of the Foreign Secretaries had gone. Anthony replied that no progress had been made. The P.M. seemed put out. His feeling that things had gone wrong came back. He said no more.

Tonight after dinner the P.M. sent for Walter Monckton[2] and asked him his view of the Russian attitude on reparations.

'The idea of Germany as a single unit has vanished. Instead, we have Russian Germany divided from British Germany by a line drawn by God knows whom, on no economic or historic grounds. What do you think of that?' said the P.M.

Monckton answered that he did not like it, but what was the alternative?

'The Russians,' the P.M. continued, 'have stripped their zone and want a rake-off from the British and American sectors as well. They will grind their zone, there will be unimaginable cruelties. It is indefensible, except on one ground: that there is no alternative.'

---

[1] The fifth meeting of the conference on July 21 had developed into an acrimonious dispute over the western boundary of Poland. The Poles had taken possession of East Prussia (a quarter of Germany's arable land), displacing more than 8 million Germans, whom we should have to feed. Stalin kept reiterating that at Yalta nothing had been agreed about the western frontier.

[2] Sir Walter Monckton, United Kingdom delegate, Allied Reparations Commission.

His voice was very grave.

'I prayed the Americans on my knees not to hand over to the Russians such a great chunk of Germany, at least until after the Conference. It would have been a bargaining counter. But they would not listen. The President dug in. I shall ask Stalin, does he want the whole world?'

The bargaining counters have gone. But that was not all. The P.M.'s health has so far deteriorated that he has no energy left to seize his opportunities. Bridges and Leslie Rowan tell me that a great deal depends here on Anthony, because the P.M. is not mastering his brief. He is too tired to prepare anything; he just deals with things as they come up. And he has, of course, quite a respectable excuse for dodging decisions. For he said at Hendaye that he would be only half a man until he knew the result of the election. In fact—he makes no bones about it—he intends to shelve the really big decisions until he knows what has happened at the poll. Moreover, I doubt if his heart is in this business. A profound study of the life of Marlborough has left him with a conviction that anything is better than discord among allies. Certainly at Moscow last year he seemed more concerned to keep Russia in step with the democracies than he was with the fate of the Poles.

Bridges agrees with me that the P.M.'s method of jocular bluntness is the right method of tackling Stalin. It is necessary to be rude in a measure. But when Winston has had the best of things in argument he sometimes does not seem to mind very much who gets the prize. Stalin's tenacity and obstinacy have no counterpart on our side. He knows exactly what he wants, and he does not mind how he gets it. He is very patient too and never loses his temper. Indeed, the Russians are courteous in conference. It is rather like a game of poker, with Joe trying to bring off a big bluff. Truman is like a Wesleyan minister who does not know anything about the game and is not very sure whether it is quite nice for him to play at all, but who is determined, if he does play, to make his full weight felt.

The P.M. predicted that the Germans in our zone will become increasingly pro-British; it will not so much be necessary to hold them down as to hold them back. Of course, we shall be charged with being pro-German.

'I am not frightened of that. The Labour Party won't mind; the Conservatives might, but I can deal with them. I am indispensable to them.'

July 23, 1945

When I went into the P.M.'s room this morning he was breakfasting. I found Sawyers mopping the table by the bed; the P.M. had upset his pineapple juice. Sawyers took a long time and the P.M. got impatient.

'That will do, Sawyers; you can do that later.'

But Sawyers went on mopping. At last the P.M. burst out:

'Oh, leave it, Sawyers, leave it. Come back later.'

Immediately Sawyers had left the room the P.M. turned to me with great solemnity:

'I am going to tell you something you must not tell to any human being. We have split the atom. The report of the great experiment has just come in. A bomb was let off in some wild spot in New Mexico. It was only a thirteen-pound bomb, but it made a crater half a mile across. People ten miles away lay with their feet towards the bomb; when it went off they rolled over and tried to look at the sky. But even with the darkest glasses it was impossible. It was the middle of the night, but it was as if seven suns had lit the earth; two hundred miles away the light could be seen. The bomb sent up smoke into the stratosphere.'

'It is H. G. Wells stuff,' I put in.

'Exactly,' the P.M. agreed. 'It is the Second Coming. The secret has been wrested from nature. The Americans spent £400 million on it. They built two cities. Not a soul knew what they were working at. All scientists have been busy with it. I have been very worried. We put the Americans on the bomb. We fired them by suggesting that it could be used in this war. We have an agreement with them. It gives the Americans the power to mould the world. It may displace fuel; a fragment gives 800 horse-power. If the Russians had got it, it would have been the end of civilization. Dropped on London, it would remove the City. It is to be used in Japan, on cities, not on armies. We thought it would be indecent to use it in Japan without telling the Russians, so they are to be told today. It has just come in time to save the world.'

I asked what would happen if the Russians got the idea and caught up. The P.M. replied that it was possible, but they wouldn't be able to do it for three years, and we must fix things up in that time. The Americans and ourselves, he said, were the only nations with principles.

I asked what would happen if Germany gets on to it. The P.M. said:

'They were working on it during the war, but—' with a smile, 'you can't produce this overnight; we shall find out their preparations. Fire was the first discovery; this is the second.'

I own I was deeply shocked by this ruthless decision to use the bomb on Japan. I knew I was hopelessly illogical. From bows and arrows to bullets, and shells, and gas-shells, and gas, to a torpedo which might send a thousand men to the bottom of the sea; and finally, to an atomic bomb; there could be no one point when the process of destruction becomes immoral. It was all to no purpose. There had been no moment in the whole war when things looked to me so black and desperate, and the future so hopeless. I knew enough of science to grasp that this was only the beginning, like the little bomb which fell outside my hut in the woods near Poperinghe in 1915, and made a hole in the ground the size of a wash-basin. It was not so much the morality of the thing, it was simply that the lynch-pin that had been underpinning the world had been half wrenched out. I thought of my boys.

Rowan came into the room and I found myself listening to his conversation with the P.M. as one hears the voices around when going under an anaesthetic, voices very far off and not like real people. I went out and wandered through empty rooms. I once slept in a house where there had been a murder. I feel like that here.

All day, preparations have gone on for the dinner tonight. The P.M. feels that he has discharged his duty as host if he provides plain good fare and gives his guests plenty of elbow room to get at it. The sappers have made a great table to seat twenty-eight, but how, he demands, do they know how many it will take? He will not, he insists, have more guests than the table will seat comfortably, even if he has to cancel some of the invitations already sent out; so six of us rather self-consciously sat in the chairs—Tommy was Stalin, and I stood for Pavlov—until at last the P.M. was satisfied that there was plenty of room for all. As it is, two Ministers, Lord Leathers and Lord Cherwell, not to mention the Solicitor General, Sir Walter Monckton, have been sacrificed to give elbow room to the rest.

Half an hour before the appointed hour fifteen of the OGPU[1] marched through the gate in single file, carrying their tommy-guns as if they were about to use them. They vanished to take up positions behind the house. And then came the three national leaders with their captains, who had survived the miscalculations of six years of world war.

I sat next to Admiral King.[2] By contrast with Marshall, who has been a steadfast friend of England, King has always been very

[1] The Russian organization for the investigation and combat of counter-revolutionary activities. Founded, 1922.
[2] Chief of American Naval Operations, 1942–5.

critical of us. His war is in the Pacific, and the conflict with Germany has been to him only a tiresome distraction. However, he made himself very pleasant to everyone and agreed that Britain and America were the only Powers in the world capable of disinterested action.

Innumerable speeches, as usual, punctuated the meal. The P.M. spoke of Truman in a happy little speech, and the President, in his reply, said that when he found himself chairman without any experience of these conferences he was almost overwhelmed. He felt very timid, but he hoped he had been fair, and he would try to be so in the future. When he sat down, Stalin got up at once and extolled Truman's modesty. This is an old trick of Stalin's to divide the democracies. He will not learn that the P.M. is jealous of no man, and that his generous temper is one of the graces of our time. While the P.M. was praising Truman, King whispered to me:

'Watch the President. This is all new to him, but he can take it. He is a more typical American than Roosevelt, and he will do a good job, not only for the United States but for the whole world.'

As the night went on the P.M. became more and more carefree, and it was in the most glowing terms that he spoke of Stalin, ending, as at Teheran, by calling him Stalin the Great. Then Stalin got up, and with a few perfunctory words of thanks—even in Russian his words rasped out as if he were impatient and rather contemptuous of this smooth stuff—went on to speak of Japan. He has usually got something at the back of his head, and tonight it was clear that it was Japan. Stalin said it would not be right to allow Britain and America to shed their blood there without help from the Soviet Union. When Stalin sat down the P.M. rose to propose a toast, but he did not refer to Stalin's speech. Rowan tells me that the P.M. is not really keen on Russia coming into the war with Japan because of the demands she will make on China; anyway, he isn't going to seem pressing.

At the end of dinner I noticed Stalin on his feet with a menu in his hand, collecting signatures. Winston growled, 'This means signing twenty-eight menus,' but for some reason all these hardened, sophisticated, wandering men began to take their menus round, and the P.M. himself sent Sawyers round with his. There was a shortage of fountain pens, and the consequent borrowing and general movement seemed to break the ice of formality and to generate a very friendly spirit. Brooke brought his card to me:

'You must sign when we have travelled together so many times.'

From anyone else that would mean little, but it is very unlike Brooke's reserved nature, with his dislike of gush, to make an observation of this kind. Anyway, his friendliness gave me pleasure, for as the years have passed I have come to respect his character, his complete integrity, his contempt for flattery, his indifference alike to praise and blame, and his great longing for peace. He said to me tonight:

'I have felt that every day of this war was taking off a month of my life.'

Stalin took his own menu around. At first he had been a little sticky; now he was smiling and most amiable. More than once he got up and walked into the next room, where the band of the Air Force was playing, and stood listening. 'Could they play something light?' he asked.

The P.M. put through a call to Max tonight and asked whether he still took the same view of the result of the election. Max replied that minor corrections might be necessary. The figure of a hundred was not sacrosanct, but, broadly speaking, he had not altered his estimate. The P.M. would have a comfortable majority. Winston invited Max to come to Downing Street on Thursday morning, when the results would be coming out, and to stay to lunch; Brendan was coming.

July 24, 1945

The P.M. went to visit the President in his tropical Air Force uniform, but the wind had gone round to the east, and he came back very cold and out of humour.

'I'm sick of the bloody Poles. I don't want to see them. Why can't Anthony talk to them? If I have to see them I shall tell them there is no support in western Europe for a puppet Polish state, the tool of Russia.

'Tommy,' the P.M. burst out irritably, 'I really think General Montgomery ought to do something about our water.'

(Since the main was torn by a falling tree we have had no water.)

'Can't they bring a water cart and fill the boiler from it by a hose?'

Tommy hadn't thought of this. The devilled chicken, too, was wrong; the P.M. doesn't like chicken 'messed about.'

Two very stiff whiskies and a brandy dispersed the black clouds, and at the end of luncheon he was all quips and smiles. 'Charles, will you transfer your services to Attlee?' I was driven to protest, but he held out his hand affectionately: 'Ah, my dear, I was only joking.' Presently he began to nod; it was more apparent to him than ever that it was Anthony's job to see the Poles. I pressed him to rest before the conference, which had been fixed for five o'clock. He asked if he might take a 'red.'

'I feel quite different,' the P.M. said when he awoke after a short sleep. Sawyers kept looking at his watch. 'You're going to be late, sir.'

After the conference I dined with Rowan; he was full of the P.M.'s tussle with Stalin. There had been a real set-to, and the P.M. had been superb. All the petulance and irritation, to which we are accustomed when the bath water is cold or the food is not to his liking, are shed when he comes to play a part in public. Like the boxer, he has learnt what happens when he loses his temper; long experience has taught him a kind of self-discipline in debate. He does not just blurt out the first thing that comes into his head.

Truman was firm, too. The Russians could not introduce their particular form of government into countries liberated directly or indirectly by all the Allies and then expect America and Britain to recognize those governments. This was his view today. It would be his view tomorrow. The P.M. said that in one country our representatives were restricted and shut in; it really amounted to internment. Stalin retorted that the P.M. was indulging in fairy-tales. The P.M. at once replied that it was one way of conducting a debate, to represent what the other side said as just a fairy-tale. Rowan said Vyshinsky was perspiring freely and was plainly unhappy. Birse, the interpreter, was sure that Vyshinsky was in for a real dressing-down from Stalin. The Russians were having a bad day. Stalin saw that they were getting nowhere, and said that their points of view were so different that the discussion must be adjourned for private debate.

Rowan said that the P.M. had asked him afterwards whether he had been too rough with the Russians.

'I told him he wasn't rough enough with them, at any rate when they talked about the Turks.'

In one afternoon the Russians had asked for a say in Algiers, a colony in North Africa and for the Dardanelles.

The P.M. has been helped by the atmosphere of this Conference, which is quite different from that of Teheran and of Yalta. There, Stalin was at pains to secure Roosevelt's backing. The President, without a word to the Prime Minister, would declare that the Russian case was most reasonable, and that it would have his support. What could Churchill do? But here, at Potsdam, it was soon plain that Roosevelt's death had changed everything. Truman is very blunt; he means business. His method is not to deploy an argument, but to state his conclusions. It reminds me of 'Wully' Robertson in the First War—'I've 'eard different.' The President is not going to be content to feed out of anyone's hand: he intends to get to the bottom of things, and when Stalin gets tough Truman at once makes it plain that he, too, can hand out the rough stuff. The Allies are not in the mood to do all the giving. It is even possible to speak critically of the Russians.

And the P.M., Rowan says, rubs his eyes to make sure that he is not dreaming, chortles, looks very pleased and is quick to give President Truman vigorous and measured support. And how adroit he is!

Tonight, when he was full of Truman's praises, the P.M. said:

'If only this had happened at Yalta.' There was a long pause. 'It is too late now,' he said sadly. He knows that the time to settle frontiers has gone. The Red Army is spreading over Europe. It will remain.

July 25, 1945

Winston told me this morning that he had had an unpleasant dream:

'I dreamed that life was over. I saw—it was very vivid—my dead body under a white sheet on a table in an empty room. I recognized my bare feet projecting from under the sheet. It was very life-like.' He mused: 'Perhaps this is the end.'

Chapter twenty-eight

The big blow

London, July 26, 1945

Today as I walked along Pall Mall to the College of Physicians, where I was lunching, I met Jock Colville. He said there had been a landslide 'like 1906.' Brendan, Harold Macmillan and other Ministers were out.

After the Comitia, when Fellows were having tea in the hall of the College, Dorothy brought me the three-o'clock results given on the wireless, which I read to them. They were so taken aback they stood there in complete silence. One Fellow so far forgot where he was as to emit a low whistle. A little later the four-o'clock results confirmed the rout.

I walked down to the Annexe. The P.M. was with Alan Lascelles; I wrote him a note. He sent out a message that he would like to see me. He was sitting in the small room next to the secretaries', where I had never seen him before, doing nothing. He was lost in a brown study. He looked up. 'Well, you know what has happened?' I spoke of the ingratitude of the people. 'Oh, no,' he answered at once, 'I wouldn't call it that. They have had a very hard time.'

I expressed my fears that it might end in Stalin's being given too much of his own way. But the P.M. replied that Attlee and Bevin would stand up to Stalin: 'I do not feel down at all. I'm not certain the Conservative Party could have dealt with the labour troubles that are coming. It will be said Max brought me down,' he mused, 'but I shall never say that. He is far harder hit by this result than any of us.'

I said what I could to comfort him: that there was great unrest in the country; that demobilization, housing and unemployment would add to it; and that it was inevitable that the Government in power would get the blame. I said that I had dreaded the next two years for him. I think this brought him a little comfort, but he said noth-

286

ing. At last he spoke. 'The public will be staggered when they hear tonight at nine o'clock that I've resigned. Labour will be in for four years at least. They may make it difficult for the Conservatives to come in again. But I think the financial consequences of their policy will be their undoing. This is not necessarily the end.'

I said that if he went abroad for health or other purpose I would like to go with him as I had done during the war, and that I should be hurt if he did not make use of me. He rose and thanked me for what I had done for him. 'If it hadn't been for you I might not be here now,' he said with tears in his eyes.

He blamed no one. He was very sad as he talked quietly about what had happened. I left him, for I did not want to add to his distress by showing my own feelings. For some time I have had a growing disquiet that he has lost touch with the way people are thinking; but I was not prepared for this debacle. I was so sure that we should return to Berlin that I left my luggage there. Now I must arrange for its recovery.

July 27, 1945

This morning, calling at the Annexe at 9.45, I found everything strangely quiet. The place seemed deserted. Sawyers told me before I went to his bedroom that Winston had been giddy before retiring. But when I went in he said at once: 'I'm very well.' He spoke very quietly; he was sad but quite composed. He had been 'stunned by the result.' He felt there was 'some disgrace in the size of the majority.' If it had been thirty or forty it would have been different. The soldiers had been noticeably cool when he opened the 'Winston Club' in Berlin. They had been told to cheer, but it was obvious that they had voted against him. The Army, he went on, had had a big say in these events. At his age there could be no question of a come-back. I asked him if he was going to take a holiday.

'There is no difficulty about holidays now,' he said with a wistful smile. 'The rest of my life will be holidays. It will be worse in three days, like a wound; I shall then realize what it means. What I shall miss is this'—pointing to the red box full of papers. 'It is a strange feeling, all power gone,' he mused. 'I had made all my plans; I feel I could have dealt with things better than anyone else. This is Labour's opportunity to bring in socialism, and they will take it. They will go very far.'

I asked him about his plans. He is going to Chequers tomorrow till Monday, when he will go to Chartwell. He rang for Tommy. When he came he did not say, 'I shall go to Chequers,' but, 'Would

287

it amuse you to come for the week-end?' I said to him there would be a reaction. 'Yes,' he agreed, 'it will begin now; they will lose by-elections.'

August 2, 1945

Went to Claridges after breakfast to see the P.M. For five years we have known him by no other name. I found him in the pent-house, on the sixth floor, with the sun streaming into his bedroom. It was very cheerful; but he said at once: 'I don't like sleeping near a precipice like that'—pointing to the balcony. 'I've no desire to quit the world,' he said with a grin, 'but thoughts, desperate thoughts come into the head.'

He spoke of his reception in the House yesterday when the Conservatives sang 'For he's a jolly good fellow.' 'There's no doubt about the solid support of the party. I've never been cheered like that at any time, and there was no victory to cheer.' Winston is strangely *naïf*. Of course the Party cling to him for self-preservation, like a lifebelt. After all, without him, what's left?

'America will not feel the same about Socialist Britain. Cripps tried to undo the impression Laski[1] had made. Attlee and Bevin and those who worked with me in the war will not allow chaos if they can help it; they are strong men. But there are grave dangers threatening our poor country. My indigestion is very troublesome. I've started my breathing exercises again.'

Yes, he had 'private worries.' He must see how he could live. He had had the most dazzling offers. For instance, twenty thousand pounds from *Time* and *Life* for four short articles; a pound a word.

'But it's no use. The Government would take it all. I'm not going to work when they take nineteen and six out of every pound I earn. I've taken a second "red" the last five nights. Does that matter? I take them when I wake in the night. If I don't, I begin to think, and then I can't get to sleep again. If Aneurin Bevan becomes Minister of Health, will there be private practice? Will you be able to look after me?'

He looked up at me like a puzzled child. At this point Mrs. Hill came in and asked if he would take a trunk call that he had put through to Lord Camrose.

August 8, 1945

It is a fortnight tomorrow since we heard. Winston has been very brave and gentle under the blow. Before it fell he did not see that the nation was no longer in the mood to accept everything he told

[1] Harold Laski, Chairman of the Labour Party, 1945–6.

them. The result of the General Election gave him back his sight. Once in the First War I stayed in a ruined farm with a wounded officer until he died. His life had not been careful, and his face had become fleshy. As the days followed one another and nothing but water passed his lips, his face became thinner and thinner, until at the end the features had regained the chiselled refinement of his youth. Since the election it has seemed to me that Winston has been purged of the frailties which have prevented so many of his immediate colleagues from fully accepting his greatness—and when you get beneath the self-indulgence which he has allowed himself throughout his life, there is a fine character, staunch and truthful, loyal and affectionate.

Now he has the more difficult task of swallowing the bitterness of second thoughts. When I called on him at Duncan Sandys's flat in Westminster Gardens I found him sitting in his silk vest on the edge of the bed, looking at the floor. I asked him how he was sleeping. He said he kept waking about four o'clock in the morning and had to take a 'red' to get to sleep, or 'futile speculations' filled his mind.

'It's no use, Charles, pretending I'm not hard hit. I can't school myself to do nothing for the rest of my life. It would have been better to have been killed in an aeroplane, or to have died like Roosevelt. After I left Potsdam, Joe did what he liked. The Russians' western frontier was allowed to advance, displacing another eight million poor devils. I'd not have agreed and the Americans would have backed me. I get fits of depression. You know how my days were filled; now it has all gone. I go to bed about twelve o'clock. There is nothing to sit up for. What is that knocking? Will it go on all day? I can no longer stop it at will.'

He hates whistling, or the sound of knocking, and someone used to rush off to silence the blasphemous sounds. I asked him once more about his plans. He wanted to get back to Chartwell. He had got his paints out. He thought he might go to the south of France about the first week in September; it was all under Eisenhower's command. Ike would be glad to let him stay there indefinitely. Perhaps he wouldn't come home until the autumn session. He'd leave that to Eden. 'If I'm ill you could fly out.' With a wry smile, 'I think the Government would arrange that for me.' Sawyers came into the room; Winston waited until he went out.

'They want me to go to Australia and New Zealand, but I haven't the heart or strength or life for it. They keep offering me the freedom of places, but I won't bother.' Under his breath he muttered something about ingratitude. 'If Eisenhower will have me, I think I'll go to the Riviera. I don't mind if I never see England again.

Ah, Charles, blessings become curses. You kept me alive and now——'

He turned his back, and when he looked at me his eyes were full of tears.

August 15, 1945

Dorothy and I went to the Lords to hear the King's Speech. Hamar Greenwood[1] said to me that there was no fall comparable to the fall of a Cabinet Minister: at one moment exercising great power, at the next a nonentity. 'There's Sam Hoare,[2] he's very disgruntled; he feels he was bundled away to Madrid for five years and ought to have been made Viceroy of India and a Marquis. You'd be surprised,' Greenwood rattled on, 'how many members of this House began either as merchants in the City (they provided the money and financed armies) or as members of the legal fraternity. These people are intensely interested in the cut and thrust of the competitive life, the drama of the struggle for power and wealth. It is quite a different world from the scientific life or the life of the professions.'

August 23, 1945

Called on Winston at Westminster Gardens. He was in quite good form. Mrs. Hill tells me he is much rested. But he said: 'It has been a horrible experience. When I left St. Paul's on Sunday there was a lot of cheering. No Minister got any. But what's the good of it all? I don't know where I stand with the public. I have not even ceased to reproach myself for wasting time whenever I play a game of cards. I find I do not want to sleep in the afternoon now. You ought to put your mind to that and what it means. I needed the afternoon sleep then; I don't seem to now. I am very happy at Chartwell. I can paint for three or four hours without getting tired. I'm just touching up old pictures, a new sky perhaps. Yes, I was standing all the time. I think I must get some sort of high stool so that I can paint sitting. I am going to Italy—to Alex—on the first of September.'

August 26, 1945

I read today a letter of Chekhov: 'There is a sort of stagnation in my soul. I explain it by the stagnation of my own personal life. I am not disappointed. I am not tired. I am not depressed, but simply everything has become less interesting.' I feel like that.

[1] Viscount Greenwood, former Conservative Minister.
[2] Viscount Templewood, Ambassador to Madrid, 1940–4.

Chapter twenty-nine

The beginning of convalescence

September 1, 1945

Winant telephoned to me in his pleasant, diffident way: 'Would you like to help me?'

It was not Winant but Sarah Churchill who needed help. She may have some difficulty, it is thought, in getting leave from the Air Force to go with her father to Italy. Winston would be away a month, and it would help if I said that she ought to go to look after him. I was not sure whether Winston would like his health used as a pretext, and, as Sarah shared my doubts, Winant in the end agreed that it would be better to apply for leave on other grounds. Winston has never had any compunction about taking Mary or Sarah away from their units to accompany him on his travels—nor did he ever hesitate to ask the captain of a battleship, or an Army chieftain, to put them up. His word was law then, none dared to dispute it. But now that he has come down in the world they have to ask for leave like any other member of the Forces. There is hurt enough in his change of fortune without this. I telephoned to Clemmie and asked her if Winston was quite happy going off to Italy without me. She said at once she was sure he was, that he was very well and I need not worry. But after I had gone to bed I was awakened by the telephone bell. It was Clemmie; she had told Winston what I had said, and he had rather jumped at the idea that I should go with him; it would, she said, be a great comfort to her too.

September 2, 1945

We left Northolt this morning in Alex's Dakota and arrived at Milan after a flight of five and a half hours. All the time Winston remained buried in a printed copy of the minutes which for five years he had sent out month by month to the Chiefs of Staff and the Cabinet. Even during luncheon he went on reading, only taking his eyes from the script to light a cigar. I drove with him to the house on Lake Como that had been prepared for him.

'People say my speeches after Dunkirk were the thing. That was only a part, not the chief part,' he complained. 'They forget I made all the main military decisions. You'd like to read my minutes, Charles.'

I asked him had they worn well. He smiled comfortably.

'They are mine. I can publish them.'

He was still going over the minutes in his head.

'Brookie was covering the retreat to Dunkirk with three divisions; Bulgey Thorne, commanding one of them, suddenly found himself faced with a large number of tanks, and thought to himself: This isn't too good, it may go hard with our fellows. Then the tanks had suddenly disappeared; they had gone to finish off Calais. I had given orders to the Calais garrison to fight to the last man, to give time for the troops to embark at Dunkirk. This saved the situation. Calais made the evacuation at Dunkirk possible.'

Winston's face became set and resolute as he followed the drama.

'If Calais had surrendered, those tanks and the troops around Calais would have turned on our men retreating to Dunkirk, and they would probably never have got away. It was my decision. When I made it I had a feeling I was going to be sick.'

He stopped and turned to me.

'Tell me, Charles, how does emotion stop the stomach digesting?'

Winston continued:

'At one time I thought we should be lucky if forty thousand men got away. Next morning my price went up. The small boats taking away our army; it is an epic tale.'

Winston lisped as he followed the men down the beaches into the water until, breast-high, they stretched out to sea, like a black pier under the gathering night.

Major Ogier, the officer from the 4th Hussars, sent to meet us at the airfield, had been at Dunkirk, and during dinner Winston questioned him closely. He wanted detail, facts.

'What took you off the beach?'

'A destroyer, sir.'

'How long were you on the beaches?' Winston persisted.

After two days a destroyer had sent boats to take them off and finally landed them at Ramsgate. Next morning they found themselves at Bristol with a great crowd of other units, but every single man had eggs and bacon for breakfast. As Ogier talked, Winston nodded vigorously and began to speak of 'the magic carpet' by which

292

this great host was collected from Dunkirk and distributed, overnight as it were, all over the country.

I made him tell again how he called his Ministers to his room at the House of Commons and told them how the fate of the Army in France was in the balance. 'But even if things come out against us, if not a man returns, we shall fight on. At that at least half of them jumped up from the table and came running to my chair and patted my back.' It was like that in 1940.

When he talks of the deliverance of Dunkirk, Winston has the invasion at the back of his mind. 'It was my job,' he said, 'to keep the Germans out.' He had, in fact, good reason to be exhilarated and uplifted by the Army's escape.

'Dunkirk was a turning-point. In a month after their return to England these men became a formidable army. It was one thing to plan an invasion of England before Dunkirk, with a hundred thousand men; quite another when perhaps half a million would be needed to break down the defences of this army.'

We were sitting on the balcony after dinner looking across the lake at the lights twinkling out of the darkness. It brought back to me the Embassy lawn at Cairo and the talks with Smuts. I said so. There was no response. Then after a long pause Winston murmured:

'Smuts sent me two heartfelt telegrams after the election, but I haven't answered them.' A pause. 'I was offended by the telegram he sent Attlee about his "brilliant victory." Brilliant indeed.' His voice rose. 'If he had just congratulated him on his victory it would have been different. Why brilliant?' The word stuck in his gorge. 'It wasn't brilliant at all.'

He looked across the lake for a long time in silence.

To turn his thoughts I asked him about Portal's future.

'If I'd gone on I'd have made him a Governor-General. He has everything which is needed. But what is the use of all these ifs?' he said impatiently.

The conversation lapsed again. His cigar smoke went straight up. I watched it vanish.

'I have a very difficult time ahead,' he said half to himself.

I said I hoped he'd write and give politics a rest. He replied that he wasn't in the mood for writing. 'Besides,' with a smile, 'I shan't write while the Government take all you earn. Dr. Johnson said that only a fool wrote when he wasn't paid for writing.'

He reverted to the election. He had hesitated for a long time whether to wait until the autumn, as the Labour Party had suggested. It was discussed by the Cabinet, but most of them felt it would be difficult to go on with the Labour Ministers undermining everything that was done.

'But,' Winston added, 'Hudson[1] didn't agree. I remember he interjected from the far end of the table that he didn't think the Prime Minister ought to be pressed when he was so reluctant. I believe, too, he was thinking of the harvest. Of course, the autumn would have paid us, as things turned out. The Jap war would have been over and I should have had another six months. I enjoyed it so much,' he added half to himself; but he went on: 'We have had some luck too.'

I tried again to turn the conversation. 'Will Russia be a nuisance in the future?' I asked him.

He answered: 'Russia has altered her tune since the atomic bomb. She sees she can't just do what she likes with the world.'[2]

He got up and went in. In the first room he entered there was a great glass bowl which became a fountain when it was inverted. He sat down and watched it. In his soft black hat, dark overcoat, white duck trousers and bedroom slippers, he made a strange picture as he gazed at the bowl.

'Marvellous,' he muttered. 'Turn it on again. I really call it remarkable.'

At last he went to bed.

September 3, 1945

We had planned to set out about ten o'clock to reconnoitre the surrounding country for a scene which Winston could paint; however, it was noon before we set off. As we drove by the lake, he kept his eyes open for running water, or a building with shadows playing on it, but we stopped for a picnic lunch before he had found what he wanted. The 'picnic' arrived in a covered shooting brake with his chair and a small table. A score of Italian peasants gathered in a circle and watched us eat. He was in high spirits.

'The greatest change in my condition that I notice is that I need do nothing I don't want to. I need not get up if I don't want to, and yet the days seem to pass speedily by.'

He went on with a whimsical look,

[1] R. S. Hudson, Minister of Agriculture and Fisheries.

[2] Two atomic bombs were dropped on Japan, the first on Hiroshima on August 6, 1945, and the second on Nagasaki, three days later. The Japanese offered to surrender on August 10, thus preventing the need for an Allied invasion and the presence of Russian troops. Russia did not declare war on Japan until a few days before the capitulation.

'The world is so full of a number of things
I'm sure we should all be as happy as kings.'

When he was satisfied that he had found something he could put
on canvas, he sat solidly for five hours, brush in hand, only pausing
from time to time to lift his sombrero and mop his brow. When
he had done, I could only hope that he would come to no harm as he
drove in an open car through the chilly night air, while he nursed
his hat.

After dinner Winston was ready to talk of anything; he only mentioned the election once. Duff Cooper, he said, had a devil of a temper. When he got into gear his veins stood out, he looked as though
he was about to have a seizure. Once someone told Duff that he was
the worst Secretary for War in living memory. 'How dare you say
that?' Duff had hissed. 'How dare you say that,' he had repeated
with intense passion, 'in the presence of Jack Seely?' [1] Winston
made guttural sounds as he savoured the full humour of Duff's remark. He did not want anyone to miss the point, 'You see,' he
added, 'Seely was there.' At that he gave a great yawn; when we
thought he was about to go to bed he broke into a hymn and sang
three verses of 'Art thou weary.'

September 4, 1945

All morning Winston has been immersed in his minutes. He has
not looked at them for a long time; now he wants to know how he
comes out of it all. When you go into his bedroom he looks up, but
he does not put down his bound copy. It is as if he was saying: 'Yes,
yes, but I'm very interested. Could you return?' He is finding his
role of prophet, as painted in these telegrams and minutes, very
reassuring and gratifying.

Luncheon was put forward to 12.45, and when it was over
Winston went off in a motor launch to a spot which he had chosen
the day before. I did not go with him, and I had just come into
the house, after bathing in the lake, when an officer arrived. He
was, he explained, the C.O. of the 4th Hussars. He had obviously come to stay. I told him Winston was out. We talked in a
desultory way for a time. He was a typical cavalry soldier of the old
kind, very conscious of the fabric of English society and of the anatomy of the horse. He had driven four hundred and fifty miles from
Austria in two days to meet Winston. Yesterday his chauffeur had
driven him over a bank with a ten-foot drop while they were

[1] Secretary of State for War, 1912–14.

travelling at fifty miles an hour. The car had turned a somersault, but no one was hurt save his batman, who had a cut on the chin. The Colonel did not seem put out at all by this experience. He had found me writing, and he was plainly anxious not to get in the way. I could find no servants. They were, I think, asleep. When at last we had discovered his room he retired, to emerge later in a very smart gabardine uniform. He was keyed up for the meeting with the P.M. Winston, he said, had once invited him to dine at No. 10. On four occasions the P.M. had inspected the Regiment during the war. No other Colonel had such a record. About 8.15, as we stood gazing down over the terrace to the lake, the launch came in sight. The Colonel smoothed his hair. Far below us we could see Winston landing; we watched him walk slowly up a path till he disappeared from view, down some steps which led to a lift that saved the climb to the house. Suddenly, while we were talking, Winston entered the room. He walked up to the Colonel, who instinctively stood to attention.

'Your name?' he asked, with a conciliatory smile.

I was sorry for the Colonel. He was disappointed, of course, that Winston had forgotten he was coming, but, after all, he knew that he had many things on his mind. What he could not understand was that Winston had failed to recognize him.

Winston took a canvas from Ogier and planted it where he thought the light was good. Standing back he gazed at his work:

'There is too much cloud, but they are flocculent. Oh, I haven't finished the water. I agree. There's no light in it at present. I'm not ashamed of it,' he said. 'I'm delighted I can make pictures after six years. I'm entirely concentrated on painting. I don't want to discuss anything else.'

Then Winston strode upstairs as if the Colonel was done with. But during dinner the four-hundred-and-fifty-mile drive and the somersault came out. Winston was interested and even touched by this odyssey.

'You mean to say you have come all that way to see me, and risked your life in this accident?'

The situation was entirely retrieved. The Colonel became one of the family. Winston told how his regiment had set out to win the regimental polo; he said that he had allowed no mere military considerations to interfere with that ambition. It had seemed more important to him than anything in his life, more exciting than anything in the war. The Colonel followed every word of this confession with affectionate pride. If it had been possible, Winston would have risen in his estimation; that this great man should attach the same importance to horsemanship as he had always done gave him a comfortable feeling of reassurance. Winston turned to me:

'He's like Alex, don't you think?'

The Colonel and the C.O. were in full accord.

Two canvases had been propped against the wall near Winston's chair, where he could contemplate their points. He kept turning to them, nursing his head as he planned improvements.

'I'm sorry I cannot draw. You must have it in you and start young to draw faces. I wish I could.'

Sarah had risen to look at the pictures from another angle. He gazed at her slender form clad in a dark dress with a long skirt.

'Why do men let women wear short skirts?' he questioned. 'Look at the toe just peeping out from the skirt. You shall sit for me for half an hour tomorrow, Sarah.'

He continued gazing at her, weighing how he would put her on the canvas. 'Don't break up the party,' he appealed to Sarah, who was moving about the room. And then for ten minutes on end he gave an epitome of Robert Graves's *The Golden Fleece*. Graves sent him all his books, and he had read the lot.

'He gets the atmosphere. Hercules is a real figure.' Then he summarized the book. 'It's not easy going at first, but you can't leave it alone till it's finished. That is the triumph for a book. While the war lasted I could only read a page at a time. Now it is different. I can get on with a book. What about a little music?' he demanded of Ogier. 'The Volga Boating Song? What's that, I can't give it a name, but it's an old friend, "Humoresque"? Well, anyway, let's have it again. Now, what about the "Blue Danube" once more? Do you remember, Charles, we had that with Uncle Joe in that film at the Kremlin?'

September 5, 1945

In a sense Winston is tough, yet he is hardly ever out of my hands. His eyes, his ears, his throat, his heart and lungs, his digestion and his diverticulitis have given him trouble at different times. Some little thing goes wrong and apprehension and impatience do the rest. And if his doctor cannot bring relief, well, he ought to. This morning he sent for me. He had discovered a swelling in his groin. He was keyed up and waited anxiously while I made my examination. When I told him he was ruptured he seemed relieved it wasn't anything worse, but he immediately fired at me a stream of questions. Was an operation necessary? Would it become strangulated? Would it get worse? How long would it be before he got used to a truss? Why should he get a rupture at his age, when he hardly took any exercise? Brigadier Edwards, the consulting surgeon for the Army in Italy, said he would get him a truss in Milan, and now all is set fair again. Besides, Winston has been painting well today, so tonight he is all smiles.

Then a soldier who had recently returned from Vienna gave a sombre account of that city under the Russians. Winston listened in gloomy silence.

When I went to his room to settle him for the night he was reading his minutes. The war was over, he was out of it all, but as he read his mind went back to the great crises when everything was at stake. He lived again the Battle of Britain. Though it was after midnight he made me sit down. 'You see, Charles, it was very nearly the end of everything.'

I have heard him tell this story many times. He always picked the same day, September 15, when he went to Fighter Command at Uxbridge. Winston sees everything in pictures. I could feel the tension in the operation room, fifty feet underground. I could see Park[1] walking up and down giving his orders. And then, as more of our fighting squadrons were put in, more of the little electric bulbs on the great blackboard glowed red. All the bulbs were red now, all our squadrons were in the air. Park was standing still. At last, unable to control himself, the P.M. turned to him: 'How many more have you got?' 'I am putting in my last,' Park replied. The two men waited, but nothing happened. The Germans, too, had put in their last. As the P.M. climbed the stairway the All Clear sounded.

When he got to Chequers he went straight to his room, where he slept for nearly four hours. This was reported to me. It had never happened before. They were uneasy. Perhaps he was not well. Next morning I asked the P.M. if he felt 'all-in' when he left Park. When he did not answer, I asked him how Park was standing up to the strain. He looked blankly at me; he had not thought about him. The fate of individuals mattered no longer. I suppose you come to think like that when you carry his burden of responsibility.

When I left Winston I wrote:

'This is worse than the Somme. In Trones Wood I remember a man saying, "There won't be many good fellows left when this business is over." The chance of coming through seemed small. But we were all in it, part of the show. Now one is only a miserable spectator. Every day the missing mount up; men who might have gone a long way in life, and perhaps done something memorable. I cannot get

[1] Air Vice-Marshal Keith Park, Commander of No. 11 Fighter Group.

these pilots out of my mind. We simply cannot afford to go on using up the pick of our people like this. The First War bled the country white, and here we are, at it again.'

September 6, 1945

We have been six days without a single letter, telegram or newspaper; they seem to get held up at Naples. If this had happened in the old days, what a terrific uproar Winston would have made! Telegrams would have been sent off, peremptory orders flashed back, abashed officials would have read, 'I will not be treated like this.' Now he hardly seems to have noticed the absence of news for, as he confessed tonight, he had found the solution of his troubles in his paint-box, just as he had thirty years ago when he was thrown out over the Dardanelles.[1]

In adversity Winston becomes gentle, patient and brave; always magnanimous to his enemies, he is content if he is justified by the event. But when the sun shines his arrogance, intolerance and cocksureness assume alarming proportions. At Hendaye, before the blow had fallen, hardly a day passed without some rather childish outburst of petulance, whereas nothing of the kind has marred the even serenity of these autumnal days. However, his sanguine spirit will not let him accept defeat for long, and it is plain from his conversation that he has made up his mind to cut his losses. He will not spend the rest of his days brooding on the past. Whatever happens, nothing can hold up for long the stream of ideas that rush bubbling through his head. And if his thoughts keep turning to the past, it is not to the election, which he scarcely mentions, but to the war and the tremendous events of those 'wonderful years.' All his life, he has come to believe, was but a preparation for that epic struggle—the grand climacteric of his career—and naturally the chief actors in that drama are much in his mind.

Particularly Stalin; for in Winston's imagination he is already one of the great figures of history. On the other hand, apart from some passing tribute to Roosevelt, he seldom seems to allude to him in his conversation. In Washington, perhaps for a week or more, Winston would immure himself in the White House, where he would talk to the President for hours at a time, but he never tells us of Roosevelt's views, nor are we regaled by what he said, or by stories

[1] The failure of the Dardanelles campaign in 1915 had serious political repercussions. Before the evacuation had been decided, Asquith's Liberal administration was superseded by his Coalition Government. Churchill, the chief architect of the venture, resigned from the Cabinet and went to France to command an infantry battalion.

about him. The cast of Roosevelt's mind—I am thinking of his preoccupation with social problems and the rights of the common man—struck no sparks in Winston's mind. The war was all they had in common. Whereas Stalin was a type Winston had not met before; he interested him, notwithstanding his deliberate rudeness and his rough speech. 'In spite of everything I'd like that man to like me.' They are Winston's own words, addressed to us in August, 1942, and they explain much that is otherwise obscure. Stalin's stories, his ways, his habits, kept leaking out in Winston's talk; the man had caught his imagination, so that the P.M. had looked forward to the meetings in the Kremlin. Tonight he told us of a conversation with Stalin that I had not heard before. It was late at night, after Winston had dined in the Marshal's private apartments. Stalin asked: 'Why are you afraid of us Russians? You need not be. We have no intention of conquering the world—though we could if we wished,' he added. Uncle Joe had never been so frank before.

'You see,' Winston said, 'we'd both had a good deal to drink. I wanted to say to Stalin, "Don't you be too sure. Ribbentrop said something of the sort to me before the war. But England is a curious country. We have a way of finding the world on our side, and the world is a big place." But everything had to be translated, and before I could say what I wanted to say, Stalin had gone on to speak of something else. Stalin had never been so candid before. The American armies were vanishing, ours were dwindling, there seemed nothing to stop the Russian armies marching where they pleased. And then the atomic bomb altered all that.'

September 7, 1945

Winston had already chosen a spot where a great willow cast its shadow over the placid lake and in the background a small yellow building caught the sunlight; and it was there this morning, armed with paints, brushes and canvases, that he took Alex. They talked of paints; Alex preferred to make his own greens; Winston spoke of the 'sombre, sepulchral finality of black.' Alex painted for three hours, then we came back in the motor-boat, leaving Winston still at work.

Later Alex asked how de Gaulle had fared in America. Truman, it would seem, was not prepared to be very friendly, but de Gaulle had for once played his cards well and appeared to have got on well with him.

When Winston had gone to bed Alex said he had been very happy to have him as his guest.

'He has done a lot for me, and now it is particularly nice to be able to do something for him when he cannot possibly do anything more for me.'

September 8, 1945

Golfed in the morning and got back a little late for luncheon, but in time to hear Winston on the Boer War. Alex asked him about Buller. Was he a good General? Winston hedged. But he went on to tell how they had secured an important height and Buller was urged to pursue the beaten foe. 'Pursuit be damned,' Buller said with emphasis: 'Why, we wanted this place badly, and if we pursue they may return.' Somebody asked him if a few squadrons of cavalry might follow, and Buller grudgingly agreed; Winston went with them, to meet the starving defenders of Ladysmith. We heard once more how Lord Granard had made Buller promise that if he ever went on a campaign he would take him with him. Granard had great wealth. He picked some of his very best champagne, and to ensure that it was not stolen, labelled each of the six cases 'castor oil.' When it did not arrive, Granard grew anxious and telephoned to the base. Enquiries were made and the answer came back: 'Cases cannot be traced. Probably used in hospitals, but am sending six similar cases.'

After luncheon Alex departed. As he drove away, Winston stood on the doorstep, waving after the retreating car and shouting: 'Remember Friday. Don't forget. Do try and come.' A smiling Alex waved back, gracious but noncommittal. So tonight we are a family party, Winston, Sarah and I, with Ogier and the officer in charge of the guard. In the old days I should have been fearful lest he should be bored, but everything is different now. As he says, he has not been so happy for a long time. Of course there had been high moments of glorious exultation after some victory, but they did not last.

This quiet, serene content is something new. That it is more than a passing phase of his convalescence I can hardly credit, for Winston is not built on these lines. Nevertheless, Winston told me today:

'With my painting I have recovered my balance. I'm damned glad now to be out of it.'

He looked for a long time across the lake, and then he added:

'I shall paint for the rest of my days. I've never painted so well before. The papers seem to bore me; I just glance at them.'

The pictures were placed where he could gaze at them as he dined. I told him a story—always a foolhardy thing to do. He listened, but his eyes were on the pictures.

'That new colour they found in Milan is wonderful. I've got it in the roofs of the houses.'

After dinner he asked for gramophone records. Ogier, who is musical, put on Edward German's *Merrie England*, but he would have none of it.

'Dreadful,' he exclaimed. 'Give me something with a tune in it.'

Then he began to waltz with Sarah. He went round for quite a long time, with a mischievous twinkle and half-suppressed smile.

'You boys, do you dance?'

Tim, who is in charge of the Guard, had gone straight from school into the Army. He didn't dance.

'When I was young,' Winston continued, 'I didn't either. It was a great mistake.'

He began to recite from *Childe Harold*. He spoke about Byron's life, but his mind is not really analytical. He never says anything about people which throws new light on them; he only tells me what they did on such and such an occasion. He spoke of Macaulay's orations as having been the greatest inspiration of his life and quoted a few tags.

And then he gave us a tremendous chunk of Pope, to whom he generally turns when I begin to quote the things I love and best remember. His face was pink, his eyes twinkled, he was a child again, radiantly happy. It was nearly two o'clock before he went to bed.

September 9, 1945

A wet day, and Winston has had to fall back once more on touching up his canvases in his bathroom, which is also his studio. When I went to his room in the late afternoon I found him in a sombre mood.

'I am very depressed,' he said; 'The papers'—pointing to a lot of newspapers littering his bed.

At that moment Sawyers came into the room and he said no more. Sarah told me later the Press had got into the house he has bought in Hyde Park Gate,[1] and, finding it was being redecorated in a manner denied to lesser folk, had made a song about it. All his good spirits seemed to have evaporated. He sighed heavily, sitting on the edge of the bed as if he was too exhausted to rise and dress. But during dinner he began to recover his morale. The flies were troublesome. He rose from the table with a mischievous glint in his eyes; then, biting his lip as if he was about to spring on some animal, he raised

---

[1] 28 Hyde Park Gate, Churchill's London house.

his napkin and for a moment stood poised, ready to strike, before with a smack he destroyed a fly on the wall. Soon, armed with our napkins, we joined in the assault. Every time a fly fell dead its corpse was placed on the table, until there were thirty dead flies laid out in a line.

The records were brought out; the 'Blue Danube' reappeared. Winston led Sarah on to a space which Ogier had cleared, and they gravely waltzed round the small area.

Then Winston had an idea. On the wall there was a picture representing a lake and its wooded shore. There was no light in the picture. Winston would repair its artistic shortcomings. But the picture had been let into the wall. At Winston's suggestion, Ogier got up on a chair and finally, as the plaster fell on the floor, the picture in its frame was wrenched from its socket in the wall. Then Ogier prised open the glass which covered the painting, and Winston, seizing the panel, bore it in triumph to his bathroom. Sarah had doubts about this assault on the property of the absent steel magnate; it was just doing damage for the fun of the thing, the kind of thing the Russians and Germans do. With a little encouragement from me, she hurried after her father to lodge her protest. It was waved aside. Winston was already busy with his brushes. It was after midnight; there was no more to be done, so I went to bed.

In the morning Sarah told me how the picture had been transformed; a sunset had been introduced, while the water gave him a chance to use the new paint which lit up whatever it touched. It was great fun, she said, forgetting her first reaction. But second thoughts often come to Winston's rescue. He isn't one of those people who instinctively do the right thing. On the contrary, he often does something foolish, but long experience has taught him a little caution. It occurred to him now that if people heard of this exploit it might be used against him even more effectively than the decorating of his new house. With turpentine he proceeded to remove every trace of the painting which he had superimposed on the dull, lifeless composition; the picture was secured again in its socket in the wall, and, except for a few small white holes on the light-green wall, where plaster had fallen, no one will suspect the assault.

September 10, 1945

Winston came back from painting, a little down because it had not come off. He began dinner in a subdued mood. The biggest blunder in his life had been the return to the gold standard. Montague Norman[1] had spread his blandishments before him till it was done,

[1] Governor of the Bank of England, 1920–44.

and had then left him severely alone. He had married a distant
relative of Winston's, 'a good looker, who was too good for him.
Norman wanted a viscounty, and when he was given only a barony
he was quite sulky for a time and didn't go near Clemmie at the opening of Parliament.'

Gradually Winston's spirits revived. He spoke of Ireland. He
thought if he had gone on he would have been able to bring her back
into the fold. Anyway, as far as he was concerned, there would
always be a candle burning in the window for the wandering
daughter.

September 13, 1945

A slight relapse in morale this morning. The election is again in
his thoughts. Perhaps it is the weather; anyway, Winston has kept
to his room all day, painting in the bathroom. The arrival of Montag,
who represents Switzerland in Paris as Fine Arts Commissioner,
helped to dispel the gloom. Winston has asked him to stay for a few
days, and hopes that Montag will give him a few tips about painting.
Montag, if he did not arrive laden with spices, came with a lot of
beautiful brushes and twenty small boxes, each containing four or
five tubes of paint. Winston said it must have cost his visitor sixty or
seventy pounds. He was like a child, squeezing out a little paint
from each tube, one after the other, on to his finger-tip, to savour the
colour. After dinner Montag talked a great deal: his theme was that
the decadence and fall of a nation can be predicted by the state of its
art. Winston has seen too much of the world to take such a thesis
very seriously.

Before he went to bed there was a message from Alex that his days
are so full that he is sorry he cannot pay us a second visit.

Winston spoke of the chivalry of war. It was to be found in the
best units of the German Army. He turned to Ogier:

'You must have seen it?'

Ogier agreed he had. Winston leaned towards him, curious and
interested.

'Tell me about it.'

He wanted concrete instances to sustain the faith that was in him.
But Ogier gave none. He simply said that the SS had destroyed
chivalry. Winston was disappointed. He told about a tank which
had done a fine bit of work, but was at last compelled to surrender,
and spoke with admiration of the chivalrous behaviour of the Germans. His eyes filled with tears when he said that the warriors of the
Middle Ages would have been horrified at things we had done. Two
officers of the Naval Division saw some German tanks approaching

over a flat space, at least two thousand yards in width. Our troops had only just arrived at the spot. There had been no time to arrange for artillery support. The two officers got out of the trench and walked towards the German tanks. They had to cross a thousand yards of level ground. They had only pistols and ten Mills grenades. The Germans disdained to waste their fire on two men, who perhaps were merely coming to surrender. The two men were allowed to approach until it was too late for the tanks to fire on them. They threw grenades into both tanks, where they exploded. Out came four scientists in white coats, with their hands up. The officers just shot them; they had not come all that way for nothing.

'Terrible things are done in war,' Winston added reflectively.

Chapter thirty

A year of recovery

London, January 4, 1946

When a man is in the seventies, he throws off the effects of a surgical operation very slowly, very imperfectly. He appears to recover, but things are not the same as they were, and in the end his life may be shortened. The result of the General Election last summer left a mark on Winston which I can only liken to the scar of a major operation. It is true that he came safely out of hospital and went abroad for a period of convalescence, and that now he has come back ready for work. But it is a different Winston. The supreme self-confidence of the war years has been undermined, something of the old *élan* has evaporated. The wound appears to have healed, but there is left an ugly scar.

Winston—incredible as it may seem—is out of a job, looking for something to do, anything to keep his mind away from the past. He asked me this morning if I would be prepared to issue something to the Press which could be used both in America and in England.

'There are lots of flies buzzing round this old decaying carcass. I want something to keep them away. I want sun, solitude, serenity and something to eat'—a pause and then a grin—'and perhaps something to drink.'

But what he really wants is something quite different. Looking up at me, he said:

'I think I can be of some use over there; they will take things from me. It may be that Congress will ask me to address them. I'd like that. Our Parliament can't. I'm a controversial figure, but they might. It's a funny position. I feel I could do things and there's nothing to be done. I'll go to Florida, avoiding New York; it's too cold there at present to go through the streets with one's hat off.'

And on top of this gnawing sense of frustration the humiliations of old age vex him. Not that the old man is impatient or unreasonable; he is in fact much more gentle these days.

He murmured something about his gratitude for all the trouble that had been taken, and then, just as I was leaving, he asked me about his eyes. When they began to bother him he had been told that ingrowing eyelashes were acting as a mechanical irritant and were the cause of his conjunctivitis. At first he found satisfaction in this diagnosis, and relief when they were removed. But at Yalta he had burst out:

'My eyes are no better, there must be something else causing the trouble. Surely it should not be beyond the resources of medicine to get to the bottom of this conjunctivitis.'

So, on our return, Whiting [1] was called in consultation. He came armed with a kind of telescope which threw a powerful light on the P.M.'s eyes, making the smaller lashes more visible. But the bright light hurt his sore eyes and presently, rising from the chair, he stalked over to the fire, with his face full of displeasure and the hurt, sulky look of a child. Whiting thought the inflammation was due to a microbe and that the lashes only contributed to the trouble. He said so without any finesse. Whereupon the P.M. exclaimed:

'Do you mean to say I've had a bug all this time that hasn't been found?'

Whiting proved right. In the tears microbes were found, which rapidly vanished with a penicillin ointment. And now, after some months of peace, his eyes have begun to trouble him again, and this time the microbes have been found to be insensitive to penicillin. The new situation defeats even Winston:

'I have brought all my wits to bear upon this problem. It's like this: these bugs are the sons and grandsons of the sensitive ones; do sensitive bugs breed insensitive sons? And how long do they remain insensitive? We must ask Fleming.'

His instinct is to think everything out, and then he is quite sure that he knows all about it—far more than any doctor or soldier or sailor can tell him.

*

I have found these notes in my diary, undated, but written later, at different times.

My task as Winston's doctor has become more difficult now that he has left Downing Street after his defeat by Attlee. During his convalescence by the shores of Lake Como he had made up his mind to banish the election from his thoughts, and I did not clearly

[1] Ophthalmic Surgeon to the Middlesex Hospital.

understand my new role until we got back to London. Here he kept running into his colleagues, who talked to him about the election, until it became plain that if the wound had partly healed in Italy it had now broken down.

The entries in my diary after we left Como record what he said to me about the 'blow.' I find in the margin of the first page the words 'delayed shock' and on the next page the words: 'What are his colleagues up to?'

The dust of the election had scarcely settled when whispers were heard in the inner circle of the Tory hierarchy that Winston needed a long rest. He ought to get on with his book; it was his duty; no one could write the history of the war as he could. Prefaced by elaborate protestations of admiration and respect, his colleagues cautiously advanced the same theme to me, though in all kinds of circuitous ways.

For one thing, the election had brought home to them that Winston had lost his hold over the country. He was no longer a political asset. There were, too, more personal reasons for their rancour. When he was Prime Minister Winston had at times been pretty rough with the Cabinet. Mackenzie King described to me what he had seen:

'Churchill was very domineering; he cowed his colleagues. I have seen him actually cruel to Mr. Attlee. He had a way of stifling discussion when it was critical and when it did not agree with his views. Then the emotional stuff was brought out, there were tears in his eyes and he carried his colleagues with him.'

This overbearing attitude of Winston's, he continued, prevented other members of the Cabinet giving of their best. Worst of all, he forgot not only the names but even the faces of respected members of the Party.

In short, with the war behind them the Tory leaders were no longer prepared to stomach his summary methods. It seemed almost indecent, but he was beginning to get on their nerves. They would have liked to get rid of him, I fancy, if they had known how.

It sounded a formidable indictment, coming from his supporters, and some of it had no doubt percolated through to him—though his critics often lost their speech in his presence. At any rate, he said half to himself: 'They are very unkind; they were not like this in the war.' But Winston is a political animal. They were only leaving a sinking ship, and that is, after all, what happens in politics. He did not take it too much to heart.

The country's verdict was another matter. It seemed to him that all his actions had been called in question. His record in the war was submitted to the nation, and it had not given its approval. He confessed to me that the size of the Labour majority had made him rather ashamed. The political scene was transformed, and he was still dazed by what had happened. This was an older, less confident Winston.

I tried to argue that it was only the swing of the pendulum, but his mind was elsewhere. When, however, I told him of the Gallup polls carried out at intervals throughout the war by the *News Chronicle* he gave me his attention: 'Tell me about them.' I said that two questions were put to the readers. To the first, 'Who do you think should be responsible for the conduct of the war?' there was only one answer: 'Winston Churchill.' The second brought out their hostility to the Tories. He interrupted: 'I don't understand.' I told him that all the time the percentage of voters who wanted a Tory Government after the war was steadily falling. He had been listening intently. And then, as he mused, the light went out of his face. For five years he had enjoyed the trust and affection of the whole country, and then, in a night, the confidence of his countrymen was withdrawn. Why had they deserted him in the hour of victory?

An even more disturbing thought was eating away his peace of mind. He had always looked to posterity for a just appraisal of his work. Had he, he wondered, been a little too confident about the verdict of history?

Winston, as far as I could tell, had at no time sat down to think out for himself the reasons for his defeat; nor, as far as my knowledge goes, did he discuss it with others. Rather, he wanted to forget this very disagreeable experience; to blot it out of his mind for ever. However, it could not be put aside as easily as that. The years in the wilderness, when he was alone in the world, and the hand of every man seemed against him, have seared his mind indelibly. He turned away with dismay from a future where he would once more find himself at variance with the world. He brooded over his repudiation by his countrymen until it began to prey on his mind, so that I was troubled about his future.

I was troubled because he seemed to be sinking into a state of melancholy that I could not fully explain. I knew that he was beginning to feel his years, and that his physical powers were on the decline, which alone can completely change a man's outlook. Winston himself was sure that he was despondent because he was nearly spent.

'I'm pretty well played out. I imagine when one folds up like that, this kind of business hits one harder. Is anything known about these things, Charles?'

But was there not something more behind this despair? Could it be that the shock of his defeat had stirred up the inborn melancholia of the Churchill blood? Brendan, I remember, told me of Winston's mood in 1915 when he had to leave the Government because he was held responsible for the failure of the attack on the Dardanelles. According to Brendan, Winston kept on saying to him—often several times in a day—'I'm finished. I'm finished.' The same cloud of despondency hung over him, then, when he was, after all, a young man.

Looking back, I still find it difficult to explain the spirit of acceptance with which Winston, belligerent by nature, met these baleful events. It is so out of character. My diary records:

'It sounds very strange, but Winston is yearning for a peaceful life. Five months have gone since the election and he has had to learn piecemeal how some of those who love him and have his interests at heart believe that his defeat was good for the country. That hurt. "If only," he murmured to me one day, "I could be sure that they were all wrong." '

A later entry takes it further: it records a scrap of conversation between Winston and the Prof.

Lord Cherwell: 'If you had been in power we should not now be in such a mess.'

Winston: 'The Government has had great difficulties. They have done things no Conservative Government would have dared to do.'

Lord Cherwell: 'What things?'

Winston: 'Direction of labour and rationing of bread and potatoes possibly. The General Election was a blessing in disguise. But they are going to have a war with Russia.'

Those days brought me very close to Winston:

'Winston grows in adversity—in 1940 he was twice the man he became in 1944. Now the arrogance and self-assertion have gone, and there is left a deep humility. He even wonders if it has not all been for the best. There is not bitterness in his soul. At a time like this he blames no one. Not a small or petty thought seems to enter his head. He has remained untarnished by the dusty world in which he has spent his life.'

He proved a wise friend to those of us who had to swallow our own feelings and get on with the job. While the war lasted, Aneurin Bevan[1] let no chance slip of attacking the Prime Minister, often in

[1] Bevan was the leader of the Labour left wing.

bitter and wounding words. Winston found it difficult to understand the mentality of anyone who did not support the war, and impossible to forgive those who criticized his conduct. Bevan—Winston would spit out the 'van' that there might be no confusion with Bevin, whom he liked as a man and trusted as a politician—was just a 'squalid nuisance.' Now he was Minister of Health in the Labour Government, and it was my task, as President of the Royal College of Physicians, to see a good deal of the Minister, and to advise him on many matters. Almost from the first day of our partnership he insisted on calling me by my Christian name. After my years with Winston I began to feel my position equivocal. I did not, of course, take my cares to Winston, who had enough of his own. But one day he said to me:

'It is your duty, Charles, to work in with this fellow Bevan. I hope you will not allow our friendship to interfere with your job as President.'

When the electorate turned its back on Churchill he was told that people abroad were dumbfounded. Did not the occupied countries of Europe revere him as the man who had delivered them out of bondage? Even Molotov, when at Potsdam he learnt the result of the election, went white. 'What does it mean?' he asked. 'What will happen?' 'Very flattering,' Winston grunted, 'because I had had the devil of a row with him.' As for the Americans, the result of the election remained to them inexplicable and even wanton.

Some of Winston's countrymen shared this bewilderment. Was it wise to replace Churchill by Attlee? But England as a whole had been prepared for change by the war, and Winston had come to hate change. While the struggle lasted the country was ready to put up with a dictator, but when peace came people wanted to have more say in things. The feeling grew that Attlee and the Party he led were in closer touch with their problems and in fuller sympathy with their aspirations than Churchill, with all his dazzling achievements, could be. They found it difficult to picture Churchill, accustomed to unquestioning obedience, dealing happily with labour disputes at a time when the workers were in a mood to strike against their own leaders. They could not persuade themselves, as they might have liked to do, that Churchill was the man for this particular job.

The trouble was that so many people felt like that about Winston. I learnt from Lascelles [1] that he had told the King after the election that Winston was not the man the country needed for the work of reconstruction; Lascelles said that the result was best for Winston and

[1] Sir Alan Lascelles, Private Secretary to the King.

best for the country. But the King found it difficult to break the war-time habit of turning to Winston for advice. When I called at 28 Hyde Park Gate, to see if all was well for the trip to Florida, I noticed an open letter on the little table by the bed, with the address in red lettering and in the big type of Buckingham Palace. Perhaps Winston followed my eyes; anyway he said:

'The King wants me to look through his speech for the State Banquet to the U.N.O. delegates.'

No. 10 had sent the speech to Buckingham Palace, who had sent it to Winston.

'Things seem pretty upside-down,' Winston grunted.

What he cannot get over is that the country has got rid of him only to put Attlee in his place. Clem Attlee puzzles him. He cannot make him out, no one in his experience of politics has been quite like him. For one thing he cannot follow the working of Attlee's mind, any more than he can understand what is in the heads of those for whom Attlee speaks. Winston's temperament and up-bringing make it difficult for him at any time to share the hopes and fears of the middle class. To make confusion more confounded, here, apparently, is a typical specimen of that section of the com-munity which holds the most advanced and, in Winston's eyes, even subversive views about society and the Empire. Perhaps Winston is too old to bother about these new ideas which are fermenting so unpleasantly in the political world. They make him impatient. He is so young in some ways, so old in others.

And he makes the not uncommon mistake of belittling what he cannot explain. When Attlee was abroad Winston quoted to me, with a mischievous smirk, the quip, 'When the mouse is away the cats will play.' He seems to accept without question that Clem is a dim little man, who has been washed up by a tidal wave and left high and dry, with great power which he does not know how to use.

Those about Winston make no effort to correct this surface im-pression. They are happy when they can distract his mind for a little, and comfort him by recounting some long story of Mr. Attlee's ineptitude. It is not all guile and make-believe on their part, for Mr. Attlee remains an enigma to the Tories. For one thing, they know very little of him, and then what they do know fails to fit the part of Prime Minister as it has been played for the last five years by Winston Churchill.

*

June 27, 1946

It is nearly a year since the election. Winston told me today he could do a good deal without getting tired.

'Yesterday I dined out and sat talking till two o'clock, and on my way home I saw a light in the Commons and found them sitting. I listened for half an hour, and then I made a very vigorous speech. I don't see why the Government shouldn't be beaten up. They've made an awful mess of this bread business. By August or September there may be no bread in the shops. They are very worried about it. Why, if we'd failed to bring in the wheat we should have been for it.'

For the first time, perhaps, the thought of a come-back flashed through his mind. He poked his nose in my face as he stopped pacing the room:

'A short time ago I was ready to retire and die gracefully. Now I'm going to stay and have them out.' With great vehemence: 'I'll tear their bleeding entrails out of them. I'm in pretty good fettle,' he went on in a more subdued tone. 'The Jerome blood.'[1]

'You would,' I mocked, 'ascribe to natural causes what is due to my art.'

'Ah, no, Charles,' he said warmly. 'I saw Alexander Fleming about my eyes. He wasn't interested in me as a patient, but in a very unusual bug in my nose, a staphylococcus, which was very resistant to penicillin.' With a grin, 'The bug seems to have caught my truculence. This is its finest hour.' His face clouded. 'I asked the Government for a plane to go to Metz—the French want me to take part in a function there—and the Government said yes, if I was prepared to pay £200. Rather shabby, wasn't it? Of course it couldn't be called a public duty, though the Foreign Office said it would do good and are in favour of it.'

July 6, 1946

When I called on Winston today he seemed in poor heart—one of his black moods.

'I'm fed-up,' he said. 'Victory has turned to sackcloth and ashes.'

August 8, 1946

Winston is happy at Chartwell, as happy as he can be when the world has gone all wrong. I found him in the studio, the walls of which are covered with his canvases. When he had greeted me he climbed on to a big chair on a kind of platform, and surveyed the

---

[1] Leonard Jerome, Churchill's American maternal grandfather; died, 1891.

313

canvas he was painting, which was at the other end of the square room.

'My desert is too hot,' he said descending from his throne and applying a white paint with a few bold strokes of a fat brush.

I said he had been busy.

'Yes, it gives me something to do—an occupation.' He paused to take in his handiwork. 'And I must have an occupation. Elliott Roosevelt has been writing a foolish book; he attacks me.'[1]

He advanced to the easel and made two or three quick strokes with his brush.

'I don't care what he says,' he added almost absentmindedly and with his eyes glued to his picture. 'He's not much of a fellow. Elliott says I delayed the cross-Channel invasion of Europe for two years.' He turned to me. 'A short time ago I asked Monty whether we could have invaded France before we did. Monty answered: "It would have been madness. We could not have done it without the landing craft." '

Winston seemed to be thinking more of the picture than of Elliott Roosevelt. This was the real Winston, magnanimous, refusing to be ruffled by the small change of politics. The telephone rang. It was Clemmie summoning us to lunch. He put on a waterproof over his boiler suit, and walked very slowly up the slope to the house. I admired the fine setting.

'Ah, you should see it when the sun is on the Weald.'

He stood still to get his breath. I asked him how he had been.

'Two nights ago I was arguing with Randolph at two o'clock. We got heated. I bellowed and he counter-bellowed, and I felt things weren't right here.'

He pointed to his heart. I asked him if it was pain. He hesitated.

'No, but I was conscious of my heart; it was like the ghost of what happened at Washington when I tried to open the window. But I'm very well if I keep within my limits. I think I can make plans for some years yet. I feel much better than when I was Prime Minister.'

Winston did not seem to expect me to intervene. When he came to the house he pulled himself wearily, step by step, up to his workroom, where he picked up a little book and asked me if I would like it. I looked over his shoulder at the title: *Secret Session Speeches by Winston Churchill*.

'It has just come from America. I'm very pleased with it.'

The secretary spoke to him of 'Baby Winston.'[2]

[1] Elliott Roosevelt, *As He Saw It* (Duell, Sloan & Pearce, New York, 1946), p. 253.
[2] Son of Randolph Churchill; born, 1940.

'Why do you call him "Baby"? He is six years old.'

'Master Winston,' she corrected herself in a subdued voice.

They came to tell us that lunch was ready. There were just the three of us. Winston spoke gloomily of the future.

'You think there will be another war?'

'Yes.'

'You mean in ten years' time?'

'Sooner. Seven or eight years. I shan't be there.'

I asked him if it would be between Russia and her satellite countries and the Anglo-Saxon countries.

'Yes, with France and Scandinavia and Belgium and Holland on our side.'

I wondered how England could take part in an atomic war when she was so small. He said:

'We ought not to wait until Russia is ready. I believe it will be eight years before she has these bombs.' His face brightened. 'America knows that fifty-two per cent. of Russia's motor industry is in Moscow and could be wiped out by a single bomb. It might mean wiping out three million people, but they would think nothing of that.' He smiled. 'They think more of erasing an historical building like the Kremlin.'

His cigar had gone out; he fumbled in his pockets for a match.

'The Russian Government is like the Roman Church: their people do not question authority.'

I made some passing reference to Potsdam. 'Ah,' he said sadly, 'that was when the blow fell.'

He said nothing for a little, and then observed, half to himself:

'It was a blow.'

At length he rose from the table.

'Let's see if there's any news,' he said as he strode into the secretaries' room.

October 24, 1946

Called at Hyde Park Gate. Winston is full of his speech in the Commons on the danger of the Russian Army, which has not been demobilized.

Winston: 'The situation is grave.'

Moran: 'You mean there might be war in two or three years' time?'

Winston: 'Perhaps sooner than that, perhaps this winter. They have two and a half million men in the occupied countries, and we have about twelve divisions. They could march to the Atlantic in a few weeks, practically unopposed. They've got forward dumps of arms everywhere. The Swiss are most perturbed. Only the atomic bomb keeps the Russians back. They're making rockets to fire on us when they get to the coast.'

Moran: 'I doubt whether there will be war.'

Winston: 'I don't think there will be.'

Moran: 'At any rate conscription isn't an answer to this threat; if we are to be formidable it must be by mobilizing our scientists.'

Winston: 'We must have men.'

I was about to tell him of the dearth of recruits taking up science during the war, but I saw that he had lost interest in the subject. He wants people to listen to him, not to argue with him; he has learnt nothing from the election. I found Clemmie in her room. She told me that Camrose was pressing Winston to get on with his memoirs. They ought to be ready by Christmas 1947; after that they would not be worth so much. Several Oxford dons, she said, had agreed to devil for Winston. She thought the book would be a good thing; at any rate it would prevent him wandering over the Continent collecting honorary degrees.

November 30, 1946

St. Andrew's Day at Eton is often a chilly festival. On this occasion Collegers and Oppidans taking part in the Wall game were, as usual, so caked from head to foot with mud that they had become indistinguishable. To the agnostic it is a poor game; for minutes on end the bully pushed and writhed, like a lot of maggots when a stone is moved; then from beneath this quivering, steaming scrum a brown figure crawled on hands and knees, and as if fearful of the light rushed to get its head down again. Claude Elliott[1] was there in gum-boots and top-hat, and the Lawrences,[2] just back from Nuremberg. When I said to her that we were going to Winston's seventy-second birthday party in the evening her face lit up as she said: 'I do envy you your party.'

Fifteen sat down to Winston's birthday party. We were summoned for eight-fifteen, but in the manner of the house it must have been nearly nine before dinner was announced. Brendan proposed Winston's health. He spoke in hyperbole and went on saying the same thing for quite a long time. Winston was much moved when he got up to reply; a big tear gathered beneath his left eye. His emotions are always near the surface, but they are never manu-

---

[1] Claude Elliott, Headmaster, later Provost, of Eton.

[2] Sir Geoffrey Lawrence, later Lord Oaksey, presiding United Kingdom judge at the Nuremberg Trials, and his wife.

factured. He said very simply that it was a comfort to him at the end of the journey to have around him those for whom he cared. Then he exclaimed:

'But we are the past, and that is done with. Mary is the future.'

He went on to speak, very shortly, of her coming marriage, and sat down; the old man at his affectionate best. Mary said she hoped, with Christopher,[1] to found another English home, and went on to speak of what she owed to her own home, which would always be the greatest influence in her life. When the ladies had retired, Brendan belittled Smuts. Winston retorted:

'My faith in Smuts is unbreakable. He is a great man.'

Later someone referred to Winston's book, when he said:

'I should like to put down, without malice and without vanity, what happened.'

The butler came in and asked Winston if he could get the table ready for Harry Green, an actor, whose thought-transference stuff had gripped Winston. I retired with Green to a room, where he gave me a pencil and paper, and asked me to put down some serious thought. He then left the room. I wrote, 'Shall I write another book?' and folded the paper up several times. When he came back he took it from me, but without undoing it, held it against my forehead and repeated what I had written. Winston also retired and wrote: 'Shall I go to Chicago in the spring?' He was astounded when Green repeated this. Leslie Rowan then went out and asked: 'Shall we be at war with Russia within ten years?' Green not only got the words right, but went on to say, 'No.' Whereupon Winston pointed out that he was much impressed by the fact that he had got Leslie's words right, but he was not at all impressed by his views as to whether there would be a war with Russia or not. Winston found it easier to swallow magic than the conjurer's claim to views, as if ordinary folk ought not to have views at all.

In the past twelve months his spirits have risen and his vigour has come back. He has put vain regrets away; once more there is a purpose in life. He is very happy at Chartwell, farming and painting and dictating his book. In short, it has been a year of recovery.

[1] Christopher Soames was at this time Assistant Military Attaché, British Embassy, Paris.

Chapter thirty-one

A preview of old age

February 22, 1947

Winston telephoned to say that he was 'wheezy.' I said I would call on him, but he answered: 'No, I'll call on you.' His brother, Jack,[1] was in a poor way, and when he and Clemmie visited him they would be next-door to me.

Winston was sad about Jack. He has a tender heart.

'He may not get through this turn. As you get older these things seem less tragic. In any case, there is not much time left.'

But it would be 'like the lash of a whip across my bare and quivering heart.' For a time he was silent, and then he said: 'Jack may go out with the tide.' Jack's malady had eaten into the wall of the main artery of his body, causing an aneurism, or bulging, which throbbed under his breastbone like a great engine. He knew that at any moment it might burst and kill him. But he went his way as if he had no care in the world. Every night during the war he dined in the Annexe in a mess set up for Tommy and the secretaries, and was the life of the party.

Winston sat gazing into the fire. 'You know, I'm six years older than Jack.'

He got up abruptly.

'I cannot help being interested in politics; the Government is doing so much harm. Of course, it's all anticlimax.'

He cannot shake off the world of affairs.

February 23, 1947

Winston has just telephoned. 'Jack is dead. I was with him a quarter of an hour before. Yes, he meant a lot to me. I thought you would not mind my telephoning you. Good night, my dear Charles.'

[1] Jack Churchill, younger brother of Winston Churchill.

June, 1947

It is nearly two years since Winston sent for me one morning because he had discovered a swelling in his groin. After examining him, I said that he had ruptured himself. Next day we began to search for a truss; the search has gone on ever since, with small success. Lately the hernia has got much larger, it is increasingly difficult to control with the truss, and is hardly ever out of his mind. He seems to look on it as a particularly humiliating hint—anyway to those who can read—of the impermanence of things. The very integument which confines his vital organs has, he protests, given way; it can, of course, be patched, stitched and strengthened to hold for a little longer, but only for a time.

Dunhill[1] rather funks an operation on a man of his age and eminence. He is a simple soul, though a fine craftsman, and regards Winston with awe and reverence as the man who saved this country from defeat. He won't hear of any question of payment whenever I have called him in to see Winston; he sees him at any time of day which suits the patient, scratching all his other appointments without a word, and he cut his summer visit to Norway by nearly a fortnight to fit in with Winston's arrangements. It is an attractive side to his character, but I am not sure it is a sound attitude for a doctor towards a patient. The only safe rule is to treat Winston exactly like any other patient. I had at last to put a blunt question to Dunhill: was there any real chance that he would be able to live the rest of his life without an operation? Dunhill thought it most improbable, and I decided forthwith to push Winston to a decision, so that the operation might be done while the going was good. If he must have it done, now is the time. So, after months of indecision, a date has been fixed.

Even now Winston havers; he would make a last determined effort to get used to the truss and put up with the skin irritation. When I thought I had persuaded him that he would get a good dividend for the small risk he was taking, a new trouble arose. With his liability to contract pneumonia, the surgeons are apprehensive of complications after the anaesthetic; they are jibbing at his cigars. At last they screwed up their courage to tell him that in men over seventy statistics proved that pulmonary complications after an anaesthetic were seven times more common in smokers than in non-smokers. Winston declared positively he could give up smoking whenever he liked; he would certainly not smoke for a fortnight before the operation if that was what the doctors wanted. It is true

[1] Sir Thomas Dunhill, Sergeant Surgeon to Her Majesty Queen Elizabeth II.

that he did make a feeble and abortive attempt to keep his word; then he decided to cut down the number of cigars to half; finally, he contrived to see Dunhill alone, and soon persuaded him to say that if Winston didn't mind the extra risk he, Dunhill, didn't.

I marvel how he dominates men. Like a ventriloquist, he puts words into the mouths of his dolls, the doctors. Then we had a skirmish over the place where the operation was to be performed; Winston made a strong plea for his own house, but this time the surgeons stood their ground. So it is all fixed for Wednesday, June 11. I went down to Chartwell on Sunday to see if anything was wanted, and had to submit to a close cross-examination. What anaesthetic would be given? Would it be injected into his veins? How long would it be before he went off? I said, before he could count fifteen. Whereupon he at once asked: how did the anaesthetic cause unconsciousness? Would he be very uncomfortable afterwards, and if so for how long? Would he have much pain?

He arrived at the nursing home with two big volumes of Macaulay's essays as a solace. I found him immersed in them on the morning of the operation. They soothed him, he said. He asked me to pass him the other volume, when he began to read from Macaulay's review of Ranke's *History of the Papacy*:

'There is not, and there never was on this earth, a work of human policy so well deserving of examination as the Roman Catholic Church. The history of that Church joins together the two great ages of human civilization. No other institution is left standing which carries the mind back to the times when the smoke of sacrifice rose from the Pantheon, and when cameleopards and tigers bounded in the Flavian amphitheatre.'

He went on reading, savouring the opulence of the language, so much of it pure Winston, while Thomas Dunhill leant over the end of the bed to catch the words, his lips parted with pleasure, not so much in Macaulay's measurement of the achievement of the Catholic Church, as in pure joy at his fortune in hearing a great historic figure talk and pay tribute to another master of words. 'A fine piece of English writing,' Winston concluded, as he closed the volume. 'A fine bit of word painting.'

An operation for hernia can be, and usually is, a simple affair, but a surgeon never can tell what difficulties may confront him when he opens a belly. Winston was on the table for more than two hours. Adhesions, the legacy of the operation for appendicitis years ago, made technical difficulties. I could see that Dunhill, his assistant and the anaesthetist were engrossed in their job; but I was only an idle spectator, and as time passed and the twenty minutes the operation was to take became an hour, and then two hours, I kept glancing at the anaesthetist; and when from time to time he put his hand under the white sheet to feel the pulse I wondered if everything was all right.

Winston, however, experienced little discomfort after the operation, though he did say on the third day that it seemed 'a frightfully long time since the operation, almost before the last war.' He confessed now that he had not liked the idea of surgery, though he had said nothing. One thing interested him: he found the day before the operation that he had discarded thoughts of any kind, his mind was just vacant, 'as I imagine it is before you die.'

When Winston is well he does not think about his health, but when he is ill, particularly when he is in pain or has a temperature, he becomes impatient, and frets if his doctor seems content to be only a spectator of the course of his illness. He welcomes any active treatment, he likes to feel something is being done, and he is puzzled by my scepticism about drugs. Once, apropos of nothing, he suddenly said, with a mischievous smirk:

'Charles does not believe in any medicines, but he thinks it's only decent to put a label on before the end.'

He is always poking fun at my preoccupation with exact diagnosis. 'You are so desperately negative, Charles,' he complained. Every time he gets a cold in the head and finds his temperature is up he becomes apprehensive; those three attacks of pneumonia are always at the back of his mind.

December 7, 1947

It has been plain for some time that Winston is becoming restive. He cannot persuade himself that he is serving a useful purpose in opposition, nor for that matter does it add to the attractions of the Front Opposition Bench that most of his colleagues are so anxious to push him off it. If he were in office it would be another matter. Then he could put away his books and, with half a dozen clever young men to do the donkey work, feel that he was doing something really worth while. Of course he is right. For, like his father before him, he is at once more sober and altogether more responsible as a Minister with Civil Servants around to steady him and keep him on the rails. I was therefore not at all taken aback when Winston announced that he was stale and had decided to go to Marrakesh.

'I don't need rest. I like my mind to be active. But psychologically one needs change from time to time—different lights, different scenes, and especially different colours. Colour plays a great part in life.'

321

He mused for a little.

'Look at the greys and browns of a miner's life.'

When he spoke of miners it seemed to put the next general election into his head. He thought if there was an election now it would come out fifty–fifty, and that would mean a coalition. But he did not think there would be an election yet; perhaps it would not come for two years. He would not be too old then, he thought. Meanwhile he must get on with his book. But how could he do this while he was leading his present life? It was then that he realized he was stale. Soon he had persuaded himself that he must be free for a time from the distraction of the House of Commons—that is, if his book was to have a chance.

Clemmie had been doubtful about Marrakesh. It was so remote if he were taken ill. However, Winston, brushing aside her doubts, went off in high spirits. He liked change, and at first, Sarah wrote, the holiday was a great success. Each morning he had dictated in his bedroom, so that in the afternoon he could go off to the mountains with his paint-box and a clear conscience. But when luncheon was at an end he would loiter for a long time in the garden of the hotel, dozing in the sun, and when at last he arrived at the appointed place in the foothills there was not time to finish his picture before the sun went down and a chill night air crept up out of the valley.

When the inevitable cold in the head came in retribution it hung around and would not go; and worse still, a low, smouldering fever persisted; and his doctor seemed so vague about everything. Winston began to say: 'I wonder, if Charles were here, whether he would find a patch on my lungs.' He was not happy in his mind, and one day he telephoned to me in London. The line was bad and he is a little hard of hearing; presently he rang off impatiently, but our Embassy in Paris had talked to him. They left me in no doubt that he wanted me to go. That was how one morning Clemmie, Dorothy and I set off for Marrakesh in a 'Dove' which Brendan had procured.

Winston greeted my arrival by holding out both his hands in an affectionate gesture. I had come a long way to help him, and he was all agog to hear my verdict. There was not much amiss, and when I had satisfied him that he had not got pneumonia he seemed to forget all about his illness. He began to come down to the restaurant for luncheon and dinner, and in a day or two had taken up his life just as it had been before he took to his bed a fortnight ago.

At night he would read aloud to us a chapter of his book, and when pressed he would read another. Winston is too self-conscious to read well, but that did not seem to matter. What would he pick out of this first volume, which he would have liked to call *The*

Downward Path? What did he think was most vivid and arresting? He began with the fighting in Norway. The indecision and pusillanimous nature of these events would not in any case have commended them to Winston, but his distaste for the whole episode had been sharpened by the feeling that if he had been Prime Minister it would have happened differently. Roger Keyes had come down to the House in full Admiral's uniform, with all his medals, and had denounced the Government for their cowardice. He asked only to be allowed to attack, to force a landing. But Dudley Pound hated him, and Winston said that if as First Lord he had given Keyes the command there might have been resignations; the price was too high for this particular risk.

This will be stuff for the serious student of war. Winston's next chapter, however, will grip the most casual reader. It tells how Chamberlain resigned and Churchill was invited to form a Government. Winston called his account a proem. He did not want to alter it. He could add a lot more detail, but it was better as it stood. Winston went on:

'I was summoned to No. 10. Halifax was there already. I could see from what the Prime Minister said that he wanted Halifax to succeed him. He looked across the table at me, but I said nothing, and there was a very long pause. Then Halifax said that it would be difficult if the Prime Minister was a peer. I could tell that he had thrown in his hand.'

Brendan Bracken had described the scene to me and explained why Winston said nothing. Early in the evening of May 9, 1940, word reached Brendan that Winston had come to an agreement with Lord Halifax that he would act as his second in command if Halifax became Prime Minister. Brendan thought this would be disastrous, that if it were carried out we should lose the war. He went about London searching for Winston. At one o'clock in the morning he found him. 'You cannot agree to this,' Brendan spluttered, but Winston was obdurate; he said that he could not go back on his word. 'Well,' Brendan persisted, 'at least you must promise you will not speak first when you get to No. 10. Promise?' At last Winston said he would promise. Brendan went to his bed mollified. He knew that Winston would keep his word, and he knew that when Halifax spoke first he would have to suggest Winston as Prime Minister.

I was thinking of Brendan's story when Winston broke in:

'Halifax's virtues have done more harm in the world than the vices of hundreds of other people.'

Chamberlain had at least believed in Munich. Halifax did not, for the Foreign Office had drilled the facts into him. But he weakly agreed.

'And yet when I meet him, I can't help having friendly talk,' he added reflectively.

'When I was appointed Prime Minister,' he went on, 'it was an immense relief; I could discipline the bloody business at last. I had no feeling of personal inadequacy, or anything of that sort. I went to bed at three o'clock, and in the morning I said to Clemmie, "There is only one man can turn me out and that is Hitler."' '

When the chapter was at an end, Clemmie looked serene; we were all silent while, for a time, he turned the pages of the American edition. Presently he looked up brightly.

'June the 6th, 1940, was one of the most fertile days of my life. I put down on paper everything that we should need for a successful invasion of France. I did this two days after Dunkirk. Dr. Johnson said: "When a man is going to be hanged it concentrates his mind wonderfully."' '

He looked up at me to see if the point had gone home.

'It was a pretty grim moment, but it's all down here—the tank landing craft and the Mulberry Harbours.'[1]

It took his mind back to the drama of those days.

'They were very wonderful,' said Winston half to himself.

Dorothy asked: 'Which year of all your life, if you could relive one twelvemonth, would you choose?' Winston: 'Nineteen-forty every time, every time.'

He seemed miles away, and then he said:

'I wish certain people could have been alive to see the events of the last years of the war; not many: my father and mother, and F.E., and Arthur Balfour, and Sunny. Sunny and I were like brothers. I have stayed for months with him at Blenheim.'

Winston had given chapters of his book to a dozen different people to read: to the Prof. and to Henry Luce, the head of *Time* and *Life*; to Lord Camrose and to Walter Graebner, and to Sarah. And here was Clemmie, pencil in hand, giving her views. She thought he had used initials too much. They would convey nothing to the average

---

[1] Churchill was entitled to a measure of complacency. He actually described these landing craft and the Mulberry Harbours in a paper to Lloyd George bearing the date July 7, 1917, nearly thirty years before the Normandy landings. The tanks were to be transported in special ships and landed in flat-bottomed boats, the bow of which was designed as a drawbridge so that the tanks could crawl ashore on the beaches. They were to be used in a scheme Winston had prepared for the capture of the Friesian Islands of Borkom and Sit. This is the work of a creative mind.

324

reader. Winston ought to replace these initials by the full name of the organization in question. He looked up impatiently with a pained expression. He doesn't really want criticism; he wants reassurance.

But he had asked for help, and I lay awake for a long time turning over possible pitfalls in my mind. His books before the war were immensely readable, but there was now a danger that he might be too anxious to convince posterity that he was right in everything, and that, in consequence, some of his text might be indigestible.

A later entry offers another explanation of the diffuseness of Winston's text. I asked John Masefield: Was the artist in Winston swamped by the statesman anxious to justify his war decisions to posterity?

Masefield: 'Dr. Johnson said: "Abundance, Sir, is a mark of genius; we praise a crab-tree if it gives much fruit." Winston is a natural force, a volcano, big and dynamic. His *World Crisis* had order and method. But he has been through an ordeal few other men would have survived. He is tired. And the first thing to go in this exhaustion is the power of selection. He is inclined to repeat himself, the sense of proportion is gone. He needs a winter's complete rest.'

Masefield prescribed Arizona. Winston was only to paint sunsets and the cactus plant. Was this diffuseness a mere passing phase, the result of exhaustion, as Masefield held, or did it mark something more permanent, the oncoming of old age?

If *The Gathering Storm* is too diffuse, if Winston is too old, too worn or too taken up with posterity, it is too late to rewrite the book after another pattern. If big cuts are needed, Winston is the last man to make them.

He has borne a crushing burden of responsibility and he has been conscious, as I can testify, that he was answerable for men's lives. It is inevitable that he should feel impelled to justify his actions. In his book Winston seems sometimes to have given more thought to this than to the texture of his prose.

Even in the books he reads he is groping for reassurance. And he has come to judge those in which he figures, not on their merits, but entirely by their attitude to himself. His opinion would change overnight if he found that they were not 'fair' to him.

One day at Marrakesh I picked a book off his bed. It was *The Real Lloyd George*, by Sylvester, who had been his secretary for a number of years.

Winston: 'I wouldn't read it. It's poor stuff. I cut him when we met in the House.'

325

Moran: 'You've read the book?'

Winston: 'No, but I think I shall. I want to find out what happened when Lloyd George saw Hitler.'

Two days later I found that he had read the book and had changed his mind about Sylvester.

'He's not as bad as I thought. I shan't cut him in future.'

His train of thought was not difficult to follow. Lloyd George had said some outrageous things about him. Winston was 'lacking in judgment,' and '*is no leader,* of course he is not. I know him so well. It is true he is an excellent speaker, but this is not everything. *Look at the Dardanelles.*' Winston had underlined with a blue pencil the words I italicize here. Perhaps, after all, Lloyd George deserved what Sylvester had given him.

Certainly Sylvester had been very fair to Winston, who liked the references to himself and the figure he cut. In particular, the way Lloyd George had been completely taken in and bamboozled by Hitler interested and pleased him. He, Winston, had not fallen into the trap which Hitler had contrived.

He got up and went to the window. Without turning round, he said:

'Can you tell me, Charles, why he died? Lloyd George, I mean. There did not appear to be anything wrong with him; things just came to an end.'

Winston went on to speak with scorn of the farm-cart funeral. His view of life remained romantic. He would like to be buried like a soldier. 'Very well, dear,' Clemmie interposed soothingly, 'you shall be buried like a soldier.'

Was this intolerance of criticism just another sign of an old man's testiness? It is often quite irrational. 'Roosevelt,' I once said to him, 'doesn't give me the impression of a powerful intelligence.' He disagreed emphatically, affirming that he was a man of great judgment. But when, thinking it fine praise, I told him that Frances Perkins had quoted the President as saying that Winston had a hundred ideas a day and that four of them were good, he blew up: 'It is impertinent of Roosevelt to say this. It comes badly from a man who hadn't any ideas at all.'

If Winston is intolerant of criticism he will go out of his way to provide ammunition for his critics. He spoke of the sequence of Conservative businessmen who in late years had been Prime Ministers: Bonar Law, Baldwin and Neville Chamberlain; and expressed the view that they had not been a success. He spoke scornfully of Bonar Law as a narrow, doctrinaire Glasgow profiteer, and of Baldwin in terms so inaccurate that even Camrose demurred. On this slender basis of their supposed incompetence, Winston—as a political thinker he is *naïf*—impulsively built a theory that politics was a whole-time job to which men should devote their lives. It was a priesthood, a profession. He, Winston, felt vaguely that there should be some test which members of the House of Commons must pass before taking their seats.

This particular digression startled me, for he is no longer fertile in ideas. Last year his failure as Leader of the Opposition could be put down in the main to lack of tact and to his indifference to the opinion of others. But now it is more the sterility of his mind that bothers thoughtful people. The once-teeming brain has run dry. Even when it is argued that the Conservatives ought to have a policy he grows impatient. The job of the leader of the Opposition, he says, is to attack the Government—that and no more.

He has not even an alternative to Communism, and he seems to resent anyone who has. I rashly asked him what he meant when he said during dinner that Communism would triumph if there was 'no settled design' put forward by the other parties in the next twenty years. He answered:

'If you think I have an alternative scheme of life, I have none. I believe in ordinary men being allowed to live their lives in their own way. If you have an alternative scheme for young people'— he was now shouting—'you ought to lead; you ought to state it now and I will pull it to pieces.'

I said I had no intention of arguing the point; it would only put his temperature up, and with that I left the room. A repentant 'Good night' was shouted after me.

Winston is ageing, and it is perhaps inevitable that he is very gloomy about the future. The optimism of the war years, which made it impossible then to think of him as an old man, has oozed out through his wounds, and he has given up planning new worlds. He does not pretend that he is interested in a future he will not live to see. His work is done; he is living in the past. The story of that past begins for me with a small boy playing with his tin soldiers on the floor of his nursery at the Little Lodge in Dublin.[1] He would end as he began. And then his buoyancy would return and he would make it plain that war was the story of the human race. At no time in the history of man had there been peace for long. He did not believe that this was the last war. Sometimes he was even more

---

[1] Churchill's father, Lord Randolph Churchill, lived in Dublin at 'the Little Lodge,' a stone's-throw from the Viceroy's Lodge, where his father, the Duke of Marlborough, lived as Lord-Lieutenant.

precise. Except at harvest-time, when self-preservation enjoins a temporary truce, the Pathan tribes are always engaged in private or public war. 'The life of the Pathan is thus full of interest.'

On one point Winston has always been clear. He has reaffirmed it so many times that the very words have stuck in my memory: 'As a nation we want nothing; we will take nothing. We entered the war for honour.'

As he talked, my mind went back to the first war I could remember. As a boy I remember reading in a paper that South Africa had been given to the Boers. It seemed a shocking thing to do. I lay awake in the long dormitory that was full of moonlight, listening to a corn-crake, and wondering what could be done about it.

Now Winston in his old age has come to feel like that about the Colonies. Listening to him laying down the law, his case seemed so strong until Smuts whispered: 'It's not quite so simple as that.' But Winston never seemed in doubt. The Empire had been cast away 'by a hideous act of self-mutilation, astounding to every nation of the world.' He was particularly shocked because the attack on the British Empire had come not from without but from within. But now the war was over, the poor Hindu had got what he wanted and the Foreign Office complained ungratefully that Mr. Churchill had left them nothing to bargain with.

So old faiths were reaffirmed, while old friends and old enemies were remembered, as he sat basking in the sun.

'Wells is a seer. His *Time Machine* is a wonderful book, in the same class as *Gulliver's Travels*. It is one of the books I would like to take with me to Purgatory. Dalton's a swine.'

He spoke of him with violence; then he mused:

'And yet of all those who served in the Coalition Government under me, he wrote the most charming letter of thanks.'

Camrose: 'Dalton is a traitor to his class.'

Winston: 'Roosevelt said to me, "They say I am a traitor to my class. I expect they say the same of you in England." I told him that in England we have no classes.'

Winston was in full spate. He went on:

'If ever it comes to the triumph of the Communists, I hope that some people will have the guts to resist. I am prepared to commit a crime'—he spoke more quickly and with emphasis—'to throw a bomb among the most subversive people. I'm not afraid of death.'

Clemmie (*quietly*): 'Have a little more brandy, Winston.'

When he spoke of Clemenceau my mind went back to his own words, written a long time ago in *The World Crisis*:

'Clemenceau embodied and expressed France; as much as any

single human being, miraculously magnified, can ever be a nation, he was France . . . he left me with the impression of a terrific engine of mental and physical power, burning and throbbing in that aged frame . . . but he was seventy-four years of age.'

That was written in 1920, when Winston was forty-six. He had always been precocious, and it was in early middle life that he came to write his own epitaph.

Part five

The Prime Minister falters

Chapter thirty-two

The first stroke

I left Winston at Marrakesh in December, 1947, living in the past and impatient of change. I could see then that he was sliding, almost imperceptibly, into old age. There is an undated entry in my medical notes that must have been written early in the New Year:

'When I examined Winston's retinal arteries with my ophthalmoscope, I found definite hardening of the vessels, but not more than one would expect after the stress of the war years. There is plenty of evidence that his circulation is sluggish.'

It did not affect his tenacity of purpose. He kept his nose in his book, *The Second World War*, though a certain diffuseness in the second volume could be ascribed to his years. After Marrakesh there is a gap in my diary for eighteen months.

August 24, 1949

Dr. Gibson telephoned from Monte Carlo this morning:
'I think Mr. Churchill has had a stroke. I would like you to see him as soon as you can.'
When I arrived at the airfield at Nice, Max told me what had happened:
'He was playing cards at two o'clock this morning when he got up and, steadying himself with his hands on the table, bent his right leg several times as if it had gone to sleep. "I've got cramp in my arm and leg," was all he said. He kept closing and opening his right fist. Then he went on playing, but when he woke this morning—it would be about seven o'clock—the cramp was still present. A little later he found he could not write as well as usual. Dr. Gibson was called, and he got on to you. It's a true bill, I am afraid,' Max added after a pause. 'But let's go and see him.'
With that he took me to his bedroom. When Max left us Winston

333

said: 'I am glad you've come; I'm worried.' I could find no loss of power when I examined him; his grip was strong. Later, when he squeezed paints out of their tubes, he could not do it as well as usual. Max had told me that he was not sure whether his speech was affected. Winston was certain that it was not, and there was nothing I could detect. I asked him about his writing. Reaching for his pen, and steadying a bit of paper against a book, he wrote very slowly and carefully:

'I am trying to do my best to make it legible. It is better than it was this morning. W. Churchill.'

He handed me the paper, which shivered as he held it out—I felt he was watching my face as I read it.

'What has gone wrong, Charles? Have I had a stroke?'

'Most people,' I explained, 'when they speak of a stroke mean that an artery has burst and there has been a haemorrhage into the brain. You've not had that. A very small clot has blocked a very small artery.'

'Will I have another?' he demanded at once. 'There may be an election soon. An election in November is now more a probability than a possibility. I might have to take over again.' He grinned. 'It feels like being balanced between the Treasury Bench and death. But I don't worry. Fate must take its course.'

His memory did not seem to be impaired. He was quite calm, though perhaps a little fearful.

Moran: 'Do you notice anything different?'

Winston: 'Yes, there seems to be a veil between me and things. And there's a sensation in my arm that was not there before.'

Moran: 'What kind of sensation?'

Winston: 'Oh, it's like a tight feeling across my shoulder-blade.'

I told him he had done enough talking and that I would come back later. When Max heard the verdict he at once said:

'Oh, he must go on with things; he wouldn't agree to rust out.'

It hardly seemed the time to make decisions of that kind. The Press, Max said, were waiting at the gate.

'You must say something to them. It is no use,' he insisted, 'trying to fool them. You were seen at the aerodrome. They are all agog.'

He handed me a message which he had concocted. It was ingenious, but I was sure it would only excite their suspicions.

'Why say anything at all? Tell them that I am your guest for a few days, that I've brought my golf clubs. We'll produce him in a day or two, and that will convince them there is nothing wrong.'

Max wasn't persuaded, but when he saw my mind was made up he said no more.

August 25, 1949

Winston is never content with a diagnosis, he demands an explanation of the pathology of every malady; it must all be reasoned out. This morning I had to expound how the tracts, as they pass down from the surface, or cortex of the brain, to the spinal cord, come together at one point at the base of the brain, so that a small haemorrhage there can result in an extensive paralysis. At that point the tracts, or nerve paths, passing to the muscles are situated in front of the nerves carrying only sensation. He had had the great good fortune that the small vessel blocked had not touched the motor area, so that there was no paralysis; it had only cut off the nutrition of certain central cells concerned with sensation, and that was why he had a sense of tightness over his shoulders.

'Sensation doesn't matter,' I said.

He interrupted: 'Life is sensation; sensation is life.'

*

But he soon came to think he had had a lucky escape, and that what had happened belonged to the past. And when some days later he lunched at the Hôtel de Paris, and everyone rose to their feet as he entered and no one noticed anything, he gained confidence. He was, to be sure, irritable at times. Next day, when we dined at another restaurant where the service was slow, he said in tones which carried that he had never been in a worse restaurant. And when an American lady at another table came across and asked him to sign her menu he exploded. Could he not have even his dinner in peace? He wanted to get home, but he had misgivings that when he got out of the aeroplane in England the Press would notice that he did not walk straight. He devised a plan—I suspect with Max's assistance—by which the Press would be sent to Northolt while he arrived at Biggin Hill. It seemed a mad thing to do, and would have given rise to all kinds of stories. Eventually I managed to scotch this plan. When, however, we arrived at Biggin Hill and he saw all the photographers with their cameras, he was certain they would notice that something was wrong with his gait, and he waved them away with an angry gesture. A little later at Chartwell he said to me:

'I'm not the man I was before this happened. I had to see Cripps at No. 11 about devaluation.[1] It was an act of courtesy on his part. He was cool and debonair, but I was in a twitter. I shall never be able to believe a word Cripps says in future. Why, only in

[1] September, 1949. The pound was devalued by the Labour Government from 4·03 to 2·8 dollars.

July he said he would sooner die than do this; now he says it will be an advantage.' And then his face brightened: 'When I arrived at Downing Street there were five people; when I left there were five hundred.'

Winston was in his seventy-fifth year. The shock of the election, coming right on the top of the strain of the war years, had done him no good. However, as the months passed I think my fears were half forgotten; he seemed to get back his interest in life, vigour returned and he appeared to put the past behind him, so that his stroke took me completely by surprise.

This is the beginning of trouble. He will not give in without a great struggle, but there can be only one end to it. How long it will last is only guesswork; he might hang on for some years yet, but this is certain: my task is just beginning.

January 24, 1950

Five months have gone by and nothing has happened. Winston has been so buried in the third volume of *The Second World War* that my fears had been set at rest until this morning when he sent for me. I went at once. He told me:

'About an hour ago everything went misty. There was no warning. I could just read, with difficulty. What does it mean, Charles? Am I going to have another stroke?'

I reassured him:

'You seem to get arterial spasms when you are very tired.'

He looked up sharply.

'You mustn't frighten me.'

In fact, I am more frightened than Winston. This is a grim start to the racket of a General Election. [1]

February 5, 1950

An election like this might well flatten a younger man, and I keep wondering how Winston is wearing under the strain. It was very late last night when he got back from Leeds, but when I called at Hyde Park Gate early this morning I found him reading the *Manchester Guardian*.

'Did Leeds tire you?'

'Oh, no, Charles. Speaking to five thousand people through a microphone is no more tiring than talking to a hundred. It doesn't bother me. I'm not overawed by them. I've got used to it. But I do

[1] The Labour Government decided to dissolve Parliament on February 3 before the Budget. The General Election was held on February 23, 1950, and resulted in the Labour Government majority being cut to 6.

worry over what I say and what I don't say. I felt invigorated by the meeting, brutalized as I am by fifty years of it. Of course, when it was all over I was tired.'

He appeared absorbed in his own thoughts. Then he muttered: 'I'm glad I've not to live my life over again. There is a dreadful degradation of standards.'

February 6, 1950

I went to Winston because Miss Sturdee[1] told me that he was taking on more speeches. After Manchester he is going to speak for Randolph at Plymouth and at Oldham. I wanted to persuade him that it was not necessary to stump the country making speeches. I tried to say that broadcasting had made other forms of appeal to the electorate of secondary importance, that argument had been replaced by little word pictures which humble folk would remember. Morrison had said that if food subsidies were taken away it would mean to a woman with two children that she would have to pay fourteen shillings more a week for her food. That went home to people. It must be met by similar methods. I saw he was hardly listening. He isn't going to learn any new techniques; he isn't interested in them.

'We, too, have our broadcasters,' was all he said.

I begin to see that we must let things take their course. I must be sensible. After all, if anything does happen he would prefer to go out fighting a general election, with plenty of cheering and booing and heckling.

May 25, 1950

Winston is quite sure that the tightness over his shoulders has increased. He can't get the stroke out of his mind. To reassure him I called in Russell Brain.[2]

'The cells in your brain,' he explained, 'which receive sensory messages from your shoulder are dead. That's all. It's a bit of luck that sensation only is affected.'

He seemed relieved by Brain's air of finality, and began talking about his dyspepsia. For ten years he had been 'tortured' by it; then he heard of Courtlandt MacMahon's name.

'He cured me by his breathing exercises. Why, after his third visit there was an enormous difference in the whole structure of the body.'

---

[1] Secretary to Churchill.

[2] Sir Russell Brain, later Lord Brain, President of the Royal College of Physicians.

June 21, 1950

Took Winston to Negus[1] for increasing deafness. He found that the higher notes were lost.

Negus: 'You won't be able to hear the twittering of birds and children's piping voices.'

Winston: 'Are you going to hurt me?' He was watching Negus as he fiddled with his tuning forks. 'You must tell me if you are.'

Negus: 'Can you hear a clock ticking in your room?'

Winston: 'I won't have a ticking clock in my room.'

[1] Sir Victor Negus, consulting surgeon to Ear, Nose and Throat Department, King's College Hospital.

Chapter thirty-three

The King's illness

I am unhappy about things. When the struggle for power is at an end and his political life is over, Winston will feel that there is no purpose in his existence. I dread what may happen then, and it is my task as his doctor to put off that day as long as I can. On the other hand, if he wins this election [1] and goes back to No. 10 I doubt whether he is up to the job. In the fourteen months since my last entry he has lost ground and has no longer the same grip on things and events. Moreover, his cares multiply.

September 18, 1951

When I saw Winston a fortnight ago he told me he had been shocked by the King's appearance. He questioned me closely about him. I explained that I could judge only by the bulletins, but they were rather disturbing—there was a possibility of cancer of the lung. Winston listened with a grave and anxious face. Tonight at eight o'clock he telephoned me saying a bulletin would be read in the nine o'clock news, intimating that 'investigations showed structural changes had developed in the King's lung.' What did it mean? I asked him who had signed the bulletin; I wanted to know if a chest surgeon was included.

'I can't remember. It will be in the nine o'clock news,' he said. 'Would you give me a ring when you have heard it? Don't mention the King. Just refer to your friend.'

He repeated this twice before he rang off. When I heard the news, I knew before I telephoned that he would expect me at Chartwell.

'How long will you take?' he asked.

'Forty minutes, about,' I answered.

'Do come.'

[1] Another General Election was to be held in October, 1951.

I found him playing cards with Randolph. The room was half in darkness; the light of a solitary lamp near the small card-table fell on the green baize. He put his hand down at once.

'Ah, Charles, come and sit here. What do you make of it?' he asked anxiously.

'I don't like it at all,' I said. 'The doctors would not have used the bronchoscope if they had not been worried about a possible cancer. But much more disturbing is their failure to say a single word of reassurance after the bronchoscopy. And why do they go into details in their brief bulletin? Why tell us that the Queen is returning to London, that Queen Mary has called at the Palace and stayed an hour and a half, and that the Prime Minister has seen the King? Surely this is to prepare the public. Why nine doctors?'

He picked up a bit of paper and handed it to me. Price Thomas [1] had obviously carried out the bronchoscopic examination. I said that my fears had been strengthened by an article in the *Sunday Express* on the King's health. Plainly someone had given Max information; the article talked of an operation and hinted that it was cancer.

Winston, almost absentmindedly: 'Max said he knew someone behind the scenes.'

Randolph interrupted several times, eagerly asking questions, until Winston said:

'Oh, do let Charles finish his argument.'

He was very grave, and said: 'If it's cancer, can he recover? How long can it go on?'

I told him what I could, and he turned it over in his mind slowly and painfully.

'Poor fellow. I'll pray for him tonight,' he said.

I told Winston that when I was with him at Monte Carlo the Duke of Windsor had taken me into the garden and explained how Queen Mary had come to him in distress during his father's illness; she had expressed the hope that Lord Dawson [2] would not try to prolong his suffering by keeping him alive once it was certain there was no chance of his recovery. To comfort Winston, I explained that if the King's doctors could do nothing, they would at least concentrate on making him as comfortable as possible and would not allow his life to become intolerable. He said at once:

'That is all very well with an ordinary patient, but it does not

[1] Sir Clement Price Thomas, chest surgeon to Westminster and Brompton Hospitals.

[2] Lord Dawson of Penn, physician in ordinary to King George V.

apply to the Monarch. Under the Constitution, the duty of the King's doctors is to prolong his life as long as possible.'

Why, he asked, had the doctors used the words 'structural changes'?

'Because,' I said, 'they were anxious to avoid talking about cancer.'

'But why?' he persisted.

I told him of the strange case of a member of the Royal Family who had cancer of the gullet. But the Royal Family were not, in those days, supposed to suffer from cancer, so his doctor was careful that no reference was ever made to the nature of the illness from which he died. In consequence, as it was known that the Prince drank, it was widely assumed that this was the cause of his death.

Winston's thoughts were already far away. He did not return to the card-table. He was very sad. The sense of history surrounding the throne of England and the mystery of death fanned the flame of his imagination. The demise of the sovereign seemed to him like a revulsion of nature. He sat there, brooding darkly upon it; his countenance was overcast, he appeared hardly conscious of my presence. He stood gazing at the little tanks full of small tropical fish; he began to feed them, checked the temperature of the water and bubbled air into the tanks. To do something—anything—always brings relief when his thoughts are bursting.

When I took my leave he insisted on coming down the stairs to see me into the car. In the hall he took me aside, and spoke of the election:

'I don't know why I should do this at my age, but they need my name.'

I asked him if the King's illness would affect the date of the election. He thought it might. Until this happened, he had thought of October 20. And yet, he reflected, there was no reason why there should be a postponement. The King would not wish it. He had been worried about the political situation for some time. A cold wind came out of the darkness: Winston was flushed.

'Go in; you will get a cold.'

And with that I left him; the drive went dark as the great door closed with a clang.

*

September 20, 1951

Winston telephoned after breakfast that he had had a very important letter. Where was I? At Marshalls?[1]

---

[1] Marshalls Manor, Maresfield, Lord Moran's home in Sussex after the war.

'Then could you run over? I'd like that.'

Winston had a letter in his hand from Lascelles, the King's secretary. He put it down and was silent for a time.

'He says that the King has a growth in his lung. It means an operation—on Monday. The King did not know that Lascelles was writing to me. Poor fellow, he does not know what it means.'

Winston questioned me about the implications of the letter. He seemed distracted, and told me that he was 'all of a twitter.' He 'got like that sometimes.' This was an older Winston. It was not his habit to get in a twitter during the war. He said that he had a lot on his mind.

He meant the election. I said to him that if things went well, he would have to think out how he was going to get through his work. He retorted:

'Oh, well, we're not there yet. Besides, I live most of the day in bed; dictating directives would be just like writing the book.'

I asked him, with misgiving, about the part he intended to play in the election campaign. He would have to write the Conservative manifesto, he said, and make a couple of broadcasts and perhaps five speeches up and down the country.

'I shan't overdo things, Charles.'

He said Labour had made such a mess of things in the hospitals that they were employing far more laymen—more secretaries, more typists—than in the old days. I told him that I had brought him a few notes on the Health Service. He put them in his pocket without reading them.

'We don't want detail,' he protested impatiently. 'We propose to give the people a lighthouse, not a shop window.'

He was very restless and did not seem able to settle to anything; he kept walking up and down the passage at Chartwell. 'Have the photographers gone?' he demanded—he didn't want them to see me. He came back into the studio.

'I shan't be able to finish them,' he said, with a glum look at three canvases.

'It's a big job to take on at my age,' he continued, 'but there's no alternative. It's my duty.'

He strode to the secretaries' room.

'Has anything come in?' he asked.

We were back in the war years again. And when I came out of the house there was the old feeling of activity, the Press cars, the sense of things afoot. But we were ten years older.

Chapter thirty-four

Back to No. 10

September 29, 1951

Winston: 'The reports are good, we ought to win. Max is talking about a majority of a hundred and fifty, or at any rate a hundred.'

Moran: 'You surely don't take Max seriously as a prophet? He has no judgment in these things.'

Winston (*scowling*): 'The circulation of his papers runs into millions; he must know what people are thinking.'

Moran: 'Anyway, he has been completely off the map in the last two elections.'

Why do I argue with him? Shall I never learn that Winston likes to have around him sanguine, hopeful people? If they are of good heart, and make the best of things, he will not count it against them if their calculations prove to be ill-founded.

Max may be right, but the Tories are full of doubts. On all sides they are saying that Winston is too old and will never take advice—and surely he needs good counsel, for men who measure their words speak gravely of the economic position of the country. Last night J. J. Astor[1] said to me:

'We've had a mouthful of green sea-water; we've got to keep afloat.'

Everything that the doctors dislike in the Health Service they put down to me. They have heard that a certain politician, who is in their bad books, may be given office if the Conservatives win the election, and it is even going round that he will be the new Minister of Health. They come to me as if I could help. 'Why don't you tackle Mr. Churchill? He won't listen to the likes of us.' They only smile in a knowing way when I protest that Winston will not ask my advice before he appoints a new Minister of Health. That, I suppose, explains how I came to blurt out to Winston what was in

[1] John J. Astor, chief proprietor of *The Times.*

my mind. I had not got far when a secretary brought in the early editions of the evening papers. He picked up the *Standard* and handed me the *Star*.

'Let's see the news,' he said.

'That's the trouble. You will never listen to anybody.'

'I've done a lot of listening in my time,' he mused.

I was uncorked and bubbling over.

'If you appoint this man as Minister of Health you will affront the doctors. I do think it would be a mistake.'

It seemed to come out involuntarily. I was shocked by my own violence and want of reason. Winston looked up quickly:

'I've no intention of giving him any appointment at the Ministry of Health. We mustn't count our chickens before they are hatched.' He added in a kindly way: 'I've never seen you upset before, Charles. You mustn't let anything I say upset you.'

'Tell me,' he went on, 'what they are saying. You won't offend me.'

'Oh, it would take a long time and you are busy.'

'Now, Charles, you cannot say there's a lot of talk, and leave it like that. You must make out your case.'

I told him what McGowan [1] had said; that he could talk to Attlee about industry, but that Winston would not listen to him; that Winston tried to go on running everything himself as he did in the war; that he ought to retire.

'Who said that?' he demanded.

'A friend of yours,' I answered.

No one in their senses would fire stories at Winston, but I saw that for once his curiosity was aroused.

'He wasn't speaking for anybody,' Winston grunted.

'I'm not so sure about that; a good many want you to retire. But there! You know political life better than I do. Everything is in a mess, and you'll need a Cabinet of all the talents to carry people with you.'

He lit a match and held it under the end of his cigar.

'We're not going to have just the old gang as you call them. But the time hasn't come yet to parcel out the posts.'

I wanted to end the conversation.

October 11, 1951

Winston will argue of course, but he is aware that there is something in what people are saying. Behind his bluff he is eaten up with misgivings. This morning when I arrived at Hyde Park Gate they

[1] Lord McGowan, Chairman, Imperial Chemical Industries.

told me: 'He was all in last night when he got back from Liverpool,' where he had gone to make an election speech. And when I went to his room, before I could say anything he admitted:

'I had a considerable reaction yesterday. I was glad I had nothing to do today.'

He had been impressed by the X-rays; it was a 'wonderful machine.' Turning to MacKenna,[1] he said:

'Immediately I had it I felt the benefit; I believe they will cure the bloody itching over my shoulders. I would like another dose today.

'*The Times* is very favourable to me, more so than it has been for a long time.'

He told me how Liverpool had cheered him, and as he spoke of the 'love and affection of the people' his eyes filled with tears. 'There was rapture in their eyes. They brought their children. I'm not conceited,' he said, 'but they wanted to touch me.' He spoke humbly, as if he was just an instrument of the Almighty.

When MacKenna rose to take his leave, Winston asked me to stay. As the door shut he said that he had a 'muzzy feeling' in his head:

'Oh, it's nothing to do with alcohol; it comes on generally before luncheon. Aspirin helps it. If it's due to the circulation in my head, can't you think out something, Charles, that would be more effective than aspirin?'

He sat huddled in his chair, gazing gloomily at the carpet.

'I am not so sure as I was that I shall be able to see things through.'

I was disturbed that he said as much; it was not like him. He knew that the incident at Monte Carlo, when his arm suddenly became 'funny,' was a notice to quit the world. In a few days he would be seventy-seven.

'I'm not afraid to die,' he said after a time, 'but I want to do this job properly.'

I told him I knew of no nostrum that would rejuvenate the circulation in his head. If he wanted to stay the course he must cut out things; he could not do everyone's job as he had done in the war; nobody wanted it. He interrupted:

'If I win the election I shall take on the Ministry of Defence.'

I retorted that he ought to get that idea out of his head. He had never felt any desire to share with anyone the burden that he carried in the war. But now things were changed; he was an old man. I tried to argue with him. He answered that he had asked Portal to do it, but Portal had replied that he would do almost anything for

---

[1] Mr. R. M. B. MacKenna, dermatologist, St. Bartholomew's Hospital.

Mr. Churchill except to get involved in political life. He would have liked Alex to take it on, but he was not free.[1]

I wondered what was passing through his mind. He has always coveted office, probably he always will, but why does he want to be Prime Minister when, as he knows, he is not the man he was?

'You look tired and sad, Charles,' he said, interrupting my thoughts.

October 15, 1951

Today at twenty minutes to one o'clock Winston telephoned to say that he had a temperature.

'What is it?' I asked.

'Oh, ninety-nine degrees,' he answered, 'but it may go up tonight.' He was leaving Euston at one o'clock.

'Could you come and see me at the station?'

Ninety-nine degrees was nothing, but there was the question of morale, for he is always impressed by a temperature. I asked him if he would like me to come with him to Huddersfield.

'I would like that very much, Charles.'

I found him apprehensive, but when the train had started and I took his temperature it was normal. He was rather disconcerted. Was the thermometer wrong? Was it all a false alarm? Would my plans be badly upset?

Winston asked me in the train to vet his speech, but I knew that my function was to comfort and reassure; it was too late to reconstruct.

We drove to the meeting from the train. There were seventeen hundred people in the hall; a thousand of them Conservatives and seven hundred Liberals. Some, when they could not get admission, had said, 'No seat, no vote.' The P.M.'s speech was in no way exceptional. When he stuck to his text his voice was strong and he spoke with vigour and conviction. But he kept introducing asides, and this he did in a very uncertain and hesitant manner which was anything but impressive. Winston, of course, is a born writer, but in speaking it is only by blood and sweat that he has become as effective as he is. Lady Violet Bonham Carter,[2] on the other hand, has the address of a natural orator. When he had done and she began to speak he sat apart on the platform as if he were by himself; his head had sunk into his shoulders, and in the hard light of the hall his face and scalp appeared devoid of hair; the monolithic lines

---

[1] Field-Marshal Alexander was Governor-General of Canada, 1946–52.

[2] Lady Violet Bonham Carter, daughter of Herbert Asquith, Liberal candidate for Huddersfield West, was supported by Churchill in the absence of a Conservative candidate.

of the great skull and jowl were somehow familiar; yes, he was like
Mussolini. His eyes gazed vacantly into the distance out of the
expressionless mask of a deaf man. There was a political meeting
going on, but he was not part of it; only when the laughter in the
hall caught his ear would he turn for enlightenment to his neighbour,
and twice he took out his watch and looked at it in a puzzled way,
as if these speeches were going on for a long time.

When it was all over we returned to the train, where we sat down
to a late supper—Winston cheerful and talkative, as is his way after
a speech. The deaf old man, who only an hour ago sat by himself
on the platform, huddled up and forlorn, was gone, and in his place
we saw a rejuvenated Winston, with his pink face and his boyish
spirits. His political agents and advisers had vanished, his worries
had resolved, and in the little family party of Lady Violet and Lord
Layton,[1] he could relax and allow his thoughts to go back to the
past. Lord Layton spoke of his orderly administration.

'You don't often get the credit for this, Winston,' he chuckled.

Winston smiled his gratitude. Layton felt things were going well;
he might even venture a little.

'Tell us, Winston, what was your biggest mistake—what do you
yourself consider now was your biggest mistake in the war?'

'I've no doubt at all,' Winston replied at once. 'Not going to
meet Truman after Roosevelt's death. During the next three months
tremendous decisions were made, and I had a feeling that they were
being made by a man I did not know.'

There was a long pause, and then he added:

'It wasn't my fault. I wanted to cross the Atlantic. But Anthony
put me off. He telegraphed from Washington that they did not
want me.'

He could say what he liked now, he could throw caution to the
winds, and to Lady Violet he freely admitted that for his part he
wanted an independent Liberal Party. If the Tories and Liberals
were united on a social policy, then he would have no fear of
Socialists, but he did fear the vulnerability of the Tories if they were
alone. The truth is that he is not happy with diehard Tories, any
more than was his father before him. Lady Violet was bitter about
the National Liberals.[2]

[1] Lord Layton, Deputy Leader of the Liberal Party.

[2] The Liberal Party joined Ramsay MacDonald's National government in 1931,
but was soon split over the Government's tariff reform proposals. The Free Trade
Liberals left the Government in the following year, but Sir John Simon remained
with the National Government along with his Protectionist followers. They
became known as National Liberals, but soon became difficult to distinguish from
Conservatives.

'Now, Violet,' Winston gently interposed, filling her glass with champagne with a whimsical pucker, 'you mustn't be too hard on them. I have only managed to live so long by carrying no hatreds.'

It is indeed true: he is completely without rancour. I asked what Max was up to.

'Oh, he flits about everywhere. He wants the jockey to win, but he hates his horse. The Tories,' Winston added sadly, 'hate him and he hates them. Max says we shall get a bigger majority than we deserve. If we are beaten,' mused Winston, 'I shall retire. There is a kind of argument going about that I am too old. I don't feel old, and I don't think I look old, though I'm on my way to eighty.'

He had received assurances from several men prominent in trade-union circles that if the country gave a definite, unequivocal verdict they would respect the constitutional issue.

His mind wandered back to the war. He had 'had great influence over President Roosevelt until about three months before Yalta; then he ceased to answer my letters.' Winston defended the President; he was not to blame for Yalta. Stalin was the villain. He spoke of the tragedy of Potsdam, of giving Russia all that she demanded 'instead of having a show-down' as he wished, which would have prevented a third world war. He was bringing forward evidence in his book that he had taken steps to postpone the demobilization of certain units until we got a satisfactory solution. 'Of course,' he added, 'Russia might not have taken all this lying down.'

It was after midnight; everyone but Winston appeared a little jaded, but he was eager and gay, and talked all the time. Lady Violet said she must go to bed.

'Ah, no, Violet, not yet.'

She put her hand on his shoulder.

'I must, Winston, I'm so tired.'

He rose reluctantly and the party broke up. When we were alone he began telling me how some Catholic bishops had come to see him. The Labour Party had made them promises, and they came to him to see what the Conservatives would do. Winston had said to them: 'This is not a spiritual way of doing things.' They had a look, he said, of the other world.

'I belong to this world,' he paused, 'but . . .' I waited. He did not finish the sentence.

October 27, 1951

Winston has crawled back into Downing Street—his majority over all other parties is eighteen. After all the talk of a majority of a hundred and fifty it must be a great disappointment to him. But when I asked one of the secretaries whether he was upset by the figures, she replied: 'Oh, I don't think so; he's relieved he is in.'

November 8, 1951

Found Winston in poor spirits.

'I have had to fill seventy-five offices—it has worried me, particularly the junior appointments. If anyone is left out, it is probably the end of his political hopes. You know how unhappy it makes me to hurt others.' He sighed deeply. 'The last fortnight has been more tiring than anything in the war. There were great decisions then, of course, but I was swept along by events.'

November 9, 1951

The election has played the devil with Winston's hearing; his deafness has been much worse during the past fortnight. 'It is a bloody nuisance,' he said sulkily. I advised him to see Victor Negus, but he preferred to call in another ear surgeon, who had good hands and a reputation for skilful technique. Both have attended him in the past. Winston's man always has an explanation for everything; above all, he always does something. So Winston likes him. He will send for him just before he has to make a speech; he pops in and sprays his throat (with normal salt solution); it seems to give him confidence that his voice will not fail. Negus, on the other hand, is dour and taciturn, with the scientific habit of mind, which is rare in any doctor, but particularly rare in this branch of medicine. I have complete confidence in his opinion, but he has made no impression on Winston—just as Wavell made none, and for the same reason. The two men ran true to form. Winston's man saw him first. He did not wait to test whether his hearing was in fact worse; the deafness was, he said, probably due to wax. But when he syringed his ears no wax was found.

November 10, 1951

This morning I brought Negus to No. 10. In the car I said to him: 'Why should Winston's deafness suddenly get much worse?'

'That's the point,' he answered. 'It may be that when I test his hearing with an audiometer I shall find no deterioration at all; he may be suffering only from fatigue of his perception, due to the

349

strain of the election. If so, his hearing will soon improve, and his deafness will be no worse than it was when I tested his hearing eighteen months since.'

And so it proved to be, but Winston was not impressed. He remains faithful to his cheerful and talkative empiric.

Chapter thirty-five

An American journey

The Queen Mary, *December 30, 1951*

The lady after whom this ship is named was talking to a friend who had forgotten something and was looking for her spectacles. They could not be found, and her old bones grumbled when she attempted to rise from her chair.

'The disabilities as one gets older, Ma'am, are horrible.'

'Damnable,' said the old Queen.

Ten years have gone by since we first travelled with Winston in the *Queen Mary*. Yet tonight we might be back again in the war; the P.M. is still talking and there, opposite to him, is Pug, still listening to him with his mouth open, as if he would not miss a syllable, uttering the same throaty, gurgling sounds of mirth. Pug, anyway, has not changed. Everything else seems different. The indomitable spirit of the P.M. of those years, battling against a deadly threat to the world's freedom, is now struggling only with the humiliations of old age and with economic problems that are quite beyond his ken.

Jock brought in a paper which he handed to the P.M.

P.M.: 'In all my life I have never seen so bewildering a situation.'

Eden: 'It is complicated.'

P.M.: 'Bewildering. And this war could easily have been stopped. At Locarno[1] it was nearly stopped. Russia would have fought at Munich.'

Moran: 'Isn't that true of both wars?'

P.M.: 'Oh, no, Charles. The first war was different, it would have been difficult to prevent it. The French were out for *revanche* and the Germans for glory, and England said, "We don't want to fight, but

---

[1] Locarno Pact—a series of agreements in 1925 between Germany, Britain, France, Italy and Belgium to keep the peace in Western Europe. Germany renounced the use of force to effect frontier changes in the west and agreed to arbitration in her eastern border disputes.

by Jingo if we do." There was a lot of glory about. Even I'—and there was a mischievous smirk—'with my very different feelings, was thrilled. You know, Anthony, if a grandson of the Kaiser had been left on the throne after 1918 Hitler would never have seized power. But it's no use saying this to the Americans. The only King they think of is George III. Look at Austria. Why, all the countries which threw off her yoke, Czecho-Slovakia and the rest, have suffered endless, cruel tortures.'

The Prof. wondered whether in Washington he would get any information about the manufacture of atomic bombs.

P.M.: 'The Labour Government spent a hundred millions on atomic research without telling anyone, without any Parliamentary sanction whatever. Their Party knew nothing about it. I could not have done it. How was it done? Oh, they just divided the money between seven or eight departments. And they called me a war-monger!' he said angrily. 'Tell me, Anthony, about Roger Makins.[1] You like him? He is good?'

Eden: 'Yes, I think he is very able. But the Prof. here knows all about him.'

Prof.: 'He passed into the F.O. at the top of the list after a brilliant first at Oxford. He is a Fellow of All Souls.'

Eden (*smiling*): 'And he's sensible in spite of that.'

January 1, 1952

All the P.M.'s party, the three Cabinet Ministers, Norman his valet, his two detectives, the Prof.'s cook—were summoned last night to go to his sitting-room at ten minutes before midnight to toast the New Year. When the clock had struck twelve times the P.M., whose thoughts seemed a long way off, pulled himself out of his chair, put down his glass and, crossing his arms, began to shout Auld Lang Syne. When this had been sung he tried to give the note for 'God Save the King.' Then he resumed his seat as if his part in the proceedings had been safely accomplished. After a little the room began to thin—youth went off to dance—till none were left but the Prof., Pug, Slim[2] and Norman Brook. For some time the P.M. sat lost in his thoughts and no one spoke.

'I cannot tell you,' he said at last, 'how much happier I shall be when I have worked out the substance of what I shall say to Congress. The speech might not come off,' he mused, 'but I shall do my best whatever happens. I feel bewildered in my mind. The three thousand

[1] Sir Roger Makins, Deputy Under-Secretary of State, Foreign Office.
[2] Field-Marshal Sir William Slim, Chief of the Imperial General Staff, 1948-52.

seven hundred millions of pounds which was to be spent on re-armament has gone up to five thousand two hundred millions. We have not stopped the rise in wages. Anyway, I'm not going to beg.'

He sat glowering at the carpet.

'We shall have to make great sacrifices,' the P.M. murmured without looking up. Then his face brightened. 'How much would it mean to the country,' he asked, 'if everyone gave up smoking? I would not hesitate to give up my cigars.'

He got up and I went with him to his room.

'I have done very little today,' he said as he kicked off his slippers so that they skidded along the floor. 'I am not so good mentally as I used to be. A speech has become a burden and an anxiety. Tell me, Charles, the truth. Am I going slowly to lose my faculties?'

He asked me to take his pulse; it was rapid and irregular.

January 4, 1952

'It was late last night,' the P.M. admitted, 'when I settled in; I am glad I shall have a light day. Discussions don't tire me. I should look forward to every hour of this trip but for these two speeches. They hover over me like two vultures. What to say worries me. I dip into the well whenever anything is needed and generally find something there, but it does not come as freely as it did; it is harder work.'

'What is today?' he asked. 'The fourth? On the seventh the terrible announcement will be made.[1] People will be told that, if we go on spending as we are doing, by June there will be no money left. I'm glad I cannot be held responsible for it,' he said gravely. 'Never in my life have I faced an ordeal of this kind. It is worse than 1940. In Washington they will feel we are down and out. We have to tell them that if the rearmament is not spread out over a longer time the nations of Western Europe will be rushing to bankruptcy and star-vation. When I have come to America before it has been as an equal. If, late in the war, they spoke of their sacrifices we could retort by saying that for a year and a half we fought alone; that we had suffered more losses.' He sighed deeply. 'They have become so great and we are now so small. Poor England! We threw away so much in 1945.'

I tried to argue that it was in the interests of America to meet us

---

[1] The announcement of a large fall in our dollar reserves was made on January 7, and further import cuts, reductions in rations and other restrictions were imposed on January 29, when Parliament reassembled.

halfway. If the P.M. failed in his attempts to stabilize our finances, there would be a swing to the left in England and we should give up any attempt to rearm, so that Germany would be thrown into the arms of Russia. He did not agree. If England and Western Europe pulled out, America would rearm Germany. America alone could defeat Russia. I turned the conversation to his speech. He seemed a little happier about it; he was picking up points from the discussions.

January 5, 1952

A driving rain kept me below until the last minute, and when I came on deck I saw three tugs, the *Mary Moran, Gertrude Moran* and *Alice Moran*, preparing to pilot the great monster to her berth. I wish I were as sure of my bearings as I try to guide my master on his journey. When we landed he was delivered up to the Press, who were tumbling over one another to get at him. After the P.M. left the shed I drove with Leslie Rowan to the aerodrome. Nobody, I suppose, saw more of the P.M. during the war than he did—he was his private secretary until the General Election of 1945, and his ability is such that everyone seems confident that he will one day be head of the Civil Service. I asked him whether he noticed many changes in Winston.

'Oh, yes,' he answered rather sadly, 'he has lost his tenacity; he no longer pushes a thing through. He has lost, too, his power of fitting in all the problems one to another. Of course in the war he would run a pet scheme, but it was always fitted into the whole plan. And he forgets figures. In the war he never did. Why, the other day I mentioned a figure he had used in the House of Commons. "Did I?" he asked, puzzled. Besides, the problems are different now. Questions of economics. He was not brought up on such things.'

I asked Leslie if he had noticed any physical changes. He seemed surprised that I should ask such a question.

'Yes, of course.'

'How?' I persisted.

'Oh, the way he walks—slowly, like an old man. Even his handling of the Press Conference today was different. It was good, of course, but not so good as it used to be in the war.' Leslie smiled. 'But he can still coin phrases. He referred yesterday to the Standing Group who deal with a future war as "Chiefs of Staff vitiated by the intrusion of the French." '

We drove between two lines of sandwich-men bearing boards: 'England bleeds Americans.' 'Money for Imperialists, but none for

Veterans.' They were Irish, or perhaps Communists, picketing the Cunard Pier. At the airfield the P.M. climbed slowly into the air-craft 'Independence,' lent by the President. During the short flight he appeared absorbed in the newspapers, but when we came down outside Washington he looked up and said:

'It is fifty years since I came here first. Mark Twain was my host.'

The world was full of his exploits then, like his escape from the Boers, and the Americans were eager to hear his story. They are still interested in him. He picked up his hat and gloves in one hand and his gold-headed cane in the other and stood at the head of the ramp, gazing down at President Truman and his Administration, who were waving to him from the tarmac. The feeling that things were about to happen came back; he pricked up his ears; he did not feel so old, after all.

It had been arranged that the visit to Washington should begin with a trip on the President's yacht on the Potomac River, but this afternoon a bitter wind caught the breath, and when the time came his little party gazed doubtfully at the grey, bleak prospect; rather anxiously they wondered how the Prime Minister's party manners would respond to such a searching test. However, we were quite wrong, and those of us who welcomed the returned reveller, when he appeared at the Embassy in the small hours, were startled to find something like the Winston we had half forgotten. He was full of the evening.

'Oh, I enjoyed it so much; we talked as equals.'

Franks:[1] 'It was a good beginning.'

Eden was more cautious. Truman, who had been very lively before dinner, had, it seemed, never opened his lips until the coffee appeared. They debated whether this had any significance. The P.M. brushed aside their doubts:

'There were twelve of us round a table, the guidance of the world was in our hands, not for domination but to work for the good of mankind.'

It was not, it seemed, that they had reached agreement on any specific issue, but rather there had been an atmosphere of friendliness which had given him pleasure.

'I do hope,' said the P.M., 'that Anthony will meet the Americans over China, which really does not matter to us. Then they in turn might meet us about Egypt or Persia, which matter a lot. After all, what Conservative in England is in favour of Chinese Communists?'

[1] Sir Oliver Franks, British Ambassador in Washington, 1948–52.

But the Foreign Secretary held his peace, and a few minutes later he said firmly that it was time for bed. When we were alone in his room the P.M. talked with animation. Then his face fell. On January 7 the adverse trade balance would come out. 'It will do a lot of harm.'

January 7, 1952

At breakfast this morning there appeared to be some disquiet about the rigidity of the American attitude. The P.M., according to Norman Brook, is so glad to be in Washington that he'd be happy even if they threw bricks at him. He doesn't mind rough stuff in the course of discussion; in fact, he rather likes it. But Eden is more sensitive, he seems to take it more to heart.

There was a discussion during luncheon—it went on till half-past three—in the course of which Mr. Churchill attacked with some heat the decision to give the command of the Atlantic to an American.[1] The C.I.G.S., the First Sea Lord[2] and Pug Ismay in turn urged him to accept the plan; we had got everything, they argued, that really mattered, for in a war the First Sea Lord would really be in control. They were particularly anxious to avoid putting up the back of the American Navy, which had taken criticism from the P.M. in the most generous spirit, just because it was Mr. Churchill. Franks interjected in his cool way that it was an issue which only counted on paper. But the P.M. would have none of it.

'I realize,' he said, 'that England is a broken and impoverished power, which has cast away a great part of its Empire and of late years has misused its resources, but these fellows bungled the U-boat war, and had to come to us for help. America may know far more than our Navy does about combined "ops" in the Pacific, between their Navy and Air Force, but she knows very little of U-boat warfare. You have urged me to do this fake without any explanation to public or Parliament. I will not do that. It must all come out publicly.'

The First Sea Lord went away to draft a modification of the plan. He wanted to meet the P.M.'s views, and when he returned he handed a paper to the P.M., but he would have none of it. Once more McGrigor retired, resolved to make a great effort to straighten

[1] It was informally agreed before Churchill took office (1951) that the supreme command of the Atlantic should rest with an American. The Atlantic Command (Saclant) was established finally on April 11, 1952, under Admiral Lyndon McCormick, U.S. Navy.

[2] Admiral of the Fleet Sir Rhoderick R. McGrigor, First Sea Lord and Chief of Naval Staff (1951–5).

things out, and after a time he appeared with another draft. He wanted the P.M. to say that he did not agree with the principle of the Atlantic Command, but must accept the commitments of the last British Government—as in so many other things.

'Why,' said the P.M. indignantly, 'go and tell that to Portsmouth and Plymouth and see what they think. The announcement that an American was to command in the Atlantic, coming only a week after the appointment of Eisenhower, was a great shock to the public. Attlee did not realize its significance, nor did Shinwell.' [1]

There was an awkward pause. And then the P.M. turned to his Service Chiefs, saying:

'I would have liked to agree with you, at a time when I am pre-occupied with my Congress Speech, but I cannot give up my convictions. If I had I should not be here.'

He got up from the table and went to his room. Leslie Rowan complained that Winston could no longer see things in perspective. (Brooke used the same words during the second conference at Quebec in September, 1944.) One day he was ready to fight to the last ditch to get his way about the Atlantic Command—it seemed to him that our national prestige was at stake—the next day he did not appear to care what four hundred million Chinese thought of England; the ferment in the Far East hardly seemed to interest him. I did not attempt to argue the point with Rowan. I was glad that the P.M. would have time for a short sleep before his next meeting at five o'clock.

When I went to wake him at half-past four I found that he had not slept, but it was restful, he said, to lie in the dark. He was unhappy, he told me sadly.

'For five years these officers have had no lead. They have got into the way of agreeing to anything. There is a deadlock over the Atlantic Command. I may have to submit. I might have to say to the Americans: "I am sorry you will not release me from the agreement with the Labour Government." '

Once more he spoke of the feeling of inequality; it was a canker in his mind, he grieves that England in her fallen state can no longer address America as an equal, but must come, cap in hand, to do her bidding. His reflections in the dark had taken a sombre turn, and he went on to talk of the defeat of the Pleven Government:[2] the

---

[1] Emanuel Shinwell, Minister of Defence, 1950–1.

[2] René Pleven, head of the French coalition government (July, 1950–February, 1951). The ninth of a series of ten coalition governments (November, 1946–July, 1951), all of which were variations formed from the 'Third Force' of Socialists, Radicals and Republican People's Party (M.R.P.).

French were an extraordinary people to do this when a 'coherent attitude' was needed. I asked him if he thought Eisenhower would be nominated by the Republicans. His face lit up:

'Ike has not only to be wooed but raped.'

January 8, 1952

I had gone to my room before luncheon, when the Ambassador put his head through the door. He began by saying he was afraid he had been a poor host, and then he came to the point. He does not want the P.M. to outstay his welcome in Washington; while he is here Truman and Dean Acheson[1] would have him on their minds. The Ambassador had seen signs that he might stop on. He ought to get away by the 19th. If he wants to stay longer it must be in New York—not Washington.

Franks is unlike anyone here. For one thing, he does not seem tired. The clarity of his pronouncements reminds one that he is a scholar, the product of a discipline to which no one here except the Prof. has been subject. He is, too, an exile, only waiting for his release to return to Oxford, so that no man is his master—and he thinks for himself. As the P.M.'s host, he is at once firm and polite. He thinks only Clemmie can persuade the P.M. to retire. He hopes she will not try. He was not a politician, he said, but he hoped this government might stay in office for three years. I said the P.M. felt the inequality with the United States.

'Yes,' Franks interjected, 'the humiliation.'

I doubted whether it could be changed until we had put our house in order economically.

'Exactly,' he snapped.

No one else here would have used that word; everyone seems to dislike precision as they would a commitment. Franks agreed that if the P.M. had no knowledge of economics, at any rate he would have the guts to tell the people the truth when the solution of our financial problems had been given to him. Not that he thought poorly of Eden, who, he said, has good judgment in spite of appearing a little on edge—in fact, in spite of his façade.

'Yes, the Prime Minister is tough,' Franks rapped out; 'after a rough night he eats a breakfast like a boy—surely no one at seventy-seven can require so much. Come,' he said, 'it is time we went down.'

Franks is an individual; he says things which those of us who have worked in a team refrain from saying. He said to Eden before we sat down to luncheon:

'The Foreign Secretary this morning was not allowed to answer

[1] Secretary of State in President Truman's Administration.

for foreign affairs. If I had been Foreign Secretary I should have been very angry.'

Eden: 'I was angry.'

The only guest at lunch was Senator McMahon, Chairman of the Senatorial Atomic Energy Committee. The P.M. sent for the original document which set forth the terms of agreement with President Roosevelt about the atomic bomb.[1] When it was brought to him, he handed it to McMahon. The Senator read it.

P.M.: 'We have been grossly deceived. There has been a breach of faith.'

The Senator: 'If we had known this the Act would not have been passed. Attlee never said a word.'

P.M.: 'No. The Americans are not an unjust people. I've learnt a lot during the voyage. I had not read many of the papers since I came into office.'

It was now three o'clock, and Franks tried to persuade the P.M. to adjourn to the drawing-room to allow the servants to clear the table.

P.M.: 'Cannot we sit here a little longer? I regard this time after lunch as an island of peace in a stormy sea.'

Tonight he said he would not come down to dinner; he would rest in bed. He had slept for more than an hour and felt refreshed, but he said:

'I am still weary. Why, Charles, since I left London I have been kicked about; I hardly know night from day; it's all right for a younger man, but I am an immense age. It's not so much going to meetings, it's thinking out what you say.'

Down below, Eden, Franks and Roger Makins sat picking the communiqué to pieces.

'Every paragraph,' Eden complained, 'begins "The Prime Minister . . ." or "The Foreign Secretary was instructed . . .". No one instructs me. The Prime Minister and I are colleagues.'

Makins: 'It ought to be "we." '

So it was changed, but when the communiqué was taken to the P.M. he was scornful. They had 'clothed themselves in wool and fed on pap.'

'Take it away,' he said. 'I can make nothing of this.'

[1] Roosevelt and Churchill agreed at the Quebec conference, 1943, that Britain and the United States should exchange their information on the technical developments of atomic weapons. In 1946, however, Senator McMahon, who was unaware of the agreement, sponsored a Bill in the American Congress which severely curtailed this mutual exchange. The Labour Government failed to press home British rights in this matter and the Bill became law.

January 9, 1952

The P.M. has developed a habit—I cannot put a date to the tendency—of making a spot diagnosis of a man, a kind of surface impression, which is rather disconcerting; he will dismiss from his mind quite considerable folk if the first impact is unfavourable. Roger Makins, Norman Brook and I lunched with him on the train to New York, when he spoke scornfully of the First Sea Lord's ineffectiveness. He had no grasp of things. Before him he remembered a long line of First Sea Lords; they had all been great sailors. The P.M. falls for swashbuckling fellows—it is not necessary to ask which he admired more, Beatty or Jellicoe. Vian had impressed him at Bristol—'at least he has fire in his belly; if he had been with us when the Atlantic Command was discussed things would have taken a different turn.' Norman Brook interjected that McGrigor had a great reputation in the Navy, but the P.M. pursued his own thoughts. If Vian was brought in as First Sea Lord perhaps McGrigor could be given the Portsmouth Command. 'We must go into this,' he said with an air of finality. He spoke about Troubridge turning away from the *Goeben*, and then excusing himself by saying he had not enough fuel. He was told to use up all he had and he would be towed back. Jellicoe himself had a streak of this—three times in the Battle of Jutland he turned away.

'When a man cannot distinguish a great from a small event he is no use. Now Slim is quite different. I can work with him.'

When Slim says something which he thinks matters his jaws snap together like a steel trap, while McGrigor is so diminutive, so hesitating in his address, that the romantic Winston Churchill, who keeps a small bust of Nelson in his room at Chartwell, is quite put out. He has never possessed any gift for the measurement of men. Now he seems ready to scrap his First Sea Lord, whom he met for the first time on this voyage, merely because he did not support him on this issue, in which the P.M. is in a minority of one.

On the outskirts of New York the P.M.'s host, Bernie Baruch,[1] boarded the train.

'Bernie!' Winston exclaimed as he hurried up the saloon to greet him.

For the moment it appeared as if he was about to embrace him. What manner of man is this, I wondered, who is acclaimed by other men in the States as completely disinterested? He wants nothing for himself, so it is said, and all recent Presidents have been glad to turn to him for advice. At any rate, that was the position; I am not sure whether it still is. Bernie Baruch is a Jew, now in his

---

[1] Bernard Baruch, American financier and adviser to successive Presidents.

eighty-first year, but neither his years nor his deafness appear to cut him off from his fellows: his intense interest in people is undiminished and his alert features keep relaxing into a friendly smile. It is as if he said: 'I don't know what you are saying, but I am sure you are having great fun and I want you to feel quite at home.'

Winston cannot be bothered as a rule to introduce his friends to his 'circus,' but tonight during dinner he seemed to feel he would like others to know more about Bernie.

'Can I tell them about your early days?' he enquired.

Bernie smiled. Perhaps he heard the P.M.'s question.

'Bernie's fortune,' the P.M. said, 'began this way. One day, it was a Friday, the eve of the Jewish Sabbath, he saw the opportunity had come to make his fortune. He instructed his broker to buy heavily. But next day he was torn in his feelings; he always spent Saturday with his mother; he determined to keep to his custom and deliberately cut himself off from the market, declining all telephone calls. Then when the sun had gone down and the Sabbath was at an end, he found he had made seven hundred thousand dollars in a day.' The P.M. loved the story. 'If it had not been for the Jewish Sabbath,' he said, 'you would probably have cashed in and sold at, say, a hundred and fifty thousand dollars. You would not have hung on.'

Once only was the pleasing harmony between the two men in danger. Britain ought to be consulted, the P.M. contended vigorously, before an atomic bomb was sent off from airfields in East Anglia. Baruch at once broke in:

'But a considerable proportion of our bombing personnel are in Britain, and they would in that case be subject to your veto. If that is maintained it might be wise to withdraw them.'

The P.M. (*with some vehemence*): 'If the American Government take the line that they need not consult us, then they had better begin removing them now. Have you seen our agreement with Roosevelt?'

Baruch: 'No, I haven't.'

P.M.: 'It laid down that neither America nor Britain would release bombs without the consent of the other Government.'

Baruch: 'Cadogan made no objection.'

The P.M. thought the Russians were frightened of us and that there would be no war, but he spoke of October, 1952, as if it might be touch and go. Baruch agreed.

January 10, 1952

Today Bernie summoned three pundits of the Press to lunch with the P.M.; he wants him to get the feel of opinion before he addresses

Congress. There were General Adler and Sulzberger of the *New York Times*, and Daniel Longwell, who holds *Life* together under Henry Luce. We had hardly taken our seats when the P.M. said without warning:

'What other nation in history, when it became supremely powerful, has had no thought of territorial aggrandizement, no ambition but to use its resources for the good of the world? I marvel at America's altruism, her sublime disinterestedness.'

All at once I realized Winston was in tears, his eyes were red, his voice faltered. He was deeply moved. Sulzberger broke the silence.

'I think, Prime Minister, it was hard-headedness on our part. I mean it was thought out, not emotional. Anyway, I hope it was, because emotion soon passes, whereas a thought-out plan might last. What view is taken in Britain about German unity?'

P.M.: 'I always felt in the war that we must strike down the tyrant, but be ready to help Germany up again as a friend. I have been doubtful about a European army only because I was concerned with its fighting power. It will not fight if you remove all traces of nationalism. I love France and Belgium, but we cannot be reduced to that level.'

And then the P.M. began to plead for a token American brigade, or even a battalion of Marines, to be sent to the Suez Canal.

P.M.: 'Now that we no longer hold India the Canal means very little to us. Australia? We could go round the Cape. We are holding the Canal not for ourselves but for civilization. I feel inclined to threaten the Americans that we will leave the Canal if they don't come in.'

General Adler: 'Could not America be invited to send this token force? If this is not done, I doubt if Congress will play.'

P.M.: 'I want it as a symbol that it is a United Nations project. Stalin was responsible for the United Nations and for the coming together of the two great English-speaking peoples; without him it might not have happened for generations. The architect of the Kremlin "builded better than he knew."

'Since Persia, the Egyptians have felt that America would not support Britain.[1] A token brigade would convince them they were wrong.'

---

[1] When Persia nationalized her oil industry and with it the Anglo-Iranian Oil Company on May 2, 1951, the Americans failed to support the British Government's protest.

Government House, Ottawa, January 11, 1952

The P.M. has been looking forward to his stay with Alex, who has a great hold over his affections, and his interest was quickened when General Templer arrived in order to be vetted for the command in Malaya.[1] After the business of the First Sea Lord, we are all a little apprehensive about Templer's fate. Alex was quite sure he was the man for this job of rooting out the Communist guerrillas from the jungle and Monty, too, had sent a letter, so we are hopeful that all will go well. Before I went to bed Templer told me he had talked with the P.M. for two hours.

'Winston began: "I am an old man. I shall probably not see you again. I may be sending you to your death." When he said this he almost broke down. And then he said to me: "Ask for power, go on asking for it, and then—never use it." At the end the P.M. smiled: "Here am I talking to you for all this time when I have two speeches on my hands." '

Templer turned to me:

'What is there about this man which no one else has?'

He did not seem to expect an answer, and I had none to give. He began to talk of his task in Malaya.

'The military problem is nothing. The police question can be set right; the civil service difficulty can be solved. What we have to do is to get the Malay and the Chinaman, with their different languages and religions, the followers of Confucius and of Islam, to say: "This is our country." '

Then Templer spoke of morale.

'There was something wrong with the British soldier in the last war; he would not have stood up to what happened in the First War. Are we going soft as a nation? But I feel it can be put right. The death penalty is necessary.'

He went on to recount a night operation:

'We were crossing a swollen river under heavy fire. I collected twenty men who would not face it. I told them that they would have to carry ammunition up a slope raked by fire. They wouldn't do it. I said I would return in an hour and then they would have to do it. In an hour they still refused. I had them court-martialled for mutiny. But at that moment I was whisked away to Anzio, and six

[1] At the end of the war well-armed Communist guerrillas, who had led the opposition to the Japanese, turned on the British in Malaya. A series of atrocities culminated in the assassination of Sir Henry Gurney, the High Commissioner of the Malayan Federation, on October 6, 1951. He was succeeded by Sir Gerald Templer.

weeks later, when I tackled Alex, he said: "They cannot be condemned to death now, the delay has been too long." So no example
was made. Twenty-five divisions could have produced similar
examples. You have studied these things. What is the explanation
of this decay in morale?' he said, turning to me.

When I got a chance, I put Templer's question to Winston. He
gave me a look as if I had accused him of spitting in church. He
did not believe in all this stuff about nerves.

'But,' I persisted, 'surely courage has a social significance? A
man who is ready to risk his skin is an unselfish man. Suppose, for
the sake of argument, that the morale of the Army in this war was
not as good as in the First War, then it means that men on the whole
were not willing to behave as unselfishly.'

He gave a great snort.

'You've got some very queer views,' he said angrily and, taking up
a book, he began to read.

I always give myself a black mark when I get drawn into an argument with Winston.

January 14, 1952

The P.M. said to Templer during luncheon:

'General, your doom will be announced tomorrow. It is a big job
if you bring it off. Good luck to you.'

Whereupon he turned away to his left-hand neighbour and spoke
no more to him. Alex rose. The General, he said, was an old friend,
and in his judgment the Government could not have got a better
man. He invited us to drink the General's health. Templer said
to me under his breath:

'I need not say anything, need I?'

But I could see that the P.M. was looking at him and expected him
to get up.

Templer said simply: 'I know nothing of this job. I will do my
best because I recognize its importance.'

When he sat down the P.M. raised his glass to him, murmuring
something about his 'dangerous mission.'

All day the P.M. has been working at his speech. He has a feeling
that he can add something even now which might make all the
difference. I think he must have infected me with his doubts and
hesitations. Anyway, tonight when he rose to speak at the dinner
given by the Prime Minister of Canada, I was so worked up I
might myself have been making the speech. We had no need to be
jittery. The fervour of his reception was a tribute, not to anything
he had to say, but to his own corner in the hearts of the Canadian

people. Afterwards he sat all crumpled up, but happy, receiving, like a Pope, the homage of the faithful. They were brought up to him one by one, and he gave them his hand, beaming upon them.

'Now,' he said to me, 'I'm not afraid of the Congress speech. When this speech is safely over it's more than half.' He turned to the Prof. 'Don't despise little things. I mean to appeal for a thousand young men to come over here to cut wood, so that we can build ten thousand houses above what Parliament has arranged. They'll have just enough wages to keep them going. And the same with steel. These are flash-lights in the sky.'

The representatives of the Press came up to him and said things which gave him pleasure. Later in his bedroom he said to me:

'They have never let me down. No friend has ever betrayed me.[1] I have come to believe in the brotherhood of man.' A whimsical smile flickered over his face. 'Now I'm making another speech.'

And with that he settled in his pillow.

January 16, 1952

Washington once more. This speech has become an obsession; it has hung over him, like a dark cloud, since the day we left England. At first he seemed to be on the verge of panic whenever it came into his mind. And then, as day after day he became familiar with the issues he must handle, as over and over and over again they were discussed by experts in committee after committee, he began to see what he ought to say. The experienced speaker knows when he has got what he wants, and so as time went by the P.M. became calmer, less irritable; the prospect of standing up before Congress no longer worried him. Once he went so far as to admit he thought it would be all right on the day. If the speech had been made a week ago he might have been jittery. Now there are moments when he even looks forward to it. I find that I am no longer jumpy, as I was in Ottawa. He will bring it off.

When the P.M. is not thinking of his speech to Congress he seems preoccupied with the security of his country.

'In 1940,' he said, 'three-quarters of a million Germans would have been needed to give invasion any chance of success; in 1941 the number had risen to a million and a half. If Hitler had turned on all his factories to making landing craft . . . If . . .' He thought 1941 was the critical year for invasion. 'If,' he mused, 'the Almighty were to rebuild the world and he asked me for advice I would have

---

[1] 'In all my life I found no friend but he was true to me'—*Julius Caesar*. One often catches Shakespearian echoes in his speech.

English Channels round every country. And the atmosphere would be such that anything which attempted to fly would be set on fire.'

The P.M. went on to speak of war with Russia. Americans in Washington appeared anxious that Russia should know what the position was. There were detailed preparations for atomic bombing, the routes for aeroplanes. It was thought that in a month to six weeks three-quarters of Russia could be immobilized. He discussed the three American Chiefs of Staff with Roger Makins. Makins said it was a terrifying thought that three men could press a button to start another war. But the P.M. dwelt on the elemental forces in America: they were enormous; the preparations for war in the past eighteen months had been striking; in three years they would be irresistible.

If, however, the P.M. appeared for the moment to take the prospect of war with Russia rather lightly, he is obsessed with the precarious existence of Britain. There were, he said sadly, fifty million inhabitants, and we produced only enough food for thirty million; the remaining twenty millions must depend for food on our ingenuity in selling our exports. No great power had been so precariously balanced, poised on the pinnacle of Victorian greatness. There would not be time for emigration to help. 'Poor England,' he said with a sigh. He keeps returning to this; it seems to haunt him.

Winston asked Franks about Cripps. Was it true that when he was staying at the Embassy three years ago, at the time of devaluation, Cripps rose at 5 a.m. and ran round the garden with nothing on?

'Nothing?' repeated Winston. 'Not even bathing drawers?'

The First Sea Lord, the P.M. said, had sent him a very fine paper on the Atlantic Command.

'I shall use it tomorrow when I go into action. I suppose,' he reflected, 'he wrote it himself.'

The First Sea Lord was recovering some of the ground lost at first contact.

January 17, 1952

Gladstone might have taken Congress off its feet with a vision of the better world for which the American people were striving, but Winston is not built that way; he must take the problems which interest Congress, and seek to persuade Members to see them through British spectacles. This he did as well as it could be done. He began by setting their suspicions at rest:

'I have not come here to ask you for money to make life more comfortable for the British people. Our standards of life are our own

366

business, and we can only show our native and enduring strength, and keep our self-respect and independence by looking after them ourselves. I have come here to ask you not for gold but for steel; not for favours but for equipment.'

Britain could no longer bear the whole burden of the defence of the Suez Canal.

'We do not seek to be masters of Egypt. We are there only as the servants and guardians of the commerce of the world.'

He went on to speak of deterrents against a third world war. In solemn tones he admonished members of Congress:

'Be careful above all things not to let go the atomic weapon until you are sure and more than sure that other means of preserving peace are in your hands.'

Members had kept their heads—only now, when he spoke of the atomic bomb, was there any real warmth in the applause. But it is election year. Many members were conscious that the eyes of those in the galleries were on them, watching what points in the speech they applauded; they could not respond to his sentiments just as they felt; so they listened in silence while Winston went grimly on his way. (There would be no more elections for *him*. One thought alone gripped his mind: he was fighting for the survival of his country.) Winston has always had the feel of his audiences in America, even when he has lost touch with his own people, and now he ended as they would wish:

'Bismarck once said that the supreme fact of the nineteenth century was that Britain and the United States spoke the same language. Let us make sure that the supreme fact of the twentieth century is that they tread the same path.'

As he resumed his seat there was great applause, as there had been when he rose; whatever they might think of his views, they wanted him to know that he was a favourite son of America in his own right.

When it was done the P.M., flushed and happy, was like a man who has been granted a reprieve. He slumped back in the car, gazing vacantly out of the window; his cigar had gone out; he yawned contentedly. It had gone well, he thought; anyway, they had been very kind before he left the Senate. General Marshall, who had come by air from South Carolina specially to see him, awaited him at the Embassy. Winston was deeply touched; he admires Marshall as a great soldier. He hurried to take both his hands.

Marshall: 'It was a great success, Prime Minister.'

P.M.: 'I think they liked it. All the great speeches in history have had a simple theme; mine had not. I had to take a number of points. Lloyd George used to say that oratory is the art of successful dilution. I never hurry; it is a great mistake. Truman says a hundred and forty words in a minute. It's too fast. You must speak slowly, and you must not be afraid of repetition.'

Marshall, turning to us: 'The most wonderful speech I have heard the Prime Minister make was at Carthage; it was an inspired speech—and there is no record of it. The amphitheatre was full of troops, many in kilts, and then when he stopped the soldiers swept down upon him and he disappeared among them.'

General Marshall knew that every speaker, when he is back in his seat, has the same craving; he wants to know, in Mr. Churchill's words, if he has hit the target. They could now talk of other things.

Marshall: 'What is said here in America is criticized by a million critics, but what is said in Russia has no critics. That is a terrible difference.

'Our basic training is sound, but you need some good professional soldiers to stiffen the "dull mass" of conscripts—your words, Prime Minister.'

P.M.: 'Glorious mass.'

Marshall, regarding Winston with a whimsical smile: 'That is politics.'

January 19, 1952

Today the P.M. is lying fallow. As the train bowled along towards New York he sat looking out of the window. I could not help noticing this, because usually he is impatient to do things, to read the papers, or play cards, or to dictate. Even when he is working on a speech or his book he cannot sit and think things out, he just says aloud what comes into his head, and then at the end he will take the typescript and correct and recorrect it many times. As his mind wandered lazily over the past, from time to time he dropped unconnected fragments. To piece these together appeared to be too much trouble; besides he was too tired to pursue any subject for long; he could not concentrate on anything.

'Baldwin was a remarkable man. I like to make people do what I wish. Baldwin liked to do what they wanted. But he was a great party organizer.

'I loved dining with Joe Chamberlain; he was a sparkling animal, attractive and fascinating, but he was a disrupter'—there was a pause to light his cigar—'a bad element. The Conservative Party was mad to adopt the raw doctrine of Imperial Preference.[1]

[1] After the Imperial Conference of 1902 Joseph Chamberlain managed to per-

'This visit to America has been a gamble. But it has come off, I think. It will do a lot of good. We have taken up old friendships and made new ones. I like Truman fearfully.'

I regretted that he had not persuaded Peter Portal to be Minister of Defence, and wondered if he still felt that Peter 'had everything,' for often with the P.M. to be out of sight is to be out of mind. The P.M. assured me that nothing would induce Portal to leave life in the country. This means that Portal has lost ground since he refused to be Minister of Defence.

There will be three hundred thousand houses next year. He would like each of them to have a little garden, because people at home love flowers. The Americans, he claimed, have no gardens to speak of; the climate is against them.

'I stuck up for the Socialists in Washington. I always get on with Attlee.'

Then the old king business bobbed up.

'When Hindenburg went, then was the time to introduce a prince. There is a gap in Germany when they have no monarch. It was in that gap that a terrible monster, Hitler, appeared. There was a German, I can't remember his name, who came to Chartwell before the war. He was writing a life of Stockmar.[1] The German said that the Generals would turn out Hitler if Britain took a strong line; if she did not, then Hitler would prevail. In 1943 this man was involved in an attempt on Hitler's life and was arrested. After the war he again visited me at Chartwell. I asked him if he was still engaged on his life of Stockmar. He answered that he was. He had received permission to inspect the archives at Windsor. I asked him what he thought of the present German Government. He replied it was not suitable for Germans. They needed a monarchy.' Then the P.M. reverted to conversation in scraps:

'At one time I could have passed an examination in Kipling's writings. My mother was a very patriotic American. When an American horse won the Derby she went about waving a small American flag.'

He looked at the ring on my finger and said it was too tight.

'Do you take it off? Not for forty years?'

---

suade the Tory Cabinet that closer political union of the Empire would come only with tariff preferences, and more particularly the purchase of dearer grain from the Dominions. The prospect of an increase in the price of bread and other goods was a factor in the landslide Tory defeat in 1906.

[1] Baron Christian Friedrich von Stockmar (1787–1863), Anglo-Belgian statesman and unofficial counsellor to Victoria and Albert (1840–63).

He said he took his ring off one finger and put it on another every night before going to sleep.

'Truth is so precious, it should be accompanied by an escort of lies. I told that to Stalin at Teheran; when it was translated he was delighted. I am no good as a conspirator. I talk too much——

'My poor papa died on January 24, 1895. It is a long time ago.

'When I was in Lloyd George's Government I wanted to bring in radical reforms in Egypt, to tax the Pashas and make life worth while for the fellaheen. If we had done that we might be there now. When you learn to think of a race as inferior beings it is difficult to get rid of that way of thinking; when I was a subaltern the Indian did not seem to me equal to the white man.'

Was he, too, having second thoughts? Was the India of his youth, Kipling's India, a mistake, after all? Had he been wrong about the Empire? He had gone out to grass. When he went to his compartment to rest I had a feeling of relief that we were at the end of our journey; an hour later when I called him he said he had slept like a stone.

'I am still very tired,' he said as the train stopped at New York.

The Queen Elizabeth, *January 26, 1952*

It was eleven o'clock in the morning. The P.M. was asleep in his cabin, with his arm across his face, when he woke up with a start.

'I have been dreaming; it was extremely vivid,' he said.

'What did you dream?' I asked.

'Oh, I could not walk straight or see straight.'

He threw off the clothes and got out of bed, and very deliberately walked across the cabin to see if he could walk straight.

What have I learnt about the P.M. during this American visit that I did not know before? He is still better informed than any of his Ministers on any question affecting the Armed Forces of the Crown. It had taken a long time to settle the Atlantic Command, and his obstinate refusal to yield had provoked even members of his own little party. But in the end he salvaged more out of the dispute than anyone thought possible. British anti-submarine forces were, he argued, the key to action in the Atlantic, and he insisted that our naval staff should retain control of any action fought within the 'hundred-fathom line'—Shinwell, he said with contempt, had never heard of the line.

'Our writ will run in the western approaches; two hundred miles west from Plymouth and the St. George's Channel; a hundred and fifty from Belfast and the Mull of Kintyre and more than a hundred miles from Scapa Flow.'

No other man could have achieved so much when the Americans were disposed to give so little.

But Winston's mind is only alert when England's security is at stake, as an old man can remember only the past. There are gaps everywhere in his grip of events—when China was the subject of discussion you could see that he had not got the facts in his head. The old appetite for work has gone; everything has become an effort. And how full of qualms he has become! In 1940—when the world was tumbling about his ears—he did not worry over anything. Now that he is Prime Minister and there is peace he seems to worry over everything. Moods come and go. He is not the same two days running. Is he finished?

Yet in Washington he is still a man apart. They can see, of course, that he is very old and rather deaf. But they still believe in him and in him alone among British politicians. There is something in this man which they do not find in other men. What is it?

Chapter thirty-six

In which I practise my calling

February 7, 1952

King George VI is dead. Before the Prime Minister made his broadcast on the death of the King he sent for his ear man to syringe his throat. Often before, C. P. Wilson had been summoned for the same purpose, but this time it was different. This is what he said to me:

Wilson: 'Usually he has made some light remark, perhaps "Another brandy would do no harm," but now he asked abruptly: "What is the time?" "Twenty minutes to nine, sir," I replied. "No, it's seventeen to nine," he rapped out irritably. "We must hurry." I sprayed his throat with normal saline. When I had done he stalked out without a word. "He is terribly upset, sir," the valet said. "But nothing to lunch-time. Then when he was reading his speech he broke down." After the broadcast he came out of his study and without looking to the right or left made for the Cabinet Room, where he shut himself in.'

The P.M. had spent the whole day preparing his broadcast. He told me about it.

'It was short, but much was expected and much had been said. I wanted to make it a little different. It was only a week ago when I saw the King at the airfield when the Princess left. He was gay and even jaunty, and drank a glass of champagne. I think he knew he had not long to live.' Winston brooded for a time. 'It was a perfect ending. He had shot nine hares and a pigeon a hundred feet up, and then he dined with five friends and went out in the night. What more could any of us ask? I hope, Charles, you will arrange something like that for me.' He smiled. 'But don't do it till I tell you.'

He seemed to have done, and then he added:

'No institution pays such dividends as the Monarchy. Why,

Canada is quite touchy about being called a Dominion, but look what happened when the Princess went there.'

February 12, 1952

Tonight at six-thirty the P.M. will have his first audience with the young Queen.

'Terrific things are happening,' Winston murmured. He spoke of his broadcast; there were letters from all kinds of people. They had liked 'walking with death.' There was nothing original in it, but it seemed 'to help people.' The troops at the funeral had had to wait fifty-five minutes, but no one had fainted or fallen out. He seemed to think this strange and unusual, and connected it vaguely with the occasion. A card, attached to the Government's wreath, bore the inscription: 'For Valour.'[1] Lord Athlone[2] told me that it was in Winston's handwriting; he said the Royal Family loved the words.

February 21, 1952

This evening, when I was about to go down to dinner, the telephone rang; it was Winston's voice. Usually the secretary calls me to the telephone before he comes.

'Where are you, Charles? I'd like to see you.'

I looked at my watch; it was seven-forty. I got into a taxi. 'Take me to 28 Hyde Park Gate.' Was the P.M. going to consult me about the new Minister of Health the papers were talking about? It was not his custom to telephone like this just before dinner. Was anything wrong?

The taxi pulled up at 28 Hyde Park Gate. A strange face opened the door.

'I want to see the Prime Minister.'

'This is the Cuban Embassy, sir. The Prime Minister left here some time ago. He is at 10 Downing Street.'

When I got to No. 10 I found him sitting on his bed in his boiler suit. He looked at me intently as if he were interested in me and wanted to know what I was thinking—so different from his usual detached and almost absent-minded greeting.

'I am glad you have come. I took up the telephone when I woke an hour ago, and I couldn't think of the words I wanted. Wrong words seemed to come into my head, but I was quite clear what was happening and did not say them. This went on for about three or four minutes. Then the operator asked, "Do you want the Private Office?" What does it mean, Charles? Am I going to have a stroke?

---

[1] 'For Valour' is the inscription on the Victoria Cross.

[2] Brother of Queen Mary. Governor-General of Canada, 1940–6.

If this happened again I'd have to pull out. It might come on in a speech. That would be the end. My pulse was all right,' he said, putting his finger on his radial artery. 'Take it now, Charles.'

I told him it was good and regular.

'Is the blood pressure up? Bring your instrument tomorrow and see if it's up. Can you do anything?'

I said I would get some trinitrin medicine.

'What will that do?' he enquired.

'It dilates the vessels and brings more blood to the spot.'

'Will it do me any harm?' he asked a little apprehensively. 'It won't burst an artery? Tell me, Charles, what happened? Why couldn't I find the words I wanted?'

I explained that some of the small vessels in his head had gone into a state of spasm, contracting so that the circulation to the speech centre was diminished.

'You'll have to pull out or arrange things so that the strain is less.'

He listened attentively and then said:

'I keep having to make important decisions, terrible decisions. It never stops. It is worse than the war.'

He rose.

'What shall I say if I run into Clemmie?' I asked.

'Oh, come, we'll go and tell her everything. She's in bed with a cold.'

He told her what had happened. She listened in silence; she was grave but quite composed. He offered to send me home in his car, but I thanked him and said I would walk some of the way. I wanted to do a little hard thinking. In the past I have taken great risks when I let him carry on at Washington after the heart-attack, and again at Monte Carlo, two and a half years ago, when he had a stroke. But now something must be done.

This might, of course, be the first warning of a stroke; if it were I could not help, events would settle themselves. In a few days, however, we could put that behind us. Then if no clot formed and it was only spasm of the arteries, in a man whose cerebral circulation was no longer what it was, we should be faced with a difficult decision. Ought he to resign, or could we do anything to patch him up for a little? With a vote of censure hanging over him, and the prospect of a row in the House over the Budget, I knew he would hate pulling out at this moment. Aneurin Bevan and his gang would say that he had run away from trouble, for, as the P.M. put it, there was a lot of venom about. I knew, too, that he had set his heart on seeing the young Queen crowned before he gave up office. That it was a bad time for Anthony to take over was clear to him; he would be held responsible for the unpopular austerity measures. Was the P.M.

374

more likely to get a stroke in the next six months if he carried on? No doctor could tell; it was mere guess-work. Even if I went to him and said, 'You must get away from this grind or you will have serious trouble,' it would get us nowhere. The P.M. is not easily frightened off his course. I was beginning to see that it was not the moment for him to go.

February 22, 1952

When I had slept on things there seemed only one course to take. If the P.M. comes safely through the next few days I've got to square up to him after the Budget and persuade him to be sensible. He won't listen to anybody, and I don't overrate my chances, but it is my job as his doctor. I think I know the turn of his mind as no one else does. I shall hate doing it, but it's the only thing I can do for him.

It was in that frame of mind that I called at No. 10 this morning. He had had a good night and was in the mood to look upon the incident as closed. Perhaps it did not mean very much, after all. Anyway, I saw that he didn't want to talk about it and I got away in a few minutes. Downstairs I sought out Jock Colville. He has come back from the Foreign Office to share with Pitblado the duties of Principal Private Secretary to the Prime Minister; he is a friend of the family, knows Winston's ways, plays cards with him for hours at a time—and idolizes him. There is not much gratitude in the political world, and my first care must be not to put sharp weapons into the hands of anyone who might use them to hurt him. I wanted to hear from someone in the Cabinet whether the duties of Prime Minister could be cut, and I have no doubt that the man to make me wise is Lord Salisbury. His complete detachment and single-mindedness, with his lack of personal ambition, give me a comfortable sense of security. I told Jock what had happened, and asked him to arrange an appointment with Salisbury.

Two hours later I was shown, with Jock, into Lord Salisbury's room at Gwydyr House. I said my piece: I asked if the Prime Minister's work could be lightened.

'A Prime Minister cannot shed his responsibilities,' Salisbury replied.

Jock thought the Honours List and Ecclesiastical preferment might be done by Salisbury with Harry Crookshank. Perhaps even the Budget proposals could be simplified and summarized a little more before being shown to the P.M.

Salisbury: 'Of course, I don't know how far they are peptonized already.'

Jock: 'I hate to be disloyal, but the P.M. is not doing his work. A document of five sheets has to be submitted to him as one paragraph, so that many of the points of the argument are lost.'

I pointed out that this had happened in the last years of the war when Martin, Rowan and Bridges in turn had complained that he was not mastering his brief.

Salisbury: 'His work seems to vary enormously from day to day.'

Jock: 'Yes, that's true. Only yesterday I simplified something and he burst out, "Can't I read?" He was right on the spot.'

Salisbury: 'Another time in the Cabinet he will talk about something for two and a half hours without once coming to the point.'

Jock: 'Yes, Egypt, for example.'

The real difficulty, I said, was that he hated delegating anything.

Salisbury (*sympathetically*): 'We are all the same; the more tired we get, the more we seem to feel we must do the thing ourselves.'

As they talked I saw that even if Winston were willing to turn over a new leaf all this tinkering would come to nothing. Then Salisbury said suddenly:

'Of course he ought to go to the Lords—oh, yes, remaining Prime Minister.'

Jock: 'Eden would lead the House and would be virtually Prime Minister. In 1952 no one but Winston could be Prime Minister in the Lords. He would be the grand old man of politics, coming down from time to time and making a great speech to their Lordships.'

Salisbury felt sure he could go to the Lords and remain Prime Minister.

'We are beginning to see light,' he added cheerfully.

My heart leapt; this was a solution that had not occurred to me. But Jock's face had become serious.

'He won't do it,' he said gloomily. 'I did once suggest to him that he should go to the Lords, and thought at first he was taking it seriously, when he said: "I should have to be the Duke of Chartwell, and Randolph would be the Marquis of Toodledo." I saw that he was laughing at me.'

Salisbury, ruefully: 'No, I am afraid he regards us in the Lords as a rather disreputable collection of old gentlemen.'

They fell to discussing who could put it to him. No one has the least influence with him; he does not listen to any of the Cabinet. The Prof.?

'Oh,' said Jock, 'he'll listen to him on guided missiles, but not on politics. He does listen to Christopher Soames, he has a great affection for him.'

Winston is still remarkably quick at spotting a plot. A loose word, and he will tumble to everything. The conversation was ceasing to be helpful. I listened to them, but I knew in my heart that it would not work.

'There is only one person,' I said at last, 'who could get him to do this, and that is the Queen.'

They thought it a good idea.

Salisbury: 'Things are beginning to take shape.'

Jock: 'There is one person—and only one—I'd like to consult—Tommy Lascelles.'

Salisbury: 'Yes, he might help, and he's as close as the grave.'

When I saw Lascelles this afternoon at Buckingham Palace I began by admonishing him that if, when I had done, he felt that the P.M. ought to retire, he must forget what I had said; for if I could not help my patient I must see that nothing I said did him hurt. With that prelude I told my story.

Lascelles followed carefully what I said, without a word of comment. At the end he said:

'Well, listening to what you have told me, I would say at once the Prime Minister ought to resign and be content to be the elder statesman in the Commons or the Lords—better perhaps in the Lords. I have been expecting for some time to see you in this room. It is true that sometimes the Prime Minister is all on the spot, and then I say to myself: Why am I worrying? But at other times he doesn't seem able to see the point of a discussion.'

The conversation was not taking quite the line I had intended.

'Don't you think,' I said, 'he is still useful to the country? Unpopular decisions have to be made over finance; he will make them. I can't see most of the politicians I know risking the displeasure of the electorate. Besides, this is not the moment for Anthony to succeed. He would get all the blame for the Budget and it might even be felt that he had pushed Winston out.'

Lascelles seemed impressed by this line of thought. Then Jock intervened. The P.M., he said, had told him a few days ago that he would like to hang on until the Coronation in May of next year. After that he would resign. Lascelles appeared to agree that if we could bring him through this year it would be the best plan.

'Of course nobody,' he reflected, 'but Winston could go to the Lords and remain Prime Minister, but he could. He is a law to himself and is still a great figure in the country. He might of course, in that event, have to get rid of some of the Peers in the Cabinet, Leathers and perhaps the Prof.—that is a question of detail. But how are you going to get him to the Lords?' he enquired dubiously.

377

Jock: 'He once refused the Garter. Now he thinks he'd rather like it. It would fit in with the Lords.'

I interrupted at this point:

'Winston isn't worldly. If you want him to do this you must prove it is for the sake of Eden or the country or the Queen.'

Lascelles: 'Yes, that's true; he isn't worldly.'

Jock then brought up my idea about the Queen, but Lascelles said he did not think anything would come of that.

'If she said her part, he would say charmingly: "It's very good of you, Ma'am, to think of it——" and then he would very politely brush it aside. The King might have done it,' Lascelles added thoughtfully, 'but he is gone.'

Various names came into his head; he dismissed them one by one, though for a moment he hesitated when he said 'Pug.' It was at length agreed that nothing should be done till the Budget was over; we should only add to his worries if we brought this up now—we must gamble on nothing happening in the next few days. Then I am to deliver a medical ultimatum that he cannot go on at the present pace, that he must either throw in his hand or in some way cut down his work. Lascelles wanted me to go to him and say outright that he must go to the Lords, but I maintained that he would listen to me on the medical argument, but that when I began on politics he would switch off. Jock agreed. I said I would try and get him into a state of mind so that he saw something must be done—it is for others to suggest that something. Lascelles agreed reluctantly. Then he seemed to go back upon the plan; the P.M. ought to resign if he were not fit to carry on. I dealt with this.

'Very well,' he said. 'I shall hear from you in ten days' time and know what success you've had.'

February 23, 1952

This morning I called on the P.M. at Chartwell. I did my stuff and was out of his room in five minutes. I knew he did not want to talk about what had happened, but I knew, too, that it was there at the back of his mind; he had been warned—and Winston is still quick enough to take his leads. He was subdued. If he was left to himself there was still a chance that he would listen to reason. For my part I had no desire to talk; it might only do harm. Jock told me on the telephone that the P.M. had been discussing the Defence debate and that Jock thought it was a good opportunity to 'put in a word.' So he had suggested that the P.M. should leave the Defence speech to Anthony Head.[1] The P.M. turned on him like a flash:

[1] Secretary of State for War.

'Have you been talking with Charles?'
Jock had brazened it out, but he was shaken.

Chartwell, February 25, 1952

Found the P.M. chastened, but still uncommunicative. Another of his black swans had been killed in the night by a fox; he would have to make totally different arrangements. His speech was finished.

'I have to make my own speeches; what they give me is silly stuff. The country,' he mused, half to himself, 'is divided into two equal parts. If they worked together they might survive. But they won't; they are set on tearing the heart out of each other.

'I knew something had happened when I could not get my words on the telephone. I didn't like it. I was frightened. Oh, not frightened,' he corrected himself, 'I'm not frightened of anything. But I'm all right now. Why, you couldn't tell by examining me that anything had happened.'

He wanted me to tell him that he could put the incident at the telephone out of his thoughts.

'But the fact remains you've had notice to go slower.'

'I don't mind dying in harness,' he said rather defiantly.

'That won't help anyone,' I said. 'You've got a certain stock of energy, mental energy, and you can either spread it out over a period of time or just use it up recklessly—and in that case it won't last long.'

He didn't even frown at me, he seemed to feel that if he tried to argue the facts were against him. Anyway, I'd planted the seed, and to change the subject I pulled out my stethoscope and began to examine him. I have not given up hope yet.

February 26, 1952

When the P.M. had replied to Herbert Morrison's speech in moving a vote of censure he wentto h is room in the House, and I joined him.

'I was alarmed at lunch-time; I seemed to have no wits, and I was very tired and shaky before getting up to speak, but I felt stronger as I got under way. Now I feel quite all right. How did it go?' he asked eagerly. 'I feel it has gone well. Morrison was really very feeble. Where is Christopher? Send for him. He will know what the Lobby thinks.'

Christopher said the speech had been well received; the point that the Labour Government had spent more than a hundred millions on manufacturing an atomic bomb without disclosing it to the House, and then called the Conservatives war-mongers, had gone particularly well. And the disclosure that Morrison was committed to reprisals if our aeroplanes in Korea were attacked by planes from central airfields in China was a most effective thrust. Christopher did not seem so certain what view members would take of the P.M. using a Cabinet document. Winston pooh-poohed this; he had been at the game for fifty years, and knew what could be done. I advised him to go home and have a bath and dine before returning to the House. But he said he would return to the House for a short time. He really wanted to know what people thought of his speech. He was excited. His pulse was 112. I have a feeling that the chance of translating him to the Lords has gone.

February 27, 1952

I called at No. 10 about half-past five, hoping to see the P.M. before he retired for his rest. But I learnt he had already gone to his room. I opened the door very gently, but the curtains had been drawn and the room was in darkness. I closed the door as quietly as I could, but Norman said he had only just settled, and went in and asked him if he would like to see me; he said yes. I found him animated, very different from the subdued Winston whose future has never been out of my mind since the difficulty with the telephone.

'You know, Charles, yesterday was a great success; the papers have been most kind. Attlee came up to me today after Questions and was positively gushing; he asked me about the Queen. He seems to have been pleased when he was found out manufacturing his atomic bomb like a good patriot. I think he's made up his mind to cut away from Bevan. But it doesn't seem to fit in with their vote of censure on me. Now there are new troubles—new decisions,' he corrected himself.

February 29, 1952

Visited the P.M. after breakfast. He said:

'Since the speech I have felt better and more cheerful about things. During luncheon that day I was stupid, dull and muzzy, and I wondered if I could make a speech at all. But we put them on their backs,' speaking with animation. 'Why, it was one of the meanest things in public life to withhold from their followers their commitment over Korea, and then bring in a vote of censure on me. I only quoted Cabinet directives, not Cabinet documents.'

I asked him if a long Cabinet tired him.

'Oh, no, I get excited; my appetite thrives on what it feeds on.

I get muzzy in the head about lunch-time, and then I get better as the day goes on.'

He once more stressed the innumerable questions that came up for decision: the future of the B.B.C., for example. He had not been able to get off to sleep yesterday afternoon as he had always done. Could I not give him something to 'curl him up'? I saw again that the telephone incident had been relegated to the past. The success of his reply to Morrison and the way the vote of censure had fizzled out had given him a little breathing space; he has got back his nerve.

'Perhaps,' he said, 'I was hardly awake when I telephoned.' With a smile, 'You can't expect to live for ever.'

March 6, 1952

Called at No. 10 at nine this morning. The P.M. was full of the debate in the House.

Winston, reproachfully: 'You ought to read the papers. They are very interesting, if you like politics. The Bevan group sat all together in one part, and Attlee's supporters were gathered together in another group. There they were, glowering at each other. The split might deepen and lead to a coalition. I should not be against it. I would retire if necessary.'

I asked him if he had been less tired. He answered:

'If I don't get my sleep in the afternoon I cannot sit up late and work. I get muddled and tired.'

March 12, 1952

The game is up; nevertheless, I decided to warn the P.M. and put it on paper that he might absorb it.

My dear Prime Minister,

I have given careful thought to the significance of the little disturbance when you went to the telephone on February 21st. It was of the same nature as the sudden mistiness which you had within a fortnight of the Leeds speech in the 1950 election, namely due to spasm of the cerebral arteries. And these were first cousins of the blocking of a little artery at Monte Carlo in August, 1949. All three point to some instability in the cerebral circulation, which must be increased by excessive mental effort. On the other hand if it were possible to lighten the load without giving up being Prime Minister, which on medical grounds would not be wise at the moment, then you ought to be able to carry on more or less indefinitely. Of course if you would like confirmation of my interpretation of events, we could get Russell Brain at any time, but they are really capable of no other explanation.

If there is any point that I have not made clear, I will of course come at any time you want. I feel sure that you would like the medical facts put down for your consideration. When I saw Clemmie about your deafness I told her my view.

Charles.

I explained to Clemmie what I had done.

My dear Clemmie,

There seem to me to be two dangers attendant upon this letter. Firstly, that he may resign, and it is our medical experience that to take a man out of a very active mental life into retirement is often—I might almost say always—accompanied by profound changes. And I would dread them here.

Secondly, that he may just take no notice. In this case we have to remember that it is not really putting the whole case when he talks about dying in harness. What one dreads much more is an attack which leaves him disabled.

I have not the slightest doubt that though there are risks in any course, to remain Prime Minister and to go to the Lords for a year or so is much the safest course medically.

I know it would be a sacrifice on his part, but I am sure it would be best for the Monarch, the country and his successor, and I think the country would look on it as a noble gesture, paving the way for the succession.

Charles.

March 13, 1952

Clemmie telephoned:

'He was not angry when he got your letter; he just swept it aside. I mentioned the Lords, but he would not consider it. Charles, I'm glad you wrote. It may do good. Instead of going to the House this afternoon and listening to Mr. Thorneycroft,[1] he has gone to bed.'

But I am under no illusions. We have failed.

March 23, 1952

A week ago the P.M. said to me:

'I got your letter. I don't want you to worry. You really needn't. One has got to die some time.'

At that moment MacKenna came into the room, and that was the end of my attempt to translate Mr. Churchill into the House of

[1] President of the Board of Trade.

Lords. I was sure I should hear no more of it; but today when I called at four o'clock he said he was just about to lie down and asked me if I would come to his room. As he undressed he said:

'I have noticed a decline in mental and physical vigour. I require more prodding to mental effort.' He smiled. 'I get a good deal of prodding. I forget names. I might even forget yours—people whose names I know as well as my own. I'm as quick at repartee in the House as ever I was. I enjoy Questions there. Do you think I ought to see Brain?'

I replied that it was no use seeing him unless he was ready to take his advice. The P.M. himself thought it would be a bad thing if he retired now. I said Brain would certainly advise cutting down what he had to do. He protested that he already devoluted a good deal of work. Rab[1] and Anthony, for example, did a lot—and they worked in a broad field. There were others, such as Lord Salisbury. He had worries, of course. He was worried over Egypt, and whether we were going to be blown up, and whether we should be able to solve our financial problems, and about houses and food.

'I'm halfway in my seventy-eighth year, and one can't expect to live for ever. I really don't think you need worry. I soon get tired physically; when I have fed the robin and the swans, and perhaps walked three-quarters of a mile, I have had enough. I dislike standing, except when making speeches.'

Then he began telling me about a poor woman whose husband had left her three lorries, and the local council, which was dominated by Labour, restricted the radius over which they could be used. He was very angry about it. It appeared that even Parliament could do nothing without legislation. He had just had a meeting with Leathers and others, lasting an hour and a half, and they were going to bring in a Bill. He took up the telephone.

'The Private Office. Pitblado? Will you get Christopher to come across, and tell him what has been done? Tell him in detail. He has been very fully into this.'

Twice I made a move. I told him he would not get to sleep if he roused himself. But each time he said:

'No, sit down. I want to talk.'

Now I rose and made for the door, and he settled in the pillow.

---

[1] R. A. Butler, Chancellor of the Exchequer.

Chapter thirty-seven

Muddling through

April 16, 1952

'This miserable cold has settled on my chest,' the P.M. telephoned this morning. 'Bring your stethoscope.' When I listened to his chest it was like a musical box.

'I have not much in reserve,' he said. 'How shall I know if it develops into anything?'

Winston seemed in poor spirits. He wanted to go to Newmarket, where two of his horses were running; as long as he has no temperature, he feels he can ignore anything that may be wrong with him. I told him there was a risk in going to Newmarket, though the risk was small. When I had said my say he picked up the house telephone and began talking to Clemmie, who was in her room.

'Charles is with me; he says there is not much wrong and sees no objection to my going, but I don't think I shall go. I've lost heart.'

It was not like him to admit defeat, and I was seeking an explanation when I met Miss Sturdee on the stairs. She told me Mrs. Churchill had taken a strong line about Newmarket.

'He couldn't get any harm, Lord Moran, could he? He would meet all his buddies who have horses running, and get away from his worries.'

April 18, 1952

From Chartwell last night word came that he had made up his mind to take part in the debate in the House on railway fares; he was coughing, and they were not happy about him. I found him, however, in better spirits, he spoke indeed with animation. His pulse and temperature were normal—he had taken them himself. When I had listened to his chest he said: 'Well, is there anything there?'

I told him that he was better in himself, but that he was still full of bronchitis. He threw himself cn his face.

'Listen again, my dear Charles,' he demanded. 'You may have examined me at a bad moment. I can't believe there's much wrong when I feel so much better in myself. Now, Charles, it's no use you telling me not to do things; you don't know what I must do. *The Times* has a stupid leader on the Government's action. You haven't seen it? Oh, well, don't bother to read it.'

I told him I wasn't interested in politics; my job was to tell him the medical position.

'Well, what is it?' he demanded.

'The trouble is in your tubes now—the larger tubes—if you take care of yourself it won't go lower down. If you don't it may spread to the smaller tubes.'

'Is that halfway to the old trouble?' he asked. Without waiting for an answer, he said cheerfully: 'Anyway, I shall be all right tomorrow. Come and sound me. Come to luncheon—and bring Dorothy.'

April 19, 1952

The P.M. sat in his place, glowering at his plate. This transport muddle has driven the threat of another attack of pneumonia out of his head. Leathers[1] was bright and apparently untroubled, but Maclay's[2] face was drawn, his cheeks sunken—he appeared to be a sick man. The P.M. said:

'When I was told I had no power to alter these fares, fury arose in my breast. I was not responsible for this rise in fares, but I am getting all the blame. I feel I must protect the people from these nationalized industries.'

He turned to Maclay, who seemed too tired to listen:

'This is a great issue, more important even than steel. It's a great opportunity. We have a very strong case.'

Presently Lord Leathers, perhaps stimulated by my presence, or it may be to get away from the depressing transport talk, said across the table:

'When I was forty-six I began to get headaches which lasted sometimes as long as three weeks; they were so severe that I was left prostrate. I saw all kinds of specialists, but I got no better. Then in despair I was persuaded by a friend to see his osteopath. I went without faith. He said to me, "Get up here," indicating an elaborate

---

[1] Lord Leathers, Secretary of State for Co-ordination of Transport, Fuel and Power, 1951-3.

[2] J. S. Maclay, Minister of Transport and Civil Aviation, 1951-2.

surgical table. "Now put your head under my arm, like this"—he was a big fellow, perhaps six foot three. Then he began turning my head this way and that, with great rapidity. "I'm breaking down adhesions," he said. Finally, he gave a terrible wrench, there was a loud click—I thought he'd broken my neck. But I have never had a headache since.'

He looked at me in a challenging manner. The P.M. leant forward eagerly:

'Now, Charles, I call that a very remarkable story. You really ought to put aside your prejudices and go into it.' He turned to Leathers: 'A year and a half ago I went to an osteopath without telling Charles, and he knocked me about, but I was not a pin the better. I suppose it all depends on what is wrong with you.'

They were waiting for my answer. But I had no mind to be drawn into an argument with the P.M. and Leathers on faith healing. It seems strange that a man who is a director of 52 companies can be so credulous. At the first opportunity I took my leave.

The Government seems to blunder out of one crisis into another. The weakness in the P.M.'s administration has taken everybody by surprise, and people say that if John Anderson, now Lord Waverley, had been in charge of the home front, as he was in the war, none of this confusion would have arisen.

June 1, 1952

Lunched with Lord Waverley at West Dean. While I was waiting for an opening he asked me:

'How long have you known Winston?' 'Oh,' he said, 'that's not a long time. I have known him since 1906, when he was Under-Secretary to the Minister for the Colonies, Lord Elgin.'

Winston, he said, had marked a document, 'I can take no responsibility for this measure.' Underneath, in a lady-like hand, Lord Elgin had written, 'I take responsibility.'

'Winston,' Waverley ruminated, 'was not autocratic, he was really quite humble; he would go over what had been done with an open mind.'

'He needs wise men round him,' I added.

Waverley interrupted: 'That's not enough; he must have congenial men about him, like Freddie Guest.'

I said I thought Winston was unhappy: the political ground on which just now he had to make runs wasn't his wicket. Waverley agreed.

'He was not happy in the old days when he was at the Treasury, and now, faced by economic questions, he is not at his ease. And

386

his colleagues,' Waverley went on, 'are not happy either. Leathers has not learnt to handle an assembly like the Lords.'

I said: 'Winston will need all the help his friends can give if he is to come through with any credit. If you'd been a Minister,' I ventured to affirm, 'this transport muddle would never have occurred.'

Waverley looked down his nose and said nothing—he looked like a prim elder of the kirk.

'He needs you in the Cabinet,' I persisted.

Waverley said quietly that he could not afford to join the Cabinet.

June 2, 1952

Today at Chartwell I found the P.M. in an amiable mood and said to him:

'If I had had to make a Cabinet when you did I'd have begun, I think, with Waverley.'

'I asked John,' he retorted. 'I couldn't do more. He said he was over seventy, and that if he joined the Government he would not be able to get a job when he left office. He couldn't afford to give up his present posts, which brought him in a good income, and take office at £4,000 a year.'

June 3, 1952

I was on my back in hospital when the House of Lords debated commercial television.[1] Yet as I read Hansard I was conscious of the long shadow of that gaunt old covenanter, Lord Reith, across its pages. I could see him as he rose in his place like another John Knox to scourge the infidel. 'I am slow of speech,' he began, 'reluctant to waste your Lordships' time and my own.' He claimed no credit at all for what had been done when he was Director-General of the B.B.C. during the first sixteen years of its existence. He had tried to do as he had been taught in the Manse of the College Church in Glasgow. He believed that he was peculiarly helped in plan and execution. Of the worth and consequence of British broadcasting, its flower and essence, he spoke with pride: today it commanded the respect and the admiration of the whole world. 'What grounds are there,' he cried, 'for jeopardizing that heritage and tradition?' It was a betrayal and a surrender; that was what was so shocking and so serious, so unnecessary and so wrong. 'Need we be ashamed of moral values or of intellectual and ethical objectives? It is these that are here and now at stake.'

[1] House of Lords, May 22 and 26, 1952.

Then as I read on I could picture Lord Halifax, a lank wraith of a man, with his withered left hand hidden in a black mitten, rise. He declared that no gloss could conceal the fact that a fundamental issue had been raised and that a vital principle was being touched by this concession to the claims of commercial and sponsored television. 'I think,' he said, 'that it is profoundly wrong.' Where it was the practice abroad, experience had condemned it. Opinion there was satisfied that it meant a lowering of standards. 'I do not think,' Lord Halifax said with great solemnity, 'it is possible, except at your peril, to ignore that mass of experience.'

There followed Lord Radcliffe,[1] who made a declaration of his faith. 'Let me say with what deep dismay I regard this proposal and how grave I believe is the decision to allow sponsored television programmes in this country. It is the level of culture of this country that you are needlessly putting to the hazard.'

*

All that day and the day after those who have authority in the House, one after another, voiced their anxiety. In what they said there was a note of urgency. The future of our country depended upon the education of our masters—it was a race against time—and yet we were ready to blunt the instrument which alone could reach the mass of the people. It would be found in every home, shaping opinion, moulding national character. Some of the younger members of the House, it is true, spoke brightly in support of the Government. Perhaps they had a feeling they were moving with the times. But when the Lord Chancellor[2] rose to end the debate, as far as argument could settle the question it was already settled.

The speech from the Woolsack went a long way to restoring the spirits of the Party, or at any rate of such as had followed the lead of the Government. But those who had spoken in the debate—the men who count in the deliberations of the House—were not concerned with making debating points. They were preoccupied with the effect of television over the years upon the minds and lives of their fellow citizens, the importance, to borrow Lord Kirkwood's words, of somehow educating our people to understand the meaning of the vital problems which come before them. Nothing else seemed to matter.

[1] Lord of Appeal in Ordinary, 1949–64.
[2] Lord Simonds.

I could not speak in their support, but I wrote to *The Times*:

June 3, 1952

Sir,

The Lord Chancellor's defence of sponsored broadcasting in the House of Lords was no doubt good politics, and, if he had to speak to a brief, it would be unreasonable to quarrel with his polemics.

Illness kept me from attending the House and it may well be that to those who listened to his persuasive speech, the analogy between the freedom of the Press in Milton's day and such freedom of the air as we can hope to see appeared closer than it did in the cold print of Hansard. After all, the Lord Chancellor was summing up against the evidence—if experience of sponsored broadcasting in other countries can be called evidence—and in opposition to the considered opinion of all three parties, at any rate of those to whom the House turns for guidance in such an issue. Reading the speeches of Lords Halifax, Waverley, Radcliffe, Samuel, Jowitt and Reith, one realizes how difficult it must be to dispose of such cumulative disquiet by mere dialectic, however effective, particularly as they were supported by every committee and Royal Commission which had reported on the subject. It was plainly no ordinary occasion, and the Lord Chancellor must have felt that the Government were looking to him for succour. They certainly did not look in vain.

'Trust the people,' he proclaimed. It is a fine sentiment to be sure, though when the Athenians argued that all men are created equal, it seemed to Plato 'like being flippant about serious things.' Nevertheless we can all subscribe to it if only with qualifications. For after all, carried to its logical conclusion, it destroys the case for a second chamber. And the working philosophy of the Tory creed itself postulates, according to Arthur Balfour, no more than a kind of delaying machinery to give a chance for second thoughts. Besides, it must have occurred to the House that every argument the Lord Chancellor used could have been advanced with equal force when broadcasting was first given a charter. Was he arguing that we should now be better off if the Reith dynasty had been cut out and broadcasting had been sponsored from the outset?

We have not heard the last of this issue. Meanwhile the debate is dead and gone and I am only concerned to point a moral. The Lord Chancellor quoted Cromwell, though there are other of his sayings more apposite to this hour. The Protector stiffened the purpose of his followers by a religious appeal, and England, General Smuts once said to me, is waiting now for such another summons. He believed that without faith we send our soldiers limping into battle, and that the life of the craftsman in his workshop is robbed of its true meaning. The Lord Chancellor rather sniffed at the 'Holier than Thou' attitude of some peers, but it is precisely because the average English-man is sensitive to this kind of criticism, that the fumbling in this debate for a more serious approach to things made so deep an impression. It will linger in men's minds when the debate itself has been forgotten.

I am, Sir, Your obedient Servant
Moran

Some days later Lord Reith said to me: 'I wrote to Winston the day after the debate, but he has not answered. I always thought he was a courteous man. I said I had not seen him for ten years and would like to talk to him about it. I was shocked at the Lord Chancellor's speech.' His gaunt, scarred face expressed his grief and his alarm. England was going headlong to the devil, and his soul yearned to do something for the shattered state of the country.

The next morning I found Clemmie in Winston's room, when the following conversation took place.

Clemmie: 'Have you read Charles's letter in *The Times*?'

Winston: 'It is not a subject I feel very strongly about. I do not worry about it as I do over the solvency of the country.'

Moran: 'But is not the issue fundamental?'

Winston (*peevishly*): 'I don't see why it is fundamental. It is not at all fundamental.'

It was plain that he did not want to discuss the question; he was not interested in abstract issues. And then, on the spur of the moment he said:

'But I am against the monopoly enjoyed by the B.B.C. For eleven years they kept me off the air. They prevented me from expressing views which have proved to be right. Their behaviour has been tyrannical. They are honeycombed with Socialists—probably with Communists.'

He spoke hotly; his detachment had quite gone.

'I first quarrelled with Reith,' he went on, 'in 1926, during the General Strike. He behaved quite impartially between the strikers and the nation. I said he had no right to be impartial between the fire and the fire-brigade. The nation was being held up. It did not matter so much to me, as the Columbia Broadcasting Corporation was ready to let me speak at any time, and would pay me £500 for doing so. But it might have happened to others.'

June 20, 1952

The P.M. was dictating a memorandum when I called at No. 10. He sent out a message: would I make myself comfortable in the drawing-room for a few minutes? He would not be long. Then he forgot all about me. It might have been an hour later when a secretary discovered me. Winston seemed quite upset about it. He had never done this before. He said his memory was 'awful.'

I asked him how he had been. He looked up wearily:

'As well as I can be. I'm not what I was—not mentally over-flowing. I don't want to dictate a memorandum,' he smiled. 'Of course I have written some quite serious papers.'

I asked him if he had any plans for a holiday.

'What can I do?' he answered a little impatiently. 'I cannot go abroad as the guest of *Life* while I am Prime Minister. I must find some interest.'

'Do you mean your book?'

'Oh, no; I must superintend things at Chartwell. I don't mean I am going to cut down trees—I promise you I won't do anything foolish—but I can direct others cutting them down. I don't know why, but I love Chartwell; somehow it's home to me.'

The P.M. gloomily contemplated the papers on his bed-rest.

'It is a most perplexing time, much worse than the war. All talk and no co-operation. Attlee and his people are behaving badly—currying popularity by attacking America. It's easy to pick out things there to attack in an election year.'

All this, of course, does not mean that Winston is thinking of retiring. It is his way of seeing if, as his doctor, I can help. He can't talk about his disabilities to anyone else. It seems, too, to relieve his feelings to go over the difficulties he has to overcome with some-one not in the political world, though my part is only to listen; he does not want my views. But there is no weakening of purpose.

'I told the 1922 Committee,'[1] Winston continued, 'that they must trust the Government and that they must trust me too. I said they could be assured that I would not stay if I found I was failing physi-cally or mentally. They took it all right. There is no movement to get me out. Anthony is absorbed in his work at the Foreign Office. It would be madness to move him.'

The P.M. thought his health was better than it has been for some time. He was not so stupid in the head in the middle of the day as he had been five months ago.

[1] A committee set up in 1922, comprising all back-bench Conservative Members of Parliament.

'Now, Charles, it is nearly three years since the trouble at Monte Carlo. Did you think then that I should be here now?'

He put his hand on my arm.

'You found the pulse good? I can still hold my own in the House. I can put anyone on his back if it is necessary.'

It is no more than the truth. His answers at Question Time in the House of Commons, particularly to Supplementaries, have the old merit of unexpectedness.

He seemed to want to talk, and rambled on in a way that was not at all like him in the early morning. It became obvious that he wanted to persuade himself that he was fit to carry on.

'I drink a great deal,' he said, 'it keeps me going. Oh, not too much, Charles.'

Last night, he returned from the 'Other Club'[1] hilarious (Camrose took him home), and at Chartwell on Sunday Jock said the P.M. spoke of his pranks at Sandhurst; Jock had not laughed so much for a long time.

July 30, 1952

When I entered his bedroom this morning the P.M. threw the morning papers on the floor in great disgust. I knew from the set of his jaw that he was looking for trouble. I asked him, was he rested?

'Yes,' he answered grimly. 'I'll knock hell out of anyone. You would think, from the way Attlee's supporters carry on, that they weren't responsible for the awful mess we found. There will have to be more cuts to keep the country from bankruptcy.'

In the afternoon I went to the House of Commons to hear him speak on rearmament. He had a very noisy passage, but what could he expect when he deliberately trailed his coat to Shinwell? I left the Chamber with Alex, who is now Minister of Defence. He said he would be glad to be done with it all.

'I would never have taken this job on if I had known what the House of Commons was like. They shout at each other. I think, Charles, it is lamentable. Do you consider that the English people have deteriorated? I don't believe the House was like that before the war.'

During tea Trenchard supported Alex; he thought it wrong that

---

[1] F. E. Smith and Winston Churchill founded the 'Other Club' in 1911 in a fit of impatience with 'The Club.' The Other Club had a strong hold on Churchill's affections, and on more than one occasion when he was abroad and Lord Moran had to persuade him that he was not fit to travel to attend a dinner there was a stormy scene.

the Commons should treat Winston like that, he had done so much for the country. At that point the waitress gave me a bit of paper. It was a message from Jock. He was rather worried about the Prime Minister. He had been very shaky after his speech. He looked grey.

'Could you pop over—but you must not say I sent for you—he's in his room in the House of Commons.'

I found him slumped in his chair with a whisky and soda.

'I didn't tell them anything,' he said, smiling.

'Are you tired?'

'Oh, no, I feel quite well.'

This racket in the House, day after day, is doing him no good, but he can no longer do without it. He will go on squandering what is left of his capital until he goes bankrupt.

August 29, 1952

Lunched at Chartwell. The P.M. told me that Washington does not want us to 'gang up' against Persia.

'It is the kind of language Roosevelt used about Russia during the war. But Truman is very friendly. It is Harry and Winston.'

He talked of many things, ending with his views on the duties of family life. He did not think that celibacy, as imposed by the Roman Catholic Church on priests, could be right. I reminded him how he had been impressed during the election by the other-worldliness of some Roman priests who had come to see him.

'Kelly here is a Roman,' the P.M. interrupted. He was afraid I might say something unguarded. 'God is the Supreme Creator,' he mused. 'He is good—but I am not certain about a future life after death.'

September 30, 1952

The P.M. was back from his holiday at Monte Carlo and says he feels better for it; he has more vigour. 'I had no money to gamble at the tables, but I did three pictures while I was away, and worked five hours every day at my book.'

In France he got a second wind. He said to me today:

'The Government position is stronger than it was a year ago. I have not yet decided when to resign. It might do me no good when the curtain is down.'

Then, as if the subject were closed, he added:

'I am going to Balmoral tomorrow. I felt I ought to see the Queen. I have not seen her for two months.'

November 13, 1952

I asked the P.M. how he had slept. 'I dream a lot. Why do I do that? The dreams are always pleasant, so that I am sorry when I wake. I want them to go on. They are extremely complicated. I dreamt last night about ten cigars. They were of enormous size, and each had attached to it a piece of paper with the history of that particular cigar.'

The unmistakable signs of old age are at last apparent; they seem to bother him, and yet he has no intention of giving up. This is an unequal contest, and I shall hear more of it.

He pushed away his plate and rang a bell, when Walter came in with a particularly big pear and a glass of orange juice.

'You know Fred Woolton?[1] I want to talk to you about him. You know he has been ill?'

The P.M. had forgotten that when he heard Lord Woolton was seriously ill he had been much concerned and had sent for me. He was, he said, very fond of Fred, and had been very much upset when told how gravely ill he was. But the political mind is essentially practical. The work of the Lord President of the Council would be greatly increased by the Coronation, and the Prime Minister had a growing feeling that Woolton would not be up to it.

P.M.: 'I don't believe he can be fit in four months' time, but I don't want to discourage the poor man, and put him back perhaps, by writing and asking him to put his office in my hands. I know he wants to do the Coronation. He likes pomp and ceremony. Of course he will have to give up being Chairman of the Party, but that was going to happen in any case before his illness. But I would give him a step in the Peerage. He wants that. Can you help me about him, Charles?'

December 2, 1952

Pitblado telephoned asking me to call at No. 10; he did not think that it was about the P.M.'s health. When I got there it was about Arthur Deakin. Tom O'Brien and Will Lawther[2] had spoken to the P.M. about him; they were worried and said that he had something wrong with his bladder and was in hospital.

'When I mentioned your name and that you might help,' said Winston, 'they shook hands with each other.'

I asked the P.M. if Deakin was in the Manor House Hospital.

'Yes, that's where he is. This is political,' he went on. 'Deakin is

[1] Lord Woolton, Lord President of the Council.
[2] Deakin, O'Brien and Lawther were all trade-union leaders.

a very important person. I told what you had done for Tom Williams, when he was Minister of Agriculture.'

The P.M.'s friendliness to the trade-union leaders is an obvious move, but their response to his advances is interesting. They know, when they dine with him at No. 10, that it will do them no good in the Party. But they cannot help liking him. He doesn't seem to them at all like other Tories. I remember that Ernie Bevin had a great affection for 'The old man.'

I asked the P.M. how he was. 'Oh,' he replied, 'as well as I shall ever be.'

Part six

Never give in

Chapter thirty-eight

A new lease of life

February 18, 1953

P.M.: 'Yesterday I was worried about my chest when I asked you to call, but I think my cold is subsiding. The poor Cabinet has been afflicted. Lord Salisbury has gone away for a month. He is one of those in my orchestra whose note I value.'

Moran: 'He is, of course, full of sense, but he has got a bee in his bonnet about the reform of the House of Lords.'

P.M.: 'We may revoke the Parliament Act,[1] if they are not too timid. Everyone is timid nowadays. It is all appeasement. I don't like it.'

His mind went back to the old conflict of 1911 with the House of Lords. He spoke with great severity of their conduct at that time.

P.M.: 'In a few minutes they had undone all we did in a session.'

Moran: 'Attlee, it seems, wanted to hold a conference on the reform of the House of Lords; at any rate he did not wish to return a direct refusal, but after Jennie Lee [2] had spoken the meeting turned it down.'

P.M.: 'We may do better on our own. At any rate we should restore the two years.'

Moran: 'It's too late. All this will lead to the abolition of the House.'

P.M.: 'I doubt that. The public are, I think, more friendly to your House than you imagine.'

The House of Lords means nothing to him. The history of England, its romance and changing fortunes, is for Winston embodied in the Royal House. He looked at a new photograph of the Queen. She was in white, with long white gloves, smiling and radiant.

[1] The Liberal Government's measure in 1911 to reduce the power of the House of Lords after the latter's persistent baulking of the administration's Bills.

[2] Jennie Lee, M.P., wife of Aneurin Bevan.

'Lovely,' he murmured, 'she's a pet. I fear they may ask her to do too much. She's doing so well.'

'I feel,' he said, 'that if I retired now it might do me a lot of harm. I could, of course, write another book. I might divide what I have between those near to me, and go abroad for five months in the year —Jamaica perhaps. But I might dislike what the Government did when I had left it, and I might say so, and there might be the hell of a row.

'I must not trouble you, Charles, to come with me to America. But I am very grateful for your generous offer. I think I'll take a chance this time. I suppose something will happen to me some day. It's bound to. But I'm not in bad condition. I haven't seen you since I replied to the vote of censure. I was glad to leave things in the House like that, because it showed them I was as good as any of them. Our people were cheering all the time, while most of the Opposition sat silent. I told them just what I thought of their charge of war-mongering.

'I hate this foggy stuff,' he grumbled, 'I never go out. I stay most of the time working in bed. They are saying, Charles, that I am going to get something out of Ike.[1] Well, we mustn't pitch our hopes too high. But I might. And if I did it would be good for this country and for America too.'

February 19, 1953

Found the P.M. absorbed in George Orwell's book, *1984*.

'Have you read it, Charles? Oh, you must. I'm reading it for a second time. It is a very remarkable book. But you came to tell me about poor Smith. You know, Charles, I don't like psychiatrists. One of them said that insulin produces a state of coma, and when I asked if there was any danger in the treatment, he talked of "irreversible coma." (With great contempt:) 'Irreversible coma, indeed, when he means death.'

Moran: 'I saw Woolton in the Lords today.'

P.M.: 'He looks a wreck. Fred himself told me the doctors gave him up. He was not fit, they argued, for a general anaesthetic. So they could not explore his chest for an abscess. And then a young surgeon came along. He used a local anaesthetic and plunged his knife into Fred's side so that matter gushed out. Fred said to him: "You are the most brutal surgeon I've met," but from that moment he began to get well. Do you know, Charles, about the Duke of Newcastle and the Glove?

[1] General Eisenhower was elected President of the United States on November 4, 1952.

Moran: 'No.'

P.M.: 'Well, as Lord of the Manor of Worksop he had the privilege of giving the Queen a glove when she is crowned. But as the Manor has been made a company, the Committee of Privileges has decided that it reverts to the Crown. I asked them to give it to Woolton. It is a dignified little ceremony. He will like it.'

Lord Woolton had passed from his mind, when there came to him, as an afterthought, the kindly idea of a consolation prize—of the Glove. Perhaps it may comfort Woolton when he thinks of the fat part in the ceremony he had to relinquish through illness.

The P.M. asked me today if he could see another eye specialist.

'I have stuck to Juler for so long,' he told me, 'because he did discover the ingrowing eyelashes when no one else did. At that time my eyes were so bad I could not read, even official documents. But he is stumped now, and we must change the bowling.'

February 24, 1953

Yesterday the P.M. spat up a little blood, so this morning I packed him off, vigorously protesting, to be X-rayed. I am sure nothing will be found, for he is just now in terrific form.

P.M.: 'What is this they are saying about smoking and cancer of the lungs?'

Moran: 'It is not proven.'

P.M.: 'You always give me a careful answer.'

Moran: 'You have smoked all your life, and I have never tried to make you give it up.'

A smile lit up his features.

'When I think of all the great causes you have championed, I think you were wise not to add that to your labours.'

For some time he has been hanging on to power while his strength was failing. And now, without any apparent reason, he seems to have taken a new lease of life.

'I'm much better than I was a year ago,' he said gaily. 'I can bite now, really hard.' And he snapped his jaws together. 'After our trip to America I was in poor form. Gladstone[1] lived to be eighty-eight; I might go on another eight years. If I do it will be very tiresome for those who manage my finances. Things are already getting very complicated. You see, Charles, during the war I retired from business, but by the end of the war I had become notorious; and all sorts of things, such as film rights and the copyright of my books, gave me quite a bit of capital. For the first time in my life I was

[1] William Ewart Gladstone (1809–98), retired from office as Prime Minister on March 3, 1894, and died four years later from cancer after a painful illness.

quite a rich man. But the income-tax people take it all. I let Hyde Park Gate for £2,000 a year—2,000 sixpences.'

I have said there was no reason for this renaissance, but it can be traced back, I think, to the day when Eden went sick and the P.M. took over the Foreign Office. Since he became Prime Minister he has been submerged by one economic problem after another, to which he could see no obvious solution; in this field he was ill at ease, and his discomfort became plain to his colleagues and to the House. And then suddenly he found himself at the F.O. dealing with questions which were familiar to him, engaged in work which he could do as well as anyone. He was more sure of himself; he had long ago learnt how to handle the House; now he was also master of his theme.

P.M. 'Anthony has aged a lot. When Rab goes to America I shall be Chancellor of the Exchequer—not that I shall do much—and also Foreign Secretary.'

Moran: 'Good Lord.'

P.M.: 'Oh, you needn't worry. I enjoyed myself yesterday. I managed things like I used to do. I was able to put my spoke in on three occasions. First, Slim. You'll hear more of this. Oh, yes, he has a hell of a face. Then I saw Gromyko.'[1]

The P.M. grinned.

'One touch of nature makes the whole world kin; my recipe with him, Charles, was a little, but of course not too much, geniality. Thirdly, the amnesty to the deserters. They have been on the run for eight years, have not seen their wives and have been reduced to all kinds of fraud. The Queen was very keen on this. The Government was responsible, the Service Departments were against an amnesty. They all squawked about it.'

This, I think, pleased him most, but he has been generally on the war path; letting some fresh air into stuffy rooms in Whitehall and laying down the law about the Coronation arrangements.[2]

'I'm doing some scratching and clawing. They were going to charge everyone in the Abbey—three thousand of them, the elect from all over the place—sixteen shillings for sandwiches. I stepped in and stopped that. The people in the stands at Hyde Park Corner, by Byron's statue, will be there from seven in the morning till five in the evening. They were seeing to their sanitary needs, but doing nothing for them in food and drink.'

A great grin prepared me for a sally:

'Looking after their exports while neglecting their imports. And why?'

[1] Andrei Gromyko, Soviet Ambassador to the Court of St. James's 1952–3.
[2] The Coronation of Queen Elizabeth II was to take place on June 2, 1953.

A look of withering scorn crossed his face.

'Because alcohol had not been drunk in the royal parks for a hundred years, they were to have nothing to drink. I altered all that. Even the people not in the stands will have booths.

'Then that poor old Florence Horsbrugh [1] has been making all the educational world her enemy. She wanted a reduction of 10 per cent. in the grants for adult education. All to save £250,000 out of £2,000 million. Besides, these are the very people who ought to be helped—because they are helping themselves, far more than a stodgy boy of fourteen, sulkily doing his lessons. She would have hit the picked people. . . . I get the most agreeable dreams—the detail is beautifully done. I get the sense of being in a scene or situation.'

He looked once more at the photograph of the Queen.

'Lovely, inspiring. All the film people in the world, if they had scoured the globe, could not have found anyone so suited to the part.'

Then he began singing a hymn. '"Yet nightly pitch my moving tent a day's march nearer home."[2]

'Do you remember when Monty gathered his staff officers round him in the Desert after El Alamein, I gave them this hymn? But in my dreams it seems to get mixed up with horses.'

March 7, 1953

The P.M. feels that Stalin's death [3] may lead to a relaxation in tension. It is an opportunity that will not recur, and with Anthony away he is sure he can go straight ahead. He seems to think of little else. He is much incensed by the *Daily Mirror*'s remarks about Stalin and describes it as 'dancing on his tomb.' The *Mirror*, for its part, complains of Mr. Churchill's 'crocodile tears.'

The time has gone when he had the strength and energy to go into every subject in detail. I wish he would get rid of some of the drudgery by devoluting it. For instance, he has just made a speech on defence which has taken him a week to prepare, though Head could have done the donkey work for him.

The P.M.'s task might be easier if he had not so many lame ducks. He questioned me today about Leathers, who is the worse for wear and chafing to resign. Leathers dislikes party politics, affirming that war service was different. The truth is that he cuts a poor figure in the Lords, and he knows it.

[1] Miss Florence Horsbrugh, Minister of Education.
[2] Hymns A. & M. (1889), No. 231.
[3] Stalin died on March 6, 1953.

April 24, 1953

This morning Winston is in good heart.

'I'm really wonderfully well, Charles. Everyone around me is going down. Anthony will be away for months. His doctors are divided, and they are saying that he may have to have another operation. There would not be any danger, but they would like to get him in better condition before anything is done. I have asked him to go to Chequers. Anthony would like to keep an eye on things at the Foreign Office, but I won't let him. I cannot deal with a sick man.'

I knew that this was the P.M.'s way of telling me that he meant to go on with the Foreign Office all the time Anthony was away.

'You could no doubt do this for a short time as an emergency measure,' I told him, 'but to burden yourself with the F.O. for an indefinite period, perhaps for months, is surely not wise.'

'Oh, I like it,' he answered. 'It doesn't add as much work as you think. You see, I've got to keep an eye on foreign affairs at any time. Yes. I have been hunted. I am making my speeches out of my head at present. They seem to go all right.'

But he said this as if he was not at all worried, and there is a general feeling that he is in better fettle, which, of course, gets back to him. Yesterday Swinton said to me:

'What have you done with your man? He is full of energy and doing well too.'

All the same I am not happy about him. To add to the grievous burdens of the First Minister in this fashion is surely folly. I feel certain we are riding for a fall, but when I plead with him all he says is: 'Oh, don't go on like that, Charles.'

He told me he was going down to see the Queen tonight.

'I'll tell you a secret,' he said this like a schoolboy. 'You mustn't tell anyone. She wants me to accept the Garter. I refused it before. But then the Prime Minister had a say in it. Now only the Queen decides.'[1]

April 28, 1953

P.M.: 'This is interesting. We had a hundred and ten Cabinet meetings in the past year; while the Socialists had only eighty-five in a year—and that in a time of great political activity. I am a great believer in bringing things before the Cabinet. If a Minister has got anything on his mind and he has the sense to get it argued by the Cabinet he will have the machine behind him.'

[1] Winston Churchill was made a Knight of the Garter on this day and became Sir Winston.

He pushed away the bed-rest, making the breakfast china rattle.

P.M.: 'Anthony is to have another operation tomorrow. Is there any danger, Charles? He is yellow. He pulled up his shirt to show me his incision. I did not want to see it, but it turned out to be quite healed.'

Moran: 'It's not Anthony I'm bothered about. You know I don't fuss, but you are asking for trouble. I don't believe you can go on like this.'

And then, to my surprise, he admitted that he was torpid. That is something new.

'But I'm all right,' he asserted. 'I'm sleeping well. Of course there are plenty of Foreign Office complications. I have lived seventy eight years without hearing of bloody places like Cambodia.'

With a whimsical look he strung out half a dozen strange-sounding names.

'They have never worried me, and I haven't worried them.'

May 28, 1953

It is a month since my last entry. There are times when I have not had the heart to record the details of his struggle to do his job. He is, of course, fighting it out inch by inch, but it is a losing game. I asked him this morning how he was weathering the racket.

'Yes, it is a racket,' he allowed, 'and I'm getting older. I miss Anthony. He's going to Boston on the 5th June in a special Canadian aircraft for his operation. Poor fellow.'

He was silent for a time, and when he spoke again he was determined to be cheerful.

'The Cabinet is very helpful. They have confidence in me. Rab is good. I would rather go to the Abbey for the Coronation in a big car with large windows than be hidden away in a box of a carriage. Besides, the 4th Hussars, who are providing an escort for me, have never before escorted a motor vehicle—the two things do not go together. But I must ask the Queen and find out what she wants.'

I told him that his speech in Westminster Hall had gone well. He smiled with pleasure.

'No one else could have done it. It had all to come out of this poor nut. The private office can't help in this kind of thing. I was particularly pleased with the bit about the American constitution. I was bold, too, about the conflict between the Crown and Parliament—a hundred yards from Cromwell's statue; the dirty dog, I never liked him. Oh, the Queen liked my speech. Paul Reynaud was quite right not to try to form a Government in Paris. But it is a

405

pity. He has meddled in great things—though he got the worst of them.'

June 9, 1953

'I wouldn't say this to anyone else,' one of the entourage said this morning, 'but isn't it strange that as Winston gets older and more entrenched in people's affections, he gets vainer? There is a lot of work at present, and we are often at it till two or three in the morning. And yet he wastes an hour every night in reading the newspapers. He goes through all of them with care to find something about himself.'

June 16, 1953

'We don't know anything for certain about Bermuda,'[1] the P.M. said. 'My telegram to Ike crossed with one from him. I wanted him to stick to the date fixed for the conference, when the Frogs would come into line. But Ike says we must not hurry them; it will pay good dividends to be patient. Dividends,' he repeated scornfully. 'The bloody Frogs can't make up their minds. With the German elections coming on they are playing party politics in Paris; every little party playing their own game, each with an ideology of their own. They don't care for anything but their own petty intrigues. It is lamentable for poor France. And now the King of Cambodia has bolted on them. Ike only thinks of France. He does not give a thought to our difficulties. The eyes of the world are on us—people are beginning to talk; they wonder what all the delay means. Dulles[2] is a terrible influence. Ike now wants to postpone the conference for a fortnight to give the French a chance to settle down after the election. And every day it's getting hotter in Bermuda.'

Horace Evans tells me the news of Anthony is not too good; his future is uncertain.

June 23, 1953

When I saw the P.M. today he seemed played out—as he was at Cairo before the Carthage illness. I thought his speech was slurred and a little indistinct. Twice I had to ask him to repeat what he had said. He said the Foreign Office was very hard work. I asked

---

[1] Intended three-power conference between Britain, France and the United States at Summit level, to discuss the upkeep of military forces in Western Europe. Churchill's illness caused the meeting to be postponed from June to December, 1953.

[2] John Foster Dulles, President Eisenhower's Secretary of State.

him must he really carry the burden of the F.O. until the autumn? He said he must. I told him I was unhappy about the strain, that it was an impossible existence and that I hoped he would find he could do something about it. He grunted and picked up some papers. Before I left No. 10 I sought out Pitblado to tell him that I was worried about things.

Chapter thirty-nine

Stricken down

June 24, 1953

About half an hour after midnight the telephone awoke me. It was No. 10: would I go and see the Prime Minister at nine o'clock the following morning? The girl at the No. 10 exchange said no more, and it was not till this morning that I learnt of their failure to get me on the telephone. They had given me up at last and left a message with the girl.

Jock told me that at the dinner for de Gasperi[1] the P.M. had made a brilliant little speech, all about Caesar and the Legions. When the guests were beginning to withdraw Christopher noticed that the P.M. was trying to stand up; before he could go to his assistance Winston suddenly flopped back into his chair. He hurried to him, and, seeing that Clemmie was watching him anxiously some distance away, he told her that Winston was very tired.

'Oh, we must get him to bed then,' she answered.

Christopher interposed: 'We must get the waiters away first; he can't walk.'

While Jock was recounting this, Christopher came into the room. He mentioned that the P.M.'s speech was indistinct; it was difficult to understand what he said. Jock added that others had noticed the P.M.'s plight.

'I think they thought he had had too much to drink.'

Jock was sure his speech was affected; the articulation was only distinct when he made an effort. When I was satisfied that I should get no more out of them, I went to his room.

'Ah, Charles, I thought you would never come.'

I could see that the left side of his mouth sagged; it was more noticeable when he spoke. I got him out of bed to see how he walked. He asked me to open the door of his wardrobe, which is lined with

[1] Prime Minister of Italy.

a long mirror; he wanted to see for himself how he got on. He was not very steady on his feet, and once I jumped to his side, thinking he would fall. When he was back in bed he said:

'I would not like to walk to my seat in the House of Commons with members watching. What has happened, Charles? Is it a stroke?'

I told him I would tell him what was wrong when I had examined him. There was no loss of power of the hand or leg that I could detect, even by delicate tests. After I had finished my examination he said. 'I want to know everything.' I explained to him that the circulation in his head was sluggish; there was spasm of a small artery. It belonged to the same family as the incident at Monte Carlo in August, 1949. He said he thought that was the trouble. I asked him if he would like to see Sir Russell Brain. He did not answer. He seemed to be trying to work things out.

'I want to know, Charles, where I stand and what this means.'

I said I would return in the afternoon. After luncheon he telephoned me. I could understand everything that he said.

'You spoke of Russell Brain. Do bring him when you come.'

I advised Brain to be firm, the P.M. might want to do things. There will be lots of people buzzing round, but we must sit tight until we know where we are. In a few days the position will be plainer. When Brain had done, the P.M. questioned him. Then I came to the point. I told him he must not go to the House for Questions. He argued about this, saying he liked Questions. Then he sent for Jock and asked him how many questions there were; which were for him and which were addressed to the Foreign Secretary. Were they important?

'Oh, bring them and let me see.'

While Jock was out of the room I felt I must act before he committed himself. I said I could not guarantee that he would not get up in the House and use the wrong word; he might rise in his place and no words might come. He listened in silence. When Jock came back he read the Questions. 'They are not very important,' Jock added, and the P.M. seemed to agree. Finally, he said abruptly that he would not go to the House.

June 25, 1953

No improvement in his speech, and he is, if anything, more unsteady in his gait.

'I don't feel like managing the world'—there was a long pause—'and yet never have they looked more like offering me it. I feel, Charles, I could do something that no one else can do. I was at the

409

peak of my opportunities, exchanging friendly messages with Malen-kov [1] and Adenauer.'[2]

'You meant to send them messages?'

'No, I have done already. I have stretched out a hand to grasp the paw of the Russian bear. Great things seemed within my grasp. Not perhaps world peace, but world easement. I feel I could have changed the bias of the world. America is very powerful, but very clumsy. Look at this Syngman Rhee [3] business. I could have made her more sensible.'

His speech was becoming blurred and more difficult to follow. He lay back on the pillow as if he were too tired to go on. Once more I pressed him not to attend the Cabinet, and when he became obstin-ate I said that the left side of his mouth drooped and I did not want him to go among people until he was better. They would notice things, and there would be talk. After I had gone Christopher took up the good work; and the P.M. in the end gave up the idea and left about noon for Chartwell. When I dined with Lord Camrose he showed me a letter Jock had sent him explaining, at Winston's re-quest, what had happened. Camrose urged me to get him to Ber-muda at any cost. He must rest, and the voyage would cut off his work.

June 26, 1953

'Look, my hand is clumsy,' the P.M. said as I entered his room at Chartwell.

Transferring his cigar to his left hand, he made a wavering at-tempt to put it to his lips.

'It is so feeble. Hold out your hand, Charles.'

And with that he tried to touch the tips of my fingers with the corresponding fingers of his own hand.

'I'm not afraid of death, but it would be very inconvenient to a lot of people. Rab is very efficient up to a point, but he is narrow and doesn't see beyond his nose. If Anthony were standing by the door there, and I was here, and a telegram was given to him in-volving a decision, well, in nine cases out of ten we should agree.'

When he had done I examined his left hand and arm. There was some loss of power in the left grip—and this had developed since yesterday, three days after the onset of the trouble. I do not like

---

[1] Chairman of Council of Ministers, U.S.S.R.

[2] Chancellor of the Federal Republic of Germany.

[3] President of the South Korean Republic. His objections to the peace terms and demands for the release of anti-Communist North Korean prisoners brought a temporary halt in the Paris Conference 1953.

this, the thrombosis is obviously spreading. He knew that his hand was weaker, and he complained, 'I am having great difficulty in turning over in bed.'

'Two days ago,' he reflected, 'I wanted to take the Cabinet. Now I couldn't. I have scratched Bermuda. It will not come out until Ike replies to my telegram.' He handed me the telegram he had sent to Ike.

I drew up a medical bulletin:

'For a long time the Prime Minister has had no respite from his arduous duties and a disturbance of the cerebral circulation has developed, resulting in attacks of giddiness. We have therefore advised him to abandon his journey to Bermuda and to take at least a month's rest.'

Brain and I signed this. But when we had gone Rab Butler and Lord Salisbury altered it, and persuaded the P.M. to agree to their wording:

'The Prime Minister has had no respite for a long time from his very arduous duties and is in need of a complete rest. We have therefore advised him to abandon his journey to Bermuda and to lighten his duties for at least a month.'

They may well be right, that is of course if he comes through. For if he recovers and wants to carry on as Prime Minister, then the less we say about a stroke, the better for him. But will anyone who knows the P.M. credit that he is willing to take a month's rest merely because his doctors thought he was overdoing things? And besides, if he dies in the next few days will Lord Salisbury think his change in the bulletin was wise? It is a gamble.

June 27, 1953

'I'm getting more helpless. I shall soon be completely paralysed on my left side.'

That was what he said to me this morning.

'I don't mind. But I hope it won't last long. Will the other side be paralysed? Why, it might last for years. Tell me, Charles, is there no operation for this kind of thing? I don't mind being a pioneer. Anyway, it is clear now that we made the right decision in abandoning Bermuda.'

I got him out of bed, but he could hardly stand.

Last night I noticed that he was dragging his left leg. Now it is obvious there is some loss of power, so that the foot drops and the toes catch the carpet. He cannot walk now without two people helping him, though in his wheel-chair he can propel himself from room to room. He paused before his portrait in the blue drawing-room:

'It is the picture of a very unhappy man, painted after the Dardanelles by Orpen. He thought I was finished.'

June 28, 1953

Max Beaverbrook came to lunch. We got the P.M. into his chair at the head of the table before the others appeared. Max was noisy:

'Oh, Winston, you are not as bad as you were in 1949, and you got over that in a very short time. You'll soon be a different man, won't he, Charles? I didn't believe the Trades Union Congress could be managed by any politician, but you've done it. You've got Labour muddled; they've lost the initiative.'

P.M.: 'I think we ought to let the House have a free vote on sponsored television. Are you agin, Max?'

Max: 'Oh, yaas.'

P.M.: 'I'm not taken in by the Russians, but before the British people are committed to another long struggle, I wanted to be sure there was nothing in their recent change of attitude.'

He spoke with tears in his eyes. Then his face lit up and for a little time something of the old vigour of speech came back while Max poured out his soft talk. But I could see the P.M. was getting very tired and that it was time to break up the party. Clemmie had arranged that he should be carried to the swimming-pool to see the grandchildren bathe, but he asked me to take him back to bed. He insisted on getting out of his chair, and we helped him to his room; his good foot coming down on the passage with a noisy stump, while the toes of his left foot dragged along the carpet. When we were alone he slumped upon the bed.

'A week ago I was thinking of running the world—and now——' He shrugged his shoulders. 'When I sit still I feel quite well.'

He looked ruefully at his foot, and then he remembered I had told him that other arteries—what doctors call the collateral circulation —would take on the work of the blocked vessel.

'The blood ought to be getting round the back streets by now. What have you got to say about that, Charles?'

I brought Max to say goodbye, warning him to stay only a few minutes, and then rejoined Clemmie. She told me Winston had said to her: 'I hope I shall either improve or get worse.'

'Even when he is well,' Clemmie went on, 'Winston likes to be surrounded by people petting him and doing things for him.'

I went back to the P.M. His mind wandered to the night when it happened, to No. 10 and the de Gasperi dinner.

'I made quite a good speech impromptu, and then ten minutes after I was like this.'

He turned to Max with a grim smile:

'Today I have knocked Christie[1] off the headlines except in the *Empire News*.'

Max feels all Fleet Street knows what has happened and that it is foolish not to issue bulletins which approximate to the truth. He went away saying he would compose one and telephone me. With all his astuteness, he is obtuse in these matters. If the P.M. is to carry on till October before he hands over to Anthony, I now agree with Salisbury that the less we say about strokes the better. I have a feeling things have taken a turn for the better. It is true that he cannot walk without support, and has little power in his left leg; nor will he admit that there is any real improvement in his hand. But whereas yesterday he sat about doing nothing, as if he had no energy to read or talk or even to think, when I went into his bedroom about six o'clock this evening, he said:

'I have become involved in *Phineas Finn*.'

He is back in his normal mood, and what is left is a physical disability.

Tonight Brendan dined with us. He can draw the P.M. out, and has a kind of explosive cheerfulness which seems to help. The P.M. said that he had only read one book in the first six months of the war—*Journey to the Western Isles of Scotland*, by Dr. Johnson. He admired Johnson. Then Brendan got out of him that he went to the Atlantic Charter Meeting with E. M. Forster's *A Passage to India*.

Winston has learnt to take what Max says with a pinch of salt.

'He poured out floods of optimism as he always does, saying I should soon be in full harness again.'

The P.M. owned that he felt more friendly to the Russians than he had done at some periods of his life. When I pondered on this I remembered a saying of G. M. Young, that there is no better way of bringing a decade or a generation into focus than to ask what they were most afraid of and what they did about it. The fear of another war has occupied men's thoughts since the end of the last war. And in their hearts they feel that the P.M. can do more than anyone else to avert another catastrophe. Winston knows that he is speaking, not for the Tory Party, but for the whole country, and as he watches the slow spread of this creeping paralysis, he is haunted by the lost

[1] John Halliday Christie, responsible for the murder of at least six women.

413

opportunity. He realizes that little men are tied to their texts, that he alone can break down the wall of suspicion which shuts off Russia from the West.

When Brendan had gone he rang a bell:

'Bring me the Queen's letter and my reply. I want you to see, Charles, what I can still do.'

Jock had told me he had suggested to Tommy Lascelles that the Queen should write to the P.M. in her own handwriting. She did.

June 26, 1953.

'My dear Prime Minister,

'I am so sorry to hear from Tommy Lascelles that you have not been feeling too well these last few days.

'I do hope it is not serious and that you will be quite recovered in a very short time.

'Our visit here is going very well and Edinburgh is thrilled by all the pageantry. We have been lucky in having fine weather, but I fear that it is now raining after a thunderstorm.

With all good wishes,
Yours very sincerely,
Elizabeth R.'

The P.M. himself was thrilled by this letter. He showed me his reply, which more than rose to the requirements of the situation. Written only five days after his stroke, it seemed to me a remarkable document with its poise, proportion and sense of detachment. I took heart that he could do so much.

In his letter he recalled the circumstances in which he had been stricken down; he spoke of his plight as he lay in bed as if it had happened to someone else; he told Her Majesty that he was not without hope that he might soon be about and able to discharge his duties until the autumn, when he thought that Anthony would be able to take over.

Lord Waverley has told us that he was able to detect in Winston's composition a streak of humility that had somehow escaped the scrutiny of his friends, and in Winston's approach to the Throne his sense of history invested the Monarch with a certain mystique, so that he always spoke of the Royal House with touching reverence.

June 29, 1953

Camrose came to lunch. He took me aside.

'It's a tragedy, Charles, Beaverbrook being his first visitor. The Conservative Party loathe him so. If it had been Brendan it wouldn't have mattered.'

Camrose talked to the P.M. about the final volume of his book; some of the telegrams about the P.M.'s reluctance to give ground to the Russians before Potsdam were, he said, tremendously effective. If only Winston could tell the whole story. But apart from the book, Camrose never seems to have much to say to him. It sometimes appears that he is overawed by the great man. But he sat with him on the lawn for a long time. I left them, and in the rose garden came across Clemmie. She asked if Camrose had gone. I said no; I wished he would, as I thought the P.M. was getting tired. At this Clemmie burst out:

'If you had more courage you'd tell him so.'

June 30, 1953

Still no bulletin. Max rang up and pressed for something. He got excited. The fact is that while Clemmie vehemently asserts that the P.M. should retire now, he wants to carry on until October; and it won't help him if we tell the public that he has had a stroke.

The Prof. to luncheon. He has developed diabetes. When he asked the P.M. how he was, Winston answered with a touch of levity:

'I eats well and sleeps well and drinks well, but when I get alongside any business I go all of a tremble. I could do without smoking but not without my liquor; that would be a sad impoverishment.' His face became grave. 'It is extraordinary between night and morning that I should go like this—a bundle of old rags. To be different from other people, and yet I feel quite well. What did you work at last night, Charles, when we went to the film? I only work,' he said, 'when I want to. I must be lured by pleasure, spurred by excitement.'

He spoke of the French with contempt—five years of ignominy, and they have enjoyed every hour of it. With a great effort he turned over in bed.

'I am a hulk—only breathing and excreting.'

He got up for luncheon, but when he had talked for a little with the Prof. he felt weary and, calling for his wheel-chair, went back to bed. Norman Brook came to dinner. Winston likes him, and they talked away for a long time. Jock got the P.M. going about Antwerp[1] —'a very exciting experience.' Then he told us of the mutiny over demobilization at the end of the First War. They came to him at

[1] Early in October 1914 Churchill, then First Lord of the Admiralty, went to Antwerp in an attempt to persuade the Belgian Government to delay their evacuation of the port. Antwerp fell on October 10. It is possible that the five-day prolongation of Antwerp's resistance was a crucial factor in depriving the Germans of a decisive victory that autumn.

the War Office and said that this was a serious mutiny. The soldiers were dissatisfied with the regulations for demobilization; they felt it was not being done fairly. They had gathered on the Horse Guards Parade, and things looked ugly. Winston asked: 'How many troops have we to deal with them?' They answered, a battalion of the Guards and three squadrons of the Household Cavalry. 'Are they loyal?' Winston asked. 'We hope they are,' was the doubtful answer. 'Can you arrest the mutineers?' 'We are not certain.' 'Have you any other suggestions?' They had none. 'Then arrest the mutineers.' He stood watching from a window over the parade ground. He expected firing to break out any minute. But the mutineers allowed the Guards to surround them.

We asked the P.M. what he did when the mutineers were under arrest.

P.M.: 'Oh, I changed the system of demobilization overnight: the first to join was the first to be demobilized, and any man with a wound stripe or a decoration could go when he wished. This removed their strong sense of injustice. It was one of the best things I did.'

Brook asked him about Glasgow.

'David Kirkwood[1] asked that they should be given separate machinery to make shells. I arranged this, and soon they were producing shells at a quicker rate than anyone. That was the beginning of my friendship with David.'

Still thinking of mutinies, he said:

'Haig wanted to shoot eight or nine of the ring-leaders of the Calais mutiny.[2] But I would not agree in peace-time. They got two years.'

He rambled on, wondering why butterflies were not so numerous as they once were. After the war he would have arranged for clouds of butterflies. The love of flowers and affection for animals were two of the noblest qualities of our race. You did not find gardens in America. You can live a long time with a geranium.

Once more he told how one of our tanks at the end of an engagement had to surrender to the Germans, and how the Germans saluted them and complimented them on their courage in the fight.

'That is how I like war to be conducted,' the P.M. said.

'I'm finished,' he said sadly, 'but a week ago I had big plans. My influence everywhere had never been greater. Nehru and Adenauer were very friendly. Of course I knew that I was taking risks by my advances to the Russians. I might have taken a big toss.'

[1] Lord Kirkwood, formerly M.P. for East Dunbartonshire.
[2] British soldiers mutinied in January, 1919, as a result of slow demobilization.

Alas, he will keep thinking of what might have been. He had given the final volume of the book to Norman Brook to read. He questioned him now about it. Would anything in it cause offence to the Americans?

'If I am going to die, then I can say what I like and take the view that I believe to be right. But if I live and am still Prime Minister, then I must not say things which will anger Ike.'

July 1, 1953

Christopher, finding the P.M. bright-eyed and alert, said encouragingly:

'You are going to get quite well.'

P.M.: 'Yes, but I don't know how much difficulty I'll have in getting back my position.'

'You see,' Christopher added dryly, 'he has not given up hope of a come-back. I don't know what Clemmie will say.'

July 2, 1953

When I saw the P.M. at Chartwell this morning, he said:

'You will look in on your way back from London?'

So I dined there. Harold Macmillan was the only guest. He has curiosity and talked well when the P.M. gave him the chance. Winston spoke of death. He did not believe in another world; only in 'black velvet'—eternal sleep. He kept taking up different subjects and then dropping them, almost at once, as if he could not be bothered to go deeply into anything. He spoke of some African chiefs drinking beer, armed with staves, inflamed with alcohol and inspired by liberal principles—the old love of words—and then of Buddhism, 'a Tory religion.' He used not to believe in rationing or in any other device which would lead to bureaucracy, but Sam Hoare had converted him. He drifted on. Lord Rosebery had written a vivid account of Gladstone's last Cabinet.

'By comparison,' Winston concluded, 'my reign has been considerate and reasonable.'

When I took him to his room I asked him the history of a badger's skin hanging on the wall.

'Oh,' he said, 'I was returning one night from the Other Club, rather hilarious, when just outside the gates there was a bump. I got out and saw a badger fighting for breath. I took it in my arms. They said it had killed one of my swans; but there was no proof, and in any case I forgave it.'

When I rose to leave he said, 'Oh don't go, Charles.' He was

417

rather excited and not ready for sleep. I got away half an hour later and was opening the door at Marshalls when I heard the telephone ring. It was the night nurse. The P.M. wanted to speak to me.

'My leg has been twitching for the last hour,' he said, 'the arm too has twitched a little. What does it mean?'

I comforted him, but my mind is ill at ease.

July 3, 1953

The report this morning is reassuring. He had slept well once he got off, and according to Jock, seemed in good spirits. It is strange that no one around the P.M. seems able to grasp what is the exact nature of his disability. This is not an acute illness from which he may recover completely. He will never again be the same man he was before the stroke, because the clot in the artery has cut off some of the blood which went to his brain and was the ultimate source of all his activities. So his brain is always anaemic, and when the circulation flags a little, then he has no zest for work and cannot face detail, or his leg twitches, or something of the kind. He is really living on a volcano, and he may get another stroke at any time.

Chapter forty

Fighting back

July 3, 1953

Winston has discovered Trollope. I asked him if he had read anything by him before; he said, 'No.' Clemmie explained that he had always been so busy with his own plans that he had had no time for reading.

'It is the same,' she said, 'with a lot of things. Why, Charles, when Winston took up painting in 1915 he had never up to that moment been in a picture gallery. He went with me—do you remember, dear?—to the National Gallery, and pausing before the first picture, a very ordinary affair, he appeared absorbed in it. For half an hour he studied its technique minutely. Next day he again visited the gallery, but I took him in this time by the left entrance instead of the right, so that I might at least be sure he would not return to the same picture.'

He spoke of the Westminster Election.[1]

'At the head of each of my committees was a Conservative, who was helping me in defiance of the orders of the Central Office. Families were divided. It was most exciting.'

Suddenly the P.M.'s voice broke and tears streamed down his face.

'Since this happened I have been very lachrymose. At parts of

---

[1] Churchill left the Liberal Party because they had combined with Labour to defeat the Baldwin Government. Labour in consequence came into power. In 1924 a by-election occurred in the Abbey division of Westminster, a Tory stronghold. Baldwin was determined to have nothing to do with Churchill. Winston decided to challenge this, and stood as an anti-socialist candidate in opposition to the official Tory. The Tory caucus were furious, and all the resources of the Party were mobilized to ensure his defeat. Churchill lost, but only by forty votes. It was a moral victory. Baldwin saw he could not keep Churchill out, and nine months later, when the Tories were returned to power, he was given the safe seat of Epping, and made Chancellor of the Exchequer.

Phineas Finn I became very tearful, though it is not at all a moving story. Will it go on, Charles?'

'What happened at the election?'

'Oh, we were beaten by forty votes, but it did good. Baldwin learnt my hold over the Tory Party. I expected he would give me office in 1935. He had spoken to me in friendly terms before the election.'

Jock: 'Was India the reason?'

P.M.: 'Oh, no. India was over by then. But the war-monger business had begun.'

Jock: 'As far back as that?'

P.M.: 'Yes. Baldwin was receiving Baptists and that sort of person, and he gave a pledge to the Peace Society.'

Jock asked about the eleven years in the wilderness.[1]

P.M.: 'I was quite happy at Chartwell. I was making £20,000 every year by my books and by journalism. I wrote *Marlborough* and finished *The World Crisis*. I think I will go and rest now.'

I went with him to his room. As he got into bed he smiled at me mischievously:

'There will be a bloody row if I get well. And it does not seem impossible.'

Franklin Roosevelt had been dead seven years, he reflected.

'I always looked up to him as an older man, though he was eight years my junior. I am no longer really interested in public affairs. Oh, yes, I mean that. You see, Charles, you must be right in it, or interest flags.'

He told me a story I had not heard before.

'When I was a subaltern I was sitting on a couch with a girl at a kind of dance hall in Oxford Street; my legs were crossed, and a big fellow, as he went by, caught my toe. I did not move my feet, and next time round the big fellow caught my foot and pulled me round the floor by it. When I got up I rushed at him. I remembered no more till I found my head in a spittoon in a corner of the room. He turned out to be a retired pugilist. That is the only time I remember being knocked out like that. It wasn't painful. Of course, my creed is when a man hits you, you must in honour hit back. Next morning I had a thick head, the only time in my life I have had a headache.'

When he noticed that I was examining a long chart on the wall, depicting the results of the U-boat struggle throughout the war, he said:

---

[1] 1929–39. Shortly after the Conservative defeat in 1929, Churchill resigned from the Shadow Cabinet. He was not given office again until the war broke out. Throughout the 1930s he was deeply distrusted by both the major political parties.

'You see, up to Pearl Harbour we had got it in hand; then when America came in her merchant fleet was almost too easy a target. Look how sharply the losses rose.'

Next to the chart there was a print of the great statesmen of the First War.

'It was painted by Sir James Guthrie,' the P.M. explained, 'I never heard of him either before or since, but it is a fine composition. I like it. Arthur Balfour is the key figure. Guthrie has put me in the centre of the picture; it is a little out of focus, for I was in low water then.'

He rose and walked across the room to the picture. There were sixteen men in it.

'I'm the only one left alive,' he reflected.

I glanced at two photographs, one of his father and the other of his mother, with several of Clemmie in many positions, and Mary and Sarah. Over his bed was a painting of a room.

'That is the dining-room of my mother's last house. It was furnished by her—she had a remarkable gift for this. My mother's coffin rested there the night before burial.'

Alongside a print of the Battle of Blenheim was a photograph of the balcony at Buckingham Palace on Victory Day. The King and Queen and the two princesses stood by his side. His old humility where the Royal Family was concerned came out: they had been kind enough to sign the photograph, he said. Stalin's portrait had been replaced by three paintings of his horses in desperate finishes: Colonist, and 'the poor horse' which won a race and then died. I was on the point of asking what happened to Stalin's photograph when, turning round, I saw he was deep in *Phineas Finn*.

July 4, 1953

A good day. Full of spirits. He can walk a short distance and says that each day he will do a little more. During dinner his retirement in October came up.

'I shall do what is best for the country.'

Clemmie: 'Of course, dear, I know you will.'

P.M. (*with a whimsical smile*): 'Circumstances may convince me of my indispensability.'

There it is: he has no intention of retiring if he can help it. All afternoon he has sat on the croquet lawn reading under his sombrero, hardly once did he look up; it was some time before I discovered that he had fallen asleep. During dinner he spouted some verses which he said expressed exactly the Socialist point of view. They were from *Punch*, perhaps fifty years ago. He thought they were called 'Reflections from St. James's Park.' Then he quoted from Longfellow—at length. Afterwards there was a film about the siege of Malta, which gave him pleasure.

July 5, 1953

The night nurse reported that his leg had twitched for nearly an hour, but it was not so severe, and he did not mention it to me. He can walk alone now.

Monty came to luncheon and stayed to dinner. He arrived with a theme. If, he argued, Western Germany rearmed, they would be with the West. But this isn't going to happen. Germany, according to Monty, will be united before she is armed, and he wants this united Germany to look to the West and not to the East for allies.

Monty: 'What I fear is an alliance between Russia and this united Germany. Russia would give them back what they have lost. Her change of tone is all propaganda designed to bring this about.'

Moran: 'Is the Foreign Office alive to this?'

Monty: 'I very much doubt it. I know Strang;[1] he is a routine fellow. Prudent no doubt, but without vision. There are too many routine people in the Foreign Office. Without a moment's thought he strung off the names of three ambassadors who were 'wet, weak and needed a weed-killer. What is needed is vision. The F.O. ought to make an intensive study of the problem. They ought to be ready with a thought-out plan which could be put into operation the moment Germany is united. I think it is most important that a man with a strong personality should be posted as our ambassador in Paris when Oliver Harvey retires. He will retire very soon.'

Monty produced two documents which he gave to the P.M.

'They give my views on this problem.'

The P.M. began skimming through them. When he had done he put them down.

'They are very important papers. My own mind has been moving along the same lines.'

At this point the P.M. rang for a secretary and asked for Volume VI of his book, *Triumph and Tragedy*. It was brought to him in chapters. He became immersed in the long galley sheets. At last he extracted one of the chapters.

'Read this,' he said, handing it to Monty. 'That is the most important telegram I have ever sent. It was dated May 12, 1945 and addressed to President Truman, pleading that we should not give up the part of Germany we occupied to the Russians until we had

[1] Permanent Under-Secretary of State, Foreign Office, later Lord Strang.

422

made a firm agreement with them. Truman replied that we had given our word. I argued that this did not hold under the new circumstances, because the Russians had broken their word over Vienna.'[1]

Monty read the telegram and put it down; then he read it again.

'That was the first mention of the Iron Curtain? All these telegrams,' he said, 'ought to be published. People think we are winning the cold war. It is not true. We are losing it—thirty love. The Big Three ought to have met earlier; Potsdam was too late.'

P.M.: 'Yes, June, 1945, or May.'

Monty: 'This all began at Casablanca. Unconditional surrender meant that Russian troops would invade Germany, and once that was decided we ought to have made certain we'd be first in Berlin, Vienna and Prague. It could have been done. If Alex's command had not been weakened he would have got to Vienna.'

Moran: 'Wasn't the shortage of landing craft throughout the war a crucial factor—a fatal handicap?'

Monty: 'Yes, that is true.'

P.M.: 'I warned the Americans before Potsdam not to withdraw from any of the part of Germany we occupied until we had a satisfactory understanding. They would not listen. And they will not listen now when I warn them about Germany. At Potsdam I wanted Prussia isolated and Germany divided horizontally and not vertically.

The P.M. gave me a telegram about Austria, dated June 14, 1945. 'Read that.'

Monty: 'What is our policy in Korea? It is no good making war without a policy.'

P.M.: 'If I were in charge I would withdraw the United Nations troops to the coast and leave Syngman Rhee to the Chinese. But the American public would not swallow this. Korea does not really matter now. I'd never heard of the bloody place till I was seventy-four. Its importance lies in the fact that it has led to the rearming of America. That may have saved the peace of the world. And Indo-China, too, does not really matter. We gave up India. Why shouldn't France give up Indo-China?'

Monty (*demurring*): 'Indo-China matters strategically. If Indo-China goes, Siam goes too. And then Malaya would be in danger.'

P.M.: 'We could hold the Isthmus.'

Monty: 'Yes, perhaps we might.'

P.M.: 'It's Germany, not Korea, that matters.'

---

[1] Mr. Churchill's 'Iron Curtain' telegram, dated May 12, 1945, pleaded with President Truman for an understanding with the Russians, 'before we weaken our armies mortally or retire to the zones of occupation.' See Appendix (2) pp. 795–6.

Later, on the croquet lawn, Monty appeared in a new light as he expanded in the sun. It was as if he had only come into the world with the war, and wanted to hear from Winston all about the political figures of the years between the wars.

Monty: 'Tell me about Baldwin. Was he a bad man?'

P.M.: 'He was a much greater figure than G. M. Young[1] makes him out to be.'

Monty (*without waiting for the P.M. to finish*): 'And what about Chamberlain?'

P.M.: 'Baldwin thought Europe was a bore, and Chamberlain thought it was only a greater Birmingham.'

Monty: 'I knew nothing of Ramsay MacDonald.'

P.M.: 'He was a pertinacious Scot who made the Parliamentary Labour Party.'

Monty: 'And Bonar Law?'

Clemmie: 'If you want the truth about him you must listen to Winston and then to Lord Beaverbrook and strike a medium. Winston did not like him.'

Monty, who had taken off his coat, called for it as a night breeze came up out of the valley; a little later he added a blue pullover. Winston said, 'You would like a bath before dinner?' Monty answered that he never took a bath before dinner; he would catch cold. Then Monty had a little tiff with Clemmie.

Monty: 'I have a boy on my staff who wants to give up soldiering and take up politics.'

P.M.: 'Was he a good soldier?'

Monty: 'You know I have only good people on my staff. Yes, he is a brilliant boy. They asked me for a recommendation. In it I told them he had been used to soldiering and telling the truth, and would be out of his depth among politicians, who do a lot of lying.'

At this Clemmie sprang at his throat. She did not know why he should speak like that of politicians. He had said this not once but twice in one afternoon. It was bad manners to say this to the Central Office. Monty wouldn't like it if they wrote in that way about the Army. Monty laughed a little awkwardly.

July 6, 1953

A bad day; the P.M. does not feel on the top of things.

P.M.: 'I can understand death or illness, but not this. I had a busy, scheming brain once, and now'—pointing to his head—'it's

[1] G. M. Young, *Life of Baldwin.*

empty. Today we should have been at Bermuda. The punch seems to have gone out of the movement. I should have said things to the French no one else could say. They want the best of all worlds— not to fight in the war, but to remain a great power.'

Strang (*mildly*): 'They have, sir, put blood and fortune into Indo-China for better or for worse.'

P.M.: 'Either they must sign E.D.C.[1] or we must adopt punitive measures.'

When they had gone, I went with the P.M. to his room. He sat on his bed and began to give me Longfellow's 'King Robert of Sicily.' He went on and on without apparently hesitating for a word. I asked him when last he had read the poem. He answered: 'About fifty years ago.' 'Wait a moment,' I said, and went in search of a copy of Longfellow. When I found it and had taken it to his room, I said:

'I believe your memory is as good as ever it was, but I want to be sure.'

I asked him to repeat the lines while I checked the words from the text. Wanting to come out with credit, he entered into the spirit of the test:

> '*Robert of Sicily, brother of Pope Urbane*
> *And Valmond, Emperor of Allemaine,*
> *Apparelled in magnificent attire,*
> *With retinue of many a knight and squire,*
> *On St. John's Eve, at vespers, proudly sat*
> *And heard the priests chant the Magnificat.*
> *And as he listened, o'er and o'er again*
> *Repeated, like a burden or refrain,*
> *He caught the "Deposuit potentes*
> *De sede, et exultavit humiles";*
> *And slowly lifting up his kingly head,*
> *He to a learned clerk beside him said,*
> *"What mean these words," The clerk made answer meet*
> *"He has put down the mighty from their seat,*
> *And has exalted them of low degree."*
> *Thereat King Robert muttered scornfully,*

---

[1] E.D.C. was the stillborn European Defence Community or European Army. It originated in France and Germany in late 1950 after Mr. Churchill had called at Strasbourg in August of that year for 'the immediate creation of a European Army under a united command in which we should all bear a worthy and honourable part . . . in co-operation with the United States and Canada.' Successive Labour and Conservative Governments in Britain did not feel able to take part, and it was finally killed when it was rejected by the French Assembly in 1954.

> " ' Tis well that such seditious words are sung
> Only by priests and in the Latin tongue,
> For unto priests and people be it known
> There is no power can push me from my throne !"
> And leaning back, he yawned and fell asleep,
> Lulled by the chant monotonous and deep.
>
> When he awoke it was already night ;
> The church was empty and there was no light,
> Save for the lamps, that glimmered few and faint,
> Lighted a little space before some saint.
> He started from his seat and gazed around,
> But saw no living thing and heard no sound.
> He groped towards the door, but it was locked ;
> He cried aloud, and listened, and then knocked.
> And uttered awful threatenings and complaints,
> And imprecations upon men and saints.
> The sounds re-echoed from the roof and walls
> As if dead priests were laughing in their stalls.'

This may perhaps give critics pause, if the day should come when he is harshly judged for sticking to his post. Here and there he got a word wrong: priests became monks and lamps candles; perhaps half a dozen words out of three hundred and fifty. The stroke has not touched his memory. I told him so. He brightened and smiled.

He is confiding in no one, but he means to carry on if he is able, and the question whether he will be able is hardly ever out of his head. This is his secret battle. There are moments when he does not want to do anything, when a dreadful apathy settles on him and he nearly loses heart. But he always sets his jaw and hangs on.

July 7, 1953

Lord and Lady Salisbury to dinner at Chartwell. For two hours the P.M. expounded his views on the international situation, until the acting Foreign Secretary was fully briefed for his visit to Washington; and this the P.M. did without obvious fatigue.

July 8, 1953

There is some gain in the strength of the left foot and an obvious improvement in his 'attitude to life,' to use his own words. During dinner Winston leant towards Clemmie:

'You will not be angry with me, dear, but you ought not to say

426

"very delicious." "Delicious" alone expresses everything you wish to say. You would not say "very unique." '

Whether Clemmie respected his loving care for language I cannot tell, but she turned his flank, choosing her own field of battle. She began with a disarming air of innocence.

'In *Phineas Finn* you took people *out* to dinner, not *in* to dinner.'

This acted as a preface to a discourse on manners, in which Clemmie did all the talking and Winston took in every word. Men lit a woman's cigarettes, but did not necessarily listen to her conversation. Winston listened with curiosity. The small change of good manners was to him a foreign currency.

He had read three chapters of *Jane Eyre*, and had been 'arrested' by them. He rose and walked to the lift with an occasional lurch. New possibilities were opening up. He would entertain the Jockey Club to dinner at Downing Street. Mr. Baldwin had been host to the King and Queen at dinner before he resigned. Mr. Churchill would like to follow that precedent. Other engaging adventures passed through his mind. The suspicion of a smile advertised his thoughts.

July 9, 1953

The P.M. was still asleep this morning when I called at half-past nine. He said rather apologetically:

'I went on reading *Jane Eyre* till two o'clock this morning. It got hold of me. Funny that my education in Victorian novels should begin when I am nearly eighty.'

I had Pope in my hand.

'What are you reading? Ah, when I used to quote from him it was usually from his *Essay on Man*:

> '*Vice is a monster of so frightful mien,*
> *As, to be hated, needs but to be seen;*
> *Yet seen too oft, familiar with her face,*
> *We first endure, then pity, then embrace.*
> *But where the extreme of vice was ne'er agreed:*
> *Ask where's the north? at York 'tis on the Tweed;*
> *In Scotland, at the Orcades; and there,*
> *At Greenland, Zembla, or the Lord knows where.*
> *No creature owns it in the first degree,*
> *But thinks his neighbour further gone than he;*
> *Even those who dwell beneath its very zone,*
> *Or never feel the rage, or never own;*
> *What happier natures shrink at with affright,*
> *The hard inhabitant contends he is right.*'

His face lit up.

'Ike will come.'

'To London?'

'Yes, if he gets into an aircraft he doesn't mind if the journey is two hours or eight. He has done a lot of flying.'

'Would the people mind?' I asked.

'Oh,' said the P.M., his eyes filling up, 'he'd be worshipped if he came over here, almost to the point of idolatry. Clemmie would give him Irish stew. He likes that.'

'I meant, would the American people mind his coming to London?'

'Oh, they would not mind very much. Of course, they always fear being got at by the snobbery of the Court.'

July 10, 1953

I asked the P.M., while he was waiting for his breakfast, what he made of the dismissal of Beria from the Communist Party,[1] as an enemy of the party and of the Soviet people. We had come to think of the head of the Russian secret police as one of the ruling triumvirate, on the same level as Molotov and Malenkov.

P.M.: 'Beria—Siberia. Strange things are happening there. It is very significant and supports the line I have taken. The Russians were surprisingly patient about the disturbances in East Germany. The aggressive party in the Kremlin must have said: You see what comes of giving in, this is the result of concessions. But they had not the power to arrest Malenkov. At a conference of the Big Four he would have welcomed me particularly.'

The P.M.'s eyes dilated, he spoke eagerly.

'I would have met them more than halfway. It might have meant a real U.N.O., with Russia working with the rest for the good of Europe. We would have promised them that no more atomic bombs would be made, no more research into their manufacture. Those already made would be locked away. They would have had at their disposal much of the money now spent on armaments to provide better conditions for the Russian people. I trust the opportunity may not slip away. I have not given up hope of attending a Four Power Conference in, say, September. Do you think, Charles, I shall be fit by then?'

I asked him if he had read an article in the *Spectator* on his oratory.

[1] After Stalin's death (March 6, 1953) Beria became one of the four Deputy Prime Ministers as well as Minister for Internal Affairs. He was dismissed on July 10, 1953, for 'anti-party and anti-state activities,' and executed after his trial for treason on December 23, 1953.

'I am not an orator,' mused Winston. 'An orator is spontaneous. The written word—ah, that's different. You write: "There exists some uncertainty as to his whereabouts." You say: "Where is he? Does he exist?"'

Moran: 'What do you mean when you say that great orators are spontaneous and you are not?'

P.M.: 'Oh, they indulge in a great deal of dramatic art.'

Suddenly he spouted with great feeling a speech by a countryman against towns.

Moran: 'Who said that?'

P.M.: 'I did. I just made it up. A hundred and fifty years ago dramatic art was conspicuous in great orators. It was my ambition, all my life, to be master of the spoken word. That was my only ambition. Of course you learn a lot when you have spoken for fifty years, and as a result of my great experience I no longer fear that I shall say something in the House of Commons which will get me into a hole. In my youth I was always afraid of that. But that is only competent speaking. Oratory is repetition. Lloyd George and Bevan are carried away by their feelings. I'm not. I run short of something to say.'

Moran: 'I suppose that was why Lloyd George criticized your choice of words?'

P.M.: 'What do you mean?'

Moran: 'Lloyd George said you were more concerned with the sound of words than with their effect in influencing a crowd. John noticed that you use unusual, bookish adjectives: that for example, you wrote of Mussolini's invasion of Abyssinia that his conduct was "at once obsolete and reprehensible." '

P.M.: 'Ah, the b's in those words, obsolete, reprehensible, you must pay attention to euphony.'

Moran: 'You are very fond of eighteenth-century phrases. I catch the same cadences in your books and in your speeches. They seem to owe something to Gibbon and Macaulay, just as Asquith's style was moulded by the writers of antiquity.'

P.M.: 'Oh, I have not read much, though I have written a lot.'

I read to him Rosebery's description of the way in which Lord Randolph prepared his speeches. But the P.M. had stepped out of the confessional and was now just talking. He grumbled that he did not get forty-eight hours' seclusion in which he could think out what he was going to say.

Moran: 'You are supposed to be a bad patient, but you have behaved very well in the last fortnight.'

P.M.: 'I feel I have done my bit.'

429

He changed the subject abruptly.

'I find *Jane Eyre* very exciting. It is a wonderful book. I'm so glad I have read it.'

July 11, 1953

I drove over to Chartwell from Marshalls in the late afternoon. When I asked him how he was he lifted his left arm above his head and turned on the switch of the reading lamp.

'I could not do that yesterday. Come, we will walk in the garden and you will see what I can do.'

He insisted on walking without assistance. We picked our way over great stepping stones across a little pond—I felt he must fall, but nothing happened. The detective produced a tin of squirming maggots, and the P.M. fed the goldfish with them. He called for a chair and, flopping into it, said:

'I'm better, but I'm not entirely recovered yet. I get very weary. You must give me some strength, Charles, before I can do anything. At present I keep dropping off to sleep.'

He seems bent on attending a race meeting at Lingfield in a week's time. I explained that he would have to be helped to his box, but he insisted; his mind was set on it. Somehow this must be stopped.

'It does not matter,' he argues, 'what people think of me now; it's what I can do in the autumn that will count. If in two months' time I can do a good broadcast and say something which the others can't say, it will be all right. People will ask: Is the brute competent? If he is, they will prefer me to others. If he isn't—well, that's different.'

Suppose he is obstinate and appears in public now, everyone will know he has had a stroke. He thinks that does not matter. I believe it matters a great deal. When people hear someone has had a stroke they feel that something has happened in the head which leads to paralysis and some deterioration of the mind. The man may perhaps go on living for a while, but for serious things he is finished. When the P.M. wrote to Ike he said he had a stroke, that he was completely paralysed and that his speech was affected. I don't know why he went into all this detail. It was quite unnecessary. When I reasoned with him, trying to persuade him not to talk of a stroke and of paralysis, he repeated the word 'paralysis.'

'But I like the word,' he persisted.

Some sense of the drama and of the poignant part he had to play in it was at the back of his mind. He is so unlike anyone else.

July 12, 1953

The nurse telephoned that the P.M. did not feel so well when he woke this morning. He was much stiffer, particularly in his back muscles. She thought he was worrying about it. I told him it meant nothing; that in his walk in the garden, balancing himself and correcting the weakness of the left side, he had made excessive use of muscles he does not generally use. Thus reassured, he banished it from his mind. But he complains of 'immense fatigue.'

'Can't you give me a tonic, Charles? Something to get rid of this horrible sense of exhaustion?'

I asked him what he could do. He rang for a secretary and asked for a memorandum which he had just dictated for Lord Salisbury, to be sent through the Ambassador in Washington.

'The thought is good, but the words are slovenly. I show it to you not to extract your political views, but in order that you may know what I can do.'

The document began by saying that the Cabinet tomorrow would consider the postponement of E.D.C.

'I do not object to the postponement, though I believe E.D.C. would have made the French less troublesome and Soviet Russia more disposed to work with me. The French want the Four Power talks to be carried out under such conditions that nothing will come of them. They are resolved to prevent German rearmament. And the Americans are behaving like fools. Dulles particularly. They want to make enemies of Russia and to stir up her satellite states. That can only lead to war. Malenkov is, I feel, a good man. I wish I could meet him. If we'd got E.D.C., then we could have spoken to Russia from strength, because German rearmament is the only thing they are afraid of. I want to use Germany and E.D.C. to keep Russia in the mood to be reasonable—to make her play. And I would use Russia to prevent Germany getting out of hand. It sounds cynical. The underlings don't want a Four Power Conference at this highest level; they want a meeting of the Foreign Secretaries. Nothing will come of that. In the war we decided the mood and they worked out the detail. It won't work in any other way.'

The document ended with a sympathetic understanding of the difficult task Lord Salisbury had undertaken. 'Try to get a Four Power Conference. It will give great satisfaction.' The P.M. knew we were at a 'turning point of the world,' and as he lay there, half the man he was, I thought of one of his heroes, Nelson, lying mortally wounded, listening to the roar of the cannon on deck and wondering what was happening in this battle that would decide the fate of the world.

'Poor Anthony will be relieved at this,' the P.M. said grimly. 'He must have thought I would go on for ever.'

July 13, 1953

P.M. in good form, though his leg twitched for an hour last night. But the problem we have still to face is not the paralysed arm and leg, for it already appears that there will in the long run be no loss of power in his limbs, it is the fatigue on any exertion, whether physical or mental, that may remain as a permanent handicap. There is, too, another disconcerting relic of his illness: he is liable to become emotional, so that without warning, as he is saying something or reading a book, in his own words he 'blubs like a child.' I found him reading Trollope's *The Prime Minister*.

P.M.: 'I find the difference between those days[1] and the present time interesting.'

Moran: 'In what way?'

P.M.: 'Oh, they mixed up society and politics. What happened at the Carlton and Reform Clubs mattered to the Prime Minister then, and the House of Lords had a lot of power. Though the franchise had already been extended, public opinion had less power then. The wife of the Prime Minister filled her house with a week-end party of forty-five people, and the talk influenced the course of events. On one occasion the Leader of the House went for a walk with the Prime Minister; he suggested that they ought to have a policy, to bring in two or three measures, instead of just drifting along, and the Prime Minister was affronted. Another time the Leader of the House was not asked to dine with the Prime Minister, and there was a serious bust-up.

'I have loyal friends,' the P.M. reflected, implying that there was little loyalty in Trollope's world.

Moran: 'How is Ike doing?'

P.M.: 'The Americans want to hold a Four Power Conference at a lower level. The Foreign Ministers might meet. Dulles is ambitious to be one of the big figures of the world. And' (sadly) 'I am not in a position to make a fuss. But the Russians may refuse. Bidault's only aim is to prevent the conference doing anything.'

There was a message from Clemmie that she would like to see me before I left. I found her concerned with his progress.

'How long do you think he will have to have two nurses?'

[1] 1876.

I said it was too early to say. Had Winston any views? Clemmie smiled.

'Winston is a pasha. If he cannot clap his hands for a servant he calls for Walter as he enters the house. If it were left to him he'd have the nurses for the rest of his life. He would like two in his room, two in the passage. He is never so happy, Charles, as he is when one of the nurses is doing something for him while Walter puts on his socks.'

July 14, 1953

Found the P.M. on the croquet lawn. He was weary.

'Talking tires me,' he said.

I was told that Max had come to luncheon and had been shouting at him for two hours. He wanted a general election. But the P.M. has learnt at last that Max is not a reliable counsellor where elections are concerned. He has no intention of going to the country.

'I am tired of making decisions,' he told me. 'I am taking a holiday. Doodling and reading novels.'

Jock said that he showed the P.M. this morning a number of Foreign Office telegrams, which a month ago would have riveted his attention. Now he hardly glanced at them. He had lost his zest for work. Yet he has not given up hope that he will get well and carry on just where he left off when he was struck down.

'In two weeks,' he said, 'I may be very different, but I do not know if I shall be able to seize power as I exercised it when the Foreign Office was in my hands.'

He had a short waterproof over his greatcoat and a rug drawn over his knees. When he had been reading for some time big snorts came from under the big sombrero, which had tilted forward. Then he awoke, gazed around with a dazed look and, raising himself in his chair, began to talk.

'I dislike weakness, but I do not think anything that has happened in Egypt so far justifies wholesale measures.[1]

'I am disappointed with events in America. They've bitched things up. The Foreign Ministers are to meet in the autumn: Bidault, Dulles and Molotov.'

He lapsed into thought. At length he said:

'I'm turning over in my mind saying something serious to Ike. I want to make clear to him that I reserve the right to see Malenkov

---

[1] General Mohammed Neguib forced King Farouk of Egypt to abdicate at the beginning of the year. The country was declared a Republic on June 18, 1953, under Neguib's leadership.

433

alone. It's no good seeing the Russians after the Foreign Ministers have drawn up agreements.'

He went indoors to telephone to Rab, to tell him of his misgivings, but I do not know if Rab was able to console him.

I talked to Jock as we drove from Chartwell to London. I reminded him that Maynard Keynes had written that Churchill went wrong over the Gold Standard, because he lacked instinctive judgment to tell him what was wrong. Jock thought this might be true, but that if Keynes had known him better he might have added that from time to time he seemed to recognize instinctively, before others, that some course of action was right. For example, giving South Africa back to the Boers. An opportunity of the kind might soon occur, Jock went on, to give self-government to the Gold Coast. He smiled.

'I am afraid the P.M. will not be interested in the inhabitants of those parts.'

Jock told me of an occasion when he was leaving the House of Commons with Tommy Lascelles after a debate in which Winston had taken a prominent part. 'There may be two opinions of him as a politician,' Lascelles said thoughtfully, 'but there can be only one of him as a poet.' 'You know,' Jock continued, 'the lines in *The World Crisis* with their tribute to those who fell at the Somme. And then there is what he said about Neville Chamberlain when he died.'

This is what he wrote about the Somme:

'A young army, but the finest we have ever marshalled; improvised at the sound of the cannonade, every man a volunteer, inspired not only by love of country but by a widespread conviction that human freedom was challenged by military and imperial tyranny, they grudged no sacrifice however unfruitful and shrank from no ordeal however destructive. Struggling forward through the mire and filth of the trenches, across the corpse-strewn crater fields, amid the flaring, crashing, blasting barrages and murderous machine-gun fire, conscious of their race, proud of their cause, they seized the most formidable soldiery in Europe by the throat, slew them and hurled them unceasingly backwards. If two lives or ten lives were required by their commanders to kill one German, no word of complaint ever rose from the fighting troops. No attack however forlorn, however fatal, found them without ardour. No slaughter however desolating preventing them from returning to the charge. No physical conditions however severe deprived their commanders of their obedience and loyalty. Martyrs not less than soldiers, they fulfilled the high purpose of duty with which they were embued. The battlefields of the Somme were the graveyards of Kitchener's

434

Army. The flower of that generous manhood which quitted peaceful civilian life in every kind of workaday occupation, which came at the call of Britain, and as we may still hope, at the call of humanity, and came from the most remote parts of her Empire, was shorn away for ever in 1916. Unconquerable except by death, which they had conquered, they have set up a monument of native virtue which will command the wonder, the reverence and the gratitude of our island people as long as we endure as a nation among men.'[1]

And this is what he said of Neville Chamberlain:

'At the lychgate we may all pass our own conduct and our own judgments under a searching review. It is not given to human beings, happily for them, for otherwise life would be intolerable, to foresee or to predict to any large extent the unfolding course of events. In one phase men seem to have been right, in another they seem to have been wrong. Then again, a few years later, when the perspective of time has lengthened, all stands in a different setting. There is a new proportion. There is another scale of values. History with its flickering lamp stumbles along the trail of the past, trying to reconstruct its scenes, to revive its echoes, and kindle with pale gleams the passion of former days. What is the worth of all this? The only guide to a man is his conscience; the only shield to his memory is the rectitude and sincerity of his actions. It is very imprudent to walk through life without this shield, because we are so often mocked by the failure of our hopes and the upsetting of our calculations; but with this shield, however the fates may play, we march always in the ranks of honour.

'Whatever else history may or may not say about these terrible, tremendous years, we can be sure that Neville Chamberlain acted with perfect sincerity according to his lights and strove to the utmost of his capacity and authority, which were powerful, to save the world from the awful, devastating struggle in which we are now engaged. . . . Herr Hitler protests with frantic words and gestures that he has only desired peace. What do these ravings and outpourings count for before the silence of Neville Chamberlain's tomb? Long, hard, and hazardous years lie before us, but at least we enter upon them united and with clean hearts. . . .

'He was, like his father and his brother Austen before him, a famous Member of the House of Commons, and we here assembled this morning, members of all parties, without a single exception, feel that we do ourselves and our country honour in saluting the

[1] *The World Crisis*, 1916–18, Part 1, pp. 195–6.

memory of one whom Disraeli would have called "an English worthy."[1]

July 15, 1953

There is no noticeable change in the P.M.'s condition. Speaking with a kind of detachment he said:

'I don't think I shall ever get well, but I shall not make any decisions until September. Anthony will mew a good deal.'

He spoke rather irritably to the nurse, and then he added:

'As patients get better they get more ill-tempered. I must warn you of that.'

And he beamed at her. He was troubled often with fluids going down the wrong way. Turning to Clemmie after one of these bouts of coughing, he said:

'You see, dear, we have a turnstile in our throat, and it is so arranged that traffic is bound to go the right way, until things go wrong.'

He showed me a memorandum that he had written on helicopters. When they were 300 feet from the ground or less, if the engine cut out or the propeller came off there was a nasty crash. His memorandum contained suggestions to meet that contingency; the propeller was to be hollow, and in the hollow there was a parachute. He had sent his paper to the Prof. for his comments.

July 16, 1953

Decided to see the P.M. in the morning after breakfast, before he was tired. As I entered his bedroom he was speaking with vigour into the telephone.

'I have never allowed my private communications to the President to be submitted to anyone, in the war or since.'

He paused and listened.

'Oh, I have no objection to Lord Salisbury seeing my message. Yes, show it to him. Tell him I wish him to see it before it goes. Tell him I think he has done very well in the circumstances—no, in face of great difficulties, in face of Bidault and Dulles. Ike ought to know I do not agree—— Oh, I agree of course, but that I do not approve of what has been done about the Four Power Conference.'

He put down the telephone. The massage lady, whose ministrations had gone on intermittently throughout the conversation, now made a spirited effort to persuade him that as his left side was weak he must hold the walking-stick in his right hand. He insisted it must

[1] Mr. Churchill in the House of Commons, November 12, 1940.

be in his left and not his right hand. Christopher joined in and demonstrated the point by walking across the room.

'You see, you swing your arms.'

P.M. (*with a grin*): 'That is optional.' Then impatiently, and with an air of finality: 'I have thought it out.'

There was no more to be said. She was cowed into silence. He turned to me:

'I think I ought to have a new eye lotion. I am a great believer in change.'

Christopher followed me when I left the room.

'How do you think he is? He seems up and down. Yesterday Cox, you know, the fellow who advises about the garden, came to lunch. Winston was tired and uncommunicative. He had a fit of coughing when he was drinking his brandy. When he got his breath he said to Cox, "I am only concerned with changing the guard properly and with dignity. It must all go smoothly. Then I shall live here—I hope not for long." It was,' Christopher continued, 'very embarrassing in the presence of Cox, who had been told nothing. And then tomorrow morning he will be quite perky and absorbed in planning what he will do in the autumn.'

July 17, 1953

I found him struggling with *Wuthering Heights*. He said:

'I find it difficult to follow—rather confused. The narrator . . .'

He is better and has more grasp of things.

July 18, 1953

Found the P.M. in the blue drawing-room at Chartwell engrossed in *Wuthering Heights*. He looked up as if to say: I'm really very interested. Do you think you could find anything to do for a little? What he did say was:

'Charles would like some tea.'

And so I was parked out for a time with Clemmie and Duncan Sandys. When they had gone I went over to his corner, and with an effort he put down the book, holding out his wrist for me to count the pulse.

'I am dominated by this book; fascinated by its confusion. It is altogether exceptional. What is my pulse?'

Ike is in disgrace, and there was scorn in his voice when he said:

'Apparently Ike is like a king; he can't deal with detail. There was no nonsense of that sort about Franklin Roosevelt. Of course, Dulles is at the bottom of this.'

I was told that before I came the P.M. had been very belligerent, and that in disposing of Ike and others he showed something of his old fire.

July 19, 1953

A bad day. Apathetic. When I got to Chartwell about five o'clock Walter told me that he had just woken up.

P.M.: 'My legs feel tired, not refreshed as I had hoped. Is this a recession, Charles?'

His speech was very slurred; more than once I had to ask him to repeat what he had said. Annoyed with this, and determined to correct the slurring, he spat out 'lazy' with great emphasis.

'I could not at present conduct the affairs of the Government of the country. That is obvious. Yet the physical recovery is good.'

He threw his legs out of bed and walked to the bathroom to demonstrate how much better his walking was. In the bathroom a bar had been put by the side of the bath; grasping this, he stepped into the empty bath and then proceeded to lever himself down till he sat in triumph, with only his silk vest on his person: 'I couldn't have done that a week ago.'

'I have a horror of a day wasted, when there is nothing at all to show for it, when one has achieved nothing. Even to read a fine book, which one has not had time to read before, is something; or perhaps one does a little work on the book.

'Dulles lied when he said Ike did not want to do detail; when I saw him six months ago it was Ike himself who suggested a conference at Stockholm. Of course the Russians may refuse to attend a conference on these terms. They would like me to visit them, I think, to spite America—not that I would ever split from the Americans.'

Moran: 'Is Ike really fitted for his present job?'

P.M.: 'Well, in the war he had a very genuine gift for friendship and for keeping the peace. But I decided in the States six months ago that he was really a Brigadier.

'I had a nice letter from Augustus John. Yes, I like him; he used to lunch here and keep an eye on my painting.'

July 20, 1953

I was prepared to hear this morning that the P.M. had been in poor form when Rab came to dine with him last night. But nothing of the sort. According to the office he was in excellent spirits. Indeed, Rab said that he was astonished by the progress he had made in the course of a week. It became plain that Rab did not rule out a come-back. The P.M. beamed at me.

'They said I was very good with Rab.' His voice became stronger.

438

'I am again a forceful animal. I could kick people around this morning.'

He has got back his self-confidence. I asked him what attitude the Party would take in the House of Commons on the debate on foreign affairs.

'Oh,' the P.M. answered, 'they are going to stick by my statement of May 11.'

July 21, 1953

Winston may be confident, but he was all agog to hear about Rab's speech on foreign policy. 'You weren't in the House?' There was a note of reproach in his voice. He wanted to know what Rab had said of him and how he came out of it all. He rang his bell, and when Miss Gilliatt appeared he told her to telephone Christopher. When he could not be found, he demanded a word with Jock. But Jock was on his way home. So in the end the Chief Whip was called to the telephone. His verdict on Butler's speech was that it was rather tame.

'He doesn't seem to have brought it off,' the P.M. murmured.

I don't know why the P.M. is making all this fuss about Rab's speech. He does not usually bother his head about his colleagues' opinions. But now things are somehow different. What the Party is thinking has come to matter. At Margate they will decide his future. 'I must know where I stand,' he grumbled.

Miss Gilliatt came in with a letter from the President.

'A new letter? That is interesting.'

When he had read it he handed it to me:

'Dear Winston,
'Many thanks for your letter.
'In the first place let me say how greatly I rejoice at the report of a great improvement in your health. Your own country, and indeed the whole world, can hardly spare you even in semi-retirement, and I rejoice that you expect to emerge in full vigour in September.
'I have a feeling that it is dangerous to talk generalities to the Russians unless and until their proposals for Germany and Austria show that we can depend on them. I like to keep talks informal with those I can trust as friends. That was why I looked forward so much to Bermuda. But I do not like talking informally with those who only wish to entrap and embarrass us. I would prefer, at any rate in the first instance, to leave the initial approach to the Foreign Ministers on limited and specific lines. . . .'

439

There followed a paragraph to the effect that as President it was difficult to leave America.

'. . . I greatly look forward to your reappearance in September.

With warmest regards,

Ike.'

'A nice letter. He is very friendly. The Russians feel my illness is a put-up job. Christopher sat next to Malik[1] at a dinner. He said: "Mr. Churchill knew he would get a rebuff from the Americans, hence his illness." I think I must see Malik sometime. Ike takes a very cautious line about Russia.'

Sat next to Alex lunching at the House of Lords. He said to me in his confiding way:

'Now, Charles, you know Winston better than anyone. Can't you get him to retire?'

I suppose this is in the thoughts of many people.

July 22, 1953

Found the P.M. in poor form. Speech very slurred, and he is walking badly. Camrose, who had come down to see about Volume VI of the book, said to me:

'He will never go back to the House.'

Only once was there a glimpse of the Winston we have known. He began quoting poetry—Pope—and for a little time his manner became animated, his voice strong, his eye alert. Camrose was astonished at his memory. The P.M.'s thoughts went back to his nursery days: he was very happy with his old nurse, till he was sent to 'penal servitude.' That was his description of his life at his prep. school at Brighton, where he was from his eighth to eleventh year. He said that at the school there were volumes of *Punch*, and that he would pore over them and their story of what had happened in recent history. Then his thoughts came back with a jerk to the present. He could not get out of his head the opportunity that had been lost at Moscow. Dulles was 'clever enough to be stupid on a rather large scale.'

He sat brooding; at last he looked up.

'I made an exhibition of myself today. I get maudlin. It seems a feature of this blow. Why am I like this, Charles? I'll have to go. The trouble is, it is easy to go, but it's not so easy when you find them doing things you don't approve of.'

I said the general opinion seemed to be that Rab had not held the House in his speech on Foreign Affairs.

[1] Jacob Malik, Soviet Ambassador to the Court of St. James's, 1953–60.

'Ah,' he said, 'it's easy to hold out bright hopes as I did. It's more difficult to apologize to the House when they do not come to fulfilment. I've not enjoyed July. I've not had much fun. If the rest of my life is to be like this I hope some means may be found of accelerating——'

He stopped short, and abruptly took up a book and began to read.

July 23, 1953

This morning the P.M. handed me a typed message. I read:

'Monsieur Bidault told the Council of Ministers that the P.M. is suffering from complete paralysis, and that though he retains his intellectual lucidity, he is incapable of moving without assistance. Mr. Eden is cutting short his convalescence in order to fly home.'

Moran: 'Is that in the French Press?'

P.M.: 'Yes, and in all the bloody American papers.' (*Grinning*) 'They are issuing a correction.' (*Fiercely*) 'I don't care what they say. If a month from now I appear and can walk and talk all right, that will shut them up.'

He jumped out of bed and, walking across the room, climbed on to a chair and stood erect without holding on to anything.

'What do you think of that?' he asked defiantly.

Christopher came into the room.

Christopher: 'The Press—even the television people—are going to be at Downing Street in force tomorrow. Why not go direct to Chequers and cut out London?'

P.M. (*a little inconsequently*): 'But I want to sit again in my chair in the Cabinet Room.'

Christopher: 'You can do that on your return from Chequers in a fortnight's time.'

P.M.: 'Very well, we'll go direct if Charles can get Brain to come to Chequers.'

Christopher grinned with pleasure at his unexpected docility.

P.M.: 'I think, Charles, Salisbury was right to alter your bulletin. It was better to say I needed a month's rest than all that business about a disturbance of the cerebral circulation. I didn't like that.'

Moran: 'No, you preferred saying you had a stroke. Salisbury and Butler took a chance, and it came off. But doctors are not there to gamble. They issue bulletins to gain time.'

P.M.: 'I don't follow.'

Moran: 'When a man has a stroke, for two or three days you can't tell what is going to happen. He may go out.'

P.M.: 'What do you mean? Go out?'

Moran: 'Die, of course.'

P.M.: 'Oh, I see.'

Moran: 'If you had perished after we had said a rest was necessary the public might have thought you had got a pretty long rest. In fact, they would not have thought Salisbury's bulletin clever at all. The gamble came off—for the time. But we have not finished with explanations.'

I saw that he was not listening.

Chequers, July 24, 1953

The P.M. moved from Chartwell to Chequers today. He loves Chartwell, though there is nothing there except a rather ordinary house—and the Weald. But Clemmie insisted that the servants must have a rest, or they would leave. The country around Chequers looked enchanting in the evening light, and the long gallery brought back a lot of war memories.

When I went to his room to see if he was tired he began at once about the Russians. He said they had refused to work with us in Europe.

P.M.: 'The Americans were simple-minded to expect them to do anything else. They want the Kremlin to give up the part of Germany they themselves gave up to Stalin.'

Moran: 'What is the next step?'

P.M.: 'Perhaps I may take it if I can learn to walk properly. Would you come with me to Moscow? I knew you would, my dear Charles. We have travelled a good many miles together.'

I wonder where it will end. Sir Russell Brain, a careful, prudent physician, puts the P.M.'s chance of coming back alive from a trip to Moscow as low as fifty–fifty. Excitement might bring on another stroke, or at any rate leave him unable to play his part when he got there. But if he knew the odds I am sure he would take them.

P.M.: 'You look very solemn, Charles. What are your thoughts?'

Without waiting for an answer, he continued:

'My plan for dividing Germany horizontally and not vertically was the right one. Prussia would have been treated politely but severely; there would have been a gathering of states on Vienna—Bavaria and the rest.

'Rab had a bad headache during the Foreign Office debate, poor fellow, he seems to have had only an indifferent day. He made the mistake of telling the House that we had done well at Washington.[1] And now everyone can see we didn't. Lord Salisbury agrees with

---

[1] R. A. Butler had accompanied Eden to Washington for talks with the new Eisenhower Administration (March 4–7, 1953).

me. When dealing with powerful allies we have to take the best we can get, not what we want.'

Moran: 'How are you getting on with Trollope? You're reading *The Duke's Children?*'

P.M.: 'Oh, the Duke was a silly man. He objected to his daughter getting married to a perfectly respectable man. His only sin was that he was not a nobleman and had no money. So much in those days depended on whether a man had money.'

During dinner Clemmie told how at a luncheon given by the French Ambassador, she had sat next to Lord Halifax.

'Edward seemed to suggest that Winston was a handicap to the Conservative Party. At last I turned on him. "I don't know what you are getting at," I said rather hotly. "If the country had depended on you we might have lost the war." Edward was furious and demanded an apology.'

As she recalled the scene she laughed aloud.

'Later he talked to Winston, saying I ought to apologize. Winston replied he hoped I'd do nothing of the sort. You see, Charles, Edward Halifax has been spoilt. Baldwin was largely responsible.'

Winston went on to recall an incident in 1911 when he was at the Admiralty.

'A.J.B.[1] called on me. He leant against the mantelpiece' (the P.M. does not often notice that kind of thing) 'while I told him of some of my plans in the event of war, particularly of an expedition into the Baltic. I remember what he said. "Winston, I believe your hour has come." That was 1911,' the P.M. pondered, 'and it wasn't till 1940 that I had a chance.'

Chequers, July 25, 1953

The P.M. has come to no harm from the journey and is in good form. He has put on a special show for Sir Russell Brain.

'When I can walk without a limp, then we can let the movies do their worst.'

Brain thinks he may recover 90 per cent. physically. But he is less certain about his ability to concentrate. He doubts whether he will be alive in a year's time. Winston told Brain:

'I don't like concentrating, unless I'm excited or irritated.' Then with a gush of hope: 'I don't see why I shouldn't recover as I did at Monte Carlo. Do you see any reason, Charles?'

The P.M. kept his eye on Brain, who had not, of course, transmitted his forebodings, and, when he said nothing, began to question

---

[1] Arthur James Balfour, then leader of the Conservative opposition.

him closely about the prospects of becoming less tearful. Brain said cautiously that the tendency might get less.

'I was always a little blubbery, but now when I read anything, it moves me. I care so much about some things. I have decided to hold a Cabinet when I return to Chartwell in a fortnight's time. All the invalids would be present—Eden, Macmillan and myself.'

Moran: 'Why be in a hurry? I am against an early Cabinet. Someone will make a speech saying how glad they are to have you back, and you may break down.'

I fancy this went home and we may hear no more of this Cabinet.

P.M.: 'Anyway, October 10 is the annual Party meeting at Margate, and I must make a speech then or get out.' Pointing to his forehead: 'I feel there is a small bit of the brain which has been affected by this business and may, if I use it too much, crack. Of course I know it's pure imagination—not scientific medicine,' and he put his hand affectionately on my shoulder. 'Eden is coming on Monday. Perhaps it would be better, Charles, if I saw him alone. It is a delicate business. You might come in the late afternoon and stay to dinner. I don't think I shall commit myself when I see Anthony. I don't like being kicked out till I've had a shot at settling this Russian business.'

He leant towards me:

'You realize, Charles, I'm playing a big hand—the easement of the world, perhaps peace over the world—without of course giving up proper means of defence. If it came off, and there was disarmament,' he lisped in his excitement, 'production might be doubled and we might be able to give to the working man what he has never had—leisure. A four-day week, and then three days' fun. I had my teeth in it. I have become so valuable that they would allow me to do it in my own way. I must be right, of course—but I need not be busy—others would do the work.

'What is happening in Germany is very important. You've not seen it in the papers? It was in the *Telegraph*. The Germans are taking my line. They want a Locarno. America must be ready to attack Germany if she should attack Russia, while if Russia is the aggressor America would declare war on her.'

The thought of this better world, where the United Nations would at last keep the peace, left him in tears. He could not speak for some time. Then with an effort he took refuge in levity:

'I am trying, Charles, to cut down alcohol. I have knocked off brandy'—the coming sally made him smile—'and take cointreau instead. I disliked whisky at first. It was only when I was a subaltern in India, and there was a choice between drinking dirty water

444

and dirty water with some whisky in it, that I got to like it. I have always, since that time, made a point of keeping in practice.'

But since the stroke he has discovered that alcohol does him no good. It makes his speech more difficult to understand and fuddles what is left of his wits; and yet he does not attempt to control his thirst. 'Is alcohol a food?' he enquires inconsequently.

July 27, 1953

When I dined with the P.M. at Chequers he was full of vigour and talk. I found him in bed, though he was already late for dinner, absorbed in *Candide*, in an English translation. He looked up:

'This is an extraordinary book, Charles, have you read it? "The best of all possible worlds" philosophy is attacked with measureless satire. I'm excited about what will come next. Listen,' he said with a grin, turning to the famous passage on syphilis:

'The next day, as Candide was walking out, he met a beggar all covered with scabs, his eyes were sunk in his head, the end of his nose was eaten off, his mouth drawn on one side, his teeth as black as coal, snuffling and coughing, and every time he attempted to spit, out dropped a tooth.'

Walter came into the room.

'Dinner is ready, sir.'

He took no notice, but went on reading with gurgles in his throat as he savoured Pangloss's explanation to Candide how he had been reduced to this miserable condition.

' "Oh, Pangloss," cried Candide, "is not the devil the root of it?" "Not at all," replied the great man, "it was a thing unavoidable, a necessary ingredient in the best of worlds; for if Columbus had not, in an island of America, caught this disease which contaminates the source of generation, and frequently impedes propagation itself, and is evidently opposite to the great end of nature, we should have had neither chocolate nor cochineal." '

As he put down the book reluctantly he sighed:

'I'm burning to get on with it.'

'Have you never read it before?' I asked.

'No, my life has been too full of things to read much.'

While he was dressing I asked him which of the three Trollope books he liked best. He replied without hesitation, '*The Duke's Children*.'

'Why? Oh, because it is a good picture of an extraordinary world that has gone. The Duke is, of course, a poop; a Liberal he calls himself, yet he is so narrow-minded.'

445

The P.M. was in no hurry and gave me a chunk of the *Ingoldsby Legends* by 'a great rhymster.' After that he recited with gusto:

> *'Life is mostly froth and bubble,*
> *Two things stand like stone—*
> *Kindness in another's trouble,*
> *Courage in our own.*

'Yes. Adam Lindsay Gordon. Come, they will be waiting for us.'

After dinner, when we were alone, he went on talking for a long time.

'I had a greater opportunity before the blow than I ever had since I became a Member of the House of Commons—if only, Charles, I had the strength. I'm a sort of survival. Roosevelt and Stalin are both dead. I only am left. People say: "He means us well, all this is within his reach."'

'We have had a leisured class. It has vanished. Now we must think of the leisured masses. Why not? It isn't impossible. When there is no longer a risk of war a lot of money will be set free, it will be available to provide leisure for the people.'

It was the old hankering for a romantic role. War had been his hobby. Nothing had been to him so consistently stimulating. But that was gone and done with. And now, with his life running out, it was in his mind to end as a maker of peace among men; in this, his final role, he would appear before the world as, perhaps, the only hope of breaking the cold war.

And this was not just a dramatic curtain to his long life with all its vicissitudes. His generous heart seems, as the days pass, to be flushed with kindly thoughts about all mankind, even about the Germans. He has always admired them, they are a great people. He admired their Army, and would have liked, he once said, to go to Germany to appeal to young Germans to wipe out the disgrace of Hitler and of the cruel murder of the Jews. There is so much to do and time is getting short.

'Before I lead the British people into another and more bloody war, I want to satisfy my conscience and my honour that the Russians are not just play-acting. I believe they do mean something. I believe there has been a change of heart. I have talked with two Popes. What do you think we talked about? Bolshevism!'

I asked him why Roosevelt had been so friendly to Stalin. But he did not answer my question. It is not easy to draw him out. He thought that the hydrogen bomb accounted for a certain arrogance in the Americans. He did not want them to be arrogant.

July 28, 1953

Dined at Arlington House with Max and Brendan. It became obvious that this was planned to pump me; they wanted to find out what I really thought about Winston and what advice I shall give him about his future. Max as a preliminary tried to fill me up with champagne. I asked him point blank how he saw Winston's future.

'Oh, he ought to retire,' he said without any hesitation. 'Attlee will attack him presently; they will say it is a government of invalids, and there will be trouble too in his own party.'

Besides, Max thinks he will break down in the House if he comes back. I let Max do the talking.

I asked the P.M. whether he had discussed with Anthony what was going to happen in October about the succession. Was Anthony in a patient frame of mind?

'Oh, he didn't mention it,' the P.M. answered, 'and I didn't expect he would.'

July 30, 1953

David Maxwell-Fyfe[1] and his wife were at Chequers when I lunched there. David has won the solid goodwill—perhaps I might say the affection—of the House of Commons, by his simple, straightforward honesty and his kindly nature. They have learnt that when he does a job it is done once and for all. But these are not the particular qualities that make a man congenial to Winston. Today David sat next to the P.M., almost in silence, unless Winston spoke to him.

The P.M. seems to have more energy. Miss Gilliatt says he is clamouring for work. That, of course, is an exaggeration, but it does mean that he is willing to look at some papers which the private office has collected. He himself is sure that he is gaining ground, though he made this cryptic remark:

'I have a feeling I am only half in the world. It is a curious feeling. Adlai Stevenson[2] lunched here yesterday. I like him.'

At times he wonders whether Ike's election was a good thing for us—or for the world. Perhaps, after all, we should have been better off with Stevenson and the Democrats.

---

[1] Home Secretary and Minister for Welsh Affairs, later Lord Kilmuir.

[2] Democratic candidate in the American Presidential election in 1952. Defeated by General Eisenhower.

August 5, 1953

I found the P.M. closeted with Moir, his solicitor, when I arrived at Chequers for luncheon. He told me later that he had learnt from Winston that Randolph was to be his biographer. But the P.M. had other things on his mind this morning. We had hardly taken our seats at luncheon when he turned to us (Lennox-Boyd[1] and Leathers were the other guests) and asked if we had read the article in *The Times* on Beria's fall. Leathers thought it sounded well informed.

'Who wrote it?' the P.M. asked.

'Isaac Deutscher.'

He had not heard of him.

'If it is true, I do not want to make Malenkov's acquaintance. It would serve no purpose. In this man there can be no strength and no sense of decency as we understand it.'

To the P.M. this event seemed to blast all his hopes, his castle in the air came clattering down. He had decided that Malenkov was a good man—after all, there must be decent Russians—and now, apart from any question of decency, what was left of his plan? If it was possible to overthrow Beria so easily, what guarantee is there that Malenkov cannot be displaced with just as little effort? What was the good of meeting him if, the day after, he, too, might be swept away?

One thing Winston thought could be salvaged from the wreck.

'If our conciliatory attitude does no good abroad it may help at home.'

He meant that it had convinced the public that his Government was resolved to end the cold war if it was given half a chance. In their mind he had become associated with a determined effort to ease world tension and to avoid at all costs a third world war. The thought of Malenkov came back. What had become now of his plan for meeting the Russians in Moscow? It seemed as if the last excuse for hanging on had been snatched from him.

I went with him to his room. He sat heavily on the bed:

'I did want to last until next year. The party meeting is on October 10; Anthony may not be fit by then. He looked very frail when he was here; and I thought he seemed subdued. It would not be fair to Anthony to let Rab take it. Of course, everything depends on whether I can face October 10. I could not walk up the floor of the House of Commons at present. You must help me, Charles.'

Leathers brought me back to London, talking about himself all the time. In his conversation he cuts a bold figure. He had said to

[1] Minister of Transport and Civil Aviation; later Lord Boyd of Merton.

Winston, 'I cannot accept this, or do that.' In fact, he is quite meek and does what Winston tells him.

August 8, 1953

Lunched at Chequers. Rab Butler and Salisbury there. Butler, like an Asquith, is rather too impatient with pedestrian folk. He has more staying power than Anthony, but at present he lacks what people call the 'common touch.' They complain, too, that he will back a horse both ways. He seems none the worse for the grind while the P.M. and Anthony were away ill. He does not get worked up like Anthony. Of course, he is aware of the danger of racing the engine, but he says he has 'a normal family life and does not feel the strain.' After we rose from the table the P.M. stumped on to the lawn.

Butler (*turning to the P.M.*): 'Have you read what Somerset Maugham says about Burke? Burke uses short sentences, so unlike you. I suppose you were influenced by Macaulay.'

P.M.: 'Yes, Macaulay was a great influence in my young days; and Gibbon.'

The P.M. began to recite the opening lines of the fourteenth chapter of the *Decline and Fall*.

P.M.: 'I have been reading Forester's book about 1814. He has the art of narrative; it is only the harmonious arrangement of facts.'

Something was coming. His grin broadened.

'I made an attack once in the House on Arthur Balfour. I made a tremendous onslaught on him.' Here he declaimed, with great vigour in his voice, the climax of his attack, culminating in the accusation, which the P.M. hissed out, 'You hold this House in contempt.' 'A.J.B., speaking very quietly, "No, I have no contempt for the House, only for some of its members." ' Winston chortled at Balfour's hit. 'I have in my life concentrated more on self-expression than on self-denial.'

He likes this aphorism and often repeats it in conversation.

Butler: 'Alex[1] has been very helpful in the reduction of expenditure on the Armed Forces.'

P.M.: 'There will be trouble if the Air Force is weakened.'

Butler: 'It's the Navy that will be cut.'

P.M.: 'If I had been returned in 1945 I would have introduced a constituent assembly for India. Of course, they might have got rid of us anyway, but I'd have liked to try.'

He told how some Indians had been treated with contempt.

'If we had made friends with them and taken them into our lives

[1] Earl Alexander of Tunis, now Minister of Defence.

instead of restricting our intercourse to the political field, things might have been very different.'

August 9, 1953

The nurse telephoned this morning that yesterday, when Sir Winston was playing croquet, he hit the ball hard, and then, hurrying after it, became very short of breath—he was cyanosed, she added. But Jock said he was in fine form at night, hilarious in fact, and kept them up until one o'clock.

August 12, 1953

Arranged with Russell Brain to see the P.M. at No. 10, on his way from Chequers to Chartwell. Winston took us to the Cabinet Room. Smiling, he said:

'Pray take your seats at the Cabinet table.' He went on: 'I am not the man I was, but I have made a great improvement. I can tie my bow now. I couldn't do that a short time ago. And I can feel now if the razor has done its job. Before I couldn't feel the stubble. I am less emotional. Of course at times I still blubber. For instance, when I was told the Germans like me—after all I have done to them. But you would like to examine me. Come to my room.'

Winston lay flat on his bed in nothing but his vest.

'Would you like to take my pulse, Charles?' and he held out his arm.

Russell sat contemplating the P.M. for what seemed a long time. I became a little uncomfortable.

'I'm getting cold,' grumbled the P.M.

When Brain had finished his examination, and pulled up his chair, the P.M. said:

'You haven't tried if I can feel a pinprick.'

Whereupon Russell meekly got up and resumed his examination.

'Well,' said the P.M., looking at Brain, 'what is the position? What do you think? Have I made progress?'

'Yes,' Brain answered dryly.

'But surely, Sir Russell, you do agree I am better?'

This time Brain got as far as admitting 'considerable progress.'

'You really feel I am getting on?'

'Oh, yes, Prime Minister. I am very pleased.'

Brain is not good at patter. He did not seem to discern that the P.M. was seeking reassurance.

P.M.: 'When Walter goes out of the room I want to say something to you. The Queen has asked Clemmie and me to the St. Leger on

450

the 12th of September. And then to go on to Balmoral. I'd like to go. Oh, I've accepted. Of course, if anything happened and I am worse, I can get out of it.'

Brain rose and took his leave. When he had gone the P.M. turned to me.

'Sir Russell isn't keeping anything back? I want to know everything. He is at the head of your profession? He doesn't seem to get much fun out of life.'

I was afraid that the P.M. might underrate Brain. It is easy to do that. He has a first-rate intelligence, but it is hidden behind a rather ordinary exterior. And Winston only glances at the shop-window, he doesn't bother to go behind the counter. So far Brain has failed to impress the P.M., just as Wavell failed, and probably for the same reason. When I was searching for this, George Meredith's cautionary words came into my head:

'It is a terrific decree in life that they must act who would prevail.'

As we drove away, Brain said:

'Probably in a month's time he will be as well as he ever will be. I doubt whether he will be able to re-enter public life. If the Prime Minister goes to the Party meeting on October the 10th he might become emotional, or he might get very tired and walk away from the platform very badly, or he might even forget what he meant to say.'

Brain told me that Horace Evans had tackled him about the Prime Minister. Evans had said that his patient, Anthony Eden, complained that he did not know where he was: at first the Prime Minister had written to Mr. Eden as if everything was at an end and that he would have to take over; and now he is behaving as if nothing had happened.

August 16, 1953

When I asked the P.M. this morning how he had been since he left Chequers he replied:

'I was very depressed last night. I would have liked to see you. I nearly asked you to come over. I get anxious about myself, though,' he hastened to add, 'I don't mind what happens to me. I was conscious of my heart. How? Oh, just like it feels when you are troubled with wind. Then Oliver Lyttelton came to dinner and he cheered me up—he's an agreeable personality. I was depressed, not only about myself, but about the terrible state of the world. That hydrogen bomb can destroy two million people. It is so awful that I have a feeling it will not happen.'

Winston seems to have put the mishap to Beria out of his mind.

'I am thinking of going over to see Eisenhower. When? Oh, about September 20th. I don't mind if anything does happen to me. I should stay at the Embassy for three days. I have a lot of things I want to say to that man. I can do something with the Russians which no one else can do. That is the only reason why I am clinging to office. But I have no mental zeal. I don't want to do things. I used to wake in the morning wanting to do a lot of things. Perhaps I need a tonic. I can correct proofs, of course; that is no effort.'

He picked up a galley proof from the bed that he had been reading when I came in.

'Read that. We made an arrangement with Stalin in the war about spheres of influence, expressed in percentages. Rumania, Bulgaria, Greece and so on. Here they are in print. Read the last paragraph. It seems rather cynical, I said to Stalin, to barter away the lives of millions of people in this fashion. Perhaps we ought to burn this paper. "Oh, no," said Stalin, "you keep it." We did that, Charles, on the spot in a few minutes. You see, the people at the top can do these things, which others can't do.[1]

'The eye man—what's his name?—yes, King, of course, said to me yesterday, "You are much rested since I last saw you the day before your illness." That means something, Charles. He has been trained for years in the scrutiny of faces. Of course, I have not had a rest like this for a long time. I hope that Anthony and I will both be able to meet the Party Conference on October 10th. We would say, "We two invalids have come here to report to you." '

When I left him I heard that Clemmie wanted to see me.

'How is Winston?' she enquired, and did not wait to hear my answer. 'Of course, he has to make a very great decision in the next month—whether he goes on. He is talking now of going to America to see Ike. But Ike does not want to see him, he was delighted when Bermuda was scratched. If Winston was at his best, then he might be able to fix up something with the President in the course of the next two years, but as it is, Ike is waiting to see which way the cat

---

[1] At his meeting with Stalin in Moscow in October, 1944, the Prime Minister said to Stalin; 'Let us settle about our affairs in the Balkans . . . don't let us get at cross-purposes in small ways.' While his words were being translated the P.M. wrote out on a half sheet of paper the predominance of Russia and Britain in percentages.

Rumania	Greece	Bulgaria	Yugo-slavia and Hungary
Russia 90%	Great Britain 90%	Russia 75%	Russia 50%
Others 10%	Russia 10%	Others 25%	Others 50%

This Stalin blue-pencilled as a sign of agreement. *Triumph and Tragedy*, p. 198.

452

jumps, and whether Winston will retire. Moreover, Charles, Ike doesn't like his countrymen saying that the Prime Minister of Britain is making up the President's mind. I believe,' she continued, 'when the blow has fallen Winston will settle down to build a new life here at Chartwell.'

She keeps telling me this. She does not realize that he has no future—he must live for a little longer on his glorious past.

Chapter forty-one

Struggle for survival

August 17, 1953

I had arranged to take a small boy to the Test Match at the Oval, when I was summoned to Chartwell to see the P.M. He was apprehensive about stiffness in the back, which has been bothering him off and on for a fortnight. 'Could it,' he asked, 'develop into something which might prevent me appearing at Margate?' There are symptoms which are significant, throwing light on the course and nature of an illness, and others which are never explained, and in retrospect appear irrelevant. Such a distinction has no meaning for Winston. There is no sense, I tell him, in giving different-coloured medicines for symptoms until I know their cause. Yet he goes on demanding action. Anything that is done, however futile, brings him satisfaction. 'But surely you can do something,' he will say petulantly; and when I was driven to suggest that aspirin might relieve his 'stiffness,' if it were muscular, he said, 'I'd like that.' At once he became interested and asked how many tablets he must take and at what time.

When we had emerged from this rough and tumble he suddenly said:

'I am taking the Cabinet tomorrow.'

I said I was sorry he had made that decision. He ignored my remark. I want to gain time for him. His plan for meeting Malenkov has so far helped him to face the uncertainty of this wretched, drawn-out illness, but for the moment at any rate he has lost faith in his Moscow visit, and the real struggle for survival is only beginning. He sees clearly certain tests he must pass if he is to stay in public life.

'Have you read the *Daily Mirror*?' he asked, and rang for a secretary.

As it was handed to me, I read the big headlines on the front page: 'What is the truth about Churchill's illness?' The *New York Herald Tribune*, according to the *Mirror*, had stated that the P.M. had had a stroke in the last week in June, and that although he had made a near-miraculous recovery, those in the best position to judge did not believe he would ever again be able to assume active day-to-day leadership of his country.

'Is there any reason,' the *Mirror* went on, 'why the British people should not be told the facts about the health of their Prime Minister? Is there any reason why they should always be the last to learn what is going on in their own country? Must they always be driven to pick up their information at second hand from tittle-tattle abroad? The public is baffled and worried ... the nation is rightly concerned. The United Nations Assembly meets today to pave the way to a firm and lasting peace. It is for Britain to save the conference from futility and the United Nations from failure. She must speak with all the strength that comes from firm leadership. So long as the Prime Minister's physical fitness to lead the country is in doubt, she cannot do that. Let us know now whether Sir Winston Churchill is fit enough to lead us.'

'Five million people read that,' the P.M. said grimly. 'It's rubbish, of course, but it won't help at Margate.'

This snarling by the Press is something new. So far they have left him to fight it out alone.

'What are your plans for tomorrow?' I enquired.

'I'm having a luncheon party here for my book, and then I shall go up to London for the Cabinet at 5 p.m.'

I disliked the plan, and said so. The luncheon would be convivial and go on till three-thirty, then he would have an hour's drive, arriving at No. 10 tired, and below his best form.

August 18, 1953

The P.M. telephoned. Could I see him at No. 10 at one o'clock? That was how I learnt that he had cancelled the luncheon. I said I would rather see him after the Cabinet to see how he had weathered the discussion. But he persisted, because he wanted me to give him a sedative pill to give him sleep in the afternoon. He was very short tempered and on edge, shouting at a porter when the lift was not ready; and when we got to the bedroom he complained irritably:

'I was very well this morning. Now my head is fuddled. The noise of the car and the traffic and reading the papers on my way here tired me. I am going to have my luncheon in bed while Norman

455

Brook tells me about the agenda for the Cabinet. I must get some sleep this afternoon. What about a red?'

When I said it would only do harm by depressing the circulation, he appeared disappointed. I asked him how long the Cabinet would last. He replied:

'I shan't hurry them; it may take three hours.'

I called again at seven-forty. He was still in the Cabinet Room with a Minister, but the Cabinet itself had only lasted an hour and forty minutes. I waited for him in the bedroom. As he entered the room I knew things had gone well. He thanked me affectionately for coming.

'Well, how did it go?'

'Oh,' he answered cheerfully, 'they say I was better at the end than at the beginning. I had to settle two important things after the Cabinet, so that I was either explaining what I wanted or arguing for nearly three hours. It was very concentrated work, but I was able to dominate the Cabinet and settle things the way I wanted. I made my little jokes. Of course, one oughtn't to be nervous, but I was. I wondered how it would go. I thought about it a lot all day, whereas usually I never give it a thought till I go into the Cabinet Room. After all, it was my first Cabinet since it happened. It will be less of a strain next time.'

Norman Brook told me that he did not think any of the P.M.'s colleagues noticed anything different from an ordinary Cabinet.

'Winston let other people talk more than usual perhaps—he certainly talked less himself. No one noticed anything strange in his speech, and he walked to his seat much as he usually does.' Brook added: 'He has dipped his foot in water, and it wasn't cold; he wants to go on. This isn't the moment to make decisions about retiring.'

The P.M. had arranged to dine with Brendan at his house at eight-fifteen, but at that hour he had not got into his bath. On coming into his room he threw off his clothes, lay back on the bed and seemed disinclined to move.

'I am very tired, Charles; I don't want to do anything.'

As Brook put it, 'Tired but happy.'

Before midnight Brendan telephoned me. Winston had just left. Brendan wanted me to dine with him on Friday. He is against the P.M. going on and wants my views.

August 19, 1953

The P.M., the nurse reported, went to bed at eleven o'clock, but twitchings in both legs kept him awake until one o'clock. I found him suffering from reaction. He was not so well, he said.

456

'In what way?'

'Oh, I cannot concentrate, and I don't want to do any work; my head was muzzy this morning. I took 7 grains of aspirin. You know, Charles, it is much more effective than 5 grains. If a Cabinet can flatten me out like this, what will Margate do?'

When I had examined him I told him there was no real set-back; it was only reaction after the Cabinet, it would not happen at Margate. At once he became more cheerful and began to tell me about Persia. Mossadeq[1] had received a reverse and his Foreign Minister had been torn to bits by the mob.

P.M.: 'Gascoigne[2] came to see me this morning; he is just back from Moscow. He said that Beria's fall is a good thing. He and Malenkov were great friends, but Beria was thrown to the wolves without a moment's hesitation. They are like wild beasts. There has been no change of heart in Russia, but she wants peace.'

The P.M. showed me half a dozen numbers of a monthly magazine called *History Today*.

'Brendan tells me they sell thirty thousand copies every month. He is behind it. It is written by young historians for serious people. This is the more serious side of the nation. I find all this very encouraging. It would appear that not everyone in England reads the *Daily Mirror*. These young historians will be very useful to me. Before the war I wrote *A History of the English-speaking Peoples*, in four volumes—a million words. I will get them to check its accuracy.' He smiled. 'I've been living on the *Second World War*. Now I shall live on this history. I shall lay an egg a year—a volume every twelve months should not mean much work. I am reading another of Trollope. I find him very readable.'

Clemmie gave me tea and some advice about Winston. She said he was not so well—he was very white.

'What do you really think of him, Charles? You know about the St. Leger and Balmoral? I told him I thought he was crazy to try to do all these things.'

August 21, 1953

The P.M. in poor spirits.

He grumbled: 'I've done nothing today, yet I feel tired. Why should I be like this, Charles?'

[1] Dr. Mohammed Mossadeq, Prime Minister of Persia, was arrested on August 19, 1953, following a three-day struggle for power by the Army, whose right-wing leaders had gained influence with the Shah. Mossadeq was accused of collusion with the Communists and the U.S.S.R.

[2] Sir Alvary Gascoigne, British Ambassador in Moscow, 1951-3.

457

I suggested he was paying for Tuesday's Cabinet. He neither agreed nor disagreed.

'I've no zeal, no zest.' He smiled. 'I could never say my sibilants like ordinary people. I can only say zest by giving an expiratory snort. I can't make sibilants by putting my tongue against my teeth. . . . I am only thinking whether I can do anything to help; not what will be the effect on me—that doesn't matter. . . . My stiffness is less troublesome.'

Moran: 'I'm not worried about that.'

P.M.: 'What are you worried about?'

This question was accompanied by a searching look; he was interested in my answer.

Moran: 'Fatigue—that is our enemy.'

P.M.: 'I think I could make a speech now.'

Moran: 'I'm sure you could. What I'm not sure about is whether you would be up to a difficult job next day if you had to face something of the kind.'

P.M.: 'I had some twitching of one leg last night for a short time.'

Moran: 'Before Tuesday you'd no twitching for a fortnight. This is all part of Tuesday's bill. Now you've done it once I don't think the next Cabinet will take so much out of you.'

P.M.: 'Painting takes a lot out of me. I can't face it. Of course, what it takes is quite different from anything I have been doing. I think things in Persia are a little better.' (*Grinning*) 'Mossadeq's troubled, as I am, with being too emotional.'

Then the smile faded and he said very gravely:

'People think they can settle these obstinate world issues at one stroke. You can't do that. No one can do it. The essence of my policy is to get agreement about bits of a problem—to gain three or four years' easement.'

I asked him whether he intended to go to America to see Ike in September. He thought for a moment.

'I think I'd rather go and see the Russians. The country will be very disappointed if I give up trying to get the Russians in a friendly mood.'

Alan Hodge, a young historian, had lunched with him. Together they had looked through some of his first volume on *A History of the English-speaking Peoples*. He sighed.

'I wish I could write as I did ten years ago. Though they say the sixth volume of my book, which I call *Triumph and Tragedy*, is the best of the lot—more meat in it. Of course, the Americans will like it, because there is a lot about them. They are sometimes too confident. I have to tell them that.'

458

He took up some photographs taken yesterday for *Life* and handed them to me.

'Could you tell from them,' he asked, 'what had happened?'

August 24, 1953

I have noticed that the P.M. has become very short of breath on any exertion since his stroke two months ago, and though this is plainly due to degenerative changes in the muscle of his heart, associated with old age, I thought he ought to see Parkinson.[1] I went with him today. When Winston had gone into another room to dress, Parkinson said he was shocked by the way he had aged since he saw him four years ago; he felt quite sure he could never again act as Prime Minister. Mindful of 'Honest John's' uncompromising way with patients, I asked him not to be too gloomy. At that moment the P.M. came back into the room dressed. Parkinson told him his heart was years younger than his age, and more in that key, until the P.M. must have wondered why I had taken him to a heart specialist.

The P.M. turned to me: 'Well, Charles, we need not bother about my pump any more.'

Addressing Parkinson, he said: 'I have at the back of my mind whether or not I shall be able to take the Party meeting on October 10th. Everything depends on whether I can appear in public. I think I can, but I shall make no decision till the end of September. I shall carry on for a little,' he went on, as if his doubts had been dispelled by Parkinson's verdict. 'I'm only thinking of my work, my duty. I have nothing to gain from hanging on. I don't mind dying in harness—but I don't think I shall. I believe I shall have some warning.' Then he said: 'Well, Sir John, what can you do for me?'

August 25, 1953

Russell Brain was hardly more cheerful today than Parkinson had been. He doubts whether the P.M. will ever be able to make speeches in public or to answer questions in the House of Commons.

'Even if I am wrong and he resumes his duties in the House, I believe that in a few weeks the effort would be too much. His walking, which is still unsteady, might get worse, and he might be so fatigued that he could no longer carry on. In any case, probably a month from now his gait will be much the same, at any rate when he is tired.'

I reminded Brain that the P.M. was rather a law to himself. The second day after the stroke he insisted on walking about, where

[1] Sir John Parkinson, Cardiologist to the London Hospital.

others at a like stage would be lying in bed; his will-power may well have called into play what he calls the back streets, and we doctors term the collateral circulation. Brain agreed this had no doubt helped him. He agreed, too, that if he retired now he would probably be dead within a year. Moreover, that year in retirement must be something of an anticlimax; he would no longer find his name in the papers; he would not be forgotten, but he would have little say in the control of events. On the other hand, if he decides that he can still do a useful job of work for the country it is for his doctors to help if they can, and certainly not to hinder.

Both Parkinson and Brain were so gloomy that I decided to ask Norman Brook how the P.M. had weathered his second Cabinet since the stroke. He is full of good sense, detached, and yet friendly to the P.M. The Cabinet, I was told, lasted two hours and forty minutes, and at the end the P.M. was quite fresh; indeed, he kept bringing up matters for discussion, when it was obvious that his colleagues wanted to get away—were, in fact, leaving one by one. He was animated, spry and had no difficulty apparently in concentrating as long as the discussion lasted. After the Cabinet the P.M. remained in close deliberation with Lord Swinton[1] and Rab until seven o'clock—the delicate task of reorganization of the Government engaged their attention.

'At seven o'clock,' Brook went on, 'I understand the P.M. went to his room and, calling for the proofs of *Triumph and Tragedy*, worked on them until dinner-time. Swinton and Rab dined with him and did not leave him until one o'clock. From three in the afternoon until one o'clock in the morning,' said Brook, summing up, 'the P.M. was in continuous debate on intricate matters of government.'

I told Brook I could add a postscript to his report. I found him at nine o'clock this morning, breakfasting, and right at the top of his form. He looked up brightly as I came into the room.

'I notice I am clear-headed in the mornings now—a great improvement. Even the irritation of my skin vanished when this other business came, as if the Deity felt I could not play with two toys at the same time. I feel 90 per cent.—at any rate 80 per cent.—of what I was.'

Of course, in measuring the strain a great deal depends on the attitude of his colleagues, particularly the senior members of his Cabinet. I asked Brook bluntly:

'Does the Cabinet want him to go on?'

Brook answered that it was difficult to answer my question.

[1] Secretary of State for Commonwealth Relations.

'Some of them are, of course, interested. But when his illness began I was surprised how upset certain members of the Cabinet were—I am thinking of some of his colleagues whom I did not expect to be so friendly—and when it looked as if he might not go on, they were quite nonplussed.'

When Brook had told me this I said to him:

'There are two courses open to the P.M. Which do you think is in his interest?'

Brook confessed he had changed his mind.

'I think now he ought to go on for a while; it would probably be best for the country. As for the P.M.'s personal happiness, I have no doubt about the choice. He talked to me one day before his illness, saying he could not bear to see things mishandled, and might feel angry and frustrated. Besides all this,' Brook ended, 'I am astonished at the speed of his recovery after what had happened. In some ways he seems better than before his stroke.'

Pitblado gave me his view. He was surprised by the P.M.'s grip of things.

'He showed no signs of flagging at one o'clock this morning—indeed, I made up my mind we were going to have a very late night working at papers. At present he seems in pretty good form.'

I talked to the P.M. for a little.

'If I resign,' he said, 'I shall probably go to Barbados for two or three months.'

I asked him about his immediate plans. He answered:

'I'll go to Chequers after luncheon and I shall stay there till September 8. But I have not decided whether to go abroad in September—if my painting at Chequers is a success I shall stay there.'

He had been annoyed with one of his junior ministers, who had broken off in the middle of an important conference to join his wife for a holiday abroad.

'He pleaded tonsillitis. Very well: illness is one thing, a holiday is another. I am told that all the preparations for the holiday were made before there was any talk of illness. And this man was unknown the other day—had never held office. It's bad. I'm seeing Lord Salisbury about it.'

Having delivered himself of these strictures, the P.M. said:

'I'm clever at pushing away things and yet keeping an eye'—his eyes dilated—'on what matters. The political situation is satisfactory. Labour is divided and uncertain of its theme. We are building three hundred thousand houses; but all the time old ones are falling into disrepair, while owners will do nothing as long as rent restriction is in force. It would be cowardly not to face this challenge.'

August 26, 1953

It is now my job to try to persuade the P.M. to be sensible about his health. I do not look forward to the task. He is a poor listener unless you agree with him, and I am conscious that the time is ill-chosen to preach care. For when I entered his room this morning he said that he felt as well as ever he did; as if nothing had happened; that the Cabinet had not tired him; that he had worked without a break for ten hours without ill effects.

'It's pretty good, Charles, I don't think things are too bad.'

He has felt since his stroke that his future depends on clearing a number of hurdles, which begin at Doncaster, where he will make his first appearance in public at the St. Leger. He is quite prepared to make elaborate preparations and to have rehearsals of each crucial test. But it is not really as simple as that. I have felt from the first that he would probably rise to a special occasion. What I doubted—what I still doubt—was whether the cumulative fatigue of his onerous duties would in the end bring about defeat. Until he gets this into his head we can hardly expect him to make a deliberate attempt to nurse his dwindling capital. It is, moreover, a task foreign to his nature, for he has always been profligate of his resources.

'You are firing on four cylinders instead of six,' I began.

'Only four?' he asked in some consternation.

I explained that it was a figure of speech; there was no precision in the number.

'Suppose you have to make a journey to the North of Scotland. It isn't a question of whether you can get up the first steep hill on the road, though of course if you can't the whole journey collapses. The crux is, can you finish the journey? In other words, I can see you taking Cabinets as well as ever you did, and making speeches as effective as any in the past. But if you do this, say, on a Monday, will you be able, on the Tuesday, to transact important business, or will you be too tired? That is our problem. There can be no certain answer, no definite yes or no. All we can do is to watch the result of a Cabinet, or of the journey to Balmoral, and try to appraise the fatigue so that we can form an opinion of what you can do. That is why seeing you yesterday at noon was little help to me; whereas if I had seen you after the Cabinet I might have learnt something.'

To my surprise, he showed no signs of impatience as I unfolded my theme. On the contrary, he listened attentively to what I said with-

462

out interrupting me once. So encouraged, I went on to point the moral.

'If you decide not to resign, then you will have to think out how to do your work as Prime Minister without squandering your strength. You will have to learn how to live within your income.'

'If I go on,' he put in, 'I must do the job properly.'

'Yes, but that does not mean that you can take up the reins just where they were taken out of your hands by your illness. If you attempt to conduct the affairs of the nation as you have done before this happened you will probably fail. You would soon find yourself so weary that you yourself would decide you could not carry on. We have taken a good many risks together. But now it's my job as your doctor to warn you bluntly that if you are not willing to think out a new way of being Prime Minister, then you would be wise to resign before October.'

'I've been troubled a good deal, my dear Charles, with this decision. I am not sure the effect of giving up everything all at once would be very good for me.'

Moran: 'I'm not sure either. I must stick to the doctor's part in this business, but I am not certain that some of those I hear giving you advice have thought things out. It is easy to say that you could build up a new life at Chartwell after you retire, writing another book and seeing people you like. But would it work out that way? You might be unhappy with the way in which the Government was conducting the affairs of the nation, feel frustrated and even be tempted to criticize old colleagues in the House. You might even become, a little prematurely, part of history, while still very much alive. This isn't my job, but I hope you will do nothing in a hurry.'

With that I left him before I strayed too far from my brief.

September 1, 1953

It was half-past seven in the evening when I arrived at Chequers and found him in bed correcting proofs.

'I was frightfully well this morning,' he began, 'quite like old times. Now I feel flat. I have had to make a lot of small corrections in the book. I had left out any mention of Bernie Baruch, and I had to correct this and then fit in what I had written to the text. And all the time the bloody telephone kept ringing and I had to break off to talk about the reshuffle I am making of the Government.'

I saw he wanted to finish what he was doing, and was about to leave him, when he said:

'Will you go and get ready for dinner and come back when you have changed?'

463

On my return he was still in bed. He seemed too tired to make the effort to get up, though dinner was waiting for him. When he did get out of bed his gait was very unsteady. I asked him at what hour he had gone to bed. He admitted he had talked with Harold Macmillan and Anthony till a quarter to two.

'It won't do,' I expostulated.

P.M.: 'Now, Charles, you must not fuss me.'

Moran: 'Well, if you want to be fit by the party meeting you are not going the right way about it. I don't think you have got hold of the way Brain and I are thinking, and (mindful of Clemmie's advice) I'll put it on paper.'

'Oh, don't do that,' he said peevishly. 'I know what's bad for me. I must get into bed by midnight.'

There was no one at dinner except Clemmie and a relative living at Brighton, who had been staying at Chequers for the past week. The P.M. slumped in his chair and made no effort to talk. From time to time he sighed heavily, yawning and opening his mouth very wide, when Clemmie would pick up a fork and tap his knuckles as a rebuke for his bad manners. He took this in good part, but when at last he said something it was about blackamoors and niggers, so that he fell into further disfavour with Clemmie. She rose, saying, 'We will get the cards ready; don't be too long.'

He brooded for a while over his brandy and then, pulling himself heavily out of his chair, shuffled into the drawing-room, where he stood gazing rather stupidly at the card table.

'I'm very tired,' he said, 'I think I will go to bed.'

And without waiting for Clemmie's comment he trudged off to the private office. When he had gone, Clemmie put down her cards, and looking up at me said:

'How do you think he is?'

'Well,' I replied, 'I'd be happier if he'd give up Doncaster.'

''Why don't you tell him so?' she retorted sharply. 'Winston,' she went on, 'played a little croquet this afternoon, he played quite well —he has a good eye—but I thought he looked used up after it.'

When the P.M. did not come back, I went after him and found him dictating to a secretary. I told him that he was overtired and ought to go to bed. In a few minutes he rose wearily, swayed as if he might fall and walked unsteadily to his room. There he plopped down on his bed and rang for Walter.

'I'm going to bed,' he grunted.

Walter took off his slippers, and when with an effort the P.M. had disengaged his arms from his boiler suit, Walter tugged at his trousers till the garment peeled off. When he had discarded all his clothes he lay on his back, naked and breathing heavily. Walter then handed him his eye drops. The P.M., holding the drop bottle above each eye in turn, performed a ritual he had carried out for fifty years. Then he called for his hair-brushes, and lifting his head a little from the pillow, he brushed his head as carefully as if he had hair; and when he had done, and all the rites were completed, Walter pulled the clothes over him as he settled low in the bed, mumbling words and grunting with contentment.

September 2, 1953

The P.M. is rested after nine hours' 'beautiful sleep,' but is a little subdued.

'I am sad,' he owned. 'The world is in a terrible state. Germany is rapidly regaining strength and will soon be reunited, while Russia and America and Britain outbid each other for her favour. Read that,' he said, handing me the *Daily Mirror*. 'No, not now, take it away when you go. The Americans are very angry with us. They have lost more than a hundred thousand men in Korea, and all they hear is the Socialists bleating about China.'[1]

The *Mirror* printed a number of extracts from the American Press, all about the increasing friction between Great Britain and the United States.

'There is no hope for civilization if we drift apart,' he said to himself.

Then he began questioning me about electricity. Was it nationalized?[2]

'I don't like this strike. It seems more like a conspiracy than a strike. It is surely a new technique. Certain key electricians are called out, while the rest go on working; they pay the wages of those on strike.'

He rang for a secretary.

'Is electricity nationalized?' he demanded.

Pitblado thought it was.

'Make certain,' he said impatiently. 'Find out the exact position.'

I asked him whether the strike would hold up everything.

'Oh, no, it can't go on for long. It would cause too much annoyance and interference with people's lives. I mean to take a hand,' he said, setting his jaw. 'Walter Monckton has gone for a holiday.'

[1] Total number of U.S. troops in Korea 2,834,000.

Killed in action	27,704
Wounded	77,596
Deaths other than in action	9,429

[2] Electricity was nationalized April 1, 1948.

A wide grin told me that something was coming. 'He is worn out giving way. His deputy is coming down after luncheon. Walter told me he used to make sixty thousand pounds in a year till he came into the Government.'

'You get no peace,' I interposed.

'No, but I don't dislike it. I wouldn't do it if I did.' He corrected himself. 'I do it because I believe I can be useful.

'Do you know anything about dreams, Charles, and their meaning? I have curious, elaborate, complicated dreams. I wake, but when I go to sleep again they go on. They are too complicated to explain. Yes, they are enjoyable. Sometimes they are not at all involved. For instance, last night I dreamt of a large woman of the Eleanor Roosevelt type, and this woman was President of the United States. It was all extremely vivid, but I want to know what it means. Yes, tell me about them. I was too tired last night. It is all the detail that worries me. I can't deal with it as I did, but I am all right this morning.'

He got out of bed to demonstrate how well he could walk when he gave his mind to it; he had nothing on but a silk vest, so that, as I followed him along the passage and out into the great hall, I could see how much more steadily he walked now that he was rested.

'Pretty good, I call it. But why was I so unsteady last night? Can you explain that, Charles?'

'Probably a combination of fatigue and alcohol.'

I told him why alcohol affected his gait since his stroke. When he was tired it made his walk very unsteady. He did not think there was much in this—but perhaps my warning may bear fruit.

'Come and see how I get into my bath.'

It was waiting for him, filled almost to the brim. He stepped in, and grasping both sides of the bath, slowly sat down.

He sat back and in a few moments called, 'Walter, put in some more warm.' And then he found he could turn the tap with his foot—even with the left foot. He held a big sponge to his face while he held his head under water. All the time the water overflowed on to the floor with a slapping sound.

'Parkinson tells me that baths are bad for the circulation. What nonsense! Why, I've had two every day for fifty years. I really feel very well now.'

I asked him, when he felt like that, if he noticed any difference since the stroke. He hesitated, and then said:

'Yes, my memory is not so good. I sat between two people last night during dinner and I could not remember their names, though

466

I knew them quite well. I find it very embarrassing. I've just finished a minor reshuffle of the Government—quite important as far as it goes. The Overlords[1] are going. Leathers has wanted to resign for a long time. I only kept him by calling him a deserter. I hope there will be no leak. It is difficult to discuss it on the telephone with colleagues when they are all over the place, and keep it secret. But I like to carry them with me, and anyway it will all come out on Friday. You cannot imagine how complicated it all is—little details. Amory said he did not think he had done anything to deserve being made a Privy Councillor. I have told Anthony that he can be Foreign Minister again or lead the House; that I shall not decide anything about myself until I see how I get on, but that at present I feel able to carry on.'

He sent for a secretary.

'Has Mr. Eden had time to reply yet?' he asked.

Nothing had come from him up to date, was the answer. Mr. Eden has been too long in diplomacy to be precipitate in the expression of his feelings.

'Salter[2] will be here in a few minutes. I put him in to strengthen the economic side. I'm sure he has done his work well, but he isn't a House of Commons man. Now I've got to tell him that he will not be required after the reshuffle. I hope he'll soon join you in the other House. They are all very good about it,' he mused, '—not all. It appears that R—— goes about saying I am much slower since the stroke.' He smiled grimly. 'When you, Charles, and Dunhill persuaded me to have my operation in 1947 R—— said: "Perhaps the doctors will do what the 1922 Committee could not do—remove the Prime Minister." Yet I promoted him,' he reflected, 'in spite of what he said about me.

'And there is another uncertainty. On October 23 my book will appear. It will have a great effect on the Americans. They will learn what I tried to prevent and how far Truman is responsible; how far he botched things. Have you read my Iron Curtain telegram, Charles? It may be said that the British Prime Minister should not have said things offensive to the Russians, while he is trying to bring them into line with America. Of course, my decision at the end of September may settle this. If I go, I can say what I like, what I believe to be history. It is this uncertainty whether I

[1] Ministers appointed in 1951 to supervise groups of ministries, i.e.: Lord Woolton, Food and Agriculture; Lord Leathers, Fuel and Power; Lord Cherwell, Scientific Research and Atomic Energy.

[2] Minister of State for Economic Affairs, 1951–2; Minister of Materials, 1952–3.

go or stay which is trying, particularly when it is my own decision which will decide it.'

I wanted to make my attitude clear.

'I am not against you going on in certain circumstances, for a short time. But I am against a premature appearance in public. When you do appear, I want you to bring it off. I'm not happy about this Doncaster programme.'

He listened glumly, protesting that Doncaster would do him no harm; he would only have to walk four yards to the Royal Box; after that he would be sitting until they drove to the train.

'I have never been on a Royal train. The last time I travelled with the Sovereign was in 1915, when I went with the King to inspect a division that was going to the Dardanelles. I remember we had a very good dinner. I shall fly back from Balmoral. There's nothing in it. You need not worry.'

I said nothing and we sat in silence for a long time. Then he rang for Pitblado.

'Don't telephone Lascelles till I tell you,' he said. 'If the strike goes on, it might seem like levity to go to a race meeting. I may decide to fly direct to Balmoral.'

From Pitblado I learnt that Lascelles was only waiting for a word from the Prime Minister to send out the announcement. Winston was still undecided about Doncaster. As I was leaving he called me back.

'Have you written your name in the Visitors' Book? Do. I would like you to. I may never come back here.'

He mumbled something about: ' "Why am I loth to leave this earthly scene?"—yes, Burns.'

September 8, 1953

'I have taken a step forward, Charles. This morning's Cabinet was a considerable advance on the first two.'

That was how he greeted me when I called at No. 10 about three o'clock. 'Of course,' he went on, 'I am tired now.'

I warned him to be careful about alcohol when he went North. He smiled:

'I promise I'll be on my best behaviour. Come,' he said, 'and see the Chancellor.'

We found him waiting in the Cabinet Room. The P.M. addressed him cheerfully:

'I thought that I was all right this morning. Did you think so?'

468

Rab agreed in such a way that I felt the P.M. had really done the Cabinet well.

When I left them I had a few words with Pitblado. I asked him whether the P.M. had made a good impression on his week-end visitors. Pitblado pondered for a little.

'I think,' he said, 'Head and Macmillan left probably without making up their minds. The P.M. was older, but, on the other hand, I don't think they felt he must necessarily give up. Of course, the Chief Whip is different;[1] he sees so much of him.'

'Do his colleagues want him to carry on?' I asked.

Pitblado hesitated:

'I think Eden would be happy if he knew when the P.M. was going to retire, even if it was April. Something definite, that's what he wants. Rab is probably quite happy; he may be in a better position now than he would be if the P.M. resigned, and he has demonstrated that he is of Prime Ministerial timber.

'I have an idea, gathered from little things, that the P.M. is not certain himself what to do, but that his present intention is to carry on. Of course, this trip north may help; if anything goes wrong he may decide not to go on.

'As for his colleagues, they are bound to be influenced by what happens. If he can sail through the Party Meeting on October 10 and carry on in the House as before I don't think anyone will stir a finger. It is, after all,' Pitblado added, 'because he has so obviously been master of the House of Commons and has dealt so effectively with the Opposition since he became Prime Minister that the Party has been so docile.'

Is the P.M. really uncertain what to do? If Pitblado means that he is turning over in his mind yet once more whether he must go, no doubt he is right. But if he means that the P.M. is faltering in his resolve to stay on if he is physically able, then I am sure he is wrong.

There are times when I wonder if he is wrestling with still deeper uncertainties. For five years he has tried to justify to posterity in the six volumes of his book all that he did in the war. But have there been black hours when he has not been so sure? There was the sinking of the *Prince of Wales* and the *Repulse* and the lives of the English sailors lost in that unhappy affair. And there was—— But the mind of the man of action does not work like that. When he has taken a decision on which thousands of lives depend, he puts it away from him. How otherwise could he keep sane? He may do it crudely, so that it jars on our senses, like Stalin when he demanded:

[1] P. G. T. Buchan-Hepburn (1st Lord Hailes, 1957), Conservative Chief Whip, 1948–55.

'What is one generation?' Or he may do it by thinking at another level, like Winston when he said, 'It pays us in the air to exchange machine for machine with the Germans.' And yet, when all this is said, my doubts remain. Does the artist, for that is what Winston is, really escape so lightly?

September 11, 1953

The P.M. goes by train this afternoon to Doncaster for the St. Leger. This is his first public appearance since the stroke, and he is keyed up about it, though he may make a show of taking it in his stride. I found him in good form.

'I'll give you an exhibition,' he said cheerfully, as he threw off the bedclothes and swung his legs out of bed.

In his vest and reading jacket he proceeded to walk very carefully across the room, with a determined, concentrated expression on his face. In turning he swayed, and impatiently repeated the movement. When he reached the bed he stood on his right leg like a stork, and then on his left, when he was a little unsteady. Then he bent both knees, dropping down till he nearly sat on the floor.

'I'm pretty steady, don't you think, Charles? There is a longish walk at the station, but I think I can manage it.'

He got back into bed, and then he had another idea. Sitting on the edge of the bed and balancing his left foot above his bedroom slippers, embroidered with the letters WSC in red, he picked up a slipper between his big toe and the next.

'Not everyone could do that, even if they were all right,' he said with a touch of pride. 'Camrose came yesterday. He saw a great improvement. He particularly noticed that I was less emotional. Bill was afraid the enthusiasm of the Yorkshire crowd might move me, but'—rather scornfully—'that's not what makes me emotional. It's when I read about something—I am rescuing Joan of Arc or something of the kind. When I was looking at my *History of the English-speaking Peoples* yesterday I twice became lugubrious. Camrose went so far as to say that I'm quite all right again. He is sure no one would dream of turning me out if I wanted to go on. But I will on no account carry on if I cannot do my work properly.

'I've had some very vivid dreams, the detail is quite extraordinary. And it's all reasonable. I dreamed last night that we were on a train in Russia with all the Russian Bolsheviks, Molotov, Malenkov, Zhukov, Voroshilov; the relationship between us was so vivid and so correct. There was a counter-revolution. We had some special bombs, none of them larger than a matchbox, with a very local effect. With them we destroyed the Russians, all of them. There

470

was no one left. The counter-revolution was entirely successful. The dream went on for a long time. Can these dreams do any harm, Charles?

'They say we ought to have more young men in the House and in office. I answer: "Give me their names and I will at once see them personally." Of course, the truth is there isn't a large stock of the kind we want. Neville Duke[1] lunched with me yesterday. He is very able. I should be quite happy to have him in the Cabinet. But he might not be able to get a seat, and'—with a smirk—'he mightn't turn out to be a Conservative. I don't think we are doing too badly in the House. Of course,' he ruminated, 'there is the cost of living. I am going to have an enquiry into the amounts of the common foods that are consumed—and see how the figures compare with those of twelve years ago and six years ago. This ought to tell us something.

'I've finished the book and I've started another one which will give me occupation for another three or four years, if I live. The *History* will be a standby if I don't go on in politics.'

He was silent for a little. 'Anthony is getting better, Horace Evans reported to me. But he has to stick to a strict diet, and this prevents him putting on weight. He is still very thin.'

He rang for Walter.

'Bring me the new cigars—the Filipinos. They are very mild,' he explained, 'you hardly know you are smoking, which, of course, is the object of smoking.'

I asked him about his movements.

'In a few moments the income-tax man is coming to take away most of what I have. It is all very complicated; you have to go back before last April—and then the surtax is for another year. That hit some of the Labour people. They had to come down from £5,000 to £1,000, and then, out of their reduced incomes pay their out-of-date supertax.

'I come back on Tuesday—it only takes two and a quarter hours. Do you think you could see me between five and six o'clock? I would like that very much. Then on Wednesday there will be a Cabinet and de Valera[2] is lunching with me. I am glad it has been possible to arrange this. He is nearly blind, I am told. They'd give me a great reception if I went over to Dublin. On Thursday I go to Max for nine or ten days. Mary will come with me, but Christopher will have to come in another plane. Man and wife ought not to travel in the same plane when they have young children.'

[1] A fighter-pilot who destroyed 28 enemy aircraft in the Second World War.
[2] Eamon de Valera, head of Government of the Republic of Ireland.

September 15, 1953

'I have been worrying quite a lot about my problem—whether to give up my task. I have had a full mind. I don't want to. I'm quite clear about that. Why, in the morning I feel the same as I always did. In the last ten days I am more myself. I am better,' he went on with conviction.

'How do you know that?' I asked.

'I've got a different outlook on life now.'

I asked him what he meant. He held up his hand.

'Before, I did not coincide with myself: one hand didn't cover the other.'

Seeing I did not understand, he leant over the bed, and, taking a pencil, drew the outline of a man, very roughly, in red pencil. And then he drew another figure in blue.

'You see, Charles, one wasn't on the top of the other. My self-confidence has come back. I am more determined to go on.'

He got out of bed and walked across the room, a little unsteadily.

'You see, I am a little shaky, but I am tired now; I have done a very long day. I think in the north they felt that I was all right. I walked in the heather yesterday for three-quarters of a mile, and when I got out of the aircraft this afternoon I inspected the guard of honour and shook hands with everyone. You see I am not behaving like an invalid. I am doing everything I should normally do.

'Oh, no, I shan't overdo things in France. I shall not do anything there except my speech—thirty-five minutes perhaps. I feel now I could take on anyone who wanted to get me out. But I don't think they want me to go. I am really very popular. At Doncaster, when the Queen appeared in the box, I kept back, but when she came out and said to me, "They want you," I went into the box, and when I appeared I got as much cheering as she did.'

Winston talks like this to still the nagging fear that he is no longer fit to carry on.

'I went to church at Balmoral. It is forty-five years since I was there. Now there were long avenues of people, and they raised their hands, waving and cheering, which I was told had never happened before. I think I shall be all right on the 10th. I have important things to say that concern the country.'

'I'm not bothered about your speech to the Party meeting. That isn't the trouble.'

'What is the trouble?' he demanded abruptly.

'You were a rich man once, physically, but you've gone through a fortune.'

'How I appear in public,' the P.M. persisted, 'is what matters. I am improving. Don't you think so? And I shall have a good story to tell them. They talked of a million unemployed and there aren't any. They foretold strikes in every industry, and there is a small strike in only one. Of course there is the cost of living. I don't believe in percentages, in protein and that kind of rubbish. I believe in tons of food consumed. Three hundred thousand tons more meat are consumed than when Labour was in office. That is a solid fact. Two years ago there was a sense of crisis. People felt anything might happen. That's gone. Of course there's plenty of criticism, but it's well meaning. I don't think the Russians want trouble.'

When he made his quip that he went to Crathie church forty-five years ago I remembered that the morning papers had a photograph of the young Winston outside the same church just forty-five years ago. He was President of the Board of Trade then. What an innings he has had!

September 16, 1953

The P.M. leaves for Monte Carlo tomorrow. I found him rested after the long Cabinet yesterday.

'I was on top of the Cabinet business. We discussed the housing programme. It was clear we could not go into it all again in detail, and they took the course I advised, and were quite happy about it. Most of the time was taken over Egypt. I can follow an argument as well as ever, and I made them laugh a lot. Didn't they say anything about it in the private office, Charles? They must have heard it. When the challenge to my position is over I shall take things quietly,' he said reassuringly. 'I don't want to hand in. I am better and I shall go on. Not for long. Perhaps a year. I don't want to go to the country. It would be trading on my popularity. I have been working quite hard. No, I have done no reading. There has been no time. I have had to see a lot of people. I don't see many people as a rule—and those I see are usually the same people. I don't like seeing a lot of strangers. De Valera lunched here. A very agreeable occasion. I like the man. They talk of my taking a holiday in France. It is absurd. I don't take holidays,' he said scornfully, 'coconut shies and that sort of thing. I shall work all morning and paint all afternoon. I've finished my book.'

'The history?'

'Oh, I haven't to do much writing. The first volume is practically

473

done. All I have to do is to gather together a team of experts to correct it.'

When he had gone to his bath I sought out Christopher. He told me that the family felt that Winston ought to retire, but he had told them that it was selfish of them to want him to resign if he could help the country. Christopher questioned me about the P.M.'s future.

'I sit just behind him in the House of Commons, and I keep watching him, expecting that any moment I may have to carry him out. But I see quite clearly,' he continued, 'that he will do what he wants to do. You have more influence with him than anyone, but of course that's not very much.' And Christopher smiled on me benignly.

'You remember, Charles, when he was in bed, and it was uncertain whether he would come through, he used Anthony's illness as an excuse when he said he would have to carry on. I told you then, you remember, that if he hadn't this excuse he would find another. Well, now that Anthony's quite well enough to lead he just says: "I'm not going to retire. I shall carry on."

'The Queen told Miss Gilliatt that the improvement he had made since she last saw him was astonishing.'

Chapter forty-two

Ordeal of Margate

October 2, 1953

The P.M. returned from Monte Carlo yesterday, and I saw him this morning. Miss Gilliatt was not very cheerful about him. He had been in low spirits, and she thought his walking had not improved. Walter said that he had been very irritable. They spoke of him as abstracted and moody; he seemed to be brooding over Margate. Winston told me that he had done 4,000 words, enough for an hour's speech. I suggested that fifty minutes would do, and he did not demur. I gave him the political gossip. I do not think he took it in; his mind was on the Conference.

October 6, 1953

'I am more myself,' he said this morning. 'Do you know what is the best cure for me? Sleep. Soon, I hope, I shall have a long sleep. They have taken things lying down.'

'You mean Anthony and the Cabinet?'

'Yes. There is going to be a bloody row in Guiana.[1] You must give me something to take before my speech at Margate. Rab has an idea. He thinks I might sit on a very high stool while speaking.'

'Good God,' I ejaculated.

I discouraged him from experiments of that kind. The more everything is the same as usual the better.

'Well,' he said, 'I must try the speech out. If you could come on Thursday at three o'clock I would do everything just as it will happen on Saturday. I shall have a very light luncheon, perhaps

[1] British Guiana was given its Constitution along with adult suffrage in 1953. In April the left-wing Dr. Cheddi Jagan came to power after the elections. Fears that Communism would be allowed to spread caused the British Government to suspend the Constitution and reintroduce military government.

pâté and a dozen oysters. Then I would stand for forty minutes and say my piece and see what happens. I don't even know if I can stand that time. I haven't been on my feet for more than a few minutes on end since it happened.'

Then he gave me the peroration.

'It is a good ending, I think. Oh, yes, the speech is finished.'

For weeks now, whenever an idea came to him he would try it out on us. Yesterday when it was all in type he began to ask if they would notice anything wrong with his articulation.

'It's not at all noticeable, Charles? Of course, you must not judge me now when I am only half awake.'

He was silent for a time.

'I am going to practise my speech in front of a looking-glass, watching myself speak as I did in bygone days, long ago.'

He is resolved that nothing shall be left to chance. C. P. Wilson, his throat surgeon, will be at Margate in order to spray his throat before he speaks, while I hope to redeem my rather negative reputation as a vendor of nostrums by inventing a pill which he will take an hour before he rises to address the meeting.

When I left him I sought out Jock. I found him with Pitblado. I told them that I was sure he would bring off the speech.

'What worries me is what is going to happen then?'

'Yes,' said Jock. 'If it is a terrific success he will throw caution to the winds. "I haven't felt so well for years," he will say.'

October 9, 1953

I came back from Truro by the night train to see if the dress rehearsal had gone all right and if he was in good fettle for tomorrow. He told me all about it:

'I did everything precisely as it will be done tomorrow. The speech is now timed for two o'clock, so I had a dozen oysters, exactly two mouthfuls of steak and half a glass of champagne at noon. Then I took your pill at one o'clock. It was a great success. It cleared my head and gave me great confidence. Then promptly at two o'clock I got on my feet and went through my speech in thirty-six and a half minutes. I made no allowance for a pause. Clemmie sat behind me, so I had not the stimulus of an audience. But I know now that I can stand that time. I feel it is all right.'

I left him happy and confident, and returned to the West Country.

October 10, 1953

In the train returning from Bath I could not get Winston out of my head. I could not help fretting over him, though I knew there

476

was no sense in moping, because I could not change anything. But sometimes his terrific concentration on his immediate purpose frightens me. He is like a gambler who doubles, then trebles, his stake until all that he has depends on the turn of the dice. The P.M. has put his shirt on this speech.

'Never before,' he said as I left him, 'has so much depended on a single bloody speech. You think it will be all right, Charles?'

The Cabinet did not matter, he could deal with them. It was the Party that would decide. I tried to reassure him, but he persisted. If he could hold the meeting all would be well. If he failed in that, life for him was over.

This is something more than the old panic before an important speech. He has been living with this speech almost from the start of his illness. Only a week after his stroke—now nearly four months ago—even before the paralysis cleared up, when most people would be thinking nervously of their chance of coming through, he was turning over in his mind how he could get back to No. 10.

There were black moods, of course, especially at first, when the uncertainty preyed on his spirits. But not for a moment did he allow these moods to deflect his purpose. His mind was irrevocably set.

The bother is that Winston has made me as windy as himself about this infernal speech. I have myself spoken in that hall at Margate, and I can picture the sea of faces peering up at him. Will they notice anything different in him? Will they see that his mouth droops at the left side, that he does not swing his left arm, that his walk is unsteady when he's tired? Will they hear that his articulation is not so clear when he comes to the end of his speech?

The train was late, and it was after ten o'clock when I called at No. 10. I found the P.M. with Clemmie, Diana, Duncan Sandys and Jock Colville, listening on the wireless to the account of the day's events at Margate. A glance at the P.M.'s face told me that it had come off. Flushed, a little fuddled perhaps, he was ticking over happily. There was about him an air of complete relaxation, which one does not associate with him. He greeted me affectionately.

'The pill was marvellous,' he said, putting his hand on my arm. 'What was in it? Did you invent it? Now, Charles, I know you don't like medicines, but you see what good they can do. You must have given a lot of thought to this pill. I won't ask for it often, I promise. Perhaps once a month when I have a difficult speech in the House. Anyway, Charles, what harm would it do if I took it more often?'

When I did not answer, he went on:

'Of course if I had not tried the pill out on Thursday I should not have dared to take it, because I remember Edwin Montagu took a stimulant before a debate in the House and everything went wrong. But on Thursday it completely cleared away the muzzy feeling in my head. I felt just as I did before the stroke. It gave me great confidence at Margate. I knew I could get through without breaking down. I owe a great deal to you, my dear Charles.'

He turned to Clemmie.

'Who is that speaking?'

Duncan answered for her:

'John Strachey.[1] He is debating with Ted Leather about your speech.'

'Oh, switch it off.'

Clemmie took up the wireless and carried it under her arm into the next room. When they had gone, he said:

'Now I can sit back and get others to do the work. I shall ease off. I need only make occasional speeches. I shall not take part in the Guiana debate. I'll get Harold Macmillan to help Anthony. I may have to say something in the Suez debate, but I shall put Anthony in front. It's his business. If he likes this policy of scuttle in Egypt he must defend it.' The P.M. repeated: 'It's his affair.' He spoke with distaste.

Does Winston really mean to take things easily? He is always saying that you must attend the House of Commons regularly or you lose the atmosphere.

'I think it went very well,' he continued; 'they all said so. I have never, Charles, taken so much trouble over a speech before. I fussed over it all the time I was in France. I knew from the beginning this was the hurdle I had to surmount. It is an immense relief to have it behind me.'

A pile of Sunday papers lay in front of him.

'They are very good to me,' he murmured. 'Have you seen this in the *Sunday Pictorial*?'

'There appears,' I read, 'to be a slight twist on the right side of his face, which became more marked as his speech progressed.'

'It is not very noticeable, Charles?'

'If it were, they would have got it on the side affected,' I answered.

He picked up the *Observer* and gave me the *Sunday Times*. After a little he said:

'Shall we exchange?'

While he was absorbed in the *Sunday Times* I slipped out of the room. I wanted to find out from the office if they knew how the speech had gone down. The reports were reassuring. When his

[1] Secretary of State for War in Labour Government, 1950–1.

478

speech was at an end, the members of the conference gathered, I was told, in little groups in the passages and in the streets. There had been all kinds of rumours in the country. They wanted to know if they were true. Was it a fact that he had had a stroke? Was he finished? They went to Margate to settle finally whether he was fit to go on. Now they could see for themselves and hear for themselves. And there could be no doubt about the answer. 'He is not a bit changed, after all; he is still in good shape,' said one. 'I guess the Old Man will be with us next year,' said another.

What he said to them did not seem to matter. The points he made were familiar to me, he had tried them out on us more than once. But it seems that they were hardly mentioned in the talk outside the hall at Margate. And yet his central theme is surely a fitting curtain to the drama of his long life. For three score years he had been fascinated by war and all its ways; even in the last election his Party lost many votes because Labour had called him a war-monger. And now this astonishing man, who is about to enter his eightieth year, wants to be accepted over the world as the apostle of peace:

'If I stay on for the time being, bearing the burden at my age, it is not because of love of power or office. I have had an ample feast of both. If I stay it is because I have the feeling that I may, through things that have happened, have an influence on what I care about above all else—the building of a sure and lasting peace.'

He still has the power to express what everybody is thinking in words men remember:

'My prime thought is to simplify. The vast majority of all the peoples desire above all things to earn their daily bread in peace. The world needs a period of calm rather than vehement attempts to produce clear-cut solutions. . . . Five months ago, on May 11th, I made a speech in the House of Commons. I have not spoken since. This is the first time in my political life that I have been quiet for so long. I thought that friendly, informal, personal talks between the leading figures in the countries mainly involved might do good and could not easily do much harm.'

His plan is not dead. As Prime Minister he may still be of service to the Party as the embodiment of the common yearning for peace and for security. He will stay on 'for the time being.' It was noticed that he did not tell the conference how long that might be. But tonight, with the ordeal over and his mind at rest, he began to think aloud:

'I am interested in the scene, but I shall not make use of Margate to stay for long. Anthony has accepted the position, and there is no

479

fuss in the Cabinet. But I shall go some time next year, perhaps when the Queen returns.'[1]

Perhaps it will not be left to him to decide. What I fear is the burden of his long day. I believe that it is the House of Commons which will in the end get him down.

He had put away the papers and was, I think, going all over Margate once more, when Diana came into the room.

'Papa, you are coming over very clearly. Do come and listen.'

He pulled himself wearily out of his chair and shuffled towards the door. Clemmie beckoned me to sit beside her on the sofa.

'Who is that speaking now? Cannot I have it louder?'

Duncan explained:

'It is Ted Leather.'

'And who is that now? I cannot hear very well what he is saying.'

'That's you, papa, speaking,' Diana answered, smiling.

He leaned forward, cupping his ears.

'In the first two years of Tory Government the British nation has actually eaten four thousand tons more meat than it did in the last two years of Socialist administration.'

A broad grin greeted this.

'I ought to have said four hundred thousand. I got out of that by saying how lucky I was that I was not complicating it with percentages. Personally, I like short words and vulgar fractions.

'What's that about Germany?'

Duncan repeated the words:

'It is nearly four years ago since I said that Western Europe could never be defended against Soviet Russia without German military aid.'

'They didn't like that, but they took it,' Winston mused.

The applause went on for a long time. The way he speaks, his little tricks and mannerisms, bring back to them the war and all they owe to him. And, of course, Winston's personality dwarfs those around him. Eden and Butler fall into place and seem to grow visibly smaller when he is about.

Jock brought in a message:

'It's from the President. It came from the American Ambassador.'

The P.M. seemed to wake up as they switched off the wireless.

'Give it to me.'

Jock grinned at his impatience, adding:

'Ike doesn't know Foster Dulles's commitments, but he is sure he will be sympathetic when he gets your invitation.'

[1] The Queen was leaving on November 23 for her Commonwealth tour, lasting six months.

'We asked Dulles to come over to see Eden,' the P.M. explained. 'I have given up the idea of meeting Ike at the Azores.'

This was evidently news to Duncan.

'What about the Azores?' he asked.

'Oh,' said the P.M., 'I gave it up because it meant asking Ike a favour.'

'You're tired, dear,' Clemmie put in.

'I'm not in the least tired,' he protested vigorously, 'I don't feel like going to bed for a long time. I shouldn't sleep if I did.'

A small black kitten jumped on to his knee. It was found on the steps of No. 10 and had been taken in.

'It has brought me luck,' he said, stroking the purring cat.

He had assumed proprietorship.

'It shall be called Margate.'

Rufus, the P.M.'s poodle, had gone to bed in a sulk. The P.M. soon tired of the debate on the wireless. There was too much Strachey and Leather. Long before these inventions, he said, pushing the wireless away, the people received a broad and pretty accurate impression of what was happening, soon after it had happened. Richard III governed the country quite well, but the people had got it into their heads that he had murdered the two princes in the Tower, and so in the end he was killed at Bosworth. Winston talked for a time about Henry VIII and his wives. No one had minded them, because of the importance of an heir.

'I've sent Rab away for a week—he is very tired.' He said this as if he could not help being sorry for his Cabinet, who were always going away sick. It was time for bed.

Chapter forty-three

The P.M. relaxes

October 11, 1953

Called on the P.M. to see if he was the worse for wear. Found the black kitten licking itself on his bed. He was reading *The Dynasts*; as far as he had got he did not like it.

He hates the policy of 'scuttle' which the Foreign Office and Anthony have persuaded him to accept about the Suez Canal,[1] but tries to console himself with the fact that the eighty thousand troops can be used elsewhere, and that it will mean a substantial economy. The Foreign Office, he thinks, 'is an excellent institution for explaining us to other countries, but when its head is weak it seems to spend its time seeking agreements abroad at our expense.'

I asked the P.M. if he would have a more peaceful time with Margate behind him.

'Oh,' he answered, 'things sound less alarming around the Cabinet table than in the Press.'

Things were, indeed, very quiet. Eden, back at the Foreign Office, wasn't allowing much to go beyond him, and the P.M. is not accepting any engagements—he will not even go to Guildhall for the Queen Mother's Freedom.[2]

But it is only a lull. Jock says it is not true that they have taken things lying down. Anyway, it is not true of Eden. He is by nature not given to being disloyal. But his role as heir apparent is like that of the Prince of Wales in the last years of Queen Victoria's reign when she would not let him see official papers. I asked Jock what was likely to happen.

'Oh,' Jock answered, 'nothing much for six or eight weeks. Then

---

[1] The Anglo-Egyptian Agreement was eventually signed on July 27, 1954. All British troops were to be evacuated from the Canal Zone within twenty months.

[2] The Queen Mother received the Freedom of the City of London on October 28, 1953.

if the P.M. isn't in control of the House there would be murmuring, and the Chief Whip would have to tell him that the Party was not happy. At that point Anthony might force a show-down, or he might even resign—history might repeat itself,' Jock mused.

Anthony might strike. Somehow it is not a word we associate with Eden, but I am told that he is being pushed from behind. Presently the Party will take charge.

It appears that Rab Butler is sitting on the fence with one leg dangling on each side. He likes cricket similes. He is trying to keep a straight bat, he says. He is not trying to make runs.

'The Queen's going away from the country complicates things. The P.M. says that if he is going to retire he will do so soon, so as to give the new P.M. time to settle in before the Queen leaves the country. But he won't,' said Jock smiling.

October 20, 1953

If there is going to be a tussle with Anthony I must patch up the P.M. It is not going to be easy to put him on his feet. Yesterday he telephoned to me three times within an hour; the third time to ask if he could take a tablet of aspirin at dinner-time. He was 'so stupid.' I was in bed with a feverish cold, and he was plainly torn between the fear of picking up my cold and an urge to talk about his troubles. He said he had felt sickly all day, but when I asked him whether that was the whole trouble he admitted that it was not, that he would like to go into things with me. He does not usually say that sort of thing, and I was not very happy about him, particularly when he told me that the Cabinet would probably go on for four hours. So this morning I got a mask from Bell and Croyden, and muzzled in this fashion I called at No. 10.

Jock told me that he had been worried about him yesterday. He had been reading *The Dynasts* and kept getting fiction and reality mixed up. He was expecting Queen Charlotte to come in through the door.

'You know, Charles, I was like that,' Jock said, 'after the war when I got a kind of delayed shell-shock. The P.M. kept repeating himself. He talks about his hurdles. Margate was one, and his first appearance in the House of Commons this afternoon, to answer questions, is another. I felt he would do Margate all right, and I am sure he will get through this afternoon with credit.'

'But I am not too happy about him. He was not in very good form at the Cabinet.'

Jock thought for a moment.

'You know, he is always acting a part, but I am sure he was not acting last night after dinner when he suddenly said: "I think, Jock, we are near the end of the road." Before dinner he said that if he retired he would still have his seat below the gangway and his *History of the English-speaking Peoples* to keep him occupied. But I sometimes think,' Jock mused, 'it would be better for him to go out in harness.'

I found the P.M. reading *The Times*, while the black kitten, lying on its back, pawed the fluttering edges of the paper.

'I'm not frightened of the House of course, any more than a child is frightened of its nursery.'

October 21, 1953

As I entered No. 10 Pitblado was in the hall. He told me that he found the P.M. reading *The Dynasts* after breakfast; it would be about ten o'clock, he thought. That was quite new. He supposed it was a sign that the P.M. wasn't brimming over with energy. He had a long day before him, but it was no use trying to persuade him to give up the Trinity House[1] meeting when the Queen was going. Last night he came back from an Audience overflowing with her praises. Walter explained that the tailors were in his room preparing his uniform for the meeting.

If the P.M. was an ordinary mortal one would say that the game is up. But he will not admit that he was unduly tired on Monday, and now that they were over the P.M. said he hadn't been really worried about his first Questions in the House.

'You see, Charles, I have been so long at the game that it has become almost automatic. Besides, I am stronger. Why, I walked the whole length of the corridor to the Smoking Room and no one, I think, noticed anything.'

That is one of the difficulties in dealing with him, he won't put all his cards on the table for anyone. Perhaps he talks like this to comfort himself that he is still up to the job. To persuade others is, by comparison, a simple task.

There appears to be general agreement that the P.M. was quite himself in the way in which he handled Questions. Harvie Watt, who was his parliamentary secretary during the war, thought he had done it very well: 'much better than I expected'; while the lobby correspondent of the *Manchester Guardian*, whose sharp eyes do not miss much, was satisfied that Mr. Churchill had not suffered any change since he was last on view at Westminster. And when he announced that he had gone back on a firm pledge to the House of

---

[1] The general lighthouse and principal pilotage authority. Both the Sovereign and Churchill were Elder Brethren of Trinity House.

Commons—the pledge to restore the University seats—it seemed to be merely the recording of an act of statesmanship.

I asked him: 'Did it tire you jumping up and down for nearly a quarter of an hour answering supplementaries?'

'Oh, no, not at all; but it did make me rather short of breath.'

He picked up the *Guardian*, but when I rose to go he half put it down as he said:

'Thank you, Charles, I hope you got no harm yesterday coming out to see me. You hit the bull's eye with the pill.'

October 23, 1953

Clemmie telephoned that if my cold was really better she would like to talk to me about Winston. She had picked up influenza when she was staying with the Harveys in Paris and she was not right yet. Winston had been very glad to see her back, and then for two days he had sat at meals huddled up, without a word for anyone.

She hesitated. 'He promised me that he would retire when Anthony was fit to carry on, and now when Anthony is perfectly fit he just goes on as before. Monsieur Bidault will not come to London because he cannot get a word in edgeways. The Harveys told me that.'

A smile flickered over her tired features. She became grave again:

'You know, Christopher is very fond of Winston, and he has promised to tell me if his stock falls in the House of Commons. He has given me his word that I shall be told if they want to get rid of him. But the trouble is, Charles, that his stock has actually risen, until they say it has not been so high for a long time. Do you know what I mean by the 1922 Committee? They are very Right. Well, when they met to discuss Egypt the Chief Whip wanted Winston to open the discussion. But he refused. Anthony ought to open, Winston insisted. And then at the end he got up and gave them a tremendous wigging. They knew that he was not a Little Englander, but he told them bluntly we simply could not afford to stay in Egypt. He looked to them for support in a difficult situation, not for that kind of carping. They were tremendously impressed. The old lion could still issue from his den, and when he did his growl was as frightening as ever.'

She laughed at the thought.

'They cannot make it out at all, Charles. They have heard all kinds of rumours about a stroke and paralysis, and now he seems in better form than ever. They described how he strode up a long corridor in the House of Commons, swinging his arms as if he was twenty.'

Her pride in Winston struggled through the clouds of irritation.

'Of course he has worries. But what really upset Winston was that Walter has given a month's notice. He was very hurt about it. You see, Walter has been with him for four years, and we have been very kind to him. I am scouring London for someone to take his place. Valeting Winston is not very easy.'

And then she came to business.

'How is he really, Charles?'

I answered that I was not very happy about him.

'Then why do you not tell him so?' she rapped out sharply. 'Cannot you do something? You will wait until he gets another stroke.'

Her manner softened.

'It may not be a bad time to get him to retire. He won't let them push him out, but when all his colleagues are saying nice things about him he is much more likely to think it is time to go.' She smiled. 'Winston sent for Dr. Barnett and told him: "My wife wants me to resign, but I am not going to." Dr. Barnett thought perhaps the seed had been sown. You know, I don't want to hound him into resigning.'

October 27, 1953

When I called at No. 10 he had just finished breakfast and was reading a book. He put it down reluctantly. He had to master a difficult problem before the Cabinet met. Then perhaps two and a half hours with the Cabinet; then half a dozen questions in the House; then an audience with the Queen, and after that a deputation had come from Leeds to give him the Freedom of their City. It was going to be a long day. He gave a great yawn.

'I have been reading *Quentin Durward*. I like it very much, as much as *Ivanhoe*.'

Christopher came in.

'Have you read the paper on meat yet?'

The P.M. grunted that he was about to do so. Christopher joined me a few moments later in the secretaries' room. With his mixture of good humour and outspokenness he said:

'Considering how much a Prime Minister has to do, and how little Winston does, I think we are rather clever. I have been trying to get him to read this document on meat, but he keeps saying, "I must read another chapter" (of *Quentin Durward*). He is alert enough when he brings himself to do anything and he has been in a good mood, but, Charles, he has no zest for work. He does not want to be bothered with anything. I do not know where this will end. I cannot get him to read important papers.'

Moran: 'If you and Jock and Norman Brook agree at any time that he is doing himself no good in his job, then I will try to get him to retire.'

Christopher: 'That time has not come yet.'

Chapter forty-four

A new Winston sees visions

November 3, 1953

Called at No. 10 to find out if the P.M. was happy about the speech he is making today on the Address. He said there had been a dispute. Anthony did not want him to talk about a change of heart in Russia. He and the Foreign Office do not believe that there is any evidence that anything of the kind has happened there. The P.M. reached for the small sheets on which his speech was written out.

'This is what I was going to say.'

He read a page of his speech.

'I shall tone it down. I don't want any difference or any unpleasantness.' There was a smirk. 'The F.O. has a gift for saying that something is neither better nor worse. There is no evidence, they argue, that it is better; on the other hand, no one could say it was worse. I shall speak for fifty minutes. You will listen to me? I shall look up to the gallery.'

It was a placid Winston I left, sitting up in bed, turning over the sheets of his speech, loosely held together by a green thread. He was cheerful, and when he is in good heart before a speech I have few qualms. I met Miss Portal on my way down. She said that this is the first speech that Winston has made in the House of Commons since his stroke, but that it had taken much less out of him than the Margate address. He had taken trouble over it, of course, but he did not get worked up preparing it, and seemed happier about the way it would be received. Even Anthony's intervention was no more than a pin-prick. In the old days there would have been an explosion.

The fact is that he has greatly changed since his illness.

'Winston is positively good tempered these days,' Lord Woolton exclaimed.

488

Even his secretaries can relax, for when things go wrong they can tell him without a scene. 'He is not easily put out,' they say with an affectionate smile, as if it had always been so with him. Last week a Labour Member of the House of Commons came up to me: 'What have you done to Winston?' he asked. 'There is something serene about him.'

A discerning friend of Winston's answered for me: 'Of course he has mellowed. Thrust a man out of political life into the wilderness for eleven years and then let him be taken into men's hearts wherever they are free and what do you expect to happen? It is difficult to think ill of a world that is so friendly and so anxious to sing hosannas.' There is, of course, truth in this. Alexander Fleming had lived in obscurity and in some disfavour. His research into the acne bacillus and the Wasserman reaction had been generally discredited. He seemed to his profession to be disgruntled by criticism and by neglect; a sour, rather silent Scot. And then, on the verge of old age, he discovered penicillin. He, too, had found a place in the sun, so that it was no longer necessary to stake a claim aggressively. For he knew now that his name had a place in history. Fleming seemed to spend the rest of his days travelling over the world, making modest little speeches implying that there had been a great element of luck in his discovery. Famous universities were proud to give him an honorary degree, and everywhere he went he won men's hearts by his happy simplicity.

If, however, basking in the sun accounted for the change in Winston's attitude to life it should have taken place soon after the war, whereas his sweet temper now—those who only knew Winston in the war will scoff at the adjective—is in sharp contrast to the querulous mood that troubled Conservatives when Winston led the Opposition after the war. At that time he was always getting into a wrangle with Herbert Morrison, and seemed to make little effort to control his natural pugnacity.

When I speak of a change in Winston I am not thinking of his courage in adversity. This is, of course, first cousin to his pugnacity. And the essence of this change is that Winston has got on top of his pugnacity. For that matter he does not feel to be in adversity as he did in 1915 after the Dardanelles. Then he was full of despair; he had no future. Now there is purpose in his days, an object in life.

One day, it may have been late in August about two months after his stroke, Winston spoke of this. I said to him:

'You have been a good patient. I don't believe you felt like this in 1915 after the Dardanelles.'

'Good Lord, no,' he replied. 'I thought then that I was finished.

This is different. Get me through Margate and I will do the rest.'

I did not realize this difference at first. When he became paralysed I used to watch his helpless misery with a lump in my throat. This surely was the end of all things, and then as the days went by and he grew better it occurred to me that, apart from passing moods of dejection, he did not feel miserable at all. Perhaps no man who has set his heart on some end can be unhappy while the struggle lasts. Winston knew, of course, that life was uncertain, that at any moment he might get another stroke, but there was something to live for. To get back into Parliament, that was his aim. Even then he could think of nothing else. And, after all, he is so built that his joy in life has always come from grappling with someone, doing something, however painful the process.

Cynics in the House of Commons speak of a kind of calculated benevolence. They contend that there is nothing new in this, that since he became Prime Minister for the second time he has lost no opportunity of making his peace with his political opponents. He has discovered, they argue, that if he wants something done it is foolish to stir up faction by giving rein to his pugnacity.

And they are ready with chapter and verse. Tom O'Brien was a guest at Downing Street to meet Signor de Gasperi when the P.M. was stricken; another Labour colleague was a guest when Winston was host to M. Bidault. For that matter Winston asked me to see Arthur Deakin professionally because he was 'very important politically.' The P.M.'s policy of keeping on friendly terms with the Opposition was, in their lingo, given a shot in the arm when he set out to make friends with the Russians. He was resolved that he would not allow Party bickering to wreck his hopes of an understanding with Moscow.

The cynic finds truth too slippery to hold. For my part I am inclined to discount political motives. Even Max Beaverbrook, who in his earthy way is impatient of highfalutin motives, and draws upon his unusual knowledge of human frailty in order to account for men's actions, scoffs at all this talk of a calculated benevolence. For him there is nothing to explain. Winston, according to Max, had stolen the Socialists' clothes while they were bathing, and he so fancied himself in his borrowed finery that he had worn it ever since. Winston knows, of course, that it is not possible to ask for a coalition, but he likes to think of the House of Commons as a Council of State. He likes to speak for the whole House as he did in the war. Max harps on this, in his impish manner he pictures Winston discarding the laurel wreath of the great war leader for the cloth cap of Keir Hardie.

490

However, Max for all his astuteness is not the man to discriminate between a mere shift in Winston's political tactics and a change in his character, between what he does and what he is. Winston is, in a sense, a different being. And this change in the man himself is the direct outcome of his illness. During these interminable weeks I have been very close to him, and I am not sure that even now I have told everything. There comes a time in the lives of many men when, looking over their shoulders, they ask where they are going, and whether, after all, it is worth while.

Though Winston has been determined to get well, if it lay in his power, death must have seemed very near to him as he lay helplessly watching the creeping paralysis advancing over his body. What passed through his head I could only guess. He had always made light of religious things, but could a man of his cast of mind, in his eightieth year, with death round the corner, find peace of mind in pagan beliefs?

This came into my head one day when Winston said to me he did not feel so well. He wondered if his illness had taken a turn for the worse. He said he had made resolutions which he meant to keep if he came through. I waited, but he said nothing more. I asked him what he had in mind, but he seemed to be sorry that he had said as much, and setting his jaw abruptly, changed the subject.

At this point perhaps the reader will forgive me if I recount a personal experience. My father, then in his twenties, and a busy doctor in the West Riding of Yorkshire, was stricken by four attacks of rheumatic fever in quick succession, that left his heart crippled and compelled him to give up work. After eighteen months' rest, faced with the expense of educating his three children, the eldest of whom was only eight years of age, he bought a smaller practice and contrived somehow to do his work. As a child I was vaguely aware that something was wrong, and when I had said good night to him I used to linger on the stairs, listening, fearing that something was about to happen. Sometimes when we were playing with him he would stop to get his breath. Many years later, when I was a medical student reading for my Finals, my mother wrote anxiously that he had brought on heart-failure by bicycling up a steep hill in the Lake District against a strong wind. The doctors said that his heart did not respond to digitalis, that the dropsy was spreading and that he could not last long. She had a feeling that if he came to London something could be done. After the long and exhausting journey he became very breathless, and when I went for his medicine I found the bottle empty. I hurried to the chemist with the prescription. When he had taken a few doses out of the new bottle the dropsy began rapidly to disappear, and his breathing became easier. It transpired that he had been on an inert preparation of digitalis. When he was given the drug in an active form he seemed miraculously to recover. He lived to the age of eighty-one.

My father never spoke to me of his illness. He must have known that he had been very near to death, but what passed through his mind I never knew. It was noticed that something had happened which profoundly affected his whole nature. Did he, too, make vows in the intervals of fighting for his breath? Up to that time he had been a formidable personality, so that all who came near him were careful of their step. When things went wrong my father would hardly speak for perhaps two or even three days. I remember my mother telling me after one of these incidents that my father came of turbulent stock. After his illness, though he lived for a quarter of a century, there were no more moods; he became very gentle, very patient, a kindly old man greatly beloved by his neighbours. Before that time he never went to church or concerned himself with religious matters. But when he got about again, though he had great difficulty in kneeling, he never failed to say his prayers in the morning and in the evening. He was often in pain, but he did not whimper. This surely was no passing mood of repentance, but rather what the Methodists term a 'conversion,' which endured while life lasted. Perhaps if we could penetrate into the inner recesses of Winston's soul we might find that something of that kind had happened there after his stroke, some rearrangement of his thoughts about ultimate things.

House of Commons, November 3, 1953

In his speech in the House today we were listening to a man chastened, I had almost said cleansed, by a grim experience. What he had to say he resolved to put, as far as he was able, in the most persuasive way possible. He did not believe the nation was so divided as some people would like to make out. There were a great many things on which most people agreed. Fourteen million vote Tory, and about another fourteen million vote Socialist, and it was not really credible that one of these two masses of voters possessed all the virtues and all the wisdom, while the other lot were dupes and fools. It seemed to him nonsense to draw such sharp contrasts between them. It was difficult for specialists in faction to prevent members getting very friendly with each other. His course was clear:

'We have to help our respective parties, but we have also to make sure that we help our country and its people. There can be no doubt where our duty lies between these two.'

492

His party, it is true, was opposed to the nationalization of industry, but where they were preserving it, as in the coal mines, the railways, air traffic, gas and electricity, they were doing their utmost to make a success of it, even though (and here he beamed on the House) this might somewhat mar the symmetry of party recrimination. When he came to speak of the highly controversial subject of the repair of houses and their rents the Opposition could hardly find the heart to differ from the 'old man.'

'We have to face the fact that two and a quarter million houses were built a hundred years ago, and another two million are between sixty-five and a hundred years old. Surely this is a matter which ought to interest the whole House. If the Opposition has a counter-proposal, let them put it forward, and we shall give it our earnest attention. Would it be very wrong if I suggested that we might look into this together, with the desire to have more decent homes for the people counting much higher in our minds than ordinary partisan political gain?'

It was impossible to resist this reasonable way of looking at things. Never had his authority over the House been so obvious.

Only when the House was in this mood did he begin to unfold the great theme which he himself regarded as his valedictory message to his country. It seemed as if he was brooding on the future of the world, which he knew he must soon leave. The death of Stalin had led to the assumption of power by a different régime in the Kremlin. Might the end of the Stalin epoch lead to a change in Soviet policy, a change of heart?

'Have there been far-reaching changes in the temper and outlook of all the Russians? I do not find it unreasonable or dangerous' (though he would not say so too positively because of Anthony) 'to conclude that internal prosperity rather than external conquest is not only the deep desire of the Russian people but also the long-term interest of their rulers. It was in this state of mind that six months ago I thought it would be a good thing if the heads of the principal States and governments concerned met the new leaders of Russia to establish personal acquaintance.'

And then the thought of Anthony returned, and he warned the House that there was a risk that such a conference might end in a still worse deadlock than existed at present. Yet he could not pretend to the House that he thought it a great risk; even the hydrogen bomb made war improbable:

'The rapid and ceaseless developments of atomic warfare and the hydrogen bomb—these fearful scientific discoveries cast their shadow on every thoughtful mind, and yet the probabilities of another world war have become more remote. Indeed, I have sometimes the odd thought that the annihilating character of these agencies may bring an utterly unforeseeable security to mankind. When I was a schoolboy I was not good at arithmetic, but I have since heard it said that certain mathematical quantities, when they pass through infinity, change their signs from plus to minus or the other way round. It may be that this rule may have a novel application, and that when the advance of destructive weapons enables everyone to kill everybody else, nobody will want to kill anyone at all.'

If the bomb had convinced men that war had become impossible the resources set free could be used to enlarge the well-being of the people. The time had come to spread before the House his own splendid vision of an alternative to mass-destruction, the swiftest expansion of material well-being that had ever been within their reach or even within their dreams:

'By material well-being I mean not only abundance, but a degree of leisure for the masses such as has never before been possible in our mortal struggle for life. . . . We and all nations stand at this hour of human history upon the portals of supreme catastrophe and of measureless reward. My faith is that in God's mercy we shall choose aright.'

As I left the Chamber I was stopped by a Labour Member. His eyes were full of tears.

'He is a very great man,' he murmured. 'Can't you take him away and let him have a good long rest? The country needs him.'

I found the P.M. in his room, tired but in good heart.

'That's the last bloody hurdle. Now, Charles, we can think of Moscow.'

He gave a great yawn, opening his mouth very wide.

'Your pill cleared my head. Now I can turn my mind to other things. You do not realize, Charles, how much depends on the Russians. I must see Malenkov. Then I can depart in peace.'

His face was grey. I wanted him to go back to No. 10 to rest. But he was worked up and was all agog to hear what they were saying in the lobbies about his speech.

'The House liked it, I think. That mathematical bit was my own; it will go round the world.'

He emptied his glass and, rising with an effort from his chair, tottered out into the Lobby.

494

Chapter forty-five

Now for Moscow

November 4, 1953

This speech is a step forward. Winston has been profoundly shaken by this illness, and it will be some time before he can build up his old self-confidence. But every time he goes over what he calls 'one of these hurdles' he gains in assurance. His first appearance in public at Doncaster, his first Cabinet, the speech at Margate, the first occasion when he answered Questions in the House, and this speech, which is the first he has made in the House since his illness, each has been an ordeal which he has met without flinching. I have never felt so near to him. Most people, after a stroke, are only concerned with keeping alive. He never for a moment seems to give a thought to this. I love his guts. I believe that he is quite invincible.

It is single combat. No one, it seems, is with him in his valiant fight to seize this last opportunity of bringing about world easement. Camrose declared that Winston would never return to the House of Commons, Max said he was finished, Alex blurted out, 'Cannot you make him resign?' Indeed, I sometimes feel as if I were aiding and abetting him in a foolish course of action which must end in disaster. Then at other times he himself gets the path he has chosen in its true perspective.

'What does it matter if anything does happen to me?' he exclaimed. 'There is no disgrace in going out trying to do one's job.'

When I saw him this morning he seemed rested. He was devouring the morning papers, which were full of his speech.

'I am getting better every day, Charles. Don't you think it is a remarkable recovery? Have you ever seen any similar case? I take things for granted now which even a fortnight ago worried me. I still become lachrymose at times, and if some of the thoughts in my speech had occurred to me for the first time in the House I should have been tearful. But I'd been over it all before, so I wasn't troubled.'

This is the first time he has spoken of this affliction with detachment.

'I am thinking of substituting port for brandy. You wouldn't be against that?'

I answered that it was the lesser of two evils, whereat he grinned broadly. The smile vanished.

'Before I can go to see Malenkov the President must agree. This is very secret. I may go to the Azores. It would take Ike ten hours to fly there—or perhaps to Heaven. Only six hours for us. The *Vanguard* would be waiting for us there to provide accommodation. Of course it depends on Ike's other commitments. There will be a deadlock with the Russians, and Dulles will not be against the Azores once he sees no possibility of himself meeting Molotov.'

'When would you go?'

'Oh, perhaps in the middle of December. I might go by sea. I don't want to go to Washington as long as there is a waddle in my walk. I have decided to walk a thousand yards every day, in the garden or in the Park. I think if my muscles were toned up I might walk better. I couldn't deal at present with all the reporters at Washington.'

He caught sight of the Queen's photograph in a paper.

'The country is so lucky,' he murmured.

He held out his hand. He wanted to read the papers.

November 5, 1953

Christopher telephoned to say that they were worried about Winston's going to the Cenotaph on Sunday and standing for twenty minutes without a hat in this weather.

'I'd rather,' he said, 'Winston did two speeches than this. We have tried to prevent him, but failed. You are the only person who can stop him.'

Christopher said if I came to No. 10 at two-fifteen I should catch him before he went to the House for Questions. When I got there, Oates, one of the secretaries, went off to see who was lunching with him. He came back saying that the P.M. was alone.

'I am afraid the atmosphere is rather hostile; he suspects what you are after, and the family has already been nagging him. Besides, he is trying to mug up the Foreign Secretary's speech, against time, before going to the House.'

I expected he would bite my head off. I put my point in a few sentences.

'I think,' he responded, 'you are quite right. It would be foolish to stand for a long time without a hat in this raw November weather.

I shall get someone to do it for me. Will you have coffee, Charles, or brandy?'

But he had Eden's speech on his plate, and he was due in the House, so I made my excuses.

November 10, 1953

The P.M. has fixed up with the President to meet at Bermuda on December 4. He is quite excited about it.

'I put out my paw to Ike, and it was fixed up at once. My stock is very high. There is a feeling that I am the only person who could do anything with Russia. I believe in Moscow they think that too.'

What an asset his optimism is! It keeps out the facts. He has set his heart on Moscow, but Ike thinks it can do no good, while Anthony is as certain it will do harm. So Winston has a difficult hand to play.

'I shall go by air. It costs £30,000 if we go by *Vanguard*, and only £3,000 by air. Besides, at this time of year we might be battened down for most of the voyage. Ike wanted to keep it quiet till he was ready, but the French leaked. I have been bothered with indigestion, and have started my exercises again. I have eleven Questions today, with Supplementaries it means twenty.'

I asked him would they bother him? He made a contemptuous little gesture. Then he grinned.

'I have only to tell one man to mind his own business.'

November 12, 1953

Jock is not very happy about Bermuda. Aldrich[1] was very frank about things. He admitted that Winston's stock had fallen in the States. They don't like his views on Moscow. Nor does it help that Ike has been found out; he is no politician, he is a soldier. This means that Dulles is in charge. I feared that very little might come of Bermuda. Aldrich was afraid that this might be true.

He knows what many Americans forget: that Winston's prestige in the world is a wasting asset, in the sense that he will not be in public life much longer. When America is ready to do something he may be gone. Ben-Gurion[2] told Black Rod[3] recently that the only statesman he trusted was Winston Churchill, and Horrocks said that it was the same everywhere in the Middle East.

---

[1] Winthrop Aldrich, American Ambassador in London, 1953–7.
[2] Prime Minister of Israel.
[3] Lieut.-General Sir Brian Horrocks.

November 18, 1953

The P.M. looked up as I entered his room this morning.

'I'm not sure I'm getting any better,' he said, 'I am very stiff, and my walk is very tottery, and my body feels tired. And when I do any work my head gets tired. I am at my worst from one o'clock till about half-past three, just when Questions come up. I'm confused, so that I don't want to talk to anyone when I am lunching. From five o'clock on I am all right, especially if I get in an hour's sleep. It would have been easy to retire after Margate when I had made my speech; now I must carry on until the Queen returns in May.'

His condition is unlikely to change, and I have told him this in the plainest terms.

"I am bewildered by the world; the confusion is terrible,' he complains. 'There is the news from Egypt, and now the F.O. wants a war with Israel. Ernie Bevin apparently made a treaty with Jordan. I don't want war.'

'There were some old fellows here last night, when the Jockey Club dined here. General Baird, who is ninety-four, got up the stairs all right and made a short speech.'

The P.M. said there would be no 'Parl.' for a month at Christmas. He looked out of the window at the fog.

'I hate the winter,' he said. 'I may go to Max's house at Cap d'Ail when Parl. rises. I would like to win this by-election,[1] but I don't think we shall.'

He jerked out unconnected sentences as if it were too much trouble to pursue anything for long.

November 23, 1953

Last night, after I had gone to bed, the telephone rang. The P.M. thought he was getting a cold and would like to see me in the morning. When I arrived at No. 10 I knew from the air of expectancy in the hall that he might arrive at any moment. He elbowed himself out of the car awkwardly and shuffled down the passage to the lift. The journey from Chartwell had tired him. He said he felt chilly and got into bed, though the Cabinet was due to start in ten minutes' time. I told him he didn't give himself a chance coming up from Chartwell like this at the last moment. He grumbled something under his breath—he doesn't like criticism. But I stuck to my point. Two hours in the Cabinet would not help matters, and by the time

---

[1] Holborn, won for Labour by Mrs. Lena Jeger in November, 1953.

he got to the airport to bid farewell to the Queen he would be un-steady on his feet—I explained that I was afraid of the Press. He gave me a look: Must you really go on like this? it seemed to say.

The cold had not developed; he did not mention it. As he got warmer in bed he became more cheerful.

'I've been reading an interesting book: *The Reason Why*. I forget who wrote it. Yes, Mrs. Woodham-Smith. You ought to read it, Charles. I was much struck by it.' His eyes twinkled. 'I was naughty. I read it for eight hours at a sitting yesterday. I get bitten by books nowadays. She arranges her facts very well, but there are some that are not clear to me. If the officers were so bad in the Crimea, then the men must have been very good. And if the organization was so bad, it was good enough to land sixty thousand men, and in a few days these men stormed the Alma, which the Russians thought was impregnable. I did not know,' the P.M. continued, 'why the purchase of commissions in the Army was kept on for so long. It was to prevent men getting them who did not belong to the existing social order, and might have become a danger to it. She accounts for the Charge of the Light Brigade by the feud between Cardigan and Lucan. I'm not sure about that. Both behaved at Balaclava in a perfectly proper manner. I must read her *Florence Nightingale*.'

I told him he would be late for the Cabinet. He kicked off the blankets and then lay quite still, as if exhausted by the effort.

'I would like to go to sleep,' he murmured, closing his eyes.

Then he began to dress by slow stages. When at length he came down into the hall an attendant held his greatcoat to help him into it.

'What are you doing?' he said impatiently. 'Where am I going?'

One of the secretaries explained that the Cabinet was in the House of Commons, so that if there was a division Ministers would be in the House. He seemed to be taken aback. Anyway, he was not going to be hurried.

'Where is Walter? I want to see him before he goes.'

'I am sorry, Walter, you are leaving. It is your fault, not mine. Let me know how you get on. We shall be interested. This is my photograph.'

Then he stumped out, and those who were going with him hurried to their cars.

November 24, 1953

As I entered the P.M.'s room this morning he threw away the *Daily Mirror* with a gesture of disgust.

'They want Prince Charles to mix with working people. I

suppose they would have a ballot, and each day the successful twelve would come to the Palace. I wish we could buy that rag; it is doing so much harm.'

I picked up the *Mirror* while he got on with his breakfast. 'Why not open the Palace to the People?' was the heading. It was this that had raised his ire—there was nothing about Prince Charles.

'Poor Queen,' Winston muttered over his breakfast, 'she will be asked to do so much.'

November 27, 1953

The P.M. asked me whether I had voted in the television debate in the Lords. He thought Hailsham's concluding remarks were very true:

'The Government have not in the country a very wide balance of advantage, even if they have that. They are now antagonizing the Free Churches . . . there are many members of the Church of England who will agree with the most reverend Primate; there are the Vice-Chancellors of all the universities, and the whole educational system; and there are other bodies of organized opinion, also, who are against them.'

'I have always felt,' the P.M. concluded, 'that the Government's intervention could do the Conservative Party no good and might well do it much harm. The Tories have gained nothing by bringing up this Television question, and have certainly lost something.' His voice rising. 'I don't know what all this God-damned fuss is about. I don't care what happens. The issue does not rouse me at all. I can't understand why people get so excited about it. They want me to put on the Whips in the Commons. I am very reluctant to do so. If we don't, then what happens will not affect the Party.'

He spoke of the reform of the House of Lords. The House, he thought, would be wise to be content with influencing opinion. If it tried to get more power, then it might do itself great hurt:

'I'm not committed at all. I think a peer should be able to surrender his right to sit in the House if that is his wish, and I would like the two years' veto to be restored.'

There had been a 'fuss' in the House of Commons about officers' pensions, and he was very depressed when he returned from the House.

'I hoped Butler would be able to find some compromise, but he failed. I felt,' he repeated, 'that it was not fair to leave a question where there was so much feeling to an Under-Secretary. It was really a sense of chivalry that led me to intervene. I think that got known in the House.' His voice rose. He was not afraid of the House; his jaw set. 'I may go to America; it all depends on how things turn out.'

Canopus, *December 2, 1953*

This may be my last journey with Winston. We began life humbly enough, in an unheated Lancaster bomber, and end it, twelve years later, in high state in the strato-cruiser *Canopus*. Messages no longer pass to the captain asking at what height we are flying; 18,000 feet or 11,000 feet (both were recorded last night), it is all one to us, pressurized at 5,000 feet. Most of the seniors and quite a number of the juniors came to me last night for sleeping pills—this weak-kneed generation that needs dope for a few hours in the air.

Lunched at a table for four; the Prof. and the P.M. on one side, Anthony and I opposite. After greeting Anthony cheerfully, Winston took up his book, *Death to the French*, by C. S. Forester, and kept his nose in it throughout the meal. The Prof., who is getting deaf, could not hear what we said, so giving up the attempt to bring him in, I talked to Anthony.

The P.M., he said, was very anti-Frog. 'The French are pretty hopeless,' Anthony went on, 'but France is a geographical necessity. As for the Americans, he thought "they mistake movement for action"; as long as something is happening they are quite happy. They still loved Ike, but were beginning to have doubts about him.'

Everything Anthony said was sensible, and his judgment of men was discerning. He is not like Winston; he looks behind the façade. Looking across at the P.M. buried in his book, he said:

'They say to him exactly what they said to Neville Chamberlain, that he is the only man who can save the situation. And,' Anthony added, 'the people who are saying this to Winston are the same who said it to Neville.' He went on: 'I wanted to give up the F.O. and take some office in the Cabinet which would give me experience of the home front, but' (*smiling*) 'Winston has got used to me; he said Salisbury could not be Foreign Secretary because he was in the Lords. He was so much against my leaving the F.O. that I gave in.'

There it is in a sentence: the essential difference between the two men is exposed. If the roles were reversed it is impossible to picture Winston meekly accepting such a handicap in the climb to power. Once, it is true, Anthony brought himself to the point of resigning from the Cabinet, but day in, day out, he lacks the hard core which in Winston is hidden by his emotional nature and by his magnanimity.

Where people are concerned Winston Churchill exists in an imaginary world of his own making. Sometimes his ideas, too, have no roots in reality; the supposed change of heart in Russia may be one of them. Both as a judge of men and as a cool appraiser of events, Anthony is much sounder and more discriminating than Winston, but the personality of the P.M. and his power over words raise him into another world, which will always be closed to Anthony, who was born, and will remain, a secondary figure.

I was roused from my thoughts when Christopher appeared. He wanted the P.M. to read some briefs for the Conference, but Winston did not seem at all keen on work. We were bumping on the edge of a storm, and possibly his mind went back to the night in February, 1943, when we were crossing the Atlantic and were struck by lightning. His flying memories are not at all happy, and however he may hide it, he is full of apprehension.

The P.M. looked down. We were crossing the coast of Newfoundland, and were flying over a desolate expanse of rocks and great pools. 'Bloody country,' he ejaculated, picking up his book, while Anthony retreated into Turgenev's *A Sportsman's Sketches*. He held it so that I could read the title. 'It's Clarissa's,' he told me.

Chapter forty-six

Bermuda—hope deferred

Bermuda, December 3, 1953

A few steps lead from the balcony of the Mid-Ocean Club to the golf links. At the top I stopped to pass the time of day with a Welsh Fusilier on guard, who apparently knew me. At the bottom I found that I had forgotten my golf balls, but before I could re-enter the building I had to produce my pass to the Fusilier. When the President leaves, all these precautions will disappear.

Archie Compston was in command on the first tee. He had prospered as the professional to the Coombe Hill Golf Club. Now he winters in Bermuda as the local instructor. His flattery is as grooved as his swing. He promised Christopher, the merest beginner in the game, that if he put himself in his hands in the summer he would undertake that he emerged the winner of White's handicap.

The Americans have taken over the first floor, the French have the second and the third belongs to us. I went to the P.M.'s room to see if he was ready for dinner.

'There will be great difficulties arranging things here,' he began.

'You mean the agenda?'

'I don't like the word.'

He had been turning over in his mind the question of an atomic war. At dinner he took up the theme:

P.M.: 'There was a time when the Western Powers could have used the atomic bomb without any reply by Russia. That time has gone. How many atomic bombs do you think the Russians have?'

Prof.: 'Oh, between three hundred and four hundred. The Americans may have three thousand or four thousand.'

P.M.: 'If there were war, Europe would be shattered and subjugated; Britain shattered, but, I hope, not subjugated. Russia would be left without a central government and incapable of carrying on a modern war.'

503

There was a long silence while the P.M. brooded over his dinner plate, which he held between the forefinger and thumb of both hands. It was one of his black days, when his imagination conjures up what might happen to mankind if he fails with Malenkov.

P.M.: 'We have been living in a time when at any moment London, men, women and children, might be destroyed overnight.'

I was glad to turn the conversation.

'But does Russia want war?'

P.M.: 'I believe it is not in her interest to make war. When I meet Malenkov we can build for peace.'

Moran: 'Then who is making difficulties?'

P.M.: 'Ike. He doesn't think any good can come from talks with the Russians. But it will pay him to come along with us. I shall do what I can to persuade him. I might stay longer here than I meant, at any rate if I could persuade Ike to stay too. He is the key man in this business.'

Moran: 'I thought Dulles was.'

He took no notice of my remark.

P.M.: 'I would not hesitate to go on to Washington if that was necessary. I think, Charles, I could manage it. I don't feel old, though I have some of the disabilities of old age. My outlook on things has not changed. It is exactly what it was. In the mornings I feel the same as I always did, but I have become torpid in the middle of the day. You ought to be able to think out some line of action which would help me. This old carcass of mine is a bloody nuisance.'

He changed the conversation abruptly.

'There are some interesting people in the party—Bob Dixon,[1] for example.'

Such a remark was so alien to his usual way of thinking that I had the curiosity later to trace it to its source. Anthony had put it into his head. The P.M. does not notice whether people are interesting or uninteresting; as long as they are good listeners and are congenial to him he is content.

'The French are going to be very difficult. They will want everything and give nothing.' The P.M. grinned broadly. 'I have been reading *Death to the French*. I must get Christopher to put it away before they come. I have had a good talk with Anthony; we have clarified things.'

---

[1] Sir Pierson Dixon, Deputy Under-Secretary of State, Foreign Office.

December 4, 1953

At the dinner at Government House my neighbour, a member of one of the old families who governed Bermuda, Butterfield by name, who was at Oxford with Anthony and had dined with him the night before, said that Anthony spoke of Winston as a 'sick man,' and was worried about him. But it was Anthony who looked tired and bored during dinner. He listened with a feeble smile to the P.M., who was in great form, exchanging old memories with Ike. Anthony has behaved very well, but the role of heir apparent does not become easier. The P.M. made an adroit, unprepared, speech about America and Ike. She was out to serve, not to dominate or rule. The French Prime Minister, who was sitting opposite to me, looked as abstracted and bored as Anthony; he appeared to be dining off E.D.C.

On our return I went with the P.M. to his room, where we were soon joined by Christopher. He told us that the Press had got a full account of the first meeting and were making a great story of the division of opinion between the P.M. and the President about Russia. The P.M. seemed put out; he did not know that the Press would be informed in this way. But when Christopher went on in his loud voice about the harm it would do, Winston became impatient:

'It is foolish to exaggerate. Everything I have said will do good in England. It was all very carefully considered. I believe that I am going to be master in the discussions. Ike is a pal on the same level.'

December 5, 1953

The P.M. is less sure about things today. It appears that when he pleaded with Ike that Russia was changed, Ike spoke of her as a whore, who might have changed her dress, but who should be chased from the streets. Russia, according to Ike, was out to destroy the civilized world.

'Of course,' said the P.M. pacing up and down the room, 'anyone could say the Russians are evil minded and mean to destroy the free countries. Well, if we really feel like that, perhaps we ought to take action before they get as many atomic bombs as America has. I made that point to Ike, who said, perhaps logically, that it ought to be considered. But,' said Winston, resuming his seat, 'if one did not believe that such a large fraction of the world was evil it could do no harm to try and be friendly as long as we did not relax our defensive preparations.'

I asked him how Ike had managed to retreat from his attitude towards Russia.

'Oh, he hasn't,' the P.M. put in, 'but when we came out of the meeting he said there was a lot in what I said. Most people, when beaten in argument, become sulky. Ike is so selfless.'

I asked him what the French thought about all this. The P.M., shortly:

'I take no account of them, they are harmless.'

I lunched with the Governor. Hood[1] is a full-blooded red-faced Scot with no neck to speak of, as if he had stepped down from a Raeburn portrait for our correction. He has a fine record as an administrator, and the islanders do not want to part with him.

On my return I went straight to the P.M.'s room. When I told him where I had been he said, 'I like Hood. Would you like to be a Governor, Charles? I believe you would do it very well.' Winston does not waste much time speculating on the possibilities of those around him. It only occurred to him that I could hold an administrative post when he saw another doctor doing work of this kind and doing it well.

The P.M. complained that he was muddled and stupid. I asked him how long he had before his next Conference. He looked at his watch. 'It is at five o'clock, just an hour from now.' He said he would not bother to take off his clothes; then he changed his mind for 'even half an hour next to the sheets seems to do a lot of good.' He got out of his clothes lazily, and plopped into the bed naked, as his habit. He lay for a time as if it was too much trouble to turn over. Then, when the curtains were drawn and he had put on his black eye-shade, he settled to sleep.

As I left the room a message came from the French Prime Minister.[2] He did not feel well; he had pain when he coughed and his temperature was nearly 105°. I doubt whether he will take any more part in the conference.

December 6, 1953

This morning, as I sat beside the P.M.'s bed, he said slowly: 'The world is in an awful state, I cannot cope with it.'

I saw him again after the five-o'clock meeting.

'The presence of the French means that every word has to be translated, and in any case they cannot do anything,' Winston grumbled. 'Bidault[3] talked for an hour and a half about four villages

---

[1] Lieut.-General Sir Alexander Hood.
[2] Joseph Laniel.
[3] Georges Bidault, French Foreign Minister.

in the Saar. I went for him, telling him plainly that if American troops were withdrawn from Europe British troops would leave too. Bidault said to me, "Do not be so unkind." I did not say to him what I ought to have said: it is because of my love for France that I am unkind.'

I asked him what part Ike had played. He answered:

'Things are very easy between us. I think he trusts me. I have now had eleven hours' private talks with him. He is going to make a speech in New York on atomic bombs, which will mean that all this Bermuda business will be forgotten as unimportant.'

The P.M. has been trying to persuade himself that Ike will give way over Moscow. But he is less certain about things. He got up as if it were a great effort and went off to dine with the French, while Pug and I were the guests of Ike, supported by half a dozen of his party. After dinner Ike said:

'No one has treated me so well as Winston Churchill. He knows I love him; sometimes he takes advantage of that.'

We broke up early and I went to the P.M.'s room to wait for him. After a time he stumbled in and threw himself in his evening clothes across the bed. 'Do you mind ringing the bell, Charles?' When his servant came he appeared for a moment alarmed by the complete relaxation of the prostrate figure. 'I am very tired,' Winston groaned.

When I left the P.M. I found Norman Brook smoking his black pipe as if he had time for anything. I value his opinion because he gets hold of the facts and does not exaggerate what can be learnt from them. He knows my only concern is to keep the P.M. on his feet; he is very cautious and discreet—as Secretary of the Cabinet he must be; besides it is part of his temperament.

'During the war,' he said, 'the Prime Minister had a gift for picking out two or three things and getting them up in detail—that was his strength. He made no attempt in those days to keep up with lots of things. Now, of course, he is a lazy Prime Minister; he reads novels after breakfast. But it is much better from the country's point of view that he should stay on.'

Norman was not delivering a moral stricture, he was merely recording that the P.M.'s faculties were not what they used to be. But he did not think people noticed that the P.M. was easing off. He was doing the Cabinets all right.

December 7, 1953

It is not like Winston, when he has a fixed purpose, to admit that he is not up to the job. After a morning meeting he told me that they were discussing Egypt when an argument had suddenly occurred to him which completely changed the American view. There were other matters of a domestic nature in which his will prevailed. 'You ought not to think, Charles, that I am too tired to do my work.'

It had been arranged that the *Canopus* would return on Wednesday, but during luncheon the P.M., without any warning, announced that he would like to stay another day in Bermuda. Christopher interposed that Anthony had lunch and dinner engagements in London which he would have to cancel, whereat the P.M. blew up:

'To hell with his engagements. He's not running this show.'

When we were alone his mood changed.

'When I had a chance to speak to the President he told me he did not need converting. We ought not to pay any more attention to McCarthy than they did to Aneurin Bevan. I cannot make it out. I am bewildered. It seems that everything is left to Dulles. It appears that the President is no more than a ventriloquist's doll.'

He said no more for a time. Then he said:

'This fellow preaches like a Methodist Minister, and his bloody text is always the same: That nothing but evil can come out of meeting with Malenkov.'

There was a long pause.

'Dulles is a terrible handicap.' His voice rose. 'Ten years ago I could have dealt with him. Even as it is I have not been defeated by this bastard. I have been humiliated by my own decay. Ah, no, Charles, you have done all that could be done to slow things down.'

When I turned round he was in tears. That was the last I heard of Moscow while we were at Bermuda.

Winston seems to have lost interest in the Conference. He grunted under his breath that he did not want to talk with the 'Bloody Frogs.' That was Anthony's job. He is nearly played out, and I was relieved when he said he would get a little sleep before the conference. When he woke he noticed that the fingers of his right hand were numb. He thought he must have slept on them. I could see no purpose in disillusioning him, but I shall be glad when we get him safely home. At that moment there was a knock on the door. It was a message for the P.M. from the conference of Foreign Ministers. Could they have another half-hour?

When Anthony eventually came up to the P.M.'s room I noticed how thin and drawn his face is these days.

'We have had a hell of a time. The communiqué is giving a lot of trouble. Oh, the French are making all sorts of difficulties about E.D.C.' Anthony spoke in a tired and rather petulant voice.

The conference had met at half-past five and went on till the P.M. broke it up by sending for them for dinner. The French were led to his room, silent and self-conscious. The P.M. had done enough talking, and during dinner he sat abstracted. The conference was resumed about ten o'clock, and it was after one o'clock when the P.M. came upstairs. I did not like this drawn-out meeting, which had gone on for seven hours, but he did not appear jaded, depressed, or sluggish. He was in fact bright and good-humoured.

'Your pill worked wonders. Anthony failed to get anything out of Bidault, so he has gone to Laniel's room to see what he can do with him. It will do his pneumonia good,' he said grimly.

When Anthony appeared he collapsed into a chair. The communiqué, though weak, did, he argued, represent what had happened. Winston grunted:

'It is obvious there was no agreement between us, and that the French would not accept E.D.C. The Americans talk about pulling out, but when it comes to the time I think they will draw back from this.'

No one made a move; it was as if they were too weary to get up and go to bed. I thought it was time I saw my other patient, Laniel. His room was full of excited Frenchmen. Laniel seemed upset, as far as a stolid Norman shows any emotion. I gave him a stiff sedative, and packed the rest of them off to bed.

December 8, 1953

The P.M. is surprisingly well after yesterday's performance.

P.M.: 'The communiqué was a flop. In refusing E.D.C the French may have thrown away the last chance of saving France.'

Moran: 'The Americans will take it badly?'

P.M.: 'Oh, very badly. They may pull out, and if they do we shall follow.'

Moran: 'What will happen then?'

P.M.: 'Oh, France may become a kind of Czecho-Slovakia, a satellite of Russia.'

Moran: 'And where does Adenauer come in?'

P.M.: 'The Germans would form a secret army, but the Russians will attack them before they can do anything. But my view is that the Russians are afraid. They may listen to reason.'

Moran: 'What kind of defence could we put up if things go like that?'

P.M. (*shrugging his shoulders*): 'What the Americans call peripheral defence: Iceland, Spain, Turkey, wherever there are bases. Bidault is prepared to sacrifice his career for E.D.C. He knows it is necessary. I would like you, Charles, to go to Laniel and invite him to return in the *Canopus*.' He grinned. 'It would have the additional advantage that it would provide a reason why we took another day away from the House of Commons. Will he be well enough to travel with us?'

Moran: 'He is taking a chance. If he didn't, he could not be a candidate for the Presidential Election.'

P.M.: 'Anthony is very good with other people. His voice is so smooth and his manner so quiet, so persuasive.'

December 9, 1953

When I saw the P.M. after breakfast he told me he had had some twitching in his foot. He said he would have an easy day. The Governor would drive him round the island in the morning, and he had promised to inspect the Bermuda troops in the afternoon.

Dinner began dismally. After the soup there was steak. The P.M. blew up.

'Is there no fish? Who ordered the dinner? Christopher?'

He had never heard of such a thing. However, the efficient Henri, who had been imported specially from Calgary to look after the Prime Minister, somehow produced whitebait, almost as if it had been ordered with the dinner, and the P.M., who likes this particular dish, was placated.

There followed a long discussion about our defences against a Russian attack. Pug felt the strength of the Russians had been exaggerated. In the event of war they would have long lines of communication, and would always be looking back over their shoulders at Poland and the other satellite countries. The P.M. agreed they were probably not so strong as people thought, but even if they were only a third as strong we had no real defences in Europe to hold them back.

As long as this discussion went on the P.M. remained alert and interested. He was particularly scornful of the lack of proportion shown in the allocation of the House's time for debate—two days for TV and only one day for foreign affairs and atomic war. He might be out of date, but to him it sounded fantastic. He decided he would send a letter now to Rab about these matters and tell him when he and Anthony would speak. He rang for a secretary to take it down. But there was no one in the private office and no one in the Foreign Secretary's office. Everyone, it appeared, had gone bathing by moonlight. The P.M. became very irritable. He would never again bring only two private secretaries to a conference. At this point Anthony volunteered to take down the P.M.'s words, and it was in this manner that the letter took shape. The P.M. turned to Christopher and asked him how he thought something would go with the Party. Christopher answered at some length.

P.M. (*interrupting*): 'Oh, do please let me get on with my letter.'

Christopher (*in injured tones*): 'I thought you wanted my opinion.'

As he finished, Miss Portal put her head in, and the tension was relieved.

The talk grew thin. Pug exchanged a look of understanding with Anthony, who wanted to go to bed, but Pug was in time to agree with Winston's views on Germany. When the P.M. retired at last to his room he picked up a paper, though it was one o'clock and he was now very tired.

December 10, 1953

This is the first conference that the P.M. has attended where the Press has got hold of everything and printed it full of partisan colouring. That, anyway, is his complaint. Yesterday, while Clemmie was in the air on her way to Stockholm to receive Winston's Nobel Prize,[1] he was jumpy and worried. Then a message came. As he read it his face cleared.

'They have arrived. I hate to have people I love in the air—unless I am with them.'

After lunch a car took him to the beach, where, leaning on his stick and on a detective, he descended a steep sand dune. At the bottom there was a rock, about twice a man's height. Up this, to everybody's amazement and consternation, he proceeded to crawl. We got him down eventually and pulled and pushed him up the dune. At the top he stood getting his breath, perspiring profusely.

'I have not sweated like this since my illness,' he said. 'Take my pulse, Charles.'

There were people all round, and I got out of it somehow.

'Are you very angry with me,' he asked, looking at me like a naughty child.

He insisted on driving to the aquarium, eight miles distant.

---

[1] Sir Winston Churchill had been awarded the 1953 Nobel Prize for Literature.

Christopher said that I was against it. The P.M. had done enough. Winston dismissed such counsels of weakness and climbed into his car, while I trudged back to the Club. When I got there I found he had changed his mind and had gone to his room. I found him lying on his bed. He wondered if the sweating had done him harm. I gave him a vigorous rub-down with a rough towel and bundled him into bed. He was quite pleased with himself.

'It is a lovely spot,' he said. 'I must come here for a holiday.'

He picked up *Royal Flush*.[1]

'I think it is very good indeed,' he said, quite unaware that I had given it to him.

Soon he became absorbed in the story and I left him. I marvel at his spirits. It is a long way to come for so little.

London, December 15, 1953

When the P.M. telephoned me this morning I was already on my way to No. 10.

I asked him how things were. A faint smile flickered over his face. 'Bloody,' he answered. But he was not thinking of his health.

'There are a number of events causing me anxiety, though I am, of course, used to that sort of thing.'

He began to tell me about them:

'Dulles, who never said a word to the Frogs at Bermuda, now tells them in Paris in the plainest fashion that if they won't agree to E.D.C. America may pull out. Oh, there's no doubt about what he did say. Of course, the French cannot do anything. Their system of government is bankrupt.'

The P.M. groaned; he was very weary.

'Then I have to lunch with the 1922 Committee. They have put very strong pressure on the Government to force TV through the House, though half the Cabinet is against it. I have never mastered this subject, but I think Morrison's proposal of an all-Party conference is very sensible. I don't like meeting them when I am displeased with their conduct.

'And on top of this is the strike.[2]

'But everything would be all right if I hadn't to make this bloody speech in the House on Thursday. I did fourteen hundred words yesterday, and it seemed to come all right, but today I don't feel like doing anything.'

He smiled, putting his hand on my arm.

[1] An historical novel by Margaret Irwin.

[2] A threatened railway strike, which was called off on December 16 after negotiations.

'But I didn't send for you to tell you this sad story. I thought you might be able to put me in better shape to compose a speech and to deal with my worries. My pulse was rapid last night, now it is too slow. Is that bad? Why should it be slow when it is quite regular and not missing beats? I think it's all right, it simply means my heart is resting. Count it now, Charles. Your hands are cold; warm them in the bathroom. You ought to look after yourself. Sixty, well what's wrong with that?'

December 16, 1953

Before his breakfast Winston got out of bed and picked up his typed speech, taking it back to bed with him. The pile of morning papers was for once left untouched.

'I mustn't waste a minute,' he said. 'I'd have liked to stay until the Queen returns, but I shall probably go when the House rises.'

Does he mean this?

Tonight during dinner I was called to the telephone. It was the P.M. himself.

'I thought you would like to know about the luncheon. It was very successful. There were two hundred members of the committee present, one of our largest meetings. They were very friendly, singing "For He's a Jolly Good Fellow." I think they took what I said to them, it was quite plain spoken. I was very firm, telling them that we should not be deterred from doing what we thought was right, either by the violence of our enemies or even by the eloquence of our best friends. I dominated and conquered the committee. I spoke for twenty-five minutes. I did not prepare anything. I did not give it ten minutes' thought. Some of the Tories had been very worked up about Suez; particularly the Privy Councillor with the moustache. Names go, Charles. This man's name has been on the tip of my tongue all day. Yes, Waterhouse.[1] I tried to remember his name by repeating water-louse.'

He did not telephone to tell me this, and I waited to find the reason. Now it came.

'I must have a clear head tomorrow for my speech. Will a green send me off to sleep? Is a green as potent as a red?'

December 17, 1953

The P.M. was still sleeping when I arrived at No. 10. He had slept nine and a half hours at a stretch, with the help of a red and a green. When his breakfast came he began to wake up.

[1] Captain Charles Waterhouse, M.P.

'We had a good day yesterday,' he began, 'with good majorities. A good many decisions were taken—the bloody TV business is settled at last. Of course not all of them went the way I wanted. It was decided to ask Alex to talk to the Foreign Affairs Committee. I didn't want that. He isn't good at this kind of thing. Anthony and I generally seem to come to the same conclusions. We sent telegrams to each other, which crossed, approving Dulles's warning to France. He was quite right to tell them bluntly that if they don't swallow E.D.C. soon there will be a drastic change in American policy. Dulles,' the P.M. added, 'was better at Bermuda than we expected.'

'I shall go to the Other Club tonight. I must dine somewhere. I shall only have three-quarters of an hour there, because I must get back to the House to hear Anthony's speech.

'I may go in a month's time, or wait till the Queen returns. Probably I shall wait.'

When I left his room I met Christopher. He told me Winston had said the same to him. Christopher gave a great laugh: 'I told Winston: "You will wait till the Queen returns and then you will find a reason why you must carry on—perhaps Anthony's health."'

'What did the P.M. say to that?' I asked.

'Oh, he smiled and said: "I don't know why you should say that." '

I listened to the P.M.'s speech from the gallery of the House of Commons. He had nothing new to tell them, but it was done with verve and vigour; he explained that he must leave Mr. Bevan time to explain his journalistic exploits in Cairo. Winston's amusement was not shared by Aneurin; the venom in his thoughts disfigured his countenance while the P.M. was speaking. It was Winston in a genial mood (though his main theme was a warning to France of the consequences of rejecting E.D.C.); in Mr. Attlee's apt phrase, he was dressed up as Father Christmas, without the presents. That was what the House missed.

On my way home I called on Brendan. He took quite a different line from Christopher. He believed that Winston was seriously considering going. I asked him why he thought that.

'Well, Charles—er, er—I think Winston is—yum, yum—stung with the—er, er—idea of bringing out his *History of the English-speaking Peoples* in—er, er—three or four volumes.'

When Brendan said this I remembered that the P.M. told me that *Life* had offered him 50,000 dollars for each of four volumes to appear every year for the next four years.

'You see, Charles,' Brendan went on, 'Cassells hold the serial rights of the *History*, but—er, er yum—because they felt the terms

514

arranged before the war were no longer er, er—fair to Winston under
the altered circumstances, they have surrendered them.'

I told Brendan that I doubted whether the P.M. would resign just
to write another book.

'Er, er—probably you are right, Charles.'

December 18, 1953

'I was naughty last week,' Winston began. 'I went back to the
Other Club after Anthony's speech, and did not go to bed until
after one o'clock.'

He put down the *Manchester Guardian* glumly.

'They complain I have nothing new to tell the House. They cannot expect me to make the speech of my life every day. A speech is a
serious undertaking these days. I am not as fertile as I was. Of
course I do better when I am worked up, but I am not so easily
annoyed as I used to be; my reactions are not so quick. But after
all, Charles, I have not really had a let-up since Margate. I want
to keep my influence with the Americans. I think that is very important. They don't share my views about Russia.'

I said that the French were not likely to change their policy over
E.D.C.

'Impotence isn't a policy,' the P.M. retorted. 'What do you
think of Anthony?' he asked, and without waiting for an answer
continued: 'He seems fitter. He made a good speech in the House
last night. He hates the Tory rebels more than the Egyptians. I
may go soon. I am bored. I don't like some of the things which are
happening.'

For three days in succession Winston has played with the idea of
resignation, but I do not now believe that he will give up office until
he has to.

In the early afternoon the P.M. telephoned that he had burnt his
hand. I said I would bring Sir Thomas Dunhill. He asked if he
was well versed in the modern treatment of burns. The P.M. had
been lunching at Trinity House, where Anthony was elected one of
the Elder Brethren, when he put down his cigar on his plate so that
a box of matches burst into flame. He had some big blisters on his
left hand. I explained that Dunhill would see him before he went to
Chartwell, as I was going to Wales. He asked me the object of my
journey, and I told him: to watch a rugger match between Wales and
the New Zealanders. He did not appear to think that it was a very
good reason.

December 20, 1953

On my return from Wales I went with Dunhill to see the P.M. at No. 10. While Sir Thomas was preparing the dressings I was told that it had not been a very peaceful day at Chartwell. Christopher had been shooting pheasants when a bird came over very low and the gun on the other side of him wheeled round. Christopher saw what was happening and ducked, but the man next to him was hit in the face. Then two foals had got loose and had galloped over Clemmie's new croquet lawn, but the damage would be put right before she heard of it. A new black swan had arrived.

'If I retire, and I am seriously thinking of it, I shall be looking round for a convenient disease which will carry me off.'

At this point Dunhill said he was ready. There followed an extraordinary performance. Everything Dunhill did the P.M. criticized, advancing his own views of the manner in which the hand should be dressed and bandaged. It began when Dunhill's deft fingers were stripping off the dressings and plaster.

'Let me do it. I'm getting to know about it all.'

He gazed at the big blisters exposed.

'That shows how well my skin responds to injury.'

When the dressings were replaced he pointed out a spot which he did not think had been properly covered with gauze. Then he complained because the bandage came too far down his fingers; it made so much difference if he could move his fingers freely.

'This is the boundary line, the bandage must not come below that. Give me the scissors. I can cut away the part which comes too low.'

At last I intervened.

'You ought not to speak to the man at the wheel.'

'I'm the bloody wheel,' and the P.M. gave me a great grin. 'I really think it's still not right. Couldn't this part be done again?'

Whereupon the patient Dunhill undid much of what he had just done and started again.

'I want to wash the tips of my fingers. They are sticky.'

Dunhill said mildly: 'I washed them a few moments ago.'

When the P.M. persisted I had come to Dunhill's assistance. 'You've got water on the brain,' I told him.

He knew he was being perverse and smiled broadly.

'When I get to Chequers, what shall I do?' Dunhill suggested that when the dressing had to be changed the P.M. should go to Stoke Mandeville, but he replied that he could not think of going to the surgeon; the surgeon must come to him.

'I hope,' Winston added, 'he will accept my assistance.'

Kipling, Dunhill reminded him, wrote of the toad beneath the harrow which knows where every point goes.

'Yes, that is the point,' the P.M. said.

He lay back on the bed, closing his eyes.

'I am so sleepy. I don't know why,' he muttered.

December 30, 1953

I went into his room with his breakfast. Before I could say good morning he barked out what was in his mind. Government, he grumbled, had become more complicated than it used to be.

'You mean Labour is difficult and has more say in things?'

'Oh, no, it's worse than that, we have to consider intricate matters, valuations and that kind of thing, which never came before the Cabinets I can remember. For example, some agricultural land was requisitioned during the war as a bombing range. Now for some reason they no longer want it as a range.'

'You mean Crichel Down?'[1]

'Yes. It would seem proper in the circumstances to return it to its owner, who is asking that his ancestral acres be returned to him, with of course such compensation as may be agreed. But not at all—the government department concerned wants to take it over as Crown lands, though nationalization of land is against Tory policy. It seems to me all wrong. The land was taken for military purposes in a national emergency; it is no longer needed, and cannot be retained for some other purpose.'

He yawned noisily. 'I get very tired when I do anything. My back aches, and I don't want to tackle a difficult job. No zest. No energy.'

I said that when I last saw him he had some thoughts of retiring.

'Oh,' he answered in an offhand way, 'I'm not thinking of that. I don't want you to think I'm in a bad way. Yesterday I was as clear-headed at the end of the Cabinet as I was when it began. I sleep well; it is a great blessing. Nature ought to make some provision that as we get older we sleep more and more. A time would come when we might sleep eighteen out of the twenty-four hours, though

---

[1] Crichel Down was compulsorily purchased by the Air Ministry in 1937. It was transferred to the Ministry of Agriculture in 1950, and at large public expense the land was used for the setting up of an experimental farm. A Public Enquiry reported in June, 1954, that civil servants had been high-handed in their dealings with the original owners and that undue public funds had been spent on the experimental project. The affair led to the resignation of Sir Thomas Dugdale, Minister for Agriculture.

when we were awake we should be nearly as good as ever.' He gave a great grin. 'And then we would sleep all the time. I have just slept eight hours, and I could go off again now.' (Miss Portal told me that he had dropped off to sleep in the middle of the morning while actually dictating—more than once this had happened.)

'You haven't taken my pulse.' I felt it.

At that moment Mowlem, the plastic surgeon, who had been looking after his hand while he was at Chequers, came into the room. Winston had already related how Mowlem had told him: 'The recuperative powers shown by your hand are those of a much younger man.' That is the kind of patter Winston likes. It showed, on Mowlem's part, a good working knowledge of psychology. I had not met him before, but I knew without asking that the P.M. liked him and had confidence in his skill, so that he did not suggest that Dunhill should see him again; in the field of surgery Winston can usually spot a master craftsman. His answers to Winston's questions were clear and decisive. There were no doubts in his mind; his manner was full of easy assurance.

When we left the room Mowlem recalled the first time he saw the P.M. at Chequers; how he sat on his bed for nearly an hour while Winston talked about Omdurman. It took me about a year to reach that stage with Winston. I left Mowlem and returned to the P.M. He kept yawning, opening his mouth very wide, without putting up his hand. 'I'm not properly awake yet,' he said. 'My memory for names, Charles, is very bad; it seems to be getting worse. I shall soon forget my own name. Oh, no, my memory for details is quite all right.'

I asked him if he had read anything in the Christmas holidays.

'No,' he answered reflectively, 'I have done very little; often I did nothing at all. A man in his eightieth year'—he smiled—'does not want to do things.'

Part seven

Winston and Anthony

Chapter forty-seven

First he said he wouldn't

January 12, 1954

'Winston,' Jock said this morning, 'was always a procrastinator, a waster of time. In the war he was not so bad, but now he wastes whole days. I don't mean that he has been in bad form. Sometimes he is almost as good as ever, but these occasions are rarer, and last a shorter time.'

I told Jock that I gave Winston a pill before the last Cabinet because he did not seem able to concentrate; when I said something to him there was a long pause before he answered. With a suspicion of a smile, Jock said that this might be due to inattention; they all suffered from this. 'Sometimes at meals,' he went on, 'Winston is very apathetic. Then Clemmie gives him a rebuke, and he'll pull himself together and be quite normal.'

January 21, 1954

While I was in the Midlands the P.M. got it into his head that he was 'chesty,' and Clemmie persuaded him to see her doctor. Winston admitted that it was a false alarm, muttering apologetically:

'I get anxious about my chest.'

And then, seeking comfort:

'But my walking is better. I can stride up the Lobby of the House of Commons quite briskly if I put my mind to it. You know, Charles, I am less keen than I was on the political scene. I don't know where I am.'

I asked him if he had any speeches hanging over him.

He grinned.

'Well, I ought to have. I told Woolton that I had been reading *The Dynasts* for hours on end. He wondered how I found the time. I explained that I didn't bother about other things as much as I used to do.'

521

Winston continued: 'The *Manchester Guardian* is very fair to me. Did you see what their Parliamentary Correspondent said?' Then, testily. 'You don't read the papers, Charles. He wrote that there was clearly no physical reason why the Prime Minister should put off his harness at this particular moment.'

He handed me the paper. I read that while other Ministers snoozed or looked vacant when not answering their own Questions, the P.M.'s mind was always active. But the truth is that he no longer follows the course of events as he did. He reads a novel or plays bezique with Clemmie, or sometimes just potters.

He showed me a scar on his right arm.

'That's where I gave some skin for grafting to Dick Molyneux after the battle of Omdurman—it hurt like the devil. His death is in today's paper.'

The P.M. grinned.

'He will take my skin with him, a kind of advance guard, into the next world.'

January 26, 1954

Winston is very subdued this morning.

'I wish, Charles, I had more energy. Can't you do anything for me? I must do something for my living. The *Mirror* is suggesting I am past it, and that I ought to resign. Read it,' he growled, passing me the paper. 'Why do I waste my time over this rag? I am being bloody tame. I defer too much to other people's opinions.'

February 4, 1954

When I was in the north of England Christopher telephoned. He was worried about Winston. This was his story: 'While Winston was answering questions in the House he had to keep bobbing up and down, perhaps as many as twenty times in all, and I noticed he got very short of breath. I tried to count his respirations from my seat just behind where he sits on the Front Bench. I made them fifty in a minute. What ought they to be? What does it mean, Charles? Can anything be done?'

I explained that his shortness of breath was due to degeneration of his heart muscle associated with old age, and that very little could be done for it.

'I'd like you,' Christopher continued, 'to put a call through to Winston. Ask him how he is, and he'll tell you all about it.'

When I telephoned, the P.M.'s voice was quite clear. 'Are you in London, Charles? Leeds—oh, you're still in the north.' His voice fell. He repeated what Christopher had told me. Then he said

522

a little abruptly: 'When are you coming back?' I knew that he was not happy about things. I went straight from the station at King's Cross to No. 10, where I found him in the pillared room, playing bezique with Clemmie. When he saw me he said: 'Here's Charles,' and putting down his hand, rose from the table and came over to an armchair. Rising with difficulty from its depths, he proceeded to illustrate how bobbing up to answer questions had been an effort.

'Now, I oughtn't to have done that just before you take my pulse,' he murmured. 'I don't think I've been so well, Charles, the last two days. I must go without lunch, or be content with something light about noon.' He paced up and down the room a little unsteadily. Then he collapsed into his chair with a deep sigh.

The P.M. rose, went over to a table and, opening *Punch*, handed it to me.

'They have been attacking me. It isn't really a proper cartoon. You have seen it?

'Yes, there's malice in it. The *Mirror* has had nothing so hostile. Look at my hands—I have beautiful hands.'

It was true. Those podgy, shapeless hands, peering out from a great expanse of white cuff, were not his. I was shocked by this vicious cartoon; there was something un-English in this savage attack on his failing powers. The eyes were dull and lifeless. There was no tone in the flaccid muscles; the jowl sagged. It was the expressionless mask of extreme old age. Under this venomous drawing was inscribed this caption:

'Man goeth forth unto his work and to his labour until the evening.'

On the opposite page the editor of *Punch*, Malcolm Muggeridge, supported this attack on Churchill's decline in an effusion entitled: 'A Story without an Ending.' It was full of spleen. Writing ostensibly of a Byzantine ruler, Bellarius, he wrote:

'By this time he had reached an advanced age.... His splendid faculties ... began to falter. The spectacle of him thus clutching wearily at all the appurtenances and responsibilities of an authority he could no longer fully exercise was to his admirers infinitely sorrowful, and to his enemies infinitely derisory.'

So it had come to this. Winston was hurt. Then, with an effort, he seemed to pull himself together.

'*Punch* goes everywhere. I shall have to retire if this sort of thing goes on. I must make a speech in a fortnight's time,' Winston continued; 'it is necessary when things like this happen.'

I said what I could. While I talked he sat feeling his pulse. 'Without taking it I can feel it isn't right. It keeps missing a beat, one–two–pause, one–two–pause.' And then with a touch of impatience: 'Well, I don't care. One day there will be no pulse to be felt.'

I noticed that when he rose to get a glass of whisky he lurched to one side as if he might fall. 'Are you going, Charles?' When he thanked me for my visit he made a little affectionate gesture, though I'd done nothing. He appeared to be on the point of breaking down. 'Clemmie,' he said, 'Charles is going.' And Clemmie put down her cards and thanked me too.

February 6, 1954

The attacks in the Press, the cartoon in *Punch* in particular, are still festering in his mind.

'It is an unpleasant situation,' he said. 'All this uncertainty.'

'You mean about resigning?'

'Yes. When my work is not good enough, when it no longer entitles me to be head of the Government, when I am no longer earning my keep, then I shall go. I shall not stay a minute beyond my time.' He paused. 'I'm not sure my work is good enough.'

'But surely,' I suggested, 'some of these attacks are not entirely disinterested?'

'Oh,' he replied, 'I must not complain. The Opposition are very good to me. You did not hear Fenner Brockway in the House? He said that when I was Home Secretary in the Liberal Government before the First World War I did more for the prisoners than any Home Secretary in the last fifty years. You know, he himself was in prison for more than three years during the First War, so he knows what he is talking about.'[1]

Winston made several efforts to relight his cigar, a messy performance.

'Rab is behaving very well,' Winston said. 'The Party has great

---

[1] In commending prison reforms to the House of Commons on July 20, 1910, Winston Churchill said: 'The mood and temper of the public with regard to the treatment of crime and criminals is one of the most unfailing tests of the civilization of any country. A calm, dispassionate recognition of the rights of the accused against the State and even of convicted criminals against the State: a constant heart-searching by all charged with the duty of punishment, a desire and eagerness to rehabilitate in the world of industry all those who have paid their due in the hard coinage of punishment, tireless efforts towards the discovery of curative and regenerative processes, unfaltering faith that there is treasure, if you can only find it, in the heart of every man—these are the symbols which, in the treatment of crime and criminals, mark and measure the stored up strength of a nation and are the sign and proof of the living virtue in it.'

confidence in him. He scorns to play for popularity, just does what
he thinks is right.' Winston smiled. 'I'm the greatest hunter of
popularity of them all. Oh, not for myself. But I keep advising the
Party to make concessions. I hate giving way as much as I did in
my hot youth, but I have come to know the nation and what must
be done to retain power.'

Jane Portal tells me that he plays cards half the night.

'Bed, cards and work, that is my life now. I don't mind when it
stops. After all, one can't go on for ever.

'I've been reading *Hamlet* since I saw it at the Old Vic. I don't
think I have read it before. No living being,' he mused, 'has been
analysed like that creature of the imagination. It is a tremendous
tale.'

He looked out at the fog drifting across the Horse Guards Parade.

'Bloody world,' he murmured. 'No human being would have
come into it if he had known what it was like.'

February 7, 1954

On my arrival at Chequers, before I went to Winston's room,
Christopher took me aside. 'You know, Charles, I have noticed a
marked deterioration in Winston in the past month. He is much
deafer—keeps turning to his neighbour, asking what is he saying?
People can't help noticing it. Besides, he made a box of his speech
about the rifle. He must pull out. He mustn't meet the new Parliament as Prime Minister. You are the only person who can persuade
him he ought to go. It ought to be his friends and not his enemies
who persuade him to resign.

'You can't compete with him,' Christopher laughed. 'Why, he
said to me today, supposing I did retire, and two months later some
world event happened, and I wanted to take a hand in it, I might
be very sorry I'd pulled out. It might well be a course of events
which I could have directed and perhaps guided the country safely
through.'

Christopher gave a great guffaw, and his untidy features were
stretched with glee. 'Well, Clemmie wants to see you before you go
to Winston. If you don't agree about his retiring you'd better have
it out with her.'

I found him in bed, coughing, sneezing and damning everyone.
When I had gone over his chest I asked him would he like me to stay
the night? 'If,' he answered, 'that is not very inconvenient. It
would be nice if you would see me out of this.'

I enquired about his plans.

'I shall do some work this morning. I like to feel I am doing

525

something no one else can do. I don't think we've done badly in the last two years. The Government has been sensible if not brilliant. Doing nothing is often very important in the art of government. You see, I have influence and a store of experience which no one else has, and I can decide things at a meeting as well as ever I could.'

In these times he is for ever grappling with his conscience, trying to persuade himself that he is fit to do his job and that the country will gain if he carries on.

Is he fit to be Prime Minister? The framework is everywhere giving way, but in his outlook he seems to have aged little.

Tonight, after the ladies had retired, he told a highly flavoured story, which he had retailed to the smoke-room of the House. 'Perhaps I oughtn't to have told it. I'm not sure it conformed altogether with the dignity of my office; but,' grinning, 'they liked it very much.' He giggled like a schoolboy telling a smutty story. In some ways that's what he still is. 'If I live to be ninety,' he said, 'I don't think I could ever become venerable. Now you, Charles, look quite venerable. You would have made a good bishop. Did you ever use bad language when you were with a battalion in France in the First War?'

Randolph, who is writing a life of the late Lord Derby for Longman's, brought to luncheon a young man of that name. His talk interested the P.M. A great-uncle in the firm had given Disraeli £10,000 for one of his novels. 'How much?' Winston queried. 'Which novel did you say?' Macaulay, Longman went on, was not read now; there was no demand for his books. The P.M. grunted that he was very sorry to hear that. Macaulay had been a great influence in his young days.

Richard Aldington's book on Lawrence of Arabia, which had greatly angered Lawrence's friends, brought Randolph into the conversation. The P.M. had spoken with scorn of the author's claim that he had started out to write an ordinary biography but that facts accumulated as he went on which led him to change his view of Lawrence. Randolph could not wait till the P.M. had done. 'Will you allow me to finish?' the P.M. said, his voice rising. 'But, Father, Chester Wilmot did the same thing. As he got into his book [1] he became convinced that you were right and the Americans were wrong. He did just what Aldington has done, and you had not a word of criticism. On the contrary, you were full of praise for his book.' The P.M. ignored Randolph's intervention.

During dinner the P.M. asked the Prof. a lot of questions. Did he give lectures at Oxford? If so, how many, and what was the size of

---

[1] Chester Wilmot, *Struggle for Europe*. (Collins, 1952).

LORD MORAN
portrait by Pietro Annigoni

LORD MORAN

Portrait by Piero Annigoni

his audience? What did he lecture about? What was Metaphysics? Did he encourage the undergraduates to ask questions? The Prof. answered: 'No, their tutors could see to that.' Did he like lecturing? The Prof.'s 'No' was even more emphatic; it bored him. Besides, he was not interested in undergraduates, he did not even know them by name. The lectures he gave were more or less the same every year. 'Did you,' the P.M. went on, 'enjoy Cabinets?' 'Sometimes,' replied the Prof. in a non-committal way. 'I loved every minute of them,' the P.M. mused. It is not often he interests himself in the way of life of someone else. We were all, I think, curious.

February 8, 1954

Winston said: 'Christopher wrote to that awful fellow, Muggeridge, you know the editor of *Punch*. He knows him, lives in his neighbourhood. Muggeridge wrote back saying that he was a journalist and must do his duty as a journalist. If he held opinions he must express them; said that he was one of my greatest admirers, but that I was no longer up to the job. He instanced the scuttle from the Sudan.'

There was a long pause.

'Many people in the country may feel as he does. I never liked it. But he isn't very logical. If I went, Anthony would succeed, and he is passionately for our getting out of the Sudan.

'Most people feel that the Prime Minister is always responsible; he should insist on getting his own way. That is not my idea. I don't think he should be an autocrat. I never was, even in the war. Of course I had great powers, my relations with Roosevelt and things like that ensured this. But the Cabinet ought to have their say. There are a few occasions, of course, when the Prime Minister must have his own way or resign.'

There was another long pause.

'There are always a lot of bloody rows in politics—that's what politics is for. A lot of fires blaze up, and it's my job to put them out. You get habituated to the heat.'

Christopher intervened to say he was lunching with a friend. Clemmie was in Scotland. Winston, with the hurt expression of a child: 'What do I do?' 'Wow,' said Christopher. 'I'll scratch. You can lunch me at White's or Buck's.' The P.M. growled: 'I'm damned if I do. I hate clubs.'

February 23, 1954

Winston had thought of publishing the Mau-Mau oath,[1] but it was

[1] The Mau Mau revolt began in 1952 among the Kikuyu tribe of Kenya. The

not really fit for publication, so it was decided to put it in the House of Commons in a place where members could read it.

'It is very long. No one could have made it up if he had tried. It is incredibly filthy.' Smiling grimly. 'It was certainly calculated to impress the recipient.'

I spoke to Oates[1] before I left, suggesting that perhaps I saw the P.M. at his worst, usually in the early morning. Oates thought there might be something in this.

'Last night the P.M. worked on his speech from ten-thirty until midnight, with a Foreign Office expert, making some very good points and directing the argument. Then he went over questions for today and finally read the early editions of the morning papers. He went to bed about a quarter to one. He was really as alert as before his illness. He is generally like that in the evenings.'

February 24, 1954

When the P.M. takes up the morning papers it is not *The Times* or the *Manchester Guardian* to which he turns, but generally the *Daily Mirror* or the *Daily Worker*. Perhaps he means to get the worst over first. I think sometimes he takes these attacks on his waning powers too seriously. At any rate, he has some good friends, and they are not all in his own party. The Parliamentary Correspondent of the *Manchester Guardian* writes today: 'The Prime Minister has grown into the affections of the whole House in the most striking way in these recent months.'

February 26, 1954

Winston in good spirits.

'I like to keep on speaking terms with everyone. I like to have the Germans on my side, but I don't want to quarrel with the Russians. I want to keep in with both sides.' Grinning. 'I'm getting a bit cheeky, getting things my own way.'

He flung himself out of bed and strode—a little unsteadily—to the bathroom, and began to shave. 'Simmons,' he called out, 'bring me a whisky. Charles.' I went in. He was sitting in front of the glass, shaving. 'I've had this cold hanging round me for three weeks; now I feel I've got the better of it. I did it myself, too. My own resistance

---

leaders administered oaths of a revolting and obscene nature, often by force, upon tribesmen, who were then obliged to kill or harm Europeans or loyal Kikuyus if so ordered. Appalling atrocities were committed.

[1] One of the Prime Minister's private secretaries.

to the bugs was built up. That's why I was able to throw it off. The microbes weren't killed by antibiotics.'

March 3, 1954

The P.M. rang up.

'I thought you would like to know how the speech went. It made a profound impression on the House. I dominated them.'

March 4, 1954

I found him breakfasting. He was wide awake and positively cheerful. Well, Christopher's right after all. The P.M. hasn't waited for the Queen's return to fish up an excuse for hanging on.

'I shall stay to the end of the Session—the last days of July. You see, the Ministers have most of them got Bills—they're up to the eyes in the details, and if I went when the Queen returns it would be very inconvenient for them. Harold Macmillan[1] told me a change in the Government would affect his plans. Besides, I've got back a great deal of my activity, physical and mental. I was struck by my vigour in winding up the Debate—so was the House. A good deal of it had to be extempore. I had to pick up and answer points in the Debate. I was doubtful before the speech how far I could do this. But,' he said reflectively, 'I've been at it so long. It is almost second nature. Of course, it is a great exertion, and next day I don't feel like doing anything.'

He rang me up in the evening after the Cabinet. He had taken a pill which he called the 'Lord Moran' in the morning; did this mean he could not take my 'special' pill in the afternoon? Would they clash? Not being able to get hold of me, he had taken a chance. 'You see, I had five hours on end.' I asked him if he was very weary. 'Not at all. Now I am going out to dinner with the American Ambassador.' This astonishing creature obeys no laws, recognizes no rules. He goes his own way, and I am left to pick up the bits.

March 12, 1954

Jock said this morning that the P.M. had not been in such good form for years, and I went to his room expecting to find the sun shining. But he looked up at me without a smile and said sadly: 'It casts a shadow over your work when you are going to give it up soon.'

As I left the room, Christopher met me. He told me that Winston had read out something he had said during the war, and had

---

[1] Minister of Housing and Local Government at this time.

added demurely, 'I was very modest then.' I told him it was a very different story now, and he was much amused.

March 18, 1954

At the Pilgrim's Dinner tonight I sat next Sir Frederick Leith-Ross, who was Chief Economic Adviser to the Government from 1932 to 1946. He said: 'Winston was not a bad Chancellor of the Exchequer; only he was not certain of himself. Of course, he was not the easiest Minister to work for, but he was stimulating and full of ideas.' 'Good ones?' I asked. 'About one in twenty of them were sound,' Sir Frederick replied. 'You see Winston is really an artist. His present Government began well. Their first Budget tackled things boldly in the right way, but they relapsed. The financial position at the present time is not much better than when the Conservatives took office. Things done in the first Budget were relaxed. There will always be discontent while the cost of living keeps rising. That ought to govern their thoughts.'

March 19, 1954

'I'm going to resign at the end of June. They have all been so nice. That's what gets me. If they had attacked me I could have snarled back. I don't want to be selfish.'

He turned round and looked at me with interest. I knew something was coming. 'I don't suppose many people have survived two strokes?' Without waiting for an answer he continued: 'Of course, any day I may get another.' He grinned. 'That would solve a lot of problems.'

March 26, 1954

I found Winston quite perky, to use Jane Portal's words.

'It seems to be widely felt that I ought to be able to bring things to a head over the Bomb. I don't know when I shall retire,' he went on. 'I have to think of other people. It may sound egotistical, but I don't know what the boys will do when I go. So far they have only produced television and the muddle over Egypt and the Sudan. I am more worried by the hydrogen bomb[1] than by all the rest of my troubles put together. I may speak on it next week.

'My book comes out in this country on April 26. The American edition led to no ill-feeling. On the contrary, there are a good many people in the States, according to Henry Luce, who said that I was

---

[1] The first H-bomb was exploded by the United States on March 1, 1954, in the Marshall Islands and was equivalent to 14 million tons of TNT. Russia exploded her first device in the following September.

right and they were wrong about the Russians. The Americans don't mind admitting when they are wrong.

'Max is very busy with his Lloyd George book. He bought his letters for a song—he has a thousand which Lloyd George and I wrote to each other. One, dated January 19, 1918, warns him very plainly that the Germans will probably attack us—that was two months before the March offensive. I advised Lloyd George not to weaken the army. The book was written for Max by Frank Owen. My label for him, my dear Charles, would not be in your diagnostic vocabulary. I never liked him.

'Max and Brendan have given up smoking and drinking.' He grinned. 'They must want to live very much.'

'I can't get excited about television. I can't make out what all the fuss is about. I have never given my mind to it as I did to the hydrogen bomb, but I feel this bloody invention will do harm to society and to the race.'

'You'll speak when they debate it?'

'I suppose so,' he grunted, sighing deeply.

April 1, 1954

My cook from Ayrshire takes her political views from the *Mirror*, and when it is particularly venomous about Mr. Churchill she brings me her copy. It was half-past nine by Big Ben as I made for No. 10 to see for myself whether the *Daily Mirror*'s attack had got under his skin. When I went upstairs his valet said he had not gone to bed until one o'clock and was still asleep. Outside his bedroom there was a pile of morning papers. I settled down to get the hang of things.

On the back page, under the caption, 'What America says about Churchill now,' the *Mirror* quoted the *New York Times*: 'For the first time since Parliament reconvened last autumn, Sir Winston appeared unsure of himself and tired. This wasn't the Churchill of two years ago and was only the shadow of the great figure of 1940. . . . In his replies to questions Sir Winston contradicted himself.'

I turned to the leader in the *Daily Mirror*, 'Twilight of a Giant,' to find what the Editor was about. He dotted the i's and crossed the t's.

'The exposure of the myth of Winston as a post-war leader is now complete. . . . There are demands in Parliament that Britain should give a lead to the world in facing the horror-bomb problem. . . . That we should talk straighter and harder to America. What is Churchill's reply? . . . Old and tired, he mouthed comfortless words in the twilight of his career. His battles are past. . . . This is the Giant in Decay.'

I turned to the *Daily Worker* and the *Daily Herald*. They made poor reading. The Left had made up its mind to get rid of the Prime Minister. His great influence stood between them and power.

When Winston rang his bell I tidied up the papers and went in. It was some time before I could get anything out of him. 'I woke at five,' he told me, 'and could not get to sleep again. I began thinking of my speech for Monday, and my brain became active.' 'Have you much to do today?' 'Everything in the world,' he replied gloomily.

I made up my mind to call on Norman Brook. He would know how the P.M. was shaping under the stress of events. Brook took his pipe out of his mouth and began: 'I've seen a good deal of the P.M. in the last few days, and he seemed to be in good form, storming at the Americans and at our Ambassador, and generally rampaging; but,' said Norman smiling, 'we take that as normal. He thinks he will put Attlee on his back on Monday, and I daresay he will.'

Jock thinks there'll be a row if the P.M. doesn't retire in July. I asked Brook if he agreed. There was a long pause. 'Yes, I think I do,' he said at last. 'They are thinking of a General Election in the autumn of 1955. If the P.M. pulled out in July that would give Anthony nearly a year and a half before the election to reform the Government and to give the country a chance of seeing how the new Prime Minister and his government are shaping. They want younger men, full of energy and drive. Of course, Winston's colleagues may not say as much. They feel an affection for him, as we all do. But I think this is the state of feeling. The one thing that is definite and fixed is the P.M.'s declaration that he will not lead the party in another election.'

I repeated my doubts whether Winston would be happy in his retirement. He had so often said to me: 'I must have something to look forward to. I can't do nothing for the rest of my days.' Brook had his doubts too, but he hoped the novel-reading habit would grow. 'Though of course,' he added smiling, 'zip may go out of it when it's no longer forbidden fruit—when he can read without feeling he ought to be working—the cigarette behind the bush business.' Norman Brook is a good friend of the P.M., loyal, yet missing nothing.

April 3, 1954

Following the Boat Race in Lord Waverley's Port of London Authority steamer, the Lord Chancellor said to me that Winston seemed in good form.

Lord Simonds: 'He seems more genial and mellow and urbane

these days. The only change I notice is that he is rather indecisive, avoiding decisions.'

Moran: 'He never liked making decisions.'

The Lord Chancellor appeared surprised. He went on:

'Gerald Kelly went to Chartwell to advise the Prime Minister which of his pictures should be sent to the Academy. You know, Moran, Gerald says Winston has no idea when he is painting well and when he is painting badly. He says that left to himself he would send all the wrong pictures.

'Winston said to Gerald: "I painted that before my stroke." Of course we in the Cabinet knew all about the stroke, but now he seems to make no secret of it. For a man who has had a seizure he seems wonderfully well.'

Chapter forty-eight

The Prime Minister
loses ground

April 5, 1954

As I made my way to the House of Commons to listen to the debate on the hydrogen bomb, the idea that the P.M. was in for a rough time never entered my head.

The discussion began quietly. It was in no party spirit, Attlee argued, that the Opposition had raised the issue. They believed that mankind had, for the first time, realized what it was to live in the world of the hydrogen bomb, and that this had brought disarmament within the reach of practical politics. It had made possible a British initiative, and the Opposition was eager for a meeting of the three Heads of State in the new atmosphere to reconsider the reduction and control of armaments.

Mr. Attlee, in his speech, rose to the level of his grave theme, and the P.M. himself, when he replied, called it a 'thoughtful and inspiring speech.' He seemed prepared to carry on the high argument where the leader of the Opposition had left it: 'These stupendous facts,' he said, 'glare upon the human race,' but in 'the universality of potential destruction' he found hope. And then, when the whole House was still and silent, seemingly numbed by the tragic issue confronting the world, he shocked Tory and Socialist alike by making it a party matter, a fight to be won on points.

The P.M. did not see why the Government should be blamed because the Americans could use the bomb without consulting us. When in 1945 he quitted office our position was very different. He then told the House for the first time of the agreement which he made in 1943 at Quebec with President Roosevelt. These were the facts: America and Britain agreed that they would not use the atomic bomb against third parties without each other's consent; and they agreed that there would be a constant exchange of information. That, he said, looking at the Members opposite, was

534

how things stood when the Socialist Government came into office. It was unfair to blame him because Mr. Attlee had abandoned this agreement.

Mr. Attlee sprang to his feet, while a wave of anger and astonishment swept over his supporters. He did not understand why the Prime Minister should say the Labour Government had abandoned the agreement; they had abandoned nothing. It was the McMahon Act, passed in 1946, which prevented the American Government from carrying out the Quebec agreement. (Here Mr. Attlee's memory was at fault. The Act did not touch America's obligation to consult and inform us. That was not lost until 1948, when, as Mr. Attlee himself admitted to the House in 1951, the Quebec agreement was 'changed and altered' and a new agreement drawn up by Mr. Attlee's Government.)

At this point the P.M. could have risen and told Mr. Attlee that he protested too much, that his recollection of the sequence of events was not in fact accurate. There would have been nothing more to say. But unhappily the P.M.'s memory served him no better than Mr. Attlee's: they were both equally vague about the McMahon Act; they had both forgotten the debate of 1951. So it happened that when Mr. Attlee spoke of the McMahon Act the P.M.'s mind went off at a tangent. Instead of pointing out that the Act had nothing to do with the issue before the House, he argued that if Mr. Attlee had shown the Senator the Quebec agreement there would have been no Act. The Senator himself had told him that two years ago.[1] This seemed to raise the temperature on the Opposition benches. Mr. Attlee leapt to the box. He was flushed and spluttering with rage. It was not his job, he protested, to tell the Senator; that was the business of his own Government. I quote from Hansard:

'The Prime Minister: I did not intend—— (Hon. Members: 'What? Did not intend what?') I did not intend—— (Interruption.) I have no doubt whatever that before the McMahon Act was passed he [Mr. Attlee] ought to have confronted the people of the United States with the declaration. That is what I believe will be the view of history.'

When Mr. Churchill had charged Mr. Attlee with abandoning the Quebec agreement there had begun a disorderly scene in the House, and now the shouts of 'Withdraw' and 'Resign' made it difficult to hear what was said. 'The Right Honourable Gentleman is dragging us down to the gutter,' the member for Cardiff shouted. 'This is disgraceful,' another member bawled. Mrs. Braddock ad-

[1] See p. 359.

vised the Prime Minister to 'get out.' The P.M. floundered on, and the Deputy Speaker complained that there was so much noise that he could not hear what the Prime Minister was saying. Each time the P.M. had to give way to an interrupter, he half sat down, keeping his hand on the table and using it to pull himself to his feet, slowly and with increasing difficulty, so that he might resume his speech. Lord Layton whispered to me: 'This will bring his resignation nearer.'

The Prime Minister struggled on: 'Now let me say only——' Mrs. Braddock: 'You have said too much. The Right Honourable Gentleman should look at the faces behind him.' And indeed the Tories were in poor shape: they could not manage a single cheer for their leader; they sat mute. Sir Robert Boothby, white-faced, rose from the Tory benches and walked out of the Chamber. The Opposition cheered wildly this apparent mark of dissatisfaction with his leader.

I viewed the turn of events with growing concern. I marvelled that this man, in his eightieth year, and only half recovered from a stroke, could stand at the box for a full hour in all that uproar and tumult, in the face of such bitter hostility, and yet remain apparently unmoved. He had bungled the business. All the same, it made me very miserable to sit there watching him without being able to help. I wondered how it might affect him in the Party. Would he have another stroke? And then, as if the House was spent, its venom exhausted, the cries of 'Resign' and 'Withdraw' died down and in the lull the P.M. meandered on. When they allowed him to finish his speech in silence, in some strange way it seemed to increase my fears. All expression had gone from his voice, which quavered into the high-pitched speech of a very old man; he had somehow to get through a set piece before he sat down, and he gabbled through it as if his only purpose was now to get to the end.

When he left the Chamber I followed him to his room. He was flushed, and now that I was near to him it was apparent he was controlling his excitement. But he stoutly denied that he was tired, brushing aside my questions. He felt very well, he lisped rather defiantly. That his speech had miscarried did not seem to occur to him. 'It will be all right in the morning papers,' he said. A secretary brought the Prime Minister whisky, and he said obstinately that he would go back to the Chamber. Christopher was rushing about, asking everyone for Hansard. And when the volume he wanted was put into his hands he began fumbling in its pages. 'Give it to me,' the P.M. said impatiently. 'Give it to me. I know where to find it.' As his eye skimmed the debate of 1951 his face fell, he realized the opportunity that had been lost. 'I have been too tethered to my notes,' he said sadly. When I left him I ran into Norman Brook hurrying along the passage and looking as composed as usual. Attlee had sent for him. He, too, wanted Hansard. The two old gentlemen were documenting their speeches after the event.

In the Lobby I met Lady Tweedsmuir, a friend of Winston's. She was sad. 'Yes,' she said, 'he lost the House.' Some of his supporters were talking in groups. They had long faces, and looked at me as I passed. In the House of Lords I found the Lord Chancellor having tea with Lord Salisbury and Lord Swinton; they had been in the gallery and were very grave as they conversed in low voices. At another table sat Lord Woolton with some Tory peers. When I joined them their conversation stopped. After an awkward silence Woolton said: 'I was glad to see you in the gallery; it must have been a great strain on Winston in his state of health. It must have upset him; at least I know it would have upset me.'

I went back to the Lobby, wondering if Winston was all right. Members were asking why the P.M. took a party line. I held my peace, but the answer is not in doubt: he was going to knock Mr. Attlee through the ropes. Carefully coached by Lord Cherwell, he had come to the house in that mood. Lord Cherwell's influence with the P.M. should not be underrated. Winston says he has a 'lovely mind,' and in such matters listens to his advice. The Prof. is an intriguing figure: entirely disinterested (he did not want to be a member of the Cabinet) and without any political ambitions, this old Alsatian is a man of iron; his logic seems to rule out counsels of moderation.

But I must not lay all the blame on Lord Cherwell. If he led Winston astray it was because the P.M. wanted to go that way. Even now, at the end of his life, when the nation, regardless of party, insists on looking to him as the sagacious world statesman, brooding over the incalculable future and thinking only of broad horizons and world events, his tastes lie in the rough and tumble of the House of Commons. He loves a fight. He looks forward to the 'tu quoque' of Questions in the House, enjoying every minute of the back-chat. In short, he is still at heart the red-haired urchin, cocking a snook at anybody who gets in the way. Why should anyone be surprised that he loves bickering? When he was in opposition those around him were always praying that he would leave Morrison alone and not indulge in dog-fights, which hardly befitted the world figure of the war years. And last week, when he was preparing his speech, those who serve him at No. 10 were hoping that he would leave Attlee alone.

537

April 6, 1954

Winston's second thoughts this morning were sober and penitent.

'Things didn't go as well as I expected. When one gets old one lives too much in the past. I ought to have told the House that I was very happy the Opposition had come round to my view that the Heads of the three States ought to meet, instead of . . .'

He was silent for a little, lost in thought.

'You see, Charles, I felt it was an extraordinary act of folly on the part of Labour to throw away the Quebec agreement. For years I have wanted it published. I was irritated that we had been relegated to a position where we had no say in things. Besides, I thought that what I said might have some effect on America. But there is truth in what the *Manchester Guardian* says this morning, that it's no use crying over spilt milk.'

I asked him if he had been upset by the hostility of the Labour benches. 'Oh, no,' he answered at once, 'I felt very well. After my speech I went to the Smoke Room and had a nice talk.' He pondered a while. 'I can see I must leave it alone,' he said sadly. 'Anthony did extremely well. It gives me confidence that he can control things so well. It was his best speech since his illness.'

He got out of bed and shuffled into the bathroom. I picked up *The Times* and read that the Prime Minister's 'sense of occasion had deserted him sadly' yesterday; he was responsible that 'the proceedings had degenerated into a sterile, angry and pitiful party wrangle.' There was a feeling, not confined to the Labour Press, that by his inept handling of the debate he had played into the hands of those who insist that he is no longer fit to be First Minister of the Crown.

Chapter forty-nine

A tired mind

April 8, 1954

I was settling for a night's work when the P.M. telephoned: 'Charles? Are you in London? I would like to see you. I have had a very hard day.'

I found him in his dark-blue velvet boiler suit, drinking brandy with Duncan and Diana. It was ten o'clock, but they had only just finished dinner. He had slumped into his chair, and appeared to have difficulty in keeping awake.

He began to tell me of his talk with the 1922 Committee.

'I met them at seven o'clock. I did not feel well. When I looked at them—it was a record attendance—I had a sense of helplessness. I felt very bad. I was tottering about. And then will-power came to my rescue. I spoke to them for twenty-five minutes. They cheered me warmly when I began, and again when I sat down, treating me with great respect. The meeting was about the pay of Members of the House. They believe the public will be restive if the House votes itself a rise in wages. But I told them Tory democracy must make a gesture. It was for the good of Parliament in the long run that the salaries of members should be raised.'

Duncan Sandys, who unlike Christopher cannot follow the old man's moods, launched out into an argument that it would do the Government a lot of harm if it was thought they had brought in higher salaries of their own accord. They ought to be careful that the Opposition was made plainly responsible for the rise. The P.M. did not seem impressed by all these tactics. But if Duncan had noticed that the P.M. was restless, he did not allow it to affect his purpose. He knew his facts—if need be he would stay up all night to master them—and he thought the P.M. ought to know them too.

As Minister of Supply he had become convinced of the necessity of economy in money spent on defence. Winston interrupted impatiently: it was folly to spend eighteen millions on a carrier and then a few months later to put it in moth-balls; it created a very bad impression.

The P.M. made little pretence of following Duncan's argument, though it was clear, cogent and forcibly put. There is good stuff in this fellow—great industry and guts—and it makes me sad that Winston is only bored by his son-in-law. Of course it has always been like that with him. If a man is not congenial nothing happens. In such circumstances he will obstinately shut his eyes to unusual merit.

Diana looked at me meaningly, as if to say, 'Cannot you get him to go to bed.' When I did nothing she whispered: 'Papa is very weary.'

And then Malenkov's name came up. Mary and Christopher had lunched with the Soviet Chargé d'Affaires and they gathered that Malenkov would welcome a meeting with the Prime Minister. Winston seemed to wake up.

'I feel better. I feel quite different.'

He began to talk with vigour.

'They will say, of course, that I may get a snub. I don't care. What does a snub matter if you save the world.'

Then he said with an air of finality:

'I shall not relinquish office until I meet Malenkov.'

'Where,' I broke in, 'would you see him?'

'Oh, there would be no difficulty. Ike said once that he would like to meet Malenkov at Stockholm. I could join the Russians there. It would be a great thing if he came out of Russia to meet me.'

He did not think the Russians would object to a meeting outside Russia on grounds of *amour propre*:

'At my age, with death at my shoulder, the Kremlin cannot speak of jealousy. They know I have nothing to gain. I would pop over to America first, to make it all right with them. I know them so well, they would not think I was up to dirty work.'

His eyes became more prominent.

'The Americans know I am the greatest anti-Communist of all time. Besides,' with a mischievous grin, 'they would see I was going in any case.'

Of course, the Cabinet might try to prevent him going. It would not be easy, but he thought that public opinion would be on his side. Duncan heard all this for the first time; he warmly welcomed the plan. Could it be set in motion quickly? Everything seemed ripe for

540

it. That could not last. Winston snapped out impatiently that nothing could be done until after Geneva.

'If the conference fails, I shall pick up the bits. If it triumphs, I shall go to meet Malenkov to exploit the victory. You will come with me, Charles?'

His voice grew stronger as he thought of what might come from such a meeting.

'I would ask for something in return for being an intermediary—Vienna perhaps. Austria might be set free.'

He told me how, in 1895, he had gone to the Cuban War:

'I wanted to hear the sound of bullets. I had only £35 left after getting my equipment, but in New York the Jeromes got active and introduced me to Burke Cochran. He was an Irishman, a pillar of Tammany Hall,[1] and one of their greatest orators. I can remember what he said even now. "The earth is a generous mother. She will provide in plentiful abundance food for all her children if they will but cultivate her soil in justice and in peace."'

Twice over he mouthed the words. He grinned.

'A long time later I repeated that up and down the country so often that at last Clemmie threatened that, if I said it again, she would not come about with me. I was not twenty at the time of the Cuban War, and was only a Second Lieutenant, but I was taken to an inspection at West Point and treated as if I had been a General. I was brought up in that state of civilization,' he said, 'when it was everywhere accepted that men are born unequal. I have always had a manservant,' he reflected with a whimsical smile.

'The world is in a terrible state. I have never seen such complications. Everything is in a tangle.'

Duncan: 'Well, after all, you would rather have it like that than exist in a boring world.'

P.M. (*eagerly*): 'Oh, no, I prefer a boring world, where the young people would be safe.'

The burst of energy had spent itself. He looked very tired. I tried to persuade him to go to bed. But he said he would go down to the Cabinet Room and do some work; besides, he must see the early editions of the morning papers. At last he agreed to go to his room if the papers were taken to him.

[1] Democratic Party Organization in New York linked with the big business houses of the Eastern sea-board at the end of the nineteenth century.

April 9, 1954

When I saw Winston this morning he said:

'It is sad about the loss of the Comet.[1] So much of our reputation abroad seems to depend on them.

'The result of the by-election[2] is disappointing. It is bad; we thought we might win.'

He grinned.

'It distresses me more than the Comet.'

He came back to Bevan and his friends, who were saying that America, unless she changed her tune, would have to 'go it alone.' He became very grave. Bevan's line was full of danger.

'I think she might retire from Europe, and rely on peripheral defence, or she might declare war on Russia and blow her to pieces. It will be two years before Russia will be able to take her bombs to America.'

I asked the P.M. what would happen to Germany if there was war between Russia and the United States.

'Poor lambs, they would be over-run and our neutrality would not save us. I wanted America to have a show-down with the Soviet Republic before the Russians had the bomb.'

April 12, 1954

The big idea still quickens Winston's pulse. He said today:

'I am told that if a thousand hydrogen bombs were exploded the cumulative effect on the atmosphere might be such that the health, and even the lives, of the whole human race would be affected. I would like to know if that is true. I want it investigated. If it proved true there might be in the world a new common interest in preventing these explosions.'

April 14, 1954

He lit a match and held his cigar over the flame.

'Poor Boothby, everyone is attacking him because he walked out while I was speaking.'

The P.M. can afford to be generous. It appears that there has been a sharp reaction in his favour. The *Observer*, for instance, puts down the explosiveness of the debate to strained nerves. The Old Man seems to have nine lives.

[1] The loss of two Comet airliners in rapid succession during the early months of 1954 dashed hopes for the ascendancy of the British aircraft industry. The whole fleet was grounded, and a special enquiry showed that metal fatigue was the cause of the disasters.

[2] On April 8 Labour held Edinburgh East with an increased majority.

He stopped rambling and became very solemn.

'I am thinking again about the question of retiring. I don't see why I should go. Yesterday I developed great strength. I talked more than anyone else in the Cabinet. I guided, collected opinions and expressed my views. It went on for three hours, and at the end I was fresher than most of them.'

April 28, 1954

After Anthony had flown to London from Geneva on Sunday, the Cabinet on his advice said 'No' to Dulles, who wanted to intervene in Indo-China. The P.M. said to me this morning:

'It is no good putting in troops to control the situation in the jungle. Besides, I don't see why we should fight for France in Indo-China when we have given away India. It would have given me pleasure to fight for Britain in India. We think we can hold Malaya even if Indo-China falls.'

He became more vehement.

'The French want us to look after France in Europe while America watches over her Empire. It just won't do. They are making E.D.C. impossible.'

He told me how he had prepared his speech for the House.

'The F.O. sent a mass of verbiage, Foreign Office clichés. It would have shocked the House. They only wanted to hear that we had no commitments.'

'It was woolly stuff?'

'No, not woolly, but they think they can hide behind a cloud of words. I tore it all to pieces. I took an hour and a half over it. I am slower than I was. But it is all in my head, I have a grip on the whole situation. I told the House that we must not let the Dien Bien Phu[1] battle mar the sense of world proportion. They liked that. We have the confidence of the House. I was going to make a ten minutes' speech at the Albert Hall on May 1st. Now I shall make it half an hour and deal with this situation.'

As he said this he jutted out his jaw.

'When I go I shall be bored doing nothing. I don't think it will do my health any good, but——'

He stopped. He looked very sad, as if life were over.

'This is a secret which you must tell to no human being. It might increase the danger to the Queen. I am going out to Gibraltar to meet her. I shall come with her in the yacht across the Bay. I am

---

[1] Situated in Thai country west of Hanoi. The post was occupied by French paratroops during the Indo-China war. After a fifty-five-day siege, it fell to the Vietminh on May 7 and led indirectly to the end of the war (July 21, 1954).

an experienced sailor. Then I shall go to America, perhaps ten days later. It's not yet fixed up. Ike can't fix anything till he is certain that Dulles will be there to hold his hand.'

He told me how Bevan had driven into a van and had then driven off; how a man in a car, with his wife, saw what happened and hopped out, taking Bevan's number as he drove off. The police came up and questioned this man, and he gave the number of the car, without knowing that Bevan was in it. It turns out that the man was a relation of Attlee—a chance in a million. The P.M. grinned broadly.

'If only I had been at Chequers that week-end it might have been the beginning of a coalition!'

I suggested that it was a poor way of doing things, to drive off.

'Oh, no,' Winston said; 'it might have happened to anybody.'

A handsome saying, bearing in mind what he thinks of Bevan.

'Did the Cabinet tire you?'

'No,' he answered. 'It amuses me.'

I walked across to the House, where I met the Lord Chancellor. I spoke of days when there was more leisure to think things out. 'Yes,' the Chancellor agreed. 'How true that is. I am a new boy in politics. After a lifetime in the Law seeking justice and truth, if that doesn't sound priggish, I have a feeling all the time that we are doing things looking over our shoulder at the voter.'

May 4, 1954

Winston said this morning with an air of finality:

'I shall go in July, unless of course more unexpected developments occur which makes me indispensable. I no longer find life attractive. There is no fun in it. People,' he added gloomily, 'are too base or too stupid to master the new ways of the modern world.'

If he had little or no say in things was it worth while to go on? He had never seen foreign affairs so complicated.

'Have you read, Charles, Stirling Cole's speech in the *Manchester Guardian*? You know, he succeeded McMahon as Chairman of the Atomic Energy Committee. He says that one plane on one mission can today carry more destruction than all the bombs carried by all the Air Forces of all the Allies and all the Axis nations during the six years of the war. We cannot at present defend ourselves against an atomic attack. We should not even have time to evacuate the great cities. Cole says that there is worse to come, that in three or four years from now Russia will be able to launch a saturation attack against us which will make retaliation impossible.'

Winston pondered for a little, his voice became stronger.

'There is one gleam of hope: revolutionary changes are taking place in the science of defence.

'Two high-ranking officers in the American Army told me yesterday that they had not read Cole's speech. If a man reads nothing else he should read that.'

The P.M. went on to speak with concern of the tension between the United States and Britain.

'The danger is that the Americans may become impatient. I know their people—they may get in a rage and say: Bevan is right. Why should we not go it alone? Why wait until Russia overtakes us? They could go to the Kremlin and say: "These are our demands. Our fellows have been alerted. You must agree or we shall attack you." I think it would be all right. There is fear in the Kremlin. If I were an American I'd do this. Six years ago in my Llandudno speech I advocated a show-down. They had no bombs then.'

He spoke of Dulles.

'He is a dull, unimaginative, uncomprehending, insensitive man; so clumsy. I hope he will disappear.'

To change his thoughts I asked him about the book.

'Ah, more copies have been sold of it than of any other book except the Bible.'

He smiled.

'I am not competing.'

May 7, 1954

'I am not going to Gibraltar,' Winston began this morning. 'There is too much work to do. Our majority was down to three. So many of the Party seem to be ill. I shall meet the Queen on Friday in a destroyer.'

May 8, 1954

Winston telephoned after dinner: 'I am streaming and I am having no treatment. Are there no quack remedies for a cold, Charles? I would like to try them. Is there no new spray I could use? What about another Dover's powder tonight?'

I advised him to go to bed. 'No,' he retorted with vigour, 'I am not going to bed. I want to go to a film. I feel quite well, I have no temperature. Why should I go to bed?'

I asked him if he would like to see me.

'Yes,' he replied, 'I'd like that.'

The visit was not really necessary. No fever, no cough. Just apprehension.

545

May 9, 1954

Saw the P.M. at Chartwell in the middle of the afternoon. 'Well, what about your cold?' Winston deliberately made some wheezing sounds for my benefit. 'Listen with your stethoscope—if you have brought it,' he added with a smirk. I listened to his chest and reassured him.

He said he was worried about the Queen at Gibraltar, he would not be happy till he heard that she had left for England. It was probably nerves on his part, but there might be demonstrations and even explosions.

'I was,' he continued, 'reading Hans Andersen's fairy-tales when Pitblado came into the room, and I gave a hell of a jump. Why do I do that? I never used to start like this.'

As I was leaving him I stopped to look at a small head of Napoleon. 'Ah, that was the most beautiful countenance from which genius ever looked upon mankind.' 'Someone said that,' Winston mused.

May 10, 1954

Exactly an hour was spent this morning in deciding whether he would go to London to answer a question by Bevan in the House on the proposed Security Pact for South-East Asia.[1] He sent for Pitblado, who handed him a paper. 'It is the Foreign Secretary's advice about dealing with this question; he sent it from Geneva.' At last I said: 'If you do not take care of your cold you will infect the Queen on Friday.' That went home, and he decided that he would not go to London. 'I get nothing out of Anthony. I don't know what is happening,' the P.M. murmured. This is a new tune.

May 14, 1954

To No. 10 today to see if the P.M. was fit to meet the Queen. At least that was my purpose. But it soon became clear that his mind was made up already. 'I am going to carry out the plans I have made,' he said. 'At my age it can do no harm to be in the open in this warm weather. It would be different if it were cold and boisterous. Besides, I have a lot of important business with the Queen.' But he had his own doubts. He asked me if his cold was still infectious? Would he give it to the Queen? He did not appear to

---

[1] The South East Asia Defence Treaty was signed on September 8, 1954, and set up SEATO as an Asian complement to NATO.

be interested in my answer. Then he shot at me quickly: 'If I did get more harm, what would happen? Would my cold go down into the smaller tubes?' He became more cheerful. He would be back at No. 10 at half-past one tomorrow. He asked me to lunch with him. 'You shall give me medical advice, and I will give you some nourishment.

'You are not pleased with me, Charles?'

'Oh, I don't know about that; there is a risk that this cold will settle on your chest. But it isn't a great risk, and I'm not going to waste time by presenting a minority report.'

He grinned broadly.

'My dear Charles, you know I always listen to your advice.

'I woke very early. I'm not sleeping as well as I did. Perhaps Providence, in view of the long sleep into which I must soon fall, does not deem it worth while to trouble over details. After all, does it matter so much whether I sleep six or eight hours? I fancy my mind is too active, it will not be put to sleep. There are so many grave matters calling for decisions. The French are dreadful—Laniel with his majority of two. If they had extended the period of conscription to two years the war in Indo-China might now be over. As it is, the real fighting was done by the Germans in the Foreign Legion. They were magnificent.'

As I left his room, Jane Portal said Chequers wanted me on the telephone. It was Clemmie. 'Is that Charles? Have you seen Winston? Do you approve of his going to meet the Queen? The Royal Family do not like picking up colds. They always keep their engagements. The Queen is very fond of Winston, but she will not be at all pleased if she catches his cold. Besides, there is the danger to himself. What do you think about that?' I saw no purpose in nagging. He knew the risks—such as they were—to the Queen and himself. He himself must make the decision. Clemmie did not seem to agree.

May 15, 1954

Mary, Christopher and their son, Nicholas, were in the middle of luncheon when I arrived at No. 10. Mary explained that they had to be at Buckingham Palace by 2.30 p.m. I decided to wait for Winston. He arrived late.

'How is your cold, Papa?' Mary asked at once. I was relieved when he said: 'Certainly no worse; on the whole I should say it is better. You were right, Charles, to oppose my going. I ought not to have gone.' He grinned. 'My behaviour was wrong, but your predictions were wrong too. I was on the bridge for an hour and

547

a half, and it was pretty draughty most of the time, but I have an idea sea air does a cold good.' 'Did you stand all that time?' asked Christopher. 'Oh, no, the Queen was kind enough to direct a chair to be brought for me.'

'Is she well? How did she look? Has she really enjoyed the trip?'

'I could not detect,' Winston answered, 'the slightest evidence of strain. When I came from the bridge to the saloon I did not at once recognize a masculine figure in khaki trousers. It was the Queen, who had taken off her coat. Prince Philip came in. "Come and meet your mother," he said to her. She laughed. "How can I, like this?" She is so completely natural.'

'Did you do much work with her?' Christopher enquired.

'There was no opportunity. We had a film, a very poor film, called *Maggie*. The cinema was very cold. I held a cushion to my chest like this, I was so chilled. I had never been up the river before. The Duke knew all about its history. I must get Lord Ivanhoe'— he paused—'yes, Lord Waverley, to take Clemmie.'

'Lord Moran will have port,' he said to the butler. 'Oh, yes, Charles, Stilton is wedded to port; let no man put them asunder. That terrible fellow has given you water,' he said contemptuously.

Winston handed me a letter from the President. He wants the P.M. to go to America on June 18. The letter ended: 'With warm regards, as ever, Ike.' 'You see, Charles, he wants a discussion between the two of us. He is very friendly.'

Christopher had spent the morning at Epsom and was full of the promise of one of Winston's horses. It had put up a great gallop. 'We have had nothing like it since the days of Colonist.[1] I put on £10 each way for you. It's running today.'

I said that a horse's legs were poorly adapted to meet wear and tear. Winston broke in:

'I don't know why, Charles, you, who know so much about Nature, should attack her so unfairly. When she designed a horse she never meant her to carry a man. You say a horse never lasts any time in a campaign. The unfortunate beast carries, besides a trooper, his saddle, and equipment and arms, a matter perhaps of fifteen stones.

'You did not think of that,' he said slyly, as he put his hand on mine in a disarming way.

Montague Browne[2] came in. 'It's time, sir, you went. You are

[1] 'Colonist II'—winner of the Jockey Club Cup, the Winston Churchill Stakes, the White Rose Stakes and second in the Ascot Gold Cup (1950).
[2] Anthony Montague Browne, Private Secretary on secondment from the Foreign Office.

due at the pier at two fifty-five.' The P.M. looked at his watch. 'Oh, there's plenty of time,' he said, pouring out another glass of port.

May 18, 1954

I asked the P.M. how his statement to the House on security and South-East Asia had gone. 'Very well,' he thought.

'Dulles lays down what he considers the minimum we must do if we are to hold the Communists, though he makes it sound terrible. But it is necessary that someone should stand up to them.

'The House was pleased at Anthony's appeasement. I like it up to a point, but only up to a point. He keeps away from me. Of course, he sends telegrams, but they are so involved; in half an hour's conversation we could clear up everything.'

May 21, 1954

Yesterday, Winston admitted, was a rough day: a long Cabinet with some difficult problems. He grinned broadly, and I waited for what was to come.

'I was determined that the Committee should agree to a free vote in the House on Members' pay. They were then certain to lose.'

He became serious.

'It is all wrong when members go about scratching a meal here and a meal there. Do you know, Charles, that a large number, perhaps as many as a hundred and twenty, of the Members of the House have less to live on than a coal-miner? Some of them, poor devils, are not sure of a square meal. When I think of the power and grandeur of their situation I am certain that it is most dangerous to keep them in poverty; it is just asking for trouble.

'They are very decent people when you know them. Of course, they are tiresome at times. One of them rose and proposed the motion that there should be no increase in the payment of Members until Old Age Pensions were put on a satisfactory basis. I said, "What clap-trap." As if the two questions had anything in common.'

His voice rose till he was half shouting.

'How absurd to link them together. The cost of increasing Members' pay would amount, at most, to £250,000, while the Pensions would mop up forty or fifty millions. Besides, if things go well we might get both. I got my way in the end; I am not afraid of them, and they know it.'

He contemplated his breakfast.

'I mastered them, though I was not very good. But they were very friendly after the meeting.'

Montague Browne, when I saw him, put the matter rather differently. The meeting of the 1922 Committee had not gone very well.

'The P.M. left here,' Montague Browne continued, 'with a definite idea in his head as to how he would run the meeting, and the speech he was going to make to them. But the meeting in fact went quite differently, and when the P.M. worked off on them the speech he had prepared it wasn't really to the point. You know, Lord Moran, he will play bezique, instead of mugging up whatever is coming up. Yesterday, for example, he knew that the Chancellor was going to the Committee, and he ought to have talked it over with him, but he gets absorbed in cards.'

Winston, on the other hand, had a good word for bezique:

'It is strange, you have to use your brain, but it is a different part. I find it restful. It takes my mind away from things. I lunched the Home Secretary. You know, I don't like seeing people I don't know well.'

'They tire you?'

He grinned.

'No, they bore me. I like familiar faces round me. Christopher, for example. He is very good.'

While he talked to me he bound round his cigar a ribbon of what appeared to be brown paper. 'It's an anti-slobber device invented by one of the jewellers. I cannot use it in public, or they would ask me what it was for.' A broad smile lit up his face.

'Anthony has had no experience at all of Home Affairs. He has always done the Foreign Office, and done it well. But I don't know how he will get on with all the Home stuff.'

May 25, 1954

'I am near the end,' he said.

I had nothing to say, and he went on:

'I am glad now it is the end.'

I could not let this pass.

'But you aren't in bad shape?'

'Ah, Charles, when you see me in the morning I feel strong and capable. Though even now my back aches as if I had had a hard day's hunting yesterday. And I have a tired mind.'

He yawned, opening his mouth very wide.

'I have got to make a speech to those bloody women in the Albert Hall on Thursday. It will take me four or five hours to knock together, though I shall only be on my feet for twenty-five minutes. I have cut it down to that. Of course, I can still do administration; my great experience helps me in that. I can force myself to do anything. It is the lack of desire, Charles, which worries me.'

We sat for a time in silence, Winston staring gloomily into space.

'There is no let-up at all; everyone wants to see me. I am a specimen, a kind of survival. I wish things were quieter in the House and that the world was more at rest. I hardly walk at all now. I have not been out for a month, except to go to the House or to Chequers.'

He pushed away his bed-rest, stretching his arms and yawning again.

Chapter fifty

Anthony had better accept

May 27, 1954

'There is a good deal of depression.'

'But surely the debate on Members' pay went as you wished?'

'Yes, I got my way, but I am depressed at the general bloodiness of things. I cannot see why anyone should want to quarrel with America. She stands alone in the world against Communism. The difficulty is how far we ought to go in restraining her from taking risks which we cannot share.'

His face lit up. 'I am seeing Billy Graham at noon and the Duke of Windsor at twelve-thirty.'

When I called at No. 10 this afternoon, to see if Winston was very tired after his speech at the Albert Hall, I was told that he had gone direct to the House of Commons. There I found him in his room in a cheerful frame of mind. The speech had gone well, he said.

'I was in command. My voice was hoarse yesterday—you know, I still bring up a lot of phlegm—but your namesake is very good; he did his job well.[1] After he had sprayed my throat my voice was loud, resonant and commanding.'

Winston said this with great vigour and verve, as if to say: that was how I did it.

'They had passed a resolution the day before against the payment of Members but I talked to them very straight, telling them they'd got to have it.'

He seemed lost in thought for a little.

'Anthony would not have liked it if he had been present. I was in the saddle; there was no sign of inferiority or failure. I can still make a great speech.'

I asked him whether Anthony was becoming impatient. 'Oh, of

[1] C. P. Wilson, ear, nose and throat surgeon to the Middlesex Hospital.

course,' Winston replied. 'He'd like me to go.' Then he added quickly: 'I don't mean he'd like me to come to any harm.'

He grinned: something was coming. 'Woolton was down to make a short speech, but the lady who was in the Chair doesn't like him, and she had arranged with the organist that immediately I sat down he was to play "God Save the Queen." Oh, no, I'm not tired. I could have gone on for an hour; I spoke for thirty-eight minutes. But what is wrong is that I should make such a bloody fuss over this speech.' I suggested that he had had a worrying week. He mused. 'My relations with Anthony——' he began and stopped short. 'The President and I consider Dulles and Anthony as a junior grade.' He said nothing for some time. 'Yes, Anthony would like me to go.'

June 2, 1954

As I approached Winston's bed he threw away the *Daily Express* with a sharp gesture of impatience. 'Max's paper attacks me in one column about the payment of Members, and on another page prays me to banish the idea of retiring.

'Stanley Baldwin, just before he resigned, proposed that members should be given an additional £200 every year, a sum equivalent to £500 now—and the unemployed could be counted in thousands then.'

His mind went back to the House of Commons.

'I despise these people's shifts and turns. The world deserves all it gets if it acts from fear. What else could I do?' he demanded hotly. 'Thirty Tory Members were determined to vote for the increase in pay, whatever happened.'

He mused for a time.

'I think they would be hard put to it if I go. My experience enables me to make a great many decisions quickly. You don't want me, Charles, to retire on health grounds?

'Anthony tells me nothing. He keeps me out of foreign affairs, treats them as a private preserve of his own. Now he doesn't want me to go to America. I don't mind. I'm ready to go alone.

'I shan't get a sleep this afternoon. I have a pretty full day. Two Cabinets with the Derby in between. A friend of Clemmie's dreamed some time ago that Lavengro would win the Derby. She put two pounds on this horse when it was forty to one. I think I shall back Lavengro. After all, a dream is a great thing. No one had heard of this horse then, while lately it has become more and more prominent in the betting.'

Pitblado met me in the passage. He told me that the P.M. had had a letter from Anthony which irked him. Pitblado smiled. 'They irk each other. Of course,' he continued. 'I can see the Foreign Secretary's point of view; when you are struggling against odds at Geneva[1] it is a nuisance to have a fixed engagement in Washington.'

June 4, 1954

Pulvertaft took a swab of the P.M.'s eye, which looked red and angry. When he had gone, Winston passed me the *Daily Mirror*. 'There is a serious row in the Party about this payment of Members. It is a crisis.'

'What will happen?'

'I can't tell. It depends on what attitude we take—whether we give way. The Cabinet has been in on everything. Nothing has been done without consulting them. Of course, Anthony has been absent a good deal, but he agreed with the line we took.'

His voice rose in anger: 'If they do nothing for Members who are worried about their income, I shall resign. I'm not going to run away. I don't mind a row with some of the bloody fools among the Tories. They didn't care a bloody damn about Old Age Pensions before this came up. Now it serves their purpose to think of them in connection with the pay of Members. I had made up my mind to go at Whitsuntide, until Harold Macmillan said it would be very inconvenient for members who had Bills to put through the House. Then I decided to resign at the end of the session. If I stay longer it will be because of this controversy over pay,' and he jutted out his jaw and looked very fierce.

I asked him if all this affected his visit to America. 'I shall know more about that after I've seen Anthony,' he replied. 'I could go alone, of course. Anthony doesn't want that.' He thought for some time. 'I may not go.' I said I wished he could have a short let-up; a little peace. He said grimly: 'We've had our peaceful time. Now there is going to be trouble. Geneva is hotting up. Things are not looking well. It appears to be a crisis. We can do nothing,' he said sadly. 'We have no weapons. We can only bleat: "Please do not harm us. We are powerless."'

'If nothing comes out of Geneva,' I said, 'it will not do Anthony any good.'

'Oh,' Winston said quickly, 'it's not his fault. He has made a tremendous effort.'

---

[1] The conference met on April 26, 1954, to discuss the peaceful settlement of the Korean question and to restore peace in Indo-China.

Cherkley, June 6, 1954

Max said Winston was out of step with the Tories about the payment of Members. I asked him if he thought the P.M. was worried about it. 'Not at all. Not at all,' Max shouted.

June 10, 1954

I found a message from the P.M. by the telephone: 'The Prime Minister would be grateful if Mr. Edgar King[1] and Lord Moran could call at 3 p.m.' We found him in his bedroom.

'My eyes are very troublesome,' he grumbled, 'worse than they have ever been.' He lay down in his frock coat on the bed (he had been at the Trooping the Colour in the morning). When King went to the bathroom Winston fixed me with a keen look. 'This will mean more work for me. Everything had been arranged. I was to go at the end of July. I was very happy about things. It was just a case of transferring the burden to Anthony's shoulders as smoothly as possible.' His voice became strong and resonant. 'Now it's a case of a world crisis. I could not leave the Government in an emergency such as this. It is not,' he added quickly, 'that I want to hang on to office for a few weeks more. But I have a gift to make to the country; a duty to perform. It would be cowardly to run away from such a situation. It would be wrong to think of the convenience of the Party now, to do something just to make it easy for Anthony to succeed, something which would allow him to get into the saddle before the Tories meet in the autumn. The Tories themselves would not wish it.' He paused. 'I don't know, of course, what view Anthony will take of this.' His jowl protruded as he said in firm tones: 'I'm in office, I'm master. I cannot plead that my health is so bad I ought to resign. My duty is plain. I shall postpone my visit to America for a week. Anthony would probably be able to go on the 17th, but he can't be sure, and the President himself suggested a postponement.'

June 15, 1954

Went to No. 10 to see if the P.M. was any the worse for the Garter ceremony at Windsor. He looked up and began turning over a pile of the morning papers. 'There is a very good picture of me in the *Yorkshire Post.* You haven't seen it? I can't put my hand on it. Oh,' he said, leaning over the bed, 'it's there on the floor. I haven't looked so dignified for a long time. The scene in the chapel was lovely.'

[1] Ophthalmic surgeon to Moorfields Eye Hospital.

It had been a long day. 'I began at eight o'clock,' he continued, 'and went on till after midnight. I had to climb a great many stairs up to the Chapel and afterwards in the Castle; and there was a lot of standing, and I'm no good at that. In addition, I had an audience with the Queen. There were some very important matters I had to tell her. Of course I was weary—physically tired—at the end of the day, but my head was quite clear. I could have gone on working when I went to bed. I'm sure I have more vigour than I had, Charles. There is no doubt in my mind about that.

'I'm not thinking of retiring, at any rate till September. I have written to Anthony that I do not intend to resign at present. I don't know if he has accepted it. He'd better.' The P.M. looked very grim. 'Could I tell them,' he added as an afterthought, 'that you thought I was as well as before the stroke?'

I advised him not to use the expression 'stroke.'

'But I like the word,' he said obstinately. 'Of course I know that I'm nearly eighty and that I may get another stroke any day. My heart may stop at any time, but my health is certainly no excuse for evading all these great issues, just because one doesn't know the answers. I'm not going to quit. It would be cowardice to run away at such a time. No,' he said with great emphasis, 'I shall certainly not retire when any day anything might happen.

'It is not'—and his voice rose—'as if I were making way for a strong young man. Anthony seems to be very tired. I detect strain in his telegrams. Sometimes he sends three thousand words in one day—and there is nothing in them. For instance, he wanted to change all the arrangements that have been made with Ike. He said Dulles had been very difficult and had attacked him. They showed me the account of what had happened, but it had to be pointed out to me how it could be taken as an attack on Anthony. Why, one of the incidents,' the P.M. said scornfully, 'happened a quarter of a century ago. I said I would not change my plans.' There was a pause and then the P.M. said quietly: 'He submitted. Look up my May 11 speech, Charles, and you'll see how I gave a warning that nothing can come of these talks at a lower level. They go on, day after day, endlessly. The Foreign Office keeps on splitting hairs. There is no one to say: "Bloody well go and do it." When I read what had happened at Geneva I felt a great sense of defiance. It was just like the war.'

June 17, 1954

The P.M. seemed in great heart this morning. 'The idea of a visit is a great success,' he began. 'It has been very well received. You saw what Ike said about the bridge over the Potomac river?' He picked up the *Daily Express* and read:

'The existence of a bridge over which thousands of persons travel daily isn't news. But if the bridge falls it is instantly news. We are trying to keep the bridge between this country and Britain strong.'

'I like that. And *The Times* is very friendly. I'm in control of the machine again. There is no one who has the cheek to suggest that I should go at the present time.'

His eyes were much better. King was in high favour. 'The bug has been been knocked on the head. I make my own defences quickly against infections.' As I was leaving he said: 'I'm glad you are coming, Charles. It will be very hot in Washington—it's over 100° there now, but I'll see you are comfortable and I'll insure you in case anything happens while we are in the air.'

Chapter fifty-one

The one consuming purpose

June 24, 1954

Soon after we left Heathrow in the strato-cruiser *Canopus* I dined with Winston, Anthony and the Prof. Anthony did most of the talking. He was critical of the present administration in the United States. Speaking generally, they were not so intelligent as Truman's administration; this lack of *nous* was particularly noticeable in the State Department. Foster Dulles acted foolishly when he walked out of the conference at Geneva; it was a miscalculation on his part; at any rate it failed to produce the effect he anticipated. It was stupid of the Americans to hold aloof; they hardly exchanged a word with the Russians, and never spoke to the Chinese. 'You cannot expect,' Anthony continued, 'to get anything out of people if you won't speak to them.' Winston grunted approval. 'I say "Good morning" to the member for Ebbw Vale,[1] but I cannot claim that I feel very friendly to him.'

Anthony believes that the Russians and the Chinese could be separated if only the Americans would not insist on boycotting the Chinese. At present, it is true, the Russians and the Chinese work together, and Anthony gave us an amusing illustration of this.

'Molotov came to me one day and insisted that he must open the discussion. I was in the chair and said to him: "You can't be the first speaker, for I have already got a name down." Molotov obstinately refused to give way. At last I said to him: "The name of the first speaker is Chou En-lai."[2] Molotov appeared very surprised; he had no idea, he said, that Chou En-lai intended to speak; he would certainly not stand in his way.'

---

[1] Aneurin Bevan.
[2] Chinese Minister for Foreign Affairs.

SIR ANTHONY EDEN

'China is a more formidable power than you will admit, Winston. Unlike the Russians the Chinese do not seem to be frightened by the hydrogen bomb. Perhaps they don't know much about it.'

It was difficult to tell how far Winston was following this dissertation. He has always been sceptical of China as a great power, and when Roosevelt used to say that it was better to be friends than enemies with a country of four hundred million souls, he would listen in silence, but later he spoke scornfully of 'little yellow men.' It would seem that he has scarcely moved an inch from his attitude towards China since the day of the Boxer Rebellion.[1] In truth he is not interested. What matters to him is the situation in Washington. 'How,' he asks, 'can we expect them to see our point of view if we start nagging?' He was disturbed by Anthony's conversation, though he was resolved not to get into an argument with him.

The P.M. bottled up his misgivings, so that I could not detect a vestige of ill-feeling between the two men as they talked during dinner; they were gay and communicative. Winston was particularly cheerful, looking incredibly young, his face pink and unlined, his manner boyish and mischievous. Anthony had been to Wimbledon, and his face was reddened by the sun, but he looked tired. He told us that he had found the six-hour sessions at Geneva very fatiguing, especially when he was in the chair. Winston did not appear much interested in his account of Geneva. Perhaps, in the plane, he had difficulty in hearing what Anthony was saying.

The P.M. always claims that Anthony and he agree on most things in the field of foreign affairs, though it is not often very noticeable; they don't seem, for instance, to have much in common about Suez, or China, or in their approach to Americans. It is true that Winston has appointed Anthony as his heir—after all, someone has to follow him—but he still regards him as a young man, and is not much influenced by his views.

Besides, when Winston's mind is set on something he can think of little else. He has always felt that the future of the world is bound up with the union of the English-speaking races. Now, at the end of the long day, nothing else seems to matter. He is going to America— he thinks it may be his last visit to his mother's native land—to see if anything can be done to narrow the rift about Moscow that is opening up between the two countries, and here was the Foreign Secretary bleating about what was wrong with the Americans. Later he confessed to me his misgivings. 'I hope Anthony won't upset

[1] The Chinese attempt to oust foreign influence from their country (1899–1900). After the massacre of many Europeans and Chinese Christians an international relief force re-established law and order.

559

them; they are so kind and generous to their friends.' He changed the subject rather abruptly.

Picking up my book, General Spears's *Prelude to Dunkirk*, he began: 'Hell knows no fury like a woman scorned. Spears used to love France; now he hates her. Some while ago I stipulated that he should not publish anything for a certain time. The time is up. I haven't read the book, but I expect he has made up for lost time.'

Winston was gazing out of the window at the clouds below.

'I wish flying had never been invented. The world has shrunk since the Wrights got into the air; it was an evil hour for poor England.'

He sighed heavily and turned from the window. He was tired now, and when he spoke his remarks were of a desultory and personal nature, as if he no longer felt equal to connected discourse; calling the steward, he demanded caviare. He grinned broadly.

'Do you remember, Charles, when Joe offered it to Stafford Cripps and he wanted to know whether it was eggs or fish? He said he could take it if it was eggs. Stalin didn't know which it was; he said he didn't worry about such questions.'

At last the P.M. called for his servant and prepared for bed.

June 25, 1954

No one, save Winston, seems to think that much will come out of this visit to Washington. Christopher says the Americans are hopping mad with us. There will be some straight talk, and Winston will be disappointed: he won't get what he expects to get. But surely, I tried to argue, Ike is friendly? 'He doesn't count,' Christopher rapped out. Winston, for his part, has never been a Doubting Thomas. He seems to have taken a new lease of life since we left London. At ten o'clock this morning by English time he called the steward and ordered him to take away the whisky and to bring champagne. Then he proceeded to make a meal off caviare and toast, though he had had a hearty breakfast only an hour before.

Four hours later the *Canopus* made a bumpy landing. We all waited for Winston. Presently he appeared, shuffling down the space between the seats of the aircraft. Christopher reminded him that he was wearing his spectacles, whereupon he stuffed them in his pocket without putting them in a case. Then Christopher said something in his ear, and he took the unlighted cigar from his mouth and handed it to the detective, while Anthony watched, with a grim smile, all these preliminaries to taking a curtain.

Before we landed, the P.M. handed me a sheet of notepaper: 'You might like to read it. That's what I shall broadcast. It's simple

560

and clear,' he said. When he left the microphone on the airfield a way was made for him through a throng of photographers. Then the procession of cars began to move, and gathering speed rushed down the road, all the police sirens wailing, so that there was a great screeching sound. Every car on the road, when it heard the summons, pulled up obediently to the side while the high priests of democracy passed by.

When the evening came I made a point of arriving at the White House before the P.M. began to dress for dinner. He was with Anthony. Christopher came out with an important air and admonished me in his loud voice: 'You know, Charles, Winston has been in conference without a break since he left the airfield at nine o'clock this morning.' He said this as if I were personally responsible. However, when I saw the P.M. my doubts were at once dispelled. His eyes were full of life and he was in tremendous spirits. He turned to me solemnly:

'The day has been an incredible success. It is astounding how well things have gone. Whatever cropped up, we seemed at once to agree on the principle which ought to guide us in seeking a solution.'

There was a long pause, then the whites of his eyes began to show between the pupil and the upper lid, and speaking with suppressed excitement he said:

'This may lead to results which will be received by the world with a gasp of relief and amazement.'

He appeared to believe that Ike liked his idea of meeting the Russians. He would go with Anthony. 'It's my show entirely. I have been working for this for a long time.' I asked him when he would go to Russia. 'It might be in July,' he answered, as if he were parting with the information reluctantly. He asked me not to discuss this with anyone. 'I tell my young people,' he explained, 'they must not talk about it, and I don't want to set a bad example.' He asked the hour. 'Oh, I've plenty of time.' Then he lay on his bed, and Kirkwood, his valet, brought him hot packs, which he held to his eyes, that were red and watering. As last he got into his bath, holding an enormous sponge as a fig leaf. 'Kirkwood,' he shouted, and without waiting called out in more peremptory tones, 'Kirkwood, turn on the hot tap.' He dressed very slowly, trying on one or two white coats in turn. While he was still deliberating which to wear, Anthony came in and commended his smart appearance. 'We ought to go,' he said mildly; 'the President will be there before us.'

Marshall invited me, when dinner was over, to sit beside him. The strain of the war on soldiers in high places had been grievous; it had taxed his strength until, as he told me at Quebec in the summer of

1943, his heart was 'all over the place.' What happened to him after he came back from China [1] I do not know, but it appears that some time ago he had a serious operation, and I was told that he could no longer concentrate for long on anything.

Now he lives in the past, so that we talked of the war for some time. He spoke of Winston with a kind of affectionate pride, telling me how he had been against the invasion of Normandy, though in the end he had animated and inspired the whole venture. Marshall affirmed, with an indulgent smile, that it had been part of the task of the Chiefs of Staff to wean Winston from wrong strategic conceptions—a point Alanbrooke made more than once. He did not tell how by the force of his character he himself dominated the Combined Chiefs of Staff during the war and prevented Winston getting his way with Franklin Roosevelt.

Great men are two a penny in wartime. It is not that there are more of them about: just that the public is in the mood for the grand epithet. And so, as far as I can follow military history, the admirals and generals have always been allowed to bask in the sun, that is if they won their battles. Their characters hardly seem to count; small busts of Napoleon and Nelson keep Winston company in his bedroom. And yet in this war no one, I suppose, thinks of a general as a military genius dictating the course of events by his craft. It is what Marshall was, and not what he did, that lingers in the mind—his goodness seemed to put ambition out of countenance.

The President came over and sat down and talked to Marshall about the war. It seemed to be his lot in life to do jobs that he did not care for, and he made no secret of the fact that his duties as President came under that heading.

June 26, 1954

Why Winston was so cock-a-hoop yesterday I cannot tell, unless he has come to some understanding with Ike about meeting the Russians. I can think of nothing else that will explain his mood. If he can only talk with Malenkov he is sure things will happen. This idea has completely taken possession of him. It has indeed become an article of faith and is never out of his head for long.

To hold off the threat of war until it is no longer worth while for anyone to break the peace—that is the only thing left to him now, his one consuming purpose. Without it there is little meaning in life. In his heart he has a great fear: he dreads another war, for he does not believe that England could survive.

He was talking to me yesterday of the war:

[1] Marshall visited China from December 1945 to February 1946.

'They were terrific times, and yet I am more anxious now than I was then. My thoughts are almost entirely thermo-nuclear. I spend a lot of time thinking over deterrents.'

It is his belief—and this he holds with a fierce, almost religious, intensity—that he, and he alone, can save the world from a frightful war which will be the end of everything in the civilized globe that man had known and valued. And, he keeps saying, time is short.

No doubt there are other instincts at work. For one thing, Winston's mind is practical; he is, as he will say, a political animal. He knows that to bring about a lasting peace with Russia is now the only plausible reason for hanging on to the leadership of the Party. If there was no change of heart in the Kremlin, if a policy of peaceful co-existence was only a myth, it would be difficult to justify his holding on to power in his eightieth year, when he has not completely recovered from his stroke.

He has not forgotten the Socialist taunt of 'War-monger.' It hurt him then, it hurts him now. They had to admit that he had been a great war Minister. He would show them that he was as great a peace-maker. He would like, he once owned to me, to end his days with that final, resounding triumph, which would round off his story in war and in peace. And yet, when the P.M. presses for a meeting with Malenkov, he is not altogether thinking of himself. It is not just the old craving for personal distinction. I have learnt, where Winston's motives are concerned, to keep repeating to myself: 'Winston is not worldly.'

An idea that stirs his imagination can still drive that crumbling frame to surprising exertions. He knows that the longing for peace represents the deepest feelings of the country. Only yesterday he confessed that he would like once more, before he went, to speak for England as he had done in the trough of the war, if that would avert another war. He stopped and I saw that he was in tears.

But before he can do anything with Moscow it is necessary to bring the President into line with his plan for pacifying the world. That is really why he has come to Washington. He does not underrate the difficulties of his task. America does not trust the Soviet Union. She cannot forget Stalin's duplicity; she cannot believe that a Russian promise is worth the paper it is written on.

I had tossed about in bed piecing together what Winston had told me, so that when I went to the White House this morning I somehow expected to find him worried and irritable. He was reading Spears's book and looked up with a smile: 'It was two o'clock before I went to bed,' he confessed. 'You were then twenty-four hours out of bed,' I put in.

'I do not feel at all tired. There is something in the magnetism of this great portion of the earth's surface which always makes me feel buoyant. Take my pulse. I don't think I am any the worse for two of the most strenuous days I can remember.'

Dulles is the key man in this business, and I asked Winston where he stood.

'Dulles wants to be friendly, and after all,' he added dryly, 'why I came here was to make friends.'

Roger Makins,[1] also, had a good word for Dulles, saying: 'He is very friendly, and is, too, quite intelligent.' For a year Roger has been trying to persuade Anthony that any change would be for the worse, that from our point of view Foster Dulles is a better Secretary of State than anyone else in the running for the post. It appears that the President saw Anthony yesterday in order to try to blunt the sharp differences between him and Dulles, while Winston is to see Dulles today to carry on the good work.

When there are such great issues at stake the P.M. cannot understand why Anthony should go out of his way to find faults in the Americans. He is particularly annoyed that he should choose such an occasion to have a row with the Secretary of State. Does he not realize that without the United States Britain is alone?

All the long afternoon I kept wondering how Winston was weathering the day. I determined to go to the White House while he was dressing for dinner and see for myself. I found him rather flat. He is suffering from a reaction from the unusual exertions of the last few days and is very weary. He felt his speech to about thirty members of Congress had gone well. It was quite unprepared, 'Unpinioned on the wing.' He asked Christopher what reports had come in from the 'Congress ferret.' But it appeared that the ferret had not yet returned. However, Hagerty, the President's Press Secretary, said the speech had made a great impression on all the Congressmen, and had gone with a swing. The P.M. seemed much relieved. He complained that the English papers were badly informed. He exclaimed impatiently:

'Why, they draw a picture of Anthony and me meeting angry and unsympathetic Americans, the exact opposite of the truth. I have never known them so friendly.'

He picked up the *Manchester Guardian*.

'Look at this in a sober journal. It speaks of a "bleak background." That is all wrong. I feel in my bones things are getting better and better.'

After dinner Ike came over and took a seat beside the Prof. and

[1] At this time British Ambassador in Washington.

me, and without any preliminaries began to talk of serious things. 'Freedom itself means nothing unless there is faith.'

He did not think the particular form of religion mattered, he had never attached much importance to ritual, but there must be faith. Then he rather abruptly changed the subject.

At eleven o'clock Winston rose and asked the President if he might be excused; he must make up the six hours' sleep he had lost through putting back the clocks.

When he got to his bedroom he slumped heavily into a chair and did not seem to have the energy to get into bed. He admitted he was 'all in.' 'The bedroom,' he complained, 'is very hot and airless. Is my pulse all right, Charles?' At last we got him into bed. 'Now I'm flat on my back, take it again; it may not be so quick.' He did not want me to go, and I sat for some time by his bedside. I shall be glad when we get him on the boat.

June 27, 1954

The P.M., after a long night's rest, had forgotten his misgivings. When I urged him to fit things in so that he might get a sleep in the afternoon he said shortly: 'I shan't have time for a sleep. Besides I shall only lie down if I need sleep. I feel quite well. I am not at all tired.' He had telephoned Jock at a quarter to nine in an injured tone, complaining that he had no papers and no news. Jock left his breakfast and hurried to the White House. After a two-hour film of the Queen's journey we returned to the Embassy and were sitting down to luncheon when a messenger arrived from the White House. A certain document could not be found; the Prime Minister wanted it at once. Jock, who had just arrived at the Embassy, got up from the table and returned to the White House. When he reappeared forty minutes later he said quietly: 'I would not mind if he had looked at the paper when I gave it to him.'

Tea with the Prof. Certainly he is nothing if not logical; he began at once to tidy up the situation, as if he were spring cleaning his study at 'The House.'[1] He had had a straight talk with Bedell Smith.[2] There were, according to Lord Cherwell, only two courses open to us. We could have a show-down with Russia—the Prof. was not against this; on the contrary, it might in the long run be better than glaring at each other for forty years, counting bombs. Bedell Smith was horrified at such a thought. 'Very well then,' persisted the Prof., 'we must learn to exist side by side with Russia.' But Bedell's idea of co-existence was to draw a line, and if the Communists crossed it, well, they must take the consequences.

[1] Christ Church, Oxford.   [2] General Bedell Smith, Chief of Staff to Eisenhower.

'Ike,' said the Prof., 'would like to be a constitutional monarch, keeping outside politics. He is suspicious of politicians, fears they will make him do things he does not want to do. The American Constitution,' the Prof. concluded, 'does not work when the President abdicates.'

Then he told me how the President had gone off to the Presbyterian Church this morning to pray for the country. Dulles also is very devout; he is a great figure in the Presbyterian world. The Prof. referred to their faith with amused tolerance, as one might talk of someone who believed in ghosts. He believes Winston will have done a good job of work at this Conference if it is made clear that we shall line up with the Americans whatever happens. The Prof. rose and walked very gingerly to his room. He has been warned by his doctor that his heart is not what it was and that he must go slowly.

When I had changed I went to the White House and found the P.M. in his room. He began at once about the need for more time in order to tidy up what had been done during the Conference. He would like to come back to Washington after Ottawa, work for a couple of days and then return to England by air. It would be much better than wasting the time at sea. Christopher argued that the P.M. had still a day and a half before he must leave for Canada. But Winston blew up. 'It's not enough. Great things hang on what we do here.' He stumped off to the bathroom. 'Charles!' he called out, 'Christopher!' He was lying flat in his bath, with only his nose and mouth out of the water. 'I don't want you to think I'm ungrateful. I know you arranged the sea trip for my good. But I have to think of more important things than my health.'

Winston came into the room in his bath towel. 'Is Mr. Eden back yet?' he demanded of his servant. He went on talking of what he would gain if he had more time in Washington. Then he shouted: 'Kirkwood! Mr. Eden must be back. Oh, go and see. Christ! I hope they haven't quarrelled and killed each other,' he added with a grim smile. But he was not really amused at all; he was on edge about the result of Anthony's meeting with Dulles.

The door opened. 'Can I come in?' It was Anthony's voice. Winston jumped up and advanced towards him with outstretched arms. 'Anthony, my dear, tell me what happened.' Before I withdrew I heard enough to know that the interview had gone well. 'We talked about a number of things,' Anthony began, 'E.D.C., Egypt, with I think very good results.' Winston relaxed, and subsided heavily into a chair.

*

It was late when Ike rose from the dinner-table and the party broke up. I followed Winston to his room. He was not at the top of his form. I think the English papers had upset him. He handed me the Saturday issue of the *Manchester Guardian*. He had underlined in red ink a statement by Alistair Cooke: 'Sir Winston has never yet managed to have a talk alone with President Eisenhower.' 'What absolute nonsense,' he snorted. 'A most inaccurate statement for such a sober paper. Why, I have spent about three hours every day talking to the President alone.' Christopher came into the room. 'Do you know that fellow, Cooke?' he asked. 'You do. Well, you might get into contact with him.' 'I'll telephone him now,' said Christopher rising. 'No, no, not now,' Winston shouted after him, 'and not from here.' It was not a friendly article. I read that there had been a ritual cheer for Sir Winston Churchill at the airport, but that there was more interest in the feud between Mr. Eden and Mr. Dulles. Sir Winston was 'ageing fast.' There were two columns of this stuff on the front page under the provocative heading, 'Mr. Eden steals the limelight.' It is not perhaps surprising that the P.M. had said to Christopher, 'He has got his facts all wrong. I am not jealous,' he added quietly. 'I have no need to be jealous.' Christopher went off to bed. Winston admitted he was very tired; he sat in his vest on the edge of the bed, like a spent runner. 'You have had a good day,' I said. 'All the Conference seems to me one day,' he answered; 'it never stops. Don't go, Charles, your presence is always a comfort to me.' At last he settled, ordering Kirkwood to turn over the pillow so that it was cool to his head. 'Au revoir, Charles.' I said 'Goodbye' as I was leaving the room. He corrected me: 'Don't say "Goodbye." Do come and see me when I wake in the morning— I suppose I shall wake. I may feel better then.'

June 28, 1954

An argument broke out about Guatemala[1] while we were dining at the Embassy. Bob Dixon, who had been Anthony's private secretary and is now our representative at the United Nations in New York, isn't the man to take unnecessary risks. Yet he maintained that America had been grossly inconsistent. She had supported the kind of policy in Guatemala which she had condemned as immoral when practised by the Soviet Union in Greece or Korea.

---

[1] Revolution broke out in Guatemala on June 18, 1954, after anti-Communist forces had entered the country. The rebels were supplied with American arms through Honduras and Nicaragua.

It was the most flagrant act of aggression against a small state. Winston, speaking as from the Bench, said:

'A great principle only carries weight when it is associated with the movement of great forces.'

It was important, he said, to keep a sense of proportion.

Raising his voice: 'I'd never heard of this bloody place Guatemala until I was in my seventy-ninth year.'

'Come now, Winston,' Anthony interposed mildly.

The P.M. took no notice. 'We ought not,' he continued, 'to allow Guatemala to jeopardize our relations with the United States, for on them the safety of the world might depend.'

'But Prime Minister, this is a moral issue,' Bob persisted. 'It is surely a question of right and wrong.'

The P.M. gave a great snort. Bob Dixon got very red in the face, but he seemed unable to stop arguing with Winston, though you don't have to be a diplomatist to sense how unprofitable such an argument can be. Every sentence began 'But, Prime Minister.' Anthony listened demurely, though it was plain he was on Dixon's side. From time to time Roger Makins gave a great guffaw. At last I said that, without taking sides, I thought there would be general agreement that Guatemala was not sufficiently important to allow it to interfere with the night's rest. I got up, and Lady Makins, who had joined the party, backed me up.

Winston was wide awake and reluctant to go to bed. Everybody else had risen, but he remained slumped on the couch. At last he levered himself out of his seat, and I took him to his room. 'You know, Charles,' he expostulated, 'I feel very lively; I don't know whether it is the magnetism of this country or your pills.'

'I hope you did not get cold sitting on the balcony in the chill night air.'

'Portico, not balcony, Charles.' A mischievous smile softened his correction.

I reminded him how, in one night as it were, Arthur Balfour brought England to the side of America when she was threatened with war by Spain.[1] 'I'm sure the F.O. of that day found a dozen reasons—no doubt very good reasons—for supporting Spain.'

'Exactly,' said Winston with conviction, 'very true.' It may be, of course, that it was not quite as simple as that. 'I don't want to go to bed,' the P.M. grumbled. 'I don't feel tired. I shan't sleep.'

[1] Anglo-American relations were improved by British diplomatic sympathy with the United States during the Spanish–American War 1898.

June 29, 1954

'Do you agree,' I had asked Lord Samuel one day, 'that Winston is not interested in theory?' Samuel thought for a moment before he answered. 'He is certainly not attracted by principles, as were John Morley and Balfour and Asquith. Winston asks: Will it work in practice? I don't think,' Samuel continued, 'he has ever taken any interest in speculative thought, in philosophy or religion.'

All the same, at times I have caught him musing on the art of government. It was at the back of his mind today when the Ambassador invited Dean Acheson to luncheon to give the P.M. an opportunity of learning the point of view of the Democrats. Winston, however, did all the talking; Dean Acheson's opinions did not appear to interest him.

France, the P.M. said with conviction, would do no good until she faced certain constitutional changes. They must get rid of proportional representation, and go back to the two-party system. Then he turned to America.

'If I were a member of Congress I would seek to change the system whereby none of the Administration are elected.'

He beamed at Dean Acheson.

'I think a great deal of the importance of an Opposition; if one party is more or less permanently in power it means half the nation is irresponsible. Why,' said Winston, warming to his theme, 'look what Britain owes to Labour in opposition. I am not thinking of the things they did when in power, such as bread rationing, which no Tory Government dare touch, but look at the risks Attlee and Morrison are taking now in backing E.D.C. when their Party dislikes it so much.'

The P.M.'s interest soon flagged.

He, alas, is always so taken up with his own thoughts that he is not really interested in what other people are thinking. He turned to Acheson and asked him about Egypt. Hardly pausing for an answer, he began to give his own views.

Ottawa, June 30, 1954

Washington took a good deal out of Winston, and he was already tired when he arrived last night at Ottawa. After his wonderful *tour de force* at Washington we had expected great things, but when faced by a string of questions at the Press conference at noon today he was listless and appeared jaded. At the end he got very sentimental over Canada and her connection with England, but there was more strength and life in his voice when he went on to speak of

Canada's future and her boundless resources. She was the master link of Anglo-Saxon unity. This phrase was hammered out in the air on the way to Ottawa.

When he had done, the spark died out as suddenly as it had come to life, and it was in a very subdued mood that he sat down to luncheon with the High Commissioner. And then, as he put it later, 'with the help of some liquor I came to.' He did not talk a great deal, but seemed at peace. When, however, we returned to the hotel he struck a very bad patch, one of his black moods, sombre and full of dark thoughts. His voice had become querulous. He snapped at Jock, and bit the head off anyone who came near him. He would be glad when this bloody broadcast was over. He has always got worked up before an important speech, and now to his fears and apprehension was added a rather alarming degree of exhaustion. He seemed all in. He told me he had tingling in his cheeks. Did it mean anything? He asked me to take his temperature. 'I sat in the sitting-room between two fans half an hour ago. If I caught a chill, is it too soon to produce a pain in my chest?' He decided to play bezique, and then got very fussed when they told him there was only half an hour left and he had not yet finished his broadcast.

I left him; there was nothing I could do. The corridors of the hotel were lined with excited people, and from the steps of the hotel a great crowd swelled out into the streets beyond. Washington likes Winston, but it takes him very calmly. These Canadians were different. They were wildly excited. He belonged to them, and they had a feeling that they might never see him again, that he had descended into Ottawa out of history to say 'Goodbye' to them. I went to his car, which was open, and put up the windows, and as I was doing this there was a burst of cheering. He was flushed and perspiring freely as he came down the steps after his broadcast; he paused to wave to the crowd and then clambered clumsily into the big Cadillac.

All the way to the Country Club, where he was to dine as the guest of the Canadian Prime Minister, crowds lined the road, waving frantically and smiling their affection. As his car drove off there was loud cheering, and I could see that Winston was greatly moved. I ran back to my car, and as the cheering grew in volume Winston levered himself out of his seat in the well of the car and with some difficulty perched himself on the body behind. There, with his hat in one hand, he held up the fingers of the other in the victory sign. Anthony had followed his example, and from my car some way behind they had the appearance of two marionettes acknowledging the cheers of the people with sharp, jerky movements of their arms. When the crowd thinned and the cheering died down Winston felt the chill night air, and putting on his hat subsided into the well of the car. Then as the car passed through a village there was more cheering and more crowds, and once again he hoisted himself, so painfully, on to the body of the car.

During dinner Winston became very happy. The broadcast was over, and he had not broken down. That had always been at the back of his mind. He had dreaded it, feeling that it would be something of a disgrace. Anyhow, he had got through and now he could relax. Mr. St. Laurent,[1] who sat on his right, looked a very tired man and made little attempt to talk to the P.M. But Winston was full of life and fun and beamed on everyone. The chicken broth particularly pleased him; he could not get it made like that at home, and they had paid him the compliment of providing the particular brand of champagne he likes—Pol Roger. At times he seemed to sit in a kind of stupor. Then he would wake up and raise his glass to Howe,[2] and talk with great animation. He said he did not want the party to break up; he was very happy. Anthony leant over; they were getting late, he said, they must set out for the airfield soon. Winston took no notice. It was a quarter-past eleven before we left the ground at Ottawa. In the air Winston kept talking of the kindly greeting the people of Ottawa had given him. 'I purred like a cat,' he said, 'I liked it very much.'

R.M.S. Queen Elizabeth, *July 1, 1954*

It was an immense relief last night to get Winston safely on board. I felt all day as if I were watching a patient with high fever which was only kept in bounds by cold sponging. Nowadays one does not ask whether a speech went well, but only, 'Is he all right?' It has come to that. Just to get through is an achievement in itself. A trip like this, though he loves every minute of it, makes great calls on a person of his temperament, it taxes his resources—and they are no longer there.

The Prof. and I decided to go to the veranda restaurant on the sun deck to keep a table for the P.M. We waited for some time, and then the buzz of conversation stopped suddenly as the P.M. came through the door. He appeared, very small and stooped and all huddled up as he walked, not very steadily, towards the table where we were seated. There, collapsing into a seat, he said contentedly, 'It's good to have nothing to do.'

But presently his brow clouded. 'It's abominably hot here,' he exploded. 'I don't know why I was persuaded to come by sea. We

---

[1] Prime Minister of Canada.
[2] C. D. Howe, Canadian Minister of Trade and Commerce.

should have been at Chartwell now if we had gone by air as I wanted. Is there no fan?' he demanded in angry tones. 'Cannot you open a window? They are fixed. Good God! The sun is beating on me through the glass. It is quite intolerable. I shall never come here again.' By this time everyone in the small restaurant was looking at him and listening, for his voice carries. 'This is very embarrassing,' Christopher said. Jock appeared uncomfortable. The P.M. got up and stalked to another table, and when this proved to be no better he rose and moved to a third, where he slumped down, in the sulks. 'He seems very apprehensive about himself,' I said to Jock, 'all on edge.' Jock answered that he was not surprised. 'Things with Anthony are coming to a head. Anthony is on edge too; he does not know how to put it to Winston.'

July 2, 1954

This morning, after eight hours' sleep, his pulse is 72, and soft like that of a young man; he is positively benign and, incredible as it will seem to those who know him, lazily content. When I asked him if he had any speeches on the stocks he replied that he was not going to do anything for the present, except, of course, urgent telegrams. 'After all, Charles, that is why I came by sea, to get some rest. I do not think I shall retire at the end of the month. I don't think Anthony expects me to. He is contemplating a holiday—poor Anthony, he needs a change.' Winston said this as if it would be very inconsiderate to interfere with the Foreign Secretary's plans by resigning prematurely.

'I'm planning to go to meet the Russians, if they would like it. I shall draft a telegram to Molotov this morning. Anthony is not against it. He would come with me.' Speaking more quickly he went on: 'Ike has crossed a gulf of thought. He has taken a very important step. He has made up his mind that Communism is not something which we must at all costs wipe out, but rather something we have got to learn to live with, and alongside—peaceful coexistence.'

I told him of a saying of Pitcairn—a great physician in his time— that the last thing a doctor learns is when to do nothing and to leave things to nature. His eyes lit up. 'Yes, exactly.'

At that moment Jock came in, and when he saw me made to withdraw. 'Don't go,' Winston said. 'I want you. You haven't shown my Molotov letter to Anthony?' Winston did not catch Jock's answer. 'You say you have not?' he reiterated. 'I have not,' Jock repeated, almost shouting the 'not.' 'Good,' said Winston, 'I will show it to him myself. Come back, Charles, and lunch with me.'

Everyone appeared to be in high spirits when we began luncheon and there was a hum of animated conversation, a rare event at Winston's table. The P.M., it is true, did not apparently hear much that was said, and from time to time he turned to Anthony for enlightenment. But he seemed in good heart, and was amused when he was told a joke. 'I'm going on deck,' Anthony said at length. Winston then said something to him which I could not hear. The rest of the conversation was not at all difficult to follow.

Anthony: 'Oughtn't you to consult your colleagues before sending a letter to Molotov? I think you should tell them before taking this important step.'

Winston: 'Oh, during the war I always claimed the right to send messages to the President without any censorship. I put a communication to Molotov on the same level.'

Anthony: 'But it is a new principle.'

Winston: 'Is it? I am only asking Molotov if the Russians would like me to visit them. If they say "No," well the matter is finished, and I need not bother the Cabinet.'

Anthony: 'And if they say "Yes"?'

Winston: 'Well, in that event, if my colleagues do not approve, I can easily get out of it by telling Molotov that they do not agree.'

Anthony: 'That would be rather rough on the Russians. Besides, if it should get about before Geneva finishes the Americans would feel annoyed.'

Winston: 'It need not get about. The Russians are able to keep secrets.'

Anthony: 'They are certainly able, but will they be willing? That is quite another matter.'

Among those who went with Winston on his wartime travels, none ventured to argue with him in this fashion, and as Anthony and Bob Dixon were often in his company then, it means, I fear, that people no longer speak under their breath in the great man's presence. While this was passing through my head I became conscious that Christopher was making signals that we should leave them alone to fight it out.

July 3, 1954

'It is difficult,' said Winston as he stepped into his zip-suit, 'to find new interests at the end of one's life.' Not that he tries very hard to overcome the difficulty. The effective use of words and the exercise of power make up his life now, as they have done for more than half a century. He asked me if I had read Harold Nicolson's *Public Faces*. 'A very remarkable book,' he said, 'because, written in 1932, it is all about the atomic bomb.'

573

During dinner and afterwards until he went to bed at midnight Winston kept reverting to the prospect of a meeting with the Russians. Turning to Anthony, he enquired, 'Do you think they will answer "Yes"?' Anthony thought they would agree, unless there were internal difficulties. At Geneva he had seen Molotov every day; usually, it was true, about procedure, what should go on the agenda and things of that kind; not perhaps, Anthony conceded, about matters of high statecraft. But he had been very agreeable; he might help. Anthony thought that there was no doubt that Molotov had mellowed since the war. He discussed things as if he wanted to smooth over difficulties, not to make them. Winston said:

'I am counting on the Russians wanting a better time; they want butter, not bombs, more food, more comfort. For forty years they have had a pretty rough life. They may have given up dreams of world conquest, and be ready for peaceful coexistence. Anyway, Ike has crossed the gulf which separates a mission to destroy Bolshevism from living side by side in peace. I must admit that I myself have crossed that gulf. I would like to visit Russia once more before I die.'

July 4, 1954

'I've had a lovely sleep,' Winston began while waiting for his breakfast. 'Eight hours is my proper ration. I took two reds; the drugged feeling they leave is very agreeable. I had dreams, but I cannot remember them. They soon faded.

'I shall retire on September 18th. I would have liked to go on, because I have everything at my finger-tips. They are fools,' he said impatiently; 'I can do it all so much better than anyone else.'

He changed the subject abruptly.

'Have you read the *Ocean Times*? Adenauer is demanding that France should ratify the European Defence Treaty. I am glad he has spoken out. The French are a disgrace. When they gave up in 1940 they wanted us to surrender too. We picked them out of the gutter, and now they think of nothing but themselves all the time; living in a welter of intrigue, they never seem to think of their country.'

'Will you go to Moscow before September?' I asked.

He picked me up. 'Vienna is the place I have in mind. I shall try and persuade the Russians to sign an Austrian treaty. If that came off people would whoop with joy. I might pay a courtesy visit to Moscow after Vienna—perhaps staying forty-eight hours. It has been my most strenuous week for many years. I did not know whether I could stand up to a strain of this kind, but I set my will to work. Coming at the end of this trip, I felt the broadcast at

Ottawa most. I consider that my answers to questions at the press luncheon at Washington—all spontaneous, without any preparation—was the greatest triumph of my career.'

I thought the P.M. seemed silent and preoccupied during dinner; he made no attempt to join in the conversation. But gradually he thawed and began to talk of the First War; of Plug Street[1] and the Battle of the Somme; and then, skipping a quarter of a century, how he had asked Bernard Freyberg the number of his wounds, how he answered 'thirty-three,' and had stripped and shown Winston the scars; and how he had bathed from Monty's caravan in the desert. This exchange of memories led to a very friendly atmosphere; it was difficult to believe that Anthony and the P.M. had any differences. Even when a telegram was given to Winston which brought up the projected visit to Russia, the discussion was mild and harmonious.

'After all,' said the P.M., 'both Ike and Foster Dulles have given their approval; they put it on paper in April of last year. They said that if the Prime Minister wished to make a "solitary pilgrimage" to Moscow, though they would not advise it, it was all right by them. Do you remember the message ended: "Of course you have the right to go whenever you wish."'

Anthony, who all along has been strongly opposed to such a visit to the Russians, once more bowed to Winston's tenacity and strength of will. He put it like this: 'When, Winston, you saw the President in Washington only a week ago you discussed everything but the date of this visit. You spoke to him then of a reconnoitring patrol, and you could send a message now to Ike saying that you proposed to go to Moscow as part of the patrol and would keep him informed of what happened.'

Winston is glad now that he took Anthony's advice and consulted the Cabinet about the visit to Molotov. The Government had agreed, with a few minor modifications, and a telegram had been sent to Molotov; he was now waiting for an answer. Anthony thought the odds on the Russians agreeing to a visit by Winston were 6–4 on, and perhaps 10–1 against a later meeting of Molotov, Eisenhower and the P.M. 'It may fail,' said Winston. 'If it does, then with a clear conscience and an easy mind I can go to my Maker.'

At that moment Miss Gilliatt appeared and handed the Foreign Secretary a telegram. He read it twice. Then, putting down his cigar on a plate, and half turning in his seat as if he wanted to concentrate more on the telegram, he began reading it again. It was

[1] British nickname for Ploegsteert village in Flanders. Churchill commanded the 6th Royal Scots Fusiliers when holding the line which ran through Ploegsteert.

from Roger Makins. The Ambassador was worried by the storm suddenly raised in the United States by a speech of Senator Knowland,[1] who appeared to insinuate that the Prime Minister and the Foreign Secretary had gone to Washington to get Communist China admitted to the United Nations against American wishes. The Ambassador pleaded for a disclaimer. He wanted the Foreign Secretary to say that it had hardly been mentioned in the discussions in Washington, and that there was general agreement that this was not the moment for China's admission to be considered.

Anthony handed the telegram to Winston without a word. When he had read it he looked up and said to Anthony: 'It is curious that only this afternoon, after I had read the press extracts, I got out of bed and went to you with exactly the same point as the Ambassador makes. I agree with Roger,' Winston said.

'I don't,' Anthony retorted with some warmth. 'It would be an intolerable position if the F.O. had to make a statement every time Senator Knowland attacked Britain.'

'Roger's telegram is too long, of course,' Winston put in, in his most accommodating manner. 'Why not, in six lines, say that you do not propose to support China's application for membership of the United Nations at this moment while they are still at war, and in fact the aggressor nation? Then when the whole question comes up it can be judged according to the circumstances existing at the time.'

Anthony thought this point was too technical and too subtle.

Neither the P.M. nor the Foreign Secretary would give an inch; they kept on reiterating the same points. At last Jock intervened: 'Why not ask Ike to say at his Press conference that the matter to which Senator Knowland referred had hardly been mentioned at the Washington meeting?' The argument became so sharp that Christopher beckoned to us, and we rose and left the room. Almost at once Winston came into his bedroom, where we had retreated. He mumbled that it made things very difficult when Anthony could not distinguish between a big and a small issue. It was a row over nothing. Another Guatemala. The P.M. was worried. After all, the Ambassador is Anthony's man. Jock repeated his suggestion of Ike and the Press conference. But when the P.M. went on mumbling as he paced his cabin Jock saw that nothing was to be gained by argument and slipped away.

Christopher, however, began the argument all over again. I whispered to him that it would be better to adjourn the discussion, whereupon, taking my hint, he said: 'Wow! I'm going to bed.'

[1] Republican Senator for California.

The P.M. lay flat on his back, mumbling away. I kept silent. He said again that he was very worried, though I could not see why he should get into a stew if it was a small issue. 'You can go into this in the morning,' I said mildly. 'It is nearly two o'clock.' The P.M. on such occasions is like an alarm clock; you must let him run down before there is quiet. The voyage had been doing him good; it was a complete rest. He had admitted as much, and had said this morning that he was reconciled to a ship, and here we were, having a pitched battle in the small hours of the morning. How could he expect to get to sleep when he was upset like this? I left him still mumbling.

July 5, 1954

I was late in waking, and went at once to the P.M.'s room, not without some trepidation. Vaguely—it did not come down to details —I had a feeling that last night's fracas could have done him no good. I found him placidly reading a novel. He had had a beautiful night. How many hours' sleep? 'Oh, I went off when you left the room, and did not wake till half an hour ago.' Winston seems, to a doctor's eyes, to be designed on lines quite different from the rest of mankind. Part of the difference I ascribe to some kind of shock absorber which is not included in the make-up of most men. As for Anthony, he confessed to me that he had taken aspirin 'for the strain.'

Lunched with Anthony and Tony Rumbold;[1] Winston was not mentioned once.

For our last dinner on board Christopher had taken counsel with the chef, and between them they had planned a tremendous feast; but it was not the unusual repast so much as the change in the climate that pleased me. Last night I lay awake going all over the unpleasant altercation between Winston and Anthony, and it was with some apprehension that I had looked forward to another uncomfortable sitting. But tonight everything was different. Winston was in his most benign mood. He did not avoid delicate subjects; he seemed to be able to talk about them with Anthony's full approval. A topic, which last night was full of perils, was now touched so lightly that it was seen, as it were, in retrospect in a spirit of amused detachment. His words, to be sure, were not very different from those he used last night, but he seemed to have now only one purpose in his mind—to smooth over the changing of the guard.

To Anthony Winston talked as father to son, as if he were only concerned for his future happiness. Speaking very earnestly, he implored him not to quarrel with America, whether China was or

[1] Sir Anthony Rumbold, Principal Private Secretary to the Foreign Secretary.

577

was not a member of the United Nations. He spoke of himself as a link with Queen Victoria, and it was surely the historian who impressed on Anthony that influence depends on power.

'Up to July 1944 England had a considerable say in things; after that I was conscious that it was America who made the big decisions. She will make the big decisions now.'

Winston said this with an air of finality.

'We do not yet realize her immeasurable power. She could conquer Russia without any help. In a month the Kremlin would be unable to move troops. The Americans would become enraged—violent. I know them very well. They might decide to go it alone. That was what Dulles meant when he talked about an agonizing reappraisal of policy. Without their help, England would be isolated; she might become, with France, a satellite of Russia.'

Winston's voice broke, and his eyes filled with tears. And then someone mentioned Roger Makins's telegram. It seemed possible now, among friends, to discuss any subject quietly and without heat. Anthony said good humouredly that he paid a good deal of attention to ambassadors' opinions and that Roger was a very good ambassador, but he had found that the man on the spot was inclined to take local events and issues too much to heart. Winston thought we were inclined to take China too seriously; her strength had been exaggerated; she only produced two million tons of steel in a year, and steel was everything in war. Anthony revealed how he had ragged Chou En-lai about his wish to be in the United Nations. Chou became embarrassed; it was obvious that he was most anxious that China should be recognized as a member.

The storm had passed and the smell as of a garden after rain made everyone happy. We sat back and watched the P.M. pick his way, light-footed as a cat, among the pools. We were relieved, of course, by his tact, but not perhaps altogether surprised. After all, he has spent his life putting things to people and waiting to see how they take it. When he has a mind to make the effort no one can be more adroit, more skilful in a difficult situation. But Winston's dexterity in dancing a verbal minuet is nothing new to those of us who have been with him since the war began.

Tonight there was something more. As the banquet unfolded and one delicacy followed another we all sensed that something unusual had happened and that Winston was in a strange expansive mood, in which he was taking notice of his guests. He had become conscious that those who served him and waited upon his wishes had been part of his life for a long time, that they were human beings and that they were devoted to his service. This might be the last time that he would travel as Prime Minister and some of those with him now had gone wherever he had gone since 1940.

It was late now, but Winston's gaiety and good humour had spread to his guests, and there was no thought of bed. The old man bubbled merriment. Then he went back to the First War—always a sign with Winston that the weather is set fair. Anthony began reciting Persian poetry, rather shyly and without confidence. Winston was astonished and excited. 'But Anthony, I did not know you could speak Persian. I had no idea you had this gift. It is extraordinary. When did you learn this language?' I reminded Winston that Anthony had taken his Final Schools at Oxford in Oriental languages, and got a First in them. Winston knew nothing of this. Why should he? He had nominated Anthony to succeed him, but that did not mean that before he did so he had ferreted out all the facts of his life. Anthony began writing in Persian the names of those round the table, but Winston's interest in Persian poets soon began to flag. He beamed round the table; the dinner, he said, had been very agreeable, he hoped a year tonight the same people might meet and dine together. 'You, Anthony, will be able to give the party at No. 10.' 'No,' said Anthony. 'Whatever happens I will be your guest.'

I went with Winston to his cabin. When he had nothing on but a vest he suddenly remembered some lines of Pope which he could not recall when round the table. Waddling quickly across the room, he disappeared into Anthony's cabin, and through the open door I heard him say, 'I must recite to you the words I could not remember just now.'

Chapter fifty-two

The Prime Minister and the Suez rebels

London, July 14, 1954

I found the P.M. a little deflated this morning after a long and tiring day. Following a tough Cabinet, he had to wind up the debate on Suez.

'It was Anthony's policy, but I had to bear the odium of it. Nobody hates getting out of Egypt more than I do. But it's no use to us in the present circumstances. Not a single soldier is in favour of staying there. Why don't Waterhouse and the rebels see that?'

Winston turned on me:

'Oh, I'm glad somebody has some spirit left. They are right to make their protest.'

He was not angry with them. He went on:

'Mary is a fortnight overdue. It's an extraordinary business this way of bringing babies into the world. I don't know how God thought of it.'

July 20, 1954

Summoned to No. 10, I was about to go into his room when a secretary came out and said would I mind waiting a few minutes; the Prime Minister was just dictating a telegram. Pitblado, Oates and Miss Gilliatt were all bobbing in and out of his room; something unusual was afoot. As I entered his room he held out his hand in an absent-minded way, and without taking his eyes from a document in front of him said:

'There is a crisis—a political crisis—this bloody Suez business. I can't tell what will happen. I don't know. I may get my way.'

He seemed to have forgotten that he had sent for me, and went on studying the document. After a time he looked up and held out his hand: 'Thank you, my dear.'

When there is trouble brewing I like to keep an eye on him, and after dinner I called at No. 10. He was, they told me, at the House of Commons. I found him in his room. 'It is an extraordinary business, Charles, getting old.' Until a year or two ago it appears that he had not heard the 'inaudible and noiseless foot of time.' I asked him what he noticed. He shrugged his shoulders. 'Everything.' He does not watch the onset of old age with detachment; he regards it as a stab in the back when he is fighting to keep his power. With a gesture of impatience he set his jaw, if he lost he would find things to do when he resigned.

'I have my book, *A History of the English-speaking Peoples*. It is an important book. People will lap it up. I shall not give up politics. If there is an election and we are defeated, as we may be, I would seek re-election and sit on the front Opposition bench.'

Christopher wanted him to fly to Ulster to see his horse run. I think we scotched that.

'I must see Anthony tomorrow,' he said gloomily.

July 23, 1954

Winston admitted that he was very tired last night. 'You've had a grim week,' I remarked. He repeated the word 'grim' and nodded his head.

'Continual worry,' and then he corrected himself. 'I don't worry. My experience of politics is unique. It has gone on so long.'

Winston cannot get Anthony out of his head. The Tories, he said, had given him a poor reception on his return from Geneva.

'As a Party they aren't responsive. Not that anybody can be very pleased with the results of the Conference. The other side have been very squalid. I shall go soon. I don't want to go at all. If there was a strong movement, if they said: "You must not go . . ." '

He paused for a time.

'But there isn't a strong movement either way. Anthony wants it awfully. Today's Cabinet will be decisive. They must support me or I shall go.'

He began talking of Crichel Down.

'If these young men, Lord Carrington [1] and Dick Nugent,[2] resign now they will always be debited with Crichel Down. If they stay in the Government everything will be forgotten. I have only done what was just.'

[1] Parliamentary Secretary Ministry of Agriculture and Fisheries, 1951–4.
[2] Richard Nugent, Secretary Ministry of Agriculture and Fisheries, 1951–7.

July 28, 1954

I found a pile of morning papers outside his room, and a notice
'Do not disturb' hanging on the handle of his bedroom door. He
was still asleep. There wasn't a sign of a secretary or of Kirkwood.
I took the *Daily Mirror* and the *Daily Herald* from the pile and waited.
At half-past nine the buzzer went. No one answered it. It went
again, this time without stopping. I went into his room. He looked
sleepily at his clock. 'I went to bed at half-past one, so I have had
eight hours sleep.' He picked up a green pill from his table. 'I put
it in my mouth when I woke at seven o'clock, and then I took it out
again.' He plainly felt that he deserved a good mark for his self-
discipline. 'There is another crisis,' he said wearily. 'Read this,'
and he gave me the *Daily Express*. 'No, read the Leader; it's unpleasant.' I turned the page. 'A Day of Sorrow, a Day of Shame.'
Beneath these headlines I read: 'Under our very eyes, by the hand
of a Tory Government, the greatest surrender is taking place since
the Socialists and Mountbatten engineered the scuttle from India.'

'Fancy ending my career with clearing out of Egypt. I wish I
hadn't had to do it. The Opposition are dying to get at me. They
were terribly keen on evacuating the Canal, but they may combine
with the rebels just to get us out. We might be defeated. In that
case we'd have a vote of confidence in the House on Friday. We
might go to the country. I might lead. It would have to be put to
the Party. I don't know what they would do. They'd have to choose
between a doddering old man and a young, brilliant——'

He stopped short and rang his bell. When Montague Browne
appeared he said: 'Will the Queen hold the Council at Arundel?
Go and find out.' They brought his breakfast. He slashed across a
fried egg and pushed the plate away. He picked up a paper, though
he had read them all before he went to bed, and almost at once he
put it down again. 'It's the dream of Anthony's life,' he murmured.

July 29, 1954

The P.M. has complained lately that his eye is no better, and it
has been arranged that he should see Sir Stewart Duke-Elder and
Mr. Davenport in consultation. Winston said he would like that.
His dislike of strangers does not apply to doctors. Then this Suez
debate threatened to upset our plans. However, a message came
through from No. 10 that the Prime Minister would see us in his
room at the House of Commons at four o'clock. We found him in
a reasonable mood. If he was on the verge of defeat in the House
of Commons it did not seem to worry him. I decided, however, to

be at hand in case things went wrong, and when the doctors had gone I made my way to the Gallery of the House to wait for Anthony Head to open the debate. He was the ablest of the young soldiers on Winston's staff during the war, and I knew he would talk sense. He surely did. Speaking without a note, he told the House that there was no alternative to evacuating the base. The hydrogen bomb had changed the whole situation. This weapon would be used in the next war, and used too on Britain. In such circumstances our ability to send large armies overseas would be 'severely strained.' Apart from the bomb, the base would be of little use to us in peace or war if Egypt was hostile. Finally, he drew attention to Turkey's admission to NATO and claimed that this had completely altered the position in the Middle East.

Attlee, who replied for the Opposition, had a simple task. The arguments the Government were advancing to justify the evacuation of Suez were precisely those which Mr. Churchill had repudiated so vehemently and so scornfully when in opposition in 1946. He had only to give chapter and verse. When the plan to withdraw our troops was announced by the head of the Labour Government Mr. Churchill said that 'it was a most painful blow.' 'He must have been in acute pain yesterday,' said Mr. Attlee, thrusting forward his hatchet face as if he was about to cleave the Prime Minister's skull. Mr. Churchill had spoken with derision of a policy of scuttle—the rest of Mr. Attlee's sentence was lost in a tumult of Labour cheers. In the spring of 1946 Mr. Churchill had said, 'Things are built up with great labour and cast away with great shame and folly.' What, asked Mr. Attlee, would the Right Honourable Gentleman have said if the Labour Government had brought forward the present proposals? If, Mr. Attlee concluded, the Prime Minister had stood up to his own back benchers a better settlement could have been arranged than was possible now. He had refrained from doing what was right, and had now to eat humble pie.

When Mr. Attlee sat down bedlam broke loose among his supporters; for a full minute they bellowed their approval. It had indeed been a savage and damaging attack; so effective that I found my heart thumping. I hated every minute of it. Winston's face was grey and expressionless, as if he no longer knew what was happening; he was so still he might have been frozen to the bench. He was hurt, but there was worse to come.

Captain Waterhouse rose. He was the leader of the Tory rebels. The agreement[1] had been signed: 'There it is,' he exclaimed, waving

[1] On July 27, 1954, an agreement was signed in Cairo providing for the withdrawal of British troops from the Suez Canal Zone.

a piece of paper, 'and in this piece of paper we have got all that is left of eighty years of British endeavour, thought and forethought.' He turned towards the P.M. 'It must be grave indeed for him now, to have to take this decision.' Winston, who had been sitting with his head bowed, turned round quickly and looked at him. Did this rebel really know how he hated the whole miserable business?

If Winston has believed in anything at all in the course of his long life it has been in the British Empire and all that it stands for. Some of his happiest hours as a young subaltern were spent in India—and India was gone. Now this rebel was reminding him of 'The River War.' It must have brought back a flood of memories of Omdurman and the 21st Lancers and the dervish spearmen and the wild gallop in the desert; and Egypt, too, was gone. His heart was with the rebels.

'If,' said their leader, 'the electorate of this country had seen or foreseen this paper in 1951, we should not now be sitting on this side of the House.' He had to pause until the storm of Opposition cheering died away. Happily the P.M. did not seem to hear. His mind was a long way off. 'If,' Captain Waterhouse went on, 'the hydrogen bomb is making our position in the Suez Canal completely untenable, why have we been fiercely arguing for six, eight or ten months about the power of re-entry?' He did not believe these were the real reasons at all. We were becoming weary of our responsibilities, we were losing our will to rule.

That was the fear that was gnawing at Winston's peace of mind. He was not thinking at all of the defeat of the Government; did that, after all, really matter? When Captain Waterhouse had done, the P.M. rose with difficulty and, stumbling along the Front Bench, left the Chamber. I did not follow him, because I felt he would not throw up the sponge. In a few minutes he came back. He had changed his mind. I knew that he was going to speak.

An opportunity to intervene soon came. The Socialist Member for Northampton, who had risen when Captain Waterhouse sat down, made a strange charge; he roundly affirmed that an agreement to get out of Egypt had been held up by a back-bench cabal in the Conservative Party, encouraged under the table by the Prime Minister himself. The P.M. pulled himself to his feet. 'That is an absolute untruth.' Mr. Paget persisted that Mr. Churchill had let it be known that he was against evacuation. Greatly moved, the P.M. rose. He had not concealed in public speech how much he regretted the course of events in Egypt (and indeed in the privacy of his home his lamentations were loud and often repeated). But he had changed his mind because the hydrogen bomb had changed

584

the whole strategic position in the world, making thoughts which were well founded and well knit together a year ago obsolete—utterly obsolete, he repeated. It had changed the opinion of every competent soldier he had been able to meet.

Winston had spoken for four minutes—two hundred and fifty words—and I have given the substance of his speech. But in truth the Secretary of State for War had said as much in opening the debate. Why, then, was the P.M.'s intervention so effective? The answer is to be found, I think, in the fact that Winston is a poet. And it is because he is a poet that he could do what Head, with his logic, had failed to do. He could open the eyes of the House to the appalling spectacle of the first few weeks of the next war. When hydrogen bombs were falling on London, what happened at a base at Suez would not, he thought, matter a great deal. Before he sat down he had restored to the House a sense of proportion, so that they were able to measure the importance of Suez against the incredible calamities of a war of annihilation.

July 30, 1954

The P.M. was in good heart this morning. I said to him that the debate had not ended badly. He corrected me:

'It was a triumph. If I never speak again in the House I can say I have done nothing better. I dominated the House. And,' he continued, 'it was without preparation of any kind. I said they must keep a sense of proportion. If ten million are killed in London by a hydrogen bomb, Suez will not seem of much importance to those who are left alive. When I sat down I was trembling all over. I was very excited. My pulse was over a hundred for a long time after my speech. Take it now, Charles. I don't think it did me any harm. Anthony was good; he got a great reception when he sat down.'

When I left the P.M. I met the Lord Chancellor. He is a friendly soul, but was very critical of Winston's recent achievements. 'At Wednesday's Cabinet Winston didn't seem to take things in. It was painful. I said something to him,' the Lord Chancellor went on, 'which he entirely misunderstood. Oh, yes, he heard what I said all right. Then yesterday he was as lively as a cricket. Perhaps the subjects that came up were less difficult, or he found them more interesting. I am sorry for Anthony and Rab; they don't know where they are. Of course, Moran, you know more about this than I do, but surely things can't go on like this?'

Coming from the Lord Chancellor, this was disturbing. However, though he is an able lawyer, as a politician he is very inexperienced, and I wondered if Anthony had been opening his heart to him. I decided to have a word with Norman Brook. As Secretary of the Cabinet he would know if the P.M. was no longer in control; besides, they all seem to go to him when in trouble. Norman agreed that Winston made no effort at preparation; he was definitely lazy. He instanced a review of Defence policy. 'Why, it used to be his pet subject, but now when it came up he seemed to take no interest in it.' But Brook thought he still did the Cabinet 'all right.' 'It's really a *tour de force.* He picks it up as he goes along. He doesn't bother to master anything in advance. Plays bezique instead,' and Norman smiled. 'It's really this business of meeting the Russians that keeps him from going. Anthony knows this. He ought to go before Parliament meets. There might be real trouble if he hangs on beyond that. He is trying Anthony and Rab very high.'

I said that I had noticed for some time that Winston tended to exaggerate things. The first day at Washington, for example, was an 'incredible' success; and he is always telling me how he had dominated the House of Commons or the Cabinet. 'Yes,' said Brook, 'he exaggerates the public success of his visit to Washington, keeps talking about it.' He agreed with me that this was compensatory; the P.M. did it because he wanted to justify to himself his conduct in hanging on to office. It wasn't vanity—he never did this kind of thing during the war—but only an over-mastering desire to make out a case for remaining Prime Minister.

August 3, 1954

Last night Winston telephoned from Chartwell that he had started a cold in the head. He wasn't coughing and had no temperature. What could I do for him? Could he take penicillin? And what about a Dover's powder? This morning a message came that he was streaming and thought he would have to ask the Queen to cancel his audience. He would like to see me as soon as it was convenient for me to come. When I saw him he kept closing his eyes, and then, when he opened them again, he seemed for a moment not to know what was happening. 'I am tired and torpid,' he said.

I asked Jock how he thought Winston had been since Parliament rose.

He answered: 'Last night we were talking, when he said, "I'm sorry, Jock, to harp on this, only I've got to make the most difficult decision of my life." Until he makes up his mind whether to go or not he will be on edge.'

'When will he decide?'

'When?' Jock repeated, as if he was half thinking of something else. 'Well, he's supposed to have made up his mind already. Now he seems busy unmaking it,' and Jock smiled.

Chapter fifty-three

One man's will

August 6, 1954

When I got to Chartwell about three o'clock Winston was drinking brandy with Walter Graebner,[1] who had been lunching with him.

'Have you read Spears's account of the fall of France?[2] Oh, it's a hell of a book. He took down exactly what I said. He's very flattering to me. It's a picture of her downfall which no other Englishman could have drawn. Poor France. It is terrible.'

Winston made a throaty sound. 'Terrible,' he repeated.

He looked at me with a naughty smirk, like a schoolboy owning up to a scrape. I wondered what was coming.

'Did you read about the Polish stowaway? Christopher told me about him. He had the same right to political asylum as any other stowaway,' Winston said indignantly. 'I did it. It was a quarter to one in the morning, but I rang up the Home Secretary. He had gone to bed. It appeared that Lucas-Tooth[3]—you know, he's David's deputy—had flabbily agreed to this poor Pole being sent back in the ship to his doom. I got Lord Goddam[4] to issue a writ of *habeas corpus* on the master of the Polish ship to produce the Pole. I heard that the crew had been truculent when an immigration officer boarded the ship to demand the release of the man; so it was arranged that eighty police officers should go on board. I was afraid that the master might put out to sea, and we had to make plans to ensure that the law was respected. There was no one at the Admiralty. Eventually I got hold of the Fifth Lord. They wanted to ride off the ship on to a mud bank if it showed fight. I was all for firing at the propeller, that

[1] Journalist with *Time/Life*.
[2] General Sir Edward Spears, *The Fall of France* (Heinemann, 1954).
[3] Sir Hugh Lucas-Tooth, Parliamentary Under-Secretary of State, Home Office.
[4] Lord Goddard, Lord Chief Justice, 1946–58.

would have hurt no one. Clemmie had a good idea. The Pole, she thought, could be brought ashore by a crane. Immediately he was ensconced in the basket he would be on British soil, because the crane would be on the quay.'

'Who is this Pole?' I asked. 'He might be an agent of the Free Poles. Or perhaps he's a rogue.' Winston took no notice. Plainly he did not care who he was, any more than he had bothered about Peter the Painter.[1] It was Sidney Street over again.

Graebner had taken his leave and we were alone.

'I don't know what to do,' Winston mused. 'For half of the day I am determined to stay and see the business through, and then for the other half my resignation seems inevitable. I think Anthony would be well advised to be Leader of the House and Deputy Prime Minister.'

There was a long pause.

'But of course Anthony might want to be Prime Minister. I know my theme, and I don't want to give it up. I can do it better than anyone else.'

Then, apparently on the impulse of the moment, he rang a bell.

'Bring that paper,' he said to Miss Gilliatt when she appeared. 'I'm going to show you something which is deadly secret. No one except the Cabinet has seen it. I show it to you, not to get your opinion on high policy, but we have been very close together for a long time and I want you to see what I can still do.'

He handed me a paper folded like a letter, but perhaps twice the size. In the centre of the first page was a heading:

'Two Power Talks—for the consideration of my colleagues.'

On the two inner sides was his argument. There seemed nothing particularly secret in this; it was just the case for a meeting with Malenkov. The United States of America, the argument ran, knows that at present she is well on top in thermo-nuclear weapons, and that this may not always be so. She may feel that it would be foolish to wait until this advantage has slipped away and Russia, in addition to her immense army, is as well armed with atomic weapons as America. She may feel tempted to have a show-down while Russia cannot match her in the possession of these awful weapons of destruction. There is a very real risk in these circumstances of a third world war. Would it not be prudent to give his plan a trial?

I was still in the middle of his argument when he rose, saying that

[1] Anarchist leader of a group of some twenty Letts from Baltic Russia, who had come to England to set up 'a germ cell of anarchy and revolution.' His men were involved in the Sidney Street affair (see note on p. 86).

he was going to sleep. 'Bring it to me when you have done.' I was reading it a second time when Kirkwood appeared. 'The Prime Minister would like to see you, sir,' he said. I found him lying flat on his bed, with his eye-shade, though the curtains were drawn. 'You like it? I think the argument is very tight and clear. It took me two hours. Of course, I could have done it quicker once.'

I went off to find Montague Browne to return the document. 'It is remarkable that he should do this in two hours,' I said. Montague Browne explained that the P.M. had said all this to him at different times in snippets. He had just joined the bits together. I asked in the office if the Cabinet had been impressed. 'Impressed but not convinced. The F.O. dislikes it. They say if we seem to appease Russia, other countries, like France, will say let us all hasten and make our own peace with her, and we shall see the break-up of NATO. Lord Salisbury and Crookshank were very much against.'

Will Winston go in September? No one can tell. They say that the country would like him to go on. As for the Party, no two reports agree. The Tories could, of course, get him out, but I doubt if they have the nerve. They are afraid he might say: 'I wanted to go on, but they wouldn't let me. I wanted to meet the Russians, but they wouldn't have it.' The Tories are afraid that if this got about they might lose the next election. They know that the P.M. won't say this, but they instinctively don't like being exposed to such a contingency. I wondered about the Cabinet. It seems that there is a small clique which is more and more getting up against the P.M. I hear that one of them at least is bloody-minded. Most people feel that it depends on how the P.M. shapes. They find him up and down. He will do something very badly indeed, and then when everyone is saying that he ought to go, he will astonish them by some *tour de force*.

August 11, 1954

The secretary said that I should find the P.M. in the garden; I came upon him in the paddock, feeding his mare Moll Flanders and her foal by Colonist.

'Ah, Charles, we are very excited. Christopher thought she wasn't in foal to Hyperion, but last night we found she was.'

Very slowly he made his way to the car that was to take him up the hill to the house. When he got to his room he plopped into a chair. His thoughts went back to the grim struggle for survival that has become with him almost an obsession.

'I cannot help being interested in public affairs,' he said. 'For more than fifty years it has been my life, my only interest. And now

589

I am lapped up in such uncertainty that it is affecting my personal life.'

On his desk, which I have never yet seen him use, beside a pile of books, a hand moulded in copper caught my eye. It was a cast, Winston told me, of his mother's hand, and I noticed that it was an exact counterpart of his own.

August 12, 1954

I found Winston sitting over the luncheon table with Wheeler-Bennett,[1] who soon took his leave. I brought up Attlee's visit to Moscow. Usually you cannot start him off if you try, but now he gave a grunt of disgust.

'It will lose the Tories a lot of votes. I had the initiative. Now we have lost it. I might have pushed on and done something. As it is, people will think it very sensible on Attlee's part.'

He blamed Salisbury and 'that impudent Crookshank.'

'We had planned our visit to meet the Russians at the end of September as a grand climax for Anthony.'

I asked him would Attlee's visit affect this.

'Well, it has taken the bloom off the peach. There would have been an outburst of joy if I'd seen Malenkov. Now Attlee has done it.'

He said to me: 'I must take half a red and get an hour's sleep.' I refused point blank to be a party to this. 'I don't want to rebel against you,' he said affectionately, and then proceeded to cut a capsule in half, putting his wet finger in the powder. He made a grimace. 'What a horrible taste. Retribution, Charles.'

August 16, 1954

3.15 p.m. Winston was playing bezique with Jock.

'Last night I woke at three o'clock and lay awake for three hours. My mind was marvellously clear; more efficient and smooth working than it has been for a long time. Almost as it used to be. I saw plainly outlined the most important and burdensome problem I have to solve—my relations with Anthony. I don't see why he wants to take over the dregs at the fag end of parliament—only one more session before the election—when nothing can be done. I suppose he sees himself as the brilliant young leader who will change everything. But there's no money, and without money, believe me, you cannot do anything. I have told them that I am quite willing to go on for another year if they would like me to. There may be an election in May. I'd not go on after that.

[1] Sir John Wheeler-Bennett, historian and Fellow of St. Anthony's College, Oxford.

'It's not all talk, Charles. Tomorrow Woolton comes to luncheon and we shall talk Party shop. Then on Saturday I have arranged a fifteen minutes' broadcast. I shall explain things to America. And a week later I shall do another broadcast reviewing what the Government has done, and it's a good deal—fewer unemployed for one thing.'

He said this as if I were the Opposition challenging his record.

The P.M. is bothered about France.

'I shall warn them,' the P.M. broke in. 'I can do it, because I have been their friend for forty years. I have never seen such a piece of insanity as the way they are going on. America would build up a German army and make it her sword in Europe, and we might take our troops out.

'Yesterday they brought down a message about Cyprus. It seemed to stimulate me, and I made a decision at once. They were very pleased about it. You see, Charles, I'm in charge of the F.O. while Anthony is away, and I can get things done.'

August 18, 1954

Winston was sitting up in bed at Chartwell, dictating. 'Don't go away,' he said to the secretary. 'Stay in the dining-room.' He did not hold out his wrist for me to take his pulse; he had other things to think of besides his health. I had the impression that he was seething with suppressed excitement, he talked to me with vehemence, and in a loud voice, as if he were seeking to convince someone.

'I thought of sending a message to Mendès-France [1] that I would like to see him in Paris, but it occurred to me that this might look as if I was trying to put pressure on him. Then yesterday of his own accord he asked if he could come to Chartwell to see me. He's going to Brussels for the meeting of the Six Powers about E.D.C. and would come here on his way back. I'd like that. It would be a good thing if he came to England. I shall say terrible things to him—of course within the limits of hospitality. I shall arrange for a guard of honour at the airfield. I shall wrap up what I am going to say in a lot of flattery. I shall tell him that the world is not going to be ruled by the French Chamber. I shall warn him that if the Chamber rejects E.D.C. France will be alone in the world. I shall tell him bluntly that we shall go on without them. Never was such obstinacy founded on such impotence.

'I shall tell them America may pull out and fall back on peripheral defence bases in the Pyrenees, in Norfolk, in Iceland and Turkey, so that if Russia gets nasty the Americans can drop a few bombs on

[1] French Prime Minister and Minister of Foreign Affairs, June 1954–February 1955.

her. Peripheral defence.' His voice was filled with scorn. 'It means that we shall be in the target without a say in what is in dispute. I don't like that at all. I want to prevent Ike falling back on this kind of defence.'

He smiled grimly.

'It appears that the Kremlin and our Foreign Office are at one; they do not want Malenkov to meet me.'

Moran: 'But why?'

'Oh, they don't know what might come out of such a meeting. I would have kept the Russians firmly in contact with reality; there would have been no swilling champagne,' he said bitterly. 'Of course, they might have refused to meet me outside Russia, and I couldn't have gone to them, but at least I'd have made a gesture. I'd have offered to meet them, and people would have known that it wasn't our fault if there was no meeting. It is a great relief to have charge of the F.O. instead of having to argue with Anthony. I can get something done. Anthony works very hard and is most conscientious, plugging away at routine. But that's not what is wanted at the Foreign Office, where you must take up the big issues and deal with them.'

He glowered at his papers. Then he looked at me.

'I want you to help me. In the afternoon I can neither keep awake nor go to sleep. Lennox-Boyd came to luncheon, and he was haranguing us when I dropped off to sleep, sitting at the table. I hate not being able to do one thing or the other. When I rise from luncheon I have seventy-five per cent. of sleep in me; what I need is something to tilt the balance in my favour. All I ask for is an hour of oblivion—unconsciousness. I love the sensation of going to sleep. I love sleep. I don't get the kind I did forty years ago when I was at the Admiralty in the First War.'

He shut his teeth together as if he were biting something very hard.

'I've made up my mind. I shan't go. At any rate till Christmas. There may be a bloody row. I don't mind. I don't think they will gain anything by knocking me about. You must not conclude that I am just sitting still and doing nothing. Osbert Peake [1] is coming down tomorrow about Old Age Pensions. Nearly all the Ministers are away on holiday, but I shall go on working.'

'The P.M. is determined to stay,' Jane Portal said, 'and he is taking steps to see those who can affect the issue. Christopher has been very good. He knows the House of Commons and tells the P.M. what he thinks will happen. But he does not try to bully him. That's no good. It only makes him more obstinate.'

[1] Minister of Pensions and National Insurance.

'I don't know where we are going,' I said as I left her.
'Nobody does,' she replied.

August 24, 1954

When I arrived at Chartwell I was told that the P.M. was still at
the luncheon table with Harold Macmillan. Pitblado looked at his
watch. It was four-fifteen. 'I think,' he said, 'we might send up a
message that Lord Moran is here.' Macmillan soon took his leave.
When the P.M. came into the office he appeared flushed and rather
excited. 'Come, let us go to my room,' he said.

'We were talking about important matters,' he began. 'I dare say
you can guess their nature. Harold is very able and will have a say
in things if it comes to a row.'

Winston denied that he was tired.

'We must have talked for three hours, but I feel full of vigour. I
ought to write to Anthony. I have written him two letters already;
I tore them up, they were try-outs. Can I say, Charles, that you
think I am able to bear the burden? It won't do Anthony any good
if a rumour goes about that he got me out.'

It had come to that. He did not speak for a little, then he said:

'I don't think I'm selfish, but it seems foolish'—and here his voice
rose and he spoke with great animation and vigour—'to throw away
all that I have to give. I can bring Dulles here tomorrow. He says he
is ready to come. They need my flair. You saw my message to
Eisenhower?'

I suppose I looked puzzled. 'You mean Adenauer?'

'Yes, Adenauer. I mustn't confuse the two names,' he added,
smiling. 'Well, my message eased the situation. When Adenauer
received it he agreed to see Mendès-France and they got on quite
well together. Both of them can see the realities of the situation.
Why, if there were war tomorrow we would all fight under General
Gruenther.'[1]

He sat down with a flop into a chair.

'I don't know why I am such a bloody fool as to want to go on.'

August 28, 1954

This morning I found Winston more at peace about things than
he has been for some time.

'I had a very agreeable conversation with Anthony.'

'You don't mean he gave in without a fight?' I blurted out.

Winston ignored my interruption.

'I should resist and resent it if they tried to push me out. But

[1] Supreme Allied Commander, Europe.

593

everybody has been very nice. I would like to play the game,' he said after a pause. 'I want to be magnanimous and broad-minded. I shall go a year from now. I shall not lead in another election. They need my influence. Look at Mendès-France's visit. He came of his own free will. I did not ask him. Of course, the best thing would be if I could die during that year. Like poor Cys.—you know, Cyril Asquith—he said he would have his dinner in bed, and his wife went to make arrangements. When she came back he was dead.'

Chapter fifty-four

The burden of life

August 29, 1954

'All the members of the Cabinet have accepted my staying on. There won't be any trouble, I think.' Winston smiled mischievously. 'They don't know what they can do about it.' He became grave again. 'But I'm not so sure about things.'

That Winston has got the better of Anthony is, I fear, no more than a Pyrrhic victory. It is not Anthony we have to fear, but Winston's advancing decrepitude. The fact is that he is in poor shape.

'Of course, I don't attempt to work after dinner as I used to. I play bezique instead. And after lunch I sleep. It is dreadful. I shall not go on if I don't feel up to it. I don't look forward to this Session.'

He sighed deeply.

He is depressed by his inability to think things out. He realizes that the discovery of the hydrogen bomb has made drastic changes in our defence policy inevitable. Ten or fifteen years ago his imagination would have been stirred by such a challenge. Now he no longer has the energy of mind to think out a new policy. He does not want to be bothered. He can see the size of the job. He can see that he is no longer up to it. He is tormented by the thought that he might let the country down; it is eating away at his peace of mind.

'I have become so stupid, Charles. Cannot you do anything for me?'

September 2, 1954

When, about four o'clock, Winston woke from an hour's sleep he could not stop yawning.

'The world,' he began, 'is in a terrible condition. The throwing out of E.D.C. is a great score for the Russians.'

Then, waking up, his voice rose:

'The French have behaved in an unspeakable way, execrable. No thought at all for others, ingratitude, conceit,' he spat them out with intense distaste. 'I cannot feel the same about them in the future.'

I asked him if he had been surprised by the majority[1] in the French Chamber against E.D.C.

'No,' he answered, 'Mendès-France said there was no chance of getting it through.' Then, with more animation: 'But look at the swine, wasting three vital years. It was their own invention. They made us do it. My very pleasant relations with Anthony make things more difficult. I would have liked to control this business, but if I did I would be taking the bread out of Anthony's mouth after denying him the square meal he so much wanted.' He grinned broadly.

The Germans, the P.M. says, will take advantage of France's weakness. He had written to Adenauer; the letter had crossed one from him.

'I would like you to see the difference in tone between his letter and mine.'

He rang for a secretary. When the letter was brought he handed it to me.

'It doesn't need concentrated thought, it's the tone I wanted you to note. Generosity is always'—he hesitated for the word—'wise. If Adenauer had said: "We are not going to take advantage of this situation, we shall not ask for anything more than we should have got if the voting in the French Chamber had gone differently," the effect in this country and in America would have been very great. But,' he went on sadly, 'he's going to get all he can out of France's stupidity.'

He struggled into his zip-suit with Kirkwood's help.

He paused at the pond and rapped his stick against the stone pavement, when golden carp darted out of the shadows to gobble the maggots.

'They are twenty years old and will see me out; probably they will see you out too.'

He looked across the pond at the blue hydrangeas reflected in the clear water, saying half to himself:

'That pine tree would make a good background. I like it's red bark. I shall paint this. I would have done it yesterday but for the Cabinet. It's a different period of the year today,' and he turned up the collar of his coat.

---

[1] 319 to 264 with abstentions.

596

September 7, 1954

Calling on Winston in the middle of the morning at Chartwell, I found him working with Miss Gilliatt. She gathered up her papers and left the room. The P.M. went on talking and seemed in no hurry to call his secretary back.

'I'm very useful,' he said simply.

Ike had sent him a 'lovely letter.'

'He says my letter to Adenauer was exactly right. The Chancellor has been more moderate since I wrote to him; he sent me a gushing reply. I think Ike may come to London. I believe I can wheedle him. Then I shall be ready for the Russians. Of course the throwing out of E.D.C. rather bitched things. We have done badly in the Gallup poll in the *News Chronicle*: lost six points.'

I asked him if he thought that the Labour visit to China was responsible.

'Oh, no,' he answered gloomily. 'Rising prices and rents.'

And then he said more cheerfully:

'But there won't be an election this year. If the Socialists come in war will be nearer. There will be a coolness with America.'

He spoke of the trade-union vote reaffirming its belief in German rearmament with some emotion.

'They are fine fellows. That is the element which has been the strength of England for a thousand years; responsibility, constancy. "Death," Schiller said, "is so universal, it must be good!" We make too much of it,' Winston added. 'All religions do.' Then he grinned. 'Of course, I may alter my views.'

September 10, 1954

Winston was reading *The Times* when I called at Chartwell about ten o'clock. He picked up a page of the *Daily Mirror* which he had torn out, looked at it and passed it to me. I saw a big picture of Aneurin Bevan standing at the foot of a gigantic statue of Lenin.

'That might be useful to the Party Office as propaganda. It shows the fellow is a Communist,' he said with great disgust.

Winston spoke as if it was too much effort to talk clearly. Then he seemed to rouse himself. His thoughts were agreeable. What was coming now?

'I reduced the age when a man gets a pension from seventy to sixty-five. It was a great event then—so long ago. Now it is utterly forgotten. The General Council of the T.U.C. wanted to raise it again to sixty-seven. But they were defeated by a big majority. I agree with the majority. We will not let them raise the age while I am in office. Of course, if a man voluntarily wants to go on working till he is sixty-seven or sixty-eight, that's a different matter.'

He lapsed again into lassitude. His animation had gone. He did not seem to want to talk. He began fingering *The Times*. I had come, he knew, some distance to see him, and he did not want to hurt my feelings. As I rose to go, I noticed a book on the shelf which hangs against the wall; I leant across the bed and picked it up.

The Fabulous Leonard Jerome,[1] it was called. He became interested at once. 'A really remarkable man,' he began; 'he did exactly what he liked'—Winston smiled—'and he liked what he did. It's a very frank book; nothing is held back. He was one of nine brothers; with one of them he was particularly friendly; they married two sisters and built houses at Rochester connected by a bridge. I've seen it. Not that he was particularly domesticated.' A great grin signalled that something was coming. 'He was a magnificent looking man, and had a number of illegitimate children. He produced one of the most famous singers in the world. I think she succeeded Adelina Patti.' Winston took the book from me, and when he had found the place he wanted, showed me a photograph of Minnie Hawk as Carmen. 'Look very carefully at it, Charles.' Then he glanced up at the photograph of his mother above his bed. 'They're very like each other,' he added thoughtfully. 'My mother was his daughter, and Minnie was a natural daughter.' I asked him what Mrs. Jerome made of all this. 'Once,' he replied, 'meeting one of his mistresses, she said: "My dear, I understand what you feel. He is so irresistible." My grandmother lived a lot in Paris, the Paris of the Second Empire, and my mother was really brought up there.

'They were terrific times on Wall Street. It was an age of unbridled individualism. Men would deliberately decide to destroy a great company, or perhaps they would determine to ruin some great figure in the financial world. My grandfather would devote himself to work and in a short time make a fortune; then he would give up the life completely, disappearing for a year or two, generally to Europe. When he came back to New York he might have lost the fortune he had made, and at once set about piling up another. Money poured through his fingers,' and Winston held up his hand to show me how this happened. 'He generally had an income of £10,000, perhaps equal to £40,000 now. My grandfather thought nothing of spending $70,000 on a party, where each lady found a gold bracelet, inset with diamonds, wrapped in her napkin. He built enormous stables, and in front of them he planted a vast house. And then he threw up everything, and for five years became

[1] Anita Leslie, *The Fabulous Leonard Jerome* (Hutchinson, 1954).

Consul at Trieste; there he had great influence and would have liked to go on with the life.

'He founded the Jockey Club in New York,' Winston went on, 'and though he had to deal with crooks, cleaned up the Turf. He had a particular liking for sailing small yachts across the Atlantic. One day he and two of his friends each put up £30,000; they agreed to sail three boats from New York to the Needles; the first to arrive would take the prize of £90,000.' I saw that Winston was deeply stirred by the adventures of his grandfather; as he told me about him he seemed to live through it, and his voice had now become strong and full of vigour and expression. He began to draw for me a picture of New York after the Civil War, 'a turbulent place.' 'It was a time of tremendous convulsions, all the people bursting with energy and life. The four hundred governing families quarrelled among themselves, cutting this person and staring through that. They were anxious to control the *nouveaux riches*, especially the less reputable ones, trying to do what an older and more tolerant aristocracy in England had done more quietly and more effectively.' I rose to leave him, but he took no notice. He had become engrossed in his story, and did not want me to go. He had escaped into the past, right away from a world of tribulation. Searching through the book, he found the page he was looking for and showed me a photograph of his grandfather. 'Very fierce,' Winston commented. 'I'm the only tame one they've produced.'

September 26, 1954

Winston was struggling with his speech for the Party Conference at Blackpool when I saw him at Chartwell this morning. He looked up at me as if he were carrying the burden of the world.

'Bloody,' he ejaculated.

'When is it?'

'October 7. I shall go up the night before and get to bed early.'

'Anyway, it isn't a formidable hurdle like Margate last October, and you've started in good time.'

'Oh, I don't know,' he grumbled. 'I'm not looking forward to it, I've nothing to say.'

As Miss Gilliatt was collecting her papers before leaving the room, he took up a sheet of paper and gave it to me to read. It was in his own writing.

'I haven't written out a speech in my own hand for forty years. I did it because I was determined to make myself compose—I won't be beaten.'

His voice became stronger and more vehement.

599

'I'll write out the whole bloody speech if necessary. I do all my work in the mornings now—though, of course, I can preside over meetings at any time.'

While I was reading, he said in a vigorous voice:

'We must learn the lessons of the past. We must not remember today the hatreds of yesterday.'

I knew he was trying it out on me, not so much to discover what I thought about the words but rather to get an impression how they sounded to him.

'If millions of people in one country learn to hate millions in another trouble is bound to come. This fellow Aneurin Bevan is deliberately stirring up anger and passion by bringing up Germany's sins in the war. It is very wrong. My right foot feels cold.'

He threw back the bed-clothes, and taking my hand, directed it to the offending limb.

'Of course I take no exercise; I get tired at once.'

I asked him how much he could do before he felt fatigue. 'Nothing,' he answered.

I tried to hearten him by reminding him that only last week he had come through a fifteen-hour day.

'I was very depressed next day,' he said grudgingly. 'I don't know why I get depressed as I do. They gave me Lord Russell's book on German war crimes.[1] A terrible book. Have you read the *Conspiracy of Silence*? It's by an Austrian,[2] who is in Paris now, and has a preface by the man[3] who wrote *Darkness at Noon*. Yes, the Russians questioned this poor fellow for eighteen hours at a time, and if he showed any signs of exhaustion they hit him in the face. It is a terrible world.

'You know, Charles,' he said sadly, 'I have come to think Stalin very culpable. Eight million lives were lost in the famine and another seven million in the collectivization of the farms. I did not realize this.'

'Don't you remember Stalin saying "What is one generation?" '

I had caught his attention by this remark.

'Did he say that? When?'

He said nothing for some time, brooding. Then he quoted Stalin:

' "A single death is an incident of consequence and pathos, but the death of a million is a matter of statistics." '

'I want,' said the P.M., 'to leave the conference to Anthony as much as I can. He likes doing it very much and does it very well.'

In the car on the way to Chartwell Mrs. Romilly[4] told me how

---

[1] *The Scourge of the Swastika* (Cassell, 1954).   [2] M. Blizowd.

[3] Arthur Koestler.   [4] Lady Churchill's sister.

she had dined with Winston the night the First War broke out. 'Clemmie seemed crushed, but Winston was elated'—she hesitated— 'perhaps elated is the wrong word. Anyway, he was bursting with energy and excitement.' She thought Clemmie would want to play croquet if the rain held off. I told her about Monty and his croquet tactics. 'Oh, yes,' she laughed. 'You know Mrs. Attlee is almost a professional player, but Monty kept giving her instructions. At last she put down her mallet. "I know a great deal about croquet," she said. "Please do not order me about. It is quite intolerable." Monty seemed rather confused, but after a little he again began directing the game. He cannot help it. But Clemmie is very fond of him, though they have sharp tiffs at times. I suppose,' Mrs. Romilly added inconsequently, 'he is a very fine soldier.'

October 1, 1954

The P.M.'s fear that America might withdraw from Europe and 'go it alone' was not without reason. When the Nine Power Conference met on Wednesday Mr. Dulles spoke of a great wave of disillusionment which had swept over America after E.D.C. had been rejected; there was a feeling, he said, that 'the situation in Europe is pretty hopeless.' It was in this bleak atmosphere that the delegates were asked to find some means of rearming Germany that would be accepted by a majority of the French Assembly. Round the table they sat, doodling, mumbling, despairing.

Then Mr. Eden rose and told the representatives of the Nine Powers that if the conference was successful Britain would undertake to keep on the Continent the forces now stationed there; that she would not withdraw them without the consent of the majority of the Brussels Treaty Powers, including West Germany and Italy, as well as France and the Low Countries. Mr. Eden called this 'a very formidable step to take,' since it committed Britain to the defence of Western Europe. The delegates sat dumbfounded. The silence was at length broken by M. Spaak, who, turning to M. Mendès-France, said, 'You've won.' Everyone felt that the situation had been transformed and that Mr. Eden's pledge saved the conference when it seemed bound to end in a fiasco.

It was accordingly with a light heart that I entered the P.M.'s bedroom this morning, as Kirkwood backed out with the breakfast tray. But somehow the P.M. did not seem particularly elated; indeed, he seemed to take more interest in the result of the East Croydon by-election, and what the papers said about it, than in the conference. He was frankly delighted with the figures. 'Why, Charles, in proportion they are better than in the last three by-elections.' He spoke of Bevan's performance at the Labour Conference at Scarborough with distaste. 'That fellow is a gold-mine to us,' he said cheerfully. 'Such a cad.'

I brought him back to Anthony's pledge. 'It can be cancelled at any time,' he went on with a mischievous smile. 'It does not mean anything. All words. Of course I shall not say that,' he added hastily. 'But what is all the fuss about? No one in their senses thought we could bring our troops home from the Continent. No one imagined that if Russia decided to march to the West we could sit still and do nothing; if there is war we are bound to fight. We have always been better than our word. Now they are going to do exactly what I suggested at Strasbourg in August, 1950. Never,' he said, smiling broadly, 'was the leadership of Europe so cheaply won.'

I wondered why the P.M. had taken Anthony's historic declaration at the London Conference so coolly. After all, President Eisenhower called it 'one of the greatest diplomatic achievements of our time,' and Mendès-France spoke of the historic importance of Anthony's words. Is it because the idea came from Anthony? I banished the unworthy thought. The P.M. feels that the pledge at the conference has not changed anything. The French wanted our troops on the spot. It is the effect of the pledge on feeling in the Cabinet and in America that is new.

'Adenauer wants me to do what I can to strengthen and arm France.' The P.M.'s eyes opened wider. 'Germany wants a strong France,' he repeated; he did not wish me to miss the significance of Adenauer's attitude. 'I can go to Germany now. Oh, I haven't been into dates yet. All the credit is due to Anthony. He arranged everything.'

He sighed deeply. 'Now I have got this Blackpool speech on my hands. I wish it was in shape. I shall not take you to Blackpool, Charles; it would only draw attention to my health. It's different, of course, when I go abroad.'

October 9, 1954

The P.M. was abstracted, grave and uncommunicative. He was due to leave the house for Blackpool in an hour, and was going over his speech in his head. I said that it was not like last year; he would take it in his stride. He smiled doubtfully. 'I think I can harangue the bastards for fifty minutes.' He did not want to talk, and I left him.

October 10, 1954

A year ago the delegates went to Margate to find out the truth about 'The Old Man.' There had been talk about a stroke. Would he be able to carry on? they had wondered; while we in London sat on tenter-hooks dreading that he might break down in the middle of his speech. This morning, however, when I picked up the *Observer* I did not turn at once to the P.M.'s speech. When I did what I read put me in good heart. The reporter knew all about Mr. Churchill; he had got him in focus even down to the delighted little crows before the jokes. He recalled how at Margate last year the conference had bidden goodbye to Sir Winston—some of the delegates had felt a lump in the throat as they took part in an historic, a unique occasion—and here he was once more as if nothing had happened. Was the Party impatiently crying out for a change? The *Observer* was quite sure of the answer. 'The conference was endlessly delighted with him.'

Certainly it did not enter the Prime Minister's head that he was at Blackpool on approval. There was, indeed, a suggestion that as he slowly climbed the stairs to the platform he was chuckling over something. Would the delegates really like to know when he was going to retire? Well, he was not going to tell them. That was his secret. He seemed, in his own impish way, to be enjoying their bewilderment. 'At any rate, for the moment,' the paper concluded, 'the rank and file seem content that he should go in his own time and how he pleases.' After all, he seemed, strange to relate, in far better shape than a year ago.

But when I got to Chartwell and asked Jane Portal how it had gone she did not seem so sure. Opinions were mixed. Anyway, judging by the applause, it went well with the delegates. Jane smiled affectionately. 'He was as quick as ever to cover his mistakes; he said "sovereignty" when he meant "solvency," and then in the same breath added: "Quite a natural mistake to make, for the two go together very well." Of course, he fumbled for a word at times. I suppose,' she said, 'we've got used to that and hardly notice when he hesitates for his words.'

However, Jock and Christopher were 'disappointed.' Jock thought it was one of his worst speeches. 'Why?' I asked. 'Because,' Jock said, 'his delivery was so bad.' Christopher had gone down among the delegates and sensed that it was not what the P.M.'s hearers wanted. There was an election, not too far off now, and the Party was frankly worried; the public-opinion polls showed them to be doing none too well. And here was the leader of the Party singling out Mr. Attlee and Mr. Morrison, praising them because they had been consistent in foreign policy. That, of course, was magnanimous and all that, but it wasn't going to help the Conservatives at the hustings. All this highbrow stuff was, they thought, out of place at a Party conference. The P.M. was, no doubt, a very great man, but he seemed to have lost touch with the rank and file; he did not know what they were thinking.

They had gone to Blackpool hoping for news; what they wanted to hear from the Prime Minister was when he intended to retire. This uncertainty about the leadership was not doing the Conservatives as a party much good. And all they were told was that there was quite enough for both Mr. Churchill and Mr. Eden to do at the present time. In this mood what more natural than that the delegates should look for signs in the old man that would confirm their feeling that the time had come for him to go. Someone had noticed that he said 1850 when he meant 1950 (he had made the same mistake in the Cabinet), while others thought he looked tired and that his delivery was a little slow and rather halting at times. As long as he made the Opposition look small the Party would be quiet and let him carry on, but he ought to know that only success could justify his lingering on the stage.

However, if those who listened to the Prime Minister had doubts, he himself had none. 'The Tories as a party,' he once complained to me, 'aren't responsive,' but he did not feel like that at Blackpool. When I went to his room and asked him what had happened, he replied:

'Oh, it was a huge success. I was not at all tired at the end. The pill was wonderful. I felt exactly as I did twenty years ago when I could work the whole bloody day like any other man. Tell me, Charles, does it do very much harm to the constitution? It gives me great confidence.' For a time he seemed a long way off, and then he looked up: 'While Anthony has this French business on his hands how could he give it all up and take on my job?'

I did not attempt to answer this conundrum. He continued:

'There may be a strike tonight among the printers, and no morning papers, so that no one will read my speech. I hope very much that at the last minute it will be called off.'

October 14, 1954

I was taken aback when I found the P.M. in an explosive mood. He spoke bitterly of the folly of the Tories in rashly throwing away all he had to give. Something has happened. I suspect that Christopher has told him of the feeling in the Party that he ought to

604

go. My guess was on the target. The delegates might have made up their minds, but the P.M. has no intention of bowing to their will. 'If they try to get me out I will resist.' He stopped short in the middle of a sentence. He had said, I suppose, more than he meant.

With an expression of weariness he went on: 'I have got to go to the station to meet that man from Ethiopia.' So this voice out of the eighteenth century spoke of an enlightened ruler. When I repeated this ebullition to Jock he greeted it with a wan smile. 'Haile Selassie is a great man,' he said; 'one of the few friends we have got in the world.'

*

It was, no doubt, a shock to Winston when he found out that the Party as a whole wanted him to resign. But this is guess-work, for I can find no reference in my diary during the next fortnight to the political situation, apart from a grouse at the work involved in reconstructing the Government.[1] For the time being he was out of conceit with politics.

October 21, 1954

Winston was correcting proofs of his *History of the English-speaking Peoples*. He looked glumly at me, grunting: 'I have been very tired the last few days. I must not let these personal issues rattle me; reconstructing the Cabinet is like solving a kaleidoscopic jig-saw puzzle. It was all so personal, and you know how much I hate hurting people's feelings. The Lord Chancellor wasn't happy about going; did you see the ceremony when David[2] was introduced?'

He did not listen to my answer, but when he asked me whether the House of Lords thought it was a change for the better he turned and looked straight at me, waiting for my reply. The P.M.'s conscience seems to prick him about this change.

'Simonds,' he continued, 'had no political experience, though he may have been a good lawyer. Lord Salisbury wanted help; he wanted someone in the House who understood politics.' There was a long pause, and I thought the P.M. had done, when he observed: 'David always wanted it. He wanted it when Simonds got it, but I could not spare him then; he was so useful in the House of Commons, where he was most industrious.' David had worked his passage, and had first claim.

[1] A major Cabinet reshuffle took place in October. Eight senior ministers were involved.
[2] David Maxwell-Fyfe, Viscount Kilmuir (1954). Succeeded Lord Simonds as Lord Chancellor on October 18, 1954.

Norman Brook took up the story; he told me how the P.M. dislikes telling people they are not wanted any longer. 'He gets out of it whenever he can. All the juniors, for instance, who were discharged had to be seen by the Chief Whip. "You see them and explain," the P.M. said, "and I will write to them after you have done that." Salisbury was given the task of breaking to Simonds that his services as Lord Chancellor were no longer required.'

As for Lord Salisbury needing help, I said that David would not find his new job in the Lords very exacting. There are few peers who speak without notes; most of them just read their pieces. The P.M. interrupted: 'There is no one in the Commons who can get along without his script.' I asked him if the speaking in the Commons had deteriorated in the last thirty years. 'You mean the quality of the speeches?' he asked, and thought for a moment. 'Fewer spoke then. Yes, they had more personality in those days.'

'Anthony was very happy about the Garter. It was the Queen's suggestion.' A broad grin appeared as he told me of a cartoon by Low in yesterday's *Manchester Guardian*. Winston thought it a good idea that at eighty a man should get younger every year. The smile vanished. 'But it won't happen,' he muttered glumly.

October 24, 1954

Winston, it seems, has resolved to put Blackpool out of his head. If the Party is foolish enough to want him to go, it has not weakened his purpose to stay. All that it has done is to set him free from the tiresome duty of keeping up appearances and to make plain to him that window-dressing is now futile. He does not even try to persuade me that he is fit to carry on. Why should he, when the Party has decided that the time has come for him to go? Why bother now to disguise the fact that he does not want to settle down to hard work, that he has no longer any zest for anything? Why go to the trouble of preparing speeches if his audience has already made up its mind?

'I am lunching the Emperor of Ethiopia tomorrow before I go down to Chequers. I have never entertained an Emperor before,' he added with a whimsical smile. I told the P.M. that the Emperor was dining with the Archbishop of Canterbury. 'They are both Christians,' Winston observed, 'though the Ethiopians are guilty of a gross heresy.' He tried to explain what it was. 'It is something about the Trinity. The difference is between like substance and same substance.' He was not sure which the Ethiopians used, but anyway: 'Thousands have been cut to pieces for that very heresy.' He grinned. 'If I were asked about it I would say that I accept what is the law. I am no good at metaphysics.'

October 26, 1954

The P.M. handed me a paper with photographs of the Queen receiving the Italian film-stars. 'She knocks 'em all endways. Lovely she is,' and he held the picture away from him to see it better. He picked up the *Daily Worker* from the bed. 'Poison, hatred for the existing order,' he said sadly.

'The House is giving me a book for my birthday.[1] It is wonderfully got up—the College of Arms is helping—and will cost £400. But I am worried about it. There is a space for every constituency in the House of Commons, so that every Member can sign. Some may not want to sign. Of course, I haven't read it, but I know the general trend. It is full of flattering things; things no man ought to hear in his lifetime; things I should blush to read. Bunyan is brought in. I'm compared to him.

'One of the papers is getting up a subscription for a birthday present. If it's for me, so that I can do what I want with it, I would like it very much. But I don't want them to raise a sum for charity just to bring home some coloured gentleman from Jamaica to complete his education. I'd rather they did nothing. Of course, I might give some of the money subscribed to a charity that I was connected with. But I'm not a rich man. I got nothing out of those six volumes'—he jerked his head towards a shelf on the wall—'and Clemmie got nothing, except a few shillings. The children, of course, will benefit. The four volumes of my *History of the English-speaking Peoples* will bring me a great income, but the Treasury will take it all.

'I am not in favour of the present rate of taxation on earned incomes. It will destroy all incentive. People will not work as hard. Everything has become so expensive, servants, every single thing. I lunched yesterday at the House of Commons.'

'Anyway, that would be reasonable enough,' I put in.

'I paid £1 14s.,' Winston retorted. 'Oh, I had a brandy and half a bottle of hock. It is not that I have expensive tastes. I stay in bed too much to spend a lot of money. I'm not extravagant. Racing practically pays for itself. If I retired I could make a lot of money, perhaps £50,000 a year, but it would be only 50,000 shillings. If people want to subscribe to give me a birthday present I don't mind.

'I have accepted an invitation to address the Scottish National Union of Conservatives—where? Oh, somewhere in Scotland.'

He answered as if his mind were elsewhere. Thinking he meant

[1] Winston's eightieth birthday was on November 30, 1954.

in the immediate future, I asked innocently, 'What date?' He hesitated. Then he grinned. 'May 20th.'

He looked at me as if he was curious to see how I would take it.

'It is some time off,' I said. 'Six months in fact.'

November 10, 1954

The P.M. felt rather under the weather and grumbled that he had not found it easy to settle down to his speech for Guildhall. As long as I have known Winston he has taken almost excessive pains to ensure the success of an important speech. Now he does not seem to care. A good deal is left to chance. Sometimes he does not appear to be interested in what he is saying. It is true that what he said was passable enough, and he said it, too, with plenty of vigour, but there were some awkward pauses. Even when reading a speech—as he invariably does—he seems to lose his concentration, as if he were bored with it, and only wanted to get to the end. A secretary explained the pauses. 'He would play bezique instead of getting on with the speech. It was never properly prepared. That was why there were those dreadful pauses; he was not familiar with the script.'

When I asked the P.M. about his speech he answered with a touch of impatience: 'Oh, it went all right.' There was a long pause. 'Perhaps I have cared too much what people think.'

His mood changed. His birthday would be a very heavy day. He spoke very simply of the kindness of everybody. 'I am humbled,' he said, 'by what is being said. Look at that,' and he pointed to a letter from two old-age pensioners, with a postal order for 5*s*. 'I have had it framed.' A boy had sent six penny stamps. 'I have not deserved all this.'

This was not conventional modesty—indeed, Winston has never been a modest man in the usual sense. It was not the Englishman's instinctive response when praised, but rather a deep human response to a profoundly moving experience.

Chapter fifty-five

The Woodford blunder

November 23, 1954

The P.M. telephoned yesterday: 'I'm bothered about the speeches. Westminster Hall on the birthday, Bristol and, of course, Woodford tonight. I shall want three 'majors' to get me through them. I'm short of ideas, they don't come to me as easily as they did.' I asked him if he really needed a 'major' when he talked to his constituents. 'Well, perhaps not,' he agreed, 'they will be very kind to me.'

This morning, however, it seemed that his troubles were forgotten. He talked again about the subscription list. 'I don't mind telling you I'm very happy about it. I shall be able to stay on at Chartwell now.' He was pleased, too, with the result of the by-election at West Derby. 'Things are better now than they have been for a long time,' he reflected. 'Three years in office with a majority of sixteen; you know, Charles, it is a great achievement. Don't worry about me; I'm not really fussed about tonight.'

November 28, 1954

'I used to be frightened in the old days,' Winston once told me, 'that I should say something in the House of Commons and wake up and find it had landed me in trouble. That doesn't happen now. I've learned a lot; after all, I've had fifty years of it.' But Clemmie only shook her head; she is still terrified that he will put his foot in things, and will never be happy until he resigns. I suppose she is right, from her point of view. Anyway, we're in trouble again. Winston, speaking to his constituents in a girls' school at Woodford on November 23, went out of his way to give them some secret history:

'Even before the war had ended, and while the Germans were surrendering by hundreds of thousands. . . . I telegraphed to Lord Montgomery directing him to be careful in collecting the German arms, to stack them so that they could easily be issued again to the

German soldiers whom we should have to work with if the Soviet advance continued.'

What on earth made him say it? *The Times* begins a critical leader with these words, and no one is sure about the answer. Why did he want to tell his constituents about the telegram? It seems that he found everyone at Woodford full of the birthday; there was a lot of celebrating and drinking of toasts, his foresight was extolled. Then someone asked him about the Russians, and Fulton[1] was mentioned. It was good to recall that he was alive then to the threat to Western Europe. The rest is guesswork, but I think I can follow his thoughts. These kind folk spoke of Fulton, but long before Fulton he was alive to the Russian menace; that wanted bringing home to people. For only one thing mattered now—it was often in his mind—when his record came before posterity they must be fair to him. All this talk about the war having been fought in vain made him angry. At any rate, he was not to blame. To get that quite clear he had added a sixth volume to his book and called it *Triumph and Tragedy*. He would remember then how Camrose and his publishers tried to persuade him that it was a mistake to bring out another volume. But he would not listen to them. For he was resolved to make it known that he wanted to take precautions against some rather ugly possibilities as early as the spring of 1945, at a time when the Americans were still busy making friends with Stalin and had not woken up to the danger of Communism.

That, no doubt, was why the P.M. wanted to tell his constituents about his foresight in the spring of 1945, but why did he blurt it all out now? He had not, after all, given up hope of talks with the Russians, and this surely would not help matters. In plain fact, Winston had no idea at Woodford that he was laying up trouble for himself. Though he studies the papers morning and evening with some care, he never seems to know in what way the public will react to anything that he may do or say. Like Mr. Gladstone,[2] he has no gift for getting into other people's minds; sometimes he does not even appear to be interested.

It was this that used to puzzle President Roosevelt; that any politician could exist like this in a vacuum was incomprehensible to him. He himself had spent a lot of time pondering on what his countrymen were thinking—he was in the habit of trying out his

---

[1] In Fulton, Missouri, on March 5, 1946, Churchill pleaded for Great Britain and the United States to unite as guardians of the peace, and he set out frankly the menace of Soviet policies.

[2] G. M. Young, in *To-day and Yesterday*, writes: 'But of those roving explorations of other men's minds. . . . Mr. Gladstone was by temperament incapable.'

speeches on experienced politicians before they were delivered. Whereas when Winston made a speech it was a kind of one-way traffic that owed nothing to the audience.

I turned instinctively to Norman Brook to check whether Winston's detachment was as complete as I have depicted. He is so full of horse-sense that he has no time for fancy reasoning. He agreed that Winston's mind works in this way.

'He is the king-pin, of course, and he will do the job. He thinks of those around him only as menials, they do not really count. Oh, no, he is not in the least interested in any of us, or in our future. As long as we are devoted to him, and do not make bad mistakes, Winston will not think of anyone else. One man at a time has always been his motto.'

With this in mind we can now follow Mr. Churchill's thoughts in 1945. True, we are still taken aback by his ignorance of what the ordinary man was then thinking. We still find it difficult to understand how anyone can live so cut off from other people, but what he told us at Woodford no longer surprises us. Did he imagine, for a moment, *The Times* asked scornfully, that the Western peoples, hating the Hitler régime with a hatred greater than anything they had known, would understand and accept the use of Hitler's defeated soldiers to set a military barrier against the forces they still welcomed as victorious allies? Did he expect memories and emotions to fade overnight? The plain answer is that he did. Nor will he admit, even now, that what he had in mind would have split opinion in Britain and America.

However, it is no good crying over spilt milk. What everyone wants to know now is whether the Prime Minister is in real trouble or whether this is just another false alarm like the hydrogen bomb debate. Moscow, no doubt, will make a song and dance and hint that talks with Russia are not likely to come to anything while Mr. Churchill is Prime Minister. But unless this feeling is at all common in this country nothing will happen. The House of Commons will not give him much trouble unless the country takes it seriously. For it is already obvious that Attlee will not sponsor an attack on the Prime Minister on this issue unless a section of his Party forces his hand. The *Manchester Guardian* has spoken for sober opinion; it does not take the P.M.'s slip at all seriously. Sir Winston, it dryly remarks, could hardly have foreseen, when he told his constituents this little anecdote, that he would be denounced by the oddest of Press choruses—*The Times*, the *Daily Herald*, the *Daily Mirror* and the *Daily Worker*. Their common link, the *Guardian* observes, seems to be the wish to force him out of office.

What does the P.M. himself make of it all? I have not seen him since the speech, but from what I hear at No. 10 he does not seem to have taken it to heart. Anyway he went off to Bristol in good shape, and appears to be having high jinks there. Saturated with gifts, as he has been, there was a break in his voice when he thanked the students for giving him an eighteenth-century salver, 'on a day when, if you look at the papers, I am supposed to be in a bit of a scrape.' For their part they had no feeling that he was an old man; on the contrary, he seemed to be one of themselves, and two thousand young voices shouted their joy and approval. The same puckish humour marked his approach to their seniors. 'I always enjoy coming here, and I may say that I rather like wearing this robe. It was my father's robe as Chancellor of the Exchequer in 1886, and was most carefully preserved by my mother until I had the opportunity of wearing it as Chancellor of the Exchequer myself.'

Oliver Franks happened to be at Bristol that day, and he was puzzled because Winston's physical condition seems to change as quickly as his moods. 'I saw him at Buckingham Palace a few days before,' he told me, 'sitting on a sofa, apparently too weary to listen to anybody; his face was white and like a mask, his body had flopped, he seemed a very old man who had not long to live. But at Bristol he was pink, his expression was full of animation and his eyes twinkled. Perhaps you doctors can explain what happens?'

November 29, 1954

About five o'clock Jane Portal telephoned: 'Could you see the Prime Minister at seven-thirty? The Cabinet ought to be over by then. He has been sitting taking his pulse with his thumb,' she added. 'He's worrying over Woodford, and he's not happy about tomorrow.' The last of the Cabinet were leaving as I entered No. 10. I found him in the Cabinet Room, and as he came towards me his gait was very unsteady and his face was dull and without expression. 'I'm worried about this stupid mistake of mine. I was quite certain it was in my book, otherwise I would never have said what I did. And now it seems there wasn't a telegram, after all. Anyway, no trace can be found of it. I must have thought better of it. My speech ought, of course, to have been checked.' He sat for some time glowering at his feet. 'If my slip has done harm with the Russians I may pull out sooner than I intended. Take my pulse, Charles.' It was 82. When I had reassured him he brightened up a little. 'The *Daily Mirror* has declared a truce for tomorrow. They have sent £1,000 to my birthday fund. I am to be given a cheque for £140,000 tomorrow. All this leaves me very humble; it is more than I deserve.'

Montague Browne told me that the P.M. was worried about the Russians; he would like to be sure that his speech has done no harm at the Kremlin. 'That's all he cares about. He didn't seem at all depressed by the criticisms of his speech until he read what appeared in *Pravda* yesterday.' I asked Montague Browne about the telegram. It appears that Pownall [1] was asked three years ago to check this telegram to Monty for the P.M.'s book. He could find no trace of any telegram and concluded the P.M. must have decided at the last moment not to send it. I asked if Labour would be able to make capital out of the speech. 'They can and will,' he replied. Christopher added cheerfully: 'It was very stupid of Winston to say it.' As I left, the doorway of No. 10 was blocked by an immense birthday cake which two men were trying to lever into the hall without injuring any of the eighty white candles.

[1] Lieut.-General Sir Henry Pownall. Assisted Churchill in the preparation of *The Second World War.*

Chapter fifty-six

Harmony and discord

November 30, 1954

Winston Churchill is eighty years of age today—a remarkable achievement for a man of his habits. A fine disregard for common sense has marked his earthly pilgrimage. What he wanted to do he has always done without a thought for the consequences. And now he can say that he has his cake and has eaten it too. To account for his survival it is generally supposed that he has a wonderful constitution. Indeed he is unusual in the way in which he can adapt himself to circumstances; he is indifferent, for instance, to heat and cold; fatigue of mind or body he hardly knew until he was seventy; while whatever may happen overnight in the way of revelry, he wakes with a song in his heart and a zest for breakfast.

On the other hand, he is often in the hands of the doctor. It is now fifteen years since I first saw him, and in that time he has had:

(i) a heart attack in Washington just after Pearl Harbour;
(ii) three attacks of pneumonia, one of which at any rate was a 'damned nice thing';
(iii) two strokes, in 1949 and 1953;
(iv) two operations, one of which found the abdomen full of adhesions and lasted two hours;
(v) senile pruritis, perhaps the most intractable of all skin troubles;
(vi) a form of conjunctivitis unlikely to clear up without a small operation.

(I have not mentioned dyspepsia or diverticulitis, because they have never really caused worry.) To this catalogue of woe I should add that for ten years he has not had natural sleep apart from sedatives. Looking back, he seems to have been in the wars a great deal, but I treasure my battle honours: it has been possible, save for two attacks of pneumonia and some gossip about his stroke in June, 1953, to keep all this from the public, and for that matter from the political world.

When I had written so far I made my way to No. 10, bearing my small gift, Lord David Cecil's two volumes on Melbourne, bound in leather by two Poles who work in Hampstead, and one of the Duke of Marlborough's letters in French from my boys. The room was full of presents of every kind. When I had greeted him he said: 'You've played a big part in this.' He told me very simply that when he read the quotation from John Bunyan on the title page of the book of commemoration he felt very humble, and when he tried to repeat the words to me his voice broke and he could not go on.

Christopher came into the room. 'Charles has given me this book. I wanted to read it.' But Christopher took no notice of Winston's kindly gesture. The P.M. gave me his speech to read, and I was charmed by its airy grace. In the office Jane Portal told me that the P.M. had talked to Mr. Attlee about the Woodford speech and has been comforted by what he said. I went back to tell him to wear a greatcoat in Westminster Hall, a gaunt, chilly place. But he said that the Ministry of Works had fitted electric pads to the back of his chair.

When the Queen had opened Parliament I lost no time in making my way to Westminster Hall, where I had the good fortune to find an empty chair. About noon there was a sudden hush, and, shading my eyes against the sun that was streaming through the great window on to the stone stairs, I could see a little party round the Prime Minister. I stood up and looked again. Yes, Aneurin Bevan and Jennie Lee were there. The man next to me, in his excitement, caught hold of my coat sleeve.

All but twenty-six members of the House of Commons had signed the Book and had contributed to a portrait of him by Graham Sutherland; it had given him pleasure that all parties were taking part in the celebration. For it was not always so. When Gladstone became eighty the Tories held aloof. Indeed, this gathering would not have been possible before the war. Winston's part then made the House more kindly, more tolerant. To mark the universal harmony *The Times* and the *Manchester Guardian* had contrived to hit on the same heading for their leading articles: 'Eighty Years On.'

Then the drums beat out the opening bar of Beethoven's Fifth Symphony—the three shorts and a long which make V in the Morse code—V for victory, the war signal in the occupied countries that the B.B.C. was about to bring them news from the outer world—and, as the Prime Minister turned to the great gathering, the Guards

615

Band played Elgar's 'Pomp and Circumstance'. Winston was in his old frock-coat. He came forward, and as he began to descend the stairs his right leg shot out in the air before it came down on the step; he was not very steady. I held my breath, but nothing happened; he took his seat, sitting bolt upright, his hands laid flat on his knees, while wide-eyed he searched all around him.

When Winston is touched by kindness he expands to his full size, and he can no more hide the underlying goodness that is in him. Now as he faced his friends from both Houses and from all parties he was resolved to keep a grip on his emotions. He told them that they were very kind 'to a party politician who had not yet retired.' Then he uttered a note of warning:

'This ceremony, with all its charm and splendour, may well be found to have seriously affected my controversial value as a party politician. However, perhaps with suitable assistance I shall get over this reaction and come round after a bit.'

At the end of his journey he was in a mood to speak well of all men. Even Graham Sutherland was forgiven. Besides, 'You can't look a gift horse in the mouth,' he said rather sadly.

'The portrait is a remarkable example of modern art. It certainly combines force and candour.'

It had to be said; they must make what they could of it. There was a little pause, and then a gust of laughter swept the hall.

The ending explains better than I can why men love him. 'I have never accepted what many people have kindly said—namely that I inspired the nation. Their will was resolute and remorseless, and as it proved, unconquerable. It fell to me to express it, and if I found the right words you must remember that I have always earned my living by my pen and by my tongue. It was the nation and the race dwelling all round the globe that had the lion's heart. I had the luck to be called upon to give the roar.'

Mr. Attlee, who must know a good deal about Churchill by now, found exactly the right words to give him pleasure: 'You had the conception of the Dardanelles campaign, the only imaginative strategic idea of the war. I wish that you had had full power to carry it to success. You urged the adoption of the tank, the only new tactical weapon of first importance in that war.' When the P.M. heard this he looked up at Mr. Attlee as if he had only half understood, then a wry smile appeared and he suddenly nodded his head. He had done his part manfully—he had promised me he would not let his emotion get on top—but now as he stumbled through the North door into the winter day he could no longer keep back his tears.

616

December 1, 1954

When I got out of the lift at No. 10 they told me that Pug Ismay, Norman Brook and Jock were closeted with the P.M. They were concocting the P.M.'s reply to Shinwell for the debate on the Address this afternoon. I sent in a note that I had only called to see if all was well after yesterday's excitement, and that I would not bother him unless he wanted anything. But in a moment they all came trooping out of his bedroom. 'The P.M. would like to see you,' Jock said.

As I entered the room he pushed away the bed-rest, and when I came to his assistance I saw Vol. VI, *Triumph and Tragedy*, open at page 498—the Iron Curtain telegram to Truman. The P.M. asked me to take his pulse. I told him everything was all right, though he looked weary and dispirited. He glanced up at me and said impulsively: 'You have been a great comfort to me.' I promised to call again later, and with that I got up and left him.

There was no venom in Shinwell's attack on the Woodford speech this afternoon, but the P.M. was in poor form when he came to reply. Yesterday was an unusual drain on his ebbing strength; besides, he is out of conceit with himself. He knew, too, that he had not much of a case. What exactly had happened about the telegram was not clear in his own mind. His voice was tired, often he hesitated for a word, and twice I feared that he would break down. Yesterday he was at his best, today he was nearly at his worst.

However, when I was worrying about his poor showing the Speaker reassured me. 'Winston,' he said, 'knows the House of Commons, and the Shinwell business went much better than I anticipated. The Prime Minister was wise enough at once to acknowledge his sins, and the House will always forgive anyone who does this. He was very adroit.' The Speaker added that he was sure it would all die down. Norman Brook was not quite so hopeful.

The P.M.'s speech had been in three parts. The first was ragged and unkempt. 'I made a goose of myself at Woodford, forgetting what I'd done,' he confessed to me. All he had to do in apologizing to the House was to translate this briefly into Parliamentary language, but he havered on until it took up a page of Hansard.

The body of the speech, on the other hand, was effective and impressed the House. It was adroit, as the Speaker said, to put beside that ill-timed disclosure the evidence of the Prime Minister's foresight in 1945, which was, after all, the cause of all the bother. Norman Brook had spent the whole morning on the speech, and I can see him saying, 'We must get this thing in perspective.' No doubt it

617

was an indiscretion on the Prime Minister's part, but how insignificant the offence seemed when set against his prescience at that time. The Prime Minister read out to the House the Iron Curtain telegram to President Truman, bearing the date May 12, 1945, to remind members of the situation then. Our armed power on the Continent was dwindling away, so that there was nothing to prevent the Russians, if they so wished, marching to the waters of the North Sea and the Atlantic. And all this hubbub was because the Prime Minister had foreseen the peril we were in and was trying to take steps to meet it. After all, was there any other way of stopping the Russians except by arming the Germans? At any rate the House was satisfied that the menace was real enough; once more they gave him full credit for his quick sense of danger; he was awake when the Americans were still asleep. No doubt it would have been better if he had left all this to the historian, but as the Speaker put it to me: 'If Winston had always been cautious we should have lost a lot.'

At this point the P.M. should have sat down. Instead he began meandering.

There were about two hundred people at his birthday party at No. 10. All Winston's world was there, with a few thrown in for the sake of political expediency, the 'impudent' Crookshank, for example.

December 3, 1954

Found the P.M. reading the *Daily Worker* and spluttering with rage. He threw it down in disgust. While he was searching the *Manchester Guardian* for approbation, I picked it up. On the front page there was a report of a meeting of the Parliamentary Labour Party. Attlee, opening the discussion, spoke of the 'abject apology' which the Prime Minister had made to the House; he did not think it was good tactics after that to continue the argument. Some of the back benchers were dissatisfied with this course. How, they asked, could the Soviet Union trust Churchill after his duplicity in 1945? How could the party continue to press for Four Power talks if he was to represent Britain? In the end, Attlee had had to change his mind; he had undertaken to refer to the telegram in the debate on Monday.

'Take my pulse, Charles.' As I put down the *Daily Worker* he said angrily: 'Though I don't care if it isn't good. I'm going to fight this out whatever happens. Abject indeed.' He spat out the offending epithet. 'The only thing I apologized for'—the P.M. was shouting now—'was that I said I had sent the telegram without checking the facts. Anthony wants to follow Attlee. Now I shall. There might be an election if they press things. World events look worse. I

618

might go and see Ike. A night in the air is nothing to me.' When? 'Oh,' he cried impatiently, 'I can't foresee events. There might be a crisis. There might be war. Mendès-France is only thinking of keeping in office. All my sympathies are with the Germans. Adenauer has sent a big silver goblet for my birthday. You saw Stansgate[1] came out strongly on my side.' He sighed deeply and said no more.

I began to check the supply of pills, cachets and capsules on the table by his bed: Disprins and 'Lord Morans', majors and minors, reds and greens, babies and midgets, to drop into his own vocabulary. He watched me for a time, then he said: 'I have found this fortnight more exhausting than any period since the Government was formed. I shall need your help.' He had not got over the excitement of the Woodford slip, which came on the top of the birthday celebrations, and when he had put Attlee out of his head he became sluggish and uncommunicative.

[1] Lord Stansgate, a Labour peer, said in the House of Lords: 'I believe, and I think the great bulk of the people in this country believe, that the greatest measure of defence we can have is that the Prime Minister should retain his position until his meeting with the Russians takes place.'

Chapter fifty-seven

An example of modern art

For some time in talking to Winston I have avoided the subject of Graham Sutherland. It is true he told me in the early stages at Chartwell that it was going to be a remarkable painting. (It is clear now that he was then speaking of the pleasing picture of himself in Garter robes, which was soon cast aside.) But a little later, when I asked him if he liked the portrait, he only grunted, adding that he had not seen it for some time. I sensed that he did not want to talk about it. However, when I inadvertently mentioned it today no encouragement was needed to get him to express an opinion. That he should go down to posterity like that had not occurred to him. He seemed put out. He does not like criticism, written or pictorial. A lot of his time since the end of the war had been spent in arranging and editing the part he will play in history, and it has been rather a shock to him that his ideas and those of Graham Sutherland seem so far apart. 'Filthy,' he spluttered. 'I think it is malignant.'

Was Winston fair to the artist? Sutherland's intentions, at any rate, seem to have been unexceptionable. The trouble was not that he admired the P.M. too little, but rather that he worshipped him too blindly. Graham Sutherland was thinking of the Churchill who had stopped the enemy and saved England, and the manner in which, without a word of guidance, Mr. Churchill took up a pose on the dais convinced the painter that he was on the right tack. 'I wanted,' he said, 'to paint him with a kind of four-square look, to picture Churchill as a rock.' One day at Chartwell—it was either the first or second sitting—Sutherland said to me: 'There are so many Churchills. I have to find the real one.' When I learnt that he intended to paint a lion at bay I tried to sound a warning note. 'Don't forget,' I said, 'that Winston is always acting, try to see him when he has got the grease-paint off his face.' But the artist paid no heed; he painted the P.M. as he pictured him in his own favourite part. And why should Winston complain, for surely it was he who created the role? All that Graham Sutherland did was to accept the legend for the truth. Winston's overwhelming personality often discourages men with a mind of their own from saying what they think. Can we wonder that the artist had been overcome by the Chartwell atmosphere? Could we reasonably expect more from him than a surface impression? Perhaps, as he said, a national hero should not be painted in his lifetime. All the same, he has missed the story that lies hidden beneath that fierce façade.

It begins at Winston's private school at Brighton, where, so he said, the boys threw cricket balls at him so that he was frightened and hid behind trees in a copse. He wished, he said simply, to live down this humiliating memory. He was resolved that he would one day be as tough as any of them. And when he grew up he seized every chance of putting to the test his will to be tough. Once, for instance, he rode a white horse along the line in France to test his nerve, though he knew it might draw fire and bring risks to the men in the trenches.

As I listened to him I could see this sensitive boy, bullied and beaten at his school, grow up into a man, small in stature, with thin, un-muscular limbs, and the white, delicate hands of a woman; there was no hair on his chest, and he spoke with a lisp and a slight stutter. He had set out to make himself tough and unfeeling, and had sought out danger in war, and provoked violent controversy in peace, and had steeled himself to endure and even treat with contempt the affronts and injuries of life. It had not been easy. He was not cut out for the part, but he would not accept defeat. When the war came and he was cast for the part of a tough, he knew his lines. 'I can look very fierce when I like,' Winston said to me one day. But when he first found that out I cannot tell; anyway, that intimidating scowl was not to be found on his face before the war. It was made to order. He had declaimed his speeches before the looking glass, and was ready now to take the call. That was how the nation saw him; they pictured him defying the overwhelming strength of a warrior race. He liked the part, it was the role he had dreamed would fall to him, and he was soon playing it for all it was worth.

There is, to be sure, plenty of power and vigour and defiance in the coarse features that Graham Sutherland has drawn, but they do not belong to Winston Churchill. Look again at him as he is in life. Take your eye away from the fleshy folds of the jowl and look again at the bony structure of the lower jaw. It is delicate, almost feminine, in its contours; where there is massive moulding, in the brow and skull, the artist had given us only an egg-shell. The lips, too, though they often pout, are delicately moulded; in short, the coarseness of the face in the portrait is only part of the artist's romantic conception of a man of wrath struggling with destiny. It is not Winston Churchill.

December 5, 1954

I am hoping that the P.M. will get a breathing space at Christmas. He has made ten speeches in a fortnight; besides, it has been an anxious time with 'harmony and discord rolling over each other.' He has decided not to take part in Monday's debate. He would leave it to Anthony.

'It means an easier week-end for me. I shall only have a few trivial things on my hands'—his face slipped into a grin—'like making bishops.'

The P.M. is surely wise to leave things to settle down—I give the credit for this change of plans to Norman Brook. The telegram will not help Labour as much as they had hoped—and they need help badly. The climate in their camp seems to go from bad to worse. It looked for a moment as if the Woodford speech might reunite the party, weakened by dissensions, and set everything right. But it is plain now that it will all fizzle out. As for the Tories, the hydrogen bomb debate taught them a lesson. Besides, the country doesn't seem interested; it is certainly not indignant. And in any case, what can the Tories do about it? They have got it into their heads at last that no one can turn the old man out until he is willing and ready to go; the public would not stand for it, and they have given up speculating on the date of his retirement.

December 10, 1954

Mr. Wigg, the Labour member for Dudley, is very angry with Lord Montgomery, and the P.M. seems as angry with Mr. Wigg. Mr. Wigg complains that the Field-Marshal, when he left the Army, kept certain documents in his possession; the P.M. answered sharply that, as Lord Montgomery had not left the Army, the honourable member's question was ill-informed as well as ill-natured. When Mr. Herbert Morrison complained of the P.M.'s discourtesy he replied that he thought it rather unworthy to suggest that an officer of Lord Montgomery's distinction should be considered for prosecution. Therefore he thought it perfectly right to make a retort which, he was glad to see, had struck home. The last two words were bellowed at the House. In truth the P.M. is suffering from a sharp reaction after eating humble pie over the telegram.

When I saw him this morning he told me all about the scene in the House. 'There was strength and vigour in my voice. I could have shouted them down.' He thundered this out as if he wanted to convince me by giving a sample of his powers. 'I'm not afraid of the House of Commons,' he went on. 'Have I not been shouted down by both parties? It was stupid of me to forget about the telegram, but the Opposition have overdone it, and it's doing them no good. I do not remember such fierce support from the Tories as I got yesterday.'

He seemed to relax. 'Things are going very well, I think. Have you seen the *News Chronicle* Gallup Poll? Where has it gone to?' he said, sorting the papers on his bed. 'Ah, here it is. In the last week of November it showed that Labour has lost ground. All the same, I shall clear out at the end of June. Not, mind you, because I think it's good for the Party, nor for the country, but I'm sorry for Anthony. He may easily flop, though I shall protect him as far as I can.'

December 16, 1954

'I think,' said Winston this morning, 'I shall die quickly once I retire. There would be no purpose in living when there is nothing to do. I don't mind dying.' He could not refrain from that little bit of bravado; he would have trotted it out whoever happened to be listening.

Then he went on to tell me what he could still do. 'I made a very good speech on atomics. I didn't need any technical advice, though I checked it with the Prof. afterwards. I can do this kind of thing as well as ever. I can think as well as ever. But of course I get very tired.' I asked him how long his atomic speech took to prepare. He replied: 'Two spells of an hour and a half, two separate mornings. Besides, of course, a lot of arguing about it.' He told me the Speaker had given a very agreeable dinner to the members of the wartime coalition. 'It could have happened in no other country,' he reflected.

He had been given a budgerigar, but they had not yet been introduced. The empty cage was on the floor. He confessed that he had had to 'drive himself' in the past three weeks.

December 22, 1954

Winston had sent away his breakfast things. There was a birdcage on his bed and a budgerigar on his shoulder. I said to him he ought to teach Toby his telephone number in case the bird got lost. Winston received this suggestion with some throaty sounds. 'Oom, Oom, Oom, I don't know my telephone number.'

623

The withered garland

He was leaving for Chequers tomorrow and would stay there until the New Year. The nine grandchildren would be gathered under one roof. There would be no more Cabinets until the Feast of the Epiphany.

'When is that? And you call yourself an Episcopalian!'

Chapter fifty-eight

Et tu, Brute

January 3, 1955

The P.M. was sitting on the edge of the bed in his shirt.

'I feel the burden of life,' he said slowly as he got back into bed. 'I don't want a railway strike. It is silly to have this happen about nothing. I may come into it more. Besides we have been anxious about the Frogs, whether they would jump the hedge.'

He had been reading *White Ladies* by . . . he hesitated for the name.

'Yes, Brett Young. I think he's dead. He was a doctor. I picked it up by chance and found it very interesting. I must look into his books, but I don't like novels with a North Country brogue.

'How cold your hands are! You really ought to look after your circulation.'

The bed-clothes began to move violently, as if he was trying to kick them off the bed; then he reached down and produced a small blue rubber hot-water bottle.

'Warm your hands on that,' and he handed it to me. 'I've been moving about, that is why my pulse is 84. Take it again. It will be lower now. I am really quite well.'

January 5, 1955

The P.M. telephoned to tell me that one of his Ministers had discovered a marvellous pill—his wife had given him one, and he had had a lovely sleep.

'And you know, Charles, all his friends are using it. You really don't keep up to date. It is quite harmless. The French chemists' shops sell it without a doctor's prescription. What is it called? Wait a moment and I can tell you—supponeryl.'

He spelt it out letter by letter.

'Now, what about it? Can I take one?'

I said I could not answer his question until I knew what was in it, but I would find out and let him know later.

About eight o'clock the P.M. telephoned again.

'You haven't let me know as you promised,' he said reproachfully.

I replied with a touch of irritation: 'You have been getting good nights for a long time with the reds, and without any ill-effects. Why do you want to change?'

'Oh,' said Winston, 'I believe in trying a variant now and then.'

'You mean you like to change for the sake of changing.'

'Now, Charles, you mustn't be angry with me. I'd like to try one. It can't really do any harm.'

January 7, 1955

Found the P.M. very sluggish. When I asked him what had happened he did not answer at once. I was not sure he had heard what I said. Then he looked up and began: 'I took one of those things on Wednesday. I had six and a half hours' lovely sleep—it was the quality of the sleep that I liked.' He looked at me rather sheepishly and then observed half defiantly: 'So last night I took two.'

'And today,' I butted in, 'you can hardly keep your eyes open.'

'Well,' he said petulantly, 'I must have sleep.'

'It is quite unnecessary to take two of those pills—they are the equivalent of four reds. No wonder you complain that your foot twitched and that you feel too torpid to do any work today.'

'But,' he argued, 'my pulse is all right—take it. Well, what is it?'

'Eighty-six.'

The P.M. roused himself and made a gesture of impatience. 'Do you realize our anxieties during the last few days? The Cabinet waited for nine hours to get news. Why, if there had been a strike on the railways'—he was shouting now—'Ministers would have hurtled off to Sandringham to get the Great Seal on the Royal Proclamation; forty thousand troops would have been sent to various points; four trains would have run somehow from Wales to bring milk; coal production would have fallen from six million to one million tons, and with that many factories would have closed down and the production of electricity would have stopped. Do you realize all the things that were bound to happen, the change in the nation's life?'

January 9, 1955

Lunched with Harold Macmillan. He has been one of Winston's intimate counsellors since his resignation became an issue, but he is not at all happy about things. He took me into the garden and talked so freely about Winston and Anthony that I began to wonder if he had lunched me for that purpose. For fifteen years, according to Harold, Winston has harried Anthony unmercifully, lectured him and butted in on his work, until poor Anthony is afraid to make a decision on his own. Anthony apparently has taken this a good deal to heart, and has been very nervy lately.

Then Harold defended Anthony. He has been very loyal to Winston, and he is a brilliant negotiator, so quiet, so wise, so persuasive. He gave me a sample of Anthony's prowess at the F.O. 'The other day Dulles brought forward a plan that was totally unacceptable to us. I wondered for a moment how Anthony would handle the situation. But he was quite wonderful. I thought his patience would never give out. An hour went by, and gradually I discovered Dulles was changing his position. At last he brought forward another scheme, which was about the exact opposite of the first, and incidentally just what we wanted. Anthony did not rush at him and say: that's what we wanted all along. He murmured that there were parts of this plan he didn't like, and then he appeared to give way to Dulles a little reluctantly.' Harold laughed into his moustache at Anthony's guile. And then he came to the point.

'You know, Moran,' he said, as he picked up a stray spade, 'Winston ought to resign. He didn't interfere in my housing, just left it all to me. But since I became Minister of Defence I have found that he can no longer handle these complicated matters properly. He can't do his job as Prime Minister as it ought to be done. He does not direct. Of course he is still tough and he isn't bothered with principles like Salisbury.' Harold chortled as he stopped to remove a fallen branch from the path. 'When the moment comes Winston will have to decide how he goes; he has missed so many curtains, when he could have gone with everyone applauding, that it won't be as easy now.'

All this was not at all what I had expected. I have looked on Harold lately as an ally of the old man. Tory Prime Ministers have been overthrown by palace revolutions before, and the P.M., since he became aware that something of the kind was brewing, has taken counsel with his supporters—with Harold Macmillan more than with anyone else. Now, though Harold is devoted to the old man, he feels that he is no longer up to his job.

January 20, 1955

The P.M. was in the Cabinet Room reading papers. When he looked up his eyes were full of tears.

'I did not think it would happen like this,' he said sadly.

'I hate politics,' I blurted out impulsively.

'Ah, no, Charles, it's not as bad as that.'

Harold's intervention has left a bruise. The P.M. had come to depend on him and counted on his support if it came to a row. After all, it was Harold who had encouraged him to hang on. Winston called him the Captain of the Praetorian Guard. And now he has gone over to the other camp.

The P.M. changed the subject abruptly.

'I've read the book you gave me. It was interesting, but Melbourne was attached to no great cause, he just pottered along.'

I said that Melbourne had been clever at holding his Cabinet together. The P.M. thought that this could not have been very difficult. I persisted that Durham and the Lord Chancellor were difficult people to have in a Cabinet.

'Yes, Brougham perhaps,' he reflected. 'The last chapter was . . .'

I pricked up my ears. What did he think of that devastating picture of the loneliness of old age?

'I have been reading Rosebery's *Pitt*,' the P.M. went on. 'It's not very good.'

I asked him whether he thought Rosebery's *Chatham* was a better book, and whether he liked the chapter on his oratory. He answered absent-mindedly:

'Rosebery wrote about Chatham before he became interesting and about Napoleon after he had ceased to be interesting.'

January 24, 1955

Plainly there is a growing feeling among Winston's friends that the time has come for him to go. But only Harold Macmillan has had the guts to say so. I am beginning to have second thoughts. If I did not dread the future I might agree with Macmillan. Anyway he did what he thought was right, and he must have hated doing it.

I asked the P.M. if he had been doing much work.

'I do nothing,' he answered with a grin, 'that I can get out of. I am pretty skilful now at avoiding things. I don't mind dying,' he remarked a little irrelevantly. 'I have seen all there is to be seen.'

Jock had been troubled with indigestion, and the P.M. had given him my white medicine. It soothed him.

'It won't do him any harm?' he enquired a little anxiously. 'I think I must show him my breathing exercises. Before I met you I used to get a sharp pain before meals, and then afterwards a great feeling of discomfort and oppression under the heart, as if I had heart disease. I kept thinking about it. It rather got on my mind. At that time I was under a Portuguese doctor, I cannot remember his name. Yes, Lopez. He used to give me most wonderful prescriptions. There were a large number of drugs in each of them. They did me good. Then the poor fellow died. I went to his funeral and came away with'—he hesitated—'Taplow. Yes, Ettie Desborough. "What are we to do now?" I said to her. She told me of a man who taught his patients marvellous breathing exercises which helped them a lot. Courtland MacMahon was his name. You must have known him. He wasn't a doctor, but doctors thought very well of him—a dignified man. Let me show you, Charles, what happens when I get indigestion.'

He picked up a blue pencil and began drawing on a piece of red blotting paper.

'My stomach is usually a platform like this, but at times it sags and becomes a saucer like that.'

His drawing was more like the pocket of a billiard table.

'Then poisonous liquids collect in the saucer and give off foetid gases.'

These he depicted as two columns of smoke rising from the edges of the saucer.

'At that moment I do my breathing exercises. My abdominal muscles contract like this'—and he put his hands on his round belly and began breathing deeply—'so that they squeeze out all the poisonous liquids.'

The blue pencil became very active, crossing out the saucer.

'Your white medicine is a great relief, but of course my indigestion is not as bad now as it was then.' He looked up and waited for my comments.

I reached for his drawing which he seemed reluctant to give up. I took the pencil. 'As a work of art it's not bad, but it's not good physiology.'

He appeared rather crestfallen, but said nothing. He took the blotting paper from me and tore it into small pieces. He is always careful not to leave incriminating documents about. Then he waited for me to explain, if I could, where he had gone wrong. I had just drawn his stomach on the blotting paper when the door opened and Christopher put in an appearance with a handful of papers. The P.M.'s face fell. It was not that he was particularly interested in my views of his dyspepsia, but he knew that when I went he must begin work. I think that was why he talked about Jock's indigestion.

January 27, 1955

The P.M. had made a speech on Tuesday evening to the National Federation of Building Trade Employers.

'We have built a million houses. A very sensible easement of the life of the nation. I showed them my trade-union card as a brick-layer. I went on for about a quarter of an hour—it took me three or four hours to prepare, but it went like hot cakes.'

February 3, 1955

I shall be glad when this Conference is over. Winston is finding it very hard work, he owned to me today, and it's not like him to say that.

'This meeting of the Commonwealth Prime Ministers is a hell of a business. It is not at all like the old gatherings of the Dominions.'

Of course, when I said he must have been very weary after the Palace he protested at once that he was not. He does not want any-one to think that he is not up to it. Then in a few minutes he seemed to forget what he had said.

'The work is unceasing, two meetings every day, five hours al-together, and I am in the Chair the whole time. I get very weary, but I recover. Your "minors" have been my salvation.'

How is he really wearing, and is he doing the job as it ought to be done? He himself has no doubts.

'I'm taking a big part in the Conference. I have held my own, and more than held my own. You must have heard, Charles, stories of my part in the Conference?' When I was not forthcoming, he went on: 'I have led the discussions, made little jokes, given them ideas, and engaged in arguments.

'Some of the others are not lasting as well as I am; they are feeling the strain and show it. Last night Attlee came up to me at the Palace. I could see he was quivering, and then he fainted in my arms. I'm not very strong, but with Mrs. Attlee's help I got him on to a couch. Poor Attlee, he is getting old; he is seventy-two. A lot of people saw it happen. But don't mention this. Yes, it will get about, but I don't want to be the someone spreading it. I would not go but for my liking for Anthony. They will be weaker when I am gone. Anthony's foreign policy has not been very successful.'

The Commonwealth Prime Ministers are agreed that Winston is a fantastic old man. Those who saw him at the Coronation think he is in better form now. Brook, Pitblado and the office tell me that when he was saying a set piece to a big assembly, sitting down, he mumbled and havered, but on the less formal occasions he was wonderfully impressive.

I asked the P.M. about Nehru. He said to me: 'I get on very well with him. I tell him he has a great role to play as the leader of Free Asia against Communism.' I was curious to know how Nehru took this. 'Oh, he wants to do it—and I want him to do it. He has a feeling that the Communists are against him, and that,' Winston added with a grin, 'is apt to change people's opinions.

'I told the Prime Ministers,' Winston continued, 'that there were fifty thousand Chinese characters in their alphabet; six thousand of them are used by their Civil Service; three thousand by ordinary people. So the Civil Servant has to be educated for eight years. That is why, for five thousand years, the proletariat in China has been kept out of the Civil Service. They roared with laughter. It had not occurred to them in that way.'

Winston held out his finger as a perch for the bird.

'When I play with it, Rufus walks out.' As if he were addressing the bird, Winston said:

'Molotov attacked me yesterday. I hope he's as wrong about atomic bombs as he is in his facts in what he said about me. Our private information is that they haven't really got a hydrogen bomb. If they had, they would have treated us quite differently.'

Christopher had telephoned to me about Winston's health when I was out, and I asked Jane Portal what was in his mind. She answered: 'He has a fixed idea in his head about the P.M. He wants him to retire.' It has taken a long time, but he has got his way. The P.M. will go in April. Or is this, I wonder, Harold's doing?

Chapter fifty-nine

Swan-song

February 16, 1955

'I'm earning my screw in these closing minutes,' was Winston's greeting this morning. 'I work all day. I've made up my mind I shall go in April. But I'm not telling anyone. I want it to come as a surprise. So I'm spreading the gospel the other way that there is no reason why I should not carry on. I think I shall go to Sicily and work north as it gets hotter.

'What is my expectation of life, Charles?' When I did not answer he went on: 'Of course I know I may get another stroke at any moment. I'm still muzzy in the middle of the day. If I can get an hour's sleep it helps. Eddie Marsh used to go to sleep every day after lunch. However, he died quite young; he was only eighty,' said Winston with a smirk.

'When I retire I think I shall take up riding again. It would not tire me. I ride by balance. I would get a quiet horse. Of course I shan't resign if there is a war. Chiang and Chou, bloody stinkers, are shouting at each other and making war possible.' He spoke with great disgust. 'As for the Frogs, they are hopeless, quite hopeless.'

February 21, 1955

Winston was in the Cabinet Room, talking to the Chancellor, when I arrived at No. 10. After a time Jock said: 'How late can you leave here and catch your train?' As he said this the P.M.'s bell rang. He looked up at me. 'I would have stayed longer if they had pressed me not to give up my office. I shall leave things very unsettled, and my relations with the President have never been closer—fourteen years' friendship. That will vanish, and then it will be Anthony and Dulles.' He sighed deeply. 'But I have given Anthony a date when I shall go. I shall not go back on that now, barring, of course, a war.

'A week tomorrow I have to make a very important speech in the

632

Defence debate. I shall need a "major," because I want it to be one of my best speeches. Before I quit office I shall make it clear to the world that I am still fit to govern. I am going not because I can no longer carry the burden, but because I wish to give a younger man his chance.'

The idea of a valedictory message to the House of Commons has been at the back of his mind since he decided—and this time his decision is, I think, final—that he would go after the Budget. He wants to make it one of his great utterances, something the House would long remember. He wishes to demonstrate to them before he resigns that he is still able to advise the country in great matters.

'After all, I took the decision to make a hydrogen bomb, and, as I told Harold Macmillan, that is what they will concentrate on in the House.'

Miss Gilliatt appeared. 'Lady Churchill wants you to know that a carpet has arrived from the Shah and is spread out for you to see.'

'The Shah of Persia,' Winston explained, 'is lunching here today.'

March 1, 1955

I get anxious now when I am out of touch with Winston. For a week I have been making speeches in the North of England, and even when I was waiting to speak he would come into my head; I wanted to slip out to telephone to No. 10 to find out what was happening. Was he really all right? However, this morning he did not seem as tired as I had expected.

'I've taken a hell of a lot of trouble over this speech,' he began, 'twenty hours over its preparation and eight hours checking the facts. Besides, it was built on what I had already said to the Commonwealth Prime Ministers.'

He was so taken up with his script that he made no attempt to read the morning papers, which were neatly piled on his bed-rest as Kirkwood had left them. He picked up one of the typed sheets and began to try out on me some of his turns of phrase. After a little he appeared to forget my presence; he would take up one of the sheets, glance at it and then put it down again.

When Winston is cooking a speech it is never finished until it is delivered; he goes on fiddling with it, altering a word here, cutting out a sentence there, adding something that has just come into his head. I could not help him; he will be unhappy until it is over.

In the office I found Montague Browne busy preparing chapter headings for the speech. 'The Prime Minister wants them,' he explained, 'though the speech does not lend itself to them.'

'How will it go?' I asked.

Montague Browne hesitated. 'I suppose there is not much that has not been said before.'

'Why then,' I asked, 'is he so worked up about it?'

'Oh,' said Montague Browne, 'it's his swan-song.'

When I left him I walked through the Green Park to Hyde Park Corner; I wanted to straighten things out. This hydrogen bomb has got Winston down. When at Potsdam he told me about the explosion of the first atomic bomb he saw the scene as an artist, but I remember that he had not yet grasped what it meant to the world. It had not occurred to him then that it might in the long run mean the end of everything on which he sets store. The hydrogen bomb is another matter. His mind is full of foreboding, his mood dark and sombre. 'The entire foundation of human affairs,' he said in his speech, 'has been revolutionized by the hydrogen bomb.' This nagging pain is always in his head, robbing him of all peace of mind. I come upon him brooding so that he does not seem to know I am there.

'You are unhappy about the hydrogen bomb?'

'Terrible, terrible,' he repeated, half to himself. 'Nothing so menacing to our civilization since the Mongols.'

I am beginning to piece things together. Until Malenkov[1] fell he believed that he, and he alone, could help to make the Russians see reason. He would make them see that their self-interest would be served by an understanding with the West. When Malenkov went, the bottom fell out of Winston's plans.

'If we had been able to go to Bermuda, where *Vanguard* was waiting, I might have been able to persuade the President that a meeting with Malenkov would be useful. I think Malenkov would have played. Our visit might have strengthened his position and turned the scale in his struggle with his enemies. But the opportunity was missed.'

He brooded over the bed-rest on what might have been.

'Ike got into his "royal" mood and said he could not leave the country, and that sort of stuff, though his predecessors did not feel like that. And there is a new wind blowing from Russia.'

'A cold blast?'

'Yes, they are isolating Malenkov and then they will strangle him. No, my usefulness, where Russia is concerned, is gone. I wanted to give Malenkov a chance, and he has vanished.'

I had come to think that Winston's thoughts had settled into a mould. I certainly did not believe that an old man could change his way of thinking almost overnight as it were, and I was not at all prepared for the new note of urgency which the bomb had brought into his thoughts. It had not been there before, even in the war.

[1] Malenkov resigned as Prime Minister on February 8, 1955.

But this is not all. For it is no accident that he is choosing the debate on defence for his final pronouncement. It is his duty to tell the House and the nation what must be done if Britain is to survive. He is responsible. He appointed Alex Minister of Defence, partly because he liked having him about the place, but more because he was of a mind to be his own Minister of Defence, as he had been in the war. As Winston puts it in his kindly way, Alex is a soldier and he knows nothing of politics. Not that this matters, for the P.M. keeps assuring himself that he at any rate is on top of the problem. More than once in the last few months he has said to me:

'I have got it all in my head, I have got a firm grip on it. I know what must be done.'

There are, it is true, moments when he is not so sure, when he is tormented by his vision of the future. Winston is a proud man, and it hurts him to think how vulnerable, in the atomic age, a small, densely populated island like Britain has become. In these dark moments I believe he questions if he is still fit to lead and advise in these matters. At any rate, he keeps telling me that no one in the Cabinet has the same grip on the overall picture of the hydrogen bomb as he has. Sometimes it seems that he protests too much, that he is trying to square his conscience, for, of course, he knows what he can do and what is now beyond his powers. It has been very painful to watch his once confident personality now in liquidation. I hate to think he knows what is happening.

*

I was glad that I had gone to the Peers' Gallery in good time, for the House was crowded. Looking round, I saw Mountbatten in the second row rise as if he were about to leave the Chamber, and then push past me into the middle of the front row, though he could see and hear as well where he was. Winston came into the House in time to answer his Questions. Walking very carefully, he picked his way along the front bench; once he seemed to lose his balance, but recovered himself in time, and as Butler made way for him he flopped into his seat. He spoke for three-quarters of an hour, and his voice at the end was as strong as at the beginning. The speech held the House, though he seemed more concerned with his theme than with its effect on members. To Winston these occasions, when the House plans for the future, are part of English history.

'We live in a period, happily unique in human history, when the whole world is divided intellectually and to a large extent geographically between the creeds of Communist discipline and individual freedom.'

His voice sank to a whisper as he reminded the House that both sides possessed obliterating weapons of the nuclear age. He went on:

'We have antagonisms now as deep as those of the Reformation and its reactions which led to the Thirty Years' War. But now they are spread over the whole world instead of only over a small part of Europe. We have, to some extent, the geographical division of the Mongol invasion in the thirteenth century, only more ruthless and more thorough. We have force and science, hitherto the servants of man, now threatening to become his master. . . .

'What ought we to do? Which way shall we turn to save our lives and the future of the world? It does not matter so much to old people; they are going soon anyway, but I find it poignant to look at youth in all its activity and ardour and, most of all, to watch little children playing their merry games, and wonder what would lie before them if God wearied of mankind.'

A great speech, Winston has himself laid down, must have a single theme. His theme was simple. For safety Britain must rely on deterrents. That was why the Government had decided to make the hydrogen bomb. He was so absorbed in his argument that his words came without study, as he gave out his message, like some ancient clock tolling out the hours of the night over the silent town. However, the habits of a lifetime are not easily put aside. Once he found relief from the solemnity of his argument in words coined at leisure. All the countries of the world might feel so vulnerable that, cowed by fear, they might at last be content to live in peace.

'Then it may well be that we shall by a process of sublime irony have reached a stage in this story where safety will be the sturdy child of terror, and survival the twin brother of annihilation.'

It was at that moment that talks at the highest level might bring results. The mood quickly passed; once more the gravity of his theme weighed upon him. The P.M. was drawn back to the dreadful details. The House knew that if there was war Britain must be destroyed; it measured and accepted the cost. Winston Churchill, who knew that his own days were numbered, took heart that before he went he had given back to his country the leadership of the free world. When he sat down he had done what he set out to do.

What ought we to do if God wearied of mankind? That was the question that tormented him as he came towards the end of his journey. His life had been a series of gay sorties from an inviolable home into the political arena to win personal distinction; looking back, he had enjoyed every minute of the game. Here at the end was something that transcended individual combat.

Winston sat for a time listening to Shinwell. When he rose to leave the Chamber I followed him to his room. The door opened and O'Brien came in; he keeps the P.M. in touch with political opinion and with the Press. Winston turned to him eagerly:

'How did they take it? Good. I thought they might like what I said.'

He was still all agog to find out the response of the House. He seemed to be bottling up his excitement, and I noticed that he was out of breath. 'If you never made another speech,' said Christopher —and he seemed just as excited as the P.M.—'that was a very fine swan-song.' Winston's face fell.

'I may not make many more speeches in the House,' he said gloomily.

He turned to Jock and told him to have his frock-coat sent over from No. 10; he was going to see the Queen.

He caught my eye.

'It's all right, Charles, of course I'm tired, but not too tired. In fact, I'm very well. I had to do it alone; no one could do it for me. Shinwell said there was nothing original in my speech. I don't know why he should say that,' Winston complained in an injured voice. 'I couldn't——'

At that moment Clemmie came into the room and I slipped away.

March 2, 1955

When the debate was resumed today Aneurin Bevan made a clever, provocative speech. He wanted talks with Russia, but complained that at a time when the existence of this country was at stake these talks were ruled out because the United States would not allow them. The P.M. rose:

'It is absolutely wrong,' he said, 'to suggest that the course that we have followed here has been at the dictation of the United States. It is quite true that I would have liked to see a top-level conference with the three powers, and I would have liked to see it shortly after Mr. Malenkov took power—as I said at the time—to see, "Is there a new look?" . . . I prepared in every way to go over to see the President. However, I was struck down by a very sudden illness which paralysed me completely, physically. That is why I had to put it all off.'

March 3, 1955

'You saw what I said in the House about my illness?' Winston began immediately I entered the room.

'Why did you say it?' I asked.

'Oh,' he answered, 'it was impromptu. I was stung to say it by

637

Bevan. But I do not regret it. It put me right with the Party opposite, and it will do no harm in the long run, when my actions will be seen to be simple and straightforward.'

He has always wanted to tell people about his stroke. The drama of his illness appealed to him, and at the time I had great difficulty in persuading him that people in this country, when they hear that a man has had a stroke, are inclined to write him off as no longer a going concern.

The P.M. looked up from *The Times*.

'I've never had such a Press. I like what they say about the way my speech was received in America. They welcome us as a partner in defence.'

I picked up the *Daily Worker*.

'Ah, there it's all abuse and hatred,' he sighed. 'The majority was a hundred and seven and our working figure is sixteen.'

He spat out these words with tremendous contempt.

To change the subject I asked Winston what would happen in the quarrel between Attlee and Bevan.

'Attlee,' he replied, 'has been very upset, but he has come out of it with no discredit; he has shown great courage. Bevan is eructating bitterness. There will be a split; some of them may come over to us. There might be a coalition. If I had been a younger man I might have led it. But I shall not go back on my date with Anthony,' he grinned. 'I am not thinking of a come-back. At least not yet.

'It is less than a month now before I go. At any rate, by my speech I have swept away all thought that I was not competent to do my job. It will make it clear that the sacrifice I am making is a genuine one.'

Chapter sixty

Depression

It would be fitting at this point to bring to an end my account of Winston's second term of office, for when he is troubled about England's survival he appears to take on another dimension. But his struggle for his own survival was in fact not fought out at that level. Perhaps his swan-song brought home to him that he was finished and done with, a mere pawn in the great game in which he had been a maestro. Or it may be that his thoughts were turned inwards by all this talk that he was not fit for his job, so that he became conscious of his own frailty. At any rate, my diary for the next two or three weeks makes sad reading:

March 8, 1955

Last night, just before midnight, Winston telephoned. His cold had come back.

'Are you in bed?' I asked sleepily.

'No.'

'Well you ought to be.'

He had started the penicillin spray.

This morning the cold appeared to have gone, but he said:

'Would you like to warm your paws in the bathroom? I would like you to listen to my chest. I have an idea there might be something there. I took my temperature twice last night. I kept it in my mouth for five minutes on both occasions, but it was two degrees below normal. Isn't that dangerous? I have been using the menthol and cocaine spray. I let it trickle down Adenoid Avenue; it does a lot of good.'

I listened patiently to the measures he had taken, and then advised him to stay indoors. He reached for his board containing his appointments. He thought he might take my advice. It would obviously be sensible. I could see that he did not want to lunch at the Mansion House.

'There will have to be something in the Press. We must get Jock.'

He rang his bell. Jock was ready with the words: 'The Prime Minister has a cold and has been advised by Lord Moran to stay indoors.'

'Go away and put something on paper,' the P.M. said.

Jock returned in a minute.

'Directed, not advised,' the P.M. said with a mischievous grin.

'Yes,' said Jock, entering into the spirit of the thing, 'His Lordship is a very masterful personality.'

'Get on to Michael Adeane,'[1] said the P.M., 'I have an audience with the Queen and I ought not to give her the infection.'

March 17, 1955

Monty, in pyjamas, came out of Winston's room as I spoke to Kirkwood. He had not transmitted his good spirits to the P.M., who, poor devil, seemed in an ill humour: he hates going. 'There is a time to be old,' said the sage, 'a time to take in sail.' But Winston is not a sage, he has no liking for the part.

In the office I found Mary. She was concerned about her father. 'From his own point of view it would have been better,' she said, 'if he had gone on till he dropped in his tracks, but his colleagues would not agree to that. He is terribly flat, but when he resigns I think his "lust for life" will keep him going. If his big speech on the hydrogen bomb had been made a hundred years ago nothing more would have been expected of him for a long time. Now it's different. Something else blows up without warning; there is no respite. It's the detail that gets Papa down.'

March 21, 1955

'You will find the P.M. very depressed,' said Jane Portal this morning. 'He has given up reading the newspapers and sits about staring into space. They are really kicking him out.' Jane felt indignant. 'The P.M. is so kind and loyal. He doesn't think evil of anyone.' I turned this over in my mind and decided that it was the truth. It is quite astonishing after fifty years in politics.

I found him in the Cabinet Room, abstracted. He appeared to come back to the present with a jerk. 'Look at this,' he said, throwing me the *Star*. A heading gave May 26 as the date of the General Election.

[1] Private Secretary to the Queen.

'They are telling me the day I shall have to go. I wonder who gave them the date? I suppose the Party. They wanted to fix a date once and for all for the Election. The Central Office must have let it out,' he ruminated. 'I don't care,' he said impatiently.

Jock asked him if he had liked Randolph's book.[1] 'It can't do any harm,' the P.M. replied. 'My vanity led me to spend two hours looking through it—I didn't go to bed until one forty-five. Perhaps,' he added with a grim smile, 'the public will not be as interested in it as I was.'

March 23, 1955

'Did you see that shocking affair in the *Manchester Guardian*?' Winston looked at me as if he thought I could help. I knew what was in his mind. In this morning's issue there were two big headlines: 'Cabinet urging Premier to resign. His health said to be retarding its work.'

'But Winston,' I butted in, 'they are usually so friendly.'

'Oh, this was not their Parliamentary correspondent, he is very sound; it was their Lobby correspondent,' and it appears that it was all based on the conversation with one Conservative M.P. 'One,' he repeated scornfully.

'If I dug in I don't think they could make me go. But I like Anthony so much and I have worked with him so long. And he wants to be Prime Minister terribly. Several times he has tried to bring on an election because he thought it would get me out.' A wry smirk spread over the P.M.'s face. 'He might succeed in getting me out and fail to get himself in.' He spoke in a kindly way of Anthony, and then suddenly said sharply: 'But he has no business——' He stopped short. For some time he was silent. Then he spoke very sadly of political life. He had been hurt by the things Anthony had said lately. He had always liked him. After all, he chose him to succeed at a time when no one seemed to think of Anthony as a possible Prime Minister. He could not understand why he was so changed, nor what was in his mind. He had not been like this in the old days.

At times one caught a glimpse of the old truculence. He might have to go, but he would not let them trample on him. It was absurd to say he was not fit to carry on. He said hotly: 'I don't know why I am going. I feel very strong. I am really very well.' As Christopher says: 'He is terribly anxious no one should think that he is resigning on grounds of health. He has been deeply hurt by all this talk that he is not up to his job. That's why,' said Christopher

[1] Randolph Churchill, *Churchill: His Life in Pictures*.

with a grin, 'he has made up his mind he will go to Sicily without his doctor. He will show them he is in the best of health and does not need looking after.' His ways are indeed unpredictable, as they have always been. He went about telling everyone that he had suffered from paralysis, and now, a few weeks later, he is intensely anxious to persuade the country that he is in robust health. 'Do you find anything wrong with me?' he demanded, as if he were challenging me to produce evidence of his frailty.

It made him angry when it came to his ear that there was talk of Eden kicking him out. 'I have not just been drifting, doddering along, unable to decide when to go. It has been all design. Months ago I made up my mind when I would go.' He wants it to appear that he chose this particular moment to resign with only one thing in his mind: to make it easy for Anthony to climb into the saddle.

'Of course, I know when I retire I may have a reaction. For nearly sixty years I have been in political life, and I don't know what will happen when it comes to an end suddenly. But I don't mind if I die,' he added half defiantly. 'I have had a good life. I know Clemmie wants me to get out.'

March 24, 1955

Winston seems more reconciled to the course of events this morning. After all, if he himself fixed the date of his resignation it was not for him to complain. All the same, I dread the weeks that lie immediately ahead. Will he decide that there is no purpose in living when there is nothing to do? Will he hand in? Jock admits that the Cabinets will depress him until he gets out of it all. Decisions in the future will not lie with him, and in fact, all power will have gone, but Jock thinks he has been accustoming himself to this thought for a long time. I want him to take Alan Hodge[1] to Sicily to help him with his book. Winston must have something to do.

'You know, Charles, they would be wise to keep me at the top where I did very little, but where they could get my advice, which has proved very sound in practical matters lately. It has prevented some foolish, some very unwise things, being done and said. I have a feeling this would strengthen their position in the country. But these fellows—I mean my colleagues—want to get things into their own hands. And, of course, Anthony would like very much to be Prime Minister. It is natural, I suppose.'

I picked up a paper with a photograph of a smiling Anthony Eden with Nehru. Winston feels that Anthony ought to be graver, more weighty.

[1] Historian, Joint Editor of *History Today*.

'Have you seen the *News Chronicle* poll? The Tories are in a stronger position than they were.'

The P.M. himself is much concerned about the Party. He keeps wondering how they will get on without him. He telephoned me before dinner: 'I thought you would like to know that Questions were a terrific success today. There were shouts of laughter, and at the end one of the Opposition Front Bench rose and said that he was puzzled why the Tories wanted to turn out the Prime Minister. I thought you would be interested in what happened in the House.'

April 1, 1955

A letter from Winston. He has made up his mind to go to Sicily without me. He wrote on March 30: 'As I mentioned to you the other day, it would in my opinion be a mistake for me to inflict upon you the burden of coming out with me to Sicily. At this particular time it would give the appearance that I have resigned through ill-health, which is not true.'

As I entered his room this morning, he began to tell me about his plans.

'I shall see the Queen on Tuesday, then on Wednesday, after saying good-bye to the servants, I shall get out of here. I shall go to Chartwell. I love the place. I shall not go abroad until the 12th. I want to go into my private affairs, though they are not in bad shape.'

A report in the *Manchester Guardian* that he would not retire until the end of the Press strike, because he could not bear to go out of office in complete silence, had made him angry.

'It is absurd,' he said with some heat. 'As if I would alter the date of the Election because there are no papers; as if I cared a tinker's cuss what they say when I go.'

The wind dropped and he said simply: 'I don't want to go, but Anthony wants it so much.'

This evening there was a party at No. 10 for Clemmie's birthday. Winston looked tired and old. Attlee went into a long rigmarole about his trials when he was host at No. 10, how he was always sitting down with a Frenchman opposite a painting of Wellington or Nelson. The French have long memories. Curious how ill at ease Attlee is at the end of his life; when you speak to him he makes little quick, nervous movements as if he were not sure of himself. Anyway, it is pleasant to see the Attlees at the most intimate family parties at No. 10 and Clemmie kissing Mrs. Attlee. I find it comforting after Bevan and Dalton. Harold Macmillan as usual was full of good talk. It appears that he and Rab have had a pretty lively time with the two prima donnas. It seemed at times that the scenery

643

might come down on their heads. The situation was saved by the sound sense of the stage hands.

April 4, 1955

Jock told me that the P.M. was in good spirits last night and seemed reconciled to the change. Winston soon confirmed this. 'You know, Charles, how I dislike half measures. I've had enough responsibility these last few weeks to worry me and not enough to be able to take decisions. Yesterday after luncheon I felt better. I found the thought of throwing off all responsibility agreeable. I felt I didn't care a damn.' For some time he was silent, then he said in a detached way: 'Things are not very friendly—it is difficult to be friendly at the top. There is a clash of interests. I think I ought to take a minor this afternoon. I don't want to be tired when the Queen comes to dinner.'

And then, without any warning, Winston began firing questions at me:

Winston: 'As my doctor, do you think I ought to have gone before?'

Moran: 'I sometimes wonder how I shall come out of this in fifty years time.'

Winston: 'You have not answered my question.'

Moran: 'Well, last year when Max and Camrose came to Chartwell after your stroke, they asked me what was going to happen. I told them it was guess work.'

Winston: 'What do you mean by guesswork?'

Moran: 'How long it would be before you had another stroke. They both said you would never again appear in the House of Commons. I told them I had seen patients more paralysed than you were get quite well. We must wait and see.'

Winston: 'Do many people get over two strokes?'

Moran: 'They took it for granted that you were finished as a politician. I felt from the first you were more likely to snuff out if you retired.'

Winston: 'Yes, I felt like that.'

Moran: 'But Clemmie, Christopher, Max and Camrose didn't. They did their damnedest to get me to agree with them. They were afraid you would collapse in the House of Commons or blunder in the Cabinet, or make some gaffe in public. They were thinking of your reputation, while I was concerned with your health and your peace of mind.'

Winston: 'Perhaps—you were both right.'

April 5, 1955

It had been arranged that Winston's carbuncle should be treated with X-rays at MacKenna's house at half-past six, but it was seven o'clock before the P.M. turned up. He seemed in good form, said he had been petted a lot and subsided contentedly into a chair. 'All my plans,' he began, 'depend on the date of the election.'

'Haven't they decided that yet?' I asked him in surprise.

'They? It isn't *they*. I am responsible until my successor kisses hands. Not,' he added with a smirk, 'that this confers on me autocratic powers.' While he was taking off his clothes he asked MacKenna whether any microbes had grown in the culture he had taken from the carbuncle.

'Yes, plenty.'

'What were they like?' persisted Winston.

'Virulent,' answered MacKenna.

'Virulent,' repeated Winston, 'but I trust not malignant. We must use terms with precision. Tell me when you begin the X-rays.'

'They have begun,' responded MacKenna reassuringly.

While this was going on Christopher said to me: 'He's taking it very well so far; morale really quite good.' Then Winston, still smoking his cigar, shuffled to a seat with his trousers round his ankles.

Part eight

A Long Farewell

Chapter sixty-one

Good intentions

April 6, 1955

It has come at last. This afternoon Winston leaves No. 10 for good. To him it seems the end of everything. I could think of nothing to say. He threw off the bed-clothes and went to the window, where he stood looking out at the Horse Guards Parade.

'I am going to bury myself at Chartwell. I shall see no one. I have to deal with an immense correspondence. I am in a good frame of mind, unjealous.'

He grinned broadly.

'There is no doubt it does me good to be petted. I don't know what it would have been like if there had been newspapers.[1] I might live two or three years. I have been blessed with good health. My nerves are good. I don't worry about things and I don't get upset, though occasionally I may become bad-tempered.'

He fell silent; after a little he looked up.

'If it were painless, swift, unexpected. . . .' He did not finish the sentence. As long as he can do things, he keeps cheerful. Tomorrow he will go into his finances; then on Saturday he goes to Epsom. Whenever Winston is deeply stirred he instinctively turns to action.

In the hall I met Norman Brook. He said the last few days had been rather sad—Winston imputing wrong motives to everyone. 'What about Anthony?' 'Oh,' Brook answered, 'on the whole he has behaved well under considerable provocation.'

This is the end of Winston's long struggle to keep his place in politics. I suppose it had to come. But I dread the next few months. I fear he will pull down the blinds. He may read by candle-light for a while. Yet for my part it was without any particular sense of sadness that I left No. 10 for the last time. For three years and six months I have made my way to his bedroom, sometimes once in a

[1] There was a newspaper strike from March 26 to April 20, 1955.

week, sometimes twice, always going before the beginning of his day, and often he would tell me what was in his mind. It has been a great effort for him to keep going; a drawn-out struggle with failing powers. He wanted help, and he saw that I must know what he could do and what he could not do, that he ought not to keep back any of the facts. He seemed at times to open his heart, and feel the better for his candour.

And yet I wonder. Even with his doctor the habit of a lifetime was still strong, the habit of dramatizing himself. It may be that I am altogether too sceptical. Certainly at nine o'clock in the morning Winston is at his most factual. If he ever says outright what is in his mind, that is the time. When I think of all the months during which I have listened to him, and of all the things that he has said to me, it seems that this particular bedroom should have a place in my memory.

All the same, when Winston has left No. 10 I shall not associate him with that house. He does not leave his mark on his homes. After all, unless there is a Cabinet he does not get out of bed till luncheon, and unless he has Questions in the House it may be half-past three before he rises from the table. At five o'clock perhaps, or six, he will, if he can, return to his bed for his rest. Take away another two hours at the dinner-table, and what is left of the day? Why should he be interested in the furniture and fittings of rooms he hardly enters? Besides, what has seemed to matter most in his life, as far as I have had any part in it, has happened elsewhere; when he has been right up against things, it has not been at No. 10.

Before Winston left for Chartwell he said to Christopher: 'I would like to go down and see the Cabinet Room for the last time.' Perhaps his mind had gone back to the blackest days of 1940, when in that room he had told them the truth. The room was in darkness. When the light was switched on it appeared in disarray, ready for the cleaners, the chairs, shrouded in their covers, pushed to one side, the ink-pots gone. Winston looked for a moment in bewilderment on the scene, then he turned on his heel and stumbled out into the hall.

April 8, 1955

Dorothy drove me to Chartwell in time for luncheon.

'So nice of you to come and visit me in my exile,' was Winston's greeting.

'I should have been quite willing to go on giving orders as long as I had breath, but I have handled so many of these situations that I do not grudge to another his chance.'

650

He lit his cigar.

'I am in good spirits. Once my mind was made up I had a feeling of relief. I don't care a damn now. I have never found time to do the things I wanted to do. Now I shall have to look for things to fill my time.

'I've got my book. The first volume will come out in the autumn. After that I shall lay an egg a year for three years.'

'Is there much to be done on them?' I asked.

'No,' he replied, 'they could appear tomorrow. They need only a little polishing. I am not satisfied with the Tudors.'

He told me that the four volumes of his *History of the English-speaking Peoples* had been written in a year and a quarter just before the war.

'I worked at them every night till two in the morning, though at the time I was fighting for rearmament. Of course I had a team to help, but I wrote every word myself.'

'What will you do when you've done the polishing?'

'Ah, then,' he smiled broadly, 'I shall be ready to stage a comeback.'

When we were seated at the luncheon table Winston raised his glass. 'I give you the toast of Lord Horder,'[1] and he grinned mischievously. 'What is the betting on the election?' he asked gaily. 'I shall come back for it.'

Winston complained that his sense of taste was not what it had been. 'I expect, Charles, just as one's sight deteriorates, so the taste nerves are blunted by age. I think if I went now I should get to sleep; it does me so much good.' He gave me the first chapter of his *History* to read while he rested. It begins in the year 55 B.C.

Winston has received an avalanche of letters on his retirement, and Miss Sturdee has come back to lend a hand. She said to me: 'He comes into the office and asks if anything has happened, just as he used to do. You know that for years he has been inundated with "paper" and with official business. And then, all at once, as if a tap has been turned off, it has ceased. All the bustle and stir have gone out of his life. Yesterday Sir Norman Brook sent him a message by a despatch rider. Sir Winston was delighted. Not with the message, but with the messenger. It was an echo from the past.'

Someone asked Winston if he had seen a film *Carmen Jones*, in which the chief character was a Negress. Winston replied that

[1] There is an annual election for the office of President of the Royal College of Physicians. For nine years Lord Moran was re-elected President; on each occasion Lord Horder was the runner-up. Lord Moran retired in 1950. Sir Winston was under the impression that he was still President.

he didn't like 'blackamoors,' and had walked out early in the proceedings. He asked, a little irrelevantly, what happened when blacks got measles. Could the rash be spotted? When he was told that there was a very high mortality among Negroes from measles he growled: 'Well, there are plenty left. They've a high rate of production,' and he grinned good-humouredly.

April 10, 1955

'I could have stalled them off in the House and stayed for another year,' he said half to himself. 'But it would have served no purpose.'

Then, turning to me, he said:

'You've had nothing to do with my going; it was an act of free-will. I think Anthony is already feeling the strain.

'I know you think that I shall not thrive in retirement. You have had that feeling all along. I had it myself. But I am not so sure now that we were right. I have my book. Besides, I have other plans. You know this strike is causing great damage to the country and great inconvenience to millions of people. The State cannot stand by and allow this sort of thing. It is wrong that an insignificant number of people—only seven hundred men are involved—should be able to hold the community to ransom. I have been thinking of a Bill which would apply to a number of scheduled trades, where a small minority can injure the public in this way. Each man in these industries would have to sign a certificate when he began his trade undertaking to give three months' notice. In return he would receive every year five pounds from the employer and five pounds from the State, so that at the end of five years he would have fifty pounds in Savings Certificates.

'Meanwhile, before I go to Sicily I am going to read the history of the island. Clemmie says it's very interesting. Aristophanes—in a translation—is not at all dry reading; quite amusing in fact.'

London, April 27, 1955

Two hours after he had arrived at the airport from Sicily Winston telephoned:

'I'm fine, but I'd like to see you. No, it will do in the morning.'

Coming out of the lift on the seventh floor of the Hyde Park Hotel, I was directed to 708, a good room, looking down over a wide stretch of the Park in its spring dress, where I found Winston doing nothing. I stopped by the door to look at two of his pictures propped against the wall.

'I didn't find it easy to paint that cave,' he remarked. 'It isn't good, but it has depth. The other I did from the hotel garden; there is no sunlight in it, but we had no sun while we were there. Of course, I could put it in. I was delighted to find that I still got pleasure in painting. I wanted to do it.'

He gazed at his picture for some time.

'I painted with great vigour,' he repeated. 'What mattered was that I found I could concentrate for three hours—I got interested in it, and was always late for luncheon. I played a lot of cards with Jock.'

Not much, I gathered, had been done on the book.

He struck me as pale, and perhaps a little subdued.

'I have been going through considerable psychological changes,' he said. 'I have had to let things drop from my mind. I have had to shed responsibility and become a spectator. Unless there was a crisis I could not now get back to the point where I was before I resigned. I could have gone on till October if they had said, "For God's sake, don't go." But it would have done harm to trade to have an election hanging over the country. Besides, I have no desire now for anything that means effort. I have had my life—a very full life.' He grinned. 'I have got to kill time till time kills me. When, Charles, you wouldn't tell me, I asked my solicitor what my expectation of life was, and he told me four and a half years. Of course, I know I may die at any moment, but I don't care. I'm prepared for an emergency.'

His plans, he said, depended on the result of the election:

'I think we may win. If we do, but the majority is only five, I may have to attend the House; if it's forty I need not go.'

I asked him how long he would be in England.

'Until June 13 at any rate,' he answered. The Queen had commanded him to be present at the Garter ceremony at Windsor. He went on:

'I had a lovely letter from her, eight pages in her own writing. It took me a whole morning to reply. Besides, I have some horses running at Ascot and I have to see to some domestic things. My secretariat has broken up.'

I talked about the chances of a railway strike. He grinned:

'I have a car. That is the measure of my detachment from things.'

May 4, 1955

Last night Rab gave a party at No. 11 Downing Street.

I took Jock into a corner and asked him about Sicily. Winston, he said, had been in good spirits; no regrets; no looking back. He had played bezique every day for about eight hours and had painted for another four hours. Jock had happened to be passing the Hyde

653

Park Hotel when Winston drove up. He followed him to his room. Jock had found him rather flat compared with his form in Sicily.

Norman Brook joined us. Jock was upset because Winston had come back anxious to help in the election,[1] only to find he was not wanted. Winston, he said, had not been asked to do any broadcasting; Jock thought this would lose the Conservatives a lot of votes. People would say that the Tories had turned him out because he wanted to meet the Russians.

Jock turned to Norman Brook. 'What does it mean? Who is behind this?' Brook answered he had done all he could to get this decision changed, but had failed. He made it clear that he shared Jock's views. Anthony was quite friendly, he said, but he didn't want to be regarded as Winston's nominee for the Premiership. He must stand on his own feet. There was nothing else behind this decision, which had been taken at a meeting of some of the Cabinet. Jock grinned.

'Meg,[2] when she heard of this, vowed she would vote Labour.'

I said to Peter Portal: 'They're a size smaller than the old man.'

'Two sizes,' he grunted in disgust.

May 11, 1955

'Well, I'm back here again,' said Winston with a quizzical look, when I saw him at 28 Hyde Park Gate. I asked him if he had watched Harold Macmillan performing on television. I knew, of course, he would say 'No,' for he is without curiosity about other people's speeches and broadcasts. He does not share Jock's resentment that he was not invited to take part in the Tory campaign on the air. Quite the contrary, for he thinks it very reasonable that the broadcasts should be reserved for 'responsible ministers.' He talked about a good Conservative majority that would give Anthony a fine start. Now that it is all over and he is on the shelf his generous instincts have brought him, I think, peace of mind. Anthony, he explained, wanted him to appear with Harold Macmillan, but:

'All they wanted me to do, when I looked into it, was to say how good the film was and not to take more than three minutes saying it.'

The smile vanished.

'It was a paltry affair. If I'm going to use that particular medium at all I may as well do it properly.'

I asked him if he had read the leader in the *Manchester Guardian*. I told him I had it in the car, and he asked me if he could see it.

---

[1] Sir Anthony Eden, the new Prime Minister, decided to go to the country on May 26, 1955.

[2] Lady Margaret Colville, wife of Jock Colville.

The leader was headed: 'The Man Who Was.' It rebuked Eden for so pointedly ignoring the man whom he succeeded and to whom personally he owed so much. Sir Winston had been dropped as if he had become a liability; there was not a single reference to him in Sir Anthony's early speeches. After all, the *Guardian* asked, would Sir Anthony be Prime Minister at all if Sir Winston had not nursed him for the succession? And it went on to give its own explanation of this lack of generosity. Sir Anthony had to show himself as 'the new, strong, self-sufficient leader standing on his own feet.' When Winston had read the leader he looked up:

'May I keep it? I'd like to show it to Clemmie.'

'Anthony,' he added with a smile, 'has changed his tune about top-level talks; he is pressing for them now, though it was he and Bobbity[1] who were so much against them when I wanted them. I am quite cool about it all.'

He seemed lost in thought. At last he said:

'When I made that mistake and forgot about the telegram to Monty I think my usefulness with the Russians was diminished.'

He had seen Max. I asked him what line he was taking about the election, for I knew that Max had never been one of Anthony's admirers. Winston grinned.

'The last election, when I was Prime Minister, Max wanted the jockey to win, but not the horse. Now he wants the horse to win, but not the jockey. But he will support Anthony. My influence with him helps in this. I only want to help Anthony. I have no scrap of anger, jealousy or spite.'

Winston seemed to forget all about me. He has made up his mind, I think, to make the best of things. It is a small part for him, but he will make what he can of it. All the same, it will not be easy for him; to do something, to do anything, has been his life.

[1] Lord Salisbury.

Chapter sixty-two

The end of make-believe

May 12, 1955

Today, without any warning, Winston threw in his part. He could no more pretend to himself that it was all for the best when he resigned. The brave attempt at make-believe has been scrapped. He looked up as I entered the room.

'Since I retired and relaxed I have noticed a decline in my interest in things—oh, in everything. I hate London. I don't want to see people. They don't interest me. I am bored with politics. This election prevents me getting down to my book.'

In matters which did not affect him personally he had never taken much interest. Have things now gone a stage further? This had been his answer:

'I shall die quickly when I retire. There would no longer be any purpose in living.'

Since his resignation he has not once telephoned to me about his health, and when I do call on him he is quite different. He does not say to me any more: 'I want to be at my best on Tuesday in the House.' I do not find him keyed up for some exacting test—what he called a hurdle. There are no tests now, and in any case, in his own words, what does it matter to anybody whether he is or is not at his best?

May 19, 1955

'I shall be glad when this election is over,' Winston said this morning.

'You find it tiring?' I ventured.

'No,' Winston grumbled, 'boring. I am out of it all. It means nothing to me. I am only doing my duty.'

I tried to say that after the election, when he could get down to his book, things would be better. He hardly seemed to be listening.

656

'No, I'm finished. I'm only waiting.'

To turn his thoughts I told him of an article about the Presidential election in America. There seems to be no market in an election there for close reasoning; all they appear to want are vague generalities and a comfortable personality like Ike.

Winston commented drily: 'It is as well to build up a personality on a solid structure of sound argument. In America,' he went on, 'when they elect a President they want more than a skilful politician. They are seeking a personality: something that will make the President a good substitute for a monarch. Adlai Stevenson will have to build himself up gradually if he is to do any good.'

Only once did I get a glimpse of the old pugnacity when he handed me a crumpled morning paper. 'Read that.'

'Don't be daft, Sir Winston' was the leader heading. It was all about a little bickering between Attlee and Winston. When that was done with, the writer, gaining momentum, said: 'Dear old Sir Winston in fact had a rather bad day.' And in support of this printed this specimen of 'the gloriously vituperative things' that Sir Winston had thrown at the Tories in the good old days when he was helping Lloyd George to float his famous Budget. 'A party of great vested interests banded together in a formidable confederation, a party of the rich against the poor.'

The little flutter of wind died away, and in the flat calm it seemed as if he had never been interested in politics.

Chartwell, May 29, 1955

A week ago, when I tried to comfort him, he shut me up: 'To hell with everything.' He spoke in anger. This morning he is positively cheerful; with the election in his mind Winston said:

'I'm not repentant. I'm glad I went. I could have gone on, but it would have been an effort. Besides, it's a good thing to think about other people.'

There was a twinkle in his eye, then some guttural sounds, ending in a broad grin, as he added:

'Though I've not wasted much time on this in the course of my life. If I'd planned it all in detail, I could not have gone in a more fitting manner. Why, after three and a half years of Tory rule the Conservatives have come back with an increased majority, the first time this has happened for ninety years. And people say the electors are not impressed by performances. It is not true. The Americans say I only thought of the public good and paid no attention to my own affairs.

'I think television was a flop in the election. This business of just chatting round the fire,' he said scornfully, 'is all very well, but a candidate should make a pronouncement that will become part of the English language, part of English history. People ought to have to fight to get into his meetings.

'Anthony,' he said, 'has done very well in the election; he has been very restrained.'

He pondered for a little.

'It is a time for restraint, not for leadership.'

He asked if I had listened to Anthony's broadcast on the railway strike, and made me repeat what I could remember of it.

Miss Gilliatt spoke to me of his changed state.

'He has been so good tempered. Even when he had three speeches on his hands and we were looking out for storms, there was never a cross word. You know, Lord Moran, how he dislikes a new secretary. Now he has two, and he has been so sweet to them. This morning I was unpunctual, but when I said I was sorry, well, you heard how kind he was.'

Max, when I asked him about Winston's present mood, answered:

'Well, you are his doctor, and you know all about him. Since his resignation he has sent me three letters . . . very revealing letters. Moods of exultation seem to alternate with moods of depression. One moment he talks as if he was still Prime Minister, the next as if he were no longer anyone at all.'

'He still has his book,' I put in.

'Oh, yaas,' said Max, 'but what is that but anticlimax after all that has gone before.'

Max moved restlessly across the room, and went on:

'As he cannot have so very long to live, I do not hesitate to raise false hopes, if they make his outlook more cheerful.'

'What kind of hope?'

'Oh, I told him that if the majority was very small, five or even ten, then there would probably be a coalition. Oh, sure, he liked that very much. And I said that in any case his help would be needed in speaking in support of Eden's Government. He has been very hurt by Eden's neglect.'

Max, when he is not concerned to prove some theory of his own, speaks of Winston's behaviour with a certain insight; he sees that his mood changes from day to day, that his spirits rise when he thinks he has got the better of his depression. Now, when he is out of things, this may be only a poor substitute for life, as he put it, but he will fight his mood of despair inch by inch. His mind is set; he will not give way to another fit of angry impatience.

May 30, 1955

A day spent in meditation, which is not like him. He handed me
J. R. Green's *Short History of the English People* published by Macmillan
in 1874.

'Look at the print. It's bad. Green gets his chronology all
wrong. I am comforted by reading it. My account is clearer,
simpler.'

I told him that I had read Seeley's *Expansion of England* in my
youth and it opened up a new world. He looked very sad, but all he
said was: 'Now it would be Seeley's *Contraction of England*. I have
done a lot of good work on the book.'

'Alterations in the text, you mean?'

'Oh, a few. But more reshaping by arranging it in proper sequence.'

Winston stretched himself and suggested that in the garden
we should find seats out of the wind, where we should be in the
sun.

'One cannot,' he meditated, 'expect to live for ever. I would like
not to wake one morning.' He stopped short. 'No, I think I would
like to know beforehand if I'm going to die. I have had a full life
and have got a good deal out of it.'

He was rather breathless and said no more until we were seated.
Then he went on:

'I believe the spirit of man is immortal. But I do not know
whether one is conscious or unconscious after death.'

I told him what Ike had said to me, that 'freedom itself meant
nothing unless there was faith.' Winston thought there had been a
great decay in belief in his lifetime.

'It is bad for a nation when it is without faith,' he muttered.

'Isn't that true also of the individual?'

He did not answer.

'You have adjusted yourself very well to retirement.'

'Yes,' he agreed, 'the Changing of the Guard has been a model.'

There was another long pause, and then he spoke in loving praise
of Mary and of her record in the war. It had been a great happiness
to him to watch her lovely family growing up at Chartwell. He
hoped Christopher would be given office; he would run a department perfectly well. He spoke of a British Butterfly Society.

'It would aim at increasing their numbers, and it would educate
young people to be kind to them. When I was a small boy at school
we were given nets and encouraged to massacre butterflies. When
they were caught they were pinned on a board, and boys competed

659

with boys in the number of species on their board. There were Tortoiseshells and Red Admirals and Peacocks. Something, too, could be done about suitable plants for the caterpillars.'

He looked at the budgerigar perched on my finger.

'Out of that small body is produced the mechanism that made all those feathers in that pattern. All the machinery in the world could not do that.'

He got into the car to go up the hill to the house. I walked for a time in the garden. On a white stone sunk in a brick wall, that separated the kitchen garden from a road to the farm, was inscribed:

> The greater
> part of this
> wall was bu
> ilt between
> the years
> 1925 & 1932
> by Winston
> with his own
> hands.

May 31, 1955

A slight relapse. One Forbes had written a 'poisonous article,' in the course of which he said that Anthony had increased his majority while Winston's had fallen.

'It is not true,' said Winston vigorously, 'it is quite untrue.'

I asked him why he did not lie down, he seemed so somnolent.

'Ah,' he said, 'I like lying in bed, but I must not become bed-ridden. I feel very stupid,' he muttered, giving a succession of noisy yawns.

'I'm not always like this. This morning I did three hours on the book. Oh, it was simple, just rearrangement, and picking out an unnecessary passage here and there. It's thinking and composing I find difficult.'

Ringing for a secretary, he said he would like to see a list of his horses. For a long time he stood looking over the Weald, his eye feasting on the different shades of green in the evening light. At last he turned to me and said: 'I bought Chartwell for that view.'

June 2, 1955

Winston telephoned in the morning that he would like to see me; he was not very happy about things. Christopher also telephoned that he was troubled about the old man. Winston had dined with them at the farm. He was in great form, but after dinner he said he felt light-headed as if he had drunk too much. 'Of course he hadn't,' Christopher added, 'we only had a bottle of champagne between the four of us.'

'Ah, Charles, I am glad to see you,' Winston began. He said his head had felt queer when they were at dinner. However, when he woke in the night the light-headedness had gone, but in the morning his right hand was clumsy. I asked him what he had noticed.

'It is no longer trustworthy. When I think about it, it is all right. Look,' and he held out his cup without a tremor. 'But in ill-considered acts it is bad. Twice I have knocked over my cup and upset the coffee.'

He demonstrated what he could do yesterday with his hand.

'I can't do now what I did then—nothing like it.' He reached for his pen and wrote his name several times. He held the paper out to me. While I was still examining the writing he took it away from me, and was on the point of destroying the sheet of paper, when I suggested that it would be a good thing to keep it, to compare with his writing in a few days' time. Thereupon, folding the paper up and putting it in an envelope, he sealed it and scribbled 'W.S.C.' on the front.

'My writing is not good. I know that something has happened.'

As he was speaking, his cigar slipped from his mouth; he caught it so that it lay flat against his cheek.

'I don't mind a bit,' Winston continued, 'I'm not despondent. Yesterday when I lunched with Max I kept dropping my cigar and Max kept picking it up.'

When Winston tried to touch my finger with his right hand he made a circle round it, though he had a good strong grip, and when he attempted to walk I was afraid that he might fall, his right leg shot out unsteadily in the air, as if he was goose-stepping.

'Have I had another go?' he demanded.

I told him that there was a spasm of an artery.

'You mean in my head?'

It soon became plain that Clemmie and Christopher wanted me to accompany him to Chartwell and to stay the night there. Anthony, he told me in the car, had sent him a very nice letter of four sheets. He rambled on. I had to lean towards him to catch his words. Three times he popped off to sleep. At Chartwell he rejected angrily all attempts to help him up the steps. He made his way to the office in a succession of darts, bumping against the wall, first to the right and then to the left, so that it seemed he must fall. In the office he flopped into a chair.

'Anything come in?' he demanded.

661

June 3, 1955

When I went to his room this morning the notice on his door
'Don't disturb' had not been taken down; half an hour later he was
still sleeping. I began to feel uneasy and listened outside his door,
but I could not hear his breathing. I kept wondering whether this
business had spread in the night. Should I find his leg and arm
paralysed? However, when he woke he said he felt different.

'You mean better?'

'Yes,' he responded cheerfully.

He fiddled clumsily for his pen on the table by his bed, and began
writing his name. Nine times he wrote with great care and deliberation 'Winston Churchill.' Opposite the fourth of these signatures he
scribbled 'No noticeable improvement' and at the bottom of the
sheet of paper '20% down.' Just then Kirkwood appeared with his
breakfast. I was poring over his signature when he said:

'This is the thing to look at, what I'm doing now.'

He was holding out his cup at arm's length.

'Pretty good, Charles.'

When he had put down the cup his attention wandered, and his
right arm made a sudden purposeless and uncontrolled movement,
upsetting the cup, so that his fingers ended in the coffee. Looking
up, as if he wanted to say, 'There, you see, that's what I do,' he gave
his dripping fingers a rueful look.

'How they hate us,' he said sadly, handing me the *Daily Worker*.

'Read the headline, "It's up to rail bosses! T.U.C. explodes that
'inter-union' myth." They just ignore the fact that it is a dispute
between two unions.'

When he was dressed, he kept saying: 'How lucky we have been
to get the election over before the strike.'[1]

'There are two thousand engine drivers in the Forces,' said
Randolph.

'Where,' Winston broke in, 'did you get that figure?'

'The Minister of War, Anthony Head,' Randolph retorted with
an important air.

'I think they ought to be used,' Winston said.

But Randolph thought the Cabinet was wise to go slowly.

'Patience before firmness was your own motto, Papa. A little
more provocation is necessary or the N.U.R. will join the strike.

[1] The strike lasted from May 29 to June 14 and was in support of a higher wage
claim lodged by 62,000 members of the Association of Locomotive Engineers and
Firemen. The National Union of Railwaymen did not join in, and work was resumed after the issue had gone to arbitration.

Campbell has threatened that if volunteers are used to drive the trains his union will not remain neutral.'

Winston was not listening, he appeared absorbed in a daily paper. Presently he passed it to me.

'Give China Formosa. That's the point Attlee is after.'

'This Tito racket,' he said in disgust, 'the idea that this man is to hold the balance in Europe!'

Duncan Sandys is a member of the Emergency Strike Committee, and Winston admonished him during dinner to be firm with the strikers.

'What,' Winston demanded, 'is the Government doing? People will soon be asking that question.'

Duncan replied: 'We are allowing provocation to pile up, so that the public will be ready to support strong action against the strikers if necessary. If we bring in volunteers prematurely the N.U.R. engine drivers will join the strike and we shall only be worse off.'

Winston berated Duncan vigorously. Duncan looked very dour and obstinate. His father-in-law was not always very consistent. It was, after all, only a few weeks since he claimed that he had done more than anyone else to prevent a strike on the railways. Did we realize, he had demanded, what a strike meant to the country? I kept my peace until he got up at last—it was not long after eleven o'clock—and stumped to his room.

He gave me two chapters of his book to read, one entitled 'Saxon Dusk' and the other 'William the Conqueror.' 'I think you may like them. I can't write like that now.'

He sat on his bed while Kirkwood pulled off his socks and his trousers, then he took his dope, a 'red' and a 'green,' reaching quickly for his whisky to wash them down; then he anointed the inside of his nostrils with a white ointment, which he had used every night for forty years. It prevented incrustation, he said. At this point he lay flat on the bed while he held a drop-bottle above his eyes. He was now ready for the purgative which Kirkwood handed to him. 'You might wonder,' Winston smilingly conceded, 'how Kirkwood remembers everything.' Then, while he sat naked on his bed, the valet applied a calamine lotion to Winston's back under his directions. After he had drunk his soup he retired to the bathroom, where he started an electrical machine so that it made a loud buzzing sound, and sent out of a metal tube like a dentist's drill a spurt of water with which he swilled every corner and crevice of his mouth.

'Look at that water in the basin. People don't realize how much food there is in their mouths when they go to bed.'

Finally, calling for his brushes, he swept them backwards and forwards over his scalp. Now the ritual was nearly at an end. Clambering into bed, he made some sounds, half of contentment and half a groan, as Kirkwood turned off the light and Winston burrowed his head into the pillow.

June 4, 1955

'I think I am definitely better,' Winston began.

He had put his cup on the left of the breakfast tray so that he could use both hands when he lifted it to his mouth.

'Give me a bit of paper, Charles. I feel I shall write better.'

Once again he wrote out his name; four times he repeated it. Below the signatures he wrote 'I'm a very good autographer. I've had a lot of practice with other people. It's not as difficult as it seems.'

He held the paper away from him.

'Yes, the first signature is almost normal. I am better, definitely better.'

Tonight I tried, without any success, to persuade Winston that a film tires him. He insisted that he must see a thriller, *Les Diables*. He said he enjoyed a film and he was sure it did him no harm. Half an hour afterwards Christopher knocked at my door.

'Winston,' he said, 'came out of the film because his heart was pounding, and he did not feel up to much. He has gone to his room.'

There I found him stretched on his bed. He held out his wrist.

'Take my pulse, it must be 120. I don't think you'll find it too good.'

He was right. It was rapid and irregular.

'It's the first time the story of a film has upset me like this,' he continued. 'It was very exciting.'

I told him his pulse would soon settle down, and pulled up a chair by his bed. He got out of his clothes gingerly, sparing himself.

'I'm glad you're here.'

After a little, he asked me what book I had in my hand.

'Ruskin,' I answered, '*Praeterita*.'

'Ah, he writes beautifully, lovely language. Don't go, Charles.'

There was a long silence.

'Go on reading Ruskin. Don't go away.'

He addressed Kirkwood. 'Would you like to go down and see the end of the film?'

Kirkwood thanked him and vanished. When he came back he was closely questioned about what had happened to the various characters. Winston held out his wrist.

'Take it again. I think it's quieter now.'

664

June 5, 1955

'When I woke this morning,' said Winston, 'I felt master. I was on top. I was in good health again. I haven't yet made up my mind about my appointments for the next month.'

He is trying to persuade himself that the stroke which clamped down on his effort to make the best of things has made no difference. But he is not so well as he was, he cannot control his feelings as he did, and I am fearful of the days that lie ahead.

June 6, 1955

It does not seem a long time since Winston did all the talking at every meal; now he sits all huddled up in silence; he can no longer hear what is being said, he is outside the round of conversation and not part of it, though at times, it is true, when there is a burst of laughter, someone will explain to him what it is all about.

He said he would like to give me one of his pictures. I was to choose three, so that there might be an alternative if my choice fell on a picture from which he could not bear to part. I had admired a painting of a lake with trees which faced me during luncheon.

'You must have that,' he said.

When I left him his eyes filled with tears.

'I am touched by your kindness and devotion.'

With that he turned away, murmuring: 'I don't think I shall be able to do very much in the future. It is wonderful that you have kept me going for so long.'

Chapter sixty-three

Mournful gestures

June 8, 1955

Found Winston in his bath in his most unreasonable mood.

'This tickle,' he grunted, 'is quite intolerable. It kept me awake. Yes, a bloody night. The skin man has given me fourteen ointments or lotions in turn without any theory behind any of them. Just doling out some potion or unguent to keep me quiet. It's a disgrace to the medical faculty.'

As the tenure of office of Winston's adviser seemed to be threatened, I had to explain to Winston that his skin had grown old with the rest of his tissues, and that none of us could put back the clock. He gave an impatient snort. He was not convinced. I explained to him that if he were willing to cut down the number of hot baths it might help the irritation of his skin very considerably. This he regarded as an outrageous suggestion.

He was due at St. James's Palace at noon for a rehearsal of the Garter ceremony, but he was in no mood to hurry.

'I shall take my seat in the House this afternoon.'

Christopher said he would get an ovation. Winston rapped back irritably:

'I don't care a damn about that. I don't need their applause. What are those blue marks?' he asked, pointing to some bruises on his arm. 'Do you mean to tell me that all my veins are going to burst?

'I think Anthony will have to give way to the strikers. The T.U.C. have passed the buck. I don't see why the Government shouldn't negotiate before the strike ends. It would not be right to allow pique, pride or procedure to hold up negotiations. There would be no sympathy with the Prime Minister if further injuries are inflicted on the public merely on account of pique. Certainly if there is a general strike it would be ridiculous for Anthony to prance about in his Garter robes.'

June 9, 1955

When I came into his room today he said at once: 'Have you seen the *Manchester Guardian*? Attlee was very kind to me when I took my seat in the House.' It appears that when a Member caught sight of Winston advancing up the floor—he was not very steady on his feet— he cried in his excitement, 'Churchill.' At that, before anyone could check it there was an unashamed clapping of hands in the public gallery, while all the Members crowding the benches waved their order papers, cheering madly. Where would he take his seat? It could only be in the seat below the gangway alongside the Treasury Bench. It was from this seat that he had warned the nation of its danger in the years before the war. Members must have wondered what was passing through his head at that moment—the rush of memories.

When they thought of him their feelings welled over into little signals of affection. Mr. Shinwell gaily beckoned him to come over to the Labour benches. And then, when no Member dared trust himself to speak, Mr. Attlee rose from his seat and, quickly crossing the floor, took Winston by the arm, pushing him forward in front of him towards the table. Sir Winston must take the oath before him; while the whole House, seeing what was being done, rose to applaud.

Herbert Morrison, who was following Attlee, touched Winston affectionately on the back, and Winston, turning round, grasped Morrison's hand and shook it warmly. Then he signed the roll of members, writing his name for the thirteenth time in the roll of the Parliaments of Great Britain, very carefully, very deliberately—no doubt he had in mind what had happened at Chartwell.

June 10, 1955

I asked Winston what had happened at the 'Other Club.'

'Oh,' he answered, 'I don't think anyone noticed anything unusual. Have you seen anyone who was there? But I'm not so well as I was before this happened. I wonder if I shall get back where I was.'

He looked at some galley proofs.

'I get interested in the book. I can't think why Anthony is saying what he is about the strike. As if it didn't matter if the men are out for another four or five days. The public will get impatient soon.'

June 12, 1955

Christopher walked up from the farm to lunch with Winston. He is not very happy about him.

667

'Winston doesn't want to go to London. He isn't really interested in my talk about the House. It no longer holds him as it did. He doesn't mind now what happens. And you can't leave him alone. Two days ago he was lunching by himself and he dropped off to sleep and burnt a great hole in his napkin with his cigar. But yesterday he had Rootes to lunch—you know, the motor chap—and there was a most animated and reasoned conversation about the future of industry, co-partnership, profit sharing and that kind of thing.'

Christopher may be right, but Winston is full of the strike. It is the first serious issue since his resignation, and he is very critical of Anthony's handling of the situation. I remember Winston once said to me: 'If I retire what is to prevent their doing things I don't like, and I shan't be able to do anything about it?' That is what is happening now. The Government, Winston thinks, has been lulled into a feeling of security by the fact that the immediate consequences of the strike have been less than anyone thought. The development of road transport has softened the impact of the blow. But Winston says: 'We are going to pay for this in the future. We are using up our reserves.' And the sense of urgency has gone.

'If,' said Winston, 'I had been responsible I would have made a lot of the way in which the strikers had chosen a Bank Holiday to come out'—his voice became stronger—'so that the public would suffer the maximum discomfort and inconvenience. Then I'd have acted. There are two thousand engine drivers in the Forces,' he ruminated. 'It might not have been wrong to give the strikers what they originally demanded, but it's another story to give in after two weeks' shilly-shallying. It's no longer a question just of terms. All the same, if I were leading the men at this moment I wouldn't give in. This is a prosperity strike,' Winston went on. 'There is full employment, and the workers want a bigger share of the spoils.'

The old itch to do something makes him impatient. At one moment he says, 'This is costing the nation a million pounds every day, fourteen millions up to date, and it would cost only £600,000 yearly to meet their demands.' Then in the same breath he talks of the possibility of a political crisis, and the use of the Army. He handed me the *Daily Worker*, muttering 'trash' under his breath, so that he could go on reading the *Guardian*.

After a time he threw away his papers.

'I'm slovenly,' he grumbled, 'whenever I relax and make no effort.'

He asked me about my plans, which surprised me greatly. On his return from Sicily I had a feeling that he did not mind whether I called at Hyde Park Gate or stayed away. However, since this set-back he has been dreading another stroke, almost from hour to hour; he seems to want to see me every day. Yet it may be better that he should be lightly tethered to this world, for he can have no future.

'I'm writing better, much better. I think I'm over this turn,' was his cheerful valediction.

Chartwell, June 16, 1955

I found him in a corner of the rose garden which is hidden from the wind.

'I don't feel like taking part in Parliament. My head feels very full in the middle of the day. I must do away with luncheon as a social function. What is my pulse like? It was very quick yesterday afternoon.

'Bloody, those men walking off the *Queen Mary*. If I were the Cunard people, if I were in authority, I would say to the men: "We can't go on like this. We are going to lay up our ships for a month and discharge the men." They are killing the goose that lays the egg.'

Chartwell, June 17, 1955

'The Guildhall people [1] want me to make a world pronouncement on Tuesday. It's not the time for a world pronouncement. Anyway, I'm not fit for anything. I shall speak for ten minutes.'

When Winston had said this he looked gloomily across the Weald:

'And I shall worry all day over that ten minutes' speech. I'm interested in my book, that's all I care for now. I'm tremendously interested in it. If I die tomorrow the business arrangements would not be altered. It's all written. But I'd like to make it as good as I can; just taking out something here, and perhaps adding a sentence there.'

His accountant came through the garden gate.

'Ah,' said Winston, 'I shall not be very long with Lord Moran. Perhaps you would return. My finances are intricate, though not unfavourable. I have to keep moving about, when I'd like to stay here for a month. You cannot realize how much I hate doing anything.'

I tried to reassure him about Tuesday. 'We'll get you through Guildhall without any trouble.'

'Are you sure?' he said, looking at me like a child.

Hyde Park Gate, June 20, 1955

I had arranged to see Winston at three o'clock on his return from Hatfield. I found he had forgotten all about my visit, and had gone

[1] Churchill's statue in Guildhall was to be unveiled on June 21, 1955.

to sleep. They wanted to wake him, but I said I would return at six-thirty. When I came back he was sitting in the library doing nothing; Christopher was reading his speech for Guildhall.

'I'm in low spirits. Oh, I generally am now. Life for me is over. The sooner the better.'

'Wow,' said Christopher.

'I'd like to go to Chartwell,' Winston continued, 'and stay there. But Clemmie doesn't like it, and her health will keep her here. Any fun I get now is from my book.'

He had rather dreaded his visit to Lord Salisbury, but it was arranged that he should not get there till seven o'clock on Saturday, leaving Hatfield at eleven on Monday morning. That left only the midday hours on Sunday, and with a minor he hoped to get through luncheon. He thought he had got on all right, though he was walking badly. He had played twenty-two games of bezique, about seven hours' play. Christopher suggested a small alteration in his speech. But Winston did not seem interested, he said wearily:

'I think it will have to do as it is.'

I told him it was nearly seven o'clock. He had no idea it was so late.

'I must go at once. I promised Clemmie to play bezique before dinner,' but he made no move. At last I left him staring at the carpet.

June 21, 1955

Yesterday Winston appeared to be finished. He became impatient, demanding how long this must go on, and then, a moment after, it was plain that he was frightened about himself. He seemed to have given up the struggle since his stroke. Low-spirited and querulous, we could not interest him in anything. Today he is not so sure that he wants to die. The City's warm patriotism, that is as Victorian as his own frock-coat, is the medicine he needs. All the same, I was glad that this was his last public appearance If he got through this with credit he would at any rate have avoided a breakdown in public. It was in that mood that I waited in Guildhall. But immediately I caught sight of him walking slowly but steadily up to the dais I knew it was all right.

No one, I thought, would notice anything wrong with his gait. It is a good weather-vane. When he walks all right his mental processes are more or less normal. I sat back with a great feeling of relief.

Standing there on the dais beside his statue, he might have been the 'Spy' cartoon of Winston, or for that matter of his father, Lord Randolph. His white hands laid out above his groin, fingers spread

670

wide apart, thumbs uplifted, they seemed to be caressing the nap of his black frock-coat.

He did not say very much of serious import. He did not believe that humanity was going to destroy itself, though a period of relaxation of tension might well be all that was now within our grasp.

After dinner I called at Hyde Park Gate. I found him playing bezique with Clemmie, tired but happy.

'This afternoon at Guildhall,' he said, 'restored my confidence. It was a formidable ordeal. Did you like my speech? It would be easy,' he continued, 'on such an occasion to say foolish, conceited things. I carefully avoided that.'

No one is more adroit at disarming criticism of that sort by a discreet levity. He told me how agreeable to him was the prospect of his statue, resting beneath those of Gog and Magog, between Nelson and Wellington, with Pitt and Chatham. He liked it as much as he had disliked Graham Sutherland's portrait.

Then, with a toss of his head, he said:

'All is vanity. Many have done more than I have, but no one has been so kindly treated. I do not deserve it.'

I advised him to go early to bed, but he explained that he had slept for more than an hour after his return from Guildhall. Sleep did him almost as much good as a 'minor.' He thought there was something, after all, in resurrection.

'Why, if I slept for a million years I should wake up full of meat.'

June 22, 1955

Winston said cheerfully,

'I know now I can do this sort of thing. I believe Sir Russell would give me a good report.'

Guildhall has done a good job of work; he will not give in without a fight. I clutched at the opening to consolidate the gain and brought Brain to Hyde Park Gate before he changed his mind.

Without any preliminaries Winston began his story:

'Three weeks ago to the day I bumped up against the wall. I thought I was drunk, but in the morning my writing was bad. I put my signatures in an envelope, but I have left it at Chartwell.'

He reached for his pen and wrote his name several times. This he handed to Brain.

'That is like my normal writing, whereas that morning my hand lingered so that I upset things—I cannot sprinkle sugar as well even now. I wondered if it would get worse as in 1953, when I did things the day after my stroke, and I was not paralysed until the following day. But this time the other channels opened up.' He grinned. 'I'm

671

getting rather good at that. And Charles watched me like a cat, night and day, for five days. I can walk all right if I set my mind to it.'

He flung off the bed-clothes and stalked across the room. Then he stood and lifted first one leg and then the other.

'I'm still not very steady.'

Brain made a careful examination, and then sat back in his chair and said nothing. 'Charles is right,' he said at last. 'It was spasm, and now the artery has opened up again. I see no reason why you should not in a short time be as good as before.'

'You mean before I resigned?' Winston asked incredulously. 'Of course,' he went on, 'putting down responsibility is a very relaxing affair. My whole psychological position had to be changed. After my return from Sicily I had to begin my election address. The quality of thought, such as it is, was not diminished, but I had become very slow. I got it out all right in the end, but I dislike original composition. I am not ambitious any more. I only want not to make an ass of myself. I began my Guildhall address on Monday. I did 300 words in the car coming up from Chartwell, and another 300 between 10 o'clock and midnight. In the morning I finished it off only just in time. My bad time is from noon until half-past four. I am embarrassed by the midday blur.'

He complained of his memory, particularly for names. He looked at the glass of whisky by his bed.

'I keep it by me all day. Oh, it is only weak, and I only sip it. It is more a companion than a stimulant.'

Russell listened attentively to Winston's story, but offered no comment. Winston waited impatiently for suggestions, but they did not come. He had told Brain the whole story that he might get his help. He wanted to be told that his mind was not giving way. He wanted to do something. 'No,' Brain said shortly, 'there is nothing I can add to the treatment.'

Brain is an honest man, he has no patter. He told me, when I saw him to the door, that he noticed Winston a good deal changed. But of course he had not seen him for a year. There was really nothing to be said. He did not try to say comforting things. He would be more popular with Winston if he did.

Chartwell, June 26, 1955

'Sir Winston's just woken up,' said Kirkwood. But for a time he lay like a log with his eyes closed, with many toothless yawns. At last he threw off the bed-clothes, and then, as if exhausted by the effort, lay naked on his bed.

672

'I'm very feeble,' he said, still with his eyes closed. 'I can only drink and smoke—hardly anything else. I'm tired all the time. I have no physical energy. I suppose it's no good trying to do things unless one wants to?'

'After all, Guildhall didn't go badly,' I answered.

'Ah,' he responded wearily, 'I'd like to end up decently at that level. I don't want to make any more speeches. Why should I? I'm paired all this week, and anyway they are doing what I told them. You see, Charles, it's no good giving up power only to take on more work and worry. I don't want to move from Chartwell, except of course to see Clemmie. I could see that Brain thought I was finished.'

He got out of bed with an effort, and struggled into his zip suit. Then he sat down in front of a new dressing-table and pressed a button. A mirror rose slowly out of the table.

'Very clever,' said Winston. He opened four small drawers which flanked the mirror. 'I keep my medicines here. Kirkwood finds he does not lose them now. I no longer have to bother about a parting,' he said, as he reached for his hair-brushes.

He looked round. 'It's a good room to die in,' he added grimly.

'Come, will you meet me at the bottom?' he said as he got into the lift.

He crawled out of the lift and stumbled into his studio. All his pictures had gone, leaving the walls pock-marked by large nail holes.

'Where have they gone?' I whispered to Sergeant Murray. 'To the old studio down the hill,' he replied.

Winston looked round the empty room. This room and the one above it had been added to the original building and jutted out from it.

'I built this promontory,' said Winston, 'it will make Clemmie a nice drawing-room.'

I asked him if he had painted anything since his return from Sicily.

'No,' he said sadly, 'I'm not up to it.'

'Did Dorothy drive you here? Would she like to see the fish? They will have tea ready when we get back.'

When the supply of maggots was exhausted he crossed the stepping-stones with great care and stood looking down at the swimming-pool.

'Three of the grandchildren bathed there yesterday. Twenty years ago my own children used the pool.'

As we made our way back to the house he caught sight of some people peering through the open gate. He pulled himself together and walked past as he did at Guildhall, waving gaily to them. Then, as he passed out of view through the hall into the library, he flopped wearily into a chair. While Dorothy made tea I took a large volume from the shelves.

'What is it?' he asked.

'Napoleon.'

'Ah, a beautiful book. It was a present. He was a very wonderful man. I put him after Julius Caesar. Yes, he is at the top. I suppose there might be half a dozen competitors, including Marlborough, for second place.'

I showed him a coloured picture of Napoleon, sitting on a camp-stool, with his staff standing behind him.

'That,' said Winston, his voice more vigorous than it had been, 'was when he went to sleep, telling them to wake him when the troops debouched from those woods. I like to live in the past,' he mused. 'I don't think people are going to get much fun in the future.

'We have got a good horse, a two-year-old,' Winston went on. 'Have you seen the *Observer*? John Hislop—he is a good man—thinks it might come out on top.'

'You mean it might win the Derby?'

'Well, it has a chance.'

This was exciting. What a scene there would be! I could not help exclaiming: 'That, anyway, is something worth hanging on for.'

'You will come, Charles?' Winston for a moment had caught my excitement. 'It will be a bit of interest in life.' He relapsed into gloom. 'But the Derby is a long way off. A good deal can happen before that. My racing has cost me nothing. It has paid its way.'

Christopher appeared in his shirt-sleeves. He gave me a great grin. 'He doesn't play enough cards.'

Winston received this sally with a grave face.

'I'm rather a bully,' adding as an extenuating circumstance, 'I have worked hard in my time.'

Dorothy got up and held out her hand, but Winston rose and insisted on coming to the door. As we drove away he stood in the doorway waving to us.

July 4, 1955

'May I just finish these notes for my book?'

While he dictated I glanced at a pile of books by his bed.—G. M. Trevelyan's *History of England*; J. R. Green's *Short History of the English People*; *The Later Plantagenets*, by V. Green; *War in the Middle Ages*, by Oman. 'Do you read all these books?' I asked.

'Oh, no, I'm not rewriting my book. But when a difficult point arises I fatten my own account by referring to them.' 'Now,' said Winston to the secretary, 'run away.'

674

'You are staying at your country home?' he enquired. I explained that I was on my way to London and that Violet Bonham Carter was in the car. He said he would like to see her. She asked him about his book.

'That is all that concerns me now,' he replied. 'Though I'm going up to London this afternoon to vote in the House.'

She asked him what was being debated; he smiled: 'It's a three line whip, that's all I can tell you.'

July 6, 1955

'My mind,' he said to me this morning, 'works as well as ever' (a generous summing up), 'but I dislike the effort when I have to use it.' He tells me that he spends four or even five hours of the day on corrections and alterations to the book. I must ask Hodge how far these involve mental effort. As I was leaving he said that two of his fingers had gone numb—they felt quite dead— before he went to bed. 'It doesn't mean anything, Charles? I'm not going to have another stroke?'

He thanked me for coming to Chartwell. 'It is a great comfort to me, my dear. Tomorrow Henry Luce's people will be here about business in connection with the book. I want to be in good form.'

July 10, 1955

Norman Brook is staying with us at Marshalls. He has an honest mind, and is on the whole more approachable than Bridges; it is easy to understand how the whole Cabinet trust him and rely on his judgment. He is very fair to Anthony. People talk of Anthony's impatience and his moments of petulance and irritability, but generally these soon vanish, the cloud is gone and the sun is shining again. Norman thinks, looking back, that he was very patient. Winston tried him pretty hard. For a long time he would make no plan of any kind about his resignation; then when at last he did talk about it, he still refused to name any date. I got the impression that Winston did not contribute much in his last six months in office. He wasn't really up to his job. In the end he made no effort to master anything.

'What brought things to a head?' I asked.

'The Party,' Brook answered, 'had wanted for some time to go to the country. The real reason why they wanted an election was that the economic situation was as good as it was likely to be. In the autumn it might not be so good. Incidentally, the fact that they came back with a good majority proved they were right. And then when everything was fixed up Ike announced, out of the blue, that he would like to come over. His idea was that there should be a great celebration of the tenth anniversary of VE day, which he would use to bring the French up to the scratch; he thought they could be persuaded, in these surroundings, to ratify the Paris agreement. This plan did not appeal to me,' Brook went on, 'because it could not be very attractive to the Germans. Besides, nothing could have been less opportune for the Government. Winston had agreed at last to name a date in April when he would resign. Now he was sorely tempted by the prospect of a Conference with Ike to hang on. Anthony's patience at last gave way.

'"But," he said mildly. "I thought we had an understanding."

'"I cannot discuss this," Winston said in truculent tones. "It is not a matter for the Cabinet to decide."

'I suppose it wasn't,' Brook conceded. 'However, this time the Party knew all about the date, and Anthony could not have given way even if he had wanted to. So Ike was told privately that the Conservative Party had a General Election in view. Then when all this was settled, Anthony decided to take a chance and go to the country directly he took over from Winston.'

Brook was certain this was not just a trick to get Winston out; the Party believed it was the right moment to go to the country. They were sick of delays, they refused to put it off any longer. He thought for a time and then said:

'You know, if Anthony had not been ill when the P.M. had his stroke in 1953, Rab and Salisbury might have acted very differently. You see, the Party had accepted Anthony as Winston's heir; he was ill, so there was nothing for it but to carry on with Winston, however incapacitated he might be.'

Brook, too, marvelled at the strength of Winston's personality. He had begun the practice of sending a minute to a Cabinet Minister, writing across the top of the paper. It was a good plan, but no one had done it before him. When Attlee succeeded he imitated Winston's practice almost automatically. I told Brook of a conversation with Shuckburgh[1] when he was staying at Marshalls. We were talking of who would ultimately come out on top in the Tory Party, Anthony, Rab or Harold Macmillan. To my surprise, Shuckburgh, who had been Anthony's secretary said; 'If toughness is the decisive factor, it will be Anthony.' When I pressed him for his reasons, he went on:

'Of course Anthony always gave way to Winston. We were often furious with him at the F.O. He would return and say Winston had

[1] Sir Evelyn Shuckburgh, Principal Private Secretary to Secretary of State for Foreign Affairs, 1951–4.

been very nice to him and they had agreed. But this was because
he cannot bear scenes or any sort of unpleasantness. However, when
his mind is made up on a policy, no one sticks to it with the same
tenacity as Anthony.'

Brook thought well of Shuckburgh, and said he was intelligent,
exceptionally tough and thoughtful.

The conversation kept returning to Winston. I had said that
Arthur Bryant was editing Alanbrooke's[1] diaries, and that I feared
he might be critical of Winston as a strategist. Neither Alanbrooke
nor Marshall, I said, took the old man seriously in the field of
strategy. Brook thought from what Billy Collins[2] had told him that
the diaries would not be published for a long time, anyway in their
complete form. Then he rallied to Winston's side:

'The P.M. prevented any quarrelling between the three Services
and co-ordinated their work. Winston's courage in 1940 will, I am
sure, survive any criticism of his conduct of the war. He had two
valuable qualities: he never frittered away his time attending social
functions, public dinners and the like (he must have gone to only a
fraction of those Attlee attended), and he was ruthless during the
war in selecting the two or three subjects which he decided to
master.' Brook smiled. 'After the war he was even more determined
to cut down what he had to do, until in the end he made no effort
to master anything.'

I told Brook that Winston had said during the war: 'Portal has
everything,' and I asked him why Portal had fallen in his sight. A
flicker of a smile crossed Brook's face:

'Winston invited Portal to call on him; he wanted him to take on
the Ministry of Defence. Portal arrived and told him he had influenza. Winston was frightened he would get it. Portal obstinately
refused to accept office. When Winston realized he had run the
risk of picking up Portal's microbes for nothing he was very angry.
From that day the P.M. seemed to write him off.'

I tried without success to get out of Brook his explanation of the
way Winston would write off a man for good simply because he had
refused a job. I quoted Trenchard: 'Portal was as good a pilot as
he was a staff officer, a very rare combination.' Brook agreed: 'Yes,
he is a remarkable figure; he goes through life like a lone wolf.'

One day last year Lord Wavell's son, who had been given a year's
leave to put his father's paper in order, said to me: 'Why did Mr.
Churchill dislike my father?' I was about to put the question to
Brook when N—— joined us and answered my questions. It seems

[1] General Sir Alan Brooke, wartime C.I.G.S., had become Viscount Alanbrooke.
[2] William Collins, publisher.

that after the first bitterness there had been a reconciliation, so that Winston said he was not sure that he had been quite fair to Wavell in his book. At this point the official history of the war came out. Wavell was praised, he was a very fine general, and there was a broad hint that Winston had failed to discern his merits. Then Winston seemed to revert to his original verdict. 'If only,' I put in, 'Wavell had possessed something of Ismay's gift for putting himself across.'

When David Maxwell-Fyfe replaced Lord Simonds as Lord Chancellor Winston asked me what I thought of the change; he appeared uncertain how it would be taken. Winston himself, on another occasion, remarked that he liked David, but that he was a poor politician and had given him the wrong advice on Crichel Down, and on television.

Brook, who had been silent, joined in: 'David was very conscientious. What I like about him is that if you have a problem he will at once offer to help and take any amount of trouble to find a solution. He has good judgment, and when his report is ready every aspect is considered. Nothing is left out. It is pretty dull stuff, but when David has done the Cabinet doesn't want to discuss it any further, but is ready to pass on to the next item on the agenda.'

July 12, 1955

'I feel I'm breaking up quickly. I have divested myself of everything. I only want to help. I have no desire to be a rival to anyone or to be a counter-attraction. Lots of people want to see me, but I am not fit to see them.' He brooded. 'Of course if the Party had come on bended knees and said I must help them and asked me to stay I could have done it. I think I should have been up to it. I slept from midnight to nine this morning. A lovely sleep. I did not get out of bed till one-fifteen and when I had been up less than two hours I went back to bed and slept for an hour and a half. Some day soon the sleep will go on for ever. I spend most of the twenty-four hours recumbent.'

He dragged himself wearily out of bed, and sitting in front of the looking-glass, sprinkled some lotion on his scalp before he took up his brushes. 'It makes me look a little more alive,' he said. Winston rose and went to the bathroom.

Montague Browne: 'I got hold of Walter Raleigh's *Life* and his last letter to his wife. I gave them to Winston to read. He wept. "James I was a bloody man," he said angrily. And Winston didn't like Henry VIII either. He hated his cruelty to his wives; Anne Boleyn, in particular, had put up a good show.'

678

Moran: 'Winston doesn't read much. I don't suppose he read the book I gave him.'

Montague Browne: 'You mean *Melbourne*? You're quite wrong. He came into the office the other day muttering:

'"Intelligent, yes. Good looking, yes. Well-meaning, yes. But not the stuff of which Prime Ministers are made."

'I said: "But would Rab have been any better?"

'Winston looked blankly at me. "I was thinking of Melbourne."'

July 14, 1955

Anthony Eden came at five o'clock to tell Winston about Geneva. 'He wants to put his visit to me in the papers,' Winston said.

'I went to the Other Club in the evening,' Winston continued. 'A quarter to nine till a quarter to twelve. Most of them had slipped away by then, but I stayed to the end. There was some good fun. I got home at a quarter to one, tired but not unduly tired.'

'I had a good talk with Lord Goddam about Ruth Ellis.'[1]

I told Winston that some of her clientele in Soho carried knives, and that on more than one occasion she had attended the Middlesex Hospital with flesh wounds inflicted on her in the practice of her profession.

July 18, 1955

Winston said he had had a letter from Ike. 'Would you like to see it, and my reply?'

Ike was sorry that a meeting of the Four Powers at the Summit could not have been arranged earlier 'with any self-respect' on account of the antagonism of the Soviet Union to NATO. He regretted that this had prevented Winston taking part. He did not 'expect a miracle at Geneva,' but 'perhaps we may inch a little nearer to your dream of tolerance and understanding.' Ike signed the letter 'Your old friend.'

Winston's reply showed that at eighty he can still unfold his purpose in splendid fruitful sentences. One I can remember:

'It is a strange and formidable experience laying down responsibility and letting the trappings of power fall in a heap to the ground. A sense not only of psychological but of physical relaxation steals over one to leave a feeling of relief and of denudation.'

Sir John Rothenstein[2] had lunched with Winston. He did not leave until half-past four. They went round every picture in the

[1] Hanged for murdering her lover in July, 1955. The case aroused further disputes as to the validity of capital punishment.

[2] Director of the Tate Gallery.

house and in his studio. Rothenstein wanted one of Winston's pictures for the Tate Gallery.

'He will take the "Snow Scene,"' said Winston. 'Rothenstein said the Tate had waited till I was no longer Prime Minister. He wanted the picture to go to the Tate for artistic and not for political reasons. He is a good companion,' he reflected. 'Said some wise things, not all of them connected with pictures.'

July 20, 1955

This morning Winston began:

'I had an interesting dream. I was talking to Edward Grey, forty years ago. It was a long conversation. But I never can remember my dreams. They are very precise, even about detail, but they vanish.'

The budgerigar alighted on Winston's hand, and he held it to his lips. He went on:

'I can't pick up the points in conversation now. Yesterday when I went to Kempton I talked to no one but Christopher and my trainer. I avoided other people. I'm empty-headed, woolly. It's a ghastly condition. I have been making innumerable corrections in three volumes of the book. It's very confusing keeping the different periods apart. I must not do too much of it,' he said wearily, and then with a burst of impatience, 'I can only die.'

I wonder how long he can go on in this twilight state.

Chartwell, July 25, 1955

Found Winston sitting by the lake watching two men in a punt who were pulling up stakes to which wire netting was attached. 'The black swans need more food, they must have more of the lake,' he said.

Pitblado, in his London clothes, was mooning about. Anthony had sent Winston a letter all about Geneva, and Pitblado was there to fill in the picture. When he had a chance he gave me his view of Winston: 'Of course I've not seen him for some time. He is older and takes a long time to complete his sentences.' When I came back Winston said in a low voice: 'Did he ask you anything about me?'

I don't know if Anthony wants Winston to speak in the House on Wednesday in the debate on Geneva, but he is not fit to make a speech, and I did what I could to dissuade him. I asked him whether he approved of what had been done at Geneva. 'Oh, yes, at least I think so. I feel very stupid.'

July 29, 1955

Called at Chartwell on my way to Marshalls. Winston had lunched with Anthony at No. 10. Anthony, he said, was 'very sensible about things.' He was not particularly optimistic, but said the Russians had been 'simple, friendly and natural.' Winston took a long time to finish a sentence and more than once I could not follow what he was trying to say.

'I' . . . (pause) . . . 'I think' . . . (pause) . . . 'that I have' . . . (long pause) . . . 'lost my memory.' 'I'm no good . . . very stupid.'

'You mean on waking up?'

'No . . . it's more than that . . . I don't talk . . . I've . . . nothing to say . . . Anthony must have noticed . . . it. I don't care . . . I am conscious I . . . am much worse. I don't think I could make a speech now. It's extraordinary I'm not any good for anything.'

All this he mumbled as if he were speaking of someone else and was not really interested. Some of the pauses were so long that it seemed he was beginning a new sentence.

'Clemmie has made up her mind to go to Switzerland.'

'Where?'

It was some time before he answered.

'I don't remember the place, though I . . . know it quite well. Did you like the chapters I gave you?'

For a moment there was a flicker of animation. It passed. I looked at his vacant face; the skin was still smooth and pink, like a baby's skin after a bath. There is none of time's etching round the eyes. Nor could I detect a white hair, but in his mind he has rather gone to pieces.

Chartwell, August 2, 1955

I could get nothing out of Winston this morning.

'I feel . . . pretty well . . . but not much . . .'

I waited for a long time, but he went on looking at the carpet. At last I suggested 'energy.'

'Energy,' he repeated in an expressionless tone. 'Kirkwood,' he called, 'I'll have the . . .'

When he did not finish the sentence Kirkwood brought him a towel.

'No. The spray.'

Winston said: 'I can't find . . . anything . . . to say. I don't . . . make . . . conversation.'

'You mean when you are tired?'

'No . . . the whole time. I'm trying to . . .' but he left me to complete his sentence if I could. He did tell me, though he took a long time over it, that the *Daily Mirror* had offered him £3,600 for an article. 'Oh, about two thousand words.' But he wasn't going to write any article for any paper.

Christopher had telephoned twice in the week because he was worried about Winston. Was I going to see him that morning? I decided to call at the farm and tell him about things.

'He seems,' Christopher said, 'to have gone downhill very quickly in the last few days. He dined with us one night. Mary had arranged that the children should be there to make things gay and cheerful. But we couldn't get a word out of him. He seemed very depressed. And yet this week-end he was quite cheerful. One night the Prof. came to dinner. I asked him the kind of questions that would interest Winston, and he followed the conversation attentively. The next day the Kilmuirs came to lunch, and Winston took a fairly active part in the conversation. Of course, he'd had a minor before they came. That still seems to make all the difference. Do you think, Charles, anything is going to happen? Is he really much worse? I have made a list of people I think he would like to see, but when anyone comes to Chartwell he sits quite silent as if he did not hear what was going on around him.'

August 5, 1955

Lord and Lady Waverley, who had lunched with Winston, did not leave till half-past four. I saw him a few minutes after they left Chartwell. He seemed in a moribund state.

'Did you find talking to them very tiring?' I asked.

'I . . . I don't know . . . I don't know . . .' He shook his head. 'I'm afraid I gave myself away. I am a worm. I wasn't . . . like this . . . when I had the stroke. Physically I was affected, but I was able to think. I made the birthday speech (seventeen months after the stroke) and . . . the speech . . . when I came back from abroad. I wonder . . . if . . . I shall get back . . .'

He made no attempt to finish the sentence.

'You mean the control of things?' I ventured.

'No, I . . . only want . . . to be . . . myself . . . again.'

(I would not mind so much if he didn't realize what was happening.)

'At the time of your stroke you had to do things. Probably if there were an emergency now you would be able to meet it.'

'I think I . . . could,' he conceded. 'There isn't the same need to make an effort now.'

He made a little gesture as if he were saying 'What can I do about it?' Then he relapsed into a kind of trance. There was no expression of any kind on the mask-like countenance. His eyes were dull and seemed to be fixed on some distant object. For a long time he said nothing. Once or twice he closed his eyes and kept them closed for a little, so that I thought that he was about to sleep.

'I . . . don't think I shall have any difficulty in getting . . . out . . . of . . .'

I waited.

'. . . out of office.'

One of the secretaries had reported that she had noticed that he 'got confused at times.'

'I sometimes would like to see you to tell you what is in my mind. But . . .'

I waited, but he did not go on. I think I said, 'If I left you, you would sleep. It would rest you before you see Macmillan' (who was dining with him).

'I'm not afraid of seeing . . . Harold. I don't care what he says about me. I . . . can still . . . be civil. I can still . . . comport myself decently.'

He beckoned me to sit down.

August 7, 1955

Christopher says it is not necessary to warn Clemmie that Winston is not so well. She knows the position. She had thought of scratching her month in Switzerland, but decided that she must get better so that she might be ready on her return to look after him. She hoped nothing would happen while she was away. I mentioned that Winston had said he wanted sometimes to tell me what was in his mind.

'I can tell you what that is,' Christopher said grimly, 'he thinks he is dying.'

August 9, 1955

Deakin[1] told me that Winston had an illusion about the book. 'He has an idea that it should be his main interest now, but he hasn't any longer the energy to handle great masses of material. He can't enter into the rhythm of the book.' I said Winston realized that original composition, as he called it, is now beyond his reach, but he felt that he could grapple with the necessary corrections to the text. I asked Deakin about them. He said sadly that they were frankly not of much value. Deakin had not seen Winston for some months; in the past he had come only when invited. Now it is different.

We found Winston in poor heart. Proofs were scattered about the bed. Deakin said to Winston: 'How many millions of words have

[1] F. W. D. Deakin, historian, Warden of St. Anthony's College, Oxford, who helped with Winston's books.

been dictated in this room?' That took him back before the war, and he seemed happier and talked a little about his other books.

When we were alone Winston made no attempt to talk. I asked him at last how he was.

'I suffer,' he replied slowly, 'from these pauses. It . . . is the state . . . of my mind . . . that troubles me.'

He turned abruptly.

'Am I going off my head?'

August 10, 1955

Lunched with Harold Macmillan. 'Of course Winston is older,' he said, 'but when I took the conversation back to Lloyd George his memory was surprisingly good.' Macmillan asked me how long he would go on like this. I replied that was guesswork.

August 12, 1955

Winston had just gone to bed when I arrived at Chartwell at six o'clock.

'I hear you have been painting. Were you painting well?' I asked.

'Come and I'll show you,' and throwing off the bed-clothes, he stumped out of the room to his new studio, the old dining-room. There on an easel was a painting of Clemmie.

'Clemmie says she has never been painted properly, they have not come off. Do you like it?'

I asked if he had done it from memory. He answered by pressing a button, when a small lantern threw on a screen by the side of his painting a portrait of Clemmie. 'It is from a photograph of her that appeared in some paper twenty years ago when she launched the *Indomitable*. I was extraordinarily impressed by it.'

'I'm not setting up as a portrait painter, but I thought I would like to copy it.'

August 14, 1955

I got nothing out of Winston during my visit. He did not speak unless I asked a question, and then only to mumble 'yes' or 'no,' like a man talking in his sleep. I asked him 'if he had had any visitors. He said, 'Yes.' I asked him if Pug Ismay had been in form. He said, 'Yes,' without looking at me.

I learnt that Lady Violet Bonham Carter was staying in the house. I found her on the lawn. 'I saw Winston last at Clemmie's birthday party,' she said. 'I don't count the time you took me to his room for a few minutes. We had a very vigorous argument then. I

684

am shocked by the deterioration in him since then. I made a point of talking about the past: I went back to the Leicester by-election which he fought as a Liberal.' Violet poked her nose in my face: 'You know Winston left the Liberal Party at that time because he did not agree with my father's action in putting Labour into power. My father thought that if Liberals and Conservatives combined to keep Labour out of office it would embitter Labour. It was, Lord Moran, a turning point in Winston's career. But all he said was, "I can't remember . . . I can't remember these things as you do."'

Chapter sixty-four

When life was over

November 18, 1955

This morning, as I entered his room, Winston looked up glumly.

'I have to speak tonight, and I don't know what to say. I am quite impotent. I hope I get through all right. I shall only speak for five minutes.'

He was expecting Christopher, who is going to help him with the speech; meanwhile he kept looking at the small clock by his bedside. He was not interested in my ministrations, he was entirely taken up with what he was going to say. Every word is written down; all Winston has to do is to read it out. Yet he is (to quote his secretary) 'in a panic lest things go wrong.' What is at the bottom of his nagging apprehension? Sir John Simon once said to me: 'When I get up in the Law Courts I don't turn a hair. But I never rise to address the House of Commons without feeling that it is a mill-stream running away from me.' His confidence in the Courts came from long experience; he knew that what he said would be accepted. Whereas in the House he rightly felt no such certainty. Is this the explanation of Winston's lack of assurance at the end of his life? Have even the war years, when he had the House in his pocket, failed to pluck from his mind the bitter memory of his time in the wilderness?

Henry Fairlie has an article on Winston in this week's *Spectator*. He wants him to get up in the House of Commons in the course of the debate on Geneva and make another Fulton speech that would change the mind of the nation. I thought it might give a fillip to Winston's morale. He read the page slowly and then put it down without a word. He knew it was not true. He would make no more speeches that mattered. If he had to get on his legs all he could now hope for was that he would not make a fool of himself.

Chartwell, November 21, 1955

Winston had asked me to call at Chartwell on my way to London. He was reading a section of the book, now in page form. 'I have 25,000 words to write and then it is done. It might take a year, there is no hurry.' He smiled. 'No, there is a hurry. Only my book,' he went on, 'commands my ability and my interest. All the rest is drudgery.'

Without a flicker of a smile he added:

'I find the fifteenth century more interesting than the twentieth. It has more reality.'

Hyde Park Gate, December 13, 1955

When I saw Winston at Hyde Park Gate he began at once:

'There is a healthier atmosphere on both sides of the House.'

When he saw that I did not follow what he had in his mind, Winston went on:

'They are taking a firmer line with Russia and the Egyptians. I went to the House of Commons yesterday. How long was I there? Oh, I suppose about four hours, but I went back after dinner to hear Anthony.'

'Was he good?' I asked.

There was no answer.

'As usual?' I ventured.

'Yes,' muttered Winston, 'as usual. I keep losing my memory. I could not remember Anthony's name today. And now I have forgotten the name of Sir . . .'

He gazed at his bed-rest with intense concentration.

'The picture impresario. He has just gone to America largely on my business.'

Winston drummed his fingers on his bed-rest in his impatience.

'Korda, yes. Sir Alexander Korda.'

Clemmie came in.

'The tailor is waiting, Winston. You must see him, dear, before he goes.'

She turned to me.

'I am giving Winston an evening suit.'

December 20, 1955

The Ministry of Health, with unusual initiative, want to ban the use of heroin in this country. They claim that effective substitutes exist which have not the distressing effects seen in heroin addicts, that only six of sixty-two countries use this drug, and that many great

687

hospitals do not use it at all. They have asked me to see their Bill through the House of Lords. Winston has come out as a fervent defender of the drug. 'Isn't there a physician, I think his name is Douthwaite, who is against the ban? Isn't he on Guy's? Isn't that good enough?' he demanded irritably. In the debate it appeared that every other peer had a sister or aunt who owed their life to heroin. Even if the Government case had been presented with circumspection, we should have suffered defeat. As it was, we were annihilated when the Chamber divided.

When I saw Winston this morning I wondered how he would take my intervention in the heroin debate. He said at once:

'I heard you made a very good speech. Though I don't agree with you. Did the Government ask you to speak? It has done them a lot of harm. Oh, they'll drop it now. I am going to France on January 11.'

'Permanently?' I enquired.

He smiled. 'Well, semi-permanently.'

December 28, 1955

Winston looked very glum when I appeared today.

'I'm waiting about for death,' he said sombrely.

There was a long pause while he stared in front of him.

'But it won't come.'

When Winston's mind is not taken up with the imminence of death it is brooding on the safety of the Realm.

Winston's distaste for what is left to him of life makes him yearn for release; he wants to die, but he is fearful that he may leave the country without either the will or the means to defend herself.

I congratulated him on Christopher's appointment as Under-Secretary for Air.

'Yes, it will be very interesting at this time. England may be indefensible. But I think we may be able to make other countries indefensible. The Government has lost ground in the last six months. I'm glad the Chancellor of the Exchequer has gone. You see me at my best. I'm stupider . . . I . . . well, let me see . . .'

January 2, 1956

There was not a vestige of a smile when Winston looked up as I came into his room.

'I woke at four o'clock this morning with a pain in my throat, here,' and he put my hand on his neck. 'It lasted an hour, and I coughed a great deal. I wished you'd been here. I have had it

688

before. It's been going on for some time. Is it cancer?' he demanded abruptly.

Before I had time to answer he muttered:

'I don't care if it is.'

January 3, 1956

I took C. P. Wilson to look at Winston's throat. He had just arrived from Chartwell and was sitting in a chair as if he felt a great distaste for the world.

'I feel pretty bloody,' he grunted, 'I'm getting older.'

Wilson said nothing.

'I'm getting older,' he said again.

Wilson thought that the cutting off of all his activities must be a great deprivation.

'Yes,' Winston muttered, 'a lot dropped away with that.'

When Wilson had examined his throat he said:

'It is nothing serious. That is definite. There is nothing organically wrong.'

'I wasn't alarmed at all,' Winston said. But he became all at once almost cheerful. He got up and crossed the room, briskly for him. Turning to Wilson, he said with a little smile:

'Well, anyway, what's the remedy for the pain and what is causing it?'

Wilson thought that it was rheumatic. Winston seemed pleased with the diagnosis; he said he thought it was that, and that Wilson had shown discernment in divining the nature of the pain.

January 12, 1956

I asked Winston about the pain in his throat and told him that Wilson was sure it was nothing serious. He stopped me.

'I don't trouble whether it is serious, but I do if it is not serious.'

He really means this. He no longer finds any fun in life.

February 13, 1956

I asked Winston if he had been better in France than he was at Chartwell. He hesitated for a long time and then mumbled: 'I don't know.'

I asked him about his painting. He showed me a copy of a painting by Cézanne that he had taken from a book. It represented a brick-red château half-hidden by dark-green foliage. I asked him why he had chosen this particular picture to copy.

'I liked it,' he answered, 'because of the contrast between the red and the green.'

689

I told him that the Press was saying that the coming Budget was Harold Macmillan's opportunity to make a bid for the succession to the leadership of the Party.

'If he can find a way out,' Winston said, half to himself. 'There mightn't be a way out. He would have to take very unpleasant measures to make anything of the situation.'

Winston would go to the House on Thursday to vote on hanging.

'I'm a hanger,' he went on. 'It is one of the forms of death of which I have no horror. I never thought about breaking my neck out hunting.'

I marvelled at the number of books in his library that I had not read. Most of them were embellished with Lord Randolph's bookplate. 'You inherited them all? This, for example,' I said, picking out Froude's *History of England* in twelve volumes.

'I bought it,' Winston answered. 'I have read every word of it.'

February 18, 1956

I was creeping up the stairs to Winston's bedroom, having experienced of late some discomfort under my breastbone on taking stairs in my stride, when his door opened and he appeared, leaning back on Kirkwood, who was supporting him under both armpits, like an artist's dummy, while he pushed him into the passage. Winston gave me a blank, unsmiling, rather stupid look. When Kirkwood had taken him to Clemmie's room he returned explaining that Sir Winston has only just woken up. 'I had to rouse him, as he is going to see her ladyship off.'

When Winston came back into his own room he was walking very badly.

'I shall improve when I am properly awake. People must regard me as very frail. I lurch about. I don't think I shall live very long.'

When I expostulated he asked me like a child:

'Do you think I may get any better?'

He was full of the hanging debate, and even when Kirkwood had brought his breakfast he kept picking up a newspaper and reading the headlines: 'Hanging to Go'; 'By 31st. No more Hanging'; 'Wild cheers as M.P.'s decide.'

'That's the *Mirror*,' he said grimly. 'It will do harm,' he muttered. 'The Tory Party will be furious, and it will be very unpopular in the country. There will be a murder, and then people will be shocked.'

I drew my chair nearer to the bed. I could not follow his speech.

What troubled Winston was the 'unmasculinity of the island.'

'It was mad of the Tories to bring in commercial television. It is no wonder the country is going soft. My interest in politics has come back,' Winston said, as he fiddled with the papers.

I thought that the atmosphere of the House had stirred the past. I said so.

'No,' he said half to himself, 'it's the loss of masculinity, of virility, that is troubling me. I would like to speak about it in the House, to warn the country. I think I could speak clearly enough if I made the effort.'

As he said this he took great care to make every syllable clear and distinct. He shook his head sadly.

'There is no longer the necessary clarity of thought.'

February 19, 1956

Winston was drinking brandy with Brendan and Patrick Buchan-Hepburn when I called at Chartwell at three o'clock. Winston rose and took me to his room.

'My left foot twitched for three hours last night. I only got six hours' sleep. Is it dangerous? Does it mean anything?'

When I reassured him he rose and led the way back to the dining-room.

February 29, 1956

Winston is going to the House twice; he wants to vote in the Defence division.

'It is dreadful,' he murmured, and when he did not explain I asked if he had in mind the economic situation.

'No, no, dreadful,' he repeated. 'It has never been so bad.'

'You mean the country can't be defended for the moment?' He looked at me and then said sadly:

'In defence, it takes so long to arm troops with modern weapons. It takes years to change,' he muttered. 'And we've not got the hydrogen bomb yet. That's the boy. Next year we'll have it. But I think we are safe while we work with the Americans. Russia is building a navy for us to fight. But it won't be that kind of war. It's no good building submarines to blockade us. The next war will be all over too quickly for that.'

I asked him if he thought submarines were out of date.

'I should have thought so,' he said, brooding over his bed-rest.

He spoke scornfully of the 'elaboration' of our Air Force.

'They don't need half the men they've got. The three Services will never agree on anything.'

I was about to take my leave when he said:

'Don't go.'

After a long pause he said:

'Tell me, Charles, how do people die? That's what I am waiting for.' He corrected himself. 'I am waiting for my book.'

He picked up a copy of the English edition.

'You see how easily it opens, it is not necessary to break the back of the book to keep it open. I made them take away a quarter of an inch from the outer margins of the two pages and then add the half inch so gained to the inner margin. Look at it, Charles. It lies open like an angel's wings.'

Chapter sixty-five

Germany honours
Sir Winston

April 11, 1956

'Charles.' It was Winston's voice on the telephone. I asked him where he was. He answered: 'Hyde Park Gate.' He had just got in from the airport.

I found him in good heart. 'I've got back my strength.' He had slipped down from the pillow and now, taking his weight off the bed with both hands, he proceeded to lever himself back again by a succession of heaves, each accompanied by a grunt, until at last, sitting straight up in bed, he crowned his achievement by a long expiratory sigh. 'Leave me alone,' he said sharply to Kirkwood, who had gone to his assistance; it was as if he resented anyone suggesting that he could not help himself.

When I asked him how he had been in France he answered: 'I'm all right, I think. I look like living on, getting more and more useless.' When I put my finger on his pulse he said cheerfully: 'I don't think it will cause you anxiety.'

I asked Miss Pugh, who had been with him in France, if he was in good form. 'My goodness, yes. For the last three weeks he seemed twenty years younger, and now he is as happy as a child to be home again at Chartwell.'

The office sometimes finds Winston better than in fact he is. They are led astray by the uplift in his spirits when he visits the Reves' house at Rocquebrune. A few days in London, perhaps one troublesome speech, and we are back in gloom. Morale apart, time has, of course, helped. Ten months have gone since the June stroke, and the marvellous repair mechanism of the damaged brain has been at work, the side streets, as Winston calls the collateral circulation, have opened up. He can do more than he did.

April 15, 1956

Called at Chartwell on my way to London, to find out if Winston was any the worse for Friday's speech.

'How did it go?' His face fell. 'You did not read it in *The Times*?' He brushed the budgerigar off his head. I asked him if he was very tired after the speech.

'No, but it preoccupied me for three days before, three days out of my life and there's not much left. I spoke for seven minutes; not many words, I know, but it was reported in all the papers.'

'My memory is bad. I could not write my memoirs now.'

He smiled amiably.

'Fortunately that has been done already.'

He added that he could still remember poetry.

'I might speak in the House. It depends on the Budget. There are rumours of a capital gains tax. I hope they are wrong. It would be very foolish.'

April 22, 1956

Winston was sitting at a card table in his room, waiting patiently for Anthony Montague Browne. The bezique cards and markers were ready. He looked up and I could tell that he was glad to see me. He is in the mood to be pleased with the small change of political life.

Winston: 'The dinner (at No. 10) was a good show, because I was made the central figure. I sat next to Khrushchev. The Russians were delighted to see me. Anthony told them I won the war.'

At that moment Montague Browne came into the room and in his quick way picked up the thread of the conversation.

Browne: 'Could you tell which of the two, Bulganin or Khrushchev, was Number One?'

Winston: 'I've no doubt whatever; it was Khrushchev.'

Moran: 'Do you think he is a major figure, another Stalin?'

Winston: 'No, only a minor. But I am sure Bulganin and Khrushchev are in the main honest. They gave me a feeling of confidence. I am sure it is not all humbug. Their visit means something.'

Browne: 'You don't think it was a mistake?'

Winston: 'No, it will do good. At least it ought to.'

Browne: 'What are they up to?'

Winston: 'Russia is developing and getting richer. They may want to take part in the affairs of the Western nations. They may want us to help them to be better friends with the Americans. But I

694

should not be in favour of Bulganin and Khrushchev going to the States. The Americans aren't sure of themselves as we are. They might have difficulty after a visit in turning sour again with Russia.'

The Cabinet, I hear, is more critical. Winston has a busy week before him. 'I like something to do. But not too much. Often I do nothing.'

Dorothy had been talking to the policeman while we were in the house. He said there were four of them in the house guard; they did an eight-hour shift. They were told that Chartwell must be guarded night and day; they must keep awake, even when Sir Winston was away in London, on account of the number of secret documents in the house.

April 27, 1956

Winston was welcomed at Beaver Hall this morning as Grand Seigneur of the 'Company of Adventurers of England trading into Hudson's Bay.' He read his short piece, which was adequate, but wanting in animation. Then we walked across to the Skinners' Hall. There after luncheon he made a little impromptu speech of thanks which was a good deal more effective—as often happens with him. Alanbrooke said to me:

'He is a marvel. Before the Election in 1945 I said to myself: He is finished. I could not get him to decide anything. He seemed unable to come to a decision. When he had gone on waffling for two hours I said to him that there were two courses he could take. "And you know which I think is the best." But I said: "You must decide; you must choose one or the other." Winston said to me: "I can't decide. I can't make up my mind." He was burnt out, I think.'

Alanbrooke smiled.

'We were both burnt out. Anyway, we had a hell of a row for two hours. That was eleven years ago, and look at him now.'

When Winston joined us he stopped opposite me: 'That was the first impromptu speech since it happened. Before I speak I think I must jot down five or six headings; a single word would set me off.'

May 3, 1956

Winston is full of his visit to Germany. That he, the chief architect of Germany's downfall, should be their guest excites him, but he is bothered by his speech for Aachen.

'The Foreign Office brief was drivel, rubbish; what any Minister would spout. I have to say something, but it isn't easy. You see, Charles, it is an important speech. Awful,' he grunted. 'Charlemagne worked for the unity of Europe, and that is the purpose of this award. The Nazis set out to rule the world, and something went wrong.'

'They are not all dead,' I interposed. 'You will find some of them in your travels.'

'Oh,' he rejoined lightly, 'I'm a hero in Germany. It's very curious.'

I asked him if he had read the *Manchester Guardian*.[1] The editor of the weekly *Deutsche Zukunft*, a member of the Free Democratic Party, had devoted a whole page to Winston's alleged mistakes; extracts from this filled nearly a column on the centre page of the *Guardian* under two headings: 'The Misdeeds of Sir Winston; A German Attack.' The author of the article affirmed: 'Churchill did not wage war against Hitler out of any idealistic belief in freedom, but in order to maintain the balance of power. . . . Few politicians of recent years have made so many monumental mistakes as the 81-year-old British statesman.' He had done far more, it went on, to split Europe than to unite it. He had signed the Morgenthau Plan, which planned the systematic destruction of German industry, he had introduced illegal partisan warfare into territories occupied by the German Wehrmacht. Finally, he was responsible for the systematic bombing of undefended German cities. In his 'blind hatred' of Germany he had 'gambled away the British Empire and driven out the devil, Hitler, with the aid of Beelzebub, Stalin.' The Bonn correspondent of the *Guardian* introduced this tirade with the dry comment that it 'does not suggest that the award (of the Charlemagne Prize) has the general approval of the German people.'

Winston these days is not accustomed to minority reports; he read it through in silence, nursing his forehead in his left hand. When he had done he said: 'I shall have a great reception.' He had interrupted his breakfast to read the column in the *Guardian*, now he munched toast in silence. He cannot hide his feelings, and I saw he was disconcerted. As I was leaving his room he looked up: 'Is there a Leader on this?' and with that he pushed away his breakfast and picked up the *Guardian*.

May 6, 1956

It was about three o'clock in the afternoon when I arrived at Chartwell. Winston was sitting on the lawn doing nothing. It still

[1] May 3, 1956, p. 7.

seems strange to find him idling away the hours, not reading or dictating or even playing cards. I asked him about his speech for Aachen.

'It worried me,' he replied, 'but it's finished.'

He called to the policeman standing on the terrace.

'Officer, ask the young lady to bring me my speech.'

When it came he handed it to me.

'How does it read?'

I read it again before answering. I had not expected that he would take the line he did. It appeared to be a plea that the new Russia should be invited to join NATO. Winston has never shifted his position: German re-unification will only come when Russia realizes that the forces of the West have become so strong that she must accept the inevitable. Winston brushed aside my doubts, scoffing at the idea that Germany would ever take sides with Russia. 'I don't want,' he said, 'to put Germany against Russia or Russia against Germany. I want to be friends with both.'

I found Dorothy taking tea with Clemmie. Marthe Bibesco had sent Clemmie her new book: *Churchill ou le Courage*.

'It is full of inaccuracies. This is the letter I have written to her.'

The letter complained that the author had repeated an old accusation that Winston had spoken of 'This delicious war.'

'You see, Margot went about London saying that Winston used those words. Mr. Asquith was very sorry about it. Winston was very upset at the time, and went to see Margot. She apologized. I wanted the apology in writing, but Winston pooh-poohed this.'

Clemmie smiled. 'I don't really like being swept into the waste-paper basket,' and she made a little grimace.

'You know, Charles, Winston would have won the election in 1950 if it had not been for the charge that he was a war-monger. I have known Marthe Bibesco for forty years. She is a blue-stocking. Winston did not even remember what she looked like. Winston asked Violet to look through Margot's papers to see if there was any reference to him at the moment the First War broke out. All she could find was that 'Winston with a happy and confident stride went into the Cabinet Room.'

I opened the book. One of Winston's sayings was on the flyleaf. 'Because reality is better than dreams, 10.5.1940.'

May 14, 1956

I was all agog this morning to find out if Winston's visit to Germany had gone off without mishap. I went to the office on my arrival at

Chartwell. Miss Maturin, who had gone with him, said she thought there had been no mishap.

'The large crowds in the streets were silent—a few cheered—rather as Londoners received Bulganin and Khrushchev. At the Town Hall a hostile demonstration had been planned, but it rained heavily, and the only people who turned out were friendly. In the Hall itself Sir Winston spoke in English, and they did not really understand what he said, but they seemed to like his looks and were quite warm in their feelings. The papers, when they appeared, were more critical. I think they misunderstood what he said. They thought he wanted to invite Russia to join NATO, whereas what he really said was that if there had been a real change of heart and B. and K. were sincere, then he did not see why Russia should not work with the West for a united Europe. He knows you're here,' she added, so I went to his room.

Winston himself had no doubts whatever.

'The Germans were very friendly, very friendly indeed,' he repeated. 'The first night was not a success. I did not get to sleep till three. The clothes were tucked in at the bottom of the bed, which was very hard. And the sheets were coarse, and the blankets heavy. But I woke at eight and I did not feel tired. I was surprised at my own strength. I spoke without notes, except for one speech. I found things to say. I don't know what I shall do now. I felt there that I could do things.'

He knew that Christopher and I had been anxious about the visit, and he felt very pleased with himself. It had stirred up the old longing to play a part again. Had he been too impatient? Had he retired prematurely?

'What would you like to do?' I asked.

His animation vanished. His face lost its life. He came to earth with a bump.

'There is nothing to do except to die,' he answered in a low voice.

Chapter sixty-six

The flesh was weak

Chartwell, June 19, 1956

Winston is in a contrite mood this morning. He confessed, a little sheepishly, that he had walked in the procession to St. George's Chapel for the Garter Ceremony.

Moran: 'You must have been nearly all in at the end of your walk, with all those stairs and your heavy robes.'

Winston grunted: 'I had to sit down during the Service. Even when they sang "God Save the Queen" I did not stand up. My legs felt wobbly. It wasn't the length of the walk that tired me, but the way they tottered along and dawdled. I'm very much of a cripple. All I can do is a little turn round Chartwell. I used to visit the cowhouse. Now I have had to give that part up. You know, Charles, I'm not particularly interested in things.'

Moran: 'You mean in the House of Commons?'

Winston: 'No. In anything. In living. I find life pretty dull.'

Moran: 'The American reviews of the book are very friendly.'

Winston: 'Yes, pages of unending flattery. I'm busy now doing Queen Victoria.'

Moran: 'Isn't that easier than, say, Richard III? You already know so much about it.'

Winston (*musing*): 'No, that's what makes it difficult. I know too much.'

Moran: 'Are you coming right up to the present?'

Winston: 'No, no. I stop in Victoria's reign. I could not write about the woe and ruin of the terrible twentieth century.' (*Sadly*) 'We answered all the tests. But it was useless.'

Marshalls, June 24, 1956

Norman Brook is staying here again. I am not surprised that successive Prime Ministers feed out of his hand. His judgment is hardly ever at fault. He was interesting on the defeatism after Dunkirk.

Moran: 'But, Norman, I don't remember people being jumpy. Extraordinarily phlegmatic they seemed to me.'

Brook: 'I agree about the public, but there were a lot of jitters among those at the top. Brooke was imperturbable, but his Staff weren't.' (He mentioned other soldiers and Cabinet Ministers.) 'If it had not been for Winston anything might have happened. He steadied the ship.'

Moran: 'Did he contribute a great deal to the actual conduct of the war?'

Brook: 'Winston had an extraordinary capacity for seizing on things that mattered, concentrating on them and mastering them. Of course, he liked to pretend that he was looking after everything. It wasn't true. All the same, no one knew when this searchlight, sweeping round, would settle on them, so everyone worked like blazes.'

Moran: 'I sometimes wonder if Winston's habit of doing the job of all his Ministers made them feel less responsible.'

Brook: 'There might be something in that, but he animated us all.'

Moran: 'Yes, Portal made that point when Alanbrooke affirmed that in strategy Winston had contributed nothing at all.'

Brook: 'And I give Winston full marks for his long struggle to postpone the invasion of France until the American infantry was seasoned. His stubborn resistance, when the Americans wanted to get at the Germans, was quite wonderful.'

Moran: 'Winston didn't discover the Russian menace till 1944.'

Brook: 'He may have been late in tumbling to the danger, but he was, after all, the first to notice it. Anyway, far sooner than the Americans, who were badly taken in by Stalin. Look at the Iron Curtain telegram.'

Moran: 'It fascinated Monty.'

Brook: 'Winston was very cross when he discovered the boundaries of the agreed zones, and found we had already crossed our limit and had to go back. But though he tries to get away from it, he must have agreed to the zones.'

Moran: 'How do you account for that?'

Brook: 'I wonder if Winston had ever bothered to study them, or for that matter whether he had even read them. You remember, Charles, if anyone talked to him about things after the war he would say impatiently, "Cannot you see I have as much on my hands as I can deal with? Pray do not bother me with these things." '

Moran: 'What about the debit side?'

Brook did not answer my question.

'Winston has no knowledge of men,' I persisted.

Brook: 'How could he have? He disliked meeting strangers. He wasn't interested in people. When they came to see him he did not listen to them. He did all the talking. How could he find out about them?'

Moran: 'Maynard Keynes affirmed that Winston lacked instinctive judgment.'

Brook: 'If he had been like ordinary people it might have diminished his power. If he had been a sound judge of human nature it might well have interfered with his supreme virtues. As it was he was entirely self-centred, listening to nobody's views, so that in 1940 he just went straight ahead.'

Moran: 'I remember when Winston was in the doldrums after the incident of the telegram to Monty, Lord Waverley said: "After all if he'd been cautious and had taken no risks he would have been of less use to us." '

Brook (*knocking out his pipe as he smiled affectionately*): 'Winston never talks like other people. Once in Cabinet I handed him a report. He weighed the documents in his hand before he said: "This Treasury paper, by its very length, defends itself against the risk of being read." At most Cabinets he coined at least one remarkable phrase.'

Moran: 'For instance?'

Brook (*grinning*): ' "I'd rather be right than consistent." "During a long life I have had to eat my own words many times, and I have found it a very nourishing diet." '

When Norman had dug a dandelion out of the lawn with his knife he looked up:

'And yet Winston knows nothing of self-criticism.'

Moran: 'I have always been defeated when I tried to put a case to him.'

Brook: 'It was almost impossible to change his mind once it was made up. The only chance was to go to him with the news, and put your view before he had made up his mind.'

Moran: 'Nothing happened unless I had the sense to put things on paper.'

Brook: 'Yes. That meant he did not have to make up his mind forthwith. He had time to think it over.'

July 21, 1956

The political world is full of Eden's moods at No. 10; all this is known to Winston, and he is anxious about the future. He sees that things cannot go on like this for long. At the back of his mind, as I keep finding out, is the disconcerting fact that he put Anthony where he is.

August 1, 1956

Winston is very angry about Nasser's seizure of the Suez Canal.[1]

Moran: 'Nasser is not the kind of man to keep his job for long?'

Winston: 'Whoever he is he's finished after this. We can't have that malicious swine sitting across our communications.' (He said this with something of his old vehemence.) 'I saw Anthony on Monday. I know what they are going to say. Anthony asked me to treat it as a matter of confidence.'

Moran: 'What will the Americans do?'

Winston snapped: 'We don't need the Americans for this.'

Moran: 'Will you speak in the House?'

Winston: 'I might. I shall dictate something and see how it goes.'

Moran: 'Was your lunch with the King of Denmark at the Pool of London amusing?'

Winston (*grunting*): 'No. It was a damned bore.'

When he noticed I had picked up a book he went on:

'I am working at the part after the American Civil War. I read four or five books on it before I dictated anything.'

August 8, 1956

Winston came into the room flushed; he threw himself on the bed.

'It's not fair taking my pulse now. I've only just finished lunch. . . . Well, what is it? 84?'

He grinned. 'Four of them might be due to brandy.' His eye was red and angry.

'Yes,' he said with another cheerful grin, 'it's the most noticeable feature of my decline. Anthony Buchan-Hepburn . . .' he stopped short. 'I beg your pardon, Anthony . . . something Browne, yes, yes, Anthony Montague Browne. He was talking to me yesterday when I suddenly felt confused. But it cleared up all right. Nothing happened.'

Later, Montague Browne asked me what it meant. What puzzles me is that Winston's solicitor found him in very good shape this

---

[1] On July 26, in retaliation for the withdrawal of American and British funds for the building of the Aswan Dam.

morning. He was extraordinarily lucid and clear over some very complicated business.

I said to Winston that Suez seemed in a bit of a mess.

'It serves Anthony right. He has inherited what he let me in for.'

I saw he did not want to talk about Nasser. As I was leaving I met Montague Browne; he took me into the library.

'You probably think Winston is apathetic about Suez. He saw Eden on Tuesday, and he has put him right in the picture. And that inhibits Winston. He does not feel he can talk about it. I must run now. The Japanese Ambassador is coming in a few minutes to present Winston with a picture from Yoshida.'[1]

August 16, 1956

John Waverley and Ava[2] to lunch. John has been connected with Winston off and on throughout his political life, first as a Civil Servant and later as a Cabinet Minister, and he is very careful about his facts, and the conclusions that can be safely drawn from them. John pondered as I questioned him.

Moran: 'If Winston had died in 1939, before the war, what would history have said of him?'

John (*becoming very serious*): 'He had been wrong about so many things: India for example, and he was wrong on finance, and wrong about Gallipoli.'

Moran: 'Oh, come, John, surely not about Gallipoli?'

John: 'Yes, it was not the idea itself that was wrong, but Winston failed to make sure that he had enough support for it before he launched his plan. And he wasn't a very good Home Secretary. Then when he was in opposition he was isolated, and Winston needs advisers who will say to him, "Winston, you are making a fool of yourself." '

At this I could not help smiling, for John, whose firm spirit had never wavered in the bad time in Ireland and in Bengal, was no better than the rest when confronted by Winston: his valiant words died on his lips.

John: 'Left to himself, Winston's judgment was a menace. No, if he had died then he would have gone down as a failure.'

Moran: 'What about the war?'

John: 'Well, he had this wonderful gift for inspiring people. He was, too, astonishingly fertile in ideas; some were hopeless, of course, but something came out of others. And he was, as you know, a

---

[1] Shigeru Yoshida, former Prime Minister of Japan.
[2] Lady Waverley.

wonderful mouthpiece of the nation. No, I agree, he couldn't place people, and he was no good in administration unless somebody held his hand. But his imagination was a most valuable gift. And there was something . . .' (John hesitated for the word) '. . . something selfless about Winston; if an idea got hold of him he would follow it up with endless enthusiasm and energy, quite regardless of whether it was going to help him personally.'

At this point Ava spoke sharply to John. If he wanted to criticize Winston he should go to the Beefsteak or some other Club. She would have nothing said against him. Where should we be now if there had been no Winston in 1940?

During this intervention John appeared ill at ease. He now made another attempt to get the conversation back to his level.

John: 'You know, Charles, about Winston's plan for launching an appeal in October? He wants to help technology. He himself will contribute twenty-five thousand pounds. I am doubtful whether he is getting the right advice how to do it. Leathers, and not the Prof., is his adviser. The technological institute should be connected with a University and not with a local authority. Of course, this will decide in the long run whether you get a place turning out research or only a bureaucratic training place. But Winston doesn't understand the academic questions involved. His money should not be spent on bricks and mortar, but on workers' salaries and perhaps on maintenance.'

When the Waverleys left about four o'clock I telephoned to Winston. Miss Pugh told me he was asleep. I said I would be at Chartwell at six o'clock. I found him still in bed; he had not shaved, and his bed-jacket was covered with cigar-ash. I was told he had lunched off a tray. He was reading the third volume of Moneypenny and Buckle's *Life of Disraeli*.

Moran: 'Have you found it interesting?'

Winston: 'I don't know that I should read much of it if I hadn't to write about his time.'

However, he kept his forefinger marking his place . . . one gets to know these hints.

Winston: 'I want to get an idea of the years 1830 to 1860. Of course, I have some idea now, but I want to enlarge it. It's awful to have to write about thirty years when nothing happened.'

Moran: 'What about the Reform Act?'

Winston (*who did not appear to have heard what I said*): 'The American Civil War did not begin till 1861. I want to write some thirty pages about the period, beginning about 1830.'

I opened the bulky volume, which he had closed reluctantly.

Moran: 'It's a pretty solid meal; 580 pages and perhaps 350 words to a page.'

Winston (*confidently*): 'Oh, no.'

Moran: 'Well, I'll count.'

Winston: 'No, let me count.'

And he took the book from me. '340,' he said in a slightly subdued tone. 'There are six volumes and I have read two of them.'

Moran: 'It must be heavy going, old politics?'

Winston (*grinning*): 'I like old politics. A good deal of the book consists of letters; I skip a lot.'

Winston told me he had read Wells's *The Wonderful Visit* at a sitting—three hours. He denied that he had skipped a line. He could not put it down. I said to him it was a long time since he had read a book.

'Oh, come, Charles,' he protested, 'I read three on Gladstone and two on Disraeli on end. Of course, I only read books which I have to skip through in order to complete my history. I think, Clemmie, you might get me *Tono Bungay.*'

Winston is not so sure that Nasser can be written off. He is worried about Suez. He still argues that if we invade the Canal we need not stay there; when Nasser gave in we would get out. 'Anthony,' said Winston, 'wants me to speak on Suez in the House—he would like me to speak from the box.' He shook his head. 'I shall not do that. Anthony says I must be told everything.'

He is going to London later in the day. Norman Brook is dining with him. I felt happier in my mind when he told me this. Norman will give him good advice. He will tell him whether he ought to speak and if he does, what he ought to say. And I am sure that he will invest it with a proper sense of the importance of the occasion, so that Winston will not suspect that no one is bothering whether he speaks or not.

September 16, 1956

Found Winston playing bezique with Clemmie, a happy picture. They insisted on stopping the game, and Clemmie went off to bring Dorothy in to tea.

Winston: 'I don't like the way things are going. After the first debate in the House I came away encouraged, even elated. When there was danger to the country the Opposition seemed behind the Government, and Gaitskell[1] showed himself capable of playing an Englishman's part. But the second debate undid all the good; in fact, it did a good deal of harm. Gaitskell went back on things—the

[1] Hugh Gaitskell, Leader of the Labour Party.

feeling in his party was too strong for him. I want our people to take up a strong point on the Canal with a few troops and to say to Nasser: "We'll get out when you are sensible about the Canal." '

He was silent for a time. Then he said sadly: 'I am afraid we are going downhill.' The fallen state of Britain troubles him more than his own parlous condition.

Winston insisted that I must take *The Wonderful Visit* to read on my way to Spain; Clemmie rose and went over to the bookshelf, where Wells's books were. Winston directed operations from his chair. I began looking through the edition. On the flyleaf of *First and Last Things* Wells had written:

Reform Club,
Pall Mall, S.W.

'My dear Churchill,
'Here in a sort of intellectual hari-kari is my inmost self. I place it at your feet.

Very sincerely Yours
H. G. Wells.'

Clemmie invoked my aid to get Winston to persevere with a hearing aid. She got up and, speaking into his ear, said playfully; 'It's just a question of taking a little trouble, my dear. Quite stupid people learn to use it after a short time.' His eye twinkled as he put his hand affectionately on hers. He is flying to France tomorrow.

Government House, Isle of Man, October 20, 1956

The Governor called me: 'France wants you on the telephone.' When I could not hear what Winston said, he called Dr. Roberts to speak to me. Roberts was guarded on the telephone, but I gathered Winston had some kind of black-out this morning. No, he did not think it was necessary for me to see him. He was already much better. All day I have had a feeling of disquiet. When Winston telephoned, did he want to see me?

October 26, 1956

I hear from France that Winston has had an attack of cerebral spasm. During the attack he lost the use of his right leg, right arm, left side of face and Broca's area. It appears that he fell down and lost consciousness for about twenty minutes.

Chartwell, November 4, 1956

Winston was still breakfasting when I entered his room, though it was after ten o'clock. He began a sentence and then lost the thread, looking at me as though he wanted help to finish what he was saying.

'I find it difficult to write letters,' Winston complained. 'I mean to compose them. I find it difficult to do anything.'

I noticed that he was drowsy and apathetic. He gazed at me blankly, so that I was not sure whether he had heard what I had said, but when I told him that it looked as if Dulles had cancer he woke up. 'What makes you say that?' he demanded.

He pushed away the bed-rest as if it was almost too much effort. He had hardly touched his breakfast and held out his wrist. 'What is it? You haven't counted it,' he said reproachfully. Winston spoke to Wright, who let down the wooden shelf by his bed and put the bird-cage within his reach. Leaning over, Winston opened the cage and the budgerigar flew out, and fluttered twice across the room, finally perching on his head. Winston put up his hand and the bird perched on it, whereupon he drew his hand towards his lips murmuring, 'Darling.'

I telephoned to the farm that I should like to see Christopher about Winston. I found him in the hall.

He greeted me cheerfully, but soon disappeared, leaving me to Mary. As a Junior Minister he is absorbed in his job.

'I know there is nothing to be done,' Mary began. She had noticed a marked deterioration in her father when he came back from France. 'Of course, you cannot be certain what he takes in. When Anthony tells Papa something he follows it all right, but it goes in at one ear and out at the other. He doesn't attempt to work out its implications. It is just an isolated fact that has little connection with the past and none at all with the future. What I find rather sad, Charles, is that he doesn't seem interested in anything any longer. He doesn't want to do things. Mama didn't want him to make the speech at the unveiling of the Smuts Memorial, but she was sure he would not listen to her. "Are you very set, Winston," she began gently, "on this speech?" He told her, "No, I don't think I can do it." When he had sent off the telegram he seemed so relieved. He was really looking for a way out. Papa tries to get out of speeches now. It is all so different,' she added sadly. 'Of course, he varies a good deal. Last night, though we all bellowed, it seemed as if he heard nothing. And then—not very often now—he will perk up and for a short time take an interest in the conversation.'

November 11, 1956

When we were alone Winston held out his wrist.

'78? That is too fast, but it will soon come down. Let us go to my room,' he said, rising with difficulty from his chair. 'Take my pulse now, Charles. It may have fallen. 72? Why, that is normal. I'm worried,' he went on, 'about what I said to my servant the other day. I talked gibberish, as I did in France.'

I assured him that his pulse was quite good.

'Any time the bloody thing may stop,' he retorted. 'I'm not afraid to die.'

There was a long pause and then he added in a more subdued tone:

'At least I don't think I am.'

I told him that I would call in the morning.

'Do,' he said, 'I'd like that. I want you, Charles, to keep a watch on things.'

'I have a feeling of timidity about myself,' Winston confided to Brendan yesterday. Old age, by blanching the seat of reason, may cut off the fear of death even in a once imaginative mind, or it may, on the other hand, undermine fortitude, softening the will.

That Winston should own to a feeling of timidity is a measure of his decay. The mournful gestures that I have recorded were the consequence of his stroke on June 2. His plan for making the best of things then was laid in ruins. A second stroke on October 20 put an end to his project for helping the country in the Suez crisis. Each stroke seems part of a plot to destroy his reason and his will to act, leaving him more and more a physical wreck.

As I was leaving the room I picked up a book from his table.

'It's a good book,' Winston said, 'it describes very well a phase of the war. It's the diary of a woman who went to France in a destroyer, I think she went five or six times, coming back with perhaps two or three airmen whom she had helped to escape. Then the Germans noticed that she looked right before crossing the street and spotted that she was an Englishwoman. That is as far as I have read, where the page is turned down.'

Winston had read 129 pages since yesterday.

November 22, 1956

Winston's face was quite expressionless when I entered his room this morning. I took his temperature and pulse, and listened to his chest before he spoke. He told me without any bluster that he was going to dine at the Other Club. He said this with an air of great finality, and I knew that there was nothing to be gained by an argument. Clemmie repeated hotly that if he went, everyone in the constituency would know that his 'cold' was just an excuse for cutting their function last night. If Winston heard, he took no notice. After all, he had a huge majority; besides, he would never take part in another election. One thing might weigh with him. If I could get it into his head that if he took harm there was a real risk of pneumonia, I am pretty sure he would stay at home. In spite of his bravado he does not want to die.

As I rose to leave I said that if he decided to go to the club I would like him to take his temperature in the morning so that we might catch any trouble early. He glared at me. I knew my shaft had gone home. He will not go to the Other Club.

Clemmie must find me a doubtful ally. Winston is selfish, of course, he can't help it, he is just made that way, and she is trying to protect his name in the constituency. But I cannot bring myself to be hard with him now. It's little enough we can give him. Once he had plenty of enemies. Now he has none. Everyone is very kind to him, for he matters no longer. No one asks him what he thinks of a crisis. How long must he go on like this, of no use to anyone? Why should we baulk him of any fun that is left in life? Why did I intervene? Why shouldn't he go to his club? After all, he is eighty-two, and he can't expect to live for ever.

November 26, 1956

Moran: 'What made Anthony leave the country?'[1]

Winston: 'I am shocked by what he did, and I'm an Anthony man.'

Winston said this as if it had hurt him, adding in a low tone: 'I should not have done half the work he has been doing. I'd have got others to do it. He let them wake him up at all hours of the night to listen to news from New York—our night is their day.'

Moran: 'Will Anthony be able to take over when he returns from Jamaica?'

Winston (*hesitating*): 'I am very doubtful. I'd like to see Harold Macmillan Prime Minister, but they may ask Lord Salisbury. I cannot understand why our troops were halted. To go so far and not go on was madness.'

[1] On October 31, 1956, British and French troops went into action against Egypt, in order to police the Suez Canal zone. The United Nations General Assembly voted overwhelmingly against this action, and Eden was forced to order a cease fire on November 6. Eden was visibly a tired man, and on November 19 he was persuaded by his medical advisers to take a rest, and flew to Jamaica on November 23.

Moran: 'A lot of people are wishing you had been in charge.'

Winston (*shaking his head*): 'I am not the man I was. I could not be Prime Minister now. The aftermath of Suez might be serious. There may be unemployment.'

Moran: 'It is a rotten business from beginning to end.'

Winston nodded assent. 'But I'm not worrying about it.'

Is that true I wonder? Does Winston feel he is responsible for Anthony? The Prof. told me that when he was in the Cabinet he was so worried by Anthony's weakness that he spoke to Winston about it. 'I've gone too far in building him up,' Winston answered, 'to go back on it now.'

December 6, 1956

Winston: 'I was kept awake by my leg twitching. It was quite violent. I could not sleep till half-past one. It is too bad, Charles. You ought to do something about it.'

Moran: 'I don't want to give you more dope than you are taking.'

Winston (*impatiently*): 'Oh, I don't care about the future. I have no future. I must get sleep.'

Moran: 'You aren't any worse than you have been.'

Winston: 'I am certainly no better. I am weak and tired. I can't talk. I have been turning the Suez episode over in my mind. Of course, one can't tell what one would have done, but one thing is certain, I wouldn't have done anything without consulting the Americans.'

Moran: 'Why didn't Anthony go ahead?'

Winston: 'When things become known it will turn out, I think, that Anthony has been bitched, and that he wanted to go on and complete the military operation. When the Cabinet wouldn't let him he tried to resign, but they told him that he would split the Conservative Party.'

He changed the subject abruptly.

'Is it a cold night? Well, harm or no harm, I'm going to vote.'

January 12, 1957

Winston was delighted when the Queen summoned him to the palace to advise about the new Prime Minister.[1] Christopher asked him if he had remembered his top hat. 'Oh, yes,' Winston replied, 'but it's getting very shabby; as there may be more than one of these consultations in the future I must get a new one.'

[1] Sir Anthony Eden resigned as Prime Minister on January 9, 1957.

January 14, 1957

Winston had gone to bed when I arrived at Hyde Park Gate about half-past three. 'Macmillan has kept Selwyn Lloyd,'[1] I said.

Winston (*rather aggressively*): 'Did you expect that he would drop him? Lloyd stands for the position of the nation in this dispute. We haven't gone back on that. I am shocked by what Anthony did.'

He has said this to me on three separate occasions. I asked him if he had read the memoir by Sir Timothy Eden, Anthony's brother, about their father, Sir William Eden. Winston shook his head. It makes sad reading, I told him. Sir William's uncontrolled rages terrified his children, who were always on tenterhooks, fearing that they might say something that would start an explosion. A barking dog might give rise to a terrible tornado of oaths, screams and gesticulations. Sir William was a gifted egoist without any control, so that at any time there might be a terrible scene of rage and tears. Anthony did not inherit his father's instability, but it must have been a handicap to be brought up in such an atmosphere.

Winston: 'Will Anthony live long?'

Moran: 'Well, his nerves won't kill him, and if his belly was really troubling him I don't believe that his doctors would have let him go off to New Zealand.'

Winston: 'Do you think I shall be all right for a month? I may have another stroke.'

[1] Selwyn Lloyd, Secretary of State for Foreign Affairs, 1955–60.

Chapter sixty-seven

Defacing the legend

The appearance in the *Sunday Times* of the Alanbrooke *Diaries*[1] was taken by Winston's friends, that is to say by his countrymen, as an affront to his fame; but in fact it was the first serious contribution by a contemporary to the task of fitting him into his niche in history.

During the war I wrote in my diary:

'I think of Alan Brooke as one of the noblest characters in the mixed business of war; in the words of the King's Secretary, he would have made a good king.'

Unhappily, Winston did not feel like that about Brooke. There was, he grumbled, 'no give' in this Ulsterman. He was so certain in his dry way that he was right—another Stafford Cripps, as the P.M. put it. It was soon plain that they were not designed by nature to work together in double harness, and as early as the summer of 1943, at Quebec, I find in my diary the record of an explosion by Brooke at the end of a long and anxious day, so that I was fearful of a clash between the two men. It was at Quebec that the chance of an open rupture, with all its consequences, first crossed my mind. But indeed I was very wrong. The queer partnership held to the end of the war, and for this I give full credit to both men.

Brooke, when he became C.I.G.S., had been warned by Lord Milne[2] that there might be trouble ahead. Milne had foreseen that the association of two strong personalities could only succeed if Brooke was prepared to exercise an unremitting discipline of the strictest kind. This the C.I.G.S. had accepted as his own contribution to the working pact. I have that on the authority of Edward Bridges, who at Yalta expressed to me his admiration for the wisdom

---

[1] Viscount Alanbrooke, *The Turn of the Tide* (Collins, 1957).
[2] Field-Marshal Lord Milne, C.I.G.S., 1926–33.

and self-control which Brooke had shown in his dealings with the Prime Minister. It seems from my diary that I pictured Brooke then as a dour, matter-of-fact man, impatient of 'fancy reasoning,' whose quick temper was on occasion tried almost beyond endurance by his master. 'Winston,' he grumbled, 'never seems to reason anything out, he just flits from one idea to another like a butterfly in a garden.' But these isolated entries in my diary, recounting an eruption or two on the part of a man of choler, may well mislead the reader. In truth, I had no conception at the time what it meant to Brooke in daily penance to work for Winston, nor had I any inkling until now that the highly strung, sensitive, apprehensive creature we meet in the diaries was most days pulling long faces behind the iron mask he presented to the world.

Looking back, I feel that Winston is entitled to an even higher mark for carrying out his part of the bargain. For him it could not have been easy. To give way when he had set his heart on some 'gleaming' project was wholly foreign to his nature. As Norman Brook put it: 'Once Winston had made up his mind, no one could make him change it.' He would cling to his plans with astonishing tenacity. Yet time and again his pet schemes were dismissed by the C.I.G.S. with a bleak negative; they were, he would say, expensive diversions which we could not afford. I could unearth some choice samples of Winston's wrath with Brooke to set besides those quoted in the diaries. But I think that it is more to the point to record a conversation with Winston. He had said with a sly smile that if the Chiefs of Staff had not agreed with him he might have had to get rid of them. At once I taxed him with a direct question: 'Did you ever think of getting rid of Alanbrooke?' He became serious. 'Never.' There was a long pause. 'Never,' he repeated with complete conviction. Not once, as far as I know, did he over-rule him, as he so easily might have done. Throughout his life Winston devoted more time to self-expression than to self-discipline. That was one of his favourite quips, and it is in that setting that we should measure the strength of will which kept his self-control intact, and preserved for three and a half years the working arrangement with Brooke. Indeed, so well did they play their parts, while a truce was essential to the effective prosecution of the war, that I, for one, had no clear perception of the drama that was being played under our noses. Nor were Alanbrooke's closest friends any wiser; the *Diaries* came to them as a complete surprise.

When the war was over Winston felt that at last he could do as he pleased. The partnership had served its purpose, and he was content to allow the association that had sometimes proved irksome to lapse. I cannot recall a single occasion when he brought up Alan-brooke's name. It was as if he had cut this opinionated soldier out of his life and only wanted to forget him. Once, it is true, he did affirm to me, rather aggressively I thought, that he himself had been responsible for all the strategic decisions that mattered. When, how-ever, he repeated that claim in his book it became plain that he was trying to get at posterity. I do not suppose that it crossed his mind when he staked out his claim that it was bound to be unpalatable to his C.I.G.S., a professional soldier, who by virtue of his office had been held responsible for the British contribution to strategic think-ing, and that he was, in fact, asking for reprisals.

But whatever was in Alanbrooke's mind, I did not doubt that his lips would remain closed, for he was made that way. His contempt for publicity, his indifference to popular acclaim, his iron reserve appeared to be proof against all the machinations of the modern world. Like other Englishmen of his kind and upbringing, he had come to set particular store on certain inhibitions, and up till now I could have sworn that they were safe in his keeping. Then the awkward truce between the two men was broken by Alanbrooke with a resounding fanfare of trumpets.

There was a feeling of dismay when the *Diaries* were published that the legend had been scratched. Nobody, it appeared, wanted to argue about Winston's skill or lack of skill in planning the strategy of the war, though that is the crucial issue raised by the *Diaries*. Nobody was prepared to see him treated dispassionately as an historical figure. People disliked the *Diaries* because they loved Winston. There was a disposition to blame the *Diaries* because they have not done what was at no time their purpose. Alanbrooke, in his nightly jottings, was concerned with the conduct of the war, and often with Winston's part in shaping strategy. That did not require him to set forth in a balanced criticism all Winston's other qualities which will ensure him a place in history.

There was, too, a feeling of bewilderment. If this verdict on Winston's strategy was proven, how came this man, whose judgment was so fallible, to be a figure apart in the history of our time? Surely there can be only one answer: some things there were which only Winston could do, which no other man could have done. If he had been a logical man in 1940 he would have seen that his task then was impossible. As it was, like Joan of Arc, he breathed a new spirit among the people, a determination not to contemplate the possibility of defeat. But these things had nothing to do with strategy, and Alanbrooke was concerned only with Winston's strategy.

On the other hand, if a book of this kind was to be published in Winston's lifetime it is plain that Alanbrooke should have written it himself, so that he could get the feel of things and be able to measure his words. As it was, he left to Arthur Bryant the task of collecting from about a million words a mere fraction for publication, though he must have known that selection from a book can change its mood and temper. In fact, the *Diaries* leave the reader with a misleading picture of Alanbrooke. He was not really like that, his friends protested. To them, indeed, it was hardly credible that this self-effacing man, who never spoke of himself or took credit for anything in the war, should in cold print claim the landing in North Africa as 'my strategy.' There could be but one explanation: Alanbrooke was blowing off steam to his wife after hours, and what he scribbled down was not then meant for publication.

To make matters worse, Collins gave the book a tremendous boost, and everyone was agog to read it. An audience of twelve hundred, gathered at the Dorchester for a christening party, found the speakers in a subdued mood. It had begun with Arthur Bryant. He had kept pestering the *Sunday Times*, which had bought the serial rights, to change some passage for one less likely to provoke Winston's displeasure. Only now, when the book was in print, did it occur to him that these extracts, which he himself chose with such care, might affront Winston's admirers.

It became clear at the party that Bryant's panic had spread to the other speakers. Portal, Bryant and even Alanbrooke, each in turn spent most of their time trying to convince a rather sceptical audience that if the book came as a jolt, as it might, to Winston's worshippers it would in the end rather increase than diminish his stature. 'If it had not been for him,' Alanbrooke stoutly affirmed, 'the nation would not have survived the year 1940.' This was what the audience wanted, and for the first time there was some clapping of hands. Only the sailor, Andrew Cunningham, stood his ground. When he left the platform I reminded him what Alanbrooke had said to Portal of Winston's strategy. 'What did he say, Moran? I have forgotten.' 'He said that Winston had contributed nothing to the war strategy.' 'Well, anyway,' Cunningham went on in his forthright way, 'it did not amount to much.'

At the end Collins picked up a few of Alanbrooke's friends and led the way into a side room to drink sherry. They took Alanbrooke and pressed him into a chair. When he caught sight of me he beckoned to me to come over. 'I've not been very fit lately,' he began, 'my heart goes too quickly, and the doctors do not seem able to slow it down. I want you to make my peace with Winston. I have sent him a copy of the book. I explained that it was written late at night and that he mustn't take it too seriously.' Alanbrooke was speaking with animation, and I noticed that he was short of breath and a bad colour. A very sick man he seemed to me. Poor devil, the most reticent of men, he found himself caught up in all this ballyhoo of publicity when he ought to be in bed. He kept explaining to the reporters in his clipped sentences that his *Diaries* were not, whatever else they were, an attack on Sir Winston.

What did Winston make of it all? I happened to be with him when he heard for the first time that Alanbrooke was publishing his *Diaries*. It was Violet Bonham Carter, whose son Mark works for Collins, who told him. She had seen a review copy. Winston looked up quickly: 'Is it a violent attack on me?' But when the book was sent to him in France his immediate reaction was surprisingly mild; at any rate, he read it carefully, so his secretary reported, and did not seem at all put out. Perhaps like a boxer, his instinct was to make light of his punishment. He would show the world he did not care. But later at Chartwell, when he knew what people thought of the *Diaries*, he felt he could speak his mind.

I started him off when I said that it was not a very good book. 'No, no, it is a bad book, a very bad book.' I asked him if he had read the *Times Literary Supplement*. He asked me what it said. I tried to boil down the article into a few sentences: 'What,' the reviewer asked, 'do we learn from this book that we did not know before?' His answer was, 'Almost nothing.' Winston grunted his agreement. 'Nothing, for instance, about two of the outstanding issues of the war, civilian versus military control of the direction of the war and Anglo-American differences over grand strategy. Nothing of moment about the relations between Alanbrooke and Churchill. Much about Winston's dressing-gowns, and nothing about how his mind worked and how the war was won.' 'Give it to me, Charles.' He read the review carefully. 'Very good, very good,' he repeated. 'May I keep it? A very bad book.' Winston murmured, as he read the review again.

'Come,' said Winston, 'let's go down.' It was plain that the family had been demolishing the impertinent book. 'We might have won the war without Alanbrooke,' said Clemmie, 'I don't think we would have won it without Winston.' At this Winston grunted: 'He thinks he is a more important figure in the world than he is. He is not the only one who understands strategy.'

Clemmie took me aside. 'The *Diaries* came as a shock to Winston. I don't mind saying they were a great shock to me.'

The book's ill fame in the public eye and even Winston's own response to criticism could have been foretold. What was unusual in the case was the penance of the author of the *Diaries*. For it was Alanbrooke who really took to heart the rift in their relations. When it was clear to him that Winston was most deeply hurt he became very unhappy and sent him a copy of his book with this inscription on the flyleaf:

'To Winston from Brookie, with unbounded admiration, profound respect and deep affection, built up in our five years close association during the war. Some of the extracts from my *Diaries* may contain criticism and references to differences between us. I hope you will remember that these were written at the end of long and exhausting days, often in the small hours of the morning, and refer to momentary daily impressions. These casual day-to-day impressions bear no relation to the true feelings of deep-rooted friendship and admiration which bound me so closely to you throughout the war. I look upon the privilege of having served you during the war as the greatest honour destiny has bestowed upon me.'

'Did you read, Charles, what he wrote in his book? Alanbrooke wants to have it both ways,' Clemmie exclaimed.

It would surely be wrong to dismiss these *Diaries* as a series of 'petulant explosions' fired off late at night when Alanbrooke was nearly spent. For they are a faithful day-to-day record of his thoughts about the conduct of the war, and in particular of his criticism of Winston's part in shaping strategy. Alanbrooke was appalled, when he became C.I.G.S., to find no definite policy for the prosecution of the war, and even when the Prime Minister was at length converted to a long-term plan, there were always diversions, the half-digested products of Winston's impatience. Nor did Alanbrooke ever become reconciled to Winston's method of arriving at a decision, all at once and as it were by intuition, without, or so it appeared, any kind of logical examination of the problem. Alanbrooke told me that before he took up soldiering he wanted to be a surgeon. A craftsman by instinct, he knew exactly what could be done with the resources at his command, and he had the craftsman's respect for method.

Winston's judgment before the war was generally suspect. Was it as fallible in war as in peace? Alanbrooke in his *Diaries* certainly conveys that impression. The spluttering wrath of his critics will smoulder out, leaving the facts unsinged. Was Alanbrooke right?

Admiral Cunningham, in his book,[1] had already come to the same conclusion; Portal held that Winston never really understood the

[1] Admiral Sir Andrew Cunningham, *A Sailor's Odyssey* (Hutchinson, 1951).

717

effect of air power on operations, and further complained that he would focus on one spot, Sumatra or the North Cape, so that he could never see the whole picture at once; finally, General Marshall affirmed that it was an important part of the duties of the combined Chiefs of Staff to wean Winston from his strategic errors.

In time to come it should not be difficult to take Alanbrooke's measurements, but for the moment he seems to have got out of focus.

Because Arthur Bryant gave too much credit to Alanbrooke for his share in the conduct of the war—in Portal's phrase 'put too many plums in the pudding'—we should not on that account give him too little. In an important sense he was complementary to the Prime Minister. General Marshall, a friendly critic, has said that some of Winston's projects were positively dangerous and might have ended in catastrophe if they had been carried out. It was Alanbrooke's job to see that they were quietly dropped. With his feet firmly planted on the ground, he stood for a sense of proportion, for method, for good sense. If anything had happened to him I do not know any other soldier who would have stood up to the Prime Minister so effectively.

It was no easy task. The Prime Minister got his own way with everyone else: only Alanbrooke would not budge. If he sensed Winston's dislike of criticism he paid no attention to it. He could indeed be brutally frank in pulling to pieces the Prime Minister's pet projects. He would even venture to stand up to him when summoned to appear before the Cabinet, and if necessary to answer him back. In short, he kept Winston on the rails in the conduct of the war. That is his epitaph. His services in this respect will, I believe, be seen in perspective when the inner history of the war is written.

Alanbrooke was, too, a shrewd judge of men, not, I think, Winston's strongest point. I recall asking Sir Patrick Ashley-Cooper, the head of the Hudson's Bay Company, how they made use of a soldier like Alanbrooke on their Board. He told me that they had sent him on a tour of inspection of their stations in Canada and that they had been astonished by the way he had sized up the men in charge. Time had proved the accuracy of his appraisements.

The marvel is that this queer relationship between Alanbrooke and Churchill was not allowed to affect the conduct of the war. For both men, on account of their own limitations, were disposed to underrate each other.

Winston, for his part, was slow to recognize the merits of anyone who was not congenial to him. His judgments of men when he had to size up those around him—and it was a task he found not at all to his taste—were seldom impersonal. Efficiency in itself did not appear to influence his likes or dislikes. Beatty not Jellicoe, Mountbatten not Wavell, that was his form. Lloyd George, F.E., Max Beaverbrook and Lord Cherwell, these men were his cronies, in their different ways all, mark you, men of violent thought; all men with a flamboyant streak, which Winston himself got from the Jeromes. He would have been for the King, a Cavalier, disliking Puritans. Paget, Winant, Reith, he could make nothing of them, and the bloodless austerity of Stafford Cripps repelled him.

For that matter he found the rather prim, self-contained, inscrutable figure at his side no more sympathetic. He liked to do business with Alanbrooke—when they agreed—but he did not want to see too much of him out of school. If Winston did not like a man he would certainly not admire him. I asked him once: 'Don't you think that Brooke is pretty good at his job?' There was rather a long pause. 'He has a flair for the business,' he grunted. That was all he would concede. Soldiers in this country, at any rate, will feel that this is an understatement of the fact. They would readily agree that Brooke was not a Marlborough or even a Wellington; the only claim they make for him is that in the Army he is recognized as the best soldier we could produce in two wars.

Winston's inability to work in harmony with Wavell, Dill and Auchinleck, three soldiers of exceptional intelligence, drives home the point I have tried to make. There was more than a suggestion of infallibility about the Winston of the war years, and any opposition to his plans was likely to produce in him symptoms of the most acute discomfort. He had been right about the war, he knew better than anyone what ought to be done and he was determined to do what he thought was best. In that mood Winston did not find it easy to stomach strength and independence of character. In spite of Alanbrooke's self-discipline, to which Edward Bridges and others have testified, the P.M. complained that Brooke could be positively tiresome in Committee, openly opposing his views and mauling his plans. All the same, even if Brooke had been less outspoken, I doubt whether Winston would have been drawn to him as a man. It was a marriage of convenience for the duration of the war.

They had little in common. What made life worth living for one man was anathema to the other. Winston, according to Baldwin, was a soldier of fortune, and he himself admitted that personal distinction had been his aim as a young man. To do something better than the other fellow, that had been his daily purpose down the years. To gain dominion over men alike in war and peace, that would open every door in the struggle for power, and as far as he had

C C

ever thought out anything from first principles he had given his mind to this end. And then came the war.

When England, gasping for breath in 1940, turned to Winston, he was quick to discern that the people were looking for a symbol of their power to resist to the end, that he was being built up as the great national hero, that they were ready to accept him as an autocrat for the war. He liked the part—he had always dreamed of something of the kind—and he was willing now to lend a hand. Like Chatham, he was always acting.

All this was quite unintelligible to Alanbrooke. He had never found it necessary to submit to any such terms. He recoiled from the idea of gaining ascendancy over men to get his own way. The truth was that the competitive instinct had been left out of his make-up. The brutality of war horrified him, and apart from a natural yearning to practise his profession in the exacting conditions of command in the field, he was without ambition.

I do not wish to exaggerate Alanbrooke's detachment. Three times the P.M. told him that he was to be the Supreme Commander for the invasion of France and then came the cruel blow, to hear from Winston, as if it were a matter of little importance, that he was handing over the appointment to the Americans. In that moment there was revealed to Brooke the crushing indifference of these monolithic figures to the lower forms of life.

It was all very personal, as is Winston's way. If he had been a calculating politician he would have seized on to Alanbrooke's faults as they were laid bare by the war—I am not sure he is even conscious what they were. For Alanbrooke had faults. He was incurably matter-of-fact. Indeed, it sometimes seemed that he had put his mind into a strait jacket. And he was wanting in tact. He would dismiss the P.M.'s ideas in a summary fashion as far-fetched, ill-digested and not at all properly worked out. Besides, Alanbrooke was apt to forget that war is only a means to an end—a continuation of policy. In consequence, he never gave full credit to Winston for his work in keeping the grand alliance together, and in particular for his singular virtuosity in wooing the fickle Roosevelt, at any rate up to the Teheran Conference.

This brings me to Alanbrooke's gravest shortcoming: he did not get on with the Americans. His downright, direct speech, combined with his take-it-or-leave-it manner, did not help him to get his own way. It was left to Dill to bring Marshall into line, and it was Churchill, and not Alanbrooke, who prevented the President from making the war with Japan the first charge on his country's resources.

Why did Alanbrooke grate on the Americans? Before I answer

that question I shall ask another. Why did they love Dill? I saw Dill once in serious conversation with an American General. It seemed as if he could not bear to miss a single word of the American's discourse. His keen intelligence lit up his eyes as if he were saying: 'I had not thought of that before; it is all fresh to me, and so important.' Not once in the conversation did he express an opinion of his own; he did not want to talk about his own views; there would be plenty of time for that later if it was really necessary to hand on some of Winston's ideas. If the General paused to ask a question all Dill's antennae were out feeling a way to an innocuous answer. Was it surprising that the Americans loved him and that Marshall said: 'Brooke hasn't Dill's brains.'

Alanbrooke had an inborn suspicion that there might be an element of insincerity in this kind of approach. He swung instinctively to the opposite pole, throwing down his facts in the path of understanding with a brusque gesture. In his opinion it was just common sense; he had thought it all out. Not for a moment did it occur to him that there might be another point of view. Nor did he bother his head whether a soldier of another race liked what he was saying. He hurled his facts at him like hand grenades, it did not matter if they went off and left wounds. Alanbrooke's insensitive handling of his American colleagues had echoes, for it is what was American in Winston that most disturbed him.

It is an odd story of two human beings, both of whom had grown accustomed to getting their own way in life. God had been kind to them in the hour of their birth, but He had held back from both the one gift which helps men to put things into their right perspective. 'Do you think,' I once asked Lord Chief Justice Goddard, 'that a sense of humour, meaning the capacity to laugh at oneself, is a fatal handicap in life?' The Lord Chief ruminated for a time. He could think of no one like that who had been really successful. I would not say that Winston was without a sense of humour, only that it happened to be turned outwards. Turned inward, it might have become a philosophy of life and would have sweetened for him the useless days, as they repeated themselves when life was over. It might, too, have helped Alanbrooke in his dealings with that improbable man. For Winston happened to be a genius, trampling down like a bull elephant everything that got in his way.

April 10, 1957

Anthony Montague Browne telephoned this morning:

'Lady Churchill and I are rather worried about Winston, he is so quiet and uncommunicative. We wonder if anything has happened.

Could you suggest calling?' I went immediately to Hyde Park Gate.

'Anthony isn't really worried,' Clemmie began. 'It was me. I wonder whether Winston is brooding over the Alanbrooke *Diaries*? You see, this book has upset him more than he will admit. He asked me a few days ago if I had seen that thing in the *Daily Mail* about the *Diaries*. And yesterday it was the *Evening Standard*.'

She went on:

'You know Winston has become a legend. I wonder why? I think that the speeches in 1940 had a lot to do with it. When Winston enters a theatre everyone rises. The other day when our car drove up to Hyde Park Gate there was an angry man in the road quarrelling with a woman. I feared there was going to be a scene. But when he saw Winston in the car, a different look came over his face. "It's the Guvnor," he said. "Are you very well, sir?" You know, my dear Charles, I am not really angry with Alanbrooke. We must get used to criticism of Winston. I realize the poor darling cannot be a demi-god for ever.'

Clemmie smiled:

'You know as well as I do, he has some faults. The common people love him for these faults—his cigars, his extravagance. He loves Chartwell passionately. He wants the people of Westerham to like him, he has a feeling he is rather aloof. That's why he won't have the gates closed; the police have very strict orders. When he sees a crowd at the gate he will go nearer and wave to them. Sometimes he takes them in and shows them his fish. I asked him: "Are you happy?" He replied: "Yes, as happy as I can be." '

She seemed to forget about me, looking out of the window. After a time she turned round.

'Do you suppose, Charles, Winston is thinking about death?'

I asked her what had put that into her head.

'Oh,' she murmured, as if her thoughts were elsewhere, 'he suddenly said to me that he would like to go to a theatre. I was very much surprised, as you see the poor darling cannot hear what is being said on the stage. But he persisted. He was sure he would be able to follow the play.'

'It was on his mind that this might be his last theatre?'

She nodded.

I found Anthony Montague Browne in the office. He took me into the library, and when he had closed the door, began:

'Yesterday Winston said to me that he feared he was very dull. He could not think of anything to say. Then he spoke about death. He was not afraid; he would not be reluctant if it came. Five minutes later he went off to the Other Club and stayed until mid-

722

night, talking away, so that I am told he was in tremendous form.

'I collected some books for him. He found Munthe's *Story of San Michele* very readable. I do not think he has started Forester's *1812* yet. Someone found him reading Somerset Maugham and told him that Maupassant's short stories were better. I got them for him and he read them for four hours on end.

'Winston had a dream that he made a very good speech, and when he woke he felt he could. He declared he would speak on Defence for forty minutes. But after a little he realized that he could not speak for forty minutes; he could not perhaps make a speech at all. And then there was rather a flop.'

April 16, 1957

Lunched with Jock Colville at his club. I suppose nobody really understands Winston, but Jock comes as near to it as anyone. Certainly if I were at a loss to fathom why Winston did a certain thing I should go to Jock. He loves the old man, and is very sad because 'his mind seems to be wearing out before his body.' Jock went on:

'He can still deal with business. He wants to die. How long do you think he can go on like this?'

I asked Jock which of Winston's gifts had been of most value to the country in the war. He said at once:

'Winston's capacity for picking out essential things and concentrating on them.'

It came into my mind that Norman Brook singled out the same quality.

'What next?'

Jock needs a good deal of jogging to make him communicative. He pondered, but nothing happened. At last he added:

'I think his great moral courage. If something went wrong he would patiently start again at the beginning. And his vivid imagination. It was always coming to his help in the war. His magnanimity of course, and his power of inspiring everyone he met.'

Jock grinned and went on ruefully:

'He always got his way. He could persuade anybody to do anything. When he asked me to be his secretary for the second time I was determined to refuse. I knew exactly how the interview would go, and I had thought out what I should say at each turn. I would have my excuses ready. But ten minutes later I came out of the room his secretary.'

'I see all that. But, Jock, you must admit that Winston's judgment was often wrong.'

Jock was not going to admit anything of the kind.

'More than once during the war Winston would come to the right decision when everyone else was on the other side.'

'Give me an example.'

'Oh,' said Jock, 'sending the Armoured Division to Egypt in 1940 when it was obvious to us all that we needed it at home in case of invasion. And his refusal to allow any more pilots and aircraft to fight in the Battle of France; everyone wanted to send them to France. But if Winston had given way we should have lost the Battle of Britain.'

I stuck to my guns.

'Take his judgment of men. Do you really think Winston knew that Anthony Eden wasn't made of Prime Minister stuff?'

Jock took me up at once.

'One day, it would be just after Winston resigned, I went with him to his bedroom. He sat on the bed shaking his head. "I wonder," he said. And stopped short. "You wonder what?" "I wonder if he can do it. Courage," he muttered. "Anthony has courage. He would charge a square, but would he charge at the right time and in the right place?" '

Jock gave me an expansive smile.

'Yes. Suez was the answer.'

We talked of nothing but Winston. With criticism of him in full spate, I find it reassuring to listen to Jock. As I rose to go I mentioned the Alanbrooke *Diaries*. Jock had crossed in the *Queen Mary* with Sir William Dickson.[1] He was very upset by the book.

June 6, 1957

William Haley, the Editor of *The Times*, has read more widely than anyone I know. I thought it would be fun to give him a book that he had not read. Dining with him tonight, I took with me *Impressions*, by Pierre Loti, with an introduction by Henry James. I picked it up in a bookshop in Alexandria before the First War, and found that Haley had not read it. John Reith was there, the old Covenanter decked out in a crimson smoking jacket. He came across to me after dinner and without any preliminaries began:

'I intensely dislike your man, more than I have ever disliked anyone.'

Moran: 'You find Winston wanting in consideration?'

Reith: 'No. You cannot expect consideration from a Prime Minister in war. But Winston prints in his war book innumerable directives and never once lets us see a single answer. Why, he vituperated me for not doing something, though I had been trying to get the Government to do this very thing for months. And even

[1] Sir William Dickson, Marshal of the Royal Air Force, Chairman of the Chiefs of Staff Committe, 1956–9.

when I wrote to him and explained this, the same directive appeared unaltered in the next edition.'

Reith spoke without anger or vehemence, as if he were puzzled. Haley came up and, catching the drift of our talk, said that he had been reading Halifax's book,[1] and that what had struck him was the author's dislike of Winston. All through the book he is trying to put him in the dock if he can. Up till now, Winston has had things all his own way. Apart from debates in the House, hardly a breath of criticism has reached him since the war. The Alanbrooke *Diaries* seem to have loosened men's tongues. I wish they had held their peace until Winston had left us.

Marshalls, June 23, 1957

Oliver Franks is with us for Glyndebourne, and since none of his opinions is borrowed from other people, I have been seeking enlightenment on some things that have puzzled me. Did he, for example, find difficulty in reconciling the legend of Winston Churchill with some of his faults?

Franks: 'Winston has, of course, many excellencies and many deficiencies. And if you are going to measure him with that footrule, I should be as baffled as you are. But surely it is the size of the man and the way history met him, giving him an opportunity which multiplied his size, that sweeps away, for me at any rate, all difficulties of that kind. Luck you may call it. But even greater men need luck. Calvin had it; Luther too.'

Moran: 'What do you mean by size?'

Franks (*musing*): 'Well, that is difficult. Winston embodied the soul of the nation. He succeeded in being the nation, for that is what he was. In the simplified conditions of war he could be that, whereas in the more complex days of peace he never was, never could be, that. Asquith, on the other hand, as war minister, was only the chairman of a committee trying to make wise decisions.'

Moran: 'Joan of Arc, I suppose, played that role, and Chatham perhaps.'

Franks: 'Yes. And Elizabeth to be sure, at the time of the Spanish crisis and the speech at Tilbury. Winston became a prophet. We can't explain him, any more than we can understand Isaiah or Elijah. I remember early in the war attending a meeting on the roof of the Ministry of Supply when Winston addressed us. I came away more happy about things. He dispelled our misgivings and set at rest our fears; he spoke of his aim and of his purpose, so that we knew that somehow it would be achieved. He gave us faith.

[1] *Fulness of Days* (Collins, 1957).

There was in him a demonic element, as in Calvin and Luther. He was a spiritual force.'

Moran: 'It is twelve years since the end of the war. Why hasn't the legend been defaced?'

Franks: 'Nothing but a colossal blunder could have undone the work of those five years.' (*Smiling*) 'Something like an attempt to reconquer India.'

Moran: 'You thought Suez was a blunder?'

Franks: 'Oh, yes. The consequences will be felt for many years. It is as if we had lost a major battle—without casualties. We were disembowelled.'

Moran: 'What consequences have you in mind?'

Franks: 'Well. It is possible that America may meet Russia in conference without us being at the table. After the war we acted as a Great Power, though we had not the resources. A kind of confidence trick. It came off as long as the decisions we made were acceptable to the other Powers. The trouble with these island empires has always been the same: they had too few men. America and Russia can afford a holocaust, we cannot.'

Franks spoke of the importance to a politician of another life beside politics, something he can fall back on. If things go wrong in the House, Harold Macmillan, for instance, can go back to his publishing; that makes him independent.

Moran: 'Are you gloomy about the future?'

Franks: 'I think the period 1945 to 1975 may be like 1815 to 1845. We have a good many old men at the top living in the past. Macmillan tells how he was in Darlington in 1931 at the time of mass unemployment, and he was horrified by what he saw. There is a Labour leader, too, who says bitter things to the T.U.C. because for ten years his father was out of employment, and tramped up and down the Great North Road, looking for a job. They think more about this than of the last war. Nothing much will happen until a new generation takes over; we need younger men who are not obsessed with the past, men who are thinking over where they want to go.'

Winston's measurements will not, I believe, shrink with time. Oliver Franks had given the reason why. When he had gone I went to see Winston at Chartwell, full of 'the size of the man.' He was in bed, alone in the great house, reading *The Duke's Children*.

'Back to Trollope?' I asked.

'I don't know,' he mumbled, 'why you say, "Back to Trollope." I have never read him before.'

I asked if he found Trollope interesting, and he answered:

'It passes away the day.'

726

Chapter sixty-eight

Picking winners

July 4, 1957

'Winston has spent his life among charlatans and quacks.' This was Brendan's way of saying that Winston has but a poor understanding of human nature. Though he has known everybody who has counted in the last fifty years, I am perplexed to find how little he has found out about them.

Picking winners in the business of the world is a gift apart, and has nothing to do with a man's brains. Some men of great parts—Winston for example—are all at sea when they come to choose subordinates, while others with only modest talents are quite uncannily acute in probing character. I shall take only one instance. One day four of us were lunching with Anthony de Rothschild at New Court, and I remember Lord Nuffield was the first to leave. When he had gone no one spoke for a time, and then it transpired that the same thought was passing through all our heads. 'How did he get where he is?' The man on Rothschild's right, who had been rather silent, thought he might be able to help: 'If,' he said, 'the head man at Cowley leaves, next morning Nuffield appoints someone in his place whom nobody had thought of, and it always seems to work.' When I heard this it passed through my mind that it was for want of that inner prompting about men that General Auchinleck had come to grief in the desert.

A man must be born with the gift, though practice helps. I happened to be travelling by train from Sheffield to Leeds when a man entered my compartment and sat down opposite to me. His hair had been cut close to the scalp, leaving only a stubble of bristles. With his bull neck he looked like a caricature of a Prussian soldier. Judge then my surprise, as the train drew out of the station, when he produced from a bag a bottle of eau-de-Cologne which he held to his nose, off and on, during the short journey. When he got out at Leeds I hung back, to ask a young man in the corner seat what he made of him. No, he had not noticed him. Winston is like that. Born without the gift, he will not even practise, because he is not interested in people.

What Winston has missed in his life through this blind spot on his retina! How much more interesting and more complex were Stalin, Roosevelt, Harry Hopkins, Pug Ismay and Max Beaverbrook than the shadowy figures which took shape in his imagination! One day I said to him: 'Only Balzac could have made Max credible.' Winston stared at me as if I said some very foolish things.

Today, waiting in the House of Lords to pay my tribute to Lord Cherwell, I was turning these things over in my mind when Portal, who was sitting by my side on the cross benches, whispered: 'Winston was a bad picker.' I knew that this was true, though not all of Winston's friends were men of straw. After all, we were in the Chamber to give thanks for a war winner, one of the two men who held the P.M.'s hand in the conduct of the war. The other was, of course, Brooke, the C.I.G.S.

This was a war of machines, where victory—if there is any meaning in the word now—was won by our pre-eminence in the field of physics, a field quite foreign to Winston's genius. The Battle of Britain, for instance, could not have been won without radar. Someone had to interpret all this to Winston before it was too late. It was a forbidding task. Once, when Winston was in a good mood, I remember saying to him: 'If the time should ever come when England, like Carthage, is little more than a name, she will, perhaps, be remembered for two things: for her lyric poetry and for her school of physics.' Winston looked at me in a puzzled way. I persisted: 'This school of physics began at Cambridge with Isaac Newton and did not end with Lord Rutherford.' I gave it up, he was not listening.

Only the Prof. could have done it. If he had been killed it is impossible to imagine any other scientist to whom Winston would have listened. For one thing, the Prof. was a very old friend: it was nearly a quarter of a century since F.E. himself introduced them. Since then he had fought at Winston's side at a time when no one had a good word to say for the man who was 'spreading alarm and preventing an understanding with Germany.' Winston has a deep affection for the few who stood by him when he was virtually alone in the political world. He had learnt, too, to admire the Prof.'s mind and to take 'all this scientific stuff' from him before the war began.

But there was even more to it than that. There is a famous passage in *The World Crisis* in which Winston meditates on the disparity between the task set to our generals in the First World War and the gifts which they brought to its solution. Winston explains that there were no doubt more imaginative men in the Army; there were no doubt more sensitive men, there were certainly men more intellectually alert and acute; but these men in modern war are apt to crumble, and so we had to fall back on the 'blockheads' to lead our armies in France in the First German War. They at least did not lose their nerve. And here was the Prof., who had 'a beautiful brain'—he was a Fellow of the Royal Society—and yet he was apparently without nerves, and was capable of the most astonishing adventures. Winston would recount to me once more the Prof.'s exploit in his stalling aircraft:

'You know, Charles, I was very worried at that time, we were losing some of our best pilots. Their aircraft would stall and go into a nose-dive, and the pilot was always killed. The Prof., with his mathematics, worked it all out on paper. To come out of the spin safely, the pilot must pick up enough speed in a vertical dive. No one took him seriously. So the Prof. learnt to fly, and then one morning before breakfast he went up alone, wearing his bowler hat.'

Winston made some guttural sounds of mirth.

'He put his craft into a spinning nose-dive. Those watching him held their breath. It seemed certain death. But his theory worked. It is a terrific story. I did admire him so much.'

When Winston was told of the Prof.'s death, he murmured: 'He is gone and I am left to linger on.'

Before I ventured to pay tribute to Cherwell today I sought the guidance of two Fellows of the Royal Society who were associated with him in his war-work. One of those I consulted said that Cherwell completely changed the attitude of those at the top towards scientific developments. 'Modern war,' he continued, 'is probably won by ideas, and the real enemy of new ideas is always the expert. Sir Winston, with the Prof. as tutor, would not allow the expert to kill new ideas or technical innovations. Lord Swinton, who was Air Minister at the time, spoke in support. No project was too far-fetched, too novel, to be rejected outright by Lord Cherwell.

Sir Robert Watson-Watt agreed that the Prof. had an open mind. But if he did not reject outright any scheme, however fantastic it might appear, he would dissect it with a certain relish. The Prof.'s destructive criticism, according to Sir Robert, was almost certainly essential to victory, giving as an example his refusal to accept the claims of target finding made by our bomber pilots. The Prof.

demanded photographic proof. Apart from his work in harnessing science to the Allied war-effort, the Prof.'s mastery of higher physics enabled him to anticipate its use by the enemy. Sir Robert holds that this gift had more influence on the outcome of the Second World War than any of Cherwell's own inventions, or his judgment of the inventions of others, or even his personal assessment of relative priorities.

How did the Prof. get these intricate matters into Winston's head, distracted as he was by the burden of the war? When the Prof. wanted to make something clear to us he used to pull a slide rule out of his pocket, but when he set out to interpret to the P.M. what one might call fundamental research, he bore in mind the P.M.'s cry of distress: 'Can't you put it on half a sheet of notepaper?' He seemed able to reduce some really complicated scientific problem to a very simple graph, so that Winston could see at a glance the whole problem, as if he were reading a barometer. Not only was this graph intelligible, it was, I am told, very accurate, for the Prof. passed nothing on to Winston without checking its accuracy.

Did the Prof. abuse his privileged position as the P.M.'s mentor? I suppose the answer is that he did not often get the chance. Left to himself, he would no doubt have been prepared to advise the P.M. on most things, for if he was modest in speech he was not at all humble in thought. He was certain that his brain would not fail him. The P.M., however, had a shrewd idea when the Prof. could be helpful, and he did not often consult him on problems which plainly lay outside his orbit.

When he did, the results were sometimes disconcerting. Then men learnt with a start of surprise that the most violent views were hidden and disguised by the level tones of the Prof.'s voice, from which all emotion had been stripped, by the quiet, almost self-effacing manner and by the placid exterior. At such times it was noticed that every argument was driven to its last and final conclusion. In truth, Lord Cherwell was apt to forget that in public life in this country, political sense is often a surer guide than logic. Sometimes, when Winston's first impulses were sound, he was later led astray by the Prof.'s persuasive graphs, as in the Morgenthau Plan for converting the Ruhr into grassland. It followed that the Prof. was seldom a wise counsellor in political tactics; too often he was out for blood when only restraint was needed. In the debate on the hydrogen bomb, for example, he had persuaded Winston to stage a frontal attack on Attlee in order to put him on his back, when in fact it was only necessary to look up Hansard to bring about Attlee's complete discomfiture. There was a violent streak in both Winston and the Prof., and when they put their heads together I knew that we were in for trouble.

Yet I believe that historians will agree that without the Prof. a war that was won by science might have gone differently. If he did not persuade Winston to think scientifically, at least he made him sympathetic to those who did.

Chapter sixty-nine

Brendan's verdict

February 19, 1958

Last night Dr. Roberts telephoned from France: Sir Winston was feverish and coughing. This morning I flew to Nice, and when I examined Winston's chest found that he had bronchopneumonia.

The day before his illness began, Winston had lunched with Onassis on his yacht. About three o'clock Winston expressed a wish to go to the Rooms at Monte Carlo to have a little gamble. Reves suggested that they might play chemin-de-fer on the yacht instead. They played for high stakes and drank more alcohol than usual. Winston got very excited. As the afternoon wore on it was noticed that he was very white and tired. About seven o'clock Reves ventured to remind him that they had been invited for lunch. Was it not time to go home? Winston grumbled that Reves was breaking up the party. When they got home, Winston seemed 'all in.'

February 20, 1958

Looking into Winston's room about noon, I found him shivering violently, his teeth chattering. A rigor on the third day meant that the infection was spreading. I decided to change the antibiotic and get a blood count. The arrival of a French bacteriologist this afternoon led to a sharp protest:

Winston: 'Are you going to hurt me? Oh, no, I don't want that. It will hurt.'

Moran: 'It's over now.'

Winston: 'You said it wouldn't hurt. It hurt like hell.'

The Frenchman had gone about his job in silence.

Winston: 'Why doesn't he speak to me? You have told me nothing. I don't like it.'

The Frenchman smiled and held out his hand to take his leave. Winston took it grumpily without looking at him.

February 21, 1958

Winston demands to see the bulletins. 'I would be more candid and less revealing,' he complained. To Anthony Montague Browne he was more explicit. 'If I didn't push them along, nothing at all would happen.' He wants to stir up his doctors because he is bent on returning to England in time for the Other Club on Thursday.

February 22, 1958

I am not really anxious about Winston, but at 83 it is all guess-work. Perhaps if he felt ill he would be more amenable. This morning he announced that he intended to go downstairs to luncheon, although he has not yet been out of bed. Dr. Roberts, in order to dissuade him, said something about his heart.

Winston (*raising his voice*): 'It has been a comfort to me that my heart is sound and that I shall not lurch into the next world without warning. And now you talk about my heart as if it were diseased.'

Winston seemed upset. After we left the room it appears that he let himself go. 'It's bloody rot about my heart,' he said. 'I know a great deal. I'm not dependent on my doctors. I know what I can do.'

March 7, 1958

Since the meeting of the Other Club has been postponed the tension has fallen. Winston feels that his troubles are at an end, and I am flying back to England this afternoon. He plans to go home for a week, partly because he is getting bored—there is nobody exciting out here—and partly because he wants to go to the Other Club. After breakfast he got going about Suez.

'I made a great mistake giving in to them when we left the Canal. I feel responsible. All the Cabinet were for withdrawing. They persuaded me that we must get out of Suez. But if I had been in better health, if I had been stronger, we might have stayed on the Canal and all this would not have happened.'

As I was leaving the room I picked up a Bible. 'Do you read it?' I asked him. He did not answer for some time. Then he said: 'Yes, I read it; but only out of curiosity.'

March 24, 1958

Staying with the Freybergs in the Norman Tower at Windsor, I had to take my telephone calls from France in the prison room. Montague Browne rang up yesterday saying that Dr. Roberts wanted to speak to me. Since my return to England Sir Winston,

733

he said, had had two bouts of fever. I said I thought I ought to see him. At this Dr. Roberts went off to bring Clemmie to the telephone, and I was left reading the names of Cromwell's prisoners which they, while waiting to be taken to the Tower to be beheaded, had carved in the stone wall above the place where the receiver now hangs. When I had spoken to Clemmie I arranged to fly to Nice this morning.

Winston hardly looked at me as I entered his room. He said not a word. I took no notice of this wintry reception and began questioning him. He admitted grudgingly that he had been very worried on Saturday, and had wanted to see me; but now it was too late, his illness was all over. It had been noticed that Winston was yellow, but this was thought to be due to the antibiotic I had prescribed. In fact, he is suffering from obstructive jaundice, caused either by a stone or by an infection of the bile passages. I shall be glad when we get him back to England.

London, April 10, 1958

I have seen Winston twice since his return from France exactly a week ago, and on each occasion he poked fun at me as a prophet. I had urged him to get back to England in case he was stricken by a third attack of jaundice. 'Pray, at what moment may I expect this mysterious malady to appear?' He said this with an assumption of gravity, and I am bound to admit that he has not seemed so alert and free from symptoms for a long time. But when I went to his room this morning he looked glumly at me. He had a pain over his lower ribs on the right side. 'Yes,' he muttered, 'it might be the same pain that I had in France.' The car was coming for him at ten o'clock. An important gallop had been arranged for one of his horses, and he was very anxious not to miss this trial. I told him the wind was bitter, and that judging by the course of events in his first two attacks I thought he might well be running a temperature by teatime. I said this not as if I were opposed to his going, but just to bring before him a few relevant facts. Then I left him. About five o'clock Wright telephoned that Sir Winston's temperature was 100. He had stayed in bed all day.

April 11, 1958

This morning Winston did not seem to take in what I said, and he has been feverish all day.

April 12, 1958

Shepherd telephoned before breakfast: Sir Winston was jaundiced, and his pulse had gone up from 64 to 110. I asked Dr. Hunt[1] to see him with me, and took my kit prepared to stay at Chartwell. As I pulled aside the curtain that separates his room from the study, Wright and Shepherd were removing the bedclothes to get him into his vest and bed-coat. Winston sleeps naked, and I noticed that his chest and belly were bright yellow. Wright said Sir Winston had been talking rubbish; he was sure he was wandering. When I sounded him his heart was fibrillating. It looks as if we may be in for trouble.

Dined alone with Clemmie. She did not appear depressed and talked without a break. Rufus, who was stretched on the mat, began dreaming in his sleep.

'You see, Charles, Rufus has been a great failure. When Winston's dog was run over, Walter Graebner, you know who I mean, scoured the country for a poodle in the championship class. That is how he came to us. He is very highly strung. Do you know what chorea is? He had that, and the poor dog is never happy. Winston ought not to keep a dog. He hasn't the time. He will say "Good morning" to Rufus, and when Rose brings his dinner, Winston will give it to him. But nothing more. You must love and give up time to a dog and try to make him happy. Now Christopher is a dog man; he understands them, and they love him.'

Rufus began whining, and Clemmie rose from the table to wake him. She went on:

'Do you know Lord Crookshank? When Winston became Prime Minister for the second time I discovered that he was a Chamberlain man, and that he gave parties for Tories who had been admirers of Mr. Chamberlain. I thought I would try and see if I could not make him more friendly to Winston. But when I found he hated him I gave it up. I asked Winston whether he liked Crookshank. "Why do you ask, my dear? Oh, I don't mind him." You know, Charles, Winston never tries to placate men who are against him. Of course, the Tories never really liked Winston. It was Labour that made him Prime Minister in 1940.'

I was anxious about Winston and found it difficult to keep my mind on the conversation. When Clemmie left the table I crept into Winston's room in case he was asleep. He has held his own all day, and is perhaps a little more alert tonight.

---

[1] D. T. C. Hunt, senior physician, St. Mary's Hospital.

April 13, 1958

Wright came to me about noon because Sir Winston was jibbing at the treatment. 'He refuses to take the glucose. He says, sir, that it is all damn nonsense, and he hasn't drunk anything but a cup of coffee since dinner-time yesterday evening.'

When I saw Winston he burst out irritably, 'I've got my temperature down below normal. What more do you want?' 'You are still yellow,' I persisted. 'Let me see. Wright,' he shouted, 'bring me a mirror!' He gazed at himself for some time. He is still a little muddled, but there is a noticeable all-round improvement since yesterday. Only the jaundice persists.

April 15, 1958

Winston said tonight that he was planning to go to London on Tuesday—he paused to see how I took this—and to the House of Commons. I said he might manage London on that day, but I didn't know about the House. Speaking quickly and with heat, he broke in: 'I am going to the House. I am not going to be prevented.'

I held my peace and there was a long pause. Then he looked up with a suspicion of a smile. 'I am sorry. My temper is not as good as it ought to be.'

Chartwell, April 16, 1958

'I have still got the pain. It's no better.' It was with these words that Winston greeted me this morning, and I am pretty sure that there must be a small stone holding up the bile. Anyway, at his age no one is keen on surgery. Besides, he is not so yellow, and is following the Budget debate as if it really interested him. Speaking of Heathcoat-Amory [1] he said: 'He always sat opposite me in Cabinet when I was Prime Minister and he impressed me. I spoke to Harold about him. Fortunately his ideas about Amory were the same as mine.'

Winston came down to dinner for the first time since his illness. Clemmie was dipping happily into the *Oxford Book of Verse*. She pushed her plate forward to make room for it. I recalled to Winston how after his stroke in 1953 he had recited the first fifty lines of 'King Robert of Sicily' with only two mistakes. He tried to repeat the feat, but only succeeded in recalling a line or two. 'My memory,' he said sadly, 'is much worse; in the last nine months it seems to have deteriorated.' I took the book from Clemmie and turned to Arthur Hugh Clough. Winston's eyes lit up. 'Give it to me.' He looked up

[1] Derick Heathcoat-Amory, Chancellor of the Exchequer, 1958–60.

and began declaiming, but after a few words he was stumped and had to look at the book. His voice grew stronger. He used to gabble poetry; now he spoke it with fervour:

> '*For while the tired waves, vainly breaking,*
>   *Seem here no painful inch to gain,*
> *Far back, through creaks and inlets making,*
>   *Comes silent, flooding in, the main.*
>
> *And not by eastern windows only,*
>   *When daylight comes, comes in the light;*
> *In front, the sun climbs slow, how slowly!*
>   *But westward, look, the land is bright!*'

When Winston came to the last line he sat up, making a vague gesture as if he were directing our eyes to the light, as he had done, long ago, in the war. And then he slumped back, the effort had been too much for his tired mind.

After a time he rose from his chair, slowly and not without difficulty, and asked me to go with him to the study. There he flopped into a chair and sat looking into the great log fire. A warm soft glow from the red curtains fell on the shelves of books. I asked him about the dark painting that hung above the mantelpiece. 'It's Blenheim Palace.' 'And the flag hanging from that beam?' Winston's face brightened. 'That was the first Union Jack to be taken ashore in the invasion of Italy.' It is his room, and he has it to himself, except when he plays bezique. At other times he reads by the fire, often for hours at a time. Tonight Clough's words have stirred up the past. He did not want to talk; we sat for a long time in silence.

April 17, 1958

Yesterday I found Winston halfway through the second of six volumes of a first edition of *Tom Jones*, bearing the date 1749; it might have been a wedding present, Winston thought. 'I think I have got his measure,' he said, putting down the book. His interest was plainly flagging, and he was looking for another book. But today he seems to have changed his mind. I suspect he wants to know what happened to Tom Jones.

Jock arrived to dinner. He came to my room to get the hang of things before he saw Winston. Jock is full of the Churchill College which is to be built at Cambridge. Its purpose is to make known to industry what is being done by those engaged in fundamental research in science. It will do this by training a new race of techno-

---

[1] From A. H. Clough's 'Say not the Struggle Naught Availeth'.

logists in the college, cheek by jowl, as it were, with the Cavendish Laboratory. I wonder if the idea came from Winston. If it did, it is a fine curtain to a life that owes little to the scientific habit of mind; a final gesture on his part to the English people. The summons to do their best in this struggle for survival is perhaps less urgent than in 1940, but once more only Winston's voice can reach the people. Jock gave me the papers to read. An appeal is to be made next month for three and a half million pounds, and Winston will open the fund with a gift of twenty-five thousand pounds. Jock wants Winston to give a luncheon to the trustees, and asked me whether he would be able to do this.

Winston greeted Jock affectionately. I know no one who understands with such intuitive sympathy this baffling creature, who is so unlike anyone else in everything he says and does. Before Jock went to bed he came to my room. Winston had confided to him that he did not want to live. We agreed that he seemed to get little out of life. I told Jock that I often feared I was boring Winston. Jock grinned.

'When he gets very bored with me I have a special technique. I say to him: "Don't you think Napoleon was the Hitler of the nineteenth century?" Then he wakes up with a start. "How dare you say such a thing?" Winston exclaims, and it is some time before he relapses into a state of apathy. As a matter of fact, Charles, Winston hasn't got much kick out of life since he resigned in 1955.'

I lay awake puzzling why Winston finds Jock so congenial a companion. Some of his secretaries have been equally quick at detecting Winston's moods and tempers; they knew his little frailties in the manner that Max Beaverbrook can put a finger on a weak spot. In their case it was perhaps a kind of safety-first device to avert the wrath of their alarming master. They seemed to know instinctively when it was not a favourable moment to bring up some question for the Chief's decision. They knew, too, what the P.M. would do and what he would not do, and they could advise the most promising line of approach, how in a word to get him to do things in minor matters. They were, I am sure, as disinterested as Jock in their devotion to Winston's service. Jock knew all this. He knew more because he loved the artist in Winston and was captivated by the way he handled words.

Of course, Jock has ability, too, though it is not of the most practical kind. He has an ear for words when they are well handled and won a prize for Latin verse at Harrow. I have said that his ability is not of the kind to pay dividends in the market-place, but if he had to go into the City you may be sure that he would think

738

and act there like one of those directors of the Bank of England, John Revelstoke, for instance, who appear to be set up as a cautionary tale to all money-making men. I do not mean that Jock is wanting in ambition, nor for that matter would I call him unworldly. Jock was not born with an intuitive knowledge of human nature. I sometimes think I detect in him a certain lack of sympathy with more erring mortals, an impatient repugnance towards standards that are not quite impeccable, a quiet intolerance, a cold aloofness. Of course it would not be fair to expect Winston's secretary to be an Elizabeth Fry, with her warm heart and deep compassion for all shades of malefactors.

When war came, and Jock was one of the P.M.'s secretaries, important as this work was, it would have violated the code that had come down to him if he had left the fighting to others. In spite of defective eyesight, he became a pilot, and cheerfully paid the penalty in some mishaps in landing.

I wonder what effect, if any, Winston's secretaries have had on him. The manner in which anything is presented to Winston before he has made up his mind—that is the crucial point—and the time chosen to bring it forward surely plays a part in shaping things. It would be easy, I think, to underrate the part they have played in the shaping of events.

April 27, 1958

Some time later, Anthony Montague Browne came into the office with rather an important air. There was something, he said cheerfully, that he thought I ought to know. 'I suppose it sounds macabre, but the Prime Minister is concerned about what they ought to do when Sir Winston dies, and I shall have to ask him what his wishes are in the matter.'

It all began with the Queen. When word came to her that Sir Winston was ill in France, it entered her head that he was very old and very frail and might die. The Queen felt it would be the wish of her people that there should be a lying-in-state in Westminster Hall. I first heard of this when Norman Brook telephoned. His practical mind came straight to the point. 'How is Winston, because the Prime Minister is fussing about plans for his funeral?'

The Queen had told her secretary, and the secretary told Sir Norman Brook, and Sir Norman Brook told the Prime Minister. And that was how I came to be summoned to Birch Grove for drinks. After Macmillan had greeted me, he put his arm through mine and marched me off to a sloping bank of daffodils. He lost no time in coming to the point: 'How do you think Winston is? I thought he was quite alert at the Other Club on Thursday; he talked a lot and seemed to hear pretty well, that is if no one else was talking at the same time. A good deal of Winston's deafness, of course, is just inattention. And then when I met him in the Lobby he seemed very frail. What is likely to happen? One doesn't like to talk about it, but I suppose we ought to do something. I wonder what he would like done? Wellington was buried in St. Paul's. Yes, and Nelson too.' We had come to the end of the daffodils. 'Winston likes bands, I think.' And with this ambiguous remark, Macmillan hurried off to do his duty as host.

At Chartwell this morning Diana took me aside. 'What do you think of him?' Without waiting for an answer she gave me her view. 'He has aged a lot, and he is walking very badly. He went to sleep during luncheon.' There was a cold east wind, and I left Diana to get him indoors before he got harm. I followed him to the study, where with a long sigh he settled down to read *An Infamous Army*.[1] 'It is a good solid account of the three months in Brussels before Waterloo,' said Winston. Eileen Joyce, the Australian pianist, has taken Chartwell Farm where Mary used to live, and is dining with them tonight. I suggested they should ask her to play 'A Wandering Minstrel I,' but they said: 'There's not a piano in the house.'

May 8, 1958

Old men lose their hold upon life commonly in the seclusion of their homes, while in Winston's case everybody he meets tries to measure what is left of his vitality. They keep telling me how he is, that he did not take in what they said, that he was very unsteady on his feet.

At such moments, when Winston's guard is down, I hate my impotence. Yet the habits of my training call for precision. Is all this due to the dulling of his mind, or is his deafness partly responsible? Where one begins and the other ends it is not easy to say. Harold Macmillan and Jock Colville like to argue that a good deal of his deafness is due to inattention, which in his case is a form of boredom.

We have been given by accident an opportunity of measuring by an audiometer the exact degree of his deafness. Something went wrong with the wiring mechanism at the House of Commons, and Winston, who had no knowledge of this, noticed a sudden increase in his difficulty in following the debate. He was put out, and it was inevitable that his recent illness bore the blame. I seized the oppor-

[1] Georgette Heyer, *An Infamous Army*.

tunity to bring in Sir Victor Negus. Hitherto, our combined efforts to get Winston to use a hearing aid have come to nothing; he would not persevere with any instrument. Now we have had the dining-room at Hyde Park Gate wired exactly like the House of Commons. When all was ready Clemmie produced Winston. He was able to hear what she said, even when she spoke in a low voice, and was ready to admit that this was a great advance. Before he left the room he told Negus to go ahead with the wiring.

May 19, 1958

Pug Ismay has sent him the first chapters of his memoirs. It is in manuscript, and Sir Winston is fascinated. He could not put them down.

'De Gaulle,' Winston said, 'has a great chance. He is on top.[1] They have all submitted to him. It may purge French politics.' I asked him what the Algerian Committee would do. 'They will bloody well try to make trouble, but they won't succeed.'

'What about the General Strike in France?' I asked. 'Will it do anything?'

'That is the question,' he said half to himself. And then to me: 'I don't think they can do anything against men with arms.'

May 25, 1958

Clemmie said to Winston today: 'Winston, darling, do you want two nursing orderlies for the rest of your life?' He replied shortly, 'Yes, I do. I want them to remain. I want to be looked after properly.' Clemmie keeps an eye on finance; Winston never gives it a thought.

John drove me to Chartwell today. Winston was reading *Rob Roy* when we arrived. When he got up he was so unsteady that John moved quickly to his side.

'Do you find him changed?' I asked as the policeman waved us out of the gate.

'Of course, it is two years since I last saw Winston. It's his voice that has changed. It isn't recognizable. It used to have a rasping quality. Now all the tone has gone. He seems much more gentle.'

On their way home, John turned to Shirley,[2] who had come with us: 'Now think of it, that hand you shook today held a sabre at Omdurman.'

---

[1] General de Gaulle returned to power as Prime Minister on June 2, 1958.
[2] John's wife.

June 27, 1958

'You are very well, Winston.'

'I suppose I am. What the good of it is I don't know. I saw Brendan this morning.'

He stopped. I wanted to ask him about Brendan, but I feared it might upset him. Winston will not go near a hospital in the ordinary way, and poor Brendan is in a lamentable condition. We have been very apprehensive about this visit to the Westminster Hospital, and wanted it to be safely over. But Brendan so managed things that Winston did not appear distressed. It was in a steady voice that he began to tell me about it.

'Brendan was very animated. I was a quarter of an hour with him, and he talked all the time—good sense. He had a rubber tube hanging from his mouth. They feed him through it. Why do they do that, Charles?'

When I explained that his gullet was obstructed he said nothing. At last he looked up.

'The surgeons can do nothing for his kind of cancer?'

Brendan is a brave soul. The last time I saw him the hand of death was on him, but all he thought of now was to let Winston down gently. How many good deeds has this man done in the dark! For a long time he has been pressing me to write about Winston. When I did nothing he asked Moir, who is an authority on such matters, to advise me about the income-tax side of a book of this kind. He thought this might bring me to the starting-post. And all this kindness of heart in the last terrible stages of this illness. As I left I met Alan Hodge at the door. Winston had sent for him to write something about Brendan for his paper, the *Financial Times*.

July 3, 1958

I had tea with Halifax in the House of Lords. He thinks Winston's virtues were, in a sense, a handicap when we came to present our case in Washington in the war years. The Americans had never met anyone like him. He seemed to them a museum piece, a rare relic. When he told them that he had not become First Minister of the Crown in order to preside over the liquidation of the British Empire they felt that they were listening to a voice out of the eighteenth century. Later in the war, when Winston began to warn Roosevelt about Russia's designs, there still seemed to be an air of unreality about what he said, as if he was living in a remote past.

I asked Halifax point-blank: Had he seen any signs that Roosevelt was jealous of Winston as the acknowledged saviour of the free world?

He said at once: 'I'm sure he was jealous. Marshall told me that the President did not look forward to Winston's visits. He knew too much about military matters; besides he kept such shocking hours.

'No, I don't think of Franklin Roosevelt as a very great man,' Halifax added. 'He was, of course, a very adroit manipulator, without doubt a very astute politician. But what he did was to split the American people. I remember when I was in Washington a number of Republican Senators invited me to dine with them and to give them a short talk. "Before you speak, Mr. Ambassador, I want you to know that everyone in this room regards Mr. Roosevelt as a bigger dictator than Hitler or Mussolini. We believe he is taking this country to hell as quickly as he can." Even on the day of his death this bitterness welled up.'

Halifax is the only British Ambassador that Americans seem to remember; unusual men, like Roger Makins and Oliver Franks, are already half-forgotten. I cannot explain this, but I have a feeling that if I could it would tell me something about the American people. I am sure that we do not yet fully realize the influence of Halifax and Dill in America during the war. It is interesting that two men, who at the crisis of their lives were both found wanting, should later have exercised that influence on so great a scale.

July 24, 1958

A message from Brendan yesterday. He has left hospital and asked me to come to his flat at Grosvenor House. Though his nurse had warned me that I should find him a good deal changed, I was not prepared for his dreadful emaciation: the heavily built figure had become a white wraith. Even the mop of hair had gone. He walked to a chair without help, and began talking at once, as of old, while the nurse put a rug round his shoulders and another over his knees. He wanted to tell me about his illness. He had been lunching with some people when he noticed that he could not swallow properly. There were investigations, and at the end Price-Thomas told him that it was too complicated for surgery. So he had the cobalt ray. They gave him too much radiation, he thought. At this point a fit of coughing stopped him. 'There is a fistula from my oesophagus into the lungs,' he explained when he had got his breath. 'That's why I get these damned spasms of coughing. I want you, Charles, to find out for me some statistics. Does this fistula ever close? And if so, in what percentage of cases? I am not prepared to live an invalid's life, fed through a tube. If that is the position, the doctors will have to help me out of the world.' It was an old story. His doctors had not told him everything; they held out hope, but he was beginning to have his doubts. Another spasm shook him; he must come to business:

'Now, Charles, I haven't brought you here to talk about my troubles. Let's get down to something more interesting. I want to talk to you about Winston. Where shall I begin?'

'You once told me that Winston was full of apprehension,' I said. 'What made you say that? The public would think it out of character.'

'But, Charles, you know Winston better than anyone. You must know all about his fears.'

I repeated the story that Winston had told me a long time ago, how when a small boy he had been frightened by other boys throwing cricket balls at him, and he had taken refuge behind a tree, and how afterwards he had brooded on this. It was to him a shameful memory, and he was determined that one day he, too, would be tough.

Brendan took up the story. 'I was riding once with Winston and we got talking about courage. Winston insisted that it was quite wrong to suppose that men were courageous by nature. They weren't. He had always been full of apprehension, and had had to school himself to face anything. The House of Commons in particular used to frighten him. Oh, for years, perhaps up to the war. Yet, Charles, look what happened during the Abdication debate in the House of Commons. The House began yelling at him, and from all parts of the Chamber there were loud cries: "Sit down! Get out!" I broke out into a cold sweat, but Winston stood there with folded arms, very pale, but quite resolute. He was not going to give in to bullies. I went with him to the smoke-room. Members pushed away from him. There was a pair of waiters, Wright and Collins, who seeing this, stopped serving other members and went over to Winston to attend to him. Only Wedderburn—you know, Dundee—stood up for him. He came over and said to Winston: "That was the best speech you ever made in your life." I took Winston off to Lord North Street. He was miserable beyond belief; to be howled down in the House of Commons was a disgrace. But he kept saying to me he would never give in.

'There is in Winston,' Brendan went on, 'the old aristocratic contempt for consequences. Do you remember the Lord Alfred Douglas case? He was a pervert kind of fellow, and he made a series of extraordinary accusations against Winston. Winston was terribly upset, and at last he sued him. Each day he had to listen in Court to some dreadful statements. He knew, of course, the political and financial consequences if he lost the case, but he remained cool

744

and calm, while the attacks of the defending counsel became more and more bitter, more and more insulting. I can see him now, standing in the witness-box, twisting his ring round his finger; his answers were devastating. When the jury found for Winston a very curious thing happened: Winston appeared very cast down; we found that he could not bear the thought of this poor devil being sent to prison.

'You know, Winston has been so successful in controlling his fears that most people think of him as reckless. But he has had to struggle with a fearful handicap. Have you read Rowse on the Later Churchills?[1] Oh, you ought to get it; it is very well written. He says that of the last seven Dukes of Marlborough five suffered from melancholia. You and I think of Winston as self-indulgent; he has never denied himself anything, but when a mere boy he deliberately set out to change his nature, to be tough and full of rude spirits.

'It has not been easy for him. You see, Charles, Winston has always been a "despairer." Orpen, who painted him after the Dardanelles, used to speak of the misery in his face. He called him the man of misery. Winston was so sure then that he would take no further part in public life. There seemed nothing left to live for. It made him very sad. Then in his years in the wilderness, before the Second War, he kept saying: "I'm finished." He said that about twice a day. He was quite certain that he would never get back to office, for everyone seemed to regard him as a wild man. And he missed the red boxes awfully. Winston has always been wretched unless he was occupied. You know what he has been like since he resigned? Why, he told me that he prays every day for death.

'This strain of melancholy, a Churchill inheritance, is balanced in Winston by the physical and mental robustness of the Jeromes. There was in his formidable grandfather a touch of the frontiersman. When he had angered the mob he promptly put a machine-gun on the roof, which he himself could operate.'

I interrupted: 'Like the machine-gun which Winston put in the stern of the small boat which was to take him off the *Queen Mary* if she was torpedoed.'

'Exactly,' said Brendan. 'The healthy, bright red American blood cast out the Churchill melancholy. But not entirely. Winston has always been moody; he used to call his fits of depression the "Black Dog." At other times, as you know, he goes off into a kind of trance. I have seen him sit silent for several hours, and when he is like that only a few people can make him talk.'

[1] A. L. Rowse, *The Later Churchills* (Macmillan, 1958).

'Who, for instance?'

'Oh, Mrs. Edwin Montagu. She was a Stanley of Alderley. Venetia used to laugh at Winston, and take him by the scruff of the neck and tell him not to go on looking at his plate like a booby. And Mrs. Dudley Ward. She would let Winston drink a glass or two of champagne and then get him going. You knew her, Charles? Oh, she was a brilliant talker.

'Winston knew that these attacks of depression might come on him without warning, and he avoided anyone or anything that might bring them on. That's why, as you say, he won't go near a hospital, and why he dislikes people of low vitality. After all, lots of people feel like Winston. Eustace Percy wrote of British politicians after the First World War: "Gusto indeed was what we lacked; the best of us were a low-spirited lot."[1] But he pointed out that the two great exceptions were F.E.[2] and Winston. Bonar Law was a listless old cove. Only F.E. and Winston laughed aloud. Winston has always liked buoyant people around him. F.E. was his closest friend. Oh, from 1910 to 1927. You never saw them together? Well, you missed a good sight. They both had tearing spirits—that is, when Winston wasn't in the dumps—a kind of daring, a dislike of a drab existence, a tremendous zest in life. Clemmie disapproved of F.E. because she thought he led Winston into strange ways. There was no truth in this; Winston could control his drinking. When F.E. went, Max became the bogey-man. And F.E., of course, had an unattractive side; he used the giant strength of his mind to down people. Winston never did that. Indeed, he disliked personal attacks. Why, you know that if you want to remain friends with Winston you must keep a civil tongue in your head when you are talking of the Royal Family or of his father.' Brendan's words came faster. 'Lord Rosebery could make Winston talk at any time. But when he called Lord Randolph a "scug" he fell out of favour, and Winston published the life of his father[3] without Rosebery's preface.'

'I suppose, Brendan, that Winston has had many friendships?'

'Yes,' answered Brendan, 'but few deep ones. I do not mean that he is not affectionate; he would go to the stake for a friend. And I don't think he has ever lost one. You can generally tell what he finds attractive in his friends; a V.C. is in his good graces before he begins.'

'Don't you think, Brendan, that his liking for romance is just another means of switching off his sad thoughts?'

'I don't know about that,' answered Brendan. 'But he has always

---

[1] Eustace Percy, *Some Memories* (Eyre & Spottiswoode, 1958).
[2] F. E. Smith, 1st Lord Birkenhead.
[3] Winston S. Churchill, *Lord Randolph Churchill* (1906).

fallen for heroes. Winston, you know, is not a simple character.' A flicker of a smile came and went. 'If you are going to write about him, as of course you must, you won't learn much from his letters. No one, he says, but a fool writes letters for pleasure. Winston is very credulous, he has always been easily taken in. Clemmie often saved him from the charlatans he gathered round him. He is at the same time ingenuous and cunning.'

I asked Brendan what he meant by cunning.

'Oh, of course, in getting his own way. His tenacity was always remarkable. Violent, irrational, superstitious,' Brendan murmured. 'You don't think of Winston as cautious, but he can be very much on his guard.'

'Well, Charles, we began with a small boy hiding behind a tree, and I want to tell you before we end about a sandy-haired boy, a kind of portent, prepared to contradict anyone, ready to challenge the world. I want to tell you this because to understand Winston you must go back to his childhood.'

Brendan thought his bluster as a young man was a form of shyness, and told me of an occasion when Winston was lunching with Linky and the Duke of Marlborough. Linky's erudition made him feel a schoolboy; he was so ashamed of his ignorance that he made up his mind that he would educate himself. So he read and read and read. 'You know who I mean by Linky?'

'Yes, Lord Hugh Cecil. He was Winston's best man; they seemed to drift apart; perhaps they were never really buddies.'

Brendan told me that he first met Winston when he was thirty-seven years of age. He was beginning to lose some of his hair, but he had a good figure and was bursting with energy.

The nurse came in. Had I stayed too long? When I put my hand on Brendan's shoulder the spine of his scapula felt like a razor's edge. I keep thinking of him; I cannot get him out of my head.

Chapter seventy

The dying gladiator

April 13, 1959

When I called at Chartwell on my way to London I found Clemmie in the cottage, which was full of books; she explained that Winston had about ten thousand, and she was trying to reduce them by half. I sat for a time in the garden shelter with Winston. Presently he levered himself to his feet and walked towards the house. He appeared more cheerful than he has been of late, and was reluctant to go indoors.

Clemmie telephoned about eight o'clock:

'After you left, Winston went to bed. Later on he rang his bell, and when Shepherd answered it he noticed that Winston was not speaking properly. He came to me and said that he appeared confused. Winston wanted to stay the night at Chartwell, but I had to explain that there were no servants. We shall be at Hyde Park Gate by ten o'clock. Do you think you could call?'

When I asked Winston how he was I could not understand what he was trying to say to me. He knew what he wanted to say, but he could not say it. I gave him my pen and he wrote something very slowly and very carefully. I took the paper from him, but I could not read what he had written. I noticed that his little finger was white and cold. When I asked if it was painful he nodded. When I left him Clemmie took up the story:

'Winston is usually very silent in the car, but on the way to London he kept trying to say something. I was not sure whether he wanted to tell me things or whether he was experimenting to find out for himself what he could say and what he could not. When he failed to get the words he exclaimed: "Damnation! Is it a stroke, Charles?" '

I went back to his room and reassured him. He had been like this before, and it had all cleared up. I told him that in a day or two he will be all right. He said he was worried.

April 14, 1959

This morning it is impossible to detect that there is anything wrong with his speech. But Clemmie is distracted, and she has good reason for her cares. A few days ago I noticed that the pupils of his eyes did not react to light, and now there is this speech defect and the little finger; there seems no end to these wandering clots. I keep wondering what will happen next. But Winston has made up his mind to go to the Other Club on Thursday.

April 15, 1959

When Brain had examined Sir Winston he told him that a small artery had been blocked, cutting off the circulation to his speech centre for a time. But the circulation had been re-established. I had advised Russell to ask Winston if he had made any plans, and if he had, to urge him to cancel them. Winston said that he was speaking to his constituents:

'I cannot cancel it without giving a reason. I should have to tell them about this, and I could not then take part in the election. Macmillan has asked me to take some part. What does it matter if I do break down?' He broke out impatiently:

'I am quite content to die.'

Russell could think of nothing to say. He sat looking at Winston for quite a time. Then he half turned to me as if he would say: 'Cannot you do something to put an end to this visit?'

Clemmie awaited us in the library. 'Well,' she asked, 'what did he say? Did you persuade him not to speak on Monday?' Brain told her what had happened. There was a long pause. At last he said:

'Does Sir Winston worry?'

'No,' Clemmie answered. 'Winston isn't a worrier. But he is profoundly depressed. The days are very long and very dull. It was never like this in the past. He found a hundred things to do. He reads a lot, but he does not enjoy what he reads. He cannot paint now. He painted two pictures in five weeks at Marrakesh. He wants to stay in bed. Today an agreeable, amusing woman came to luncheon. Winston likes her, but at the last moment he decided to lunch in bed. He has given up America, thank God. But what about this speech? Cannot you do anything, Charles?'

April 17, 1959

Shawcross[1] told me that he drove Goddard home from the Other Club last night. He had been sitting next to Winston and said that

[1] Sir Hartley Shawcross, Attorney-General in the Labour Government, 1945–51.

it was very hard work. Winston scarcely spoke to the man on his left, and when something was said to him he seemed to connect for perhaps one or two sentences and then rang off.

April 20, 1959

Winston spoke to me about his Woodford speech.

'It needed nerve.'

'You mean you were nervous?'

'Oh, no. But if you are uncertain whether you will break down it needs nerve.'

When I left him I met Clemmie. She was gloomy about the speech. She felt after it was over that his voice was so feeble that much of his speech could not be heard.

'And once, Charles, he stumbled so that I was terrified that he was going to break down.'

Anthony Montague Browne smiled. 'As he came off the platform, Winston said: "Now for America." '

May 3, 1959

When I put a cheerful face on things this morning Winston grunted:

'I wish I was not going. I would rather stay in bed and read.'

I think it is beginning to dawn on him that to fly across the Atlantic for a few days as things are with him is a bit of a gamble. I told him he was mad to take the risk. But his mind is made up. Anything, I fancy, to break the purgatory of these interminable days. He will not take me. He cannot bear that people should think that he needs a nurse to look after him. When I said 'Good-bye' he said:

'You agree to my going?'

'Under duress,' I answered.

At this Winston gave me a faint smile.

May 4, 1959

I hear that he went off in good heart. He has a feeling that for the moment he is on the map again. Perhaps, after all, life is not quite over. But I am full of forebodings. I cannot get the thought out of my head that I may not see him again.

May 8, 1959

This morning Washington wanted me on the telephone. I was sure the worst had happened.

'He's all right,' said Montague Browne. 'But there is a black bit

MR. HAROLD MACMILLAN

at the end of his little finger. It is about the size of a pea. We had to call in a doctor. He will speak to you.'

My first impulse was to impress on this American doctor the need for secrecy.

May 9, 1959

As I drove to Chartwell I wondered how I should break the news to Clemmie. She was sitting by the black swans with Diana. She began at once:

'What is the worst that can happen?'

Before I could answer Diana broke in:

'Oh, of course, Papa might have his hand off for gangrene.'

Clemmie showed me a letter from Winston in a very shaky hand. I realized that I do not often see his handwriting. Winston spoke of Ike as a 'real friend.'

May 11, 1959

Saw Winston just before noon. He was so tired that he could hardly keep awake. Clemmie told me:

'Mr. Dulles[1] was so pleased to see Winston that he did not look ill. You see he had a broad grin on his face. I asked Winston if he looked like a dying man. He said, "No." He was emaciated of course. Winston saw General Marshall, but he could not speak. The poor man has had a stroke. I am very glad Winston went to America, though I was against the journey at first. He loved the visit. I think he wanted to go to America before he died, because of his mother.'

May 12, 1959

Took Professor Rob, the surgeon, to see Winston's finger. Pulling his chair nearer so that Winston might hear what was said, he proceeded to explain very clearly and even a little bluntly that there had been a clot in the artery of his little finger. There was a black spot because not enough blood could get to the finger. If he rested he would probably lose only a bit of the finger. The black spot was dead tissue; it might take months—even a year—to dry up and come away.

'A year! A year!" Winston repeated in a shrill voice. 'You are asking too much. I have an appointment tomorrow. I am not going to deny myself this.'

[1] He had cancer and died on May 24, 1959.

May 13, 1959

Winston was asleep when Rob and I called at nine o'clock. He gave me a sour look when we trooped in. He had made up his mind to lunch with the Prime Minister at No. 10. Max and Christopher would be there, and he was sure we meant to prevent him. Rob said there was a risk if he went, but that the risk was small.

'What is it?' demanded Winston.

'If you don't rest you might lose the hand,' Rob answered curtly.

'Oh, I see,' said Winston.

May 14, 1959

With a smirk Winston announced his intention of attending Max's annual dinner tonight. He asked Rob what were the odds that this would make his finger worse. Rob replied fifty–fifty. The Prime Minister told me that Winston arrived at the dinner in a bad temper; he sat silent, brooding. When Max saw this he made up his mind to fish·Winston out of his black mood.

'Why don't you sell your damned pictures, Winston? You can get anything you like to ask for them now. When you're gone they won't be worth two shillings apiece. I'll give you a hundred and fifty thousand down for them.'

This succeeded in rousing Winston from his stupor.

May 18, 1959

Norman Brook telephoned that he would like to see me. When I called at his office I learnt that the Prime Minister had told him to find out from me the significance of the finger.

May 24, 1959

I wanted Winston to say nothing to anyone about his finger, and gave him a finger-stall to hide the black spot. Why should he advertise his decrepitude? But I hear that he has been showing it to everyone. Today he removed the stall, and looked with a quizzical expression at the black spot. 'It's a poor sight,' he said at length. 'I have never seen anything like it before.'

Clemmie tells me that he is drowsy. He went to sleep over his breakfast, and when Shepherd came in later it was quite cold and he was still alseep.

May 26, 1959

Found Winston alone in the house at Chartwell with Miss Pugh. He was reading Macaulay's essay on Milton. There are twelve volumes of his essays, and he said that he had read the lot at one time or another.

June 8, 1959

The scene of *Der Rosenkavalier* at Glyndebourne last night, the pretty woman's farewell to all that made life to her worthwhile, has set me thinking. The audience was plainly moved by the pathos of her abdication, yet the same people remain cold and indifferent when someone who once was famous draws out his leave of the world, alone and half forgotten.

I must not become morbid about Winston, though he is never far from my mind. The people I meet at Chartwell ask about him, but do they, I wonder, try to get into his mind as he sits there in the great house, through the interminable days, often alone, waiting for the end? His job is done. Will posterity say that it was well done? I sometimes wish that he would not think so much about posterity, because it seems to bring one of his black moods.

When did he begin to be troubled about his place in history? I suppose that in the war his days were so taken up with the conduct of operations that there was no time left to live with his own mistakes. It was, however, the loss of the election in the summer of 1945 that gave me my first clue to the gnawing discomfort in his mind. He was hurt by the size of the majority, he felt that the whole conduct of the war had been called in question. When he had partly recovered from the blow he resolved to prepare his defence and to put it on paper. He must have known that he had a tired mind, but he would not be turned from his purpose. In 1949—it may have been about the turn of the year—when he was half way through the third volume of *The Second World War* it became plain that he no longer had the energy of mind to do the job properly. I tried to argue with him. Surely he had done enough, had not the time come to take in sail? 'You do not understand,' he said sadly. He could not bring himself to talk of it. Nor was it necessary.

Yet only on one occasion, as far as I can remember, did he show me his scars. It was in the summer of 1953, after his stroke, when he thought he was dying and his head was confused. Even his speech was difficult to follow; he kept trying to say something and I was able at last to pick up what he wanted to say:

'I ought not . . . I must not . . . be held to account . . . for all . . . that has gone wrong.'

He still lives in the war. On Thursday I found him with a glum face, brooding over his bed-rest. I taxed him with giving way to the Churchill melancholia. 'Why,' he retorted, 'do I get stuck down in the past? Why do I keep going over and over those years when I know I cannot change anything? You, Charles, have spent your life puzzling how the mind works. You must know the answer.' He thinks I know more than I do. Indeed, much that he has told me has been no more than a cry for help. I rack my brains, wondering what I can do. That I am so useless to him torments me.

It seemed to me that I might learn what he is going through if I knew more about other men who have lived in the sun before they had to struggle through this final phase. The great man may spend his last days in public and yet be shut off from this kind. I was thinking of Adenauer. I asked Winston if he thought that the Germans would one day make common lot with the Russians. He gave a snort and asked me impatiently where I got such strange thoughts. 'The Germans will never work with Russia after their brutality to the German wounded.' But Adenauer knows his countrymen too well to accept that kind of talk. He knows their brilliant achievements, their singular gifts and their essential instability. He is feverishly attempting to bind Germany to the West before he dies so that the knot cannot be cut or unravelled. He knows that time is short. Will he be given the chance to finish his job? Even his own party do not know what he is about, and he cannot tell them. They, of course, put it down to his unbridled egotism and to his obsession that he alone can run Germany. I tried to put the gist of this to Winston, but all he said was that I knew nothing about politics.

Not every famous man, it may be, must pass through this final phase. Poor Clem,[1] for example. No tormenting doubts seem to puzzle his brain. There is a story of Attlee that may be taken as a hint that he at any rate has been spared the tribulation of these last useless years.

Meeting him at Wimbledon, Sir William Haley said:

'Tomorrow ought to be exciting.'

Attlee: 'I'm not coming here tomorrow.'

Haley: 'I meant the debate in your Lordship's House on Capital Punishment.'

Attlee: 'Oh, I've never been interested in hanging, one way or the other.'

*

Attlee seems very bent and frail as he enters the Library of the House of Lords about noon; his head is poked forward and his legs seem to be trying to catch up with the rest of his anatomy. When he has found the book he wants, he flops into one of the big red armchairs,

[1] Earl Attlee.

wriggling down until his feet are higher than his head. I go across to pass the time of day. I like to talk to him; his mental processes seem so straightforward and untroubled. He does not seem to ask where the world is going, nor does he question what it all can mean.

Yet I am told that this diffident little man ruled his Party for six years with a ruthless hand. It appears that he was able to use these methods with a Party that was never far from the boil as the result of a plan that had been carefully thought out. Attlee argued that if there were only two men below him striving for the succession he would have to take sides. But why only two? Why not a triangle of Stafford Cripps, Ernest Bevin and Herbert Morrison? And it was in that fashion that this prudent little man planned the pattern of those years of change and unrest. It all happened as he had arranged, and when Bevin died, Bevan was at once put in his place; the triangle remained intact. Am I deluding myself about Attlee? Was he indeed so simple, after all? Was he, too, in his undemonstrative way, fighting out the same grim losing battle?

*

June 9, 1959

Is Winston's Black Dog catching? I was glad to find William Haley planted in a chair in the sun, absorbed in a book. He is staying at Marshalls, and his factual talk is the medicine I need when I am getting too introspective. I soon forgot the pains of the dying gladiator in his glimpse of an inconsequential Winston. He said that when he was head of the B.B.C. after the war he came to know that if Winston was going to broadcast he would be sure to telephone some days before. It happened, said Haley, on four or five occasions. He therefore left instructions with his staff what they were to do. Winston was sure that the B.B.C. wanted to cut down the time allotted to him. This he resented. It was not fair to him. Haley said that when Winston was given the Freedom of his constituency, Woodford, he found that the B.B.C. was only putting out his speech on the foreign service. He was quite put out.

Winston: 'I want you to know that this is a not unimportant occasion.'

Haley: 'It has given the B.B.C. great pleasure.'

Winston grunted: 'Your young men want to cut me short. I may be cut off in the middle of a sentence. It is not right. I want to disclose to the public the pang I received from the election.'

Haley: 'You know your broadcast will be heard throughout the Commonwealth.'

Winston: 'But at home?'

'My people,' said Haley, 'pointed out to me that listeners would not want to hear his speech on a Saturday afternoon during the football season. However, we got three minutes here and two minutes there by cutting down other programmes, and eventually I was able to write to Winston that we could give him twelve minutes. He expressed his pleasure and said that the B.B.C. had been very gracious.'

Winston, he went on, did not really want more time on the air. On five different occasions after the war the B.B.C. had invited him to broadcast on important national events, but each time he refused, though he took part, of course, in political broadcasts. Moreover, both Winston and Attlee were reluctant, in 1948, to take part in television. Winston gave his reasons:

'When I was very young, if one said something at Oldham that might have led to trouble if it was spread abroad, nothing happened. But now one has to weigh every word, knowing all the time that people will be listening all over the country. It would be an intolerable burden if one had to consider how one would appear, what one would look like, all over the land.'

Attlee agreed and nothing was done.

His grumbling had its roots in an old grievance: that the B.B.C. had kept him off the air before the war. Haley explained that the B.B.C. had, foolishly perhaps, handed over to the three Parties the rationing of political broadcasts, and the selection of the speakers. It was the Tory Party, and not the B.B.C., which had kept Winston off the air. However, in spite of Haley's clear explanation, the next time Winston had to broadcast the old grievance was fished out.

The truth is that Winston could not bring himself to pin the blame to the Party system, in which he had been cradled. He was sure that the intolerable wrong that had been done to him during the years in the wilderness was due to the machinations of the B.B.C.

Winston, Haley pointed out, was not always very consistent in his actions. He was thinking of the conference between the B.B.C. and the political parties after the war. He explained that the B.B.C. would have to take back the rationing and selection of speakers from the Parties.

Everyone agreed to this except Winston, who kept up his opposition for nine months, insisting that the political parties ought to do the selection of speakers. In short, he wanted to perpetuate the very machinery which had been his own undoing. When this was pointed out to him he argued that his position before the war was a very special case; it would not occur like that again.

Haley began to smile as he told me of some exchanges with Winston at the end of the Conference. The phrases he coined were an asset to the Tories. 'I turned to Winston: "I think you are troubled about the influence of Communists in the B.B.C." Winston then said his piece. When no one supported the line he took, he said: '"You, Sir William, are an antediluvian liberal, sitting on a nest of vipers, which will presently strike and destroy you."'

August 3, 1959

Lunched at Birch Grove.[1] Harold Macmillan said: 'I miss Brendan. Who will be Winston's Boswell? He should have a Boswell. He is very witty. I always hoped Brendan would be. He must have had a wonderful fund of stories about Winston. Now he's gone I can't think who could do it. We are all getting on, the people who know him, I mean.'

The Prime Minister's face twitched with mirth.

'You know Winston's remark when he heard of the illness of someone he particularly disliked: "Nothing trivial, I trust."'

The smile widened.

'And the quip about Attlee. It must have been in 1947 when Winston was making speeches in the House. You remember Winston was never quite in step with the rather revolutionary people elected in 1945. One day Attlee answered one of these speeches very neatly and sensibly. Winston got up at the end and went to his room. He was feeling depressed about things when Colonel R. came up to him.

'Colonel R.: "Don't you think Mr. Attlee's manner in the House has enormously improved?"

'Winston: "Oom, oom, oom."

'Colonel R.: "But really, sir, I can't help feeling that he is greatly changed for the better."

'Winston: "Oom, oom, oom."

'Colonel R.: "I must say one can hardly credit that it is the same person speaking, he is so much improved."

'Winston: "Oom, oom. Have you ever read Maeterlinck?"

'Colonel R.: "No, sir."

'Winston: "Well. Go and read him. You will see that if any grub is fed on Royal Jelly it turns into a Queen Bee."

Macmillan: 'Jelly is such a splendid word. And you know to this day, the Colonel doesn't know what Winston was talking about.'

Dorothy said she had received a very agreeable letter from Mrs. Clifford. Had the Prime Minister read Clifford's book[2] *The Young*

[1] Mr. Macmillan's home in Sussex.

[2] J. L. Clifford, Professor of English Literature, Columbia University.

Samuel Johnson? The Cliffords had been touring the Hebrides in Johnson's footsteps. They found a gull's egg in almost the same place where Johnson had found his egg.

Macmillan: 'Boswell's *Tour of the Hebrides* is a wonderful travel book. The best, I think. I've been reading it again. I haven't time to read new books, but I like taking up a book I know well. I like reading lives of statesmen. Of course, we all read them when we were young and decided they gave a good picture of the man and his life. But it is quite different reading them when you know the machine. I've just been reading Philip Magnus's *Gladstone*. I felt very envious. He was Prime Minister for—was it fourteen years? and in all that time he never spent less than five months of the year at Hawarden. After all, it was a long way off, much further than Birch Grove,' he added with a quizzical smile.

Dorothy asked the Prime Minister how he had kept his garden so green. Hers was brown and parched. When she wanted to cheer herself up she looked at Norman Brook's photograph of the water garden taken with the camera Khrushchev gave him.

Macmillan: 'What do you think of Norman? Do you think he looks better than he used to? I like to keep to office hours. I don't keep him up half the night. Norman has most wonderful judgment. He is always right. Pure inborn judgment, because, as I expect you know, he had no background.

'I think,' he went on, 'Eton is a wonderful school. I think you learn there to take knocks. You learn not to make a fuss if you are criticized unfairly. Everybody at school is criticized unfairly some time or other. You learn to take it as part of the day's work. You don't write home to your mother and complain. You know, Alan Lennox-Boyd couldn't have endured the last fortnight without that training.[1]

'I try to make the Cabinet laugh sometimes, to take things lightly. After all, it's no use working oneself into a state. One just does one's best, that's all one can do.'

He spoke of Winston's kindness. Winston kept him in cigars. The Prime Minister showed me one of the cigar boxes from Cuba which Winston had given him. He thought Winston had mellowed. Then he asked me abruptly how he was. The Prime Minister thought it was very unusual for a man to go on so long in Winston's state. Women did, of course. Lady Dorothy's mother did, her last two

[1] Secretary of State for the Colonies, 1954–9. Lennox-Boyd was fiercely attacked in 1959 over the Hola camp affair in Kenya, in which eleven Mau Mau prisoners died of violence. The issue caused widespread feeling in Britain, and a motion of censure was put down in the House of Commons in June.

years had been rather sad—more dead than alive. He looked over the distant prospect. He could not understand why people went abroad; England was so lovely. The country was very prosperous. People ought to be happy. He turned to Dorothy: 'Do you think they are happy?'

This was a Prime Minister interested in other people's lives and in their backgrounds. He liked young people round him, and his eye brightened as he spoke of his grandson, who had just gone to Eton.

'I asked him a very silly question: had he come across the Headmaster? As if a Lower Boy would.'

'"Well, Grandpapa, as a matter of fact I did run into him the other day. And I am bound to tell you, Grandpapa, he made a very poor impression on me."'

August 15, 1959

Winston showed me the finger with a touch of pride. The black tip had come away. 'You could not tell,' he said, 'that anything was wrong. It took three months and they talked about a year!'

October 22, 1959

I had gone to my room in the Fernley Hotel, Bath, to unpack when there was a knock on the door. The porter wanted to know if I would take a telephone call from London.

'It is Anthony. Yes, Montague Browne. I am telephoning about Sir Winston. He isn't very well. We are at Hyde Park Gate. We were talking when he yawned twice. Then he went white, face and hands, and became unconscious. I was alarmed. I thought he was dying.'

'How long was it before he came round?'

'Oh, I suppose not more than a few minutes. When he did come round he seemed dazed. He said he felt very ill, as if he had been turned upside down. I don't know if I did right, but when I couldn't get you I telephoned to Sir Russell Brain, and he'll be here any minute. I will ring you again when Sir Russell has seen Sir Winston.'

I am in the middle of a tour of meetings about merit awards in the West Country, but I must see him tonight. It doesn't sound too good.

I found Clemmie with Winston in his bedroom. 'It's Charles, Winston,' said Clemmie. A flicker of recognition crossed his face. He said nothing, but I found that he could answer my questions. As Clemmie put it, he was 'very quiet and withdrawn.' 'Winston did not recognize Sir Russell.' There was a troubled look in Clemmie's eyes as she said this. He took no heed of us. He sat propped up in bed looking at his dinner on the bed-rest; he was not interested in food. He had a quiet pulse, his colour was good and he was falling asleep as we left him. I do not think anything will happen.

October 23, 1959

This morning when Russell and I saw Winston he seemed much as usual. He did not feel ill. Russell thought his attack was due to 'petit mal', a mild form of epilepsy, the 'falling sickness' from which both Caesar and Napoleon suffered. It was not uncommon as a sequel to a sluggish cerebral circulation. Even if there was a recurrence, the risk that he would die in one of these attacks was small, but Russell did not think that he would be alive in six months' time.

October 24, 1959

Found Winston playing bezique with Clemmie as if nothing had happened. 'He is much better,' she said, watching Winston as he collected the cards. I asked him if he could detect any difference between his condition before the attack and now. He hesitated.

'If there is any difference it is for the worse.'

'In what way?' I persisted.

'It's not really a headache, but . . .'

I helped him out. 'Muzziness?'

'Yes, muzziness. Shall I have another attack?'

I asked him how he was getting on with his book.

'There's not much in it,' he grunted.

'You don't think Tolstoy makes out his case about Napoleon?'

His face lost its vacant expression and lit up in amusement. 'Oh, I put him on one side in order to read the second volume of the bloody diaries. Tolstoy must wait until I see what Brooke has to say. I was told that the second volume was worse than the first, full of venom, but as far as I have read I don't find it so. I had forgotten, my dear, that I called you a bloody old man. I apologize to you,' he said gravely.

*

Clemmie is at pains to bring Winston's friends to see him. It appears that Rupert Gunnis's[1] visit was a great success. He took him an old picture postcard of a house party with the King of Portugal and Winston in it. Winston was thrilled, and talked about each member of the party in turn. This went on till halfpa-st three. Clemmie pressed Rupert to come again, any time. 'What card will you play next visit?' I enquired. Rupert thought for a little: 'Marie Lloyd, I think.'

[1] The date of Rupert Gunnis's visit has been torn off my diary.

November 17, 1959

Clemmie telephoned.

'Is that you, Charles? I'm very worried about Winston. He had another of his attacks when he was lunching with Lord Beaverbrook. It seems that Bullock, his chauffeur—you know he is a very sensible fellow—noticed that when Winston got out of the car he lurched to the right; he would have fallen but for Bullock. I telephoned Max to ask how Winston had been during luncheon.'

'What did he say?'

'Terrible. Winston could not get the words he wanted. Apparently he realized this and kept very silent.'

When I saw him about an hour later he still had difficulty in finding his words. When I asked him how he felt he replied, 'Frightfully stupid,' but he demurred when I said that he would not be able to see Adenauer. I explained that he might use wrong words. It might be very noticeable. He turned to Montague Browne and told him not to scratch any of his appointments for the moment. 'Anyway,' I added, 'the dinner at No. 10 is out of the question.' When he looked very glum, I asked him if he would like to see Russell Brain. He did not answer.

When Russell came he sat by Winston's bedside, staring at him; for what seemed an interminable period he went on gazing very intently at Winston, but saying nothing. Winston did not look at Russell, he just sat with his eyes fixed on his bed-rest; then it seemed that he could keep them open no longer and he dropped off to sleep, waking in a few minutes with an uncomprehending, vacant and rather startled look. Clemmie came in and said that he would miss Adenauer unless we sent him a message now. Brain looked round at me as if he wanted to say: 'What do we do now?' I got up and we trooped out.

'How do you find him?' Clemmie asked Russell, and without waiting for an answer continued: 'Winston was very disappointed. He wanted terribly to see Adenauer. You see, Sir Russell, there will not be many of these occasions in the future.'

Clemmie got nothing out of Brain, but to me he was more forthcoming. His view is frankly pessimistic. The right carotid artery had been blocked before, and it looked now as if the left was affected. He thought that one day Winston would be found in bed unable to speak. 'You mean he will have a stroke in the night?' Brain nodded.

November 18, 1959

Clemmie greeted me cheerfully this morning.

'You wouldn't know anything had happened; maybe he is a little subdued. Adenauer expressed a great desire to see Winston if it was at all possible before he left London, and it has been arranged that he will come to Hyde Park Gate this afternoon. Oh, he has promised not to stay long.'

'What happened?' I enquired later of Clemmie.

'Oh, Winston was thrilled with the interview. You see, Charles, I speak German, and I think that helped.'

'Did Winston get very tired?'

'No, not at all. The first quarter of an hour he was hesitant and his voice was not very strong, though his answers were all sensible. Then he blossomed. His voice got stronger, and he asked a lot of intelligent questions. They talked a lot about the Summit Conference. Adenauer does not trust Khrushchev. He wants to keep Russia out of everything. I think, Charles, it went off very well.'

It may have been an hour after this that I saw Winston.

'I saw . . . I saw . . . that man.'

'Adenauer, you mean?'

He nodded.

November 21, 1959

Winston is more than halfway through Zurig's *Marie Antoinette*, but how much he has taken in I cannot tell. When Miss Pugh showed him some papers this morning he did not seem to take them in as he usually does. Clemmie said an extraordinary thing had happened on their drive from London to Chartwell.

'You know, Charles, Winston usually smokes like a chimney when he is in the car. Sometimes when we have to appear together at some ceremony I have had to say to him that the smoke was making me feel sick, and he has always been very good and has put out his cigar at once. But when we drove down last night Winston did not smoke at all. This is something new. Does it mean anything, Charles?'

November 30, 1959

Winston's birthday. On my way to Hyde Park Gate I bought half a pound of caviare at Harrods. His front door was open, and the house seemed in a buzz. Three secretaries (Jane Portal had been conscripted for the occasion) were opening letters. 'How are you?' Winston looked at me. His face was without expression.

'I feel very well. I hope I don't go on feeling very well. I don't want to waste time reading novels and playing cards.'

762

Perhaps he will get his way. There may be no more birthdays. While the family celebrates, he only wants to die. As I left the house, the crowd of press photographers around the door gave way a little; there were several flashes and a lot of clicks.

December 1, 1959

I sat next to Maurice Bowra, the Warden of Wadham College, at the Cheltenham Council today. He was pretty critical of the Prof., who had told him that he had buried the hatchet with Tizard.[1] But the Prof. had added, 'I know where to find the handle.'

December 6, 1959

Those who are brought up against Winston in these times do what they can to bring him back into the world. They raise their voices and shout at him, as after someone lost in the dark, and the most successful are those who fire at him a stream of questions, taking him back perhaps to some half-buried war memory. In this machine-gun technique Monty has no equal. He brings back some battle in the desert and Winston's part in its planning, so that his face brightens and he seems to come to life again for a short time.

Few woman have ever had much luck in setting Winston's tongue wagging, but Lady Limerick is tenacious and not without experience. Winston told her that he had written forty books and had painted four hundred pictures, which had gone round the world and had raised a sum of twenty thousand pounds. The question was what to do now with the pictures. Lady Limerick said that they were painted at different periods of his life. Could he fix the date when they were painted by the difference in style? Winston was sure he could. He appeared interested; Lady Limerick felt encouraged. Was it true, she asked, that he had likened de Gaulle to a female llama who had been surprised in her bath? Winston pouted, smiled and shook his head. But his way of disavowing the remark convinced me that he was in fact responsible for this indiscretion, though on reflection he might not care to have it attributed to him by the world at large. Winston had seen *On the Beach* at his cinema; he had read the book[2] twice, it was 'a remarkable work.' Clemmie joined in. She had closed her eyes; it was so horrible. 'Don't on any account,' she said, 'read the book if you are not feeling well.'

When the ladies left the room Lord Limerick took up the running. He asked about Smuts's photograph. Winston grunted that he was

---

[1] There had been a notorious feud between Lord Cherwell and Sir Henry Tizard.

[2] Neville Shute, *On the Beach.*

a fine man. Limerick rose and went over to inspect the austere face. He picked up a new picture of Ike inscribed 'From his devoted friend,' and asked about a large silver-gilt trophy. It was the Steward's Cup, Winston answered. It was his for keeps. Winston got up and stumbled to a wooden box, which he unlocked.

'There are all Marlborough's letters to the Grand Pensionary of Holland. Six hundred and thirty of them. They were given me by the Government of the Netherlands.'

Winston does not try to impress individuals, they do not really matter. It is only a crowd—the nation for instance—which stirs him to effort. However, on this occasion he did seem to say: 'Aren't you impressed? I think you ought to be. It is really a rather remarkable collection. There is in fact nothing quite like it.'

December 16, 1959

Winston, according to Clemmie, keeps dozing off all day.

'He will begin a sentence: "Where is . . .?" and then he cannot remember what he wanted to say.'

Anthony told me that yesterday Moir had seen Winston and had failed to get anything across. The arrangements for the funeral are far advanced. Winston has changed his mind; he will not be buried at Chartwell, but at Woodstock, with his father.

December 18, 1959

One day in the year I sit in the chair of a Government Committee for six hours. I read to them a list of consultants, name by name, explaining why this particular man is worthy of a merit award. And if my attention were to wander I think I should make rather a mess of things. Not long after I took the chair the telephone in the room rang. It was Winston's secretary; he had a pain in his chest. I promised to call at five o'clock when my committee ended. A few minutes later the telephone rang again. Sir Winston was very restless. Could I not call earlier? I promised to come during the lunch hour. A quarter of an hour passed, and then there was another ring. The secretary thought Sir Winston was not looking very well. I said I would go soon after midday. I said to Winston that if the pain was really bad I would give him something to relieve it. No, he did not think it was bad enough for that. Miss Pugh said: 'Poor dear, you don't know whether he is really ill or just making a fuss because he is bored.' When I saw him again after dinner he was playing cards with Clemmie and appeared much taken up with the game.

764

December 20, 1959

Norman Brook spent nearly two hours with Winston after lunch. I wondered what he would make of Winston's waning faculties. When he came out he said:

'Of course there were long pauses, and sometimes Winston began a sentence and then could not remember what he meant to say.'

'But,' I said, 'what happened when you discussed serious problems?'

'We didn't. To my mind Winston hasn't been capable of discussing anything that matters for the last six months. I just started a line, and if he didn't seem to connect I moved on to something else. I didn't do much more than make agreeable noises. The trouble, Charles, for all who love Winston, is that you feel you can't do anything to help him.'

March 8, 1960

It had been planned that Winston should join the Onassis yacht at Gibraltar, but when our plane made an emergency landing at Madrid to refuel we learnt that the rough weather might make difficulties at Gibraltar. The pilot, however, was determined to deliver Sir Winston to the Governor waiting on the airfield, and he made two abortive attempts to land; in the second Dorothy was thrown sideways, bumping her head against the window, and everything on the tables was swept off with a clatter. Then the pilot decided to make for Tangier. When, in the war, we came down through low clouds before landing at Gibraltar, Winston became apprehensive, muttering: 'I hope we shan't collide with the Rock.' Now the blanching of his brain has wiped out his fears. Though it appears that those who were waiting on the tarmac were full of trepidation, he himself did not even seem interested, only growling irritably: 'What are they doing?'

The Nairns,[1] who had heard of our plight, met us at Tangier, and a little procession of cars carried off our party to their house on the outskirts of the town. The guests for a dinner party were already arriving, their spruce evening clothes made us feel battered and dishevelled, and, perhaps, a little in the way. T. S. Eliot, one of the guests, said it would make a wonderful scene for a play. I took him over to Winston, who gazed at him in an uncomprehending way; his name evidently meant nothing to him. Eliot drifted away, and Winston was left sitting apart, looking at the carpet, a little puzzled

---

[1] The Consul-General and his wife.

perhaps about what it all meant. He could not understand why they did not announce dinner. 'I am very hungry, Charles.' Raising his voice, he repeated this, so that I was afraid Mrs. Nairn would hear. I tried to explain that dinner was waiting for us at the Rif Hotel. He seemed too tired to make a move; sunk in his chair, he took no notice of the guests who were sitting about. They had given up making conversation, though one of them said to me that they would talk about this for a long time. It was a very great occasion.

It was nearly ten o'clock when we reached the Rif Hotel. Winston at once summoned the head waiter and ordered consommé. It was a long time coming. He kept grumbling: 'What about my soup? I gave the order a long time ago.' His voice got louder: 'Oh, damn it, what are they doing about it?' However, when dinner came he gradually began to thaw. Looking out into the courtyard, he watched the gusts of wind blow up the awning so that he could see the fairy lamps swinging in the wind and catch their light reflected in pools of water left by the storm.

'Look, Charles, at the shape of that foliage. That tree is like a animal pawing the air. You see the one I mean? It has a yellow belly. And that one is just like a crouching cat.'

Winston went on to explain that he often sees the shape of animals when he looks at trees and shrubs. I told him it was very late and urged him to go to his bed. He had been travelling for more than twelve hours. 'Oh,' he retorted, 'that doesn't tire me, it's the walking.' It was after midnight when he pulled himself to his feet with some help and tottered to the door. As he left the people in the room got up and others, appearing from nowhere, gathered round the door. They began to sing 'For he's a jolly good fellow' with a fine and touching fervour. When Winston tumbled to what was going on he gave them the victory sign twice, and then lurched, very slowly, to the lift. He was still giving the V-sign when he disappeared from their sight.

Yacht Christina, *March 9, 1960*

When we were gathering in the saloon of the yacht for luncheon Ari Onassis addressed a question to Winston across the length of the table. Winston waited till he had located the direction of the sound, then he looked at Onassis with dull, expressionless eyes. 'I can't hear you,' he muttered, but he did not ask his host to repeat his remarks. He did not seem to want to talk. However, tonight Winston came to life; he appeared quite alert and ready to join in the fun.

Some of the credit must certainly go to his host, 'Ari,' as Winston calls him, in place of his proper name Aristotle. He hardly takes his

766

eyes off his august guest; one moment he will fetch him a glass of whisky and the next, when Winston finds it cool on deck, he will tuck him up in a blanket. Once, noticing hairs on the collar of his coat, he hurried away to find a clothes brush. When we were in the games room, waiting for dinner, Ari pulled his chair nearer and held a teaspoonful of caviare to Winston's lips, as one feeds a baby. Three times he repeated this little ritual. Ari has learnt bezique in order to play with Winston. This afternoon Winston took £44 off him at baccarat. They will play cards for hours, for Ari is not a great talker, and when he does get going he probably does himself less than justice. There was some talk about Sherman Adams; how Ike had to drop him on account of his misdemeanours.

Winston: 'You must either wallop a man or vindicate him.'

Ari: 'Yes, Eisenhower just allowed him to resign. You must let your nearest and dearest go to hell when they are no longer any use to you.'

I have learnt by experience not to take that sort of stuff literally; it is only the way these tycoons unship their vanity—a kind of ruthless juggernaut pose. For my part, I believe Ari to be a kindly man, a lonely soul, for all his great wealth. A tycoon, I suppose, is a man with a money-making gift that has been left out of my composition, so that I cannot discern what is unusual in him. He can see a few moves ahead of us, and yet Onassis seems a very ordinary man to be set apart. What does Winston make of him? Is it the man or the yacht that attracts him?

Ari's face is dark, his long greying hair grows wild and seems naturally to form a coif above an inch of forehead. Below is a beak of a nose. When amused Ari bares his white teeth like a dog, to the accompaniment of a harsh laugh. He is a little fellow, not as tall as Winston when they stand side by side. He wears an old blue-black sweater, and nondescript faded grey trousers, and his small bare feet are generally thrust into canvas tennis shoes.

Martinique, March 17, 1960

Waves from the choppy sea washing the deck drove us in for luncheon. After the ladies had left us Winston, Ari and I were left alone at the table.

Ari: 'Sir Winston, Sir Winston, I think the Prefet is a nice man. I liked the Prefet. I told him that Martinique ought not to depend on sugar. They must attract American capital. They must do something. When nature provides a perfect climate and enough food people sleep all day and do nothing. If the climate in the North of England had been less harsh and the soil more fertile people would not have gone to sea so much. Necessity plays a big part in what men do.'

Winston: 'You need not talk so loud, it must be a great effort. I can hear quite well.'

Ari (*lowering his voice*): 'I'm sorry, Sir Winston. If people have to work very hard for subsistence, if they have to rub their hands to keep warm, they have no time for leisure. They cannot attend to the arts. Things of the spirit, things of the soul are left out of their lives. You told me, Sir Winston, your father died very young, if he had lived to your age you might not have had to struggle so hard. Your life would have been easier, and you might not have done what you did.'

Winston, who did not appear to be listening very attentively, broke in:

'No, we were very different people.'

Ari: 'Yes, of course, you were different, but you would not have been driven on by necessity. My mother died when I was six. If she had lived I might not have worked as hard as I have done.'

Winston: 'Would you like to play a little cards instead of talking philosophy?'

Ari: 'Not philosophy, but history.'

Winston: 'They are not very different. I like living on your ship.'

Ari: 'I wish you'd return on her. You would avoid the strain of flying.'

Winston: 'It is very kind of you to press your hospitality, but I feel I ought to return to London in time for my commitments. There is the Budget, and the ceremonies in connection with de Gaulle, and the Other Club dinner—a special, rather unique occasion. I want to keep alive links with the past. I do not feel I can brush aside anyhow my relations with people of high consequence, higgledy-piggledy. I do not want to do anything more; I have had enough of power, but I should not like to lose touch altogether with these occasions. I have reduced them to a minimum.'

Ari: 'You must decide, Sir Winston. You must do what you like.'

When they left the table Ari took the captain to Winston's cabin and made him sit on his bed while various speeds were tried—thirteen knots seemed to produce the least vibration.

A flying-fish landed on the deck when we were at dinner. Louis[1] brought it in, flapping its wings. 'Put it back quickly,' Winston broke in, 'or it will die.' Clemmie says that Winston is disappointed in Harold Macmillan. He thinks that Harold ought not to have gone

---

[1] Onassis's servant.

to Africa, encouraging the black men.[1] About midnight Ari made a move. Winston was not at all ready for sleep: 'Of course, if you want to leave me, pray do not let me detain you.'

March 23, 1960

Onassis said to Winston during lunch: 'You are in a meditative mood, not talkative.' Winston: 'My mind is very empty all day.'

Antigua

On the heights above a land-locked harbour, where Nelson made his dockyard, a house had been built for the Duke of Clarence, when he was in the Navy and stationed at Antigua. Hard by the house are the Shirley Heights, which were then held in force by the military. The forts have crumbled into ruins, and the house itself is used only on occasion by the Governor. There is left about the place an air of utter peace, a feeling that it belongs to another time. Even the cries of sea-birds and the sound of the sea far below do not reach the ear. But when I said to Winston that I would like to leave my bones in those parts, he stared at me as if to indicate that I said some very strange things.

Winston was deposited in a deep chair on the balcony, and I took my seat a little apart. After a time the creaking of the cane chair stopped. I could not tell under the great brim of his hat whether he was asleep; he was so still that I got up to see if he was all right. There seemed no one about, until at length his host appeared and, screwing up courage to approach him, said he wished to know if Sir Winston would care to rest. At this, when he understood what they were about, Winston attempted to get up from his chair; they hastened to his help and took him to a room where there was a low and very broad bed, on to which he flopped and soon fell asleep.

Perhaps an hour before sundown he was called and driven around the Heights until at last he came down to the harbour, where a little ceremony had been planned at sundown. The flag was hauled down and the band of the police beat the retreat. Thereafter, with much marching and counter-marching, they played familiar hymns, ending with 'Abide with me, fast falls the eventide,' and 'The day Thou gavest, Lord, is ended.' The 'Nunc Dimittis' atmosphere that hung over the proceedings was no doubt lost on Winston, who did not leave his car. He was put out. He had wanted to be taken over Nelson's dockyard. After Napoleon, Nelson has been his idol. And

[1] During his African tour (January–February, 1960) Macmillan made his 'Wind of Change' speech to the South African Parliament on February 3, in which he asserted the British Government's opposition to Apartheid.

he could not understand why they had driven him all round the place and left no time for this. When the band had done Winston was taken back to the yacht, where he went to his cabin.

After dinner Clemmie said firmly that she was too tired for a film and was going to bed. But Winston declared that he was not sleepy and would like to sit on deck. He persuaded Dorothy to join him. She began to sing to them: first 'Forty Years On,' and then such tunes of his Victorian youth as she had picked up from me. Each of the guests with him could hum some old snatch: 'Daisy, Daisy,' 'Tit Willow,' 'Tipperary,' 'Tarara Boom-de-ay,' 'The Eton Boating Song' and, of course, his favourite 'Take a Pair of Sparkling Eyes.' Winston joined in, his eye brightened, his face lit up, he seemed for a moment to recover his old spirits. When at length they helped him to his cabin he kept humming and singing while his clothes were taken off.

*

It is eleven years since the summer of 1949 when Winston received a tap on the shoulder—a notice to quit. Moreover, in that space of time the circulation in his head had faltered many times; old age, always an affliction, had become to him a source of embarrassment— in his own words, a feeble substitute for life. My diary for those years, five of them during his retirement, is in part a sad record of the advancing signs of decay, a catalogue of lamentations over faculties that had gone.

I have explained in the preface why I thought it right to recount the stages of his decline as long as he possessed political power, and even afterwards when his advice was still sought. But there is no point in continuing the story beyond the time when it ceases to be of any historical significance. I have therefore ended it in 1960, five years before his death.

Chapter seventy-one

The reason why

What is the ultimate secret of Winston Churchill's mastery over men? That is the kind of problem which confronted Lytton Strachey when he wrote the life of Queen Victoria—for the two cases are curiously alike. The underlying element of absurdity in the old Queen's relations with Disraeli when he was her Prime Minister, and again in the matter of her body-servant, John Brown; her lofty contempt for the dictates of wisdom and even prudence in the crisis over the Ladies of the Bedchamber; her irresponsible pressure on her Ministers to declare war on Russia—it was on such things that Strachey fastened cruelly, and in his book they are exploited ruthlessly. He made it appear that her despotic temper was always threatening to precipitate a constitutional crisis or a foreign war.

Nor was Strachey more merciful to the indiscipline of her literary style, and the quotations from the *Leaves from a Journal of Our Life in the Highlands*, with their exclamation marks and underlining, invite our ridicule. Indeed, in a sense, she never seems to have grown up; the striking advances in industry and science during her reign left her quite untouched—it was as if they had never happened; while the social changes of her time, the emancipation of women and the like, only excited her violent disapproval.

We were amused, but somehow we were not altogether convinced. Then, just when the catalogue of her little absurdities was complete, it seemed to occur to Strachey that this was not the whole story, that the portrait had somehow got out of focus. He must begin again, and at that point, without further ado, he surrendered unconditionally to the terrific force of Queen Victoria's overwhelming personality. The mocking sounds were heard no more, he was content to offer meekly an explanation of the last years of apotheosis. The mordant pen scratched away until at last it had uncovered, almost by accident as it seemed, the old Queen, so that she appeared to our astonished gaze more than life-size.

She had become a legend, a symbol of her subjects' imperial power and greatness, until they saw her only through a mist of awe and reverence. And yet, through the mist, the outlines of her character were firm and clear to her humblest subject. The splendid figure fed and satisfied their imagination. Her writings, Strachey affirms, touched the hearts of the people by their simple, unaffected picture of an unsullied home life, and her messages to the nation convinced everyone of her transparent sincerity. She was indeed so truthful, so single-minded, that concealment of her thoughts was impossible. Why should she be reserved, what had she to hide? Without reticence of any kind, she talked as she wrote, all out. As we put down Strachey's book we feel that we have been permitted to see her as her people saw her, but in truth the mystery remains. For sincerity does not intimidate experienced Ministers of State. Nor, by calling her a symbol, does Strachey explain why her son in his fiftieth year stood behind a pillar, wiping the sweat from his brow, till he could pluck up courage to ask his mother if she would forgive him for being late for dinner.

I suppose that one day somebody will write the same kind of book about Winston Churchill, and he, too, may be baffled by the improbable story. At the outset he is bound to be sceptical. Here was a man who had spent a long life in politics, and yet it was said on every side that he had never known what the ordinary voter was thinking; their lives remained apart from his life. He was, too, positively Victorian in his inability to keep in step with the changing times. Victoria had been disturbed by Gladstone's passion for reform, and now Winston Churchill found himself condemned to live in an atmosphere of interminable change. It made him angry, he could see no sense in this restless search for new methods. It was not so much that change in itself was undesirable; in Churchill's eyes it was decidedly improper. It may seem incredible in years to come that anyone so aloof, so out of sympathy with the spirit of the times, could have won the hearts of a democracy. And for that matter he had marched impudently up to the frontiers of old age baulked of his heart's desire. It took a world war to overcome the handicap and make him at long last the First Minister of the Crown.

The historian will find, however, in memoir after memoir, incontrovertible evidence that in 1940, when England was without arms and naked to invasion, Winston Churchill inspired all manner of men with his own steadfast faith in victory. He will be told how, as defeat receded and victory appeared on the horizon, the story of that indomitable man captured the imagination of his countrymen. Churchill became a 'character,' and he himself was not unwilling to lend a hand in touching up the picture, for none knew better that the public must see clearly the outlines of their heroes. That he mispronounced 'Nazi' as 'Narzi' on the air was not perhaps entirely an accident; at any rate, his vast audience waited for it and smiled affectionately when it came. They would have missed the cigar and the victory sign and the scowl of defiance, and his hats, which were different from other people's, and the siren suit. He had in truth become a legend. Lytton Strachey, when he set out to explain Queen Victoria's hold over her people, singled out her sincerity as her most outstanding virtue. I have likened Winston Churchill to Queen Victoria, and sincerity is the one quality I would have chosen as most typical of him.

He was indeed the most truthful of politicians. No doubt it is an admirable quality. But it does not explain why grown men stood in awe of that formidable personality—he seemed to frighten them. Even to rouse him from his mid-afternoon sleep was something of an adventure. In matters of great consequence he often had his way without even a show of opposition.

In the great affair of the conduct of the war it must have been difficult, no doubt, to challenge his opinion, based as it was on a mastery of military detail which no other member of the Cabinet possessed. But whatever the issue, no matter who were the disputants, he was always in complete command.

The part might have been made for him. His attitude to himself, as Strachey said of Queen Victoria, was positively regal; he had an overwhelming sense of his own position as the First Minister of the Crown. He was beyond the law. Victoria had continued to correspond with Lord Melbourne when Peel became her Prime Minister, and Winston Churchill composed a speech for the King after Mr. Attlee had succeeded him as Prime Minister. Like Victoria, his despotic temper was always getting him into trouble, and it is interesting to compare her violent telegram to Gladstone after Gordon's death with Winston Churchill's angry message to the Prime Minister of Australia, who had become critical of British strategy.

But there is this difference—and it is not without significance—Victoria sent her telegram as it stood and Churchill toned his down. He was persuaded to revise his strictures on Curtin, whereas Victoria did not suffer anyone to edit her communications. No one should dictate to her when she felt so strongly and *knew* she was right. On the other hand, if Victoria often imposed her will on others, unchecked by any principle, Winston Churchill did what he wanted in the war years to an extent the old Queen would have envied. No one could influence him; if he was reproved he only grew impatient. When criticism became unusually searching, Queen Victoria would threaten to abdicate, while Winston Churchill was content to ask the House of Commons for another vote of confidence. That it should ever be implied that the Queen had done anything wrong seemed to her very wicked, while the Prime Minister, during the war, found it difficult to understand, and impossible to forgive, any patriotic and decent-minded Englishman who was critical of his policy.

Why did the country give him his head in this manner? How came it that this man, who in time of peace had been an isolated figure, trusted by no party, was, broadly speaking, allowed in the war to do as he pleased? In Smuts's words he was 'the one indispensable man.' There was in him something that was not to be found in other men. He was not, I think, a sage. He does not seem to have been a soldier of genius. He was not, perhaps, a born administrator. There is left only an extraordinary concentration on one purpose—it amounted to an obsession—on victory, whatever it might cost. It was that single-mindedness which gave him his incomparable power during the war. It is, according to William James,[1] the essential factor in greatness, for the man of genius differs from ordinary men not in any innate quality of the brain, but in the aims and purposes on which he concentrates and in the degree of concentration which he manages to achieve. This single-mindedness of Winston Churchill was admired in the First World War. Maynard Keynes, writing of *The World Crisis*, thought that his 'intense absorption of intellectual interest and elemental emotion in what is for the moment the matter in hand' was his best quality.[2]

In other times that same quality had not been at all admired. Men called it self-will then, and said he had inherited it from his father, who was wayward from boyhood, and that one day it would end his political career, as it ended his father's. It had certainly been a terrible handicap to his political progress before the war, leaving him a lonely figure in the turmoil and riot of politics. He had done what he liked all his life, and he had paid in full measure for his liberty. Men's trust in his judgment was sapped by his exhibitions of indiscipline. They thought of him as incalculable and indeed

[1] That William James's words are to the point is shown by the fact that Lady Violet Bonham Carter made the same point in *Winston Churchill as I knew him*. It used to be my custom to enlarge on this in my addresses to the Staff College on morale.

[2] J. M. Keynes, *Essays in Biography*.

774

wholly unaccountable in the things he said and did. They certainly were not prepared to let him have his own way. Indeed, if he had died in 1939, at the age of sixty-five, he would, perhaps, have been accounted a brilliant failure, a politician without a party, without power, without influence.

But when war came this life-long handicap was transformed into a fixed purpose that put heart into the nation. Winston Churchill's lonely supremacy during those years was never in question.

Could it be that his secret did not work in peace? Victoria dominated everyone who came into her presence without any assistance from war emotions, and I thought, when I first knew him, that this was also true of Winston Churchill. But did he in fact dominate men before the war? Of course, he had always been a force in public life. As far back as Mr. Asquith's Cabinet, he had, according to Lord Samuel, considerable influence with his Liberal colleagues, while his gift for pungent phrases was respected by the Tories. He had always been pugnacious and assertive, because he was built in that fashion. But it appears from such evidence as I can collect from his contemporaries that he did not dominate men before the war. Even that bull-dog look of strength and defiance is not to be found in photographs taken before the war; it was just a piece of war equipment.

Was there something, then, in the emotions kindled by a sense of danger, a change in the mood of the people perhaps, that alone made it possible for Winston Churchill to govern as a dictator, for in the war that was, in effect, what he became? I am not thinking of the herd instinct, for I do not set out to explain why millions who had never met him took him to their hearts. It is no part of my purpose to try to analyse the sources of those fugitive loyalties that bind a nation to its war-time leaders. Yet those loyalties are everywhere recognized; war itself creates a craving in the herd for a leader, and if the nation is sound at heart, the greater the peril, the more united it will be behind him, whether he be Lloyd George or Clemenceau or another made for the hour. I am thinking of something more subtle, something over and beyond the common reaction of a race in danger, something perhaps peculiar to the country's attitude to Churchill.

Besides, the case was unusual. Stanley Baldwin had prepared the country for Winston Churchill. Baldwin, it was generally thought, had left the nation without defences in order to win an election. Everywhere men were yearning for a man who would tell them the truth, however unpalatable; they were sick of politicians. In Churchill they surely found the man they were seeking.

Churchill himself has described this change in the temper of a nation at war, for which I have been fumbling, when he wrote of Lawrence: 'The fury of the Great War raised the pitch of life to the Lawrence standard. The multitudes were swept forward till their pace was the same as his.'[1] Perhaps that was also true of Winston Churchill.

It is not, however, the whole story. There was a change in the man himself—an extraordinary sense of mission appeared to take possession of him. He seemed to shed all thought of himself. In truth, he became a dedicated man. I remember he once said to me: 'This cannot be accident, it must be design. I was kept for this job.' I do not mean, of course, that his faith in himself, his feeling that he was an appointed instrument, was a religious state. Winston was not a modern Joan of Arc, exalted and inspired by voices from God. Lincoln, John Masefield told me, came to dominate his Cabinet by sheer moral force, though there was not a man in it who did not believe himself to be more intelligent and better educated than Lincoln. Masefield had a strange fancy that there was a physical element in his supremacy, for it was said of Lincoln that he could hold up a barrel and drink from the bung-hole. Likewise, during the war there were men and women—their stories are enshrined in the resistance movements of the occupied countries—who were lifted above the anguish of torture and the fear of death by a living faith in God. But Winston Churchill was not built on that rock. It was not with him a religion but rather a state of heightened perception, generated by the stir and fervour of the hour. Churchill, of course, did not reason in that way; his mind was not in any way analytical. If it had been, I should not be pummelling my wits to explain his mastery over men.

[1] Winston S. Churchill, *Great Contemporaries* (Butterworth, 1937).

Chapter seventy-two

Taking measurements

In the First War, Maynard Keynes singled out as Winston's shining virtue his intense concentration on the matter in hand. But it was because no one could match the overwhelming force of his personality that he got his way with his countrymen during the Second War.

A man of many years told me that in his experience he had encountered two, perhaps three, men who could intimidate their fellows. At the end of my life I can think of one man only who appeared to frighten other men—Winston Churchill—and in his case only in time of war. I can recall, but I cannot explain.

If Winston's virtues were more than life-size his faults were made to scale. He was not like other men. He could do nothing in moderation. Distrust of his judgment was indeed general before the war. Attlee, a man of sober speech, summed it up:

'Fifty per cent of Winston is genius, fifty per cent bloody fool. He will behave like a child.'

Lord Waverley, who had seen him at work over many years, went further:

'Someone must hold his hand or he will blunder.'

Perhaps it was the way his mind worked that made his mental processes as wayward and eccentric as those of his father. It was a mind open to ideas but often closed to reason; a mind not judicial in any sense, not logical, not analytical. He reached his conclusions by a process of intuition. Alanbrooke fretted because Winston would never reason anything out: 'He just flits from one idea to another like a butterfly.' It was, I suppose, the mind of an artist.

It did not help that he was self-educated. He got nothing out of Harrow, he grieved that he was not sent to a university. He did not at any time submit to an intellectual discipline that might have engrained in him the importance of accuracy and the advantage of systematic study. His reading virtually ceased when he went into politics; after that, he explained to me, he could not find time to read books. Winston himself was conscious of the gaps in his knowledge.

Perhaps his pugnacity led him astray. He loved a fight and looked forward to Questions in the House, enjoying the back-chat. He was still, at heart, a red-haired urchin cocking a snook at anyone who got in his way.

Men of affairs measure their steps by the climate of public opinion. But Winston was only a poor student of human nature. It is the final paradox of his case that he stands apart in English public life, towering over his contemporaries, in spite of his ignorance of human behaviour, which is, after all, what politics are about.

To tot up the items on the debit side would serve no purpose. Among his countrymen there was no one after the war who wanted to hear about his imperfections. After all, Winston had been right when it really mattered. They sensed that his greatness was not built on the exercise of his reason.

My story is about the years of conflict. Others will tell in good time of the young Winston, before he came in for the punishment of the political world and was changed by power and his will sapped by old age and disease.

Meanwhile one is conscious of a certain largeness of soul, a freedom from envy of others that I count the brightest jewel in his crown. Lord Rosebery, writing of Winston's father, claimed this as 'a real mark of superiority.' The House of Commons, which is not often wrong in the measurement of its members, gave him magnanimity. These are rare virtues in a politician, and they were not tarnished by fifty years spent in the mixed business of politics.

If he was not given to self-criticism, he was not vain. If he was selfish and self-centred, he was not worldly. It fell to Winston Churchill in the early part of the war, when Britain was alone, to make, unaided, momentous decisions which depended less on a nice balancing of strategic reasons, and more on an invincible disdain for what is weak and in itself wrong. His name will on that account always be invested in the history of the race with a certain moral grandeur.

*

In the inner world of make-believe in which Winston found reality there was no place for a weakling. He felt that he was born to govern men. The trouble was that he did not seem designed by nature for the part. At school he was an underling, bullied and beaten. He grew up full of apprehension and he spoke with a stutter. But from the beginning, the will to conquer was there. 'Never'—

they were his own words—'never give in.' There followed years of struggle and public neglect. But before the outbreak of the First World War he had learnt to disguise his natural apprehension and had managed to extirpate bouts of depression from his system.

Winston found it easier to rid himself of his inborn disabilities than to forge a weapon that would bring him personal distinction. Not that the actual shape of the weapon was in doubt. He discovered at Harrow, where he used to write essays for other boys, that he had a certain aptitude for the handling of words; he decided that he must cultivate this gift if he was to make anything of his life.

That was how he began that long apprenticeship to the art of arranging the right words in their proper order, which, with the exercise of power, was to fill his days. He was prepared to go to great pains in learning to use his tools. He got to know Gibbon almost by heart. What impressed Winston about Gibbon was not what he said, but how he said it. It was noticed about this time that this preoccupation with the forms of speech was reflected in his own sayings. These were admirable not for sagacity, not for penetration of thought, but rather for a certain adroitness of phrasing.

Winston was a competitive animal, and the desire to excel soon came to dominate his days. Already before the outbreak of war in 1939 his books had brought him a considerable measure of success. *Lord Randolph Churchill* in two volumes, *Marlborough* in three and *The World Crisis* in four had established his position as an historian. Some of his professional brethren had, it is true, reservations. The trouble was that he had not the time, apart from skimming a few manuscripts, to get up the European background of Marlborough and Queen Anne. He got, of course, the right people to brief him and to keep him supplied with material, but it was not the same thing as if he had done the work himself.

He set out, according to his critics, to write history from a personal angle, about himself or about one of his forebears. One wonders whether, if the personal slant had been wanting, Winston would have troubled to write history. He had no bias against Whig or Tory, like Macaulay. But there emerged a decided preference for a certain type of character, the pattern of the men he found congenial in his own life—Max Beaverbrook, F. E. Smith, Lloyd George—on the whole an amoral lot in their outlook. So Marlborough's moral lapses are brushed aside as those of a young cockerel. After all, was he not supreme in the two great arts of love and war?

The generality had no reservations; they found him immensely readable. He had indeed been born with a pen in his hand. He wrote with intense conviction of the exploits of his father, of his vindication of the Great Duke, and for that matter, of his own share in great events. Perhaps the truth can be found in between. Winston was a master of military and political narrative, but events had to march in the direction his case required.

When, however, Winston stood up to speak, his assurance evaporated. His heart raced and he had to use his will to still his nerves. If he was a born writer, he was very far from being a natural speaker. Nor did time make things easier. To the end of his working days he would be on edge until he was satisfied that a speech had not misfired. He had started life with one governing purpose: one day he would be an orator. How far had he achieved his end by 1939? I have recorded his answer in another place. He would not have it that he was an orator. 'It is not true,' he grunted. 'When that fellow Bevan gets up he does not know what he is going to say and where he will end. But I have every word typed in front of me.' There was a long pause. 'An orator must be spontaneous.'

If Winston was thinking of his speeches before the war I would not quarrel with him. He was never wanting in application, and in the early years of Asquith's Government his industry in the preparation of his speeches paid steady dividends. He counted in the Government of 1906, Lord Samuel told me, because of his flair for phrase-making, which made him an electoral asset. Later, when he called Ramsay MacDonald 'a boneless wonder,' the ridicule stuck. Why did this skill, which in 1906 promised to make his political fortune, bring, before the war, such modest returns?

The first duty of an orator, Hazlitt wrote, is to echo back the feelings of his audience. But Winston had no idea what was going on in their minds. He said a piece. It was a kind of one-way traffic, he thought more of the sound of his words than of their effect on his audience. It was rather a cold-blooded business, I suppose, the words picked so deliberately as in some fine balancing act, the sentences built up with cool deliberation in his own bedroom. The speech from beginning to end had been contrived beforehand, every word typed out, the very pauses marked in the script. Even his expression as he mouthed his carefully polished periods had been observed and studied before the looking-glass.

G. M. Young has lit upon a passage which makes my point.

'The government,' Winston said, 'cannot make up their mind, or they cannot get the Prime Minister to make up his mind. So they go on in strange paradox, decided only to be undecided, resolved to be irresolute, adamant for drift, solid for fluidity, all-powerful to be impotent.'[1]

[1] G. M. Young, *Stanley Baldwin*, p. 228.

It was calculated speech, handed down to him by his father. It cannot be called oratory.

No doubt the eccentricity of his judgment, another paternal gift, contributed to the lack of confidence of his countrymen. They were bewildered; they did not know what he might do next. They found him quite unaccountable, in a measure irresponsible. It is the tale of a preacher without a text. The fact is that Winston's story before the war is the chronicle of a self-centred man making his plans in order to win personal renown. He worked in the political field and must be judged by political standards. In the House of Commons he had few friends. No party wanted him. If he had died before the war he would have been accounted a brilliant failure.

*

Then came the war. Winston, unlike his father, was given another chance. This he took with both hands. But before I try to measure the impact of the 1940 speeches let us consider what Winston meant to the nation in the doubtful days after Dunkirk. Much well-intentioned nonsense has been written about him; indeed, the rich, earthy, Falstaffian figure has been so togged up that he is barely recognizable.

Norman Brook speaks with care, and this is what he said to me: 'If it had not been for Winston, anything might have happened after Dunkirk. While he was there, bargaining with Hitler was out of the question, a separate peace unthinkable.' At another time Portal spoke to me of Winston's services to the country in 1940. 'They say there was no danger that we should have made peace with Hitler. I am not so sure. Without Winston we might have.'

He was indeed made for the hour. In the extraordinary circumstances of 1940, with the hopeless inequality of Germany and Britain —or so it seemed—we needed a very unreasonable man at the top. If Winston had been a reasonable man he would not have taken the line he did; if he had been a man of sound judgment he might have considered it his duty to act differently. A sage would have been out of his element in 1940; we got instead another Joan of Arc.

It was by the 1940 speeches that Winston reached the hearts and minds of the people. Their impact depended in part on a change in the mood of the country. The England that yearned for peace, almost at any cost it seemed, was forgotten, and in men's minds there welled up a stubborn will to resist 'the monstrous tyranny of that wicked man.' In the P.M.'s words, they would rather see the country a shambles than give in to Hitler. They wanted to be told the truth. They would rather hear the worst. And the Prime Minister hurled it at them like great hunks of bleeding meat.

Winston was changed too. He became a man with a mission; absorbed in the conduct of the struggle. All other things were put away. Oliver Franks, a cool, analytic mind, spoke of him as a spiritual force. 'He gave us faith. There was in him a demonic element as in Calvin and Luther. Churchill became a prophet.'

We owe to Lord Beaverbrook a rather different interpretation. He liked to tilt at what he called highfalutin' motives. Churchill, he said, saw in 1940 that the country was looking for a symbol of defiance, and Churchill was not at all averse to giving them what they wanted. Winston, it is true, is always unconsciously playing a part. The reader may recall that when he was about to make his first public appearance at Doncaster, after his long illness in 1953, I prayed him not to get upset if the Yorkshire crowd rose to him. He said scornfully, 'That's not what makes me emotional. It's when I am Joan of Arc that I get excited.' It was his favourite part, and when he was offered the role in the spring of 1940 he proved to be word-perfect.

Chatham's enemies complained that he was a more consummate actor than Garrick. His greatest feats of oratory, they asserted, were not more than histrionic triumphs. Rosebery dismissed their carping with contempt. Chatham, he said, was swept by a great gust of passion which carried him away. That Winston was profoundly moved by the threat to England's survival is not in question, but I believe that his appeal to his countrymen to fight it out was made more passionate by his sense of the drama of this hour in history.

These famous speeches were not in fact shaped as orations, often they were no more than a business statement to the House of Commons, perhaps on the conduct of the war; it was all plain and unadorned. And then, as the Prime Minister came to the end of his script a surge of feeling that he had kept in check flooded his being, so that he began to speak in words that have become part of the common speech.

Will these speeches be read in other times? I do not say that they will survive as such--they are not like a speech of Burke, part of our literary heritage—but it is my belief that fragments of them, the few words containing his testament of faith, will be passed down reverently, as Nelson's words are known. And even if his words are forgotten, the legend of the great utterances may persist, as Chatham's unrecorded eloquence has become a matter of faith. Without them Winston cannot be fully understood. For here his nature was revealed. After all, it can hardly have been an accident that Hazlitt,

LORD MORAN OUTSIDE 28 HYDE PARK GATE

writing on Pitt's oratory, calls his essay: 'On the Character of Lord Chatham.'

One day at Chartwell Winston gave me a book containing his 1940 speeches. 'You might like to read them, Charles.' I reminded him how the genius of Thomas Gray had been set free by the death of his friend, West, and how for a time he had poured forth his grief in poem after poem. 'Yes,' Winston mused, 'for a time, but the inspiration did not last,' and he added sadly, 'It did not return.' He knew that it was like that with him. As the danger passed, the wave of emotion began to ebb; his work was done.

The war, where Winston is concerned, fell into two parts; in the period when England was alone, when there was no strategy to speak of, when it was just a struggle for survival, he will take his place by the side of Chatham as a great War Minister. No one else, as Portal said, could have done what he did then.

When, however, America entered the war, and planning began to come into the picture, it was found that his buoyant optimism—he could see only victory—had in a sense become a handicap. 'Don't raise difficulties,' he kept saying to his soldiers. He meant, 'Don't take adverse factors into account if they do not fit into your plans.' He was certain that everything would come out all right if only they went ahead. Marshall complained that Winston did not think like a soldier. 'His planning,' he added with an affectionate smile, 'was all wishing and guessing.'

And yet, when we look back we see that Winston was often right in his clashes with the President about the conduct of the war. It was Winston who wanted to postpone the Second Front until the American infantry were battle-worthy. It was Winston who wanted to avoid costly frontal attacks on the Italian Front by flanking operations, when America would not give him the landing craft. And if he was at first taken in by Stalin, he woke to the Russian designs before most people. Roosevelt never did: he was certain that he understood Stalin and that no one else did. If Stalin was given all he asked for, Roosevelt was sure that he would help to build a better world after the war. Winston was as certain that the President had invented a Russia that did not exist. But he could do nothing. He had to watch Stalin redraw the map of Europe with Roosevelt's blessing.

One thing Winston could do: he could prevent Greece from sharing the fate of the other satellites. He would salvage her from the wreck of his plans. So he sent General Scobie's Army into Athens.

'Winston was often right,' according to F. E. Smith, Winston's closest friend, 'but when he was wrong, well, my God.' He would hatch a wild plan which, Marshall told me, might have ended in a catastrophe. It was one of the tasks of the Combined Chiefs of Staff to wean Winston from these 'wild-cat schemes.'

It sometimes appeared that the schemes were left undigested because the P.M. had no time to think out their broad strategic consequences. As the months went by he allowed himself to become more and more engrossed in the details of operations, so that there was little time left for anything else. Important questions of policy were put aside without a thought. Even when victory was in sight, and he was asked at Quebec about his plans for the future of Germany he retorted impatiently: 'That can stand over until the end of the war.' While at Teheran in December, 1943, when Stalin wanted to discuss the future of Poland, the P.M. replied that it had not been considered by the Cabinet. In consequence, when the P.M. was ready to plead for the Poles during his visit to Moscow in October, 1944, Stalin was in a position to dictate his own terms.

This preoccupation with the detail of operations led to friction with his Generals. Winston was without the first attribute of a good administrator, namely the ability to pick the right man and then to let him get on with the job. He had to have his say in the preparations for an offensive, and in fixing the exact date of an attack. Wavell, Dill and Auchinleck in turn lost their self-confidence under the barrage of directives and were broken or discarded. Winston himself was broken by the unending grind, in the sense that in the last year of the war he was not half the man he had been in 1940. Once when I was much concerned with the manner in which he was dissipating his dwindling resources, one of his entourage told me with an affectionate smile that the P.M. had been giving his attention to the shape of a guardsman's hat. No one wanted to criticize the man who had saved the country in 1940. After all, it was not his judgment but his spirit that rallied the nation after Dunkirk. The instinct of the people was no doubt sound. Winston was a war winner because he animated the nation, keeping everyone on their toes and holding them to the task in hand; because with the help of three selfless men as Chiefs of Staff he prevented friction between the three Services and because, backed by Ernest Bevin, he kept Labour sweet. It was, in the main, Winston's doing that political controversy was stilled until, with victory in sight in the last months of the war, the Labour Party began to think of the coming election.

That he was not always so successful in his dealings with President Roosevelt was not primarily his fault; a more sagacious student of human nature than Winston might have been baffled by that ambiguous character. At first all went well. In the months before

America came into the war his wise handling of the President led to a friendly feeling in the White House towards a struggling Britain, and in Washington, after Pearl Harbour, to our astonished gaze a new Winston appeared. He would listen for hours—and listening did not come easily to him—to stories he had heard before. His patience—and it was not his most obvious virtue—never seemed to give out. I was in no way surprised when Hopkins told me that the President was impressed by the Prime Minister's grasp of military detail.

When things began to go wrong I cannot tell. As America came to make all the decisions that mattered and to take over the control of operations, the P.M. became sorely worried about the future. He was sure that he knew how the war could be won, and now that England's survival was no longer at stake he felt free to speak plainly about his misgivings. As time passed, it was noticed that he got more and more outspoken.

It was in the last year of the war, during the occupation of Athens by our troops, that things came to a head. There were angry exchanges between the President and the Prime Minister, and our relations with the White House became very strained.

Throughout these events, Winston was moved only by a growing concern about the conduct of the war; there was nothing personal in his differences with the President. He always maintained that Franklin Roosevelt was a very great man, and became angry when he heard criticism.

The President's feelings towards Winston were rather more complicated. To try to unravel them I shall turn to a disturbing entry in my diary of those months. Hopkins, in a temper, blurted out that it did not seem just to the President that Winston should take all the credit as leader of the Free World. Roosevelt had become jealous of Winston. Lord Halifax confirmed this when I put a direct question to him. Marshall told me about that time that the President did not look forward to Winston's visits to the White House. Winston would embark on endless discussions about his strategy, and he was always talking about the British Empire.

The sad story ended at Yalta, where Winston became impatient with the President's apathy and indifference. He did not seem to realize that Roosevelt was a very sick man.

*

The end of the war found Winston spent. 'Before the election,' Alanbrooke told me, 'I could not get him to decide anything. I said:

785

"You must decide, you must choose." Winston said to me; "I cannot decide. I cannot make up my mind."'

At the time I put this down to what he had been through. When in 1945 we flew from Potsdam to London to hear the result of the election we were certain of victory. 'It was a big blow,' Winston confided to me. Coming so soon after the strain of the war years, it seemed to light up the Churchill melancholia. I did not at once tumble to the truth: Winston was sliding almost imperceptibly into old age.

Clemmie, I think, had noticed that he was ageing. She wanted him to give up politics. If she was thinking of his reputation, it was indeed the time to go. For the ten years that followed added little to his stature.

However, it was not Winston's advancing years that made him ineffective as Leader of the Opposition. At Fulton and at Zürich when there was danger from without he was still a sure guide, and his words of warning went round the world. The truth was that his heart was not in the job. He had never been happy out of office, and as the months passed he found it more and more difficult to persuade himself that he was serving a useful purpose sitting on the Front Opposition bench. 'I feel I could do things,' he said to me in January, 1946, 'but there is nothing to be done.' When Lord Camrose found him in this mood he pressed him to get on with his book so that the first volume might be published by 1947; he was surprised when Winston did not demur.

Perhaps it was already too late. It may be that he was too old to enter into the rhythm of a book in six volumes. Five of the six volumes of *The Second World War* were, it is true, written when Winston was still in opposition. If, however, the dates at the end of each preface are set besides the dates of his four strokes or cerebral storms it will be seen that the book was written under difficulties. They are as follows:

March, 1948	Vol. I.	THE GATHERING STORM
January, 1949	Vol. II.	THEIR FINEST HOUR
August, 1949	*Stroke at Monte Carlo*	
January, 1950	Vol. III.	THE GRAND ALLIANCE
February, 1950	*Disturbance of cerebral circulation*	
September, 1950	Vol. IV.	THE HINGE OF FATE
September, 1951	Vol. V.	CLOSING THE RING
July, 1952	*Stroke*	
June, 1953	*Stroke*	
September, 1953	Vol. VI.	TRIUMPH AND TRAGEDY

The first and second volumes were written before the first stroke in 1949, but a stroke is, after all, only the outward sign of a hardening of the arteries in the head, which had been going on for a long time. If the tag is true that a man is as old as his arteries, then Winston was an old man before he began writing the *The Second World War*. On September 1, 1951, he signed the preface to the fifth volume, the book was finished—or so it seemed—and he could put down his pen for good.

On the last day of October he crawled back into No. 10 Downing Street with a majority of seventeen over all other Parties. He had expected to do better, but it was said in the Private Office that he was relieved to be once more in command. No one could explain this mood. After all that had gone before, everything was bound to be an anti-climax. Besides, at the end of the month he would be seventy-seven years of age and a sick man at that; twice already he had been warned that the circulation in his head was in a poor way. 'How long do you give me?' he demanded. And when I did not answer he owned that he was not so sure that he would be able to see things through. The Tories shared his misgivings. It was whispered that he was too old to govern and that he would never take advice.

Winston was indeed greatly changed. The old capacity for work had gone, and with it much of his self-confidence. He forgot figures. Everything had become an effort. Moreover, he was confronted by a whole series of unfamiliar problems. The country appeared to be nearly bankrupt. The situation, he kept repeating, was bewildering. Physically, too, he was changed; he walked like an old man.

In 1952 there was another disturbance of the cerebral circulation. After this it was noticed in the Office that he was not doing his work. He did not want to be bothered by anything; he was living in the past and he hated change. To us it had become plain that he belonged to another time.

But he was not to go without a fight. In June, 1953, he was stricken down, paralysed and could not move in bed. For a time it seemed that he might not come through. But on the fifth day, when most men in that plight are only fearful that they may be going to die, Winston's mind was completely taken up with his plans for fighting his way back into the House of Commons. Lying on his back he planned the steps that he must take to convince the Tories that he was fit to lead the Party. Before each hurdle there was the same numbing anxiety whether he would bring it off. If he failed he knew that it was the end of everything. He knew too that the odds were against him. But he did not falter. In the struggle to retain power Winston was fighting for his own hand, without the support of numbers, in defiance of the Party, without friends. It was his purpose to pit the strength of his will against the weakness of the flesh. This he did with a fine disregard for consequences, a complete indifference to death, so that I was drawn to him.

The year that followed was rather a sad affair for Winston's friends. It had become plain to the Party that he was no longer fit to carry out his duties as Prime Minister. Only the astonishing tenacity of the man was left. His family and his friends did what they could to get him to resign. There seemed to them no reason now for clinging to office. But he would not listen. If he went, pray what would he do? He could not bear to give up power: there would be no purpose left in life. It was only when Harold Macmillan made his position untenable that Winston recognized that he must go.

*

On April 5, 1955, Winston resigned. Ten years later he died, in his ninety-first year. To do nothing day after day, when he had done so much, is a searching test of character, and it found Winston's will undermined by age and infirmity.

After all, a good deal was asked of him. His father, Lord Randolph, had died by inches in public, but the nature of his malady left him with the illusion that he had never been so well or spoken more effectively. Winston was less fortunate. He watched helpless and in despair the creeping paralysis in his faculties. 'I made a fool of myself,' he said after a visitor had gone. 'You know, Charles, it is the state of my mind that troubles me.'

As the years went by he gave up reading. He seldom spoke, and when he did it was difficult to follow what he said. He did not seem to know his friends. We would rise to our feet as he came into the room, supported under the arms by his nurses. As they pushed him to his chair his feet made a slapping sound on the floor. Very small, almost shrunken, he appeared huddled up in the depths of a big chair. There he sat through the afternoon hours, staring into the fire, giving it a prod with his stick when the room felt cold.

If, in those sad years of mounting decrepitude, he seemed to be fearful of the future of mankind and grew to hate change and became intolerant of criticism; if he did not try to hide his distaste for what was left to him of life, I cannot forget the anguish of that time 'when he was the chief mourner at his own protracted funeral.'[1]

Winston's eightieth birthday had brought him the homage of the free world, but when at the end of November, in the year 1964, he came to the great age of ninety, the long chronicle of boredom and

[1] Lord Rosebery, *Lord Randolph Churchill*, p. 181.

despair was hardly broken by the celebrations, which were only a half-hearted affair. Those near to him made suitable noises, but they knew that it was all make-believe, and that he did not wish to live. Christmas brought excited grandchildren to see their grandfather before being despatched to the pantomime. They came to him in turn and kissed him, and it may be that he knew what it was all about.

A time was coming when it was noticed that he did not like to be left alone. One day, as I was taking my leave, he put his hand on mine mumbling, 'Don't be too long, my dear, before you come again.' In the great days when I could help him he had not said as much. I think he was a lonely man, as I suppose he had been always.

Early in January, 1965 there was a change. He still seemed to know me, but he was drowsy and confused. At half-past eleven in the morning of January 10 Howells telephoned to me. He did not think Sir Winston was so well. He could not rouse him. I found him propped up by pillows in his bed, his head bent forward, his hands laid out on the sheet, arranged for death. I lifted his left arm, and when I let it go it fell to the bed. I could not feel a pulse. His hands were cold and he was blue about the mouth. I thought it wise to warn the public in my bulletin that he had had another stroke and that his condition was critical.

But Winston had never taken orders from anyone. He had always been unpredictable; he was to be like that to the end. Day after day I was persuaded that he would be gone before the morning, but when the morning came he was still there. In bulletin after bulletin I felt I must prepare the public for his passing, until I was at a loss what to say.

From time to time the door of the bedroom was gently pushed open and one of the family would appear and stand by the bed and whisper: 'How long can it go on?' When I did not answer I was left alone in the room, listening to the sound of his breathing. Randolph came in. I got up, and as I closed the door I saw him lift his father's hand to his lips. Lady Churchill drifted through the rooms. There was no expression on her beautiful face; she seemed to be in a trance.

One night in the small hours I was summoned to his side. The nurse on duty thought that he was dying. But when I came to him there was no change. Meanwhile the world seemed to stand still, half-incredulous that this man whom they held in reverence for what he had done was about to be taken from them. The narrow street was blocked by reporters. They did not speak to one another; they appeared numbed by what was happening behind the great black

789

door. As I came out, there was a shuffling of feet as they pushed forward to catch my words.

For fourteen days he was not seen to move. His strength left him slowly, as if he was loath to give up life. On the night of the twenty-fourth of January it appeared that a crisis was at hand. His breathing became shallow and laboured, and at eight o'clock in the morning it ceased. Mary, sitting by his side, looked up at me. I got up and bent over the bed, but he had gone.

He was taken at night to Westminster, to the Hall of William Rufus, and there for three days he lay in state, while the people gathered in crowds that stretched over Lambeth Bridge to the far side of the river, to do honour to the man they loved for his valour. On the fourth day he was borne on a gun-carriage to St. Paul's. There followed a long line of men in arms, marching to sorrowful music. With all the panoply of Church and State, and in the presence of his Queen, he was carried to an appointed place hard by the tombs of Nelson and Wellington, under the great dome, while with solemn music and the beating of drums the nation saluted the man who had saved them and saved their honour.

The village stations on the way to Bladon were crowded with his countrymen, and at Bladon in a country churchyard, in the stillness of a winter evening, in the presence of his family and a few friends, Winston Churchill was committed to English earth, which in his finest hour he had held inviolate.

Appendices

Appendix (1)

Letter from Sir Charles Wilson to Lord Beaverbrook.

18th April 1941.

Dear Lord Beaverbrook,

I find this in my war diary:

Last Monday when we were in the trenches a man reported sick and I sent him back to duty. The following day he came again and again I sent him back. But the day after he was still there among the morning sick. 'It's no good, Sir,' he said, 'I can't stick it no longer.' Once more I thoroughly overhauled him; there was nothing wrong with him physically and he was sane enough. He was simply tired; but so were others. Once more I sent him back. Next day he was killed. Unable or unwilling? This man festers in my mind. I see his face weak and sulky, and watch him slouching back reluctantly to the trenches. I see him return on a stretcher, his head all swathed in bloody bandages, a yellow froth around his gaping mouth. I hear his breathing almost stop, and then rise gradually to a great heaving gasp; and this regular rise and fall goes on till there is a pause when nothing follows and after a little I know that he is dead.

That sort of thing is always happening in war; it eats into the mind. It would be intolerable if the lives of those of us past fighting were not at the disposal of the country. We do not count; our lives are nearly over. I read the brief obituary notices of those boys who go out in the air; their story has hardly begun, but you get enough to see they were the leaders of their small community, school or university. It drives one to work that this business may come to an end before all these lads are gone; every minute seems to count. Those who have reflected on war come to admire not the gaudy act performed on the spur of the moment but rather the steady resolve to see the thing through. I remember a man at Ypres whose nerve had gone, and I sent him sick, but when he got to the casualty clearing station and the war for him was over he got out of the ambulance and asked to be sent back to the Battalion. That seemed to me real courage.

That your boy—when he had done enough in the air to satisfy

793

his conscience in doing a ground job—should of his own free will return to night fighting is a superb gesture; this is the real stuff of leadership. I know what it must mean to you. I watch my own lad, now 16½, and determined to join the Air Force when he can, grow older; if he went out the meaning of life would be gone. I feel no thrill, no sense of achievement in being President, only a chance of doing something in my small field to make the machine go more smoothly, for the Ministry of Health is of more moment in a war than many think.

You say your job is finished. Surely it has only just begun. It is not numbers of aircraft that will win the war in the air. It is, of course, quality. We have to harness science to the job, and that is as yet only done in a small way. No other nation has a body like the Royal Society. Men who have creative minds, who invent and plan new things. Dale, the President of the Royal, has creative talent and yet is a man of affairs—a rare combination. I'd like you to talk with him and get to know him. Your job finishes when the war finishes. To leave it now before a solution is found to the night bomber, when things look black, is unthinkable. Scientific men of real creative genius are individualists and kittle kettle to control. I want you to go down as the man who was unconventional enough to break through convention and bring these men to the rescue. We can't win in any other way. Humour them, like racehorses, they are all nerves, anybody can scrap with them, only you could get the best out of them. Patience was the faculty which the historian put first in Marlborough's equipment of war. Think of the effect just now of the resignation of a member of the War Cabinet on the public when it is going to get a good many hard knocks; the inevitable suggestion of divided counsels. How often is it necessary for anyone engaged on a long job of work among uncomprehending people to resist resignation as an easy, emotional and impulsive escape from a tangle of difficulties and uncertainties. Your real task is not to get the better of the Bosche but of your temperament.

I'd like to see you get away from your desk at times, among the the workers of the aircraft factories. They would respond. The relations between employer and workers are as you know governed not by wages but by emotions; it is a question of psychology (cf. Rootes of Coventry). We might have even in war a new era in which this great industry was held up after the war as an example of how men can work all out and yet be content. I'll be your welfare officer if you haven't one. I remember going on a night trench raid without stretcher bearers on the theory that the men would bring back their own killed and wounded if they were satisfied that the

794

Medical Officer was willing to take the same risks as they were. It was looked on as a mad scheme, but it worked, and they brought back nine killed and thirty-nine wounded out of a party of a hundred and ten. It will always work. Where labour is restive it can only be reassured in like fashion. I'd like to live among them in a bad area and get my wife to work among their women.

I entreat you not to be angry with this didactic letter. What you do now may save the life of your boy and mine and the lads of thousands of others; more, it may win the war. That is why I have written and because I like you very much. I broke the rule of a lifetime in talking to the Prime Minister about you, not because he was Prime Minister but because I wanted him to be clear there was no health reason why you should not go on doing your job.

Be strong enough to be idle at times, even when Rome seems to burn.

Yours sincerely,

Letter from Lord Beaverbrook to Sir Charles Wilson.

19th April 1941.

My dear Wilson,

You are as good a letter-writer as you are an orator.

But it is not possible for me to continue in office.

There are three reasons that stand in the way—

(1) Influenza in March.

(2) An operation to my eye.

(3) The removal of six polypi, as a result of which I am still bleeding.

And even if I were willing to stay, I would be of no value to the Prime Minister. He does not ask my advice, nor does he need it.

As for my special responsibility, there are more aircraft than the Air Ministry can use.

And when I criticize the Air Ministry, the Prime Minister looks upon me as a quarrelsome fellow. The rumour has been circulated everywhere among my colleagues that I have a bad temper.

I can do more good outside the Government than inside. I will support them in the Lords and in the newspapers.

I admit that there is one reason, although only one, why I should not go. It would prevail if I were not sick.

In addition to being sick I am tough. The Prime Minister needs tough men around him. I hope he will always give the tough men he has got encouragement in their tough courses.

I would like very much to see Dale. I was at a dinner the other night and looked all about for him. But he was not there.

It is quite unnecessary of you to hope that I will not be angry with you for writing me this letter. On the contrary I find it a most charming and splendid letter.

Yours ever,

Appendix (2)

Churchill's 'Iron Curtain' telegram.

Prime Minister to President Truman

12 May 45.

I am profoundly concerned about the European situation. I learn that half the American Air Force in Europe has already begun to move to the Pacific theatre. The newspapers are full of the great movements of the American armies out of Europe. Our armies also are, under previous arrangements, likely to undergo a marked reduction. The Canadian Army will certainly leave. The French are weak and difficult to deal with. Anyone can see that in a very short space of time our armed power on the Continent will have vanished except for moderate forces to hold down Germany.

2. Meanwhile what is to happen about Russia? I have always worked for friendship with Russia, but, like you, I feel deep anxiety because of their misinterpretation of the Yalta decisions, their attitude towards Poland, their overwhelming influence in the Balkans, excepting Greece, the difficulties they make about Vienna, the combination of Russian power and the territories under their control or occupied, coupled with the Communist technique in so many other countries, and above all their power to maintain very large armies in the field for a long time. What will be the position in a year or two, when the British and American Armies have melted and the French has not yet formed on any major scale, when we may have a handful of divisions, mostly French, and when Russia may choose to keep two or three hundred on active service?

3. An iron curtain is drawn down upon their front. We do not know what is going on behind. There seems little doubt that the whole of the regions east of the line Lübeck–Trieste–Corfu will soon be completely in their hands. To this must be added the further enormous area conquered by the American armies between Eisenach and the Elbe, which will, I suppose, in a few weeks be occupied, when the Americans retreat, by the Russian power. All kinds of arrangements will have to be made by General Eisenhower to prevent another immense flight of the German population westward as this enormous Muscovite advance into the centre of Europe takes place.

And then the curtain will descend again to a very large extent, if not entirely. Thus a broad band of many hundreds of miles of Russian-occupied territory will isolate us from Poland.

4. Meanwhile the attention of our peoples will be occupied in inflicting severities upon Germany, which is ruined and prostrate, and it would be open to the Russians in a very short time to advance if they chose to the waters of the North Sea and the Atlantic.

5. Surely it is vital now to come to an understanding with Russia, or see where we are with her, before we weaken our armies mortally or retire to the zones of occupation. This can only be done by a personal meeting. I should be most grateful for your opinion and advice. Of course we may take the view that Russia will behave impeccably, and no doubt that offers the most convenient solution. To sum up, this issue of a settlement with Russia before our strength has gone seems to me to dwarf all others.

Index

Aachen, 695; W.S.C.'s speech at, 697

Abdication debate, W.S.C. during, 744

Abyssinia, Italian invasion of, 429. *See also* Ethiopia

Acheson, Dean, at Washington (1964), 569; on Greece, 215

Adams, Sherman, 767

Adana, 84, 86, 145, 146

Adeane, Sir Michael, 639

Adeline, 256 n.

Adenauer, Chancellor Konrad, 410, 416, 509, 577, 593, 602, 619, 754, 761; Lady Churchill on, 762; visits W.S.C. (1959), 762; W.S.C. on, 596, 597

Adler, General, and W.S.C. (1952), 362

Aegean Sea, 218

Agincourt, H.M.S., seizure of, 185

Alanbrooke, 1st Viscount. *See* Brooke, F.-M. Sir Alan

Albert, Prince Consort, 369 n.

Aldington, Richard, W.S.C. on, 526; Randolph Churchill on, 526

Aldrich, Winthrop, in London (1953), 497

Alexander, A. V., 101 n., 251

Alexander, F.-M. (1st Earl), 68, 104, 144, 173–4, 290, 297, 304, 495, 514; and mepacrine, 163–4; and the Anzio landing, 158; as a leader, 174; as Governor-General of Canada, 346, 363; as Minister of Defence, 392–3, 449, 635; at Athens (1944), 208–15; at Athens Conference, 211 ff.; at Balaclava, 233–4; at Dunkirk, 174; at El Alamein, 76–7; at Lake Como, 300–1; at Monte Cassino, 168; at Naples, 191–2; at Potsdam, 268–85; at Sebastopol, 233; at Siena, 170–2; at Yalta, 225; during First World War, 174; in Egypt, 51, 66; in Italy, 118, 120, 122, 161–74, 190–2, 391–405; in retreat from Burma, 174; in Tripoli, 87; in Turkey, 84–6; Lord Moran on, 174; on behaviour in the Commons, 392; relations with W.S.C., 170, 171–2, 173–4; suggests W.S.C.'s retirement, 440; visits post-war Berlin, 268–70; W.S.C. on, 173–4

Algerian Committee, 741

Algiers, 71, 88, 96, 98–9, 104, 164–5, 284; capture of, 77

Alexandria, 38, 239

Alice Moran (tug), 354

Allied Control Commission (Germany), 224

Alma, storming of the, 499

American Civil War, 95, 702

American War of Independence, 31, 228

Ajax, H.M.S., 209 ff.

Anatomy of Courage, The, xv, 112 n., 238; publication difficulties of, 127–8; W.S.C. on, 127

Anders, General Wladyslaw, at Moscow, (1942) 62–3, (1944) 199–200

Andersen, Hans Christian, 546

Anderson, Lady (Ava), 703–4

Anderson, Sir John (Viscount Waverley), 47–8, 121, 251, 386, 389, 414, 548, 682, 703–4, 777; becomes Chancellor of the Exchequer, 121; declines Cabinet post (1951), 387; W.S.C. on, 121

Anglo-Jordan Treaty, 498

Index

Ankara, 145

Antigua, 769-70

Antwerp, 416.

Anzio landing, 157-8, 188, 206; W.S.C. on, 188

Aristophanes, W.S.C. on, 652

Armas, Colonel Carlos Castillo, 567 n.

Arbenz, President, deposed, 567

Ardennes, 237

Armentières, 267

Arundel, 582

As He Saw It, 314

Ashley-Cooper, Sir Patrick, 718

Asquith, Cyril, 594

Asquith, Herbert (1st Earl of Oxford and), 26, 71, 156 n., 186-7, 299 n., 429, 569, 684, 725, 775, 780; W.S.C. on, 186

Asquith, Margot, 186-7; and 'this delicious war', 697; W.S.C. on, 186-7

Assheton, Ralph, 251-2, 262

Astor, J. J., 343

Astor, Lady, 58

Aswan Dam, withdrawal of funds for, 702 n.

Athens, 172, 206-15, 234-5, 237, 238-9, 783; entry of British troops into (1944), 207; fighting in (1944), 213-14; German withdrawal from (1944), 206

Athens Conference (1944), 210-15

Athlone, Earl of, 373

Athos, Mount, 238

Atlantic, Battle of, 32, 186, 261, 276, 356, 420-1; W.S.C. on, 261, 420-1

Atlantic Charter, 213, 413

Atlantic Command (Saclant), 356-7, 366; W.S.C. on, 356-7, 360, 370

Atlas Mountains, 82, 83, 156-7

Atom bomb (atomic warfare), 280-1, 294 n., 300, 359, 361, 428, 503-4; decision to use in Japan, 280, 281; Lord Moran on, 281; Quebec Agreement on, 538, 534-5; W.S.C. on, 280-1, 300, 315, 316, 361, 367, 493-4, 503-4, 505, 544-5

Attlee, Clement (1st Earl), 22 n., 64, 143, 150, 180, 251, 264, 283, 288, 293, 307, 380, 392, 399, 514, 532,

537, 569, 677, 730, 754-5, 757, 773; and TV, 756; as Prime Minister (1945), 311, 312; at Naples (1944), 166, broadcast speech (June 5, 1945), 253; faints into W.S.C.'s arms, 630; gives W.S.C. precedence at Commons oath-taking (1955), 667; Lord McGowan on, 344; Lord Moran on, 166, 643; on Aneurin Bevan's attack, 23; on the Woodford speech, 615, 618; public view of (1945), 311-12; quarrel with Aneurin Bevan, 638; speech at Westminster Hall presentation (1954), 616; speech in the hydrogen bomb debate, 534, 535; speech in Suez debate (1954), 583; visits Moscow (1954), 590; W.S.C. on, 312, 369, 634; W.S.C. on Moscow visit of (1954), 590

Attlee, Mrs., and F.-M. Montgomery at croquet, 601

Auchinleck, F.-M. Sir Claude, 719, 727, 784; dismissed from Eighth Army command, 53; in Egypt (1942), 46-53; Sir Alan Brooke on, 46-7, 53

Augustine, St., 52

Augsburg, 22 n.

Austria, 276, 352, 541

Australia, 21, 362

Azores, 480-1, 496

Baird, Brigadier-General Edward, 498

Balaclava, 225, 233-4; Battle of, 499

Baldwin, Stanley (1st Earl), 24, 326, 427, 775; on payment of M.P.s, 553; relations with W.S.C., 419-20; W.S.C. on, 368, 424

Balfour, A. J., 26, 208, 324, 389, 421, 569; supports U.S. during Spanish-American War, 568; W.S.C. on, 443, 449

Balkans, the, 161-2, 171-2

Balmoral, 393, 450, 468, 472

Balsan, Jacques, 22 n.

Balsan, Mme., 22

Baltic Sea, 275

Baltic States, 32, 193; Russian advance into (1944), 161

Balzac, Honoré de, 728

815

823